MICROECONOMICS

A Contemporary Introduction

William A. McEachern
Professor of Economics
University of Connecticut

H84 *Published by*
SOUTH-WESTERN PUBLISHING CO.

CINCINNATI   WEST CHICAGO, IL   CARROLLTON, TX   LIVERMORE, CA

MICROECONOMICS

PREFACE

Economics is over two hundred years old, but it is new every day. Each day offers a fresh batch of evidence that can be used to support or to reshape evolving economic theory. Principles texts written initially in the 1950s, 1960s, and 1970s may not be relevant in the 1990s. As Schumpeter pointed out, competition is a process of creative destruction. Evidence suggests that instructors are often looking for something new, something better. In this book, I try to convey the vitality and excitement of the discipline and to show students that economics has relevance to the "ordinary business of life." I am new enough to the task to keep it fresh, but experienced enough to get it right.

I rely on common experience to convey economic principles. Remember the last time you were in a strange neighborhood and had to ask for directions? Along with the directions you may have heard the standard comment, "You can't miss it." So how come you missed it? Writing a principles text is much like giving directions. The author's familiarity with the material can be both a strength and a weakness. It is a strength, of course, in that the author really understands the material. But is can also be a weakness if the author provides so much detail that central features get lost. The secret is to provide just enough detail. Good directions make use of landmarks familiar to all—a gas station, a stoplight, a fork in the road. Likewise, in this book I draw on experiences common to all of us—reading a report on increased inflation; choosing between a ball game and a movie; deciding whether to pack a lunch or buy a Big Mac.

Economics is too important to neglect because it seems too difficult or, worse yet, irrelevant. I try to avoid the sort of hand waving so often used in other texts to "explain" difficult topics. To present economic principles, I use what I call the "double IDEA" approach: Intuition and Insight, Displays and Diagrams, Explanations and Examples, Analysis and Application. Drawing on common experience, I begin with intuition and insight. Once students have an initial grasp of a principle, displays and diagrams are introduced to shed light on that principle. (In contrast, some books use diagrams the way a drunk uses a lamppost—more for support than for illumination.) My diagrams and displays are accompanied by explanations and examples. Finally, the principle is subjected to analysis and application. Thus, the presentation begins naturally with the student's own experience and ends with the application of an economic principle.

This clarity of presentation provides an instructor with greater flexibility in the classroom and promotes more effective use of scarce class time. The instructor can explore in greater detail a topic of special interest but need not feel hemmed in by a requirement to cover everything in the book. The book provides much running room. Moreover, the examples in the text are all fresh. The instructor can use more traditional examples in class, and they will also seem new to students.

— a review of recent developments in the labor movement

— a current, comprehensive analysis of poverty, income distribution, and welfare reform

— an explanation of wage differentials, an analysis of comparable worth, and a review of theories of profit and entrepreneurship

— a presentation of alternative theories of regulation, plus a discussion of deregulation and re-regulation

— coverage of newer topics such as contestable markets, vertical integration, the market for corporate control, rent seeking, and public choice

The treatment of microeconomics in this text underscores the role of time and information in production and consumption. It also reflects the increasing interest in economic institutions, particularly the internal organization of households, firms, and governments. For example, the recent changes that have occurred in the division of labor within the household are highlighted throughout the text. In fact, three chapters are devoted to the internal workings of economic institutions.

More generally, I try to convey the idea that most microeconomic principles operate like gravity: they work whether or not we understand them. For example, consumers need know nothing about utility theory in order to behave as if they maximize utility. They need only behave in accordance with rational self-interest.

Organization

I have written a book that flows. Chapters in many principles texts are interrupted by boxed case studies, parenthetical explanations, contrived subdivisions, qualifying footnotes, and other distractions that mar the natural flow of the story. For example, case studies in other texts are usually segregated from the chapter's mainstream, leaving students uncertain about if and when they should be read.

Each chapter in this book is divided into logical sections and subsections. Rather than simply breaking the chapter into digestible units, the organization enhances the presentation. Qualifying footnotes are used sparingly, and parenthetical explanations are used hardly at all. Moreover, case studies appear in the natural flow of the exposition. The student can thus read each chapter from beginning to end. Each chapter, rather than being chopped into a series of definitions and qualifications, tells a compelling story.

Each chapter opens with a paragraph that both motivates the chapter and describes the major sections. Chapters consist of two or three major sections, with each section typically summarized as the chapter progresses. An end-of-chapter summary gathers together the major points of the chapter.

Major features of each chapter include the following:

Captioned Exhibits. A brief summary appears along with each diagram. These captions point out the lessons to be drawn from the analysis.

Marginal Definitions. Important economic terms are fully discussed in the body of the text but are also defined in the margins.

Case Studies. As mentioned before, case studies are not set off in boxes, as in other texts, but are integrated into the body of the chapter. The student therefore has no doubt that the case studies are to be read. These could serve as a basis for class discussion.

Profiles of Famous Economists. Rather than focus primarily on biographical information, the profiles discuss famous economists' contributions to economic thought. This material complements the analysis presented in the body of the text and is positioned to follow the flow of ideas in the chapter.

End-of-Chapter Material. Each chapter closes with a summary plus questions and problems that can be discussed either in class or during weekly discussion sections. Suggested answers are provided in the *Instructor's Manual*.

Appendixes. Several end-of-chapter appendixes provide more detailed treatment of various topics. Appendix material is typically more advanced than that contained in the body of the chapter. The only exception is the appendix to Chapter 1, which is recommended for all students unfamiliar with variables, graphs, slopes, and the like. Aside from the graphical appendix, however, subsequent material does not build on the appendixes, so their use is purely optional. Including more difficult material in this way offers the instructor greater flexibility of coverage with no loss of continuity.

Glossary. Key terms are listed alphabetically in a glossary, which appears just before the index.

Supplementary Items for Students

Study Guide.   The student *Study Guide* has chapters that correspond to each chapter in the text. Each chapter includes (1) a chapter outline, including definitions of all terms; (2) a discussion of the chapter's major points; (3) "Lagniappe," which offers extensions of material in the chapter, with each extension accompanied by a "Question to Think About"; (4) a variety of questions, including fill-in-the-blanks, true/false, multiple choice, and discussion questions; and (5) answers to all these questions.

MicroGraph.   MicroGraph is a microcomputer tutorial that is available free of charge through your South-Western representative. MicroGraph's four modules illustrate key ideas in microeconomics. These tutorials can be copied and provided to students, or they can be placed in a microcomputer lab.

Supplementary Items for Instructors

Instructor's Manual.   The *Instructor's Manual* contains a chapter corresponding to each chapter in the text. Each chapter includes (1) a brief overview of the text chapter; (2) an outline drawn from the headings in the text chapter; (3) an extensive summary of the chapter's major points; (4) pedagogical tips that expand on points raised in the chapter; and (5) suggested answers to the end-of-chapter questions and problems.

Teaching Assistant's Manual.   Instructors with teaching assistants can provide each with a *Teaching Assistant's Manual* written especially for those who meet once a week with students in a discussion or quiz section. The manual contains a chapter corresponding to each chapter of the text and offers (1) a brief overview of the text chapter; (2) an outline drawn from the headings in the text chapter; (3) additional material for class discussion; (4) an indication of topics in the chapter warranting special attention; (5) additional examples to supplement those provided in the chapter; (6) "What if?" questions for class discussion; and (7) an extensive list of short-answer questions for the quizzes administered in these weekly sections. In addition to the chapter-by-chapter accounts, four appendixes at the end of the manual provide general advice on (a) presenting material; (b) generating and maintaining class discussions; (c) preparing, administering, and grading quizzes; and (d) coping with the special challenges confronted by foreign teaching assistants. Even those with previous teaching experience may find this manual helpful.

Two-Color Transparencies.   A set of acetate transparencies reproduces important illustrations from the text.

Test Bank. The *Test Bank* available to adopters contains more than 3200 multiple choice questions, with five options for each question. None of the questions duplicates those provided in the *Study Guide.* Questions are rated according to three levels of difficulty. The *Test Bank* is available in both printed and microcomputer (MicroSWAT II) formats.

Acknowledgments

This book benefited greatly from careful review by economists from around the country. They share much of the credit but none of the blame for the final product. I would like to thank the following, who reviewed substantial portions of the manuscript: Polly Reynolds Allen, University of Connecticut; Jacquelene M. Browning, Texas A&M University; Art Goldsmith, University of North Carolina at Chapel Hill; Rich Hart, Miami University; Andrew J. Policano, University of Iowa; Steven M. Sheffrin, University of California, Davis; Roger Sherman, University of Virginia; Houston Stokes, University of Illinois at Chicago; Gregory H. Wassall, Northeastern University; and Leland B. Yeager, Auburn University.

Anybody familiar with an undertaking of the magnitude knows that much help is required. I relied on comparative advantage and the division of labor to prepare the most complete teaching package on the market today. Richard Langlois authored the biographies featured throughout the text. John Lunn wrote the *Study Guide.* Nancy Fox and Alannah Orrison prepared the *Test Bank.* And David Kleykamp was my coauthor for the *Instructor's Manual.* For their cooperation and contribution to the project, I am grateful.

Finally, I owe a special debt to my wife, Pat, who provided encouragement and good cheer during the years of writing. For her patience and inspiration, I dedicate this book to her.

CONTENTS

PART 2 Introduction to the Market System 98

PART 3   Market Structure, Pricing, and Government Regulation   184

PART 4   *Resource Markets*   *290*

William A.
McEachern

University of Connecticut
M. William Breadheft

William A. McEachern is professor of economics at the University of Connecticut, where he has taught principles of economics for more than a dozen years and has developed a series of annual workshops for teaching assistants. He has also taught at Arizona State University.

He received his Ph.D. from the University of Virginia and has published several books and monographs in public finance, public policy, and industrial organization. His research has also appeared in various journals, including *Economic Inquiry,* the *National Tax Journal, Kyklos, Public Choice,* and the *Journal of Industrial Economics.* Professor McEachern has advised federal, state, and local governments on policy matters and directed a bipartisan commission examining Connecticut's fiscal structure. He has talked before more than one hundred groups and has received the University of Connecticut's Faculty Award for Distinguished Public Service.

P A R T
O N E

Introduction to Economics

THE ART and SCIENCE of ECONOMIC ANALYSIS

You have been reading and hearing about economic issues for years—the unemployment rate, the inflation rate, the price of oil, the federal deficit, higher tuition, the price of rock concert tickets. When the explanations of these issues go into any depth, your eyes probably glaze over, and you tune out the same way you do when the weather forecaster tries to provide an in-depth analysis of high-pressure fronts colliding with moisture carried in from the coast. Because of a negative experience with economics, some of you may have been dreading this course. Some of you may have had to work up your courage just to open this book.

What many people fail to realize is that economics is much more alive than the dry accounts provided by the news media. Economics is about making choices, and you make economic choices every day—choices about whether to live in the dorm or off-campus, take a course in accounting or one in music appreciation, pack a lunch or buy a Big Mac. Because you, as an economic decision maker, are the subject of this book, you know much more about economics right now than you realize. You bring to the subject a rich personal experience, an experience that will be tapped throughout the book to reinforce your understanding of the basic concepts. This chapter will introduce you to the art and science of economic analysis. Topics discussed in this chapter include:

- Scarce resources
- Unlimited wants
- Marginal analysis
- Scientific method
- Pitfalls of economic analysis

THE ECONOMIC PROBLEM

Would you like a new car, a bigger dorm room, better meals, more free time, a more interesting social life, more spending money, more sleep? Yes, you say? Even if you are able to satisfy some of these desires, others will keep popping up. The problem is that while your wishes or desires are virtually unlimited, your resources are limited. Because of limited resources, you must choose from among your many wants and, whenever you choose, you must forgo some wants.

The problem of scarce resources but unlimited wants that you confront is faced to a greater or lesser extent by the 5 billion people around the world. It is faced by taxicab drivers, by farmers, by politicians, by shepherds, by everybody. The taxicab driver uses the cab and other scarce resources—knowledge of the city, driving skills, time—to earn income, which can be exchanged for housing, groceries, clothing, trips to Atlantic City, and other goods and services aimed at satisfying the driver's unlimited wants.

Economics is the study of how people choose to utilize their scarce and limited resources to produce, exchange, and consume goods and services in an attempt to satisfy their unlimited wants. We shall first consider what we mean by resources, next examine goods and services, and finally focus on the heart of the matter, economic choice.

Resources

Resources are divided into four broad categories: land, labor, capital, and entrepreneurial ability. These resources are combined in various ways to produce goods and services. **Land** represents not only land in the conventional sense of plots of ground but all other natural resources, including rivers, trees, and minerals. **Labor** includes the broad category of human resources, including physical labor and thought processes. The talents in this category can range from those of the street sweeper to those of the brain surgeon. **Capital** represents all manufactured equipment used in the production of goods. Examples include the street sweeper's broom, the surgeon's scalpel, the ten-ton press used to print *Newsweek*, and the building where your economics class meets. This kind of capital is sometimes called *physical capital*, to distinguish it from *human capital*, which is the knowledge and skills people develop to enhance their ability to produce, such as the taxi driver's knowledge of the city's streets or the surgeon's knowledge of the human body.

A special kind of human skill is called **entrepreneurial ability**—the rare talent required to build a better mousetrap. The entrepreneur identifies the need for a new product, figures out how best to produce it, brings together the land, labor, and capital required for production, and assumes the risk of success or failure. The entrepreneur tries to discover and act on profitable opportunities. The largest firms in the world today began as ideas in the minds of individual entrepreneurs.

Resource owners are paid **rent** for their land, **wages** for their labor, **interest** for their capital, and **profit** for their entrepreneurial ability. Profit is

---

Economics *is the study of how people choose to use scarce resources in an attempt to satisfy unlimited wants.*

Land *is all plots of ground and other natural resources used in the production of goods and services. Resource owners receive* **rent** *for the use of their land.*

Labor *is the physical and mental effort of humans. Individuals receive* **wages** *for their labor.*

Capital *includes all manufactured equipment used in the production of goods and services. Resource owners receive* **interest** *for the use of their capital.*

Entrepreneurial ability *includes managerial and organization skills together with the willingness to take risks. Resource owners receive* **profit** *for their entrepreneurial ability.*

the difference between the price the entrepreneur is paid for a product and the wages, rent, and interest the entrepreneur must pay for the resources employed. Thus, we say that the entrepreneur is the *residual claimant*, who earns whatever income is left after paying for all other resources. Sometimes nothing is left.

Goods and Services

Land, labor, and capital can be combined by the entrepreneur in an infinite variety of ways to produce goods and services to satisfy our unlimited wants. A farmer, a tractor, fifty acres of land, plus seeds and fertilizer produce the good—corn. A hundred musicians, the same number of instruments, some chairs, a director, a musical score, and a music hall combine to produce a service—Ravel's *Bolero*.

*A **good** is any-thing that is scarce and valuable.*

Corn is a **good** because it is something you can see, feel, and touch that requires scarce resources and is produced to satisfy unlimited wants. The book you now hold, your last meal, and the clothes you have on are all goods. The rendition of *Bolero* is a *service* because it is not something tangible, yet it uses scarce resources and is produced to satisfy unlimited wants. Lectures, movies, and haircuts are all services.

Because goods and services require scarce resources, they are themselves scarce. Since we cannot have all the goods and services we would like, we must constantly choose among them. We must choose among better living quarters, better meals, nicer clothes, higher-quality entertainment, more late-night pizza, and so on. Making choices in a world of scarcity means that some goods and services must be passed up.

Sometimes we think of certain goods as free because they involve no apparent cost to us. Those subscription cards that keep falling out of magazines appear to be free. At least it seems we would have little difficulty rounding up about three thousand if we had to. Their production, however, uses up scarce economic resources, resources drawn away from competing uses, such as producing higher-quality magazines perhaps. You may have heard the expression "There is no such thing as a free lunch." The lunch may appear to us to be free, but it draws scarce resources away from the production of other economic goods. Without scarcity, there would be no economic problem. Goods that are truly free do not interest the economist.

Economic Actors

There are three types of actors in the economy: households, firms, and government. Households play the leading role. As consumers, households demand the goods and services produced, and as resource owners, households supply the land, labor, capital, and entrepreneurial ability to firms and to government. Firms and government are supporting actors because they try to supply the goods and services demanded by households.

*A **market** is a set of arrangements through which buyers and sellers carry out exchange at mutually agreeable terms.*

Markets are the means by which buyers and sellers carry out exchange. Markets may be physical places, such as the supermarket, department store, and shopping mall. Or markets may consist of the arrangements by which buyers and sellers communicate their intentions, such as letters, phone calls, classified ads, and radio and television ads. These market mechanisms provide information about the quantity, quality, and price of products offered for sale. Goods·and services are bought and sold in **product markets**; resources are bought and sold in **resource markets**. The most important resource market is the labor market, or job market. Think of your experience looking for a job, and you get some idea of this market.

Microeconomics and Macroeconomics

Although you have made thousands of economic choices, if you are like most people, you have seldom reflected on your own economic behavior. For example, why did you choose to use your scarce resource, time, to read this book right now rather than do something else? **Microeconomics** is the study of your economic behavior and the economic behavior of other individual decision makers who are making choices about such matters as what to buy and what to sell, how much to work and how much to play, how much to borrow and how much to save. Microeconomics examines what factors affect individual economic choices and how changes in these factors alter such choices.

You have perhaps given little thought to the factors influencing your own economic behavior, and you have probably given even less thought to the way your choices link up with the billions of choices made by hundreds of millions of other individuals to shape our economic system. Why is it that at times the economy seems fine, while at other times the billions of individual choices result in inflation, unemployment, or widespread poverty? The study of the performance of the economy as a whole is called **macroeconomics**. Whereas microeconomics is a study of the individual pieces of the economic puzzle, macroeconomics tries to put all the pieces together to focus on the big picture. Macroeconomics considers the combined effect of individual choices on the overall performance of the economy as reflected by such measures as the nation's price level, total production, and level of employment.

Just as the whole consists of the sum of its parts, the economy is ultimately driven by individual choices—people like yourself responding to changes in their economic environment. Thus, a study of the big picture—of economic aggregates such as unemployment and inflation—must begin with an understanding of the individual choices behind those aggregates.

*A **product market** is one in which goods and services are exchanged; households are demanders in such markets, whereas firms and governments are suppliers.*

*A **resource market** is one in which resources are exchanged; households are suppliers in such markets, while firms and governments are demanders.*

***Microeconomics** is the study of the economic behavior of individual decision makers.*

***Macroeconomics** is the study of the behavior of entire economies.*

THE ART OF ECONOMIC ANALYSIS

Our economic system results from millions of individuals making billions of choices in pursuit of their unlimited wants and desires. Because these choices lie at the very heart of the economic problem—the problem of allocating scarce resources to unlimited wants—they deserve closer scrutiny. Developing an understanding of the factors that shape economic choices is the first step toward developing the art of economic analysis.

Rational Self-Interest

A key economic assumption is that individuals rationally select choices they perceive to be in their best interest. By *rational* we mean simply that people behave in a reasonable way and do not consciously try to make themselves less happy or less satisfied. The economist does not claim that each individual knows with certainty which alternatives are best, only that individuals make choices they believe to be in their best interest, and that these choices are influenced in predictable ways by changes in each individual's economic conditions, such as changes in income or in prices.

This reliance on rational self-interest should not be viewed as blind materialism, pure selfishness, or greed. Your self-interest often includes the welfare of your family, your friends, and perhaps the poor of the world. But your concern for others is partially tempered by economic considerations. You are more likely to donate your old clothes rather than your new ones to organizations such as Goodwill Industries or the Salvation Army. You may volunteer to drive a friend to the airport on Saturday afternoon, but you are less likely to offer a ride if her plane leaves at 6:00 A.M. People are more inclined to give to their favorite charity if their contributions are tax deductible.

The point is that the notion of self-interest does not rule out concern for others; it simply means that concern for others is to some extent influenced by the same economic factors that influence other economic choices. The lower the cost of expressing concern for others is, the more that concern will be expressed.

Economic Analysis Is Marginal Analysis

Economic choice usually involves some adjustment to the existing situation or to the status quo. The president of the computer software company must decide whether to develop a new word processing program. The town manager must decide whether to buy another garbage truck. Your favorite jeans are on sale, and you must decide whether to buy another pair. You are wondering whether you should carry an extra course next semester. You have just finished dinner and must decide whether to have dessert.

Economic choices may involve working a little more or a little less, studying a little more or a little less, buying a little more or a little less, selling a little more or a little less. The decisions are based on a comparison of the expected marginal costs and the expected marginal benefits of the change under consideration. **Marginal** means "extra" or "additional." You, as a rational decision maker, will change the status quo as long as your expected marginal benefit from the change exceeds your expected marginal cost. Thus, you compare the marginal benefit you expect to derive from consuming dessert with the marginal cost of dessert—the extra money, extra time, and extra calories.

Marginal means "extra" or "additional."

While the change under consideration is typically small, marginal choices could involve what appear to be major economic adjustments, such as the decision to quit school and join the Marines. For a firm, a marginal choice might mean producing a new product, building a plant in Taiwan, or even filing for bankruptcy.

By focusing on the effects of marginal adjustments to the status quo, the economist is able to cut the analysis of economic choice down to manageable proportions. Rather than confront head-on a bewildering economic reality, the economist can begin with marginal choices, then see how these marginal choices affect particular markets and help shape the economic system as a whole.

Choice Requires Time and Information

Rational choice takes time and requires information. Because of this, we seldom know all we would like to know prior to making choices. If you have any doubts about the time and information required to make choices, talk to someone who recently purchased a house, a car, or a personal computer. Talk to a corporate official who is trying to decide whether to build a new plant, what new products to introduce, or whether to buy that new machine. Consider your own experience in selecting a college. You probably talked to friends, relatives, teachers, and guidance counselors; very likely you read the school catalogs and the various college guides; you may have even visited a few campuses to meet with the admissions staff and with anyone else who was willing to talk. The decision took time and money, not to mention sheer aggravation and anxiety.

Because information is costly to acquire, we are often willing to pay others to gather and digest it for us. The existence of the magazine *Consumer Reports* and stock analysts, travel agents, real estate brokers, career counselors, and restaurant guidebooks indicates our willingness to pay for information that will facilitate our economic choices.

To review, the art of economic analysis focuses on how individuals use their scarce resources in an attempt to satisfy their unlimited wants. Rational self-interest guides individual choice. Choice involves a comparison of the marginal cost and marginal benefit of alternative actions, a comparison that requires time and information. To understand when and why marginal changes are made, we must examine the impact of economic events on individual choice. The economist studies such impacts in a systematic manner called the scientific method. The science of economic analysis will be examined next.

THE SCIENCE OF ECONOMIC ANALYSIS

Consider the science of economic analysis. The first step is to identify the economic behavior to be analyzed. An attempt is then made to cut away as much unnecessary detail as possible to isolate the essential relationships. We must develop a theory or model to explain how some aspect of the economy

*A **theory** or **model** is a simplification of economic reality designed to capture the important elements of the relationship under consideration.*

works. This **theory** or **model** is a simplification of economic reality that captures only the important elements of the relationship under consideration. Theories or models are used to explain actual events.

The Role of Theory

Economic theories need not contain every detail and interrelationship. In fact, the more details they contain, the more unwieldy they become and the less useful they are. The world we confront is so complex that we have to abstract from the billions of relationships to make any sense of things.

The role of theory is usually not well understood. Sometimes you will hear someone say "Oh, that's fine in theory, but in practice it's another matter." The meaning is that the theory provides no aid in such practical matters. Individuals who believe this fail to realize that they are simply substituting their own theory for a theory they either do not believe or do not understand. In fact, they are saying, "I have my own theory, which works better."

All of us use theories, however poorly defined or understood, to operate. People who pound on the Pepsi machine that just ate their quarter have a crude theory about how that machine works and what just went wrong. One version of that theory might go: "The quarter drops through a series of whatchamacallits, but sometimes the quarter gets stuck. *If* I pound on the machine, *then* I can free up the quarter and send it on its way." Evidently this theory works well enough so that some individuals continue to pound on machines that fail to produce (a real problem for the vending machine industry). Yet if you ask these mad pounders if they have a "theory" about how the machine operates, they would look at you as if you were crazy.

The Scientific Process

The process of theoretical investigation can be understood most easily by breaking down the scientific methodology into four steps.

*A **variable** is any magnitude that can take on different values.*

Step One   The first step is to identify and define the variables that are relevant to the economic problem under consideration. **A variable** is a magnitude that can take on different possible values, such as the unemployment rate or the price of zucchini. The variables of concern become the basic elements of the theory, and they must be selected with care.

Step Two   The second step is to state the assumptions that specify the conditions under which the theory is to apply. Assumptions play a dual role in economic theories. Assumptions are employed to simplify the theory by clearing away those portions of economic reality that are not expected to have an important effect on the theory. One major category of assumptions used for simplification is the other-things-constant assumption—in Latin, the *ceteris paribus* assumption. The idea is to isolate those variables of interest, then to assume that nothing else of importance will change. For example, suppose that we are interested in how the quantity of Pepsi purchased per week is influenced by changes in its price. Since the price of Pepsi and the quantity purchased are the variables of interest, we try to rule out changes in other possible factors, such as the income of consumers, the price of Coke, and the average temperature. We thus assume the other factors to be constant.

A second kind of assumption has to do with individual behavior and is called a behavioral assumption. As noted earlier, economists assume that individual decision makers rationally pursue their self-interest and make choices accordingly. Rational self-interest is perhaps the most fundamental of behavioral assumptions. For consumers, rationality implies spending their income in a way that maximizes their expected levels of satisfaction. For producers, rationality implies making choices about inputs, prices, and outputs that maximize expected profits. These kinds of assumptions are called behavioral assumptions because they specify how individuals are expected to behave—what makes them tick, so to speak.

*A **hypothesis** is a statement about relationships among variables.*

Step Three   The third step of the scientific method is to formulate a **hypothesis**, which is a theory about how key variables relate. For example, one hypothesis holds that *if* the price of a six-pack of Pepsi goes up, other things constant, *then* the quantity purchased per week will go down. Thus, the hypothesis becomes a prediction of what will happen to the quantity purchased if the price goes up. The purpose of this theory, like that of any theory, is to make predictions about the real world.

Step Four   The validity of the theory must be tested by confronting its predictions with evidence. Testing hypotheses, the fourth step, is perhaps the most difficult step in economic analysis because data must be collected in a way that focuses attention on the variables in question, while other effects must be carefully filtered out. The test will lead us either to reject the theory as being inconsistent with the evidence or to decide to employ the theory until some other theory comes along that predicts even better. The objective of any theory is to predict better than competing theories. A theory may not be a good predictor at all times, yet it might still do a better job of predicting than competing theories.

Predictions Versus Forecasts

The predictions of a theory are not the same as an economic forecast. Economic theory might predict that *if* consumer spending increases, *then* unemployment will decrease, other things constant. This theory is in the form of a *conditional* statement. In contrast, an economic forecast might simply state that unemployment will go down next year. The forecaster might be guessing that consumer spending will increase next year and that unemployment will therefore go down. If this forecast about unemployment turns out to be wrong, the underlying economic theory may not necessarily be faulty, since the forecast was not offered as a conditional statement. The forecaster may simply have guessed wrong about an increase in consumer spending.

Remember this distinction between the predictions of economic theory and the forecasts of economists. Predictions are conditional statements of the *if-then* variety, whereas forecasts are more like guesses about what will actually occur. It is the forecaster you hear from most often in the media. And while the economist may be the most informed forecaster, keep in mind that forecasts are nothing more than educated guesses.

Normative Versus Positive Analysis

Economics is a social science aimed at predicting the effects of particular changes on human action. Economists, through their simplifying models, attempt to discover how the world works. How do people behave as a result of a change in price, income, or some other variable? Sometimes economists concern themselves not with how the world works but with how it *should* work.

Consider this statement: "If the price increases, then the quantity purchased will decrease." Compare this with "Income in the United States should be distributed more equally." The first statement is concerned with how the world works; the second, with how, in someone's opinion, the world should work. The first is called a **positive economic statement** because it is an assertion about economic reality that can be supported or rejected by reference to the facts. Positive statements do not have to be statements of theory. More generally, a positive statement is any statement that can be verified by reference to the facts, such as "Oil prices have increased" or "Blonds have more fun."

The statement about the distribution of income in the United States is called a **normative economic statement** because it represents someone's opinion, and an opinion cannot be shown to be true or false by reference to the facts. Positive statements are concerned with what *is*, while normative statements are concerned with what, in someone's opinion, *should be*. Compare "The unemployment rate *is* 7 percent" with "Unemployment *should be* reduced." Positive statements do not necessarily have to be true, but they must be subject to possible verification by reference to the facts.

Because economists hold divergent opinions about what might constitute a more perfect world, they offer alternative normative prescriptions for handling particular economic problems. The average person hears these conflicting views and thinks economists must be in disarray. Most of the disagreement among economists, however, involves matters of normative rather than positive analysis.

To be sure, many theoretical issues remain unresolved, but there is broad consensus in the economics profession about most fundamental theoretical principles—that is, there is much agreement about positive economic analysis. For example, in a survey of two hundred economists[1] 90 percent agreed

*A **positive economic statement** is one that can be proven or disproven by reference to facts.*

*A **normative economic statement** is one that represents an opinion and is not capable of being proved or disproved.*

---

[1]J. Kearl, et al., "A Confusion of Economists," *American Economic Review* 69 (May 1979): Table 1.

with the statement "A minimum wage increases unemployment among young and unskilled workers"; 98 percent agreed with the statement "A ceiling on rents reduces the quantity and quality of housing available." Both of these are positive statements because they can be shown to be consistent or inconsistent with the evidence. In contrast, there was much less agreement on normative statements, such as "The government should be an employer of last resort and initiate a guaranteed job program." Only 53 percent of the economists surveyed agreed with that statement.

Economists Tell Stories

Despite economists' reliance on the scientific method for developing and evaluating theories, economic thinking is perhaps as much art as science. Observing some phenomenon in the real world, isolating the key variables, formulating a theory to predict how these variables relate, and devising an unambiguous way to test the predictions all involve more than simply an understanding of economics and scientific methodology. These steps involve an intuition for identifying, relating, measuring, and testing theories.

Economic analysis also calls upon the imagination of a storyteller. Economists tell stories about how they think the world works. Although these are technically called theories or models, they are stories nonetheless. To tell a compelling story, the economist relies on case studies, anecdotes, parables, and the personal experience of the listener. The story about the Pepsi machine was an example. Throughout this book you will hear stories that bring you into closer touch with each concept under consideration. These stories help to breathe life into economic theory and cut down to manageable size an otherwise overwhelmingly complex economic reality.

SOME PITFALLS OF ECONOMIC THINKING

Economic investigation, like other scientific inquiry, is subject to common mistakes in reasoning that in the hands of the unwary could result in faulty conclusions. We will discuss three sources of confusion.

Fallacy That Association Is Causation

Does this sound familiar: "The stock market was higher today as traders reacted favorably to diminished tensions in the Middle East." Every weekday the evening news reports closing prices on the New York Stock Exchange, usually noting that the price movement was due to some specific event, such as a new government policy, growing (or diminished) tension in some part of the world, or announcements of some economic indicator, such as the unemployment rate. Although it is comforting to think that a movement in prices resulting from millions of individual trades can be traced to a single event, such simplifications are often misleading and even wrong. To assume that event *B* was caused by event *A* simply because *B* and *A* are associated in time is to fall into the **fallacy that association is causation**, a common error. The simple fact that one event follows another or one event occurs with another does not necessarily imply that one causes the other. Remember: association is not necessarily causation.

*The **association-causation fallacy** is the mistaken idea that if two variables are associated in time, one must necessarily cause the other.*

Fallacy of Composition

Did you ever go early to get a good place in line for rock concert tickets, only to find when you showed up that hundreds of others went early as well? Similarly, a farmer believes that a bumper crop will put an end to financial worries. The farmer does have a bumper crop, but so do other farmers, and the abundant supply gluts the market, depressing prices. You and the farmer have committed the **fallacy of composition**, which is an erroneous belief that what is true for the individual or for the part is also true for the group or the whole. You could be first in line only if others did not show up early as well. Similarly, the farmer could benefit from a bumper crop only if other farmers did not also have one.

*The **fallacy of composition** is the erroneous belief that what is true for the individual or part must necessarily be true for the group or whole.*

Ignoring the Secondary Effects

Many cities, because of concern about escalating rents, have over the years imposed rent controls on housing. After all, what better way to prevent rents from going up than to pass laws to prevent such increases? Over time, however, developers may stop building new units in the city because they cannot charge enough rent to earn a profit. Moreover, existing housing could deteriorate because owners cannot recover maintenance costs through higher rents. Thus, the quantity and quality of housing may well decline as a result of what appeared to be a reasonable public policy of keeping rents from going up.

Secondary effects of economic actions are those that develop slowly over time as people react to events.

The mistake of the policymakers was to *ignore the* **secondary effects** of this policy. Economic actions have primary effects, but they also have secondary effects that often turn out to be more important than the primary effects. Secondary effects may develop more slowly and may not always be obvious, but good economic analysis should take them into account.

Minimum-wage legislation represents another policy with important secondary effects. The initial effect of a minimum-wage law is to raise the wage of workers at the bottom of the wage scale. The secondary effect, however, often puts some of these same people out of work, particularly those with the least experience, such as teenagers. Employers do not find their labor worth the higher wage.

Politicians are usually concerned more with the primary, or initial, effects of a policy, for these are the effects that capture public attention and influence support in the next election. The secondary effects are more subtle and unfold over time, often after the next election. For example, a president facing reelection may increase government spending to give the economy a boost and to increase employment. This policy may eventually lead to higher inflation and greater unemployment, but not until after the election.

IF ECONOMISTS ARE SO SMART,
WHY AREN'T THEY RICH?

Why aren't economists rich? Well, some of them are. Some economists earn as much as $20,000 per appearance on the lecture circuit. Others earn thousands a day as consultants. Economists have been appointed to many high-level government positions, including not only positions for which they have clear expertise, such as Secretary of Commerce, Secretary of the Treasury, and Secretary of Labor, but also other positions for which the connection is less obvious, such as Secretary of State and Secretary of Defense. Economics is the only social science and the only business discipline to be awarded the prestigious Nobel Prize, and pronouncements by economists are reported in the media daily.

Despite its critics, the economics profession thrives because its models usually do a better job of making economic sense out of a confusing world than do alternative approaches. In the land of the blind, the one-eyed person is king. Leonard Silk, the economic columnist for *The New York Times*, writes: "Businessmen employ economists in large numbers or consult them at high fees, believing that their cracked crystal balls are better than none at all. The press pursues the best-known seers. While many laymen may be annoyed by economists, other social scientists *hate* them—for their fame, Nobel Prizes, and ready access to political power."[2]

But not all economists are rich, nor is wealth the objective of the discipline. In a similar vein, not all doctors are healthy (some of them even smoke); not all carpenters live in perfectly built homes; not all marriage counselors are happily married; and not all child psychologists have well-adjusted children.

Economics is a challenging discipline, but it is also an exciting and rewarding one. As you develop the art and science of economic analysis, you will begin to see things you never noticed before. You will recognize models you have been using all along and learn to devise new models to solve economic problems. And you do not need a Ph.D. to apply the tools of the trade. All you need is the realization that economic forces shape your life and the economy in ways that are predictable and important.

The good news is that you already know a great deal about economics. The less welcome news is that to make use of your knowledge of economics, you must cultivate the art and science of economic analysis. You must develop the special art of simplifying the real world to isolate the key variables, and you must be able to tell a persuasive story about how these variables relate. Moreover, you must grow familiar with the scientific process, appreciating both the power of theory and the pitfalls of economic analysis. In short, you must come to understand the special way that economists "see" the world.

---

[2]*Economics in Plain English* (New York: Simon and Schuster, 1978), 17 (emphasis in original).

This textbook describes how economic factors affect individual choice and how these billions of individual choices come together to shape the economic system. Economists do not claim that economics is the whole story or even that economic factors are always the most important. Economists do believe, however, that economic factors have an important and predictable effect on individual choice and that these choices strongly influence the way we live.

As we have said, the world is complex. To understand how the economy works, we must abstract from this complication to uncover relationships among key variables. We can express economic relationships in words, through algebraic expressions, or with graphs. The appendix to this chapter provides an introduction to the use of graphs. Since students with varying quantitative backgrounds take this course, some of you will find the appendix unnecessary. If you are already familiar with relationships between variables, slopes, tangents, and the like, you can probably just browse. Those of you with little recent experience with graphs, however, will benefit from a more careful reading.

In the next chapter we will introduce some key ideas of economic analysis. Subsequent chapters will use these ideas to explore economic problems and to explain economic behavior that may otherwise appear puzzling. You must walk before you can run, however, and in the next chapter you will take those first wobbly steps.

SUMMARY

1. Economics is the study of how individuals choose to utilize their scarce and limited resources to produce, exchange, and consume goods and services in an attempt to satisfy their unlimited wants. The economic problem arises from the conflict between scarce resources and unlimited wants. If there were no scarcity, there would be no need to study economics.

2. Economic resources are combined in a variety of ways to produce goods and services. Major categories of resources include (1) land, representing all natural resources, (2) labor, (3) capital, and (4) entrepreneurial ability. Because economic resources are scarce, only a limited amount of goods and services can be produced with them; hence, choices must be made.

3. Microeconomics focuses on individual choices in households, in firms, and in governments. Economists assume that these choices are guided by rational self-interest and involve a comparison of the marginal cost

and the marginal benefit associated with each action. Choice requires time and information, both of which are scarce and valuable. Macroeconomics studies the performance of the economy as a whole. Whereas microeconomics examines the individual pieces of the puzzle, macroeconomics steps back to consider the big picture.

4. Economists use theories or models to help predict the effect that changes in economic factors will have on individual choices and, in turn, the effect these individual choices will have on particular markets and on the economy as a whole. Economists employ the scientific method to (1) identify the key variables, (2) state the assumptions under which the theory operates, (3) derive predictions about how, according to the theory, the variables relate, and (4) test the theory by comparing these predictions with the evidence. Some theories may not work perfectly, but they will continue to be used as long as they predict better than competing theories.

5. Positive economic analysis attempts to discover how the world works. Normative economic analysis is concerned more with how, in someone's opinion, the world should work.

6. Economic analysis, if not pursued carefully, can result in faulty conclusions. Some common pitfalls are (1) the fallacy that association is causation, the erroneous belief that because events occur together or in a particular sequence they are causally related; (2) the fallacy of composition, which is the faulty belief that what is true for the individual is also true for the group, and (3) ignoring the secondary effects, which results from analysis that focuses only on the immediate effects and fails to consider the secondary effects, which are often more important.

QUESTIONS AND PROBLEMS

1. (Definition of Economics) Recently some economists have conducted controlled experiments on animals. They claim that some animals act according to basic economic theory. That is, the animals act as though they are seeking to satisfy goals subject to the imposition of external constraints. If the researcher changes the constraints, predictable behavioral changes can be observed in such animals. How does such constrained goal seeking conform to the definition of economics given in the text? Are animals different from humans when it comes to economic behavior?

2. (Resources) Determine which category of resources is applicable to each of the following:

   a. taxicab
   b. computer software
   c. one hour of legal counsel
   d. a parking lot
   e. a forest
   f. the Mississippi River
   g. a prison

3. (Goods and Services) Explain why each of the following should *not* be considered a "free lunch" for the economy as a whole:

   a. food stamps
   b. U.S. aid to developing countries
   c. corporate charitable contributions
   d. noncable television programs
   e. high school education

4. (Resources) California, New York, and Michigan have high per-capita incomes, while some other states have low per-capita incomes. Can these differences be explained by scarcity of resources?

5. (Resources and Scarcity) "The only real resource that the human race has is the human mind." This line is often used to counter arguments that society is running out of its scarce resources. Is there truth in the statement? Are the resources of land, labor, and capital being depleted faster than they can be replaced?

6. (Micro Versus Macro) Some economists believe that in order to really understand macroeconomics, one must fully understand microeconomics. How does microeconomics relate to macroeconomics?

7. (Rational Self-Interest) Classical economists maintained that society would be in some sense optimally arranged if individual members of society pursued their own self-interest. Is such a sweeping generalization possible? What about such problems as traffic jams, litter, and runs on banks? Doesn't self-interest need to be taken in the context of the aggregation of individual goals and their feasibility?

8. (Marginal Analysis) A small pizza store must decide if it will increase the radius of its delivery area by an extra mile. What considerations must be taken into account if such a decision is to contribute to profitability?

9. (The Value of Time) Economists often attempt to measure the value of time by using wage rates or average salary levels. If this measure is accurate, then the value of time in growing economies is always rising. How does the growing value of time affect the types of products and services being introduced into the economy? How might this increase in the value of time be related to the widespread use of microwave ovens, video cassette recorders, McDonald's, and automatic tellers at banks?

10. (Pitfalls in Economic Thinking) Using the discussion of pitfalls in economic thinking, identify the fallacy or mistake in thinking in the following statements:

   a. Raising taxes will always increase government revenues.

   b. Whenever there is a recession, imports tend to decrease. Thus, to stop a recession, we should increase imports.

   c. Thriftiness is a sound virtue for the family and for the nation as a whole.

   d. Capitalist economies do well in wartime because war promotes full employment and growing incomes. Hence, an economic boom can lead to conditions favorable to war.

   e. Air bags in automobiles can reduce accidental death from collision. Therefore, air bags in cars make good economic sense.

   f. Gold sells for about $400 per ounce. Therefore, the U.S. government could sell all of the gold in Fort Knox at $400 per ounce and eliminate the national debt.

APPENDIX

Understanding Graphs

Take out a blank piece of paper. Put a point in the middle. That will be the point of departure, called the *origin*. With your pencil at the origin, draw a straight line off to the right; this line is called the *horizontal axis*. Returning to the origin, draw another line up, or north; this line is called the *vertical axis*. The variable *x* often represents the value measured along the horizontal axis, with the value of *x* increasing as you move away from the origin. Similarly, the variable *y* often represents the value measured along the vertical axis, with the value of *y* increasing as you move away from the origin. The basic elements of a graph are presented as Exhibit 1. Within the space framed by the axes, we can plot combinations of the variables under consideration. For example, point *a* represents the combination where *x* equals 10 and *y* equals 5. Point *b* represents 5 units of *x* and 15 units of *y*.

It has been said that a picture is worth a thousand words. Graphs are pictures showing how variables relate. Consider Exhibit 2, which shows the U.S. unemployment rate each year since 1900. As you can see, the year is measured along the

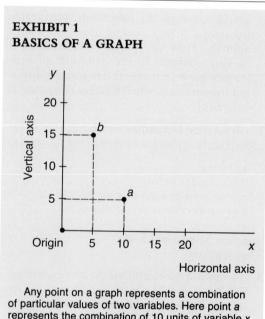

EXHIBIT 1
BASICS OF A GRAPH

Any point on a graph represents a combination of particular values of two variables. Here point *a* represents the combination of 10 units of variable *x* (measured on the horizontal axis) and 5 units of variable *y* (measured on the vertical axis). Point *b* represents 5 units of *x* and 15 units of *y*.

horizontal axis, and the unemployment rate along the vertical axis. Exhibit 2 is a **time-series graph** because it conveys how a variable, in this case the unemployment rate, changes over time.

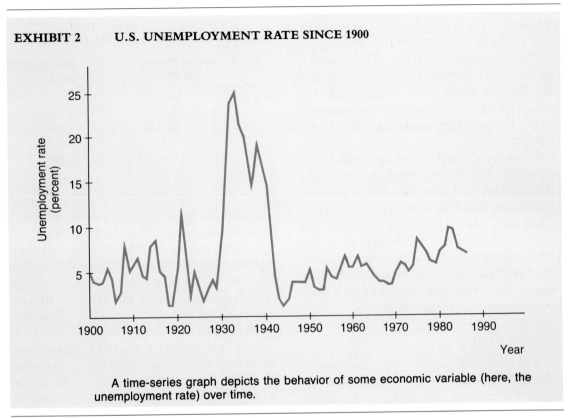

EXHIBIT 2   U.S. UNEMPLOYMENT RATE SINCE 1900

A time-series graph depicts the behavior of some economic variable (here, the unemployment rate) over time.

Source: *Historical Statistics of the United States,* 1970, and *Economic Report of the President, 1987.*

If you had to describe the information presented in Exhibit 2 in words, it would take pages. The picture shows not only how one year compares to the next but also how one decade compares to another and what the trend is over time. The dramatically higher unemployment rate during the Great Depression of the 1930s is unmistakable. Also notice that the average unemployment rate has drifted up since the 1940s. The eye can wander over the hills and valleys to observe patterns that would be hard to express in words. Thus, one role of graphs is to convey information in a compact and efficient way. This appendix shows how to construct and use graphs to express a variety of relationships among variables.

Most of the graphs of interest in this book reflect the relationship between two

economic variables, such as the year and the unemployment rate already discussed, the price of a commodity and the quantity demanded, the cost of production and the quantity produced. Graphs are a way of compressing information. Because we focus on just two variables, we must abstract from other details in the economy. With graphs we therefore sacrifice some richness of detail for clarity of expression.

We often observe that one thing appears to depend on another. The time it takes you to drive home depends on the distance to be traveled. Your weight depends on how much you eat. The amount of Pepsi purchased depends on its price. A functional relationship exists between the two variables when one variable depends on another. The value of the **dependent variable** is determined by the value of the **independent variable**. Your weight, the dependent variable, is determined by how much you eat, the independent variable. This is not to say that other factors, such as exercise and age, do not affect your weight, but we typically focus on the relationship between the two key variables, assuming other factors constant.

Many of the relationships studied in economics can be expressed as functional relationships, with one variable depending on another. The task of the economist is to isolate such relationships and determine the direction of causality. Recall that one of the pitfalls of economic thinking is the erroneous belief that association is causation. Simply because two events are related in time does not mean one causes the other.

Drawing Graphs

We will introduce graphs with a very simple relationship. Suppose you are planning a trip across the country and want to determine how far you will travel each day. You estimate that your average driving speed will be about 50 miles per hour. Possible combinations of driving time and distance traveled are presented as the schedule in Exhibit 3. The first column lists the hours driven per day, and the second column, the number of miles traveled per day. The distance traveled, the dependent variable, depends on the number of hours driven, the independent variable. We identify combinations of hours driven and distance traveled as *a, b, c,* and so on.

We can plot the combinations from Exhibit 3 on a graph (Exhibit 4), with hours driven per day measured along the horizontal axis and total distance traveled along the vertical axis. Each combination of hours driven and distance traveled is represented by a point in Exhibit 4. For example, point *a* shows that when only 1 hour is driven, only 50 miles are traveled. Point *b* indicates that when 2 hours are driven, 100 miles are

EXHIBIT 3
SCHEDULE RELATING DISTANCE TRAVELED TO HOURS DRIVEN

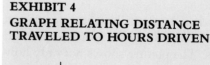

	Hours Driven per Day	Distance Traveled per Day
a	1	50
b	2	100
c	3	150
d	4	200
e	5	250

traveled. By connecting the points, we have a line running upward and to the right.

Three types of relationships between variables can be expressed: (1) as one variable increases, the other increases as well, in which case there is a **positive,** or **direct, relation** between the variables; (2) as one variable increases, the other decreases, in which case there is a **negative,** or **inverse, relation**; and (3) as one variable increases, the other remains the same, in which case the two variables are said to be *independent,* or

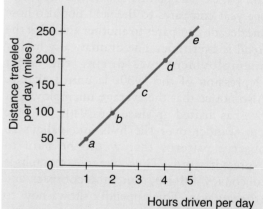

EXHIBIT 4

GRAPH RELATING DISTANCE TRAVELED TO HOURS DRIVEN

Points *a–e* depict different combinations of hours driven per day and the corresponding distances traveled. Connecting these points gives us a graph.

unrelated. The relationship between hours driven and distance traveled is positive, or direct.

An economic relationship can be stated in words, represented as a schedule, or illustrated as a graph. In later chapters we consider demand, a key economic relationship. The demand curve shows the relationship between the quantity of a product demanded and the price of that product. In Exhibit 5 we depict the relationship between the price of Pepsi and the quantity of Pepsi demanded per week. This demand curve is identified simply as *D*.

Economists measure price, the independent variable, along the vertical axis, and quantity demanded, the dependent variable, along the horizontal axis. This arrangement appears odd to mathematicians, who usually put the independent variable on the horizontal axis and the dependent variable on the vertical axis. In another context the cost of production might be the dependent variable and quantity produced the independent variable, so for consistency, economists measure dollar amounts on the vertical axis and quantity on the horizontal axis.

As you can see from Exhibit 5, more Pepsi is demanded at lower prices than at higher prices. There is an inverse, or negative, relationship between price and quantity demanded. Inverse relations are expressed by a downward-sloping curve. One of the advantages of graphs is that they easily convey the relation between variables. We need not examine the particular combinations of numbers; we need only focus on the shape of the curve.

The Slope of Straight Lines

A more precise way to describe the shape of a curve is to measure its slope. The *slope* of a line indicates how much the vertical variable changes for a given increase in the horizontal variable. Specifically, the **slope** between two points on any straight line is the vertical change between those two points divided by the horizontal change, or

$$\text{Slope} = \frac{\text{Change in the vertical distance}}{\text{Change in the horizontal distance}}$$

For short, we refer to the slope as the *rise* over the *run*, where the rise is the vertical change and the run is the horizontal change.

In Exhibit 6 we present four panels, each indicating the vertical change given a 10-unit increase in the horizontal variable. In panel (a) the vertical increases by 5 units when the horizontal distance increases by 10 units. Since the slope is the change in the vertical distance divided by the change in the horizontal distance, the slope of the line in panel (a) is 5/10, or 0.5. Notice that the slope in this case is a positive number because the relationship between the two variables is positive, or direct. This slope indicates that for

EXHIBIT 5
HYPOTHETICAL DEMAND CURVE FOR PEPSI

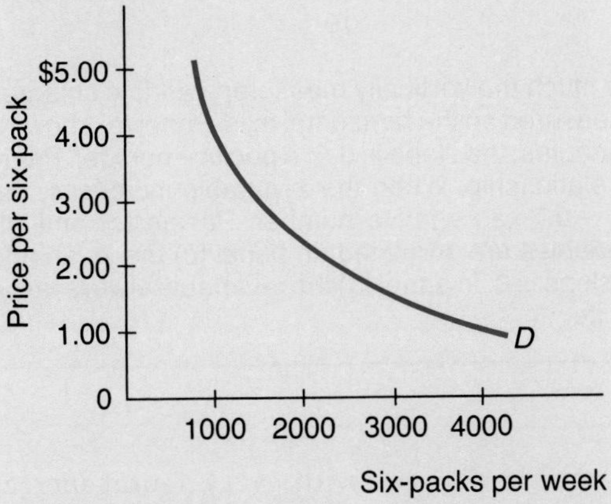

The demand curve shows an inverse, or negative, relationship between price and quantity demanded. The curve slopes downward from left to right, indicating that the quantity demanded increases as the price falls.

EXHIBIT 6   ALTERNATIVE SLOPES FOR STRAIGHT LINES

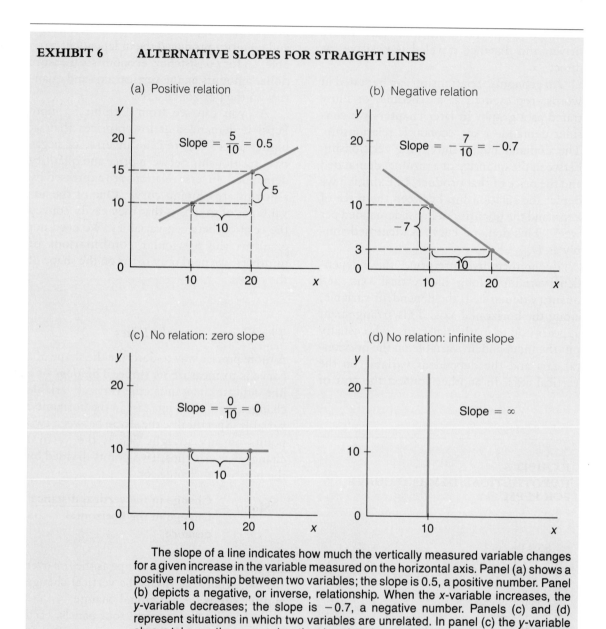

The slope of a line indicates how much the vertically measured variable changes for a given increase in the variable measured on the horizontal axis. Panel (a) shows a positive relationship between two variables; the slope is 0.5, a positive number. Panel (b) depicts a negative, or inverse, relationship. When the x-variable increases, the y-variable decreases; the slope is −0.7, a negative number. Panels (c) and (d) represent situations in which two variables are unrelated. In panel (c) the y-variable always takes on the same value; the slope is 0. In panel (d) the x-variable always takes on the same value; the slope is infinite.

every 1 unit increase in the horizontal variable, the vertical variable increases by 0.5 unit. The slope, incidentally, does not imply causality—the increase in the horizontal variable does not necessarily cause the increase in the vertical variable. The slope simply indicates in a uniform way how much the vertical

variable changes with every 1-unit increase in the horizontal variable.

In panel (b) the vertical declines by 7 units when the horizontal increases by 10 units, so the slope equals −7/10, or −0.7. The slope in this case is a negative number because the two variables have a negative, or inverse, relationship. In panel (c) the vertical remains unchanged as the horizontal increases by 10, so the slope equals 0/10, or 0. These two variables are unrelated.

Finally, in panel (d) the vertical variable can take on any value, though the horizontal variable remains constant. In this case any change in the vertical measure is divided by 0 since the horizontal value remains fixed. Any number divided by 0 is infinitely large, so we say that the slope of a vertical line is infinite. Again, the two variables are unrelated.

The Slope of Curved Lines

The slope of a straight line is the same everywhere along the line, but the slope of a curved line usually varies at every point along the curve. Consider the curve in Exhibit 7. To find the slope of that curved line at a particular point, draw a straight line that just touches the curve at that point but does not cut or cross the curve. Such a line is called a **tangent** to the curve at that point. The slope of the tangent is the slope of the curve at that point.

For example, the line *AA* is drawn tangent to the curve at point *a*. The slope of the curve at that point equals the slope of the tangent *AA*. As the horizontal value increases from 0 to 10, the vertical value drops from 40 to 0. Thus, the vertical change divided by the horizontal change equals −40/10, or −4.0, which is the slope of the line at point *a*.

Alternatively, consider *BB*, a line drawn tangent to the curve at point *b*. The slope of *BB* is the change in the vertical divided by the change in the horizontal, or −10/30, which equals −0.33. The slopes of the curve at these two points are negative because the curve is downward sloping, reflecting a negative, or inverse, relationship between the two variables. As you can see, the curve gets flatter as the horizontal variable increases, so the value of the slope approaches 0.

Other curves, of course, will reflect different slopes as well as different changes in the slope along the curve. Downward-sloping curves have a negative slope, and upward-sloping curves, a positive slope. Sometimes curves are more complex, having both positive and negative ranges. For example, the hill-shaped curve in Exhibit 8(a) shows that for relatively low values of *x*, there is a positive relation between *x* and *y*. As the value of *x* increases, however, its positive relationship with *y* diminishes, eventually becoming negative. We can divide the curve into two segments: (1) the segment between the origin and point *A*, where the slope is positive, and (2) the segment of the curve to the right of point *A*, where the slope is negative. The slope of the curve is 0 at point *A*.

An example of this type of curve could be the relationship between the temperature of a swimming pool and your enjoyment from a swim. Along the horizontal axis could be the water temperature, and along the vertical axis could be some measure of your enjoyment. At very low temperatures swimming is not much fun because the water is so cold. As the temperature increases, your enjoy-

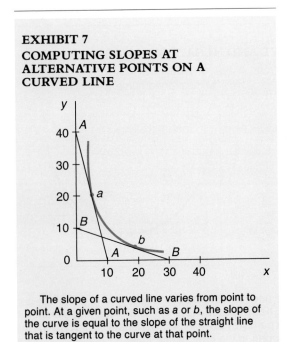

EXHIBIT 7

COMPUTING SLOPES AT ALTERNATIVE POINTS ON A CURVED LINE

The slope of a curved line varies from point to point. At a given point, such as *a* or *b*, the slope of the curve is equal to the slope of the straight line that is tangent to the curve at that point.

ment level increases. At some point, say at 85 degrees, your level of enjoyment reaches a maximum. So the value of *A* equals 85 degrees. At still higher temperatures, the water becomes uncomfortably hot, so your enjoyment level falls.

The opposite relationship is graphed in Exhibit 8(b), where initially *x* and *y* are negatively related until point *B* is reached; thereafter they are positively related. As those of you studying microeconomics will discover, this U-shaped curve is used to depict the relationship between the average cost of production, measured on the vertical axis, and total production, measured on the horizontal axis. (Lines depicting the relationship between variables are often called *curves* in this book even though they sometimes happen to be straight lines. Thus, a demand "curve" often may be drawn as a straight line.)

Of Mice and Lice: The 45-Degree Line from the Origin

As we said earlier, economists tell stories to convey concepts. We close this chapter with a playful account of country mice to illustrate some other graphical relationships. Picture a family of mice living in the belfry of a country church. Because the belfry is unheated and drafty, the temperature inside is always the same as the temperature outside. Thus, when it is 0 degrees outside, it is 0 degrees in the belfry. The outside temperature is the independent variable, and the inside temperature, the dependent variable.

In Exhibit 9 the external temperature is measured along the horizontal axis, and the belfry temperature, along the vertical axis. The relationship between the inside and outside temperatures is shown by the line drawn in Exhibit 9. Since the belfry temperature increases by 1 degree each time the outside temperature increases by 1 degree, the slope of the line is equal to 1.0. The line bisects the angle formed by the two axes so that every point on the line is of equal distance from each axis. More precisely, we say that the line is a ray drawn from the origin, forming a 45-degree angle with the horizontal axis. (By the way, the degrees measuring an angle have nothing to do with the temperature degrees

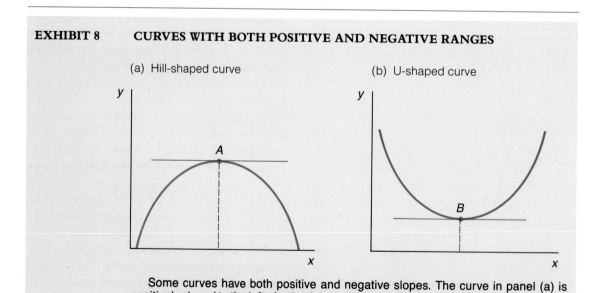

EXHIBIT 8   CURVES WITH BOTH POSITIVE AND NEGATIVE RANGES

(a) Hill-shaped curve   (b) U-shaped curve

Some curves have both positive and negative slopes. The curve in panel (a) is positively sloped to the left of point *A*, has a 0 slope at point *A*, and is negatively sloped to the right of that point. The curve in panel (b) starts off with a negative slope, has a 0 slope at point *B*, and is positively sloped to the right of that point.

EXHIBIT 9
THE 45-DEGREE LINE FROM ORIGIN

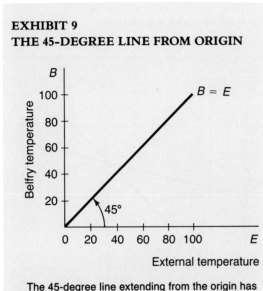

The 45-degree line extending from the origin has a slope equal to 1. At each point along the line, the value of what is measured on the horizontal axis (here, external temperature) is equal to the value measured on the vertical axis (the internal temperature of the belfry).

in our example.) Many straight lines can be drawn from the origin, but only a 45-degree line exactly bisects the 90-degree angle formed by the two axes. Expressing this line as an equation, we have $B = E$, where B equals the belfry temperature and E the external temperature.

Although the church belfry is unheated, the main hall of the church is heated in winter and cooled in summer. While the parishioners might prefer to maintain the temperature of the hall at 72 degrees all year round, keeping such a constant temperature in this drafty building costs more than the parish can afford. Consequently, the temperature in the church hall varies, depending on the external temperature, as shown by the upward-sloping line in Exhibit 10(a). As you can see, even when it is 0 degrees outside, it is still 54 degrees in the church hall. As the outside temperature gets warmer, the inside temperature increases too, but not by as much. Specifically, each 4-degree increase in

the external temperature raises the inside temperature by 1 degree.

Recall that the slope of any straight line is the rise over the run—that is, the change in the vertical distance divided by the change in the horizontal distance. Thus, the slope of this temperature function equals 1 divided by 4, or .25. This line can be expressed algebraically as

$$H = 54 + .25E$$

where H represents the temperature in the church hall and E the external temperature. Notice again that when E is 0, H equals 54 degrees. When E equals 100, H equals 54 plus 25, or 79.

In Exhibit 10(b) we again present the temperature function for the church hall, but to add perspective we also sketch in a 45-degree line indicating all points at which the external temperature equals the temperature in the church hall. Notice that the temperature function for the church hall intersects the 45-degree line at 72 degrees. When the outside temperature is less than 72 degrees, the heat is on in the church hall. When the outside temperature is above 72 degrees, air conditioning keeps the hall from heating up as fast as the outside temperature. When it is exactly 72 degrees outside, neither heating nor cooling is required.

The 45-degree line is a useful reference line when the same units are measured along both the horizontal and vertical axes. The intersection between the 45-degree line and another functional relationship identifies any instances where the horizontal and vertical variables are equal. The 45-degree line is especially useful in macroeconomics.

To finish the story, why haven't the mice migrated south to the balmy church hall? Because of the cat—a restless cat that patrols the hall, ever vigilant to the stirrings of creatures, especially mice. Why is the cat so restless? Because of the fleas, which live in the cat's thick fur. The fleas' environment is maintained by the cat's body heat at a con-

EXHIBIT 10   USING THE 45-DEGREE RAY AS A REFERENCE LINE

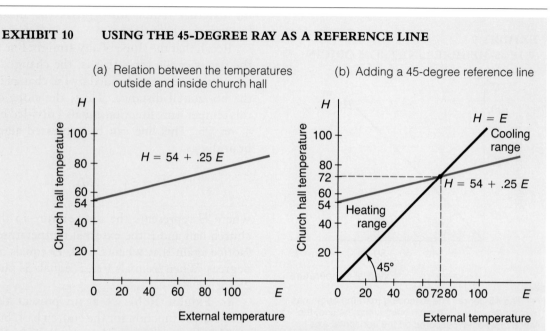

(a) Relation between the temperatures outside and inside church hall

(b) Adding a 45-degree reference line

Panel (a) is a graph showing the relationship between external temperature and the church hall temperature. When the external temperature (*E*) is 0, the hall temperature is 54 degrees. For each 4-degree increase in external temperature, the hall temperature increases by 1 degree. The slope of the line is 0.25.

Panel (b) introduces a 45-degree line showing all points at which external temperature and hall temperature are equal. The two lines intersect at an external temperature of 72 degress. At external temperatures below 72 degrees, the hall temperature exceeds the external temperature; the heating system is operating. At external temperatures above 72 degrees, external temperature exceeds hall temperature; the air conditioning is on.

stant 101.8 degrees, regardless of the temperature outside. The fleas never eat out. The relationship between the temperature on the cat's back and the external temperature is a horizontal line drawn at 101.8 degrees, as shown in Exhibit 11. We can express the relationship as simply *C* = 101.8, where *C* equals the temperature in the cat's fur. Thus, the temperature in the snug little world of the fleas is independent of the outside temperature.

**EXHIBIT 11
TEMPERATURE IN THE CAT'S FUR**

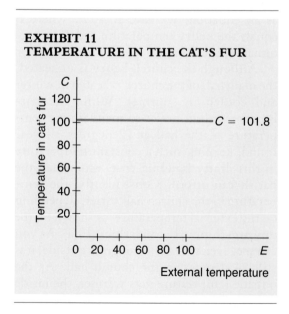

SOME TOOLS of ECONOMIC ANALYSIS

The first chapter gave you some idea of how to think like an economist. You learned that economists examine the choices that arise from scarcity. These choices are guided by rational self-interest and require both time and information. The first chapter also told you why choice is necessary, but it said little about how to analyze economic choices. In this chapter we develop the framework with which to explore economic choices—choices about what goods and services are produced, how they are produced, and for whom they are produced. Topics and terms discussed in this chapter include

- Opportunity cost
- Production possibilities frontier
- Specialization
- Comparative advantage
- Division of labor
- Economic systems

OPPORTUNITY COST AND CHOICE

The Sultan of Brunei recently moved into his new home. If uninvited guests arrive for dinner, the sultan should be able to find an extra place at the table— his new home seats forty-three hundred for dinner. If some guests need to spend the night, the sultan should be able to put them up—the place has more than a thousand rooms. For a friendly polo match the sultan has two hundred ponies from which to choose, and for a drive in the country he can choose from among his forty cars—perhaps the Aston-Martin or the Maserati will do. Several thousand members of his personal staff attend to the sultan's every need.

Opportunity Cost in a Land of Plenty

Brunei, you see, is a small, oil-rich country in the South Pacific, and the sultan's home is, in fact, a palace built at a cost of a half billion dollars and said to be the most lavish in the world. The billions of dollars in oil revenues that flow into this tiny country each year provide the sultan with a grand standard of living.

Surrounded by such opulence, the sultan would appear to have resolved the economic problem caused by scarce resources but unlimited wants. Money appears to be no object. Even if the sultan can buy whatever he wants, however, he, like the 5 billion other people in the world, has limited *time* in which to enjoy these goods and services. Consequently, the sultan, like the rest of us, must choose from among the competing uses of his scarcest resource, time.

Opportunity cost is the benefit expected from the best alternative forgone.

If he pursues one activity, he cannot at the same time do anything else. Each activity he undertakes has an opportunity cost. The **opportunity cost** is the benefit expected from the best alternative that is forgone. If the sultan chooses to play polo over his next most preferred alternative, a drive through the country in his Maserati, the opportunity cost of playing polo is the forgone benefit expected from a drive through the country.

Everybody faces scarcity to a greater or lesser extent. The sultan's scarcest resource is time, so he, like the rest of us, must choose among alternative uses of his time. This choice involves an opportunity cost because other desirable activities must be forgone to pursue the preferred choice.

Your Opportunity Cost

Every choice involves an opportunity cost. What is the cost to you of reading this book right now? It is the expected benefit you sacrificed by not spending this time on your next most preferred alternative. You could have been studying for another course, sleeping, watching TV, jogging, or whatever. Opportunity cost reflects the benefit you gave up to select the most preferred choice.

The opportunity cost of attending a football game is more than the five dollars you paid for the ticket; it includes the three hours away from your next most preferred choice. Opportunity cost includes the most attractive alternative you had to pass up. How many times have you heard someone say they did something because they "had nothing better to do"? The suggestion was that they actually had few alternatives, so they were sacrificing very little to undertake the chosen activity. But according to the idea of opportunity cost, it is always the case that we do what we do because we have nothing better to do. The choice selected at the time seemed preferable to all other possible choices. You are attending college now because you have nothing better to do. Simply put, college appeared more attractive than your next best alternative. Consider the opportunity of attending college in the following case study.

CASE STUDY

The Opportunity Cost of College

In the movie classic *Animal House*, Bluto, after hearing the news that he just flunked out of college, wailed, "Seven years of college down the drain!" College had indeed become a costly proposition for him. What is your cost per year of attending college full-time—that is, what is your opportunity cost?

What was the next best alternative you gave up by coming to college? It was probably a full-time job. Based on the experience of others who took jobs right out of high school, you likely had some notion of what your prospects for employment were. Suppose you expected to land a job paying $15,000 a year. As a college student, you are still able to work in the summer and earn $4,000. Thus, each year you are giving up a net of $11,000 ($15,000 − $4,000) in forgone earnings to attend college.

There is also the direct cost of college itself. Suppose it costs you $10,000 per year for tuition, fees, and books. This income is therefore unavailable to you (or your family) to spend on other things. Hence, the opportunity cost of paying for tuition, fees, and books is the forgone benefit you expected from the goods and services that money could have purchased. Another expense, the cost of room and board, must be handled more carefully because even if you had not gone to college, you would still have to live somewhere and eat something. In fact, you or your family would likely have incurred many expenses even if you had not gone to college, including outlays for entertainment, clothes, and laundry.

Since many outlays would have been made anyway, their cost does not represent an opportunity cost of attending college. In a sense, they are the upkeep costs that arise regardless of what you are doing. For simplicity, let's assume that these outlays are the same whether you attend college or not, so we can forget them. Thus, the net forgone earnings of $11,000 per year plus the $10,000 per year direct costs yield an opportunity cost of attending college of $21,000 per year.

The preceding analysis assumes that other things are constant. If in your view attending college is "more of a pain" than you expected the next best alternative to be, the opportunity cost of attending college is even higher. That is, if you are one of those people who find college difficult, often boring, and in most ways more unpleasant than a full-time job right out of high school would have been, then the cost in money terms understates your full opportunity cost. Not only are you incurring the added expense of college but you are also forgoing a more pleasant quality of life. If, on the contrary, you think the wild and crazy life of a college student on balance is more enjoyable than a job, then $21,000 per year overstates your true opportunity cost because the next best alternative involves a less satisfying quality of life.

Note that this analysis of opportunity cost focuses primarily on the forgone value of your next best alternative; the analysis ignores the benefits you expect to derive from a college education. Obviously, you view college as a good investment in your future even though it is costly and, for some, even painful. For you, the net benefits expected from college exceed those expected from the next best alternative, and that is why you as a rational decision maker chose the college option.

Opportunity Cost Is Subjective

Opportunity cost is a subjective notion. Only the individual chooser can estimate the expected value of the next best alternative. In fact, we can seldom truly know the actual value of the forgone alternative because by definition that alternative is passed over in favor of the most preferred choice. Thus, if you gave up an evening of pizza and conversation with friends to work on an English paper, you will never know the exact value of what you gave up. You know only what you expected. Evidently, you considered the overall benefit of working on your term paper to be greater than your next best alternative. Incidentally, one advantage of focusing exclusively on the next best alternative is that all other alternatives become irrelevant.

Calculating Opportunity Cost Requires Time and Information
Economists do not argue that individuals, when making choices, exhaustively calculate costs and benefits for all the possible alternatives. They claim only that people, in employing their scarce resources, rationally choose the alternative that promises the highest expected net benefit. Since information about alternatives is often costly to acquire, people usually make choices based on limited or even wrong information about their opportunity costs. Indeed, some choices may turn out to be poor ones (for example, you went on a picnic and it rained; the movie you selected was a bore). At the time you made the choice, however, you thought you were making the best use of all your scarce resources, including the time required to gather information about your alternatives.

Opportunity Cost May Vary with Time and Circumstance   Since opportunity cost depends on the alternatives, the opportunity cost of consuming a particular good or undertaking a certain activity will vary with time and circumstance. This is why you are less likely to study on a Saturday night than on a Wednesday night. On a Saturday night the opportunity cost of studying is greater because you have more alternative activities, and usually the expected benefit of at least one of these alternatives exceeds the expected benefit from studying. Suppose you decide on the movies for Saturday night. The opportunity cost of going to the movies may not be the expected benefit from studying because the next most preferred alternative might be attending a basketball game. For some of you, studying on Saturday night may be well down the list of preferred alternatives — perhaps ahead of reorganizing your closet but behind watching trucks being unloaded at the supermarket.

Although the idea of opportunity cost is subjective, in some circumstances money paid for goods and services becomes a reasonably good approximation of the opportunity cost of their consumption. But, as we have noted, the money cost definition may leave out some important elements, particularly the time involved. A trip to the movies costs more than the five-dollar price of the ticket; it involves the time and gasoline required to get there and back, plus the two hours it takes to watch the movie.

The idea of opportunity cost underscores what you must give up each time choices are made under conditions of scarcity. Just as resources are scarce for the individual, they are scarce for the economy as a whole. In the next section we develop a tool to explore opportunity cost for the economy.

THE ECONOMY'S PRODUCTION POSSIBILITIES

The economy has millions of different resources, which can be combined in all kinds of ways to produce millions of possible goods and services. In this section we consider a useful tool economists employ to examine the economy's production possibilities. To reduce the analysis to manageable proportions, we limit the output of the economy to just two products, food and education. We assume that the amount of resources available in the economy is fixed during the period under consideration—there is only so much labor, so much land, so much capital, and so much entrepreneurial ability. These resources combine in a variety of ways to produce food and education. We also assume that society's knowledge about how these resources can be combined to produce output—that is, society's available *technology*—remains fixed during the time period under consideration.

Efficiency and the Production Possibilities Frontier

The **production possibilities frontier** *is a curve showing all combinations of goods that can be produced when available resources are fully and efficiently utilized.*

Efficiency *is the situation attained when there is no way resources can be reallocated to increase the production of one good without decreasing the production of another.*

Given the resources and the technology available in the economy, the **production possibilities frontier**, or **PPF**, reveals the various possible combinations of the two goods that can be produced when the resources are being used efficiently. Resources are used **efficiently** when no change in the way resources are combined could increase the production of one good without decreasing the production of the other good.

The economy's PPF for producing food and education is shown by the curve FE in Exhibit 1, where F represents the amount of food produced per year if all the economy's resources are used efficiently to produce food, and E represents the amount of education produced per year if all the economy's resources are used efficiently to produce education. Points along the curve between F and E represent the possible combinations of food and education that can be produced when the economy's resources are efficiently used to produce both goods. Points inside the PPF, such as J, represent combinations of food and education that do not employ resources fully or employ them inefficiently, while points outside the PPF, such as K, represent unattainable combinations of food and education given the resources and the technology available.

EXHIBIT 1   THE ECONOMY'S PRODUCTION POSSIBILITIES FRONTIER

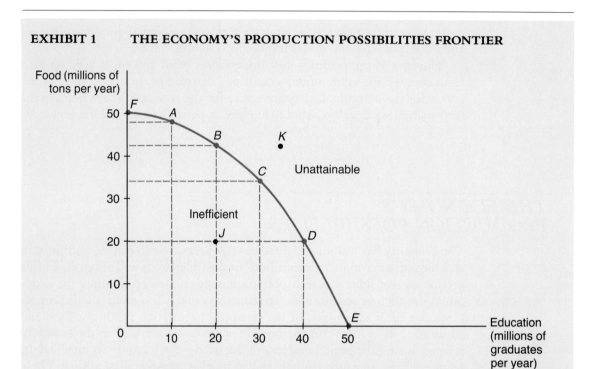

If the economy uses its available resources and technology efficiently in producing food and education, its production possibilities frontier is shown by the curve *FE*. The frontier is bowed out to illustrate the law of increasing opportunity cost: additional units of education require the economy to sacrifice more and more units of food. Note that more food must be given up in moving from *D* to *E* than in moving from *F* to *A*, though in each case the gain in education is 10 million graduates.

Points inside the frontier, such as *J*, represent inefficient use of resources. Points above and to the right of the frontier, such as *K*, represent unattainable combinations.

Notice that if you start from any point inside the PPF, such as *J*, it is always possible to increase the production of one of the goods without reducing the production of the other good. For example, from point *J* it is possible, by combining resources more efficiently, to move to *B* and produce more food without reducing the amount of education. Thus, the economy can increase the production of food by 22 million tons without reducing the amount of education produced. Alternatively, it is possible by using resources more efficiently to move from *J* to *D* and thereby increase the amount of education produced without reducing the production of food. Indeed, as you can see, it is possible to move from point *J* to any point between *B* and *D* along the PPF, such as *C,* and thereby increase the production of both food and education. Efficiency involves getting the maximum possible output from available resources.

The Shape of the Production Possibilities Frontier

Notice that any movement along the PPF involves giving up one good to get more of the other. Movements down the curve indicate that the opportunity cost of more education is less food. The PPF in Exhibit 1 is curved out like a bow. As we shall see, this bow shape indicates that resources in the economy are not all perfectly adaptable to the production of both food and education.

Although all resources are being used efficiently at point *F,* given that the objective is to produce only food, certain resources contribute little to the production of food. Some economics professors would make terrible farmers; school buildings are not easily adaptable to the production of food; some equipment used in laboratory classes is of virtually no use in the production of food. In moving from point *F* to point *A*, graduates per year increase from 0 to 10 million, but food production falls by only 2 million tons, from 50 million to 48 million tons. Thus, increasing the graduates per year from 0 (point *F*) to 10 million (point *A*) causes food production to fall very little because it draws upon those resources that add very little to food output but are quite productive in education.

The opportunity cost of more education is the food forgone. Moving down the PPF, you can see that producing additional units of education requires an increasing opportunity cost measured in terms of sacrificed food production. As the production of education increases, larger and larger amounts of food must be sacrificed because as more education is produced, the resources drawn away from food are those that are more and more important in food production.

As shown by the dashed lines in Exhibit 1, each additional 10 million graduates reduces food production by more and more. In other words, the opportunity cost of education increases as more education is produced, reflecting the **law of increasing opportunity cost**. The law of increasing opportunity cost states that as more of a particular commodity is produced, the greater the opportunity cost is of these additional units. The PPF derives its bowed shape from the law of increasing opportunity cost. For example, whereas the first 10 million college graduates have an opportunity cost of only 2 million tons of food, the final 10 million—that is, the movement from point *D* to point *E*—have an opportunity cost of 20 million tons of food.

The law of increasing opportunity cost also applies in the movement from the production of education to the production of food. When all resources in society are concentrated on education, as at point *E*, certain resources, such as tractors and cows, make little contribution to education. In fact, the cows foul the sidewalks and hallways if they are allowed to hang around the schools. Thus, in shifting resources into the production of food, little education must be surrendered initially. As more food is produced, however, resources having greater value in the production of education must be used, reflecting the law of increasing opportunity cost. Incidentally, if resources were perfectly adaptable to alternative uses, the PPF would be a straight line, reflecting a constant opportunity cost as we moved along the PPF.

*The **law of increasing opportunity cost** states that as more of a particular good is produced, the opportunity cost of production rises.*

Shifts in the Production Possibilities Frontier

When we construct the production possibilities frontier, we assume that the resources available in the economy and the level of technology are constant. Over time, however, the PPF may shift as a result of a change in resource availability or because of some technological breakthrough.

Changes in Resource Availability For example, if individuals in the economy decided to work longer hours, this decision would shift the PPF out so that more of both goods could be produced, as depicted in Exhibit 2(a). An increase in the size of the labor force, an increase in the skills of the labor force, or an increase in the availability of other resources would also shift out the PPF. In contrast, a decrease in the availability or the quality of resources would shift the PPF inward, as depicted in panel (b).

Effects of Technological Change Another type of change that could cause the economy's PPF to shift out is some technological discovery that combines available resources more efficiently. The effect of a technological breakthrough in the production of food, such as a more bug-resistant strain of some crop, is demonstrated in Exhibit 2(c). As you can see, such a development primarily increases the production of food. Exhibit 2(d) shows the result of a technological breakthrough in the production of education, such as the development of a computer program for self-instruction. Some discoveries could enhance production for both products, such as a managerial innovation designed to control the use of resources more efficiently. Break-throughs that improve the efficiency of resources in producing both products are reflected by the outward shift of the PPF in Exhibit 2(a).

What We Can Learn from the PPF The production possibilities frontier demonstrates several concepts introduced thus far. The first is scarcity: the economy can produce only so much. The PPF describes what combinations of output are possible given the resources and technology available. Some combinations are impossible unless more resources become available or better technology is developed. Because the PPF is downward sloping, the more that is produced of one good, the less can be produced of the other good. This tradeoff demonstrates the concept of opportunity cost. The bowed-out shape of the PPF reflects the law of increasing opportunity cost, which arises because not all resources are perfectly adaptable to the production of different goods. Individuals in the economy must somehow choose the combination along the PPF to be produced, so the PPF also underscores the problem of choice. The way individuals select the combination will depend on the decision-making rules operating in the economy. Later in this chapter we will consider some alternative decision-making rules that have developed in different economic systems, but first we must learn more about production and efficiency.

EXHIBIT 2 **SHIFTS IN THE ECONOMY'S PRODUCTION POSSIBILITIES FRONTIER**

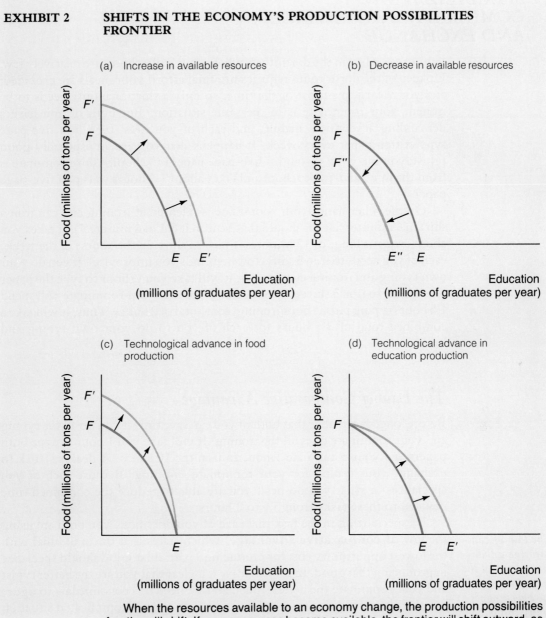

When the resources available to an economy change, the production possibilities frontier will shift. If more resources become available, the frontier will shift outward, as in panel (a), indicating that more output can be produced. A decrease in available resources will cause the frontier to shift inward, as in panel (b). Technological changes can also shift the frontier. Panel (c) shows a technological improvement in food production. More food can now be produced for any given level of education. Panel (d) shows a technological advance in the production of education.

SPECIALIZATION, COMPARATIVE ADVANTAGE, AND EXCHANGE

Suppose you live in the dormitory, where your daily chores are relatively few. Upkeep of the dorm room requires minimal effort; your meals are provided; and you wear jeans most of the time, so only a shirt or blouse needs to be ironed. Your roommate is in the same situation. But both of you have a demanding academic schedule, and each of you must turn in a five-page typewritten paper every week. It happens that you are an especially good typist; you can whip through a five-page paper in ½ hour. Your roommate is from the hunt-and-peck school and takes about 1½ hours to type a five-page paper.

On the other hand, your roommate is talented at ironing and can iron a shirt in 6 minutes flat (or should that be iron it flat in 6 minutes?). It takes you about twice as long, or 12 minutes, to iron a shirt. In the course of the week, each of you needs to iron 5 shirts (on weekends you improvise). If you do your own typing and ironing every week, it will take you ½ hour to type the paper plus 1 hour to iron 5 shirts, for a total of 1½ hours. Your roommate will spend 1½ hours typing plus ½ hour ironing, for a total of 2 hours. Thus, it will take a combined total of 3½ hours for each of you to do your own typing and ironing.

The Law of Comparative Advantage

Before long, you realize that both of you can save time if you do all the typing and your roommate does all the ironing. It will take you 1 hour to type both papers and your roommate 1 hour to iron the 10 shirts. A deal is struck to exchange your typing for your roommate's ironing. Because each of you specializes in what you do best, you are able to reduce the combined time devoted to these tasks from 3½ to 2 hours.

The law of comparative advantage says that the individual with the lowest opportunity cost of producing a particular good should specialize in producing that good.

By specializing in the task that each of you does best, you both are using the **law of comparative advantage**, which states that the individual with the lowest opportunity cost for producing a particular good should specialize in producing that good. In this example it is clear that you are the better typist and your roommate the better ironer, and we need no economic law to figure out that there are gains from specialization. In a more complicated situation the law of comparative advantage is not quite so obvious, yet there are surprising gains from specialization, as we shall now see.

Absolute and Comparative Advantage

The gains from specialization and exchange in the example above are intuitively obvious. Perhaps a more interesting case arises if we change the example so that you are not only a faster typist than your roommate but also a faster ironer. Suppose you can still type the five-page paper in ½ hour, compared to your roommate's 1½ hours, but now it takes your roommate 15 minutes to iron a shirt, compared to 12 minutes a shirt for you. In this case you have an **absolute advantage** in performing both tasks because you can do each task in less time than can your roommate. More generally, having an absolute advantage means having the ability to produce the output with fewer resources than other producers use.

***Absolute advantage** is the ability to produce something with fewer resources than other producers use.*

Does your absolute advantage in both activities mean specialization is no longer a good idea? Recall that the law of comparative advantage states that the individual with the lower opportunity cost for producing a particular good should specialize in producing that good. In the time it would take you to type your paper, you could iron 2½ shirts, so the opportunity cost to you of typing a paper is not ironing 2½ shirts. Your roommate, however, though slower at both tasks, could iron 6 shirts in the time taken to type a paper. Therefore, your roommate's opportunity cost of typing the paper is not ironing 6 shirts. Since your opportunity cost of typing the paper is only 2½ shirts, compared to 6 shirts for your roommate, you have the lower opportunity cost for typing. Thus, you should do all the typing, and your roommate, all the ironing.

***Comparative advantage** is the ability to produce something at a lower opportunity cost than other producers face.*

Although you have an absolute advantage in both tasks, your **comparative advantage** calls for specializing in the task in which you have the lower opportunity cost—in this case, typing. If you each typed your own papers and ironed your own shirts, it would take you 1½ hours and your roommate 2¾ hours to complete the tasks. Alternatively, if you each specialize according to the law of comparative advantage, you would take only 1 hour to type the 2 papers and your roommate would take only 2½ hours to iron the 10 shirts. Thus, specialization in this case saves each of you time: you, ½ hour, and your roommate, 15 minutes. Exhibit 3 summarizes the example. Even though you are better at both tasks than your roommate, you are comparatively better at typing. Put another way, your roommate, although worse at both tasks, is not quite as poor at ironing as at typing.

Don't think this is simply just common sense, because it is not. Common sense would lead you to do your own ironing and typing since you are more skilled at both tasks than your roommate. Spend a little time reviewing Exhibit 3. Try approaching the problem in terms of the opportunity cost of ironing, working it through until you are satisfied that the outcome is the same.

The law of comparative advantage applies not only to individuals but also to firms, to regions of the country, and to countries. Those individuals, firms, regions, or countries with the lowest opportunity cost for producing a particular good should specialize in producing that good. Because of such factors as geography, climate, availability of natural resources, and the education of the work force, certain parts of the country or certain parts of the world have a comparative advantage in producing particular goods. From computers in California's "Silicon Valley" to citrus products in Florida—from Apples to oranges—resources are used most efficiently when production and trade conform to the law of comparative advantage.

EXHIBIT 3
COMPARATIVE ADVANTAGE: MINIMIZING THE TIME
SPENT TYPING AND IRONING

CASE 1: You are a faster typist, and your roommate, a faster ironer.

	Hours Spent on Each Task					
	Each Does Own			**Each Specializes**		
	Type	Iron	Total	Type	Iron	Total
You	½	1	1½	1	0	1
Roommate	1½	½	2	0	1	1
	2	1½	3½	1	1	2

CASE 2: You are a faster typist and a faster ironer, but you are a comparatively faster typist.

	Hours Spent on Each Task					
	Each Does Own			**Each Specializes**		
	Type	Iron	Total	Type	Iron	Total
You	½	1	1½	1	0	1
Roommate	1½	1¼	2¾	0	2½	2½
	2	2¼	4¼	1	2½	3½

Cases 1 and 2 both show gains from specialization and exchange for you and your roommate. Each of you needs to iron 5 shirts and type a five-page paper each week. In both cases it takes you ½ hour to type the paper and 12 minutes to iron 1 shirt, or 1 hour in all to iron 5 shirts. In both cases your roommate takes 1½ hours to type the paper. But whereas in Case 1 it takes your roommate only 6 minutes to iron a shirt, or ½ hour for 5 shirts, in Case 2 it takes 15 minutes, or 1¼ hours for 5 shirts.

In Case 1 you have an absolute advantage and a comparative advantage in typing, and the time spent on these tasks is minimized if you do all the typing and your roommate does all the ironing. In Case 2 you have an absolute advantage in both typing and ironing because you are a faster typist and a faster ironer than your roommate. But you have a comparative advantage only in typing because you have a lower opportunity cost for typing than does your roommate. The opportunity cost of typing is measured in terms of shirts not ironed.

Specialization and Exchange

Barter is the exchange of one good for another without the use of money.

In the previous example you specialized in typing and your roommate in ironing, and you each exchanged your product. No money changed hands. In other words, you engaged in barter. **Barter** is a system of exchange in which products are exchanged for other products. Barter works satisfactorily in very simple economies, where there is little specialization and few different goods to trade, but for economies with greater specialization, *money* plays an important role in facilitating exchange. Money serves as a *medium of exchange* because it is the one thing that everyone is willing to accept in return for all goods and services.

Without money, specialization and exchange would have to rely on a great deal of luck. For example, suppose you make French pastry and I make braided rugs. I decide I want some French pastry. If you happen to want a braided rug, we could perhaps strike a deal, but this would be sheer coincidence. If instead you want a new sweater, then I would have to find a sweater maker who wants a braided rug. If I am fortunate enough to make such a connection, I may be able to trade the sweater to you for the rug. But what if the sweater is the wrong size or color?

Barter exchange is time-consuming and complicated. If, however, money is used as the medium of exchange, I can exchange my braided rugs for money, then use the money to buy the pastry. Money makes the exchange much simpler and involves no coincidence.

Because of specialization and comparative advantage, most people consume little of what they produce and produce little of what they consume. People specialize in particular activities and exchange their products for money, which, in turn, is exchanged for goods produced by others. Thus, people sell their specialized products in one market and buy the products of others in another market. Did you make a single article of clothing you are now wearing? Probably not. Consider the degree of specialization that went into your cotton shirt or blouse. Some farmer in a warm climate grew the cotton and sold it to someone who spun it into thread, who sold it to someone who wove it into fabric, who sold it to someone who made the shirt, who sold it to a wholesaler, who sold it to a retailer, who sold it to you. Your shirt or blouse probably went through more than half a dozen specialists on its way to you.

Division of Labor and Gains from Specialization

Think about your last trip to McDonald's: "Let's see, I'll have a Big Mac, an order of fries, and a chocolate shake." About 30 seconds later your order was ready. In contrast, consider how long it would take you to fix the same meal yourself. Preparing a homemade version of the Big Mac with all its special ingredients (two all-beef patties, special sauce, lettuce, cheese, pickles, and onions on a sesame-seed bun) would take at least 15 minutes. Peeling, slicing, and frying the potatoes would take another 15 minutes. With the ice cream on hand, you should be able to make the shake in 5 minutes. If you add in the time it takes to buy the ingredients and to clean up afterward, meal preparations would take you at least 1 hour.

*The **division of labor** is the organization of production into tasks in which people specialize.*

Why is the McDonald's meal faster, cheaper, and for some people better than one you could make yourself? Why is fast food so fast? The manager of McDonald's is taking advantage of the gains resulting from the **division of labor**. Rather than have each worker prepare an entire individual meal, McDonald's has separated the meal into various tasks and has assigned individuals to these separate tasks. This division of labor results in greater specialization of labor and allows the group to produce much more than they could have if each person had tried to do it all. Instead of having 20 employees

Adam Smith
(1723–1790)

The Bettmann Archive, Inc.

Britain in the eighteenth century was at the forefront of industrialization, but by modern standards it was still very much a developing country. It is not surprising, then, that economic thought of the time was concerned centrally with economic growth. What constitutes national wealth? Where does it come from? What can we do to get more of it? In 1776 a bookish professor of moral philosophy from Scotland answered these questions in a way that was to have a lasting effect on the way we think about economics.

Adam Smith was born in the village of Kirkcaldy, near Edinburgh. After studying at Oxford University—largely without the assistance of professors—he returned to Scotland to begin a teaching career. Smith the man was awkward and absentminded, a kind of eighteenth century nerd. But no one doubted his brilliance, and he quickly rose to prominence within the important intellectual movement now known as the Scottish Enlightenment. After publishing a well-received book on moral philosophy in 1759, Smith turned his attention to political economy. The result was a rich and scholarly treatise called *The Wealth of Nations.*

National wealth, said Smith, is not gained by amassing money at the expense of other countries. True wealth lies in the country's productive capacity, especially in the skill and ability of its workers. To increase wealth, a country must increase productive capacity, or efficiency. And, for Smith, the most potent source of increased efficiency was specialization, what he called the division of labor. The subdivision of tasks saves time, increases the level of skill, and leads to innovation. The result is "that universal opulence which extends itself to the lowest ranks of the people"—new and cheaper products and a higher standard of living for all.

How can a country secure this kind of productivity growth? Smith's answer was truly a radical one. Rather than attempting to control resources and guide investment, a country should instead rely on a set of institutions Smith called "the system of natural liberty"—what is now sometimes called *laissez faire.* By this he meant a system of rights and laws that would harness individual self-interest and allow people to take the best advantage of their localized skills and knowledge. Smith's famous metaphor leaves a vivid image: the decentralized market system allocates resources as if by an invisible hand.

Richard Langlois

make 20 complete meals in an hour by each doing it all, the 20 employees specialize and produce more than 200 meals per hour.

How is this tenfold increase in productivity possible? First, the manager can assign tasks according to individual preferences and abilities. The employee with the toothy smile and pleasant personality can handle the customers up front, while the employee with a strong back but few social graces can handle the fifty-pound sacks of potatoes out back. Second, as each individual performs the same task more and more, he or she gets better at it. Experience is a good teacher. The employee operating the cash register, for example, can better handle the special problems that arise in dealing with customers. Third, there is no lost time in moving from one task to another.

Specialization occurs when individuals confine their work to the production of a single good or service.

Finally, and perhaps most importantly, the **specialization** of labor allows for the introduction of more sophisticated production techniques, which would not make economic sense on a smaller scale. For example, McDonald's does not prepare each milkshake separately but rather mixes ingredients in a machine that shakes gallons at a time. Such machines would be impractical in the home. The specialization of labor allows for the introduction of specialized machines, and these machines make each worker more productive.

Thus, more is produced when workers specialize according to the law of comparative advantage. Specialization of labor takes advantage of individual preferences and natural abilities, allows workers to develop more experience at a particular task, reduces the time required to shift between different tasks, and allows for the introduction of labor-saving machinery.

In closing, we should note that specialization can create problems since doing the same thing eight hours a day often becomes tedious. Consider, for example, the assembly line worker whose task is to tighten a particular bolt on the cars as they pass by. Such a job could drive you crazy. Thus, the gains from breaking production down into individual tasks must be weighed against the problem of assigning workers to repetitive and tedious jobs.

THREE ECONOMIC QUESTIONS: WHAT, HOW, AND FOR WHOM?

The focus to this point has been on how individuals choose to use their scarce resources in attempting to satisfy their unlimited wants—more specifically, how they specialize their activities in accord with the law of comparative advantage. This emphasis on the individual has been appropriate because the world of economics is driven by the choices of individual decision makers, whether they are consumers, producers, or politicians.

To make sense of economic reality, however, we must observe how these individual choices tie into the entire economic system. Later in this chapter we will explore how the decision-making structure in the economy can differ from country to country, but for now we should realize that regardless of the economic structure, all economies must, through their decision-making processes, answer three fundamental questions.

What Will Be Produced and in What Quantities?

As you observe the economy around you, you take for granted the incredible number of choices that go into deciding what gets produced. For example, of the thousands of potential rock stars, which ones will make albums, and how many albums will be produced? Which fruits will be grown? Which new kitchen appliances will be introduced? Which new roads will be built?

An economic system has to determine the level and composition of society's output, and thus the system must resolve the preceding questions along with millions of other questions. Although different economies resolve these questions using different decision-making rules and mechanisms, all economies must make these decisions when confronting scarce resources.

How Will Goods Be Produced?

The economic system or, more specifically, individual decision makers in the economic system, must determine how each output is to be produced. Which resources available in the economy should be used, and how should they be combined to produce each product? How much labor should be used and at what skill level? What kinds of machines should be used? How much fertilizer should be used to grow the best sweet peas? Should the factory be built in the city or closer to the interstate highway?

Again, billions of individual decisions must be made to determine what resources are to be employed and how these resources are to be combined in producing the goods and services. We will see later that in some economic systems prices play a fundamental role in guiding such decision making.

For Whom Will Goods Be Produced?

Finally, the economic system must decide how the fruits of production should be divided among the population. Who will actually consume the goods and services produced? Should equal amounts of the good be provided to everyone in the economy? Should the weak and the sick receive more? Should goods be allocated according to height? Weight? Looks? Race? Gender? The value of resources supplied? Political connections? The question "For whom will goods be produced?" is often referred to as the distribution question, and its answer helps shape each individual's incentives to produce.

Consider your own situation. What has determined your share of the goods and services produced? Money from your parents, earnings from summer and part-time jobs, and possibly loans and student aid have been the primary determinants. In short, your income from various sources determines how much you are able to purchase. In our economic system, your income depends on who your parents are, your labor skills, how hard you work, your ownership of other resources, and the relative scarcity of your resources.

In our system you have a property right to your resources—meaning you have the right to use or to exchange these resources as you choose. You are free to sell your resources in return for income, which can be used to purchase goods and services. Thus, the kinds and amount of goods and services you receive will depend primarily on the value of the resources you can sell in the market. Other economic systems answer the distribution question differently, as we shall see.

The Interdependence of the Questions What, How, and For Whom?

Although the three questions have been addressed separately, they are closely interwoven. The answer to one depends very much on the answers to the others. For example, the answer to what is to be produced will depend on who will receive the good. An economy that distributes goods and services in uniform amounts to all individuals will, no doubt, answer the what-is-to-be-produced question differently from the economy that somehow allows each individual to choose a unique bundle of goods and services. Also, if you have a property right in your own resources, you will probably treat these resources differently than if there were no private property. That is, if you did not own the fruits of your own labor, you might decide differently about how much to work.

ALTERNATIVE WAYS OF ANSWERING THE THREE ECONOMIC QUESTIONS

Each economy resolves the three questions—what, how, and for whom?—differently. The laws about resource ownership and the extent to which the government attempts to coordinate economic activity determine the "rules of the game"—the set of conditions that shape individual incentives and constraints. Two extremes of ownership and coordination can be contrasted.

Pure Capitalism

Pure capitalism is the economic system characterized by private ownership of resources and the use of prices to coordinate economic activity in free, competitive markets.

Under **pure capitalism** the rules of the game include the private ownership of resources and the coordination of economic activity by the price signals generated in free, competitive markets. Any income derived from the use of land, labor, capital, or entrepreneurial ability goes to the individual owners of those resources. Owners have property rights to the use of their resources and are therefore free to sell their resources to the highest bidder. Producers are free to make and sell whatever they think will be profitable. Consumers are free to buy whatever goods they can afford. All this voluntary buying and selling is coordinated by competitive markets, where buyers and sellers come together and make their wishes known. Market prices guide the use of resources to their highest-valued use.

Under pure capitalism, markets direct the what, how, and for whom of production. No single individual or small group coordinates these activities. Rather, it is the voluntary choices of many buyers and sellers, responding only to their individual incentives and constraints, that direct resources and products to the highest bidder. According to Adam Smith, one of the first to explain the allocative role of markets, the economy is coordinated as if by an "invisible hand"—an unseen force that harnesses the pursuit of self-interest to direct resources to where they earn the greatest return.

Pure capitalism is sometimes called *laissez-faire* capitalism; translated from the French, this means "to let do," or to let people do as they choose without government intervention. Thus, under pure capitalism, voluntary choices based on rational self-interest are made in competitive markets to answer the questions what, how, and for whom?

Command Economy

*A **command economy** is characterized by public ownership of resources and the coordination of economic activity through centralized planning.*

Along a spectrum ranging from the freest to the most regimented type of economic system, pure capitalism would be at one end and the **command economy** would be at the opposite end. Pure capitalism is characterized by the private ownership of resources and the coordination of economic activity through competitive market prices. In the command economy, there is public rather than private ownership of resources, and coordination results from central planning rather than from decentralized markets.

In the command economy there is public or communal ownership of property. Resources are directed and production coordinated through some form of central planning. The collective will of the people is, in theory, reflected by the decisions of the central planners. These planners, as representatives of all the people, determine how much steel, how many cars, how many women's suits, how many personal computers, and how many cherry pies to produce. The central planners also determine how these goods are to be produced and who will receive the goods. In theory, the command economy incorporates individual choice into collective choice, which, in turn, is reflected in central planning decisions.

Mixed Economies

No country on earth exemplifies either type of economic system in its pure form. The United States represents a mixed capitalist system, with governments directing about a third of all economic activity and private markets about two-thirds. Even the two-thirds carried out in the private sector is often regulated by government in a variety of ways.

About 25 percent of the world's population lives in the People's Republic of China, perhaps the most centrally planned of economies. Even in China, however, workers are entitled to their wages, and with increasing frequency marketlike mechanisms are being introduced, allowing some private businesses to operate. Although the Soviet Union is primarily a command economy, a portion of the Soviet agricultural sector is allowed to function under competitive market conditions. In 1986 the Soviet Union also began permitting other limited forms of private enterprise. For the first time since the 1920s families were allowed to operate small businesses, such as restaurants and laundries.

Although public ownership of the resources usually goes hand-in-hand with centrally planned coordination, hybrid systems are developing. Yugoslavia, for example, has developed a system called market socialism, where the public ownership of some resources, particularly capital, has been combined with relatively free markets to direct economic activity. Hungary and Poland are also experimenting with a profusion of small, consumer-oriented businesses.

Finally, some economic systems are directed largely by custom or religion. Laws of the Muslim religion set limits on the rate of interest that can be earned on certain investments. The caste system in India and elsewhere often restricts the occupations available to individuals. Hence, religion, custom, and family relations play important roles in the organization and coordination of economic activity. Your own pattern of consumption and choice of occupation may be influenced by some of these factors.

Although economies can answer the three economic questions in a variety of ways, this text will focus primarily on the mixed form of capitalism found in the United States. This mix represents a blend of private choice guided by the price system in competitive markets, alongside public choice guided by representative democracy in political markets. The study of mixed capitalism such as ours becomes more relevant as capitalist economies and command economies grow more alike. Resource coordination through competitive markets will be examined in the next chapter.

SUMMARY

1. Scarcity arises because resources are limited, but wants are unlimited. Since we cannot satisfy all of our wants, we must make choices, and choice involves opportunity cost. The opportunity cost of the chosen alternative is the benefit forgone from the next most preferred alternative.

2. The production possibilities frontier is a curve that shows the productive capabilities of the economy, assuming all resources are used efficiently. Points inside the frontier result from an inefficient use of resources; points outside the frontier are unattainable given the economy's resources and technology. This frontier's bow shape reflects the law of increasing opportunity cost, which exists because resources are not perfectly adaptable to the production of different goods. Over time, the production possibilities frontier can shift in or out as a result of changes in the availability of resources or in technology. The frontier demonstrates several economic concepts, including scarcity, choice, efficiency, and the law of increasing opportunity cost.

3. The law of comparative advantage states that the individual with the lowest opportunity cost for producing a particular good should specialize in the production of that good. Specialization, according to the law of comparative advantage, promotes the most efficient use of resources. Specialization of labor enhances efficiency by (1) taking advantage of individual preferences and natural abilities, (2) allowing workers to develop expertise in a particular task, (3) reducing the time required to shift between different tasks, and (4) encouraging the introduction of labor-saving machinery in the production process.

4. All economic systems, regardless of their decision-making process, must answer three fundamental questions: What is to be produced? How is it to be produced? For whom is it to be produced?

5. Nations answer the questions differently, depending on (1) the ownership of resources and (2) the way economic activity is conducted and directed. Two extremes of ownership and

coordination are represented by pure capitalism and a pure command economy. Under pure capitalism resources are owned by individuals, and economic activity is coordinated by prices in competitive markets. In a pure command economy all resources are owned in common, and economic activity is coordinated by central planning. In reality, these economic systems exist nowhere in the world in their pure form. All countries represent a mix of both elements, with some leaning more toward capitalism and others leaning more toward a command economy. Economic systems have been growing more alike over time.

QUESTIONS AND PROBLEMS

1. (Opportunity Costs) Consider the ways in which changing conditions and time can affect the opportunity cost of going to a movie. Here are some examples you may wish to consider and discuss:

    a. You have a final exam the next day.
    b. School will be on holiday for one month starting today.
    c. The same movie will be shown on TV the next night.
    d. The school dance or concert is the same night.

2. (Opportunity Costs) "You should never buy precooked frozen foods because you would then be paying for the labor costs of the preparation of the food." Is this statement always true or can it conflict with the principle of comparative advantage?

3. (Production Possibilities) During the late 1960s and early 1970s Mao Zedong and the leaders of the Great Proletarian Cultural Revolution forced highly educated professionals in China to move to the farms and work as peasants. The action was justified by arguing that such professionals should become acquainted with honest labor because in so doing they would learn to respect the common laborer. This policy created a massive reduction in productivity, incentives, and economic growth, and it was later abandoned. How does such a policy relate to the production possibilities frontier?

4. (Production Possibilities) Two thousand illegal aliens reportedly enter the United States *each day.* The recent immigration bill will make it a federal offense to hire such illegal aliens. What will happen to the U.S. production possibilities frontier? Will all industries be equally affected? Which individuals in society will be helped, and which will be hurt?

5. (Production Possibilities) "If society decides, by way of the marketplace, to use its resources fully (that is, the economy is on the production possibilities frontier), then future generations will be worse off because they will not be able to use these resources." If this assertion is true, full employment of resources may not be a good thing. Comment on the validity of the assertion.

6. (Production Possibilities) Often there is confusion about what will shift the production possibilities frontier. For example, someone might think that a reduction in the unemployment rate shifts the PPF outward. Explain why this is *not* the case.

7. (Specialization) Discuss the strengths and weaknesses associated with the practice of having each subject at universities taught by different professors. That is, why not have one professor teach history, economics, physics, mathematics, and so on?

8. (Comparative and Absolute Advantage) In the United States some states specialize in the production of certain products. For example, over 50 percent of the apples consumed in the United States come from the Pacific Northwest. Identify states that have absolute advantages in the production of their goods and states that have comparative advantages in the production of their goods.

9. (Comparative Advantage) Corporate executives often use limousines, even though the executives are perfectly good drivers. Suppose that a certain executive is a better driver than her chauffeur. Use the principle of comparative advantage to show that the executive should still employ the driver rather than drive the car herself.

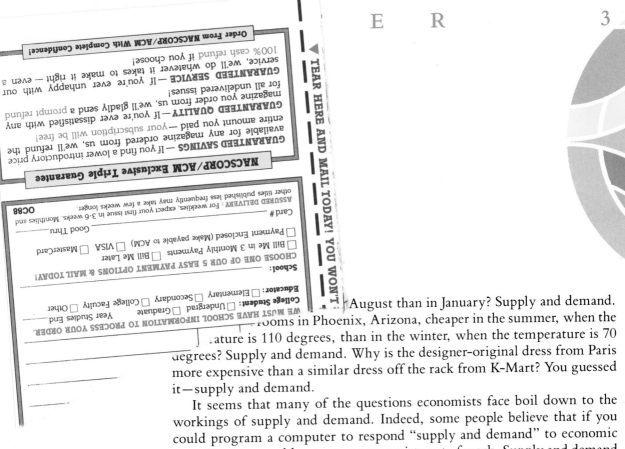

August than in January? Supply and demand. rooms in Phoenix, Arizona, cheaper in the summer, when the ~~temper~~ature is 110 degrees, than in the winter, when the temperature is 70 degrees? Supply and demand. Why is the designer-original dress from Paris more expensive than a similar dress off the rack from K-Mart? You guessed it—supply and demand.

It seems that many of the questions economists face boil down to the workings of supply and demand. Indeed, some people believe that if you could program a computer to respond "supply and demand" to economic questions, you could put many economists out of work. Supply and demand are the most fundamental and the most powerful of all economic tools. An understanding of the forces of supply and demand will take you far in your development of the art and science of economic analysis. This chapter will introduce the underpinnings of supply and demand and show how the two interact in competitive markets. As you will see, the correct analysis of supply and demand takes skill and care. The chapter uses graphs extensively, so you may want to refer back to the appendix of Chapter 1 for a refresher. Topics and terms discussed include:

- Demand
- Supply
- Markets
- Equilibrium price and quantity
- Disequilibrium

DEMAND

In Western Pennsylvania, in the middle of nowhere, is a poorly lit, run down yellow building known as Pechin's Mart. The aisles are unmarked and strewn with half-empty boxes arranged in no apparent design. The sagging roof leaks when it rains. Why would shoppers come from as far away as Maryland to put up with the chaos and the grubbiness to buy as many groceries as they can haul away? The store has violated nearly all the rules of retailing, yet it thrives, with annual sales more than four times the average for supermarkets around the country. The store thrives because it has followed one rule merchants have known for thousands of years — the store has the lowest prices around.

You as a consumer have little trouble grasping the notion that people will buy more of a good at a lower price than at a higher price. Sell a product for less, and the world will beat a path to your door. In fact, the relationship between the price of a good and the quantity demanded has been elevated to the status of an economic law. The **law of demand** states that the quantity demanded is inversely related to its price, other things constant. Thus, the higher the price is, the smaller will be the quantity demanded; and the lower the price, the greater the quantity demanded. Often we say demand reflects the quantity that consumers are both *willing* and *able* to buy at each alternative price. For example, you may be *able* to buy a motorcycle at a price of $2000 because you have enough money to pay for it, but you may not be *willing* to buy one simply because motorcycles do not interest you.

*The **law of demand** states that the quantity of a good demanded is inversely related to its price, other things constant.*

What Is Demand?

If the price of Pepsi is $1 a six-pack, how many six-packs will be demanded each week? How many will be demanded if the price is $2? If the price is $3? The answers to these questions provide a schedule conveying the relationship between the price of Pepsi and the quantity demanded. This schedule is called the demand for Pepsi. More generally, **demand** is a schedule indicating the quantity of a well-defined commodity that consumers are willing and able to buy at each possible price during a given period of time, other things constant. Because demand is calculated for a specific period of time, such as a day, a week, or a month, demand is best thought of as the *rate* of desired purchase at each possible price.

Demand is a schedule indicating the quantity of a well-defined good that consumers are willing and able to buy at each possible price during a given period of time, other things constant.

Other Prices Held Constant   Notice that the definition of demand includes the other-things-constant assumption. The reason we need to hold other things constant is that demand is influenced by factors other than the price. For example, Pepsi and Coke represent alternative ways of quenching a thirst. Therefore, the quantity of Pepsi demanded will depend not only on the price of Pepsi but also on the price of Coke, as well as the prices of other alternatives. Since we want to isolate the relationship between the price of Pepsi and the quantity of Pepsi demanded, we must hold the prices of these alternatives constant. By holding other prices constant, we are looking at the price change of one good, Pepsi, *relative to* the prices of other goods. Thus we are looking at the effects of a change in what is called the *relative price* of Pepsi. If the price of Pepsi increases while the price of other goods remains constant, the relative price of Pepsi has increased.

Demand, Wants, and Need   Consumer *demand* and consumer *wants* are not the same thing. As we have seen, wants are unlimited. You may want a

Mercedes, but at a price of $50,000, that car is likely to be beyond your budget (i.e., the quantity you demand at that price is 0). Nor is *demand* the same as *need*. You may need a new muffler for your car, but you do not buy one when the price is $100. Evidently, you believe you have better ways to spend your money. If, however, the price of mufflers falls far enough, say to $20, then you are both willing and able to buy one.

The Substitution Effect of a Price Change   Why is less demanded when the price is higher? The explanation begins when scarce resources meet unlimited wants. Many goods and services are capable of satisfying your many wants. For example, your hunger can be satisfied by pizza, tacos, cheese sandwiches, sirloin steak, or fried chicken. Similarly, your desire for warmth in the winter can be met by warm clothing, home insulation, heating oil, or a trip to Hawaii. Clearly, some ways of satisfying your various wants will be more appealing to you than others. Dining on filet mignon at a posh French restaurant would be preferred by most of you to fixing a peanut butter and jelly sandwich in your dorm. In a world without scarcity there would be no prices, so you would always prefer the most attractive alternative. Scarcity, however, is an overriding reality, and the degree of scarcity of one good relative to another determines the relative prices of the goods.

The ***substitution effect*** *is a change in the pattern of consumption caused by a price change; when the price of a good rises, other goods will be substituted for it, and the quantity demanded will fall.*

When the price of one good goes up and prices of other goods do not change, this good becomes relatively more costly. Consumers therefore tend to substitute other goods for the higher-priced good. If the price of pizza goes up, you tend to demand less pizza and more of other foods. This is called the **substitution effect** of a price change. It means that an increase in the price of one good will encourage consumers to switch to other goods. On the other hand, a lower price will cause consumers to switch from other goods to the good that is now cheaper. Remember that it is the change in the *relative price*—the price of one good relative to the prices of other goods—that causes the substitution effect. If all prices rose by the same percentage, there would be no change in relative prices, so there would be no substitution effect.

The ***income effect*** *of a price change occurs when the price of a good rises, consumers' purchasing power falls, and so they purchase less of all normal goods.*

The Income Effect of a Price Change   A rising price will cause a decline in quantity demanded for another reason. Suppose you have $30 a week in spending money and are a pizza fanatic who buys six pizzas a week when the price is $5 per pizza. What happens to your quantity demanded if the price doubles to $10? At that price you could buy at most three pizzas a week. Thus, the increase in the price reduces your *ability* to buy pizza. At the higher price, the buying power of your income, measured in terms of pizzas, declines, so you are not able to buy as many.

Real income *is measured in terms of the goods and services it can buy.*

The quantity of pizza you demand is reduced because of what is called the **income effect** of a price increase. The increase in the price of pizza has reduced your **real income**, —that is, your income measured in terms of the goods and services it can buy. More generally, as the price of a particular good goes up, other things constant, your real income declines, and because of this decline you tend to reduce the quantity of that good you demand.

The income effect of a price change will be greater for products on which you spend a large portion of your budget, such as housing and cars, than for smaller items, such as soap and doughnuts. The larger a particular good is as a percentage of your budget, the more your budget will be affected by changes in the price of that good. For example, suppose housing costs account for $300 of your $600 monthly budget. If the price of housing drops by 33 percent, other things constant, this means you could purchase the same amount of housing for $200, thus freeing up $100 in your budget to be spent on more housing and more of other goods.

Consider now a change in price for a much less important item. Suppose you eat on average a dozen doughnuts a month at a total cost of $3. This expenditure constitutes 0.5 percent of your $600 budget. A 33 percent drop in the price of doughnuts reduces the cost of purchasing a dozen doughnuts by $1 per month, thereby freeing up $1 per month, which you can spend on more doughnuts and more of other goods. As you can see, the income effect of the change in the price of housing is likely to be greater than the income effect of a change in the price of doughnuts.

The Demand Schedule and Demand Curve

The demand relationship can be expressed as a demand schedule or as a demand curve. Exhibit 1 shows a hypothetical demand schedule for milk. When we describe demand, we must be specific about the units being measured and the time period under consideration. The price is for a half gallon of milk, and the period is a month. Alternative prices are listed in Exhibit 1, along with the quantity demanded at each price. At a price of $1.25 per half gallon, for example, consumers will demand 8 million half gallons per month.

As you can see, if the price is lower, the quantity demanded is greater. If the price drops as low as $0.25 per half gallon, 32 million half gallons will be demanded per month, four times the amount demanded at $1.25. At lower prices for milk, consumers substitute milk for other goods. Remember, all prices other than milk are assumed to be constant. As the price of milk falls, there will also be an income effect, increasing the quantity of milk demanded. However, because milk expenditures typically represent a small fraction of each consumer's budget, the income effect will probably be small.

EXHIBIT 1
THE DEMAND SCHEDULE FOR MILK

	Price per Half Gallon	Quantity Demanded (millions of half gallons per month)
a	$1.25	8
b	1.00	14
c	0.75	20
d	0.50	26
e	0.25	32

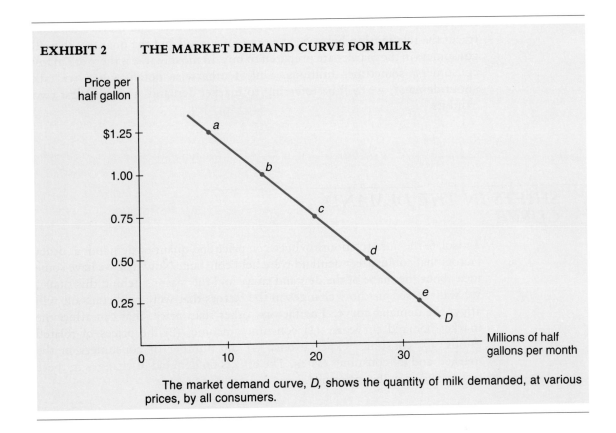

EXHIBIT 2   THE MARKET DEMAND CURVE FOR MILK

The market demand curve, *D*, shows the quantity of milk demanded, at various prices, by all consumers.

*A **demand curve** is a downward-sloping curve showing the quantity of a well-defined commodity demanded at various possible prices.*

The demand schedule presented as Exhibit 1 can also be presented as a **demand curve**. In Exhibit 2 price is measured on the vertical axis, and the quantity demanded on the horizontal axis. Each combination of price and quantity demanded listed in the demand schedule is represented by a point in Exhibit 2. Point *a*, for example, indicates that at a price of $1.25, 8 million half gallons will be demanded per month. These points are connected to form the demand curve for milk, which is labeled *D*. Note that the demand curve is downward sloping, reflecting the fact that price and quantity demanded are inversely related.

Be careful to distinguish between the demand for milk and the quantity demanded. When we talk about the demand for milk, we do not mean a specific quantity but rather the relationship between various possible prices and the quantity demanded at each price. The entire curve is referred to as the demand for milk. Individual points along the demand curve show the quantity demanded at each price — the amount consumers are willing and able to purchase if the good is offered for sale at that price. For example, at a price of $0.75 per half gallon, 20 million half gallons are demanded. When the price of milk changes, this change is expressed by a movement along the curve. Movements along the curve, say from point *a* to point *b*, are called changes in quantity demanded, *not* changes in demand.

At times it is useful to distinguish between *individual demand*, which is the demand of an individual consumer, and *market demand*, which is the sum of all the individual demands of consumers in the market. The market demand traces the relationship between the price of a good and the quantity that all consumers in the market are prepared to buy. In most markets there are many consumers, sometimes millions. Unless otherwise noted, when we talk about demand, we will be referring to market demand, as in the first two exhibits.

SHIFTS IN THE DEMAND CURVE

To isolate the pure relationship between price and quantity demanded, other factors that could affect demand were held constant. Now that we have some idea about the shape of the demand curve and the reasons behind this shape, we want to see just how changes in the factors that were held constant will affect the demand curve. The factors, other than price, that can affect the market demand curve are (1) consumer income, (2) the prices of related goods, (3) consumer expectations, (4) the number of consumers in the market, and (5) consumer tastes. The effects on demand of changes in these factors will now be examined.

Changes in Income

Demand reflects both consumer willingness and consumer ability to purchase the good at each possible price. In Exhibit 3 we have drawn the market demand curve for milk as D. The ability to purchase goods is based on income; the greater the income, the greater this purchasing ability. The demand curve, D, assumed some given consumer income. An increase in that income will normally increase demand—that is, at each price level the quantity demanded will increase. If consumer income increases, the demand curve for milk will shift to the right, as reflected by the movement from D to D'. This increase in demand indicates a greater willingness and ability to purchase milk at each price level. For example, at a price of $1 the quantity demanded increases from 14 million to 20 million half gallons per month, as indicated by the movement from point a on D to point c on D'.

Another way to understand an increase in demand is to see what happens to the price consumers are willing to pay for a particular quantity of the good. For example, with the initial demand curve in Exhibit 3, consumers were willing to pay $0.75 per half gallon for 20 million half gallons, as reflected by point b. After the increase in demand, consumers are willing to pay $1 per half gallon for 20 million half gallons, as reflected by point c on the new demand curve, which is directly above point b on the original demand curve. Thus, consumers are willing to pay $0.25 more per half gallon for 20 million half gallons. More generally, an increase in demand—that is, a shift to the right in the demand curve—means that consumers are willing to pay more for each unit than before.

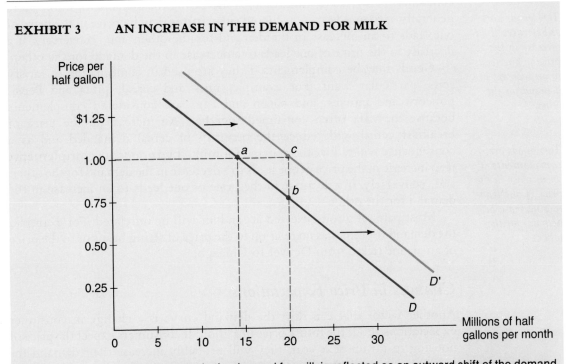

EXHIBIT 3   AN INCREASE IN THE DEMAND FOR MILK

An increase in the demand for milk is reflected as an outward shift of the demand curve. After the increase in demand, the quantity of milk demanded at a price of $1 per half gallon increases from 14 million (point *a*) to 20 milllion half gallons (point *c*). Alternatively, the shift could be interpreted as showing that the maximum price consumers are willing to pay for 20 million half gallons has increased from $0.75 per unit (at point *b*) to $1 (point *c*).

---

*The demand for an **inferior good** decreases as income rises. The demand for a **normal good** increases as income rises.*

One category of goods is referred to as **inferior goods** because the demand for these goods actually declines as income increases. Examples of inferior goods include hamburger, trips to the laundromat, and bus rides. As your income increases, you tend to switch from consuming these inferior goods to consuming normal goods (steak, your own washer and dryer, automobile or plane rides). The demand for **normal goods** increases as consumer income increases. Because the demand for milk increases when consumer income increases, milk is considered to be a normal good. Most goods are normal.

Changes in the Prices of Related Goods

As noted earlier, there are alternative ways of trying to satisfy any particular want. For example, thirst can be quenched not only by a glass of milk but also by a soft drink, fruit juice, or even a glass of water. These goods are, to a certain extent, substitutes in satisfying the particular want, thirst. The choice will depend in part on the prices of the available alternatives. Consider two substitutes, milk and juice. Obviously, they are not perfect substitutes, but an increase in the price of juice, other things equal, will encourage

*Two goods are
substitutes if an
increase in the
price of one leads
to an increase in
demand for the
other.*

consumers to switch to milk, thereby increasing the demand for milk. More generally, two goods are considered **substitutes** if an increase in the price of one leads to an increase in the demand for the other, and, conversely, if a decrease in the price of one leads to a decrease in the demand for the other.

Goods may be complements if they are used in combination to satisfy some particular want. For example, milk and cereal, pizza and Pepsi, popcorn and movies, and bacon and eggs are considered complements because they are often consumed together. An increase in the price of breakfast cereal will reduce the quantity of cereal demanded and as a consequence will reduce the demand for milk. Two goods are **complements** if an increase in the price of one leads to a decrease in the demand for the other, and, conversely, if a decrease in the price of one leads to an increase in the demand for the other.

*Two goods are
complements if
an increase in the
price of one leads
to a decrease in
demand for the
other.*

Most pairs of goods selected at random will be unrelated. For example, the demand for milk has no relation to the price of string beans or to the price of an airline ticket from Denver to Chicago.

Changes in Price Expectations

Another factor that can shift the demand curve is a change in consumer expectations about the future price of a good. If consumers expect the price of housing to go up next year, they will probably increase their demand for housing this year. On the other hand, expectations of a lower price in the future will encourage consumers to postpone purchases. Changes in expectations will have less effect if the good in question is perishable. If you expect the price of milk to go up next month, you will not buy 10 gallons today. Even in this case, though, expectations will still matter to some degree: if you expect the price of milk to go up tomorrow, you are more likely to buy a gallon today rather than your usual half gallon.

Changes in the Number of Consumers

We mentioned earlier that market demand is the sum of the individual demands of all consumers in the market. If the number of consumers in the market changes, this change will shift the demand curve. For example, if the population grows, the demand for food will increase. Even if the total population remains the same, demand could change as a result of a change in the composition of the population. For example, if the number of retired couples increases, the demand for recreational vehicles will probably increase. If the baby population declines, the demand for baby food will decrease.

Changes in Tastes

Do you like anchovies on your pizza? How about sauerkraut on your hot dog? Do you wear designer jeans? Choices in food, clothing, music, reading—indeed, all consumption choices—usually are influenced by consumer tastes. *Tastes* are nothing more than your likes and dislikes in consumption. Some people crave certain foods that would gag others. What determines tastes? Who knows? Economists certainly do not, nor do they spend much time worrying about it. Economists do recognize, however, that tastes are very important in shaping demand, and a change in tastes can change demand.

Because it is so difficult to observe a change in tastes, we should be reluctant to attribute a change in demand to a change in tastes. In our analysis of consumer demand, we will assume that tastes are given and are relatively stable over time. Only after investigating all other possible factors will we attribute a change in demand to a change in tastes. Otherwise, there is a temptation to explain any shift in demand by saying that consumers' tastes changed. For example, "Why did the demand for milk change?" "Obviously, because the taste for milk changed." There is no way to test such an assertion, so economists try to use this explanation sparingly and only after other possible changes have been ruled out.

This cautionary note is not meant to downplay the role of tastes in determining demand; it is simply a warning not to attribute the source of a change in demand to a change in tastes before carefully considering the other possibilities. At times it may be possible to trace changing tastes to specific events. For example, if health officials warn that milk consumption is linked to heart disease, the demand for milk is likely to fall. Similarly, if the common perception that only wimps drink milk develops, this perception could reduce the demand for milk.

Conclusion

A change in price, other things constant, results in a change in the quantity demanded, as reflected by a *movement along* the demand curve. A change in one of the nonprice determinants of demand, however, will result in a change in demand as reflected by a *shift* in the demand curve. There are five major determinants of demand: (1) consumer income, (2) the prices of related goods, (3) consumer expectations, (4) the number of consumers, and (5) consumer tastes. A change in any one of these determinants could cause the demand curve to shift. The distinction between a change in demand and a change in the quantity demanded is confusing at first, so be careful.

SUPPLY

Supply *is a schedule indicating the quantity of a well-defined good that producers are willing and able to sell at various prices during a given time period, other things constant.*

Just as demand is the relation between price and quantity demanded, supply is the relation between price and quantity supplied. In particular, **supply** indicates how much of the good producers are both *willing* and *able* to offer for sale at each possible price, other things constant. The relationship between price and quantity supplied is normally, though not always, a direct one—that is, more is supplied at a higher price than at a lower price, other things constant.

The Supply Schedule and Supply Curve

*A **supply curve** shows the quantity of a well-defined good supplied at various possible prices.*

In Exhibit 4 we present the supply schedule and **supply curve** for milk, *S*, showing the quantity of milk supplied at various possible prices by thousands of dairy farmers. As you can see, price and quantity supplied are directly, or positively, related. More is offered for sale at a higher price than at a lower price, so the supply curve is upward sloping.

Producers offer more goods for sale when prices are higher for two reasons. The first has to do with a *willingness* to offer more for sale at a higher price than at a lower price. Higher prices for a good mean that producers are rewarded more for production, and they naturally are more willing to produce when they are paid more to do so. The prices of other goods are assumed to remain constant when the price of milk increases. An increase in the price of milk provides farmers with an incentive to shift some resources out of the production of other goods, such as corn, where the price is now relatively lower, to milk, where the price is now relatively higher. You can think of prices as signals to existing and potential suppliers about the relative reward for producing the good. A higher milk price serves as a beacon that attracts resources from less-valued uses to the higher-valued use. Thus, as the price of a good increases, other things constant, a producer is more *willing* to supply the good.

A second reason why the supply curve tends to be upward sloping is the producers' increased *ability* to supply the good at the higher prices. Here is why the ability to supply increases. Recall the law of increasing opportunity

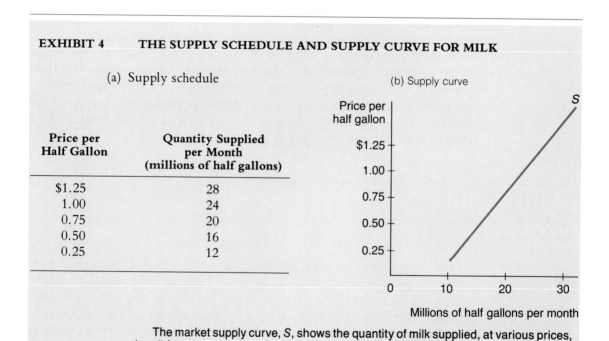

EXHIBIT 4   THE SUPPLY SCHEDULE AND SUPPLY CURVE FOR MILK

(a) Supply schedule

Price per Half Gallon	Quantity Supplied per Month (millions of half gallons)
$1.25	28
1.00	24
0.75	20
0.50	16
0.25	12

(b) Supply curve

The market supply curve, *S*, shows the quantity of milk supplied, at various prices, by all farmers.

cost, which states that as more of a particular good is produced, the greater its opportunity cost will be. Based on this law, as the quantity of a particular good increases in supply, so does its cost of production. Because producers face a higher cost of production for greater levels of production, they need to receive a higher price for their product before they are able to increase the quantity supplied. For example, low levels of milk production employ resources that are well suited to the task. As the farmer increases the production of milk, however, the additional increments of milk begin requiring resources that were better suited to the production of other goods. To feed additional cows, a farmer may have to convert a productive wheat field into grazing land. Therefore, additional output has a higher opportunity cost because it requires resources that were better suited to the production of other goods. Higher milk prices make the farmer more *able* to draw resources away from these alternative uses.

Thus, a higher price makes producers more willing and more able to increase the quantity of goods offered for sale. Producers are more willing because production of the higher-priced good is now relatively more attractive than are the alternative uses of the resources involved. Producers are more able because higher rates of production often require the use of resources involving a higher opportunity cost. Therefore, a higher price is necessary to pay for these more expensive resources.

As with demand, we distinguish between individual supply and market supply. Although we will continue to focus on market supply, keep in mind that market supply is the sum of the amount supplied at each price by the individual suppliers. Unless otherwise noted, when we talk about supply, we will be referring to market supply.

SHIFTS IN THE SUPPLY CURVE

The supply curve isolates the relationship between price and quantity supplied, other things constant. Thus, the supply curve is drawn under the assumption that no changes occur in other factors that can change supply. Such factors include (1) the state of technology, (2) the prices of relevant resources, (3) the prices of alternative goods, (4) producer expectations, and (5) the number of producers. We will consider how a change in each of these determinants of supply will affect the supply curve.

Changes in Technology

The supply curve is constructed under the assumption that the technology available to producers does not change. Recall from Chapter 2 that the state of technology represents the economy's stock of knowledge about how resources can be combined most efficiently. If some new method is devised to produce the good more efficiently, production costs will go down and suppliers will be more willing and more able to supply the good. The supply will increase, as reflected by a shift to the right in the supply curve. For example, suppose a new milking machine called The Invisible Hand has a very soothing effect on cows; cows find the new machine so udderly delightful that they produce more milk. Such a technological advance is reflected by a shift to the right in the market supply curve for milk, as shown by the shift from *S* to *S'* in Exhibit 5.

Notice that just as a change in demand could be interpreted in two different ways, so can a change in supply. First, an increase in supply means farmers supply more milk at each possible price. For example, when the price is $1 per half gallon, the quantity of milk farmers supply increases from 24 million to 28 million half gallons per month, as shown by the movement from point *a* to point *c* in Exhibit 8. Second, an increase in supply means that farmers supply the same quantity at a lower price. For example, before the increase in supply, farmers supplied 28 million half gallons when the price was $1.25 per half gallon; after the increase in supply, that same quantity is supplied for only $1 per half gallon, as shown by the movement from point *b* to point *c* in Exhibit 5.

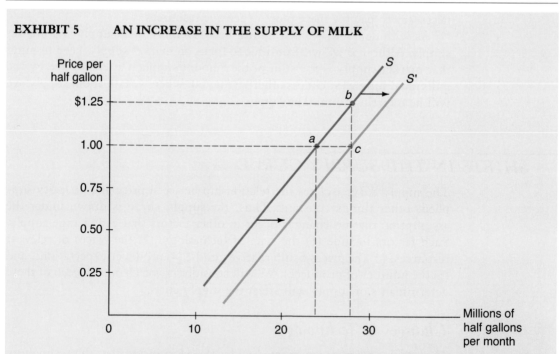

EXHIBIT 5   AN INCREASE IN THE SUPPLY OF MILK

An increase in the supply of milk is reflected by a shift to the right of the supply curve from *S* to *S'*. After the increase in supply, the quantity of milk supplied at a price of $1 per half gallon increases from 24 million half gallons (point *a*) to 28 million half gallons (point *c*). Alternatively, the shift could be interpreted as showing a reduction in the minimum price suppliers require in order to produce 28 million half gallons. Previously, a price of $1.25 per half gallon was required (point *b*); after the increase in supply, a price of $1 per half gallon is required (point *c*).

Changes in the Prices of Relevant Resources

A second change that could shift the supply curve is a change in the price of one of the resources used in the production of the good. A decrease in the price of a resource will lower the cost of producing the good and will shift the supply curve to the right, reflecting the greater ability to supply the good at each price. For example, if the price of cow feed falls, the supply of milk will shift to the right, as was reflected in Exhibit 5. On the other hand, an increase in the cost of a resource will shift the supply curve to the left, indicating that suppliers are offering less of the good at every price. For example, higher electricity rates increase the cost of heating the barn and operating the milking machines. These higher production costs would be reflected in a shift to the left in the supply curve. Again, the reduction in supply can be interpreted in two ways: when supply is reduced, farmers supply less milk at each price or supply the same quantity of milk but at a higher price.

Changes in the Prices of Alternative Goods

Nearly all resources have alternative uses. The farmer's field, tractor, barn, and time could be used to produce a variety of goods. *Alternative goods* are goods that use some of the same resources as used to produce the good under consideration. For example, suppose the production of corn uses some of the same resources as the production of milk. An increase in the price of corn raises the opportunity cost of producing milk. Because the production of corn is now relatively more rewarding, resources will shift from milk production into corn production. With fewer resources supplied to the production of milk, the supply of milk will decrease, or shift to the left. On the other hand, if there is a fall in the price of an alternative good, milk production will become relatively more attractive. As resources shift into milk production, the supply of milk would shift to the right.

Changes in Producer Expectations

Changes in producer expectations about prices can result in a shift of the supply curve. For example, at various times in recent years the Organization of Petroleum Exporting Countries (OPEC) decided to reduce their supply of oil because they expected the price of oil to be higher in the future. Their reduction in supply can be reflected by a shift to the left in the supply curve.

Changes in the Number of Producers

Since the market supply is the sum of the amount supplied by each producer, market supply depends on the number of producers in the market. If the number of producers increases, supply will shift to the right; if the number decreases, supply will shift to the left. For example, during the 1980s the number of stores renting movie videos increased, so the supply of videos for rent increased, shifting the supply curve to the right.

Conclusion

To review, there are five major determinants of supply other than the price: (1) the state of technology, (2) the prices of relevant resources, (3) the prices of alternative goods, (4) producer expectations, and (5) the number of producers in the market. You should notice that supply and demand have some similar determinants. Both depend on the prices of related goods, price expectations, and the number of participants in the market. We are now ready to bring supply and demand together.

PUTTING IT ALL TOGETHER: SUPPLY, DEMAND, AND EQUILIBRIUM

The demand curve depicts the quantity that *consumers* are willing and able to buy at each possible price. The supply curve depicts the quantity that *producers* are willing and able to sell at each possible price. Suppliers and demanders have different views of price because demanders pay the price and suppliers receive the price. Thus, higher prices tend to be good news for producers but bad news for consumers, and as prices rise, consumers reduce their quantity demanded, while producers increase their quantity supplied. How is this ongoing conflict between producers and consumers resolved?

Markets

The differing views of price held by suppliers and demanders are sorted out by the market. The market, a term first introduced in Chapter 1, is an impersonal mechanism that coordinates the decisions of many independent buyers and sellers. The market represents all the arrangements used to buy and sell a particular commodity. Markets reduce the cost of bringing buyers and sellers together and the cost of finding out what is available for sale, its price, its quality, and how it compares to other items for sale. Thus, we say

*The **transaction costs** of an exchange are the costs of the time and information required to carry it out.*

that markets reduce the **transaction costs** of exchange—the cost of time and information required for exchange. For example, suppose you want to find a summer job. One approach would be to go from employer to employer inquiring about job openings. But this would be time-consuming and would require transportation. Alternatively, you could pick up a copy of the local newspaper and let your fingers do the walking through the help-wanted ads to find out which firms need your services. These ads reduce the cost of time and information required to bring buyers and sellers together.

Markets can be broad enough to encompass the entire world, such as the market for wheat, or they can be as narrow as the competing gas stations at an intersection. Different markets provide different amounts of information about the item being exchanged, and this information is diffused, or communicated, at different speeds. For example, the stock market provides up-to-the-minute information about the price and quantity of thousands of stocks.

The coordination that occurs through markets takes place not because of some central plan but because of Adam Smith's "invisible hand." For example, most of the auto dealers in your community tend to be located together, usually on the outskirts of town. They congregate not because they like one another's company but because each dealer wants to be sure buyers can easily look over his or her car line. This common location makes it easier for buyers to go from dealer to dealer to make comparisons. For the same reason, stores group together in shopping malls. Incidentally, the car dealers locate on the outskirts of town because that type of business uses much land, and land is cheaper farther from the center of town.

Specialized Markets

Some markets are very specialized, while others are more general. In Quincy Market, a shopping center in Boston, a store called The Bear Facts sells nothing but toy bears. In a rural community outside of Boston, there is a general store where you can buy anything from a lug wrench to a pound of lamb chops. Why do some stores sell many different products, while others specialize?

Again, Adam Smith gave us the answer more than two hundred years ago when he noted that the degree of specialization is limited by the extent of the market. The larger the market is, the greater will be the degree of specialization. The shopping complex in Boston attracts millions of customers each year. Even if just a tiny fraction of them are interested in toy bears, the store can thrive. The general store, however, relies on a much smaller market—the several dozen homes scattered across the surrounding countryside—so it must offer a wider range of choice to sell enough goods to stay afloat. We are more likely to find specialty stores in major population areas than in rural communities.

Similarly, some periodicals are aimed at general readership, such as *Time* and *People*, so their subject matter and advertisements reflect this general interest. Other periodicals, such as the *American Economic Review* and the *Teddy Bear Review*, contain very specialized subject matter and advertising reflecting the narrow interests of their readers.

Market Equilibrium

Equilibrium is a situation in which the plans of buyers match the plans of sellers; no forces are present that would cause price or quantity to change.

We will examine how a market works by bringing together the market demand and market supply curves developed earlier. Exhibit 6 graphs the demand and supply of milk. The eye is drawn immediately to the point where the two curves intersect, point *e*, where the price is $0.75 and the quantity is 20 million half gallons per month.

Point *e* is the only combination of price and quantity that exactly matches the independent wishes of both buyers and sellers. At that price the quantity consumers wish to buy is equal to the quantity producers wish to sell. This combination is called the **equilibrium** level of price and quantity because

---

EXHIBIT 6   **EQUILIBRIUM IN THE MILK MARKET**

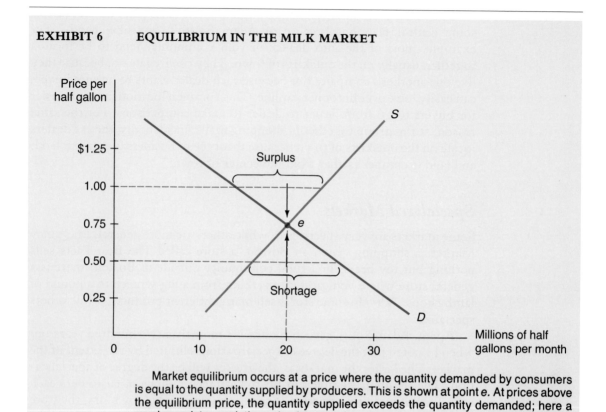

Market equilibrium occurs at a price where the quantity demanded by consumers is equal to the quantity supplied by producers. This is shown at point e. At prices above the equilibrium price, the quantity supplied exceeds the quantity demanded; here a surplus exists, and there is downward pressure on the price. At prices below equilibrium, quantity demanded exceeds quantity supplied; the resulting shortage puts upward pressure on the price.

---

once it is reached, consumers and producers will be satisfied and there will be no reason for either price or quantity to change. As we will see, there are forces in the market that will guide the market participants to this equilibrium.

To examine how the price and quantity will gravitate toward their equilibrium values, suppose the initial price is $1, exceeding the equilibrium value. According to the market supply curve in Exhibit 6, producers supply 24 million half gallons at that price. As you can see, however, at a price of $1 consumers demand only 14 million of the 24 million half gallons supplied, leaving 10 million unsold. The amount by which quantity supplied exceeds quantity demanded is called an *excess quantity supplied*, or a **surplus**. Notice that the surplus is measured at a particular price—in this case, $1.

*A **surplus** is an excess of quantity supplied over quantity demanded at a given price.*

Unless the price falls, the surplus will continue. Thus, a surplus will create downward pressure on the price level to clear the market. As the price falls, producers reduce their quantity supplied, and consumers increase their quantity demanded. As long as quantity supplied exceeds quantity demanded, there will be a tendency for the price to fall until the quantity supplied just equals the quantity demanded. This equilibrium will occur when the price equals $0.75.

What if the price is initially $0.50 per half gallon, a price below equilibrium. The quantity supplied would be 16 million half gallons per month. Consumers, however, would like to buy 26 million half gallons at that price, so they quickly empty the store shelves. The result is an *excess quantity demanded*, or a **shortage**, of 10 million half gallons. This shortage creates upward pressure on the price. As the price rises, producers increase their quantity supplied, but consumers reduce their quantity demanded. The price will increase until the shortage is eliminated. Again, the market will be in equilibrium only when the quantity demanded equals the quantity supplied. Thus, excess supply creates downward pressure on the price level, and excess demand, upward pressure on the price level.

*A **shortage** is an excess of quantity demanded over quantity supplied at a given price.*

CHANGES IN EQUILIBRIUM PRICE AND QUANTITY

Equilibrium is that combination of price and quantity where the desires of demanders and suppliers are exactly matched. Once equilibrium in achieved, that price and quantity will continue to prevail unless one of the determinants of supply or demand changes. A change in any one of these factors will change the equilibrium price and quantity in a predictable way.

Impact of Demand Shifts on Equilibrium Price and Quantity

In general, if the demand for a product increases, given an upward-sloping supply curve, the equilibrium price and quantity will also increase. If the demand curve shifts and the supply curve remains unchanged, the resulting change in price will move producers to a different point on their supply curve. Thus, equilibrium price and quantity will move up or down the supply curve as the demand curve shifts to the right or to the left. In Exhibit 7 the initial equilibrium price and quantity of milk is as depicted earlier—the price is $0.75 per half gallon and the quantity is 20 million half gallons per month.

Suppose that one of the determinants of demand changes in a way that shifts the demand curve to the right from D to D'. Any of the following changes could result in such a shift: (1) an increase in consumer income (as long as milk is a normal good); (2) an increase in the price of a substitute, such as juice, or a decrease in the price of a complement, such as chocolate chip cookies, (3) a change in consumer expectations that encourages them to buy more milk now, (4) an increase in the population; or (5) a change in consumer tastes based, for example, on a growing awareness that the calcium in milk builds stronger bones. After the increase in demand, quantity demanded exceeds quantity supplied at the price of $0.75. The resulting shortage puts

EXHIBIT 7   **EFFECTS OF AN INCREASE IN DEMAND**

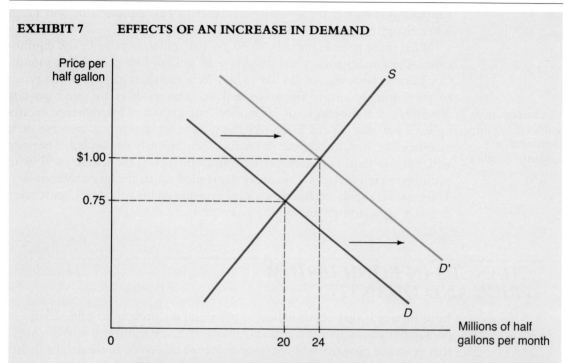

After an increase in demand shifts the demand curve from *D* to *D'*, quantity demanded exceeds quantity supplied at the old price of $0.75 per half gallon. As the price rises, quantity supplied will increase along supply curve *S*, and quantity demanded will fall along demand curve *D'*. When the new equilibrium is reached at a price of $1 per half gallon, the quantity demanded will once again equal the quantity supplied. Both price and quantity are higher following the increase in demand.

upward pressure on the price. As the price increases, the quantity supplied increases, but the quantity demanded decreases until once again the two are in equilibrium. Thus, an increase in demand increases both equilibrium price and equilibrium quantity.

In contrast, a change in one of the determinants of demand that shifts the demand curve to the left will result in a lower equilibrium price and lower equilibrium quantity. As long as the supply curve is upward sloping, any increase or decrease in demand will change equilibrium price and quantity *in the same direction* as the change in demand.

Impact of Supply Shifts on Equilibrium Price and Quantity

The impact of a change in supply on equilibrium price and quantity is not as easily remembered as a change in demand, but it is still quite simple. For a given downward-sloping demand curve, any increase in the supply of the the good will lead to a lower equilibrium price and a greater equilibrium

---

EXHIBIT 8   EFFECTS OF AN INCREASE IN SUPPLY

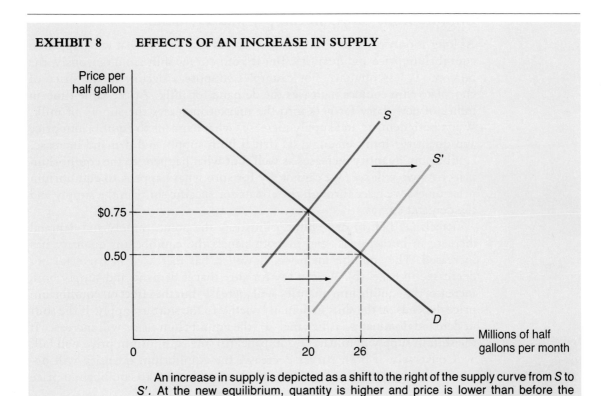

An increase in supply is depicted as a shift to the right of the supply curve from *S* to *S'*. At the new equilibrium, quantity is higher and price is lower than before the increase in supply.

---

quantity. This can be seen in Exhibit 8, where an increase in the supply of milk is shown by a shift to the right in the supply curve from *S* to *S'*.

For review, consider the kinds of changes that could shift the supply curve to the right: (1) improved technology in milk production, such as a more efficient milking machine; (2) a reduction in the price of a resource, such as electricity; (3) a reduction in the price of an alternative good; (4) a change in price expectations that encourages farmers to produce more milk now; or (5) an increase in the number of dairy farmers.

On the other hand, a change in any of these factors that results in a reduction in supply will shift the supply curve to the left, causing equilibrium quantity to fall but equilibrium price to rise. Thus, a shift in the supply curve, with the demand curve held constant, will cause equilibrium quantity to change in the same direction as the change in supply but will cause equilibrium price to change in the opposite direction. An easy way to remember is to picture the supply curve moving along a given downward-sloping demand curve. As the supply curve shifts to the left, price increases but quantity decreases; as the supply curve shifts to the right, price decreases but quantity increases.

Simultaneous Shifts in Supply and Demand

As long as only one curve shifts at a time, it is easy to say what will happen to equilibrium price and quantity. But if both curves shift simultaneously, the outcome is less obvious. For example, suppose a decline in the price of chocolate chip cookies increases the demand for milk. At the same time an influx of new dairy farmers into the market increases the supply of milk. When both demand and supply increase, what happens to equilibrium price and quantity? Intuition suggests that if both supply and demand increase, equilibrium quantity increases as well, but what happens to the equilibrium price? As we will see, we cannot say for sure what happens to equilibrium price unless we trace through the effects for specific shifts in the supply and the demand curves.

Panels (a) and (b) of Exhibit 9 illustrate the point. Supply and demand increase in both panels, and in both panels the equilibrium quantity has increased. The equilibrium price, however, has increased in panel (a) but decreased in panel (b). We can say for sure that if demand and supply both increase, the equilibrium quantity will increase, but the effect on equilibrium price depends on the shift in demand *relative* to the shift in supply. If the shift in demand dominates, as in panel (a), the equilibrium price will increase. If the shift in supply dominates, as in panel (b), the equilibrium price will fall.

Conversely, if both curves decrease, the equilibrium quantity will decrease, though, again, we cannot say what will happen to equilibrium price

**EXHIBIT 9   INDETERMINATE EFFECT OF AN INCREASE IN BOTH
                   SUPPLY AND DEMAND**

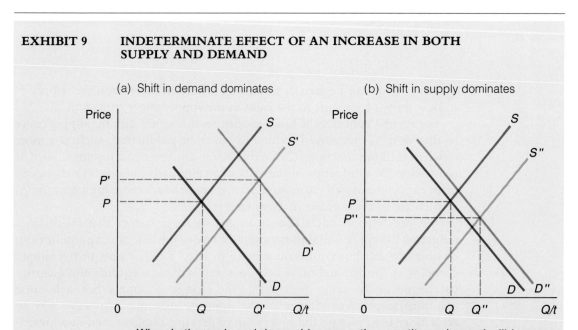

When both supply and demand increase, the quantity exchanged will increase also. The effect on price depends on which curve shifts furthest. In panel (a) the shift in demand is greater than the shift in supply; as a result, the price rises. In panel (b) the shift in supply is greater, and so the price falls.

unless we examine specific shifts. If the shift to the left in demand dominates, the price will fall; if the shift to the left in supply dominates, the price will rise. When both curves shift in the same direction, we can summarize what will happen with the following rule: if the demand curve shift is greater than the supply curve shift, equilibrium price will increase when the curves increase, and equilibrium price will decrease when the curves decrease.

If supply and demand move in opposite directions, we cannot say without reference to particular shifts what will happen to equilibrium quantity, but we can say what will happen to equilibrium price: equilibrium price will increase if demand increases and will decrease if demand decreases. For example, if demand increases and supply decreases, the equilibrium price will increase. This process is probably somewhat confusing to you, but Exhibit 10 summarizes the possibilities. Take time now to experiment with some shifts in supply and demand to develop an understanding of the process.

Although markets usually result from the interaction of many buyers and sellers, markets are seldom consciously designed by any individual or group. They naturally arise, much like the car dealers that assemble on the outskirts of town. Despite the relative simplicity with which markets coordinate the decisions of unrelated buyers and sellers, markets are not without their critics.

EXHIBIT 10   EFFECTS OF CHANGES IN BOTH SUPPLY AND DEMAND

Change in Demand

	Demand Increases	*Demand decreases*
Supply increases	Equilibrium price change is indeterminate. Equilibrium quantity increases.	Equilibrium price falls. Equilibrium quantity change is indeterminate.
Supply decreases	Equilibrium price rises. Equilibrium quantity change is indeterminate.	Equilibrium price change is indeterminate. Equilibrium quantity decreases.

Change in Supply

Markets are efficient devices for allocating scarce resources to their highest-valued use. The measure of value is consumers' willingness and ability to pay. In a market economy those who are unable to pay go without. Many people view this feature of the market system as a flaw. Some observers of the markets in the U.S. economy are troubled, for example, by the fact that although there are thousands of homeless people sleeping on the nation's streets, more than $20 billion is spent each year on pet food. On your next trip to the supermarket, notice how much shelf space is allowed for pet products—often an entire aisle. In the next section we consider some ways that government intervenes in markets to redirect production and consumption.

DISEQUILIBRIUM PRICES

A surplus triggers market forces that exert downward pressure on the price, while a shortage exerts upward pressure on the price. But markets do not adjust to equilibrium instantaneously. During the time it takes to adjust, the market is said to be in *disequilibrium*. Disequilibrium is usually a temporary phase while the market gropes toward equilibrium. But sometimes, as a result of government intervention, disequilibrium lasts a long time.

Government-Contrived Disequilibrium

Certain markets cannot freely adjust to their equilibrium values, often as a result of some government policy. In such instances the disequilibrium is more permanent and distorts the market mechanism. We will consider some of the ways that market forces can be subverted.

Price Floors   Prices are sometimes fixed at a level above the equilibrium value. For example, the federal government often regulates the prices of agricultural commodities. The rationale for interference in this market is that a freely operating market does not ensure farmers a high enough price for their products. Government officials believe that higher farm prices will stabilize agricultural markets and help prevent the family farm from becoming extinct. Farmers are also an influential voting group.

To achieve higher prices, the government sets a *minimum*, or a *floor*, on the price at which certain farm products can be sold, making it illegal to sell below that price. The effect of this minimum, or floor, on the milk market is shown in Exhibit 11, where we assume that a minimum price of $1 per half gallon has been established. At that price farmers in our simple market supply 24 million half gallons per month, but consumers demand only 14 million half gallons. Thus, the price floor results in a surplus of 10 million half gallons.

Unless the surplus is somehow eliminated, it will create downward pressure on the price of milk. So, as part of the price floor, the government agrees to buy the surplus milk to take it off the market. The federal government, in fact, spends billions of dollars each year on surplus

EXHIBIT 11   **EFFECTS OF A PRICE FLOOR**

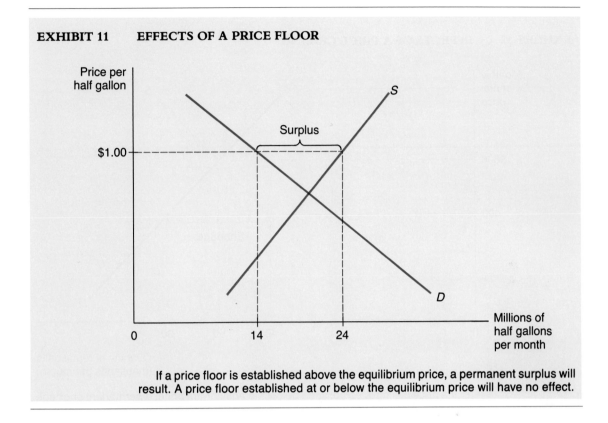

If a price floor is established above the equilibrium price, a permanent surplus will result. A price floor established at or below the equilibrium price will have no effect.

agricultural goods. The government also tries on occasion to distribute this surplus. Perhaps you have seen mounds of surplus butter in your high school cafeteria line. You may also remember hearing about people lining up for "free" blocks of surplus cheese. The government cannot give away all of the surplus, however, since that would reduce private demand and create an even bigger surplus. Consequently, the government must store most of the surplus.

Thus, the high floor price reduces the quantity demanded but increases the quantity supplied. To keep the resulting surplus from pushing prices down to their market-clearing level, the government must buy the surplus.

Price Ceilings   Sometimes it becomes an explicit public policy to ensure that prices are kept below their equilibrium values, so the government sets a *maximum*, or *ceiling*, on the price that can be charged. For example, public officials in some cities were alarmed by the rising cost of housing and imposed ceilings on the rental rates that can be charged. Exhibit 12 depicts the supply and demand for rental housing in a hypothetical city, where the number of rental units is measured on the horizontal axis, and the monthly rent on the vertical axis. The equilibrium, or market-clearing, price is $600 per month, and the equilibrium quantity is 50,000 housing units.

EXHIBIT 12   EFFECTS OF A PRICE CEILING

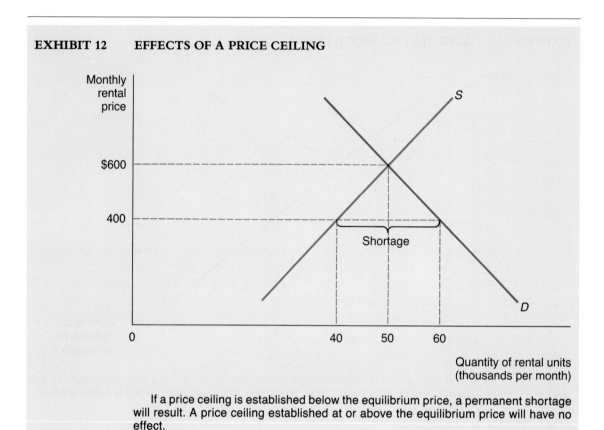

If a price ceiling is established below the equilibrium price, a permanent shortage will result. A price ceiling established at or above the equilibrium price will have no effect.

Assume that the ceiling on rents has been set at $400 per month. At that price 60,000 rental units are demanded, but only 40,000 are supplied, resulting in a shortage of 20,000 units. With so much excess demand, price no longer serves as a mechanism to ration housing units to those who value the housing most highly. Consequently, other rationing devices emerge, such as waiting lists, political connections, and the willingness to pay under-the-table charges, such as "key fees," "finder's fees," excessive deposits, and the like. If people are able to secure a rent-controlled apartment, the lease becomes a valuable asset that they keep as long as they can. Even when people move out of town, they might sublet the rent-controlled apartment.

As mentioned in Chapter 1, advocates of rent control often ignore the secondary effects that such ceilings have on the quantity of housing supplied. Nor do the available rentals go to those who are most needy. Many of the rich and famous who live at fancy addresses in New York City reportedly pay only about 20 percent of the market price for their rent-controlled apartments.

Government restrictions distort the market's ability to ration goods to those consumers who value them most highly. The problem is that artificially high prices encourage too much production, while artificially low prices discourage adequate production. These restrictions will give rise to various nonprice allocation devices to deal with the surpluses or shortages produced by the market interference. Not all disequilibrium situations are caused by government, however, as we will see next.

Disequilibrium in Private Markets

Sometimes price does not perform the market-clearing function. For example, the doorways of New York City's most "in" nightspot are often crowded with people literally begging to get in. The doorkeeper admits the strange, the rich, and the famous from among the eager group and turns away the rest. One story has it that admittance is based on shoes. You might ask why a profit-maximizing owner would follow such a rationing scheme rather than simply raising the cover charge to the point where just enough people show up each night to fill the place. The waiting crowd that gathers outside reflects the excess demand, but this crowd also represents part of the attraction of the place, so the owner does not want to set the admission fee high enough to eliminate the crowd. Also, customer enjoyment of the club depends on who else is admitted, so a large crowd provides a large pool from which to select the right mix of customers.

Although our market-adjustment model assumes the market will adjust rather quickly to equate quantity supplied with quantity demanded, often the adjustment process can take months, as you will see in the following case study.

CASE STUDY

Supply and Demand in the Cabbage Patch

It has probably been a few years since you were in a toy store, but you can perhaps remember wandering through a store such as Toys-R-Us, in awe at the selection. Such a store typically has more than ten thousand different toys to choose from, and this selection is only one-tenth of the variety of toys that the store could have stocked. Each year manufacturers add thousands of new toys to the list and drop thousands of losers. Some of these toys have tremendous staying power, such as the long-running Barbie doll (over twenty-five years in production, Barbie is older than most of you).

Store buyers must predict nearly a year in advance what will be demanded in the future because orders are placed in February for Christmas delivery. Can you imagine the uncertainty of this market? Who, for example, could have anticipated the phenomenal success of the Cabbage Patch Kids a few years back? Although more than 20 million of the dolls sold for $30 each between mid-1983 and the end of 1984, there was still excess demand.

What kind of response do we expect as a result of this disequilibrium? When the established price is below the equilibrium level, price does not serve as a rationing device, so other rationing schemes take over. The most dramatic forms of rationing were the near riots that broke out each time a store sprouted a new patch of dolls. Stores established waiting lists to allocate their monthly allotment, and the waits lasted up to eight months.

The inability of the manufacturer to keep up with the quantity demanded attracted others into the market. For example, boatloads of counterfeit dolls were reportedly pouring into the country from overseas. Some of these illegal aliens were detained at the border, but many more made it through. Classified ads also appeared, offering the doll for as much as $250. Another rationing scheme was practiced by some car dealers and furniture stores, who promised to throw in a free doll to anyone who made a major purchase. These different responses could have been predicted in a situation where the market price did not rise enough to eliminate excess demand.

Why didn't the toy manufacturer simply allow the price to seek its market level? Suppose, for example, that the market-clearing price was $60, twice the established price. Consumers may have resented paying such a high price for a doll, and the manufacturer, a producer of a variety of toys, may not have wanted to risk criticism for being an opportunist, or a "price gouger," in selling this doll.

SUMMARY

1. Demand is a relationship between the price of a good and the quantity consumers are prepared to buy. According to the law of demand, the price of a good is inversely related to the quantity demanded, other things constant. This inverse relationship between price and quantity is expressed by a downward-sloping demand curve.

2. Demand curves slope downward because of both the substitution and income effects of a price change. The substitution effect arises because a decrease in the price of one good will encourage consumers to switch to purchasing the now relatively cheaper good. The income effect arises because the real value of each consumer's income increases as the price of the good declines. Consequently, consumers are more able to buy the good as the price declines.

3. The factors other than price that can affect the demand for a product are (1) consumer income, (2) the prices of related goods, (3) consumer expectations, (4) the number of consumers in the market, and (5) consumer tastes.

4. Price and quantity supplied are usually directly, or positively, related; more is offered for sale at a higher price than at a lower price, other things constant. Because more is supplied as the price increases, the supply curve is upward sloping. Two major reasons account for the direct relationship between quantity supplied and price. First, because resources used in the production of the good are rewarded more as the price increases, the owners of these resources are more willing to supply the good at higher prices than at lower prices. Second, because the opportunity cost of producing each additional unit usually goes up as output expands, a higher price increases each producer's ability to expand quantity supplied.

5. The factors other than price that can affect the supply of a product are (1) the state of technology, (2) the prices of relevant resources, (3) the prices of alternative goods, (4) producer expectations, and (5) the number of producers.

6. Demand and supply come together in a market. A major function of markets is to provide information about the price, quantity, and quality of the item for sale. Markets reduce the transactions cost of exchange—the cost of time and information required to undertake exchange. The interaction of supply and demand guides resources and products to their highest-valued use.

7. The combination of price and quantity that exactly matches the independent wishes of

both buyers and sellers is called the equilibrium price and quantity. Once equilibrium is achieved, all consumers and producers will be satisfied. The equilibrium price and quantity will continue to prevail unless there is a change in one of the nonprice factors that determines supply of demand.

8. Markets are not always in equilibrium; it may take time for markets to adjust. During this intervening period the market is said to be in disequilibrium. Although disequilibrium is usually a temporary phase, government policies often create chronic shortages or surpluses.

QUESTIONS AND PROBLEMS

1. (Demand and Quantity Demanded) Often students are confused about what variables will shift the demand curve for a good or service. According to the text, what variables increase the demand for normal goods? Explain why a reduction in the price of a normal good does *not* increase the demand for the good.

2. (Income Effects) Often economists use the size of the income effect to classify a good or service as a luxury or necessity. What do people commonly mean by *luxuries,* and how would income effects be related to this meaning of *luxuries*?

3. (Shifting Demand) Using supply and demand curves, show the effect of each of the following events on the market for cigarettes:

   a. A cure for lung cancer is found.
   b. There is an increase in the prices of cigars and pipes.
   c. There is a substantial increase in wages in states that grow tobacco.
   d. A fertilizer that increases the yield per acre of tobacco is discovered.
   e. There is a substantial rise in the price of matches and cigarette lighters.
   f. An embargo is placed on foreign tobacco products.

4. (Substitutes) During 1973 and 1974 there was a sharp rise in the price of oil. Why should this event be related to the subsequent rise in Cadillac sales in Eastern Kentucky and West Virginia?

5. (Equilibrium) Determine whether each of the following is true or false. Then provide a short explanation for your answer.

   a. At equilibrium all sellers can find buyers.
   b. At equilibrium no buyer is willing and able to buy more than that buyer is being sold.

   c. At equilibrium there is no pressure on the market to produce or to consume more than is being sold.
   d. At prices *above* equilibrium the quantity exchanged is larger than the quantity demanded.
   e. At prices *below* equilibrium the quantity exchanged is equal to the quantity supplied.

6. (Demand) Water is essential for life, whereas diamonds are not essential for life. Yet a bucket of diamonds is worth far more (in dollars) than a bucket of water. Explain why.

7. (Supply and Demand) How did each of the following affect the world price of oil? (Use basic supply and demand analysis.)

   a. tax credits for home insulation
   b. completion of the Alaskan oil pipeline
   c. decontrol of oil price ceilings
   d. discovery of oil in Mexico and the North Sea
   e. mass production of smaller and lighter automobiles
   f. increased use of nuclear power
   g. increased fighting among OPEC members

8. (Price Floor) There is considerable interest in whether the minimum wage rate contributes to teenage unemployment. Draw a supply and demand diagram for the unskilled labor market and discuss the effects of a minimum wage. Who will be helped, and who will be hurt? Does the minimum wage make society worse off?

9. (Price Ceiling) Often a sick person will have to wait a considerable amount of time to see a doctor. How is the value of the time spent in the office, along with the price of the doctor's service, related to the market-clearing price of the office visit?

10. (Supply and Demand) Tuition at many American universities is rising each year. At some places the cost of attending school is approaching $20,000 per year. Using supply and demand, explain why this is happening. Do you think this trend will continue?

THE ECONOMIC ACTORS: HOUSEHOLDS, FIRMS, and GOVERNMENTS

The previous chapter examined the interaction of supply and demand in allocating scarce resources. Perhaps the book should have ended there since we said that most economic questions could be explained by supply and demand. However, certain details must be understood in order to apply the supply and demand framework. In this chapter we examine the three main actors in the economy: households, firms, and governments. The starring role is played by households because they supply the resources for production and demand the goods and services produced. Firms and governments are supporting actors in the sense that they try to respond to the demands of households. Topics and terms discussed include:

- Evolution of the household

- Household production

- Evolution of the firm

- Kinds of firms

- Rationale for government

INTRODUCTION

The three types of decision-making units in the economy are households, firms, and governments. Households supply resources—land, labor, capital, and entrepreneurial ability—to firms and to governments and, in turn, demand goods and services. Firms and governments supply goods and services to households, and, in turn, they demand resources. Firms supply private goods and services, such as bananas and carpet cleaning.

Governments supply public goods and services, such as highways and police protection.

The distinctions between private and public goods and services will be developed later in the chapter. For now, we recognize that public goods and services, once produced, are available equally to everyone in the economy. For example, a system of national defense protects all citizens; in fact, it would be costly to exclude anyone from the benefits of national defense. In contrast, the benefits of private goods and services are limited to those who consume the goods.

Resources are bought and sold in resource markets, where households are suppliers and firms and governments are demanders. Private goods and services are bought and sold in product markets, where firms are suppliers and households are demanders. In the product market the allocation process gives each dollar spent by the household an equal voice in deciding what private goods and services get produced and in what quantities. Public goods and services are allocated through *political markets*, which are based on the votes, not the dollars, of households. Each voter, at least in principle, has an equal voice in deciding what public goods and services get produced. Private goods and services are allocated through the market system, and public goods and services through the political system.

The structure, organization, and objectives of the three main economic units—households, firms, and governments—will be examined in this chapter. We begin with the star of the show—the household.

STARRING: THE HOUSEHOLD

Households are the key actors in the economy. Although households usually consist of several individuals, each household is viewed as acting as a single decision-making unit. The decisions of households about public and private goods determine what is produced. As suppliers of resources and as demanders of goods and services, households are required to make all kinds of choices, such as where to live, where to work, what to buy, and how much to save.

Households Maximize Utility

What exactly do households attempt to accomplish in making decisions? Households are assumed to maximize their level of satisfaction, sense of well-being, or overall welfare. For short, we say that households attempt to maximize **utility**. Households, like other economic actors, are viewed as rational decision makers, meaning that they act in their own best interests and would not deliberately select an option expected to make them worse off.

Utility is the satisfaction received from consuming a good or service.

Utility maximization is based on each household's subjective goals, not some objective standard. The subjectivity of utility allows for a wide range of household behavior—all consistent with utility maximization. Some households locate in the city; others settle down in the country. Some households are large; others are small. Some households maintain a manicured front lawn; others allow junk cars to accumulate.

A House Is Not Necessarily a Home

There are more than 85 million households in the United States. All those who live under one roof are considered part of the same household. When we think of the household, we usually think of Mom, Dad, the kids, and Rover. However, the two-parent household, though still in the majority, is less common now than it once was. In 1950 married couples made up 77 percent of households, but in the 1980s, they number less than 60 percent. The major shifts have been in the percentage of households headed by women, which increased from 8 to 12 percent, and in the percentage of people living alone or with unrelated individuals, which has climbed from 11 to 27 percent of all households. Because of these shifts, the size of the average household has decreased by about 20 percent since 1950.

Households as Resource Suppliers

Households utilize their limited resources in an attempt to satisfy their unlimited wants. They can use these resources to produce goods and services in the household, such as preparing meals or fixing a leaky roof. Alternatively, they can sell these resources in the resource market. Households supply their resources to firms and to governments and, in turn, demand goods and services. These decisions involve a complex array of choices. Consider first the role of the household as a resource supplier. Ultimately, all resources are owned by households, either directly or indirectly, and these resources are demanded by producers. Recall from Chapter 1 that households are paid wages for their labor, rent for their land, interest for their capital, and profit for their entrepreneurial abilities.

Labor is the most valuable resource owned by most households. Because the household wants to sell its labor for the highest possible wage, household members are willing to undertake activities designed to enhance the market value of their labor, such as pursuing educational programs or moving to an area of higher prevailing wages. Unfortunately, members of some households, because of poor education, disability, or bad luck, have few resources that are valued in the resource market. Also, many single parents must remain at home to care for small children. In such circumstances, society has often made the political decision that these individuals are entitled to some form of public assistance. Thus, some households receive *transfer payments* from the government. There are two kinds of transfer payments to households: (1) cash transfers, which are money payments, such as Aid to Families with Dependent Children and Social Security benefits, and (2) in-kind transfers, which are a more direct provision of goods and services, such as food stamps and free medical care.

Exhibit 1 shows the various sources of personal income received by U.S. households. As you can see, about two-thirds of personal income comes from

EXHIBIT 1
SOURCES OF PERSONAL INCOME IN 1986

Source	Billions of Dollars	Percent of Total
Wages and salaries	2282.6	65
Personal interest	475.4	14
Transfer payments	353.4	10
Proprietors' income	278.9	8
Dividends	81.2	2
Rental income	15.6	1
Total	3487.0	100

Source: *Economic Report of the President,* January 1987.

wages and salaries. A distant second on the list is interest earnings, followed by cash transfer payments. Proprietors' income is the next most important source of income, making up 8 percent of the total. Proprietors are people who work for themselves rather than for an employer—farmers, plumbers, and doctors are examples. Less than 3 percent of personal income is received in the form of rents and dividends. Thus, the majority of personal income in the United States is derived from labor earnings rather than from the ownership of such other resources as capital and land.

Households as Demanders of Goods and Services

What happens to personal income once it comes into the household? Recall that households are assumed to maximize utility. Households can allocate their income in three ways. They can spend it on private goods and services such as food and housing, called *personal consumption* expenditures. About 80 percent of personal income went to such expenditures in 1986. They can save it—about 5 percent is usually saved. Or they can pay it to the government as taxes for public goods and services. About 15 percent of personal income goes to taxes. Because decisions about public goods and services are made through some sort of public choice by all voters collectively, the individual household has little to say in such matters.

Since personal consumption represents such an overwhelming share of personal income outlays, perhaps we should look at it more closely. Exhibit 2 gives the dollar value and the breakdown of personal consumption expenditures in 1986. Note that personal spending is divided into three broad categories: (1) *durable goods,* such as refrigerators and cars, (2) *nondurable goods,* such as potato chips and soap, and (3) *services,* such as health care and bus rides. Of the amount spent on personal consumption, 14 percent was on durable goods, 34 percent was on nondurable goods, and 52 percent was on services.

The services sector is the fastest-growing area of personal spending. This sector has grown in part because many activities, such as entertainment and meal preparation, that formerly were carried out in the household are now

EXHIBIT 2
PERSONAL CONSUMPTION EXPENDITURES FOR 1986

Object	Billions of Dollars	Percent of Total
Durable Goods		
Motor vehicles	182	7
Furniture	137	5
Other	69	2
Total durable goods	388	14
Nondurable Goods		
Food	493	18
Clothing	165	6
Fuel and gasoline	93	3
Other nondurable goods	182	7
Total nondurable goods	933	34
Services		
Housing	438	16
Housing operation	178	6
Transportation	96	4
Medical care	316	11
Other services	413	15
Total services	1441	52

Source: *Economic Report of the President*, January 1987.

more often purchased in the market. In fact, enough changes have taken place in the household to make it worthwhile for us to explore this evolution.

The Evolution of the Household

In earlier times, when the economy was primarily agricultural, roles for individual family members reflected the division of labor and specialization of tasks on the farm. Parents were assisted in these tasks by their many children, who often were assigned specific functions. The household as an economic unit was much more self-contained than is the modern household. Food, clothing, and shelter were produced primarily within the household. Farm products not required for domestic consumption were sold in the market, and the money was used to purchase tools and any other special items that could not be produced by the household.

With the introduction of new seed varieties, fertilizers, and labor-saving machinery, fewer farms were needed to supply the economy's demand for food. Simultaneously, the growth of factories in the cities created an increased demand for labor in urban areas. As a result, families began migrating to the cities. These urban dwellers were far less self-sufficient than their rural counterparts.

Since World War II the economics of the household has changed in important ways. Perhaps most significant has been the dramatic increase in the number of married women in the labor force. In 1950 only about 15 percent of married women with children were in the labor force, compared with more than 50 percent today. Economists who have studied the matter argue that the greater demand for labor was the primary reason for the rising tide of married women in the work force. Many women found opportunities in the labor market more attractive than those available at home.

The rise of the two-earner household has affected the family as an economic unit. Rising wages and expanded job possibilities have increased the opportunity cost of working in the home. Consequently, less production takes place in the home, and more goods and services are demanded in the market. Child-care services, fast food, and frozen dinners have displaced some household production. Since less is produced in the home, there is less need for a division of labor in household production. The rise of the two-worker family therefore reduced the advantages of specialization within the household, which was a central feature of the farm family. Nonetheless, some production still occurs in the home. The decisions about what is produced in the home and what is purchased in the market will be explored in the next section.

SUPPORTING ACTOR: THE FIRM

As we saw, there was a time when the household grew its own food, built its own home, made its own clothes and furniture, and provided its own entertainment. Now we find that many of these goods and services are provided by firms through markets. One change already mentioned explains much of the shift of production from the home to the market. Technological developments increased the productivity of each worker and contributed to the shift of employment from the farm to the factory. The invention of the reaper, for example, allowed one farmer to accomplish what had taken many to do. Not as many farm hands were needed to grow enough food to feed a nation. Moreover, the introduction of machines in the factory made labor more productive in the factory.

Transaction Costs and the Firm

Specialization and comparative advantage explain why much production takes place outside the home. Why, however, was the firm necessary to capture the gains arising from specialization? Rather than build a table from scratch, could not a household take advantage of specialization by relying on the individual experts who grew the trees, milled the lumber, cut the wood to size, and assembled the table? No, and the reason is transaction costs. That is, if a person had to visit each of these specialists individually and strike an agreement, the cost of transacting these deals would require much information and time. These transaction costs could easily erase the gains arising from the specialization of labor.

Instead of visiting and bargaining with each specialist, you can pay someone to do the bargaining for you. You can pay an entrepreneur, who hires all the resources necessary to produce the table. Recall that the entrepreneur uncovers or discovers profit opportunities arising from the difference between what is paid for the resources and what is received from the sale of the product. Because the entrepreneur is able to contract for the construction of many tables rather than just one, the entrepreneur is able to reduce the transaction costs per table.

Before the Industrial Revolution, which began in England during the eighteenth century and spread to other parts of the world, certain activities were carried out in the home, such as turning raw cotton and wool into twine. The home served as a tiny factory specializing in the production of a specific good. Entrepreneurs relied on "putting out" the raw material to rural households, or cottages, which turned cotton and wool into finished goods. This *cottage industry* system offered the entrepreneur two advantages. First, this system shifted much of the production costs to the workers, who used their own home and their own equipment. All the entrepreneur needed was the ability to transport and store the raw material and the finished goods. Second, rural workers worked for less than urban workers because rural workers had little to do between crop cycles, so their opportunity cost was low. Most urban production during this period was regulated largely by craft guilds, which carefully limited the supply to keep their wages high.

The "putting out" system worked well for hundreds of years, but as the economy began to expand in the eighteenth century, greater demand for finished goods and rising transportation costs caused entrepreneurs to consider new ways to carry out production. The solution was to organize the work under one roof so the workers' performance could be supervised more directly. As mentioned earlier, however, this coming together of resources would not have been possible without the invention of machines far bigger than anything that had been used in the home. One hallmark of the Industrial Revolution was the organization of work in large, centrally powered factories, which allowed a more efficient division of labor and direct supervision of production.

Why Does Household Production Still Exist?

If firms are such convenient units for reducing the costs of bringing together specialized resources, why doesn't all production occur within firms? Why does some production still occur in the household? After all, activities such as meal preparation, cleaning, and child care are still undertaken primarily by members of the household, not by firms. Indeed, some people repair their own cars, paint their own homes, and perform many other tasks that could be, and in some cases are, performed by firms. Why hasn't all productive activity shifted to the market?

Like many questions in economics, these are answered by reference to opportunity cost. If a household finds that the opportunity cost of performing a task is less than the market price, the task will be performed in the household. In general, the households with the highest opportunity cost of time will hire firms to perform household tasks. Typically, the physician rather than the janitor will hire someone to mow the lawn. Consider some of the influences that at times make household production relatively more attractive than firm production.

Some Household Production Requires Few Specialized Resources   As efficient as firms are at reducing the transaction costs of bringing specialized resources together, some activities require so few of these resources that households may find it cheaper to do these jobs themselves. Sweeping the floor requires only a broom and some time and is usually performed by household members. Shampooing the rug, however, can involve expensive machinery and specialized skills, and this service is often purchased in the market. Similarly, while you would not hire someone to brush your teeth, filling a cavity is another matter. Thus, many personal tasks demand neither particular skills nor specialized machinery, so such tasks are usually performed by household members.

Some Technological Advances Have Made Household Production More Efficient   Technological breakthroughs have not been confined to the factories. Machines have entered the home as well and have made time spent in household production more efficient. The vacuum cleaner, dishwasher, and microwave oven reduce the time and often the skill required to perform household tasks. The demand for professional laundry service has declined as a result of the automatic washer and dryer and the invention of wrinkle-resistant, easy-care clothing. Therefore, some technological breakthroughs have increased the productivity of household members in performing certain household tasks.

Finally, households may choose home production because they have more control over the product than they would if they purchased the good or service in the market. For example, many people prefer home-cooked meals to restaurant food, in part because meals prepared at home can be more in accord with individual tastes.

Why Do Some Firms Specialize?

If the firm is such an efficient device for combining resources, why aren't all phases of production combined within a single firm? For example, why do many furniture factories purchase wood from other firms rather than growing their own trees? Or why do they sell their finished products to retailers rather than directly to households? Why isn't there a single large firm that produces everything? To answer these questions, we must consider the costs and benefits of coordinating activity within the firm versus coordination through markets.

While firms are convenient devices for assembling and coordinating specialized factors of production under one roof, the gains from this coordination are limited. There are bounds on the ability to monitor all the specialists, exercise quality control at each stage, and keep track of the entire process. As firms attempt to bring together more and more specialized resources, at some point the cost of this internal coordination exceeds the benefits. Then it becomes more efficient simply to purchase certain specialized inputs from other firms, letting the market handle the coordinating task of linking one firm's output with another firm's input.

The market, relying only on the profit-maximizing motives of each firm, guides resources through the intermediate steps to produce the final good. For example, consider again the the purchase of a table by a household: the household purchased the table from a furniture store, which purchased it from a manufacturer, which purchased some inputs, such as labor, directly from the household and other inputs, such as lumber and paint, from other firms. Most furniture manufacturers find it more efficient to buy their lumber from a mill than to grow it and cut it themselves.

More generally, firms often find that they are more efficient if they specialize in a single product or in a limited range of products. For instance, many seasoned travelers are wary about eating at the hotel's restaurant, despite its convenience, because of the difficulty of operating both a nice hotel and a good restaurant. Different entrepreneurs may have different abilities to coordinate resources and may have different opinions about the appropriate amount of coordination that should take place in a single firm. Hence, we observe entrepreneurs who attempt to coordinate varying degrees of specialization within the firm. That is one reason why some hotels have a restaurant and some do not.

Rather than the bulk of production taking place in the home or the household bargaining with each separate resource, these resources are brought together by entrepreneurs in firms such as factories, mills, offices, and restaurants. Firms are therefore economic units formed for profit by entrepreneurs, who combine resources—land, labor, and capital—to produce goods and services. Firms are convenient devices for reducing the transaction costs involved in hiring a variety of resources to produce a particular good or service. Moreover, by bringing resources together, firms reduce the cost of transporting the product during the various phases of production. There are limits to the gains of bringing resources together in a single firm, however, so firms tend to specialize rather than produce the final good from scratch. The market rather than the firm often serves to coordinate the intermediate stages of production, thereby linking the specialized firms.

Now that we have explored how firms evolved, we will consider the various kinds of firms.

Kinds of Firms

There are about 17 million businesses in the United States. Two-thirds of these are small farms, small retail businesses, or small services. Each year many new firms are started, and many fail. In fact, three of five new businesses go "belly up" before their third year of operation. Firms can be organized in three ways: as a sole proprietorship, as a partnership, or as a corporation. The advantages and disadvantages of each structure will be examined next.

*A **sole propri-
etorship** is a firm
with a single
owner, who has
the right to all
profits and who
bears unlimited
liability for the
firm's debts.*

Sole Proprietorships   The simplest form of organization is the **sole proprietorship**, which is the single-owner firm—Pop's corner store, the local
realtor, the family physician. Although sole proprietorships do not have to be
small, they usually are. The advantage of this business form is that the owner
is in complete control. A sole proprietorship is also easy to organize,
involving no special legal requirements. The firm simply opens for business.

One disadvantage is that the owner has unlimited liability for any debts
the business incurs. Therefore, if you are the proprietor of a corner store and
someone sues you after tripping over the front step, you could lose not just
your store, but also your house, your car, and all your other property.
Another disadvantage of the sole proprietorship is that without partners or
other backers, it may be difficult to raise enough money to make the business
a success. One final disadvantage is that sole proprietorships usually go out of
business upon the death of the proprietor.

Sole proprietorships are the most common form of business organization,
accounting for 75 percent of all businesses. Because this type of firm is
typically small, however, proprietorships generate a small portion of all
business sales—less than 10 percent.

*A **partnership** is
a firm with mul-
tiple owners, who
share the firm's
profits and who
each bear unlim-
ited liability for
the firm's debts.*

Partnerships   A more complicated form of business organization is the
partnership, which involves two or more individuals who agree to contribute some of their own resources to the business in return for a share of the
profit or loss. Law, accounting, and medical partnerships typify this business
form. A partnership is relatively easy to organize, though not as easy as the
sole proprietorship; the partners simply have to reach some accord about the
division of responsibilities and rewards. Because more than one individual is
involved from the start, partners often find it easier than sole proprietors to
raise the start-up funds necessary to get the business off the ground.

Partnerships also have disadvantages, however. Decision making can be
more difficult than with a single owner. Also, each partner is liable for all the
debts and claims against the partnership. Consequently, a partner could lose
everything because of another partner's poor business decisions. Finally, the
death or departure of one partner may disrupt the firm's continuity and could
require a complete reorganization. The partnership is the least common form
of business organization, making up less than 10 percent of all firms and
accounting for less than 5 percent of all firm sales.

*A **corporation** is
a legal entity
owned by stock-
holders, whose li-
ability is limited
to the value of
their stock.*

Corporations   By far the most complicated form of business organization
is the **corporation**. The corporation is a legal entity authorized by the state
through articles of incorporation. The corporation can be taxed and sued as if
it were a person. The owners of the corporation are issued shares of stock,
which are pieces of paper reflecting ownership. The owners of stock, or
stockholders, share in the profits of the corporation in proportion to their
ownership of stock. An owner of 10 percent of the stock is entitled to 10
percent of the profits.

A major advantage of the corporate form is that many individuals—
hundreds or even thousands—can pool their money to finance the firm. The

corporate form therefore represents the easiest way to amass large sums of financing. Another advantage is that, as a stockholder, your liability in the firm's losses is limited to the value of your stock. Thus, the most you can lose is the amount of your investment in the firm. A final advantage of this form is that the corporation has a life of its own, even if ownership of the firm changes hands.

There are some disadvantages to the corporate form as well. Whereas the sole proprietor has direct control over the firm's operation, a stockholder has less ability to determine the firm's policies because the firm may have many stockholders. Each share of stock usually carries with it one vote, so a stockholder with only 1 percent of the shares controls only 1 percent of the votes. These votes are used to elect the board of directors, who oversee the operation of the firm. Another problem with the corporate form is that because the firm is treated like a legal entity, it is also taxed like one. Profits are taxed first by the corporate profits tax; remaining profits are again taxed as personal income when they are received by the stockholders. Hence, corporate profits are taxed twice on their way to the stockholders, whereas the income from sole proprietorships and partnerships is taxed only once.

Corporations make up only 16 percent of all businesses, but because they are on average much larger than the other two forms of business, corporate sales represented 88 percent of all business sales in 1980. Exhibit 3 summarizes the importance of each kind of business in terms of total numbers and total sales. As we have said, the sole proprietorship is the most important in terms of numbers, but the corporation is the most important in terms of sales.

Nonprofit Firms

Firms can also be divided into two major categories: for-profit and non-profit firms. For-profit firms have as an explicit objective the maximization of profits. Other firms, such as a nonprofit hospital, the Red Cross, the Salvation Army, a community church, and perhaps the college you are attending, do not have profit as an explicit objective. But even these nonprofit institutions must cover the cost of the resources they employ, and they do this through some combination of contributions and charges for the services they provide. When we talk about firms in this book, we will be referring to for-profit firms.

SUPPORTING ACTOR: THE GOVERNMENT

Why does the economy need producers other than firms? Since firms appear willing and able to satisfy consumer demands as long as there is a profit in it, regardless of how strange those demands are, why not end the story here? Why is it necessary for yet another economic unit to get into the act? Well, for

EXHIBIT 3   COMPOSITION OF FIRMS BY TYPE ACCORDING TO THE NUMBERS OF EACH TYPE AND SALES OF EACH TYPE, 1980

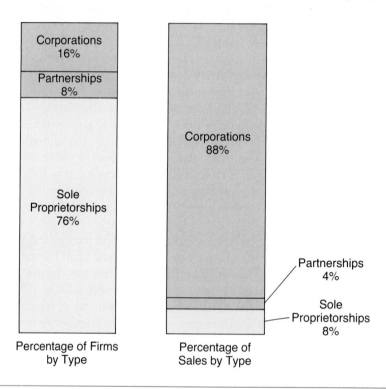

Source: *Statistical Abstract of the United States: 1984* (U.S. Bureau of the Census, 1984).

a variety of reasons, voluntary exchange through private markets does not guarantee that all demands will be met. The ways that voluntary exchange may depart from socially desirable outcomes will be explored in this section.

The Role of Government

Establishing and Enforcing the Rules of the Game   Private markets are based on people like you voluntarily employing their resources to maximize their utility. What if you were robbed of your paycheck on the way home from work each week, or what if your employer told you after a week's work that you would not be paid? The system of private markets would break down if you could not safeguard your private property or if you could not enforce contracts. Governments play a role in protecting private property through police protection and in enforcing contracts through a judicial and penal system. More generally, governments attempt to see that participants in markets abide by the "rules of the game."

Regulating Markets Although the "invisible hand" of competition generally promotes an efficient allocation of resources, firms would prefer not to face that market discipline. To avoid price competition, firms may attempt to *collude*, or to agree on a price that all firms will charge. Or individual firms may pursue *anticompetitive* behavior — unfair trade practices aimed at driving competitors out of business. For example, a large firm may sell its product in a particular region at a price below its cost to eliminate local competitors. Once competitors are gone, the price is increased. Government *antitrust laws* attempt to promote competition by prohibiting collusion and other anticompetitive practices.

Regulating Natural Monopoly Resources are usually allocated more efficiently when many firms compete rather than when the product is provided by a only one firm, or **monopoly**. Certain goods and services, however, are provided more efficiently by a monopoly than by competing firms. For example, electricity is more efficiently provided by a single firm that is responsible for all the electrical wires running through the community than by several firms that each run wires. When it is cheaper for one firm than for two or more firms to serve the market, that firm is called a **natural monopoly**. One example of a natural monopoly is an electric utility. Since a natural monopoly has no competitors, it does not confront the rigors of market competition. It could thus charge a higher price than would competitive firms. To prevent higher prices, the government regulates the operation of these natural monopolies. Government regulation is designed to ensure that the price charged consumers is no higher than is necessary to ensure the firm a normal profit, which is the profit earned by competitive firms.

*A **monopoly** is the single producer of a product that has no good substitutes.*

Natural monopoly is the situation in which one firm can serve a market more cheaply than two or more firms can.

Providing Public Goods Firms produce private goods, which are sold only to those who pay for them. Firms have little difficulty excluding those who do not pay from consuming the good. **Public goods**, once produced, are available for all to consume, regardless of who pays and who does not. For example, all residents of this country are protected by the national defense system even if some pay nothing for it. If a private firm produced national defense, households would realize that the benefits of this protection are available to them whether they pay for it or not. The private firm might have difficulty collecting payments from all households. This problem of exclusion does not occur with private goods because the firm can withhold private goods from those who fail to pay.

Public goods, such as national defense, police and fire protection, and a system of justice, once produced, are available to all. These goods will not likely be produced by private, for-profit firms since those firms cannot prevent people who fail to pay from receiving the good. Consequently, the only way the demand for public goods can be satisfied is through government provision. The government has the police power to enforce payment.

*Once produced, a **public good** is available for all residents to consume, regardless of who pays and who does not.*

Dealing with Externalities Another problem with private, competitive markets is that not all the costs and benefits of consumption or production are captured through market transactions. Market transactions reflect only the *private* costs and benefits of the parties involved in the exchange. Yet some aspects of consumption or production affect people who are not involved in the transaction. An individual who smokes considers only the private cost of smoking, not the costs imposed on others because of cigarette smoke. When a paper mill makes production decisions, it need not consider costs imposed on the nearby residents because of the foul odor of its milling process. When you decide on your education plans, you do not consider the positive benefits your fine education will have on the rest of society (for example, because you will be more productive and a better citizen).

*An **externality** is an unpriced by-product of consumption or production that harms or benefits individuals who are not involved in the transaction.*

These are examples of **externalities**, which are unpriced by-products of production or consumption that harm or benefit some individuals who are not involved in the transaction. *Positive externalities* convey benefits; *negative externalities* impose costs. Because market prices do not reflect these externalities, governments often step in to reduce negative externalities, such as factory pollution or reckless driving, and to promote positive externalities, such as quality education and proper health care. Consider positive externalities in the following case study.

CASE STUDY

Positive Externalities

The case of positive externalities is depicted in Exhibit 4, which presents the supply and demand for education. The demand curve, *D,* represents the private demand for education, which reflects the marginal private benefits obtained by individuals who acquire the education. More education is demanded at a lower price than at a higher price. But the benefits of education are not confined to those who become educated. Education confers positive externalities on other people in society in the sense that those who become more educated become better citizens, are better able to support themselves and their families, pay more taxes, are more able to read road signs, and are less likely to resort to crime to earn a living.

Thus, education confers benefits not only on those who become more educated but on others in society as well. If we add these positive externalities to the marginal private benefits of education, we get the marginal social benefits of education. The marginal social benefits include all the benefits society derives from education—both the benefits enjoyed by those who receive the education and the positive externalities enjoyed by others. The marginal social benefits curve is shown in Exhibit 4 above the private demand curve. At each level of education the marginal social benefits exceed the marginal private benefits by the value of the positive externality associated with that particular unit of education.

If education were a strictly private choice—that is, if education were bought and sold in a free market—the amount purchased would be determined by the intersection of the private demand curve, *D,* with the supply curve, yielding output level *Q.* This is the amount of education that maximizes the private net benefits from education. Beyond output level *Q,* the supply price exceeds the marginal private benefits; so those acquiring an

EXHIBIT 4 **EDUCATION AND POSITIVE EXTERNALITIES**

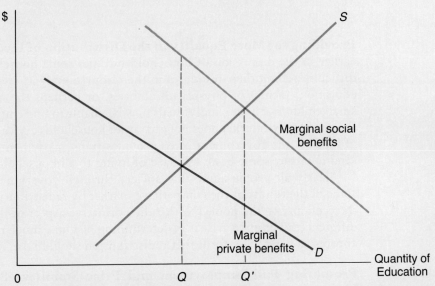

In the absence of government intervention, the quantity of education would be determined at Q, where the supply price equals the marginal private benefits of education. However, education also conveys a positive externality on the rest of society so that the marginal social benefits exceed private benefits. At quantity Q, marginal social benefits exceed the supply price, so that more education is in society's best interest. In such a situation, government will try to encourage an increase in the quantity of education to Q', where supply price equals marginal social benefit.

education would be unwilling to pay the price suppliers would require to provide that amount of education.

But is Q the optimal level of education from the society's point of view? What if one more unit of education is produced? The marginal social benefit of producing that additional unit of education exceeds the price that suppliers would require in order to provide an additional unit of education. Thus, net social welfare increases when output is expanded beyond Q. As long as the marginal social benefit of education exceeds the supply price, social welfare is improved by expanding output. Social welfare is maximized in Exhibit 4, where Q' units of education are provided—that is, where the marginal social benefit equals the supply price.

Thus, society is better off if the amount of education provided exceeds the level that would prevail if education were a strictly private choice. This is why government gets into the act. Government attempts to encourage people to acquire more education. One approach is to pass laws requiring students to stay in school until they are 16 years old. Another approach is for all taxpayers to fund the cost of education so the cost to students is free, as with public schools, or to subsidize education, as is the case with public higher education.

Providing for More Equality in the Distribution of Income   As noted earlier in the discussion of household income, some households may have difficulty selling their resources in the resource market. Because of lack of education, mental or physical disabilities, or perhaps the need to care for small children at home, individuals may be unable to find employment. Since the competitive market does not guarantee households even a minimum level of income, the government often provides transfer payments in cash and in kind to ensure some basic standard of living to all households.

Nearly all people agree that society through government should alter some of the results of the competitive market by redistributing the fruits of the economy to the poor. (Notice the normative aspect of this.) Where the differences of opinion arise is in determining just how much redistribution is appropriate and what form that redistribution should take.

Promoting Full Employment and Price Stability   Private markets provide no guarantee that the economy will always employ all the resources available or will always maintain a stable price level. The government, through its ability to tax, to spend, and to regulate the money supply, attempts to promote both full employment and price stability in the economy. The government's pursuit of full employment and price stability through its taxing and spending powers is called **fiscal policy**. Its pursuit of these objectives through the regulation of the money supply is called **monetary policy**. The implementation of these policies is often controversial; each type of policy receives extensive scrutiny in macroeconomics.

Fiscal policy is the use of government spending, taxes, and borrowing to influence aggregate economic activity.

Monetary policy is the regulation of the economy's money supply to influence aggregate economic activity.

Conclusion   Government activity directed by political markets supplements market activity. The government pursues policies to (1) establish and enforce the rules of the game, (2) promote competition in private markets, (3) regulate natural monopolies, (4) provide public goods, (5) discourage negative externalities and promote positive externalities, (6) ensure greater equality in the distribution of income, and (7) promote the full employment of resources along with stability in the price level.

The Structure of Government

The United States has a *federal system* of government, meaning that responsibilities are shared across levels of government. The state government grants some powers to local government and surrenders some powers to the national, or federal, government. As the system has evolved, the federal government has primary responsibility for the security of the nation and the stability of the economy. State governments support higher education and roads and, with aid from the federal government, assist the poor, the retarded, and those who are otherwise unable to care for themselves. Local governments' responsibilities include primary and secondary education, plus police and fire protection.

Perhaps the best way to understand government is by comparing it to something we have already discussed—households and firms. We will examine how government differs from these other economic actors.

Difficulty in Defining Objectives   Households were assumed to operate in a rational manner to maximize utility, and firms, to maximize profits, but what assumptions can we make about government behavior? What do governments or, more specifically, what do government decision makers, attempt to maximize? There was a time when elected officials and public employees were called "public servants," suggesting that their objective was to serve the public. Now, however, most economists think it naive to assume that government decision makers single-mindedly pursue the public interest, especially if doing so involves great personal cost.

One problem with focusing on the government's objectives is that there is not one government but many governments in our federal system—more than eighty thousand separate jurisdictions in all. Also, the nation was developed under a system of offsetting, or countervailing, powers among the legislative, executive, and judicial branches, so it becomes difficult to think of government as acting like a single, consistent decision maker. Even within the federal executive branch so many agencies and bureaus exist that at times they appear to be working at cross purposes. For example, at the same time the U.S. Surgeon General enforces health warnings on cigarettes, the U.S. Department of Agriculture subsidizes tobacco farmers.

Amid this tangle of jurisdictions, branches, and bureaus of government, one promising theory of behavior is that elected officials make decisions to maximize the number of votes they receive in the next election. Thus, they are *vote maximizers* who are trying to please enough voters to get elected. Another theory of government behavior distinguishes between elected officials and government employees, arguing that government employees attempt to *maximize the size of their bureau*. This theory contends that along with greater size comes a higher salary, more prestige, and more resources to be controlled. These two theories, incidentally, are not mutually exclusive; elected officials could maximize votes, and government employees could maximize the size of their bureau. Since no single theory of government behavior has gained the stature of utility maximization by households or profit maximization by firms, we leave the question about government objectives unresolved at this point.

Voluntary Exchange Versus Coercion   Market exchange is based on the voluntary behavior of firms and households; no coercion is involved. In contrast, in political markets any voting rule that requires less than unanimous consent implies some government coercion. Government follows through with a decision to collect a certain tax or to build a particular highway even if some individuals involved do not agree. Public choices are enforced by the police power of the state. If you fail to pay your taxes, you could wind up in jail. On the contrary, you are never forced to participate in market exchange. If you do not like kumquats, nobody forces you to buy them.

Absence of Market Prices   Another distinguishing feature of governments is that the selling price of the output is usually either zero or some amount below what would cover the cost of output. If you are now attending a state college or university, your tuition probably covers only about one-fourth of the public cost of providing your education. (Why do you suppose taxpayers are willing to subsidize your education?) Because the revenue side of the government budget is usually separate from the expenditure side, there is no direct link between revenue and output as there is in the market system. In the market system, if the price of a good fails to cover its cost, the good will no longer be produced. In the political system, the outlay for a particular public goods and the public revenue required to finance that good do not necessarily match, so goods may be produced even though their costs exceed their benefits.

Size and Growth of Government

In 1929, the year the Great Depression began, all government levels put together spent about $10 billion. Another way to measure the size of government spending is by looking at it as a share of the gross national product. The *gross national product*, or *GNP,* is the total value of all finished goods and services produced in the economy each year. In 1929 government spending accounted for 10 percent of GNP. Local government spending accounted for most of this, with the remainder divided between the federal and state governments. The federal government at that time played a minor role in the economy. In fact, for the country's first one hundred and fifty years the federal government's spending, except during times of war, never amounted to more than 3 percent of the gross national product.

The Great Depression increased the role of the federal government in the economy. Since 1929 the federal government's share of the gross national product has risen from 2.4 percent to over 22.5 percent. Thus, nearly one out of every four dollars spent in the United States is spent by the federal government. In contrast, only one dollar out of eight is spent by state and local governments. Exhibit 5 shows the steady growth in government spending, both in dollars and relative to the gross national product, since 1929.

All levels of government taken together either directly or indirectly account for about one out of every three dollars paid for finished goods and services in the United States. Note that state government spending increased only threefold, from less than 2 percent of GNP in 1929 to about 5 percent today. Local spending as a percentage of gross national product increased only by about two percentage points, from about 6 percent to about 8 percent today. The major source of growth has been federal outlays, particularly for Social Security and other transfer programs.

EXHIBIT 5
THE SIZE AND GROWTH OF GOVERNMENT SPENDING

Year	Total Spending (billions of dollars)	Spending as a Percent of Gross National Product			
		Total	Federal	State	Local
1929	10.3	9.9	2.4	1.6	5.9
1949	59.3	23.0	15.1	3.0	4.8
1969	286.8	30.4	17.8	4.5	8.0
1983	1178.0	35.5	22.5	5.0	8.0

Source: Advisory Commission on Intergovernmental Relations, *Significant Features of Fiscal Federalism*, February 1986.

Sources of Revenue

Where does the government's money come from? Taxes provide the bulk of revenue at all levels of government. The federal government relies primarily on the personal income tax, the state government on the sales tax, and the local government on the property tax. In addition to taxes, other revenue sources include borrowing and user charges, such as tolls and fees. Many states run lotteries designed solely to raise money. Some states also monopolize the sale of liquor—again, to raise money.

We begin our discussion of income taxes with *marginal tax rate,* which is the change in tax payment divided by the change in income. The marginal tax rate indicates how much of each additional dollar of income must be paid in taxes. A marginal tax rate of 10 percent means a person must pay $0.10 in taxes for each extra $1 in income. Since the marginal tax rate determines how much income can be kept and how much be paid to the government, the marginal rate can affect people's incentives to work.

Income taxes are of three types—proportional, progressive, or regressive. Under *proportional taxation,* taxes increase in proportion to the taxpayer's income. Taxpayers at all income levels pay the same percentage of their income in taxes. For example, if the proportional tax rate were 10 percent, an individual with an income of $10,000 would pay $1000 in taxes while an individual with an income of $100,000 would pay $10,000. The proportional tax is often called the flat-rate tax; the marginal tax rate remains constant as income increases.

Under *progressive taxation,* the percentage of income paid in taxes increases as income increases. Thus, the marginal tax rate increases with income under progressive taxation. The most important tax in the economy is the federal personal income tax. Prior to the Tax Reform Act of 1986, the federal personal income tax had fourteen separate marginal tax brackets, starting at 11 percent and rising to 50 percent. The tax reform reduced the rates to two: a 15 percent rate and a 28 percent rate. Thus, the personal income tax is still progressive, but it now has fewer rates and the difference between the bottom and top rates is not as dramatic.

Exhibit 6 shows what has happened to the highest marginal tax rate since the federal personal income tax began in 1913. As you can see, this tax has had

EXHIBIT 6   **TOP MARGINAL RATE OF THE FEDERAL PERSONAL INCOME TAX**

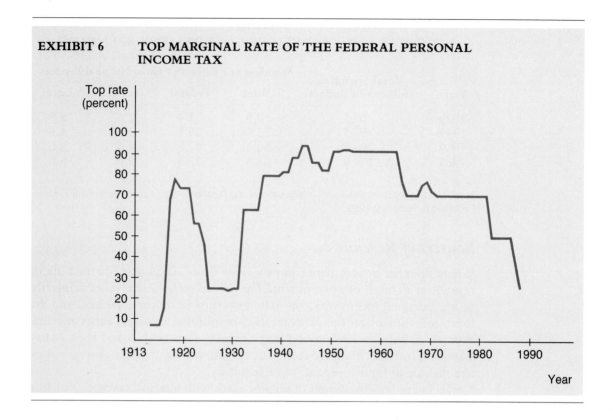

its ups and downs. The top marginal rate is lower now than any time since the 1920s. In the 1950s the government took nine of ten dollars in taxes in the highest bracket.

Regressive taxation is the third type of tax system. With *regressive taxation,* the percentage of income paid in taxes decreases as income increases. Thus, under regressive taxation the marginal tax rate declines as income increases. For example, the Social Security tax in 1987 was 7.15 percent of the first $43,800 of earnings; above $43,800 the marginal tax rate was zero.

A tax is usually justified under one of two general principles. The first is that a tax should be related to the individual's *ability to pay* so that those with a greater ability to pay are taxed more. A tax based on income or on property is often justified under an ability-to-pay rationale. The second tax principle is that of *benefits received.* The argument justifying this principle is that the tax paid should be related to the benefits the individual receives from the government activity funded by the tax. For example, the tax on gasoline is typically based on a benefits-received principle because the amount of tax you pay is linked to the amount of driving you do. Your tax is tied to the benefits you receive from the roads, and the gasoline tax usually is designated to support the construction and maintenance of highways. Thus, the benefits-received principle links the revenue side of the budget with the spending side of the budget. The trouble with the benefits-received principle is that much government activity is provided for those with little ability to pay.

This discussion of revenue sources brings to a close for now our examination of the role of government in the economy. Government has a pervasive influence on the economy, and its role will continue to surface in our discussions.

SUMMARY

1. There are three kinds of decision-making units in the economy: households, firms, and governments. Households supply resources demanded by firms and governments; and, in turn, households demand the private goods and services supplied by firms and the public goods and services supplied by governments. Households are the key actors in the economy because they supply all the resources employed and demand all the goods and services produced.

2. Most household income arises from the sale of labor, and most household income is spent on private goods and services, called personal consumption. Income not spent on personal consumption is either saved or paid as taxes. Personal consumption consists of expenditures on durable goods, nondurable goods, and services. Expenditures on services is the fastest-growing portion of personal consumption, accounting for about half of the total.

3. Firms are convenient devices for bringing together specialized resources. However, when the net benefits of organizing production within the firm are exhausted, it then becomes more efficient to allow the market to handle any additional tasks of coordinating production. The market, relying only on the profit motives of each firm, guides resources through intermediate stages to produce the final good.

4. Firms can be organized in three different ways: sole proprietorships, partnerships, and corporations. The sole proprietorship is the most common form of business organization, and the corporation the least common form. Because the corporation is typically large, corporations account for the bulk of all firms' sales.

5. The sole proprietorship is simply organized, and the owner has complete control. But because there is only one owner, it may be difficult to raise funds, plus the owner has full liability for all the firm's debts. The partnership is also relatively simple to organize, but liability is unlimited, and the firm's continuity after the death of a partner remains in question. The corporate form allows funds to be raised more easily, has limited liability, and has a life of its own, regardless of a change in ownership. However, corporations are complicated to establish, they allow little direct control by the owners, and their earnings are taxed twice.

6. For a variety of reasons, voluntary exchange through private markets yields some undesirable results. Households, through the political process, then call upon governments to correct these market failures. Government programs are designed to (1) protect private property and enforce contracts, (2) promote competition, (3) regulate natural monopolies, (4) provide public goods and services, (5) promote positive externalities and discourage negative externalities, (6) provide for greater equality in the distribution of income, and (7) promote full employment and price stability.

7. Governmental responsibilities in the United States are shared across the federal, state, and local levels. National security and economic stability are primary responsibilities of the federal level; higher education and welfare, the responsibilities of the state level; and local schools and police and fire protection, the responsibilities of the local level.

8. Taxes are the primary source of revenue to fund public programs. Other revenue sources include user charges and borrowing. A tax is usually justified based either on the individual's ability to pay the tax or on the benefits the individual receives from those activities financed by the tax. The federal government in the United States relies primarily on the personal income tax; states, on the sales tax, and localities, on the property tax.

QUESTIONS AND PROBLEMS

1. (Consumption) It is now well known that the service sector of the U.S. economy has been growing very fast. Many economists claim that this sector will provide the most new jobs in the future. What services will be important in the future, and what skills, if any, will be needed by the workers in those industries?

2. (Consumption) What factors come into play when a consumer considers buying a durable good such as an automobile or a refrigerator?

3. (Household Production) The text states that technological breakthroughs have made household production possible in some cases. What are some technological advances that have made household production of entertainment possible? How has the entertainment industry reacted to such devices?

4. (Household Production) Many households supplement their food budget by cultivating a small vegetable garden at home. Explain how each of the following may affect this kind of household production:

   a. Both husband and wife are professionals earning high salaries.
   b. The household is located in the city rather than in the country.
   c. The household is located in the South rather than in the North.
   d. The household is located in a region where there is a high sales tax on food.
   e. The household is located in a region that has a high property tax rate.

5. (Specialization) Why did the institution of the firm appear after the advent of the Industrial Revolution in the nineteenth century? What type of business organization existed before this?

6. (Corporations) Why do most large businesses organize as corporations rather than as partnerships or sole proprietorships? Must corporations always be large in terms of sales and production?

7. (Government) Economists sometimes argue over whether the government should provide a service or not. However, even when everyone agrees that the government should provide the service, it must still be decided whether the government service is best provided by the local, state, or federal government. What factors are important in determining which level of government should provide the service?

8. (Government) One of the most important government services is provided by the National Weather Service. Why isn't it possible for a private weather service to provide information and predictions about the weather? Why is it necessary to have a National Weather Service?

9. (Government) Often it is said that government is necessary when private markets fail to work effectively and fairly. Based on your reading of the text, how might private markets "break down"?

10. (Government) How are each of the following related to the various services that government is responsible for providing?

   a. the Food and Drug Administration
   b. the Pentagon
   c. the Supreme Court of the United States
   d. the progressive income tax system
   e. state-supported universities
   f. state utility rate commissions

PART
TWO

Introduction to the Market System

ELASTICITY of DEMAND and SUPPLY

As noted earlier, macroeconomics focuses on aggregate markets—on the big picture. But the big picture is a mosaic pieced together from individual decisions made in households, firms, and governments. To understand how the economy works, we must take a closer look at individual choice. In market economies the price system guides production and consumption decisions. Prices, particularly relative prices, provide producers and consumers with information about the relative scarcity of goods. In this chapter we consider how responsive producers and consumers are to price changes.

A downward-sloping demand curve and upward-sloping supply curve combine to form a powerful analytical tool. To add greater precision to our analytical ability, we must examine the shape and position of the demand and supply curves. For example, in 1986 gasoline prices fell an average of $0.20 per gallon. What happened to the quantity of gasoline demanded? You might predict that it went up, but by how much? Firms are willing to pay dearly for predictions about the impact of a change in price on quantity demanded. Likewise, it is helpful to know that an increase in the price of pork will encourage farmers to raise more pigs, but how many more pigs will be produced? What will be the effect of a $0.20 per pack tax increase on the equilibrium price and quantity of cigarettes, and what will happen to total tax receipts? To answer these questions, we need to learn about demand and supply elasticities, which tell us how sensitive the quantity demanded or supplied is to a change in price. Topics discussed in this chapter include:

• Price elasticity of demand

• Determinants of price elasticity

• Price elasticity of supply

- Income elasticity of demand
- Cross-price elasticity

PRICE ELASTICITY OF DEMAND

Producers would very much like to know what will happen to quantity demanded and to total revenue if the price of their product increases from, say, $1 to $1.25. If consumers of tacos, for example, sharply reduce their taco purchases when the price of tacos goes up, taco producers will find a higher price less attractive. Consider the two demand curves in Exhibit 1. In each case the price has increased by 25 percent, from $1 to $1.25, but the effect on the quantity demanded varies a great deal between the two panels. In panel (a) the quantity demanded drops from 100 to 95, a 5 percent decline, and in panel (b), from 100 to 70, a 30 percent decline. You can see that consumers are much more responsive to the price increase in panel (b) than in panel (a). Economists have developed a way of measuring the responsiveness of quantity demanded to a change in the price; it is called the price elasticity of demand. *Elasticity* is simply another word for *responsiveness*.

EXHIBIT 1   DEMAND CURVES OF DIFFERING ELASTICITIES

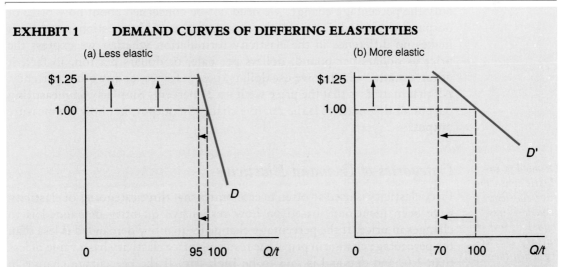

For a given change in price, the less elastic demand is, the less quantity demanded will vary. In panel (a), a 25 percent increase in price leads to a 5 percent decrease in quantity demanded. In panel (b) with more elastic demand *D'*, the same 25 percent price increase leads to a 30 percent decrease in quantity demanded.

Calculating Elasticity of Demand

*The **price elasticity of demand** measures the responsiveness of consumers to a price change; it is the percentage change in quantity demanded divided by the percentage change in price.*

In simplest terms, the **price elasticity of demand** is equal to the percentage change in the quantity demanded divided by the percentage change in price. This can be represented by the equation

$$\text{Price elasticity of demand} = \frac{\text{Percentage change in quantity demanded}}{\text{Percentage change in price}}$$

As you will recall, the law of demand states that price and the quantity demanded are inversely related. Thus, the change in price and the change in quantity will always be in opposite directions. Hence, in the preceding elasticity formula the numerator and the denominator will have opposite signs. Consequently, the price elasticity of demand will always have a negative value. For simplicity, we will use the absolute value of the elasticity, which means that we will drop the negative sign.

In panel (a) of Exhibit 1, when the price increases from $1.00 to $1.25, an increase of 25 percent, the quantity demanded decreases from 100 to 95, a drop of only 5 percent. In this case the resulting elasticity is −5 percent/25 percent, which has an absolute value of 0.2. In panel (b) the price increase is still 25 percent, but the quantity demanded falls from 100 to 70, or by 30 percent. Thus, the resulting elasticity is −30 percent/25 percent, which has an absolute value of 1.2.

Note that the relationship expressed by elasticity is between relative amounts—the percentage change in quantity divided by the percentage change in price. Thus, the focus is not on particular quantity changes. Looking at consumer responsiveness in this way washes out any effects that would be due solely to the way we define the variables. Since we consider only the percentage change, we need not be concerned about how price or output is measured. For example, suppose the good in question is cotton. It makes no difference in the elasticity formulation whether we express the price as dollars per pound, dollars per bale, or dollars per ton. In fact, it doesn't matter whether we use dollars, pesos, francs, or any other currency. All that matters is that the price went up 25 percent. Similarly, in measuring output all that matters is the relative change in output, not how we measure output.

Categories of Demand Elasticity

*Demand is **inelastic** when the price elasticity of demand is less than 1.0; it is of **unitary elasticity** when the elasticity equals 1.0; and it is **elastic** when the elasticity value exceeds 1.0.*

Price elasticity is used so often in economics that three categories of elasticity have been identified, based on how responsive quantity demanded is to changes in price. If the percentage change in quantity demanded is less than the percentage change in price, the resulting price elasticity has a value of less than 1.0, and demand is said to be **inelastic**. If the percentage change in quantity demanded just equals the percentage change in price, the resulting price elasticity has a value equal to 1.0, and demand is said to be of **unitary elasticity**. Finally, if the quantity demanded changes by a greater percentage than does the price, the resulting price elasticity has a value greater than 1.0, and demand is said to be **elastic**. In summary, demand is called inelastic if price elasticity is less than 1.0, unitary if price elasticity is equal to 1.0, and elastic if price elasticity is greater than 1.0.

Elasticity and Total Revenue

Total revenue equals price multiplied by the quantity sold at that price.

One reason producers want to know the elasticity of demand is because it tells them what will happen to their total revenue if the price is changed. **Total revenue** is the price of the product multiplied by the quantity sold at that price. We know from the inverse relationship between price and quantity demanded that changes in price and changes in quantity demanded move in opposite directions. Thus, if the price goes up, the quantity demanded goes down. The higher price means that the revenue per unit sold increases, and this will have a positive effect on total revenue. But the lower quantity demanded means that the number of units sold decreases, and this will have a negative effect on total revenue. The change in total revenue resulting from a higher price is the net result of these opposite effects. If the negative effect of a declining quantity demanded is greater than the positive effect of a rising price, total revenue will fall. More specifically, if the percentage decrease in quantity demanded exceeds the percentage increase in price—that is, if demand is elastic—then a price increase will reduce total revenue. If the percentage decrease in quantity demanded is just equal to the percentage increase in the price—that is, if demand is of unitary elasticity—then a price increase will not change total revenue. Finally, if the percentage decrease in quantity demanded is less than the percentage increase in price—that is, if demand is inelastic—then a price increase will increase total revenue.

Using the example from panel (a) of Exhibit 1, total revenue when the price is $1.00 is that price times the 100 units demanded, or $100. When the price increases to $1.25, total revenue is $1.25 times 95 units, or $118.75. Thus, if demand is inelastic, total revenue increases when the price goes up and decreases when price goes down. If demand is elastic, the opposite is true because the percentage change in quantity demanded is greater than the percentage change in price. This greater sensitivity of consumers to changes in price means that consumers are more resistant to price increases. In the example in panel (b) of Exhibit 1 total revenue goes from $100 before the price change to $1.25 multiplied by 70, or $87.50, after the price change.

As we have said, total revenue is calculated by multiplying the price times the quantity demanded. In a graph total revenue at any point along a demand curve can be seen as the area of the rectangle formed by the price, the point on the demand curve, the quantity demanded, and 0. For example, in panel (a) of Exhibit 2 the total revenue at point a equals the area formed by multiplying the price, P, by the quantity, Q. Total revenue is therefore equal to the area defined by $PaQ0$.

The three panels in Exhibit 2 highlight for the three elasticity categories the effects on total revenue of an increase in price from P to P'. As we have noted, an increase in price will have two effects on total revenue. First, total revenue will fall because fewer units are sold at the higher price; this reduction is shown in Exhibit 2 by the darker shaded rectangles. Second, total revenue will increase because the price received for each unit sold is higher; this increase is reflected by the lighter shaded rectangles.

Because demand is inelastic in panel (a), the revenue lost from reduced sales (darker shaded area) is less than the revenue gained from a higher price (lighter shaded area); hence, total revenue increases. The opposite holds for the elastic demand in panel (b), where the revenue lost from reduced sales exceeds the revenue gained from the higher price; consequently, total revenue falls. Panel (c) shows that with unitary elasticity the drop in revenue due to declining sales is just offset by the increase in revenue due to the higher price; hence, total revenue is unchanged.

Refining the Calculations: The Midpoint Formula

The discussion to this point has glossed over a tricky little problem in calculating elasticity. The problem arises because we get a different elasticity value depending on whether we move from point *a* to point *b* or from point *b* to point *a*. Consider, for example, the case where the price increases from $1.00 to $1.25, an increase of 25 percent [(1.25 − 1.00)/1.00], and the quantity decreases from 100 to 70 units, a decrease of 30 percent [(1.00 − 0.70)/1.00]. The elasticity was calculated to be 30 percent/25 percent, or 1.2. If, however, we begin with a price of $1.25 and lower it to $1.00, this

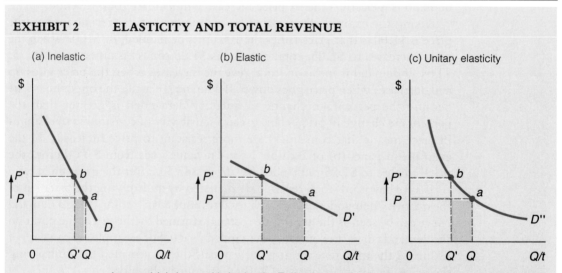

EXHIBIT 2   ELASTICITY AND TOTAL REVENUE

(a) Inelastic   (b) Elastic   (c) Unitary elasticity

In panel (a) demand is inelastic. Following a price increase, the revenue gained from the higher price exceeds the revenue lost from reduced sales; thus, total revenue increases. Demand is elastic in panel (b). After the same price increase the revenue gained from the higher price is less than that lost from reduced sales; thus, total revenue decreases. With unitary elasticity in panel (c) the two effects offset one another, so total revenue is unchanged after a price increase.

represents a price drop of 20 percent [(1.25 − 1.00)/1.25]; quantity demanded increases from 70 to 100, an increase of 43 percent [(1.00 − 0.70)/.70]. The resulting elasticity is 43 percent/20 percent, which equals 2.1.

The problem is that although the particular amounts by which price and quantity change do not vary whether we are going from the higher to the lower price or the other way around (that is, the price changes by $0.25, and the quantity demanded changes by 30 units), the *base* for calculating the percentage change has been the initial price and the initial quantity. Consequently, the base is different when we begin with $1.00 and raise the price by $0.25 than when we begin with $1.25 and lower the price by $0.25. The way economists have solved the problem is that instead of using the initial values of price and quantity as the base in calculating the percentage change, they use the midpoint between the initial value and the new value as the base. The midpoint is simply the average of the initial value and the new value. The midpoint formula for calculating the price elasticity for any change in price is

$$E_d = \frac{Q' - Q}{(Q' + Q)/2} \div \frac{P' - P}{(P' + P)/2}$$

where E_d is the price elasticity of demand, Q is the initial quantity, Q' is the quantity after the price change, P is the initial price, and P' is the new price. Thus, when the price increases from $1.00 to $1.25, the base used in calculating the percentage change is not $1.00 but ($1.25 + $1.00)/2 = $1.125. The percentage change in price is therefore 0.25/1.125, or 22 percent. And this will be the same whether we are moving from $1.00 to $1.25 or from $1.25 to $1.00.

The same holds for changes in quantity demanded. When the quantity demanded falls from 100 to 70, the base used is not 100 but (100 + 70)/2 = 85. Thus, the percentage change in quantity demanded is calculated by the midpoint method to be 30/85, which equals 35 percent. The resulting elasticity of demand is the percentage change in quantity, 35 percent, divided by the percentage change in price, 22 percent, which is 35 percent/22 percent, or 1.6. Because the midpoint formula uses the same base, the same value for the elasticity will be calculated for a price drop from $1.25 to $1.00 as for a price increase from $1.00 to $1.25.

Price Elasticity and the Linear Demand Curve

The price elasticity of demand usually varies all along the demand curve. An examination of the elasticity properties of a particular variety of demand curve, the linear demand curve, will tie together the concepts examined thus far. A *linear demand curve* is simply a straight-line demand curve. Exhibit 3 presents a linear demand curve in panel (a) and in panel (b) a curve reflecting the total revenue generated at each price along the demand curve. Total revenue, you will remember, is price times quantity demanded at that price.

In Exhibit 3(a) the price elasticity of demand is greater on the higher-price end of the demand curve than on the lower-price end. On the higher end of the demand curve any given *change* in quantity demanded is magnified in percentage terms because the quantity *level*, or base, is so small. For example, in moving from point *a* to point *b*, quantity demanded increases from 100 to 200 units. Using the midpoint formula, the percentage change is 100/150, which equals 66 percent. As we move down the demand curve, however, a change in quantity demanded of 100 units will translate into a relatively smaller percentage change because the level of quantity demanded grows larger. Moving from point *d* to point *e*, for example, increases quantity demanded from 800 to 900 units, an increase of 100 units. But because the quantity level is now greater, the percentage change is 100/850, which equals 12 percent. Although the quantity demanded changes by 100 units in both instances, this amount represents a 66 percent change in moving from *a* to *b* but only a 12 percent change in moving from *d* to *e*.

The reverse holds for price changes. At the upper end of the demand curve any given price *change* will be relatively smaller in percentage terms than the same change at the lower end of the demand curve because the price *level* is larger at the upper end. The price drop from *a* to *b* is $10, the same as from *d* to *e*, but at the upper end this amounts to a percentage change of 10/85, or about 12 percent, whereas it is 10/15, or 66 percent, at the lower end.

Putting these percentage changes together yields the price elasticity. The elasticity between points *a* and *b* is the percentage change in quantity (66 percent) divided by the percentage change in price (12 percent), which is 66 percent/12 percent, for an elasticity of 5.5. Between points *d* and *e* the percentage change in quantity is 12 percent divided by the percentage change in price of 66 percent, which yields an elasticity calculation of 12 percent/66 percent, or 0.18.

The price elasticity of demand falls steadily as we move down the curve. At a point halfway down the linear demand curve in Exhibit 3 the elasticity is equal to 1.0. This midpoint divides the demand curve into an elastic upper half and an inelastic lower half. You can observe the clear relationship between the elasticity of the demand curve in the upper diagram and total revenue in the lower diagram. Note that where the demand curve is elastic, a decrease in price results in an increase in total revenue. Where the demand curve is of unitary elasticity, total revenue reaches its peak. And where the demand curve is inelastic, a price decrease reduces total revenue.

Thus, total revenue increases as the price is reduced until the midpoint of the curve is reached, where total revenue peaks. Below the midpoint, total revenue declines as the price is reduced further. More generally, regardless of whether the demand curve is a straight line or a curve, there is a relationship between price elasticity and total revenue: a price decrease will always *increase* total revenue if demand is elastic, *decrease* total revenue if demand is inelastic, and *have no effect* on total revenue if demand is of unitary elasticity.

Three Extremes of Elasticity

You now have been exposed to a variety of elasticities based on different curves and different points on the same curve. Three other shapes will exhaust the range of possibilities.

EXHIBIT 3   **DEMAND, ELASTICITY, AND TOTAL REVENUE**

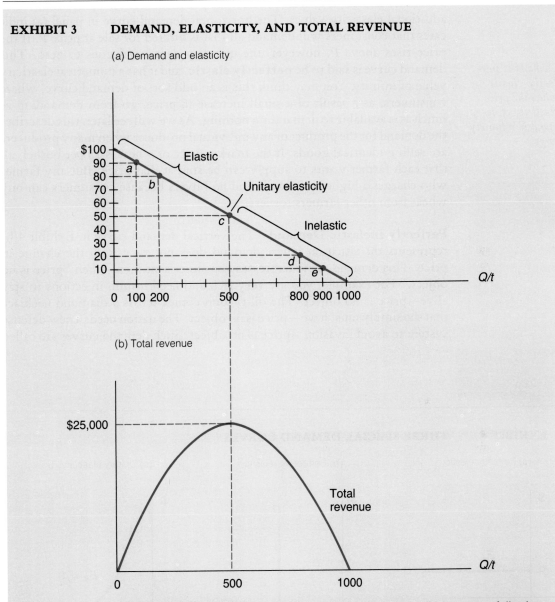

(a) Demand and elasticity

(b) Total revenue

When demand is elastic in panel (a), total revenue in panel (b) increases following a price decrease. Total revenue attains its maximum value at the level of output where demand is of unitary elasticity. When demand is inelastic, further decreases in price cause total revenue to fall.

*Demand is **perfectly elastic** when the price elasticity of demand is infinitely large.*

Perfectly Elastic Demand   The three panels of Exhibit 4 present the three additional elasticity values. The horizontal demand curve in panel (a) indicates that consumers will demand all that is offered for sale at price P. If the price rises above P, however, the quantity demanded goes to zero. This demand curve is said to be **perfectly elastic**, and it has a numerical elasticity value of infinity. You may think this is an odd sort of demand curve, where consumers, as a result of a small increase in price, go from demanding as much as is available to demanding nothing. As we will see later, this describes the demand for the product of any individual producer when many producers are selling identical goods. If the market price of wheat is $5 per bushel, all that each farmer wants to supply can be sold at that price. But any farmer who charges a higher price will find no buyers because consumers can buy wheat from other farmers for less.

Perfectly Inelastic Demand   The vertical demand curve in Exhibit 4(b) represents the situation where demand does not vary with the change in price. This demand curve expresses consumer sentiment when "price is no object." For example, you are very rich and need insulin injections to stay alive—price is no object. The oil tycoon comes across a diamond necklace that she simply must have—price is no object. The nation needs a new defense system to avoid invasion—price is no object. Such demand curves are called

EXHIBIT 4   **THREE SPECIAL DEMAND CURVES**

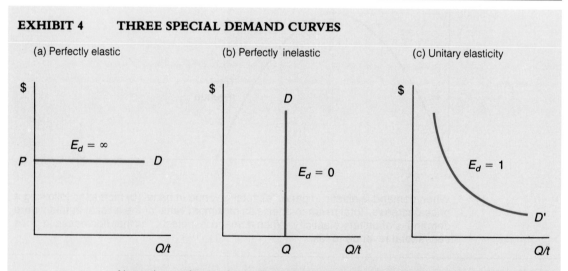

Along the perfectly elastic (horizontal) demand curve of panel (a), consumers will purchase all that is offered for sale at price P. Along the perfectly inelastic (vertical) demand curve of panel (b), consumers will purchase quantity Q regardless of price. Along the unitary elastic demand curve of panel (c), total revenue is the same for every price-quantity combination.

*Demand is **perfectly inelastic** when the price elasticity of demand is 0.*

perfectly inelastic because price changes do not affect quantity demanded, at least not over the range of prices depicted by the demand curve. Thus, the numerical value of the elasticity is zero.

Incidentally, if price rises high enough, people will simply be unable to afford the good regardless of how much they desire the good. Recall that demand reflects the quantity people are both willing and able to demand at alternative prices. For example, the wealthy oil tycoon may buy the necklace even when the price is $1 million, but if the price is $1 billion, she simply cannot afford it. Thus, a demand curve may be perfectly inelastic, but only over realistic price ranges. Perhaps we should say that the "price is no object" over the realistic range of possible prices.

Unitary Elasticity   Panel (c) in Exhibit 4 presents a demand curve that is of unitary elasticity everywhere along the curve. This means that the percentage change in price will always result in an identical percentage change in quantity. Because price and quantity changes will be equal and offsetting, total revenue will be the same for every price-quantity combination along the curve. Note that demand curves can also have an elasticity that is everywhere constant and that differs from unity.

*The price elasticity of demand takes on the same value at every point along a **constant elasticity** demand curve.*

Each of the demand curves in Exhibit 4 is called a **constant elasticity** demand curve because the elasticity is the same all along the curve. In contrast, the downward-sloping linear demand curve examined earlier had a different elasticity value at each point along the curve. Exhibit 5 brings together the five categories of price elasticity discussed and summarizes the varying effects of a change in the price on quantity demanded and on total revenue. Give this exhibit some thought and see if you can draw a demand curve to reflect each category of elasticity.

EXHIBIT 5
SUMMARY OF ELASTICITY EFFECTS

Elasticity Value	What It's Called	Effects of a 10 Percent Increase in Price	
		What Happens to Quantity	What Happens to Total Revenue
$\varepsilon = 0$	Perfectly inelastic	No change	Increases by 10 percent
$0 < \varepsilon < 1$	Inelastic	Drops by less than 10 percent	Increases by less than 10 percent
$\varepsilon = 1$	Unitary elasticity	Drops by 10 percent	No change
$1 < \varepsilon < \infty$	Elastic	Drops by more than 10 percent	Decreases
$\varepsilon = \infty$	Perfectly elastic	Drops to 0	Drops to 0

DETERMINANTS OF
DEMAND ELASTICITY

Thus far we have explored the technical properties of demand elasticity. We have not yet considered why elasticities vary for different demand curves. Several characteristics influence the price elasticity of demand for a good. We will examine each of these determinants of elasticity in some detail.

Availability of Substitutes

As noted in Chapter 3, your particular wants can be satisfied in a variety of different ways. If the price of pizza increases, you may find that other, relatively cheaper foods are close substitutes. If close substitutes are available, an increase in the price of pizza will cause you to shift to these substitutes. But if nothing else comes close to satisfying your yen for pizza, you may take the price increase in stride and change your quantity demanded very little. The greater the availability of substitutes and the closer these substitutes are, the more elastic will be the demand.

For some goods there are simply no close substitutes. When a diabetic needs insulin, nothing else will do. The demand for such goods tends to be inelastic. Because producers would like to be able to increase their price without having you switch to substitutes, they would like you to think there are no substitutes for their product. Much advertising is aimed at establishing in the consumer's mind the uniqueness of a particular product.

Proportion of the Consumer's Budget Spent on the Good

The first determinant of elasticity was based on the substitution effect of a change in price. The second determinant is tied more to the income effect of a price change. Recall that one reason a higher price reduces quantity demanded is because a higher price causes the real spending power of consumer income to decline. Because expenditures for certain goods represent a large share of the consumer's budget, changes in the price of these goods have a substantial impact on the quantity that consumers are able to purchase. Therefore, some price changes will affect demand because these changes substantially alter the consumer's real income.

A demand curve reflects both the willingness and the ability to purchase a good at alternative prices. An increase in the price of housing greatly affects the *ability* to buy housing. The income effect of higher housing prices will significantly reduce the quantity of housing demanded. Thus, the price elasticity of demand for housing will be large. In contrast, the income effect of an increase in the price of paper towels will be trivial because expenditures on paper towels represent such a small proportion of the budget. The more important the item is as a proportion of the household budget, other things constant, the more elastic will be its demand. The smaller the item is as a proportion of the budget, the less elastic will be its demand. Hence, the demand for housing, cars, and major appliances will tend to be more elastic than the demand for paper towels, pencils, and flashlight batteries.

Price Elasticity and the Definition of the Good

The number and closeness of substitutes depend on how we define the good. The more generally we define a good, the fewer substitutes there will be, and the less elastic will be the demand. For example, the demand for "food" will be less elastic than the demand for corn because there are few substitutes for food but many substitutes for corn, including a variety of other vegetables. The demand for corn, however, will be less elastic than the demand for canned corn because the consumer has more substitutes for canned corn, including fresh and frozen corn, than for corn more generally. Finally, the demand for canned corn will be less elastic than the demand for Green Giant canned corn because Green Giant canned corn has more substitutes, including other brands of canned corn, than canned corn more generally.

A Matter of Time

Consumers can substitute lower-priced goods for higher-priced goods, but this substitution often takes time. When the price of gasoline increased sharply in 1979, people began to alter their driving habits. Some adjustments could be made right away. For example, unnecessary trips and pleasure rides were eliminated immediately. In a matter of a few weeks car pools and public transportation became more popular. Fuel-efficient cars were substituted for gas guzzlers, but such replacements took several years because substitutions were linked to the normal car-replacement cycle. In fact, the quantity of gasoline consumed in the United States dropped during each of the four years following the 1979 leap in prices.

Suppose your college announces a substantial increase in room and board fees effective immediately. Some students will move off campus as soon as they can. Others will wait until the end of the school year. And, over time, fewer students may apply for admission, and incoming students will have an increased demand for off-campus housing. Thus, the longer the time period considered, the greater the ability to substitute away from relatively higher-priced products toward lower-priced substitutes.

Exhibit 6 demonstrates how demand becomes more elastic over time. Assuming that the initial price is P, D_d is the demand curve one day after a price change, D_m, one month after, and D_y, one year after. The longer the time period allowed for adjustments to price changes, the more responsive will be the change in quantity demanded for a given change in price.

If the price increases from P to P', the reduction in quantity demanded will be greater as consumers have longer to identify and adopt substitutes. For example, the demand curve D_d shows that one day after the price change the quantity consumed has been reduced very little—in this case from Q to Q_d. The demand curve D_m indicates a greater reduction in quantity demanded after one month, and demand curve D_y, the greatest reduction in quantity demanded after one year.

EXHIBIT 6   **DEMAND BECOMES MORE ELASTIC OVER TIME**

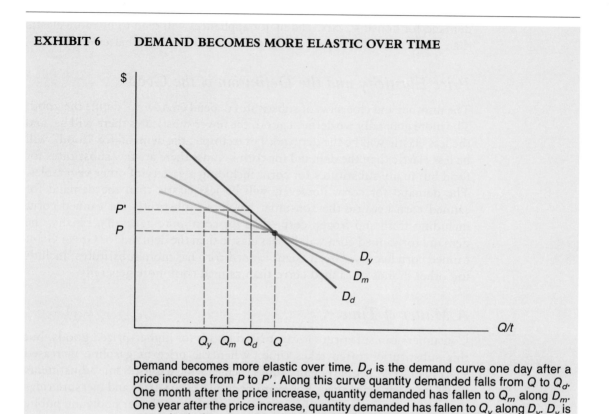

Demand becomes more elastic over time. D_d is the demand curve one day after a price increase from P to P'. Along this curve quantity demanded falls from Q to Q_d. One month after the price increase, quantity demanded has fallen to Q_m along D_m. One year after the price increase, quantity demanded has fallen to Q_y along D_y. D_y is more elastic than D_m, which is more elastic than D_d.

Luxuries Versus Necessities

Even if the price of food increases, people still must eat. They may substitute cheaper cuts of meat for steak and canned tuna for shrimp, but they will probably go without something else in their budget before going without food. Food is viewed as a necessity; people must buy necessities even if the price increases. On the other hand, a higher price for movie tickets may cause people to seek other forms of entertainment; movies may be viewed as luxuries. Similarly, higher transportation prices will encourage people to reduce their "joy rides" and to vacation closer to home. The demand for necessities will be less elastic than the demand for luxuries.

Elasticity Estimates

As a way of breathing some life into the discussion, let's consider some estimates of the price elasticity of demand for particular goods and services. As we have said, consumers substitute lower-priced goods for higher-priced goods, but this substitution often takes time. Thus, when we estimate price elasticity, we often distinguish between the short run, a period during which consumers have little time to adjust, and the long run, a period during which consumers have ample time to adjust. Neither the short run nor the long run is a uniform length of time; they will vary depending on the good in question. For example, it will take the consumer longer to fully adjust to a change in the price of housing than to a change in the price of milk.

Exhibit 7 provides short-run and long-run price elasticity estimates for selected products. Notice that the price elasticity tends to be greater in the long run because consumers have more time to adjust. For example, if the price of electricity should rise tomorrow, consumers could make some minor adjustments in their use of electricity. Over time, however, more energy-efficient appliances could be purchased, electric heat could be replaced with oil or gas heat, and other major changes could be implemented to reduce electric consumption. So the long-run elasticity exceeds the short-run elasticity. Notice also that the long-run price elasticity of demand for Chevrolets exceeds the price elasticity for automobiles more generally. Chevrolets have many more substitutes than do automobiles.

EXHIBIT 7
SELECTED PRICE ELASTICITIES OF DEMAND

Product	Short Run	Long Run
Air travel	0.1	2.4
Electricity	0.1	1.9
Gasoline	0.2	0.5
Medical care and hospitalization	0.3	0.9
Movies	0.9	3.7
Automobiles	—	1.5
Chevrolets	—	4.0

Source: H.S. Houthakker and L.D. Taylor, *Consumer Demand in the United States: Analyses and Projections*, 2d ed. (Cambridge, Mass.: Harvard University Press, 1970).

PRICE ELASTICITY OF SUPPLY

*The **price elasticity of supply** measures the responsiveness of producers to a price change; it is the percentage change in quantity supplied divided by the percentage change in price.*

Prices are signals to both sides of the market about the relative scarcity of products. High prices are a turnoff for consumers but a turn-on for producers. The price elasticity of demand is a measure of exactly how consumers respond to a price change. The same idea applies to producers. The **price elasticity of supply** measures how responsive producers are to a price change. This elasticity is calculated in the same way as the demand elasticity, but instead of using the percentage change in the quantity demanded, we employ the percentage change in the quantity supplied. In fact, we can go directly to the midpoint formula to express the price elasticity of supply as follows:

$$E_s = \frac{Q' - Q}{(Q' + Q)/2} \div \frac{P' - P}{(P' + P)/2}$$

where E_s is the price elasticity of supply, Q, the original quantity supplied, Q', the quantity after the price change, P, the original price, and P', the price after the price change. Notice that if the price increases, the quantity supplied will also increase, so the percentage change in price and the percentage change in quantity tend to move in the same direction. With changes in output and price moving in the same direction, supply elasticity is usually positive.

Categories of Supply Elasticity

The terminology for supply elasticity is the same as for demand elasticity: if supply elasticity is greater than 1.0, supply is *elastic*, if less than 1.0, supply is *inelastic*, and if equal to 1.0, supply is of *unitary elasticity*. There are also some special values of supply elasticity to be considered.

Perfectly Inelastic Supply   The most unresponsive supply curve possible is one that shows no change in the quantity supplied regardless of the change in price. Such a case is depicted as the vertical supply curve S' in Exhibit 8. Because the percentage change in quantity is zero, regardless of the change in price, the supply elasticity equals zero. This curve is said to reflect *perfectly inelastic* supply, and it describes the situation where supply cannot be varied regardless of what happens to price. This year's crop of strawberries is an example. Once the crop is grown, not another strawberry can be produced this season no matter how high the price. Any good in fixed supply, such as Picasso paintings or 1978 Dom Perignon champagne, will have a perfectly inelastic supply curve.

Perfectly Elastic Supply   At the other extreme is the case of horizontal supply, as reflected by supply curve S' in Exhibit 8. Here the producers will supply none of the good at a price below P but will supply any amount at a price of P (the quantity actually supplied at price P will depend on the quantity demanded at that price). Because a tiny increase from a price just below P to a price of P will result in an unlimited supply, this curve is said to reflect *perfectly elastic* supply, which has a mathematical elasticity value of infinity.

As individual consumers, we typically face perfectly inelastic supply curves. When we go to the supermarket, we usually can buy as much as we want at the prevailing price. This is not to say that all consumers together could buy an unlimited amount at the prevailing price. Recall the fallacy of composition: what is true for any individual consumer is not necessarily true for all consumers as a group. Even though an individual consumer faces a horizontal supply curve, it is the market supply curve that determines what price consumers as a group must pay. As we have seen, the market supply curve is typically, though not always, upward sloping.

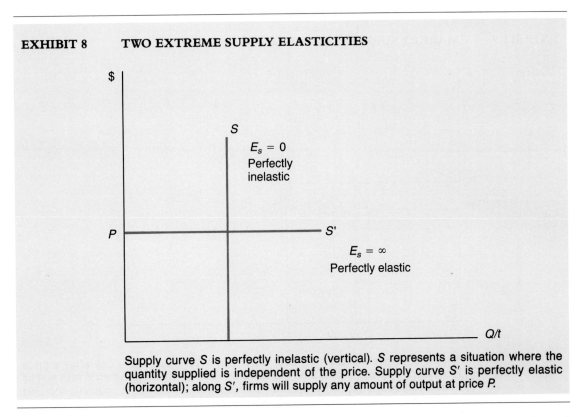

EXHIBIT 8   TWO EXTREME SUPPLY ELASTICITIES

Supply curve *S* is perfectly inelastic (vertical). *S* represents a situation where the quantity supplied is independent of the price. Supply curve *S'* is perfectly elastic (horizontal); along *S'*, firms will supply any amount of output at price *P.*

Because supply curves tend to be upward sloping, a higher price is linked to a higher quantity. Since total revenue equals price times quantity, and since both price and quantity increase as we move up the supply curve, total revenue will increase as price increases.

Determinants of Supply Elasticity

As we will see in later chapters, the elasticity of supply depends very much on how the cost of producing each additional unit changes as output increases. If the cost rises sharply as output is expanded, then the incentive to expand output offered by a higher price will be dampened by higher costs, and supply will tend to be inelastic. But if the cost rises slowly as output expands, the lure of a higher price will cause a large increase in output. In this case supply will tend to be more elastic.

An important determinant of the supply elasticity is the time period under consideration. Just as demand became more elastic over time as consumers adjusted to price changes, so too with supply. The longer the time period under consideration, the more able producers will be to adjust to price changes. Exhibit 9 presents a different supply curve for each of three time periods. S_d is the supply curve when the period of adjustment is a day. As you can see, a higher price will not elicit much of a response in quantity supplied because the firms have little time to adjust. Thus, such a supply curve will tend to be steeply sloped, reflecting inelastic supply.

EXHIBIT 9   MARKET SUPPLY FOR THREE TIME PERIODS

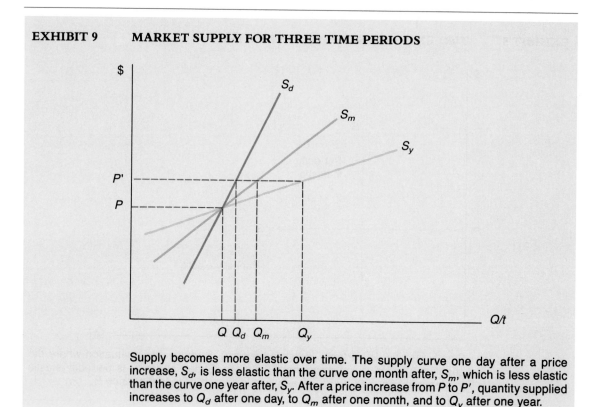

Supply becomes more elastic over time. The supply curve one day after a price increase, S_d, is less elastic than the curve one month after, S_m, which is less elastic than the curve one year after, S_y. After a price increase from P to P', quantity supplied increases to Q_d after one day, to Q_m after one month, and to Q_y after one year.

S_m is the supply curve when the time period under consideration is a month. In that time firms can more easily adjust the rate at which they employ some resources. As a result, the firms have a greater ability to vary output. Thus, the supply curve is more elastic when the time period is a month than when it is a day. The supply curve is still more elastic when the time period is a year, as shown by S_y. In a year the firms can vary most, if not all, inputs, and new firms may be drawn into the market as a result of a higher price. So a given price increase will elicit a greater response in quantity supplied for a longer period of adjustment. The elasticity of supply is therefore greater the longer this period of adjustment is.

The ability of firms to adjust to a price change will differ across industries. It may take years to increase the quantity supplied of such products as electricity, fuel-efficient cars, and prime timber. The quantity of services supplied by real estate agents, rock groups, and lunch wagons, however, seems to adjust almost overnight to changes in the price.

This concludes our introduction to the elasticity of demand and supply. One way to reinforce an understanding of elasticity is to work through an example using both demand and supply. In the next section we will show the effects of a sales tax on price and quantity and will link these effects to elasticity.

ELASTICITY AND TAX INCIDENCE: AN APPLICATION

The sales tax is the major source of state government revenue. There is much confusion about who exactly pays the tax. Is it paid by producers or by consumers? An understanding of elasticity allows us to examine the incidence of a sales tax. As we will see, the incidence of the tax—that is, who ultimately pays the tax—will depend on the elasticities of supply and demand.

Demand Elasticity and Tax Incidence

Panel (a) in Exhibit 10 depicts the supply and demand for cigarettes, where *S* is the supply curve and *D*, the demand curve. Before a tax is imposed, the equilibrium price is $0.75 per pack, and the equilibrium quantity is 10 million packs per day. Now suppose a sales tax of $0.20 is imposed on each pack of cigarettes produced. Recall that the supply curve represents the amount that producers are willing and able to supply at each price. If producers are now required to pay the government $0.20 for each pack of cigarettes they sell, they will be less willing to supply cigarettes. At each price they will supply fewer packs after the tax is imposed. Put another way, at each quantity level producers must be paid $0.20 more per pack to supply that quantity after the tax is imposed.

The tax can be viewed as an addition to the supply price, which is the price that firms must receive to supply the good. By adding $0.20 to the supply price at each level of output, the tax has the effect of shifting the supply curve upward from *S* to *S'*. The new supply curve indicates that the after-tax supply price is $0.20 higher than the pretax price at each level of output. In short, the effect of the tax is to reduce the supply of cigarettes. The demand curve will remain the same since nothing has happened to shift demand; only the quantity demanded will change.

Since suppliers are the ones who collect the tax and pass it along to the government, they at first appear to be the ones who pay the tax. But let's take a closer look. The result of the tax in this example is to raise the price to $0.90 and to decrease equilibrium quantity to 9 million packs. The shaded area represents the amount of tax collected by the government, which equals the tax per pack times the number of packs sold. Notice that the price did not increase by the full $0.20 because, though producers were willing to offer 10 million packs at a price of $0.95, consumers were not willing to purchase that many.

The higher price resulting from the tax has reduced the quantity demanded. As a result of the tax, consumers are paying $0.15 more per pack, and producers are receiving, net of the tax, $0.05 less. You can see that the original price line of $0.75 divides the shaded area into that portion of the tax paid by consumers as a higher price (the shaded portion *above* the $0.75 price line), and that portion paid by producers now receiving a lower net price (the shaded portion *below* the $0.75 price line). Thus, $0.15 of the $0.20 tax is paid by consumers as a higher price, and $0.05 is paid by suppliers as a reduction in the amount they receive per pack.

The same situation is depicted in panel (b) of Exhibit 10, with the single difference being that the demand curve, D', is more elastic than the demand curve in panel (a). Because quantity demanded is more responsive to a change in price, the suppliers cannot pass the tax increase along as easily in the form of a higher price. Hence, the price increases by only $0.05 to $0.80, and the net-of-tax receipts of producers decline by $0.15 to $0.60. Note that the sum of the price increase and net reduction to producers must always total $0.20, the amount of the tax.

From this example we can conclude that, other things constant, the more elastic the demand is, the less the tax can be passed on to consumers in the form of higher prices, and the more the tax will be absorbed by the producers. As long as consumers are unwilling to pay a higher price, producers will be unable to pass along tax increases. Also note that because sales fall more in panel (b) than in panel (a), total tax revenues are lower when demand is more elastic.

EXHIBIT 10   EFFECTS OF A SALES TAX: DIFFERENT DEMAND ELASTICITIES

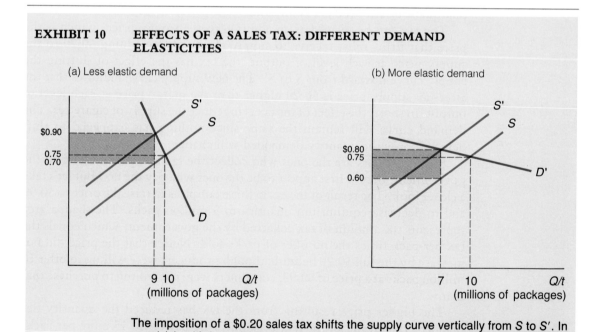

The imposition of a $0.20 sales tax shifts the supply curve vertically from S to S'. In panel (a), with less elastic demand, the market price rises from $0.75 to $0.90 per pack, and the quantity demanded and supplied falls from 10 million packs to 9 million. In panel (b), with more elastic demand, the same sales tax leads to an increase in price from $0.75 to $0.80 per pack; the quantity demanded and supplied falls from 10 million packs to 7 million.

Supply Elasticity and Taxes

The effect of the elasticity of supply on who pays the sales tax is shown in Exhibit 11, where for a given demand curve, different supply elasticities are presented. In both panels the supply curve has been shifted up by $0.20 to reflect the effect of the tax on the supply curve. The supply curve in panel (a) is relatively more elastic than the one in panel (b), so the suppliers in panel (a) are more able to pass the tax along to consumers than are those in panel (b).

Notice that the equilibrium price in panel (a) rises to $0.90—a $0.15 increase over the pretax price. But in panel (b) the price increases by only $0.05. More generally, we can say that, other things constant, the more elastic the supply is, the more suppliers can pass taxes along to consumers as higher prices.

We conclude that the more elastic the demand and the less elastic the supply, the lower will be the proportion of the tax that will be paid by consumers. Put another way, the more consumers reduce their quantity demanded in response to an increase in the price they pay and the less suppliers reduce their quantity supplied in response to a decrease in the price they receive, the less the tax is passed on to consumers and the more it is absorbed by producers.

The price elasticities of demand and supply are frequently used in economic analysis, but other elasticities also provide useful information. In the final section we will examine two other measures of elasticity.

EXHIBIT 11   EFFECTS OF A SALES TAX: DIFFERENT SUPPLY ELASTICITIES

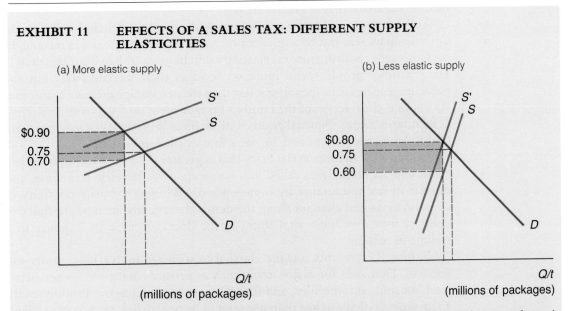

The imposition of a $0.20 sales tax shifts both the more elastic supply curve of panel (a) and the less elastic curve of panel (b) vertically by $0.20. In panel (a) the market price rises from $0.75 per pack to $0.90; in panel (b) the price rises to $0.80 per pack.

OTHER ELASTICITY MEASURES

The price elasticity of demand measures the responsiveness of quantity demanded to changes in price. We are often interested in how demand changes in response to other events, such as a change in consumer income or a change in the price of a related good.

Income Elasticity of Demand

*The **income elasticity of demand** is the percentage change in quantity demanded divided by the percentage change in income.*

What happens to the demand for certain goods if consumer income changes? In particular, what happens to the demand for new cars, dental floss, air conditioners, or bicycles if consumer income increases by 20 percent? These questions are perhaps real yawners to you, but they are of abiding interest to producers of these goods. The price elasticity of demand measures the responsiveness of quantity demanded to price changes along a given demand curve. In contrast, the **income elasticity of demand** holds price constant and measures the change in quantity demanded that results from a change in income. More specifically, the income elasticity of demand measures the percentage change in quantity demanded divided by the percentage change in income.

As noted in Chapter 3, the demand for some goods, such as hamburger and bus rides, actually declines as income increases. Thus, the income elasticity of demand for such goods will be negative. Goods with an income elasticity of less than 0 are called *inferior goods*. The demand for most goods increases as income increases. These are called *normal goods*, and they have an income elasticity that is greater than 0.

Let's take a closer look at normal goods. Sometimes demand will increase with rising income but by a smaller percentage than the increase in income. In such cases the resulting income elasticity will be greater than 0 but less than 1. For example, people spend more on food as their income rises, but the percentage increase in spending is less than the percentage increase in income. As a result, the fraction of the family's budget spent on food tends to decline as income increases. Normal goods with an income elasticity of less than 1 are said to be *income inelastic* and are sometimes called *necessities*.

Goods with an income elasticity that is greater than 1 are said to be *income elastic* and are sometimes called *luxuries*. Expensive jewelry, rare wine, and dinners in fine restaurants are luxury goods. Whereas the price elasticity of demand measured changes along the demand curve, the income elasticity of demand measures horizontal shifts in the demand curve in response to a change in income.

Exhibit 12 presents income elasticity estimates for various goods and services. Demands for major items such as private education, owner-occupied housing, automobiles, and furniture are income elastic. Products with an income elasticity of less than one tend to be necessities, such as physicians' services, gasoline, and rental housing. Note that whereas owner-occupied housing is income elastic, rental housing is inelastic, suggesting that as income rises people tend to purchase proportionately less rental housing and more owner-occupied housing.

Margarine and flour appear to be inferior goods because they have a negative income elasticity. As income increases, consumers switch from margarine to butter and from home baking to purchasing baked goods. We should add, however, that the margarine elasticity was estimated for the 1950s. Since then people have become more aware that margarine is lower in cholesterol and is therefore healthier than butter. Thus, if a study were done today, margarine may not have a negative income elasticity.

There is one more elasticity to consider, the cross-elasticity of demand, which will tell us how demand responds to changes in the price of a related good.

Cross-Price Elasticity of Demand

*The **cross-price elasticity of demand** is the percentage change in the quantity demanded of one good divided by the percentage change in the price of another good.*

The responsiveness of demand to changes in the price of another commodity is called the **cross-price elasticity of demand**. It is defined as the percentage change in the quantity demanded of one good divided by the percentage change in price of another good. The numerical value can be positive, 0, or negative, depending on the relationship between the two goods. Two particular goods can be substitutes or complements or they can have no relation.

EXHIBIT 12
SELECTED INCOME ELASTICITIES OF DEMAND

Product	Income Elasticity
Private education	2.46
Automobiles	2.45
Housing (owner occupied)	1.49
Furniture	1.48
Dental services	1.42
Restaurant meals	1.40
Shoes	1.10
Clothing	1.02
Beer	0.93
Physicians' services	0.75
Cigarettes	0.50
Gasoline and oil	0.48
Housing (rental)	0.43
Coffee	0.29
Margarine	−0.20
Flour	−0.36

Sources: T. F. Hogarty and K. G. Elzinga, "The Demand for Beer," *Review of Economics and Statistics,* May 1972; H. S. Houthakker and L. D. Taylor, *Consumer Demand in the United States: Analyses and Projections,* 2d ed. (Cambridge, Mass.: Harvard University Press, 1970); J. J. Hughes, "Note on the U.S. Demand for Coffee," *American Journal of Agricultural Economics,* November 1969; S. M. Sackrin, "Factors Affecting the Demand for Cigarettes," *Agricultural Economics Research,* July 1962; H. Wold and C. E. Leser, "Commodity Group Expenditure Functions for the United Kingdom, 1948–57," *Econometrica,* January 1961.

Substitutes   If an increase in the price of one good leads to an increase in the demand for another good, the cross-price elasticity will be positive, and the goods are considered *substitutes*. For example, an increase in the price of Coke, other things constant, will increase the demand for Pepsi, reflecting the fact that the two are substitutes.

Complements   If an increase in the price of one good leads to a decrease in the demand for another good, the cross-price elasticity will be negative, and the goods are considered *complements*. For example, an increase in the price of gasoline, other things equal, will reduce the demand for tires because people drive less as a result of higher gasoline prices and so replace their tires less frequently. Gasoline and tires have a negative cross elasticity and are complements.

In summary, when the change in demand for one good has the same sign as the change in price of another good, the two goods are substitutes; when the change in demand for one good has the opposite sign as the change in price of another good, the goods are complements. For most pairs of goods selected at random, the cross-elasticity will be 0 because the goods are unrelated.

CONCLUSIONS

Because this chapter has tended to be more quantitative than earlier chapters, you may have been preoccupied with the mechanics of the calculations and thus may have overlooked the intuitive appeal and the neat simplicity of the notion of elasticity. At its heart an elasticity measure represents the willingness and ability of buyers and sellers to alter their behavior in response to a change in their economic circumstances. For example, if the price of a good falls, consumers may be able but not willing to increase their consumption of the good. In this case the demand would be inelastic.

Elasticities of supply and demand have been calculated for all kinds of goods and services, ranging from eggs to electricity. The objective of this kind of research is to predict the effects of changes in relative prices and in income. The empirical results are generally consistent with the theoretical conclusions presented in this chapter. Some items, such as gasoline, have received more attention than others. The members of the Organization of Petroleum Exporting Countries (OPEC) have an abiding interest in the price elasticity of demand for oil. More generally, corporations spend a great deal of effort trying to estimate the price elasticity of demand for their products.

Since a corporation often produces an entire line of products, it also has a special interest in certain cross-price elasticities. Governments, too, have an ongoing interest in various elasticities. For example, what will be the effect of a 1 percent increase in the sales tax on total tax receipts? How will an increase in the income tax affect the supply of labor? Many questions can be answered by referring to particular elasticities.

In the next chapter we will examine more closely the role of consumer behavior in shaping the demand curve. We will attempt to "look behind" the demand curves to show how they are derived.

SUMMARY

1. The price elasticities of demand and supply tell us how sensitive buyers and sellers are to changes in the price. The greater the response is, the greater will be the elasticity; the less the response, the smaller will be the elasticity.

2. The price elasticity of demand equals the percentage change in quantity demanded divided by the percentage change in price. If the elasticity has a value of less than 1.0, demand is inelastic; if the value is greater than 1.0, demand is elastic; and if the value is equal to 1.0, demand is of unitary elasticity.

3. If demand is inelastic, a price increase will increase total revenue; if demand is elastic, a price increase will reduce total revenue; and if demand is of unitary elasticity, a price increase will leave total revenue unchanged.

4. Computing elasticities based on the midpoint formula ensures that the elasticity calculation between two points on a demand curve will be the same whether we are moving from a higher to a lower price or vice versa. The midpoint formula computes percentage changes in price and quantity using the average price and average quantity as the appropriate bases.

5. Some demand curves have the same elasticity everywhere along the curve. Three examples are (1) the perfectly elastic, or horizontal, demand curve, (2) the perfectly inelastic, or vertical, demand curve, and (3) the unitary elasticity demand curve. Constant elasticity demand curves, however, are more the exception than the rule. Most commonly, demand curves reflect varying elasticities for different price changes. Along a linear, or straight-lined, demand curve, for example, the elasticity of demand falls steadily as the price falls.

6. Several factors affect the price elasticity of demand. Demand will be more elastic: (1) the greater the availability of substitutes and the closer these substitutes are, (2) the larger the proportion of the consumer's budget spent on the product, (3) the more narrowly the market is defined, (4) the longer the time allowed to adjust to a change in price, and (5) the more the good tends to be a luxury rather than a necessity.

7. The price elasticity of supply uses the same kind of calculations and the same terminology as the price elasticity of demand. If costs rise sharply as output expands, supply will be less elastic. Also, the longer the time period, the more elastic will be the supply.

8. The income elasticity of demand measures the responsiveness of demand to changes in consumer income. The income elasticity of demand is positive for normal goods and negative for inferior goods. The cross-price elasticity of demand measures the responsiveness of demand to changes in the price of another product. Two goods are defined as substitutes, complements, or unrelated, depending on whether their cross-price elasticity of demand is less than, greater than, or equal to 0.

QUESTIONS AND PROBLEMS

1. (Demand Elasticity) How is it possible for many elasticities to be associated with a single demand curve?

2. (Demand Elasticity) Suppose that an executive was concerned only with maximizing the company's gross revenues. What pricing policy should be followed?

3. (Midpoint Elasticity) Suppose the initial price and quantity demanded of a good are $1 per unit and 50 units, respectively. A reduc-

tion in price to $0.20 results in an increase in quantity demanded to 70 units. Show that the midpoint elasticity from this data is equal to 0.25. A 10-percent rise in the price can be expected to reduce the quantity demanded by what percentage?

4. (Linear Demand and Elasticity) Must the elastic and inelastic sections of a linear demand curve always be of equal length? Why or why not?

5. (Perfectly Inelastic Demand) Why is it impossible for a demand curve to be perfectly inelastic for *all* prices? Consider very high and very low prices.

6. (Demand Elasticity Determinants) What happens to the elasticity of demand for automobile towing services during a large snowstorm? How might this change differ for low-income people as compared with high-income people?

7. (Perfectly Inelastic Supply) Although Picasso paintings are in fixed supply technically, what ways still exist of increasing their availability?

8. (Tax Incidence) Often it is claimed that a tax on the sale of a specific good will simply be passed on to consumers. What is necessary for this to happen? In what cases might very little of the tax be passed on to consumers?

9. (Cross Price Elasticity) Rank the following in order of increasing cross-price elasticity (from negative to positive) with coffee:
   a. mustard
   b. tea
   c. cream
   d. cola

10. (Price Elasticity) Explain why the price elasticity of demand for Coke is greater than that for soft drinks generally. How would one define the price of soft drinks generally in this case?

CONSUMER CHOICE
and DEMAND

You already know the two reasons why demand curves are downward sloping. The first is based on the substitution effect of a price change. When the price of a good falls, consumers substitute the now cheaper good for other goods because there are alternative ways of satisfying a particular want. The second reason why demand curves are downward sloping is based on the income effect of a price change. When the price of a good falls, the real incomes of consumers increase, so more of the good will be purchased (as long as the good is normal).

Because the law of demand is so important, in this chapter we present another way to derive it, a way that focuses on the logic of consumer choice in a world of scarcity. First, we develop utility analysis, which we use to predict which goods and services will be consumed and in what quantities. Then we show how this analysis relates to the law of demand. The objective of this chapter is not to tell you how to maximize your utility—you already know how to do that—but to examine more closely what you already do and to understand more fully the economic implications of your behavior. Topics discussed in this chapter include:

- Total and marginal utility
- The law of diminishing marginal utility
- Measuring utility
- Utility maximizing conditions
- Consumer surplus

UTILITY ANALYSIS

Suppose you and a friend dine together. If your friend asks how you enjoyed your meal, you might say, "It was fine" or "I liked it better than the last meal I ate here." You would not say, "It deserves a rating of 85 on the standard utility index." Nor would you say, "I liked it better than you liked your meal."

Utility describes the power of goods and services to satisfy wants. It is the sense of pleasure and satisfaction that comes from consumption. Utility is inherently subjective. The utility you derived from that meal cannot be measured objectively. You cannot give your meal an 85 utility rating and your friend's meal an 81. Each person can tell whether one personal experience is more pleasant than another, but we cannot make comparisons across individuals. Although utility is subjective, we can infer from your behavior that you receive more utility from apples than from oranges if, when the two are priced the same, you always buy apples. What determines the utility you derive from consuming a particular good?

Tastes and Preferences

The utility you receive from consuming a particular good depends on your tastes and preferences. Some goods are extremely appealing to you, and others are not. You may not understand, for example, why someone would pay good money for raw oysters, chicken livers, or country music. As noted earlier, we will have little to say about why some people like raw oysters and some do not. We simply assume that tastes are given and are relatively stable. How much utility you derive from consuming each particular good is primarily a matter of taste. As we will see, the utility you receive from different goods determines how you will allocate your income. Obviously, if you dislike oysters, you will buy none.

Although we know little about the origin of a particular individual's tastes and preferences, some people are obviously influenced by the consumption behavior of others. Evidence of this is perhaps most apparent in the fashion industry, where so-called trendsetters often establish the "in" look. Other consumption choices are also influenced by what those who are "in the know" select.

Why do some people base their consumption on the consumption of others? The typical consumer may defer to supposedly more knowledgeable consumers for advice. Young athletes may want to wear the same brand of basketball shoes as Michael Jordan or use the same tennis racket as Martina Navratilova. Manufacturers understand this and are willing to pay large sums for product endorsements. Rolex offers trendsetters its $5000 watch free just so others will notice all the famous people wearing that brand.

The other side of the coin is that some people apparently derive utility by advertising their own consumption choices, even to the point of wearing the label on the outside. Conspicuous consumption of designer jeans, Gucci handbags, and the ultimate driving machine suggest that the utility of a product is not confined to one's personal enjoyment of it but is linked to public recognition of one's superior consumption choices.

The Law of Diminishing Marginal Utility

Imagine this scenario. It is a hot day. You have just mowed the lawn and are extremely thirsty. You pour yourself a glass of cold water. That first glass is wonderful, and it puts a serious dent in your thirst; the next one is not quite as wonderful, but it is still good; the third is just fair; and the fourth glass you barely finish.

Total utility is the satisfaction derived from consuming a certain quantity of a good.

We can distinguish between the **total utility** you derived from your consumption of water and the **marginal utility** you derive from consuming one more glass. Your experience with the water reflects the most basic principle of utility analysis—the **law of diminishing marginal utility**. This law states that the more of a good consumed per time period, other things constant, the smaller the increase in total utility received from each additional unit consumed. The marginal utility you derived from each glass of water declined as your water consumption increased. You enjoyed the first glass immensely, but each additional glass provided less and less marginal utility. If someone had forced you to drink a fifth glass, you probably would not have enjoyed it; your marginal utility from a fifth glass would likely have been negative.

Marginal utility is the change in total utility derived from a one-unit change in the consumption of a good.

Diminishing marginal utility is a feature of all consumption. At times marginal utility may not decline very quickly. For example, you may be able to eat many potato chips before the marginal utility of additional chips drops sharply. For other goods the drop in marginal utility with additional consumption is more dramatic. A second Big Mac may provide some marginal utility, but the marginal utility of a third one during the same meal would be slight or even negative. A second copy of the daily newspaper would likely provide you with no marginal utility (unless you use it to line the bird cage). After a long winter that first warm day of spring is something special and is the cause of "spring fever." The fever is cured, however, by many warm days like the first. By the time August arrives people attach less marginal utility to yet another warm day. If you have any doubts about diminishing marginal utility, ask someone who has just finished a pie-eating contest if he or she would like another piece.

According to the law of diminishing marginal utility, the more of a good that is consumed per period, the smaller the marginal utility, other things constant.

MEASURING UTILITY

So far our descriptions of utility have been such words as *wonderful, good,* and *fair.* We cannot expect to push the analysis of utility very far if we are limited to such subjective language. If we want to be able to predict behavior based on changes in the economic environment, we must develop a consistent way of viewing utility.

Units of Utility

There really is no objective way of measuring utility. But suppose that someone develops a computer that can be hooked up to a biofeedback machine to measure with great precision the utility you derive from consumption. The machine was built especially for you and is based on your brain waves and body chemistry. We can use the machine to gauge the utility you derive from alternative consumption combinations. The movement of a

**Alfred Marshall
(1842–1924)**

Historical Pictures
Service, Inc., Chicago

Natura non facit saltum. This latin motto adorns the title page of Alfred Marshall's *Principles of Economics.* Literally translated, it means "nature doesn't make leaps"—in other words, change in nature is gradual and evolutionary. It is a well-chosen motto, for it sets the tone both for Marshall's conception of economics and for his own style as an economist.

Alfred Marshall was born in Clapham, England. His domineering father pushed him to enter the ministry, but the young Marshall rebelled and instead studied mathematics at Cambridge University. Soon Marshall was teaching mathematics, studying the works of the classical economists, and quietly developing his own ideas. In 1884 he was called to the Chair of Political Economy at Cambridge, a position he occupied well into the twentieth century and from which he exerted a tremendous influence on British economics. In 1890 Marshall published his *Principles*, the most important text of its age.

Marshall's concern with gradual change appears throughout the book. His approach to economic theory was fundamentally incremental. For example, one of Marshall's most important contributions is the method of partial-equilibrium analysis: don't try to examine all the complex interconnections in the economy at once, he advises; instead, look at a single market in isolation while holding all other things constant.

Marshall was something of a gradualist in his professional style as well. In 1871 several European economists (including W. Stanley Jevons in England) had proposed looking at the theory of value in a new way. The classical economists had focused on costs of production as the prime determinant of market price. These "marginalist" economists focused instead on utility—marginal utility—as the main determinant of market price. In fact, many historians call the work of Jevons and the others the "marginalist revolution." By 1871 Marshall had probably developed the idea of marginal utility on his own. A meticulous thinker and writer, Marshall refused, however, to publish his ideas until he had worked everything out to his satisfaction. Moreover, Marshall was less of a revolutionary than Jevons. He saw himself not as overthrowing the classical economics of Smith but as adding to it. The *Principles* thus combines in many ways the best of the classical and marginalist ideas. John Maynard Keynes, Marshall's most famous pupil, put it this way: "Jevons saw the kettle boil and cried out with the delighted voice of a child; Marshall too had seen the kettle boil and sat down silently to build an engine."

needle on a dial registers your utility level. We will call the units measured on the dial *utils*. **Utils** therefore are measures of pleasure, satisfaction, or utility that can be used to compare the total utility you receive from different goods as well as the marginal utility you derive from additional units of the same good.

Incidentally, you need no such machine to maximize your utility. You already do that every day without the assistance of space-age technology. If we want to examine your economic choices, however, we will assume we have this machine to measure your utility. Keep in mind that our ultimate objective is to predict the effect of certain changes on your economic behavior, and we should judge marginal utility theory on its predictive power, not on the realism of its assumptions.

In the example of drinking water to quench your thirst, suppose we hooked you up to the machine and were able to make the calculations presented in Exhibit 1. The first column lists the quantity of water consumed; the second presents the total utility, measured in utils, derived from that consumption, and the third column calculates the marginal utility of each additional glass of water consumed.

You can see from the second column that total utility increases with each of the first 4 glasses but by smaller and smaller amounts. The third column shows that you derive a marginal utility of 20 utils from the first glass. Marginal utility declines thereafter, becoming negative for the fifth glass. The total utility you derive is graphed in panel (a) of Exhibit 2. Again, because of diminishing marginal utility, each glass adds less and less to total utility, so total utility increases but at a decreasing rate. The marginal utility is presented in panel (b).

Utility Maximization in a World Without Scarcity

So how much water do you consume? Since the price of water is in effect 0, you drink water as long as each additional glass offers utility. You stop when more water provides no marginal utility. So when a good is free, you consume as long as additional units provide positive marginal utility. You stop when marginal utility is 0.

EXHIBIT 1
UTILITY YOU DERIVE FROM WATER
AFTER MOWING THE LAWN

Units of Water Consumed (8-ounce glass)	Total Utility (utils)	Marginal Utility (utils)
0	0	—
1	20	20
2	32	12
3	39	7
4	42	3
5	41	−1

EXHIBIT 2   **UTILITY YOU DERIVE FROM WATER AFTER MOWING THE LAWN**

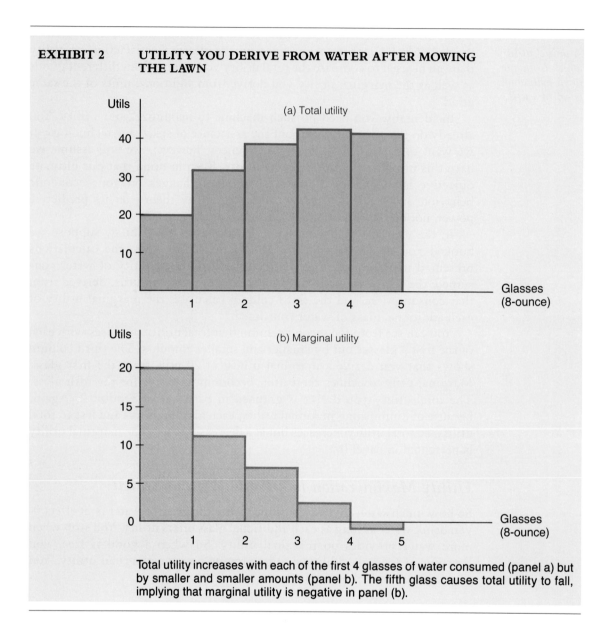

Total utility increases with each of the first 4 glasses of water consumed (panel a) but by smaller and smaller amounts (panel b). The fifth glass causes total utility to fall, implying that marginal utility is negative in panel (b).

Let's extend the analysis of utility to a world where you have only two goods from which to choose, food and clothing. Suppose the total utility and marginal utility for the alternative rates of consumption of these goods, given your tastes and preferences, have been calculated by our utility-measuring computer and are presented in Exhibit 3. You can see from columns (3) and (7) that both goods exhibit diminishing marginal utility.

Given this set of preferences, how much of each good will you consume? That depends first on the prices of the goods and second on your income. If the price of each good is 0, then you would consume as long as you derive positive marginal utility from additional units of each good. Thus, in a world

EXHIBIT 3
TOTAL AND MARGINAL UTILITY FROM
FOOD AND CLOTHING

Units of Food Consumed per Period	Total Utility (utils)	Marginal Utility (utils)	Marginal Utility per Dollar Expended (price = $4)	Units of Clothing per Period	Total Utility (utils)	Marginal Utility (utils)	Marginal Utility per Dollar Expended (price = $2)
(1)	(2)	(3)	(4)	(5)	(6)	(7)	(8)
0	0	—	—	0	0	—	—
1	25	25	6.25	1	20	20	10.00
2	41	16	4.00	2	34	14	7.00
3	53	12	3.00	3	44	10	5.00
4	62	9	2.25	4	50	6	3.00
5	68	6	1.50	5	54	4	2.00
6	72	4	1.00	6	57	3	1.50

without scarcity you would consume at least the first 6 units of each good because both goods generate positive marginal utility throughout the table. Did you ever go to a party where the food and drinks were free to you? How much did you eat and drink? You probably ate and drank until you "didn't feel like any more"—that is, until the marginal utility of each good consumed went to 0.

Utility Maximization in a World of Scarcity

But, alas, scarcity is our lot, so we should focus on how a consumer chooses in a world dominated by scarcity. To make our example more realistic, assume the price of food is $4 per unit, the price of clothing is $2 per unit, and you have an income of $20 per period. Under these conditions, how would you allocate income to derive the most utility from consumption? How would you maximize your utility?

Suppose you start off with some bundle of food and clothing. If you can increase your utility by reallocating expenditures, you will do so, and you will continue to make adjustments as long as you can increase your utility. When no further utility-increasing moves are possible, you have settled on the bundle that maximizes your utility; you have arrived at the equilibrium combination. Once you reach this equilibrium, you will maintain this consumption pattern. You have no reason to choose differently unless one of the factors that influence your demand changes, such as your tastes, your income, or prices.

There may be some trial and error in the consumption decision, but you learn from your mistakes as you move toward the utility-maximizing position. You know that food costs twice as much as clothing per period, so consuming a unit of food has an opportunity cost of not consuming 2 units of clothing. Conversely, consuming a unit of clothing requires you to forgo 0.5 units of food. Without knowing any more than this, let's see how you grope toward equilibrium.

Suppose you start off spending your whole budget of $20 on food, purchasing 5 units, which provide a total utility of 68 utils per period. Then you realize that if you reduce food consumption by 1 unit, you can buy the first 2 units of clothing. You thus give up 6 utils, the marginal utility of the fifth unit of food, but you gain a total of 34 utils from the first 2 units of clothing. Clearly, this is a utility-increasing move. Then you notice that if you reduce your food consumption to 3 units, you give up 9 utils from the fourth unit of food but gain 16 utils from buying the third and fourth units of clothing. This is another utility-maximizing move. Further reductions in food, however, will only reduce your total utility because you would have to give up 12 utils from the third unit of food but would gain only a total of 7 utils from the fifth and sixth units of clothing.

Thus, by trial and error, you find that the utility-maximizing choice is to consume 3 units of food and 4 units of clothing, for a total utility of 103 utils. This involves an outlay of $12 on food and $8 on clothing. You are in equilibrium when consuming this bundle because any change would only lower your total utility.

To make sure you understand this process of utility-maximizing choice, suppose you begin with a situation where all your income is spent on clothing. You should be able to work through the trial-and-error process of finding the utility-maximizing consumption bundle. You should once again end up with 3 units of food and 4 units of clothing. Try it. It doesn't matter where you start—the attempt to maximize utility guides you to the same consumption bundle.

The Utility-Maximizing Conditions   There is often a long way and a short way of solving a problem. We have just gone through the trial-and-error method, which is the long way. The short way is based on the knowledge that when the consumer is in equilibrium, there is no way to reallocate the budget to increase utility. In fact, as you can see in the previous example, once equilibrium has been achieved, any shift in spending from one good to another will decrease utility. A special property about the utility-maximizing combination makes it impossible to shift spending around without lowering utility: in equilibrium the last dollar spent on each good yields the same utility. More specifically, utility is maximized when the marginal utility of a good divided by its price is identical for each good purchased. If this were not so, you could always reallocate your budget to increase your total utility. Let's see how this works.

In Exhibit 3 columns (4) and (8) provide the marginal utility of each dollar's worth of food and clothing. Column (4) is derived by dividing the marginal utility of food by the price of a unit of food, which is $4. Column (8) does the same, using the marginal utility of clothing and a price of $2. You can see that the equilibrium choice of 3 units of food and 4 units of clothing yields 3 utils for the last dollar spent on either good. Equilibrium is achieved when the budget is completely exhausted, and the last dollar spent on each good yields the same utility, or

$$\frac{MU_f}{P_f} = \frac{MU_c}{P_c}$$

where MU_f is the marginal utility of the last unit of food consumed, and P_f is the price of food. The logic of this decision rule should not be overlooked. If food yields a lower marginal utility per dollar than clothing, total utility can be increased by reducing food purchases and increasing the purchase of clothing. Although we have considered only two goods, the logic of utility maximization applies to any number of goods.

A Caveat   The presentation in Exhibit 3 is correct as far as it goes, but this simple tabular approach cannot be used for examining all goods. An implicit assumption in the analysis is that the goods under consideration are unrelated—they are neither substitutes nor complements. Food and clothing satisfy different wants and can reasonably be considered unrelated. If this assumption did not hold, the marginal utility you receive from consuming one good will depend in part on how much of the other good you consume. For example, suppose we are considering your choice of water versus lemonade. If you view the two as close substitutes, the marginal utility you receive from each additional glass of water per day will depend on the amount of lemonade you consume. The marginal utility of the first glass of water will be higher if you are consuming no lemonade than if you are already consuming three glasses of lemonade per day. Thus, you cannot consider the marginal utility of each glass of water without taking into account your consumption of lemonade. By assuming that food and clothing satisfy independent wants, we have avoided the need to hinge the utility of food on the quantity of clothing consumed.

Deriving the Law of Demand from Marginal Utility

The real purpose of utility analysis is to provide information about the demand curve. How does the previous analysis relate to your individual demand for food? It yields one point on your demand curve for food: at a price of $4 per unit, you will demand 3 units. This point alone gives you no idea about the shape of your demand curve, however. It could be upward sloping for all we know.

To generate another point, let's change the price of food and see what happens to the quantity demanded. Suppose the price of food drops from $4 to $3 per unit. What will happen to your consumption decision based on the preferences already discussed in Exhibit 3? Your original consumption choice was 3 units of food and 4 units of clothing, but you will no longer consume that combination. The marginal utility per dollar of expenditure for the third unit of food is now 4 utils (12/3), which exceeds the 3 utils received from the fourth unit of clothing consumed, so you are no longer equating the marginal utility on the last dollar spent on each good. Also, if you try to maintain the original choice, you would have $3 left over in your budget because you would be spending only $9 on food. You can increase your utility by consuming a different bundle.

Based on your utility schedule as presented in Exhibit 3, you should increase your consumption of food to 4 units per period. This increase exhausts your budget and equates the marginal utility of the last dollar expended on each good. Your consumption of clothing remains the same, as does the marginal utility for the last dollar spent on clothing. But your consumption of food increases to 4 units; the marginal utility of the fourth unit, 9 utils, divided by the price of $3, yields 3 utils per dollar of expenditure, which is the same as for clothing. You are in equilibrium once again. Your total utility increases by the 9 utils you receive from the fourth unit of clothing; hence, you are clearly better off as a result of the price decrease.

Thus, when the price of food is $3 per unit, the quantity demanded is 4 units. More simply put, when the price of food falls, the quantity demanded increases. We now have a second point on your demand curve for food; the two points are presented as *a* and *b* in Exhibit 4. We could continue to change the price of food and thereby generate additional points on the demand curve, but you get some idea of the demand curve's slope from just two points. Similarly, we could generate the demand curve for clothing. The shape of the

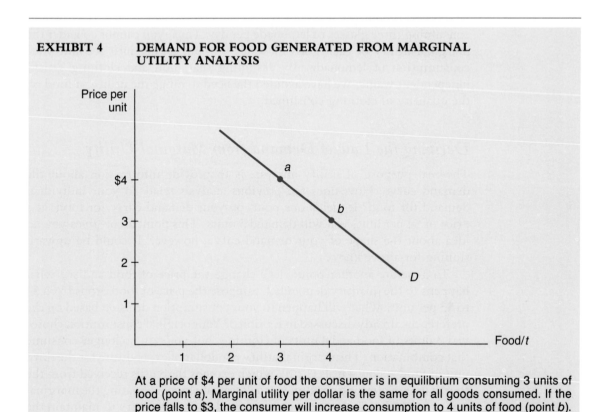

EXHIBIT 4   DEMAND FOR FOOD GENERATED FROM MARGINAL UTILITY ANALYSIS

At a price of $4 per unit of food the consumer is in equilibrium consuming 3 units of food (point *a*). Marginal utility per dollar is the same for all goods consumed. If the price falls to $3, the consumer will increase consumption to 4 units of food (point *b*). Points *a* and *b* are two points on the consumer's demand curve for food.

demand curve for food conforms to our expectations based on the law of demand; price and quantity demanded are inversely related. Incidentally, can you determine the price elasticity of demand between points *a* and *b*?

We have gone to some length to understand how you maximize utility. To understand the process, we assumed we could measure the marginal utility you derived from additional units of the good. This allowed us to construct the table presented in Exhibit 3 to analyze your consumption choices. In reality, you do not need to perform such calculations, at least not explicitly. Your tastes and preferences will naturally guide you to the most preferred bundle, given your income and the prices of goods and services. You are probably unconscious of your behavior. The force to maximize utility is like the force of gravity—both work whether or not you understand them.

Now that we have some idea of utility, we are prepared to consider consumer surplus, an application of utility analysis.

CONSUMER SURPLUS

In our example, total utility increased when the price fell from $4 to $3. In this section we take a closer look at how consumers benefit from a lower price. Suppose your demand for pizza is shown in Exhibit 5, which measures on the horizontal axis the number of medium-size pizzas demanded per month. Recall that in constructing a demand curve, we hold tastes, income, and the prices of related goods constant; only the price of pizza varies.

At a price of $8 or above you find the marginal utility of other goods that you could buy for $8 to be higher than the marginal utility of a pizza. Consequently, you demand no pizza. At a price of $7, you feel pizza is still expensive, but the marginal utility of the first pizza evidently exceeds what you could have received by spending that money on your next best alternative, which may have been a movie, some popcorn, and a Coke. A price of $6 prompts you to demand 2 pizzas a month. Apparently, your marginal valuation of the second pizza is at least $6. At a price of $5, you demand 3 pizzas a month, and at $4, you demand 4 pizzas a month, or about 1 a week.

In each case the value to you of the last unit purchased must at least equal the price; otherwise, you would not have purchased that unit. For simplicity, we say that along the demand curve the price reflects your marginal valuation of the good. The demand curve therefore shows the dollar value of the marginal utility derived from consuming each additional unit.

Consumer surplus is the difference between what a consumer is willing to pay for a given quantity of a good and what is actually paid.

Notice that when the price is $4, you receive each of the 4 pizzas for that price even though you would have been willing to pay more than $4 apiece for the first 3 pizzas. The first pizza confers marginal utility you value at $7, the second, marginal utility valued at $6, and the third, marginal utility valued at $5. In fact, you would have been willing to pay $7 for the first, $6 for the second, and $5 for the third. The total utility for the first 4 pizzas you value at $7 + $6 + $5 + $4 = $22. Note, however, that when the price is $4, you get all 4 for $16. Thus, a price of $4 confers a **consumer surplus**, or bonus, equal to the difference between what you would have been willing to pay

EXHIBIT 5   **CONSUMER SURPLUS**

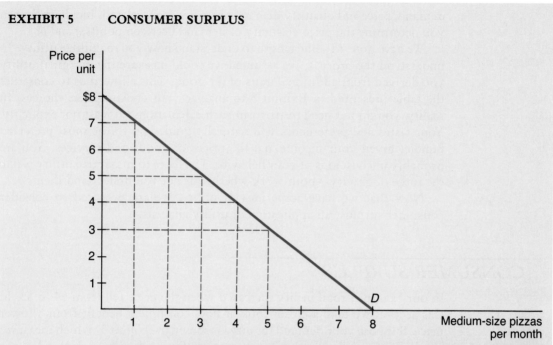

At a given quantity the height of the demand curve shows the value of the last unit purchased. The area under the demand curve up to a specific quantity shows the total value the consumer places on that quantity. At a price of $4 the consumer purchases 4 pizzas. The first pizza is valued at $7, the second at $6, the third at $5, and the fourth at $4; the consumer values 4 pizzas at $22. Since the consumer pays $4 per pizza, all 4 can be obtained for $16. The difference between what the consumer would have been willing to pay ($22) and what was actually paid ($16) is called consumer surplus. It is the area under the demand curve but above $4.

($22) and what you actually paid ($16). Put differently, the consumer surplus is equal to the difference between the value of the total utility you receive from consuming the pizza and your total expenditure.

If the price falls to $3, you purchase 5 pizzas a month. Evidently you feel that the marginal benefit you receive from the fifth unit is worth at least $3. The lower price means that you get to buy all the earlier units for $3 even though they are worth more to you than $3. Your consumer surplus when the price is $3 is the value of the total utility conferred by the first 5 pizzas, which is $7 + $6 + $5 + $4 + $3 = $25, minus the cost, which is $3 × 5 = $15. Thus, the consumer surplus is $25 − $15 = $10. When the price is lowered by $1, you are able to purchase all units for less, so your consumer surplus increases. From Exhibit 5 you can see why consumers benefit from lower prices.

DERIVING THE MARKET DEMAND FROM INDIVIDUAL DEMAND

We have now analyzed an individual demand curve. In Chapter 3 we examined the market demand curve. The market demand curve is simply the horizontal sum of the individual demand curves for all consumers in the market. Exhibit 6 shows how the demand curves for the three individuals in the market are summed across to yield the market demand curve. At a price of $5 per unit, for example, individual *A* demands 30 units, individual *B* demands 20 units, and individual *C* demands nothing. The quantity demanded at a price of $5 is therefore 50 units. At a price of $2 per unit, *A*'s quantity demanded is 60 units, *B*'s is 50 units, and *C*'s is 15 units, for a total quantity demanded of 125 units. Market demand curves show the total quantity demanded at various prices.

With certain qualifications that we need not go into here, the idea of consumer surplus can be used to examine market demand as well. We can sum each consumer's surplus to arrive at the market consumer surplus. Consumer surplus for the market demand curve is measured by the difference between the value of the total utility received from consumption and the total amount paid for that consumption. When the price is $2, each person

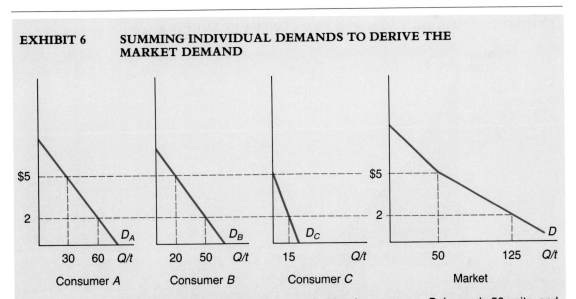

EXHIBIT 6　**SUMMING INDIVIDUAL DEMANDS TO DERIVE THE MARKET DEMAND**

At a price of $2 consumer *A* demands 60 units, consumer *B* demands 50 units, and consumer *C* demands 15 units. Total market demand at a price of $2 is 60 + 50 + 15 = 125 units. At a higher price of $5, *A* demands 30 units, *B* demands 20 units, and *C* demands nothing. Market demand at $5 is 50 units. The market supply curve, *D,* is the horizontal sum of individual demand curves, D_A, D_B, and D_C.

consumes the good until the marginal benefit of the last unit purchased equals $2. But each consumer gets to buy all the other units for $2 as well. In Exhibit 7 the darkly shaded area bounded by the price of $2 from below and the demand curve from above depicts the consumer surplus when the price is $2.

If the price dropped to $1 per unit, the lightly shaded area represents the additional consumer surplus that would be gained. Finally, you can see that if this good were free, the consumer surplus would be the entire area above the horizontal axis and below the demand curve. That consumers benefit from free goods is intuitively obvious; not so obvious is the fact that the total consumer surplus in Exhibit 7 when the price is $1 is nearly as great as when the good is free.

THE ROLE OF TIME IN DEMAND

Demand measures the desired rate of consumption at alternative prices during a given time period. An important consideration in constructing a demand curve is the time period involved, for this determines the desired rate

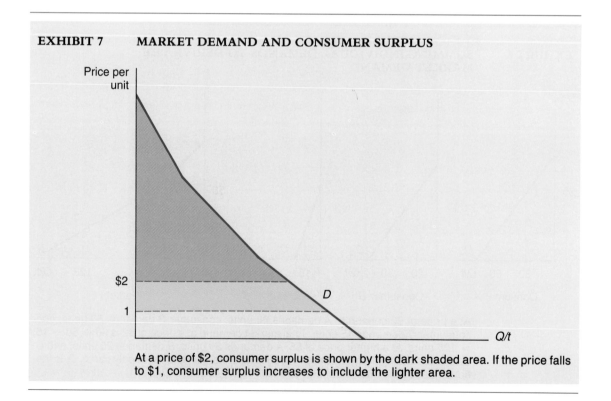

EXHIBIT 7   MARKET DEMAND AND CONSUMER SURPLUS

At a price of $2, consumer surplus is shown by the dark shaded area. If the price falls to $1, consumer surplus increases to include the lighter area.

of consumption. The longer the time period is, the greater will be the demand, other things equal. The demand for pizza is greater per month than per week or per day.

Time plays another important role in demand analysis because consumption does not occur instantaneously. Consumption takes time and, as they say, time is money—time has a positive value for most people. Goods are demanded because of the services they offer. Your demand for a lawn mower is based on its ability to cut grass; your interest is not in the mower itself but in the service it provides. Thus, you would be willing to pay more for a mower that did the job faster and saved you time. Similarly, it is not the toaster, automatic dishwasher, or bus ticket to Washington that you demand but the services these goods provide. Other things held constant, the good that can provide the same service but in less time is preferred. Consequently, the cost of consumption has two components: the money price of the good and the time price of the good.

Time is more valuable to some people than to others. The busy executive is more willing to pay a premium for a time saver than someone who is just "killing time." The money price of a good is usually the same for all consumers, but the time price of consuming that good differs across individuals, since their opportunity cost of time differs. An understanding of this difference in the value of time explains many of the consumption patterns observed in the economy. Your willingness to pay a premium for timesaving goods and services depends on the opportunity cost of your time.

Consider the alternative ways to get to Europe. You can ride the Concorde, a regular airline, or a tramp steamer. Your mode of travel will depend in part on your opportunity cost of time. Higher money costs are associated with lower time costs. The Concorde takes less than half the time of other flights, but because the Concorde is much more expensive, only travelers with an extremely high opportunity cost of time will pay such a premium for faster service. Students on their summer vacation may be more inclined to take the tramp steamer—for them the lower money cost more than compensates for the higher time cost. Busy executives, however, shepherd their scarce time much more carefully, not only in the time spent traveling but also in how travel time is utilized. Look around the next time you are on a plane or train and notice who is working on reports or dealing with correspondence.

A retired couple has a lower opportunity cost of time, so we might expect them to purchase fewer timesaving goods, such as microwave ovens and frozen "gourmet" meals, than, say, the household where both spouses work outside the home. The retired couple will be more inclined to drive across the country on their vacation, whereas the working couple will fly to their vacation destination. The retired couple will clip coupons and search the newspapers for bargains, sometimes going from store to store for particular grocery items on sale that week. The working couple will usually ignore the coupons and sales and will often purchase items at the more expensive convenience stores. Differences in the opportunity cost of time add an extra dimension to our analysis of demand.

CONCLUSIONS

This chapter presented another way to derive demand curves. Rather than relying on the substitution and income effects of a price change, we developed a utility-based analysis of consumer choice. The focus was on the utility, or benefits, that consumers receive from consumption. To observe consumer behavior, we assumed that for a particular individual, utility could be measured in some systematic way. Although some of you might be troubled by such an assumption, keep in mind that the goal of any theory is to predict. Our ultimate objective is to predict how consumer choice is affected by such things as a change in price or a change in income. We judge a theory not by the realism of its assumptions but by the accuracy of its predictions. Based on this criterion, the theory of consumer choice presented in this chapter has proven to be quite useful.

Again, we stress that consumers do not have to understand the material presented in this chapter to maximize utility. We assume that rational consumers attempt to maximize utility naturally and instinctively. This chapter simply tries to analyze that process through a model of consumer choice using utility analysis. Another way to approach consumer choice, a model based on indifference curve analysis, is developed in the appendix to this chapter.

The previous two chapters have examined demand in some detail. The next several chapters will focus on supply. We will begin our analysis of supply in the next chapter with an examination of production costs.

SUMMARY

1. *Utility* is a term used to describe the want-satisfying power of goods and services. The utility you receive from consuming a particular good depends primarily on your tastes and preferences. We distinguish between the total utility derived from consuming a good and the marginal utility derived from consuming one more unit of the good. The law of diminishing marginal utility says that the greater the amount of a particular good consumed per time period, the smaller the increase in total utility received from each additional unit consumed.

2. Utility is a subjective notion because the assessment of the want-satisfying power of consumption must be made by each individual consumer. In this chapter, however, we assumed we could measure utility for a particular individual; we were therefore able to make predictions about how changes in economic conditions, such as price and income, will affect individual choice. We cannot make utility comparisons across individuals, although we can observe that one consumer has a greater demand for a particular good than does another consumer.

3. The consumer's objective is to maximize utility. In a world without scarcity, utility is maximized by consuming goods until the marginal utility of the last unit of each good consumed is 0. In a world dominated by scarcity, utility is maximized when the final unit of each good consumed yields the same utility per dollar spent. Put another way, utility is maximized when the marginal utility divided by the price is identical for each good consumed.

4. Utility analysis can be used to construct an individual demand curve. By changing the price and observing the utility-maximizing level of consumption, we can generate points along the demand curve. As the price of a

good drops, other things constant, the consumer is able to buy all units of the good at the lower price. Thus, we say that consumers typically receive a surplus, or bonus, from consumption.

5. The market demand curve is simply the horizontal sum of the individual demand curves for all consumers in the market. With some qualification, consumer surplus for the market demand curve is measured by the difference between the value of the total utility received from consumption and the total amount paid for that consumption.

6. There are two components to the cost of consumption: the money price of the good and the time price of the good. People with a higher opportunity cost are willing to pay a higher money price for goods and services that involve a lower time price.

QUESTIONS AND PROBLEMS

1. (Diminishing Marginal Utility) Some restaurants offer "all you can eat" meals. How is this practice related to diminishing marginal utility? What restrictions on the customer must the restaurant make in order to make a profit?

2. (Marginal Utility) Consider Exhibit 3 of this chapter and suppose that each number in columns (1) and (5) is multiplied by 2. How would this affect the marginal utility in columns (3) and (7)? Would columns (4) and (8) also be affected?

3. (Marginal Utility) Is it possible for marginal utility to be negative and yet total utility to be positive? Why or why not?

4. (Consumer Equilibrium) Suppose that a consumer has a choice between two goods, X and Y. If the price of X is $2 per unit and the price of Y is $3 per unit, how much of X and Y will the consumer purchase, assuming an income of $17? Use the following information on marginal utility:

Units	MU_X	MU_Y
1	10	5
2	8	4
3	2	3
4	2	2
5	1	2

5. (Consumer Allocation) Suppose there are two goods, X and Y. Next suppose that $MU_X = MU_Y$ and the price of X is less than the price of Y. It follows from this that the rational consumer will increase purchases of X and reduce purchases of Y. Why?

6. (Consumer Allocation) Suppose that $MU_X = 100$, with the price of X equal to $10 and the price of Y equal to $5. Assuming that the consumer is in equilibrium, what must the marginal utility of Y be equal to?

7. (Market Elasticities) Compute the elasticities for individual and market demands in Exhibit 6, using the prices and quantities given. Must the market demand's elasticity be greater than each of the individual demands' elasticities? Would your answer be different if A, B, and C had identical demand curves?

8. (Time Cost and Price) In many amusement parks one pays an admission fee to the park and then one need not pay for each ride taken. How would rides be allocated in such parks? Is there an incentive for some people to sell their places in line? Why or why not?

APPENDIX

Indifference Curves

The approach used in this chapter requires us to measure utility in order to determine the optimal bundle of goods and services. In reality utility cannot be measured, so economists have developed another, more sophisticated approach to examine utility and consumer behavior—one that does not require that numbers be attached to specific levels of utility. As we will see, all this approach requires is that consumers be able to rank their preferences for various combinations of goods. We will begin with an examination of consumer preferences.

Consumer Preferences

An approach to consumer behavior that requires no specific measure of utility is called indifference curve analysis. As we will see, indifference curves capture information about consumer preferences for two goods. Specifically, **indifference curves** show all combinations of two goods that provide the consumer with the same total satisfaction or total utility. Since each of the alternative bundles of goods yields the same utility, the consumer will be indifferent about which combination is actually consumed.

We can best explain the use of indifference curves through an example. Exhibit 8 measures the quantity of food consumed by the individual per period on the horizontal axis. The vertical axis measures the quantity of clothing the individual consumes per period. At point *a*, for example, 8 units of clothing and 1 unit of food are consumed. At point *a*, the consumer is willing to give up 4 units of clothing to get 1 more unit of food. Thus, at point *b*, the individual is consuming 4 units of clothing and 2 units of food and is indifferent between this combination and the combination reflected by point *a*. At point *b* the consumer is now willing to give up only 1 unit of clothing to get another unit of food, a

tradeoff that moves the consumer to point *c*, with 3 units of clothing and 3 units of food. At point *c*, the individual is willing to give up only 0.5 units of clothing to get another unit of food. Combination *d* therefore consists of 2.5 units of clothing and 4 units of food.

By definition, the consumer is indifferent among points *a*, *b*, *c*, and *d*. We can connect these points to form indifference curve I_1, which represents all possible combinations of food and clothing that would keep the consumer at the same level of satisfaction. Since all points on the curve offer the same amount of utility, or satisfaction, the consumer is indifferent among them—hence, the name *indifference curve*. Combinations of goods along the indifference curve reflect some constant, though unspecified, level of utility.

Because both goods yield utility, more of a good is preferred to less. Thus, to keep the consumer indifferent among bundles of

**EXHIBIT 8
AN INDIFFERENCE CURVE**

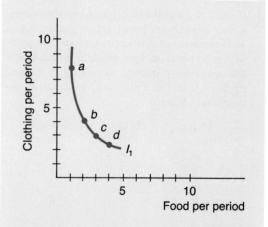

An indifference curve shows all combinations of two goods that provide a consumer with the same total utility. Points *a–d* depict four such combinations. Indifference curves are negatively sloped and convex to the origin.

goods, the increase in utility from consuming more of one good must be just offset by the reduction in utility from consuming less of another good. Thus, along an indifference curve there is an inverse relationship between the quantity of one good consumed and the quantity of another consumed. The indifference curve is therefore downward sloping.

Indifference curves are also *convex to the origin*, which means that they are bowed inward toward the origin. The slope therefore gets flatter as we move down the curve. Here is why. An individual's willingness to substitute food for clothing depends on how much of each the individual is currently consuming. At combination *a*, for example, the individual is consuming 8 units of clothing and only 1 unit of food, so there is much clothing relative to food. Because food is relatively scarce in the consumption bundle, the consumer finds another unit of food attractive and would be willing to give up 4 units of clothing to get it. Once at point *b* the amount of food consumed has doubled, so the consumer is not quite so willing to surrender clothing to get another unit of food. In fact, the consumer will forgo only 1 unit of clothing to get 1 more unit of food. This moves the consumer from point *b* to point *c*. At point *c* the consumer is even less anxious to get still more food, so is willing to give up only 0.5 units of clothing to get a fourth unit of food.

The **marginal rate of substitution**, or **MRS**, indicates how much of one good a consumer is willing to give up to get one more unit of another good while remaining equally satisfied. In moving from combination *a* to *b*, the consumer is willing to give up 4 units of clothing to get one more unit of food, so the *MRS* is 4. In the move from combination *b* to *c*, the *MRS* drops to 1, and from *b* to *c*, it falls to 0.5. Suppose that "food per period" measures meals per day. The consumer is willing to give up 4 units of clothing to get a second meal per day and 1 unit of clothing to get a third meal per day

but only 0.5 units of clothing to get a fourth meal per day.

In moving down the indifference curve, the amount of food increases, and the amount of clothing decreases. As the amount of food increases, the marginal utility of additional units of food decreases. Likewise, as the amount of clothing decreases, its marginal utility increases. Thus, in moving down an indifference curve, the consumer is willing to give up smaller and smaller amounts of clothing to get additional units of food. Consider pairs of goods more generally now, as goods *X* and *Y*. The **law of diminishing marginal rate of substitution** says that as the consumption of good *X* increases, the amount of good *Y* that the consumer is willing to give up to get each additional unit of *X* declines. Because the marginal rate of substitution of *X* for *Y* declines with an increase in consumption of *X*, the indifference curve has a diminishing slope, meaning that it is convex when viewed from the origin.

We have focused on a single indifference curve that indicates some constant but unspecified level of utility. We can use the same approach to present for this particular consumer a series of indifference curves, called an **indifference map**, for the two goods in question. Each curve in the indifference map reflects a different level of utility. Such a map for a particular consumer is shown in Exhibit 9, where indifference curves are labeled I_1, I_2, I_3, and I_4. Each consumer will have a different indifference map.

Curves farther from the origin represent greater possible combinations of goods and therefore higher levels of utility. So the utility level along I_2 is greater than that along I_1, I_3 is greater than I_2, and so on. You can perhaps best see this by drawing a line from the origin and following it to higher indifference curves. As you move out along that line, the combinations on each successive indifference curve reflect greater amounts of both goods. Since more is preferred to less,

EXHIBIT 9
AN INDIFFERENCE MAP

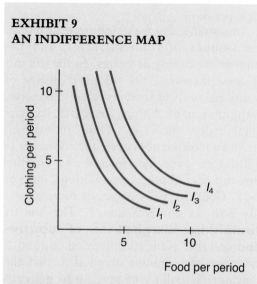

Indifference curves I_1–I_4 are four examples from an individual's indifference map. Indifference curves farther from the origin depict higher levels of utility.

negative marginal utility. Such possibilities exist, but they do not interest us because they are ignored by consumers. No consumer would knowingly increase the consumption of one good to the point where marginal utility is negative. Because we confine the analysis to cases in which goods yield positive marginal utility, our indifference curves are downward sloping.

Let's summarize the properties of indifference curves:

1. They reflect a constant though unspecified level of utility, so the consumer is indifferent among consumption combinations along a given curve.
2. Because an increase in the consumption of one good must be offset by a decrease in the consumption of the other good, indifference curves are downward sloping.

each successive indifference curve represents a higher level of utility.

One other feature of indifference curves is that they do not intersect. Exhibit 10 shows why. If indifference curves I and I' intersected at point i, then that combination of goods would lie on both indifference curves. Since the consumption of the bundle at point i reflects some specific level of utility and since point i lies on both curves, then both curves must reflect this same level of utility.

A line from the origin intersects the curves at points j and k. Combination k reflects more of both goods than combination j. Since more is preferred to less, k must be on a higher indifference curve than j. But we already said that because the two indifference curves intersect at i they must be of equal utility. Because the curves cannot reflect both identical utility and different utility, we conclude that the curves cannot intersect.

We have not considered consumption combinations where one good provides

EXHIBIT 10
INDIFFERENCE CURVES DO NOT INTERSECT

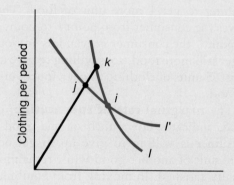

Food per period

If indifference curves crossed, as at point i, then every point on indifference curve I and every point on curve I' would have to reflect the same level of utility as at point i. But point k is a combination with more food and more clothing than point j and so must represent a higher level of utility. This contradiction means that indifference curves *cannot* intersect.

3. Because of the law of diminishing marginal rate of substitution, indifference curves are also bowed in toward the origin.
4. Indifference curves do not intersect.

Given a consumer's indifference map, how much of each good will be consumed? To determine how much will be consumed, we must find out the prices of the goods and the consumer's income. In the next section we will focus on the consumer's budget.

The Budget Line

Suppose the price of food is $4 per unit, the price of clothing is $2 per unit, and the consumer's budget is $20 per period. If the entire $20 is spent on clothing, the consumer could afford to buy 10 units. This consump-

tion choice is reflected by point C in Exhibit 11, which lies on the vertical axis and indicates that 10 units of clothing and no units of food are consumed. Alternatively, if the entire $20 is spent on food, the consumer could purchase 5 units, a possibility reflected by point F, which lies along the horizontal axis. The **budget line** connects points C and F and represents all possible combinations of clothing and food that could be purchased given the consumer's budget and product prices. You might think of the budget line, CF, as the individual's consumption possibilities frontier.

You will recall that the slope of any line is the vertical change divided by the horizontal change. At point C the quantity of clothing that could be purchased equals the consumer's income divided by the price of clothing, or Income/P_c, where P_c is the price of a unit of clothing. At point F the quantity of food that could be purchased equals the consumer's income divided by the price of food, or Income/P_f, where P_f is the price of a unit of food. To get the slope of the budget line, we divide (minus) the vertical distance (Income/P_c) by the horizontal distance (Income/P_f), as follows:

$$\text{Slope} = -\frac{\text{Income}/P_c}{\text{Income}/P_f} = -\frac{P_f}{P_c}$$

So the slope of the budget line equals the food price divided by the clothing price; in our example this is $-\$4/\$2$, which equals -2. The slope of the budget line indicates what it costs the consumer in terms of forgone clothing to get another unit of food. The consumer must give up 2 units of clothing for each additional unit of food.

As we know, the demand curve shows the quantity that the consumer is willing and able to buy at alternative prices. The indifference curve indicates what the consumer is *willing* to buy. The budget line shows what the consumer is *able* to buy. We must therefore bring together the indifference curve

**EXHIBIT 11
THE BUDGET LINE**

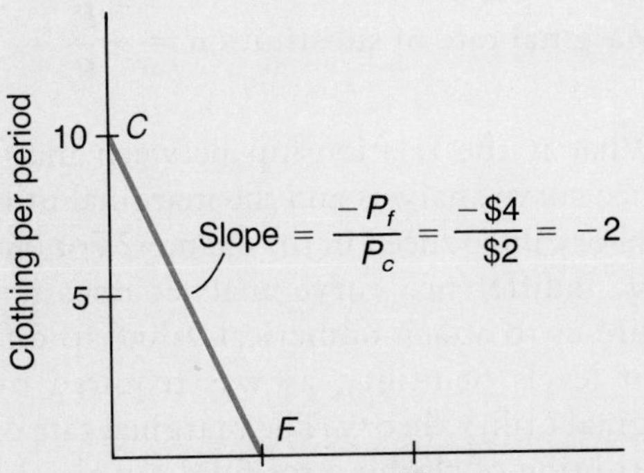

The budget line shows all combinations of food and clothing that can be purchased at fixed prices with a given amount of income. If all income is spent on clothing, 10 units could be purchased (point *C*). If all income is spent on food, 5 units could be purchased (point *F*). Points between *C* and *F* represent combinations of some food *and* some clothing. The slope of the budget line is –2, illustrating that the cost of one unit of food is two units of clothing.

and the budget line to find the quantity demanded at a particular price.

Consumer Equilibrium at the Tangency

We have assumed that consumers attempt to maximize their utility. We know that indifference curves farther from the origin represent higher levels of utility. The consumer's objective therefore is to attain the highest level of utility possible, given prices and the consumer's income. The utility-maximizing consumer will select that combination along the budget line *CF* in Exhibit 12 that lies on the highest attainable indifference curve. Combination *a* consists of 8 units of clothing costing a total of $16 and 1 unit of food at $4, for a total outlay of $20. Thus, point *a* is on the budget line and therefore is a combination the consumer is able to consume, but *a* is not on the highest attainable indifference curve. Given prices and income, the consumer depicted in Exhibit 12 maximizes utility at the combination of food and clothing depicted by point *e*, where indifference curve *I₂* just touches, or is tangent to, the budget line. This utility-maximizing consumption bundle consists of 4 units of clothing totaling $8 and 3 units of food totaling $12; so this combination thus exhausts the $20 budget.

Since the utility-maximizing combination is the best the consumer could do, point *e* is also an equilibrium outcome. Thus, there will be no tendency for the consumer to change this consumption pattern unless something else changes, such as prices or the consumer's income or tastes. The slope of the indifference curve equals the consumer's marginal rate of substitution—that is, the amount of clothing the consumer is willing to give up to get another unit of food. As we have already seen, the slope of the budget line, *CF*, equals (minus) the price ratio, which is − $4/$2, or − 2. Since the isoquant is tangent to the budget line at the equilibrium point, the marginal rate of substitution of clothing for food along the indifference

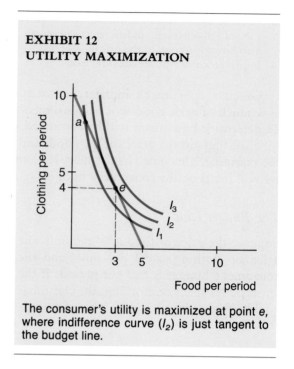

EXHIBIT 12
UTILITY MAXIMIZATION

The consumer's utility is maximized at point *e*, where indifference curve (*I₂*) is just tangent to the budget line.

curve must equal the slope of the budget line, or

$$\text{Marginal rate of substitution} = -\frac{P_f}{P_c}$$

What is the relationship between indifference curve analysis and the marginal utility theory introduced in the chapter? For one thing, indifference curve analysis does not require us to attach numerical values to different levels of utility, as was required by marginal utility theory. The marginal rate of substitution of clothing for food can also be revealed by the marginal utilities of clothing and food, provided earlier in the chapter. Exhibit 3 indicated that the marginal utility provided by the third unit of food was 12 utils, and the marginal utility provided by the fourth unit of clothing was 6 utils. Since the marginal utility of food (MU_f) is 12 utils and the marginal utility of clothing (MU_c) is 6 utils, the consumer requires 2 units of clothing to give up one unit of food. Thus, the marginal rate of substitution of clothing for food equals (minus) the ratio of food's marginal utility (MU_f) to clothing's marginal utility (MU_c), or

Marginal rate of substitution $= -\dfrac{MU_f}{MU_c}$

The results can now be generalized to say that the slope of the indifference curve equals $-MU_f/MU_c$. Since the slope of the budget line equals $-P_f/P_c$, the equilibrium condition using the indifference curve approach can be rewritten as

$$-\frac{MU_f}{MU_c} = -\frac{P_f}{P_c}$$

which can be easily rearranged to show that

$$\frac{MU_f}{P_f} = \frac{MU_c}{P_c}$$

This equation is the same equilibrium condition for utility maximization that was derived in the chapter using marginal utility theory. The equality says that in equilibrium the last dollar spent on each good yields the same utility. If this equality does not hold, the consumer will adjust consumption until the equality does hold.

Effects of a Change in Income

We have established the equilibrium consumption bundle for a particular consumer given that consumer's income and product prices. What happens if the consumer's income changes? Suppose, for example, that the consumer's income is cut in half from $20 to $10 per period, yet prices remain as before. Exhibit 13 shows the effects of this reduction of income on the equilibrium bundle consumed. Since income falls but prices remain the same, the new budget line is parallel to but below the old budget line, shifting from CF down to $C'F'$. Because of the decrease in income, the budget now buys

less of each good. If the entire budget is devoted to clothing, only 5 units can be purchased; if it is devoted to food, only 2.5 units can be purchased. The consumer once again maximizes utility by consuming that combination of goods that is on the highest attainable indifference curve—reached in this case at point e' on indifference curve I'. The fall in income reduces the consumer's ability to purchase goods, resulting in a lower level of utility.

Effects of a Change in Price

What happens to equilibrium consumption if there is a change in price? We begin at point e, our initial equilibrium, in Exhibit 14 (a). At point e the individual consumes 4 units of clothing and 3 units of food. Suppose that the price of food falls from $4 per unit to $3 per unit, other things constant. A fall in the price

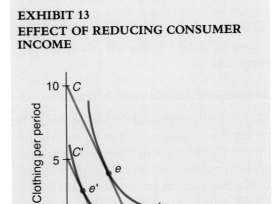

EXHIBIT 13
EFFECT OF REDUCING CONSUMER INCOME

A reduction in income causes an inward parallel shift of the budget line. The consumer is back in equilibrium at point e', where indifference curve I' is tangent to the new, lower budget line.

of food from \$4 to \$3 means that the consumer could purchase nearly 7 units of food if the entire budget were devoted to food; this maximum is identified as point F''. Since the price of clothing has not changed, however, 10 units of clothing remains the maximum amount of clothing that could be purchased. Thus, point C remains fixed, but the budget line rotates out to point F''.

After the price change the new equilibrium position occurs at e'', where the quantity of clothing consumed remains at 4 units, but the quantity of food increases from 3 units to 4 units. Thus, in accord with the law of demand, price and quantity demanded are inversely related.

Exhibit 14 (b) shows how price and quantity demanded are related. Notice that the quantity of food is a common measure on each horizontal axis, so in each panel we can show the effects of a change in the price of food on the quantity of food demanded. Specifically, when the price of food falls from \$4 per unit to \$3 per unit, other things equal, the quantity of food demanded increases from 3 units to 4 units. Since the consumer is on a higher indifference curve at e'', the consumer is clearly better off after the price reduction.

Income and Substitution Effects

We originally explained the law of demand in terms of an income effect and a substitution effect. We have now developed the analytical tools to examine these two effects more precisely. Suppose the price of food falls from \$4 to \$2, other things equal. The maximum amount of food that could be purchased with a budget of \$20 per period is 10 units, as shown in Exhibit 15, so the budget line rotates out from CF to CF^*. As you can see, after the price change the quantity of food demanded increases from 3 units to 5 units. The consumer benefits from the price drop, as reflected by the increase in utility.

Through careful analysis, the increase in the quantity of food demanded can be di-

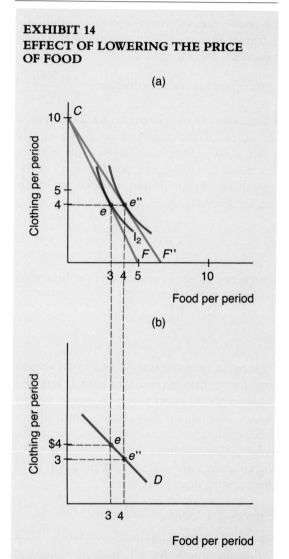

EXHIBIT 14
EFFECT OF LOWERING THE PRICE OF FOOD

A reduction in the price of food rotates the budget line outward in panel (a). The consumer is back in equilibrium at point e'' along the new budget line. Panel (b) shows that a fall in the price of food from \$4 per unit to \$3 leads to an increase in quantity demanded from 3 units to 4. Price and quantity demanded are inversely related.

vided into the substitution effect and the income effect of a price change. When the price of food falls, the ratio of the price of food to the price of clothing changes, as reflected by the changed slope of the new budget line. Suppose, for the sake of exposition, that the consumer tries to maintain the same level of utility after the price change as before. The sort of experiment we envision is for the consumer to maintain utility at I_2 by adjusting the consumption bundle in response to the change in the price of food relative to clothing. The consumer would increase the quantity demanded until a point is reached on indifference curve I_2 where the indifference curve is just tangent to $C^\#F^\#$. The budget line $C^\#F^\#$ keeps real income at the old level of utility but revises relative prices to reflect the price changes. Thus, we adjust the consumer's income line to reflect new prices but at an income level that keeps

the consumer on the same indifference curve, or at the same real income.

What we do is to hold the level of utility constant at I_2 but change the relative prices and observe the consumer's new bundle. The consumer increases the quantity of food purchased, moving down along the indifference curve I_2 until point $e^\#$ is reached. At that point, the initial indifference curve is now tangent to a budget line $C^\#F^\#$, which is parallel to CF^* since it is drawn to reflect the new set of relative prices. In moving down the original indifference curve to $e^\#$, the consumer purchases more food and less clothing. This change in quantity demanded reflects the *substitution effect* of the lower price of food. The substitution effect always in-

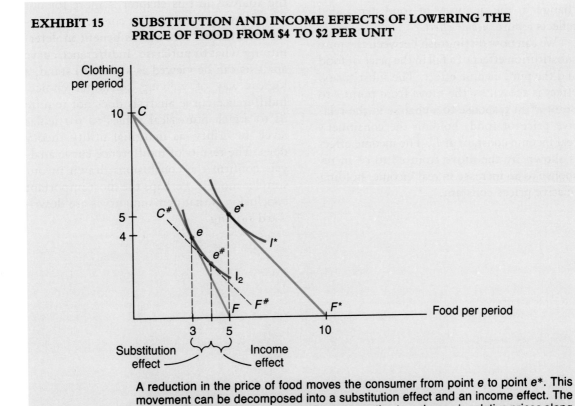

EXHIBIT 15   **SUBSTITUTION AND INCOME EFFECTS OF LOWERING THE PRICE OF FOOD FROM \$4 TO \$2 PER UNIT**

A reduction in the price of food moves the consumer from point *e* to point *e**. This movement can be decomposed into a substitution effect and an income effect. The substitution effect (from *e* to *e*\#) reflects a reaction to a change in relative prices along the original indifference curve. The income effect (from *e*\# to *e**) moves the consumer to a higher indifference curve at the new relative price ratio.

creases the quantity demanded of the good whose price has dropped. Since consumption bundle $e^{\#}$ represents the same level of utility as consumption bundle e, the consumer is neither better off nor worse off at point $e^{\#}$.

But at point $e^{\#}$ the consumer is not spending all the income available. The drop in the price of food has made more income available for both clothing and food, as shown by the expanded budget line CF^*. The consumer's real income has increased because of the lower price of food. As a result, the consumer will be able to attain point e^* on indifference curve I^*. At this combination, consumption equals 5 units each of food and clothing. Because prices are held constant during the move from $e^{\#}$ to e^*, the change in consumption is due solely to a change in income, holding prices constant. Thus, the change in the quantity of food demanded reflects a pure *income effect*.

We can now distinguish between the pure substitution effect of a fall in the price of food and the pure income effect. The substitution effect is shown by the move from point e to point $e^{\#}$ in response to a change in the relative price of food, holding the consumer's real income constant at I_2. The income effect is shown by the move from $e^{\#}$ to e^* in response to an increase in real income, holding relative prices constant.

The overall effect of a change in the price of food is the sum of the substitution effect and the income effect. In our example the substitution effect accounts for a 1-unit increase in the quantity of food demanded, and so does the income effect. Thus, the income and substitution effects combine to increase quantity demanded by 2 units when the price falls from \$4 to \$2. Incidentally, notice that as a result of the increase in real income because of the lower price of food, clothing consumption increases as well—from 4 units to 5 units in our example.

Summary

Indifference curve analysis sharpens our focus on consumer choice, but consumers need not be aware of this analysis to make rational choices. As we have said all along, the analysis in this chapter is more for our benefit in trying to predict consumer behavior than for the consumer's benefit in determining what to purchase. Indifference curve analysis can be viewed as a place to stand, a logical way of viewing consumer choice. Indifference curve analysis does not require us to attach numerical values to particular levels of utility, as marginal utility theory does. The results of indifference curve analysis confirm the conclusions drawn in our simpler models. Perhaps the most important conclusion is that demand curves are downward sloping.

COST and PRODUCTION in the FIRM

Each year hundreds of thousands of firms enter markets in the U.S. economy, and nearly as many leave. Millions of firms make choices about what goods and services to produce and what resources to employ. These firms must make plans while confronting uncertainty about consumer demand, resource availability, and the intentions of other firms. The lure of profit is so strong, however, that eager entrepreneurs are always ready to pursue their dreams.

The previous chapter explored the consumer behavior underlying the demand curve. This chapter will examine the producer behavior underlying the supply curve. More specifically, we examine a firm's production and cost of operation as a prelude to an analysis of supply.

In the previous chapter you were asked to think like a consumer. In this chapter you will be asked to think like a producer. You may feel more natural as the consumer (after all, you make purchases every day). But you know more about firms than you think because you have been around them all your life—bookstores, video stores, McDonald's. And though you probably have not yet managed a firm, you have some idea about how they operate. Topics discussed in this chapter include:

- Explicit and implicit costs
- Increasing and diminishing returns
- Short-run costs
- Long-run costs
- Economies and diseconomies of scale

COST AND PROFIT

As noted in Chapter 4, the firm brings together resources to produce whatever can be sold for a profit. Profit is the difference between the firm's total revenue and its total cost—that is, the difference between the total revenue received from the sale of output and what must be paid to resources to attract them from their next best alternative use. One problem is that the accountant and the economist do not see eye to eye on the appropriate definitions of cost and profit.

Explicit and Implicit Costs

To the economist, all costs are opportunity costs—the value of resources in their next best alternative use. Resources hired by the firm must be paid what they could earn in their next best alternative use, which is their opportunity cost. For resources purchased in resource markets, their cash payment becomes a good approximation of their opportunity cost. Some resources, however, are owned by the firm (or, more precisely, are owned by the firm's owners), so there is no direct cash payment for their use. For example, the firm does not pay rent to operate in a company-owned building. Similarly, Mom and Pop, the owners and operators of the corner grocery, usually do not pay themselves an hourly wage. The use of both types of resources—those owned by the firm and those purchased in the resource markets—represents an opportunity cost to the firm, although these costs are handled differently by the accountant.

Explicit costs are opportunity costs that take the form of actual cash payments.

Explicit costs are the opportunity costs that take the form of actual cash payments to resources purchased in resource markets—wages, rent, interest, insurance, and the like. The accountant has little trouble calculating these costs. In addition to these direct cash outlays or explicit costs, there are also **implicit costs**, which are the opportunity costs to the firm of using resources owned by the firm or provided by the firm's owners. Examples include the use of a company-owned building or the time and capital of the firm's owners. Like explicit costs, implicit costs involve an opportunity cost to the firm, but unlike explicit costs, there is usually no cash payment and no entry in the firm's accounting statement, which records the firm's revenues, costs, and profit.

Implicit costs are opportunity costs of using resources owned by the firm or provided by its owners.

Alternative Measures of Profit

Consider the distinction between implicit and explicit costs for a particular firm. Wanda Dealer is an aeronautical engineer who earns $30,000 a year working for the Flybynight Aircraft Company. On her way home from work one day she gets an idea for a rounder, more friction-resistant airplane wheel. She quits her job and scrapes together $20,000 in savings to buy the equipment necessary to begin production. She hires an assistant and starts producing the wheel in her garage, calling her business The Wheeler Dealer. Sales are slow at first—people keep telling her she is just trying to reinvent the wheel—but her wheel eventually gets rolling.

Accounting profit is total revenue minus explicit costs.

When Wanda and her accountant examine the company's performance for the year, they are quite pleased. As you can see in Exhibit 1, after paying the assistant's salary and covering the costs of raw materials, The Wheeler Dealer shows an accounting profit in 1987 of $40,000. **Accounting profit** equals total revenue minus explicit costs—those cash outlays that take the form of payments to nonowners of the firm.

What accounting profit ignores is the opportunity cost of Wanda's own resources used in the firm. First and most important is the opportunity cost of Wanda's time. Remember that she quit a $30,000-a-year job to devote herself full-time to her business, thereby forgoing that salary. She also invested in the firm her own savings of $20,000, thereby forgoing the 5 percent interest those savings earned—interest amounting to $1000 per year. Plus she now must park on the street because her garage is being used in the business. Suppose she would have been willing to pay $100 per month to park her car in a garage. Thus, the opportunity cost of using her own garage for the business is the forgone benefit valued at $100 per month, or $1200 for the year.

Economic profit is total revenue minus all costs, explicit and implicit.

The forgone salary, forgone interest, and forgone garage benefits are all called implicit costs because, although no actual payment is made, the business uses resources that have these opportunity costs. Subtracting implicit costs from accounting profit yields **economic profit**. To the economist, economic profit is a better measure of profit because economists conceive of profit as total revenue minus all costs—both implicit and explicit. In Exhibit 1 economic profit equals accounting profit less implicit costs, or $7800.

What would happen to the accounting statement if Wanda had decided to pay herself a salary of, say, $20,000 per year? Explicit costs would have increased by $20,000, implicit costs would have decreased by $20,000, and accounting profits would have decreased by $20,000. What would not change is the economic profit because it already takes into account both implicit and explicit costs. This is the beauty of the economic way of thinking: it focuses on the opportunity cost of resources, not on accounting definitions.

There is one other definition of profit that is relevant to the analysis: the profit required to induce the firm's owners to employ their resources in the firm. When all resources used by the firm are earning their opportunity cost,

EXHIBIT 1
ACCOUNTS OF WHEELER DEALER
1987

Total revenue	$75,000
Less explicit costs:	
Assistant's salary	15,000
Material and equipment	20,000
Equals accounting profit	$40,000
Less implicit costs:	
Wanda's forgone salary	$30,000
Interest forgone on savings	1,000
Forgone garage rental	1,200
Equals economic profit	$7,800

Normal profit *is the accounting profit required to induce the firm's owners to employ their resources in the firm.*

the firm is said to be earning a **normal profit**. Wanda's firm is earning a normal profit when the accounting profit equals the salary she gave up at her regular job, the interest she gave up on her savings, and the benefit she gave up from using her garage for parking. Thus, when her company earns an accounting profit of $32,200 per year—the opportunity cost of the resources capital, labor, and entrepreneurial ability Wanda supplies to the firm—the company earns a normal profit. Economic profit equals any accounting profit above a normal profit, so the $40,000 in accounting profit earned by Wanda's firm can be divided into (1) a normal profit of $32,200, which is a profit sufficient to cover the opportunity cost of all resources employed by the firm, and (2) an economic profit of $7800, which is a profit over and above what these resources could earn in their next best alternative use. The accountant's definition of profit therefore can be divided into normal profit and economic profit. As long as economic profit is positive, Wanda will be better off running her own firm.

PRODUCTION AND COST IN THE SHORT RUN

Keep in mind that the ultimate aim of this chapter is to examine the forces underlying the supply curve. The supply curve describes the relationship between the price of a product and the quantity producers are willing and able to offer for sale. Therefore, our discussion of production will focus on a relationship between cost and quantity produced. Two considerations will be of most importance: the cost per unit of output and the way cost varies with changes in the rate of output.

Costs Under the Golden Arches

Suppose a new McDonald's has just opened in your neighborhood, and its business is booming far beyond expectations. The manager responds to the unexpected demand by quickly hiring more workers, but the restaurant still cannot seem to handle the demand. The parking lot is always packed, and cars are backed up into the street waiting for a space. The manager recognizes the need for a drive-through window, but the construction will take six months, disrupting business in the process.

Variable resources *can be quickly varied to increase or decrease the level of output;* ***fixed resources*** *cannot be easily varied.*

Fixed and Variable Inputs   McDonald's, like other producers, combines resources in an attempt to satisfy consumer wants. Adjustments in some resources, such as in the number of workers, can be made rather quickly. Not surprisingly, such resources are called **variable resources** because they can be quickly varied to increase or decrease the output level. Adjustments in other resources, however, take more time. The size of the building and the stock of major machinery cannot be easily altered; these resources are therefore called **fixed resources**.

Short Run and Long Run   When they discuss the time required to adjust resource use, economists distinguish between the short run and the long run. In the **short run** at least one resource cannot be varied. In the **long run** all resources can be varied. The short run is a period so short that only the variable resources can be adjusted, not the fixed resources. Output can be varied in the short run by adjusting variable resources, but the size, or scale, of the firm is fixed in the short run. In the long run, however, all resources can be varied. The amount of time required for a long-run adjustment will vary from industry to industry because the nature of the production process varies. Earlier we mentioned that the number of lunch wagons could be adjusted more quickly that the number of electricity-generating power plants.

*In the **short run** at least one resource cannot be varied; in the **long run** all resources are variable.*

The Law of Diminishing Returns

Before we discuss the cost of production, let's focus on the link between resources and outputs at McDonald's. Let's assume that the fixed capital is already in place—the building with a drive-through window is complete, the machines for shakes, fries, and burgers are in place, and the golden arches are up. First, we will consider the production decision in the short run. To simplify the analysis, let's assume that labor is the only variable resource and that the unit of output is a meal consisting of a burger, fries, and a shake.

Exhibit 2 presents some hypothetical data showing the relationship between the amount of labor employed and the quantity of meals produced per day. The first column shows the units of labor employed, from 0 to 10. The total number of meals produced at each level of employment is in the second column. The last column shows the **marginal physical product** (**MPP**) of each worker—that is, the amount by which the total product changes with each additional unit of labor.

Marginal physical product is the change in total physical product when the usage of a particular resource changes by one unit.

Increasing Marginal Returns   Consider now what happens as we add units of labor to the fixed amount of capital. Nothing is produced without labor, so when the quantity of labor is 0, the number of meals produced, or the total physical product, is also 0. If only one worker is employed, that worker spends much of the time taking customer orders and filling these orders by running from the shake machine to the grill to the frying pit. As a result of the time involved in adjusting to the different tasks, the specialized machines cannot be used very efficiently, so the first worker is able to produce only 30 meals per day.

When 2 workers are employed, total production more than doubles to 80 meals because less running around is necessary. The marginal physical product as a result of adding a second worker is 50 meals. With the addition of a third worker, each worker is now able to specialize on an individual machine; hence, each worker is more efficient. The total physical product of 3 workers is 140 meals, which is 60 meals more than is produced by 2 workers. Because the marginal physical product increases with each additional worker, **increasing marginal returns** is experienced by this firm as each of the first 3

Increasing marginal returns occur when marginal physical product increases with each additional worker.

EXHIBIT 2
THE RELATIONSHIP BETWEEN UNITS OF
LABOR AND MEAL PRODUCTION
(Hypothetical Data)

Units of the Variable Resource (labor/day)	Total Physical Product (meals)	Marginal Physical Product (meals)
0	0	—
1	30	30
2	80	50
3	140	60
4	190	50
5	230	40
6	260	30
7	280	20
8	290	10
9	295	5
10	290	−5

workers is added. Increasing marginal returns result because additional workers can make better use of the fixed resources, so McDonald's benefits from the specialization of labor.

Diminishing Marginal Returns   The addition of a fourth worker adds to the total product, but not as much as was added by the third worker. As additional workers are added, the total product increases by successively smaller amounts, as reflected by the declining marginal physical product in Exhibit 2. With each additional worker, the advantages of specialization decrease. Indeed, with 10 workers the working area becomes so crowded that workers distract one another and get in each other's way. As a result, the total product actually declines when a tenth worker is added, so the marginal product is negative. "Too many cooks spoil the broth."

According to the law of diminishing marginal returns, the more of a good consumed per period, the smaller the marginal utility, other things constant.

Beginning with the fourth worker, the **law of diminishing marginal returns** takes hold. That law states that as additional quantities of the variable resource are combined with a given amount of the fixed resource, a point is eventually reached where additional units of the variable resource yield a smaller and smaller marginal physical product. The law of diminishing marginal returns is the most important feature of firm production in the short run. Evidence of diminishing returns is abundant. In your own studies the productivity of your first hour of studying is likely to be greater than that of your fifth hour at one sitting. Doctors, viewing themselves as the fixed resource, try to increase total product by hiring assistants and renting offices with more treatment rooms. But the marginal product of these variable inputs evidently shows diminishing returns because doctors seldom hire more than two nurses or rent more than a few treatment rooms. In agriculture, if marginal product continued to increase indefinitely, you could grow the world's supply of vegetables in your backyard simply by adding more and more labor and fertilizer to the fixed plot of land. The law of diminishing marginal returns is a key aspect of production, and, as we will see next, is an important determinant of firm cost.

The Total and Marginal Physical Product Curves

Panels (a) and (b) of Exhibit 3 illustrate the total physical product and the marginal physical product, reflecting the data in Exhibit 2. Note that as long as the marginal physical product curve is rising—that is, as long as there are increasing marginal returns—the total physical product curve increases by increasing amounts. But as the marginal product begins to decline—that is, when diminishing marginal returns occur—total product still increases but at a decreasing rate. At the output level where marginal product becomes negative, the total product curve actually begins to turn down.

EXHIBIT 3   **THE TOTAL AND MARGINAL PHYSICAL PRODUCT OF LABOR**

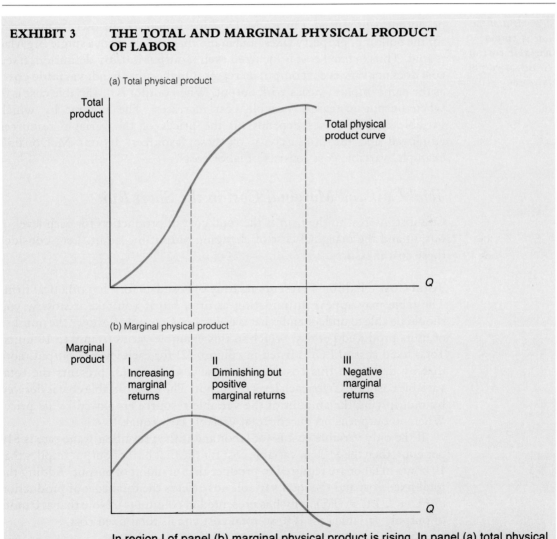

(a) Total physical product

Total product

Total physical product curve

Q

(b) Marginal physical product

Marginal product

| I | II | III |
| Increasing marginal returns | Diminishing but positive marginal returns | Negative marginal returns |

Q

In region I of panel (b) marginal physical product is rising. In panel (a) total physical product is increasing by increasing amounts. In region II marginal physical product is decreasing but is still positive. Total product is increasing by decreasing amounts. When marginal product equals 0, total product is at a maximum. Finally, in region III marginal product is negative, and total product is falling.

For purposes of exposition, we divide production in the short run into three stages: (1) increasing marginal returns are experienced by the firm during stage I; (2) diminishing but positive marginal returns are experienced during stage II; and (3) negative marginal returns are experienced during stage III.

COSTS IN THE SHORT RUN

Fixed cost is independent of the rate of output; variable cost increases as output increases.

Thus far we have spoken only about physical units of input and output. Now let's consider a firm's costs. Costs can be conveniently divided into two categories: fixed cost and variable cost. A firm must pay a **fixed cost** even if no output is produced. Once a McDonald's is in place, its owners must pay for the building, property taxes, and maintenance even if not a single Big Mac is sold. Thus, a fixed cost is incurred even if output is 0. By definition, fixed cost does not vary even if output increases. On the other hand, **variable cost**, as the name implies, varies with output. When output is 0, variable cost is 0; when output increases, variable cost increases. The amount by which variable cost increases depends on the prices of the variable resources employed and the productivity of these resources. In our McDonald's example, variable cost consists of labor costs.

Total Cost and Marginal Cost in the Short Run

Of most interest to the firm is the total cost of production for each level of output and the marginal cost of changing output by 1 unit. Let's consider these cost measures.

Total Cost   Exhibit 4 presents an array of cost data for a hypothetical firm. The table may appear intimidating at first, but if you take it slowly, you should be able to understand what is going on. Column (1) shows the number of units produced per day, which in this example varies from 0 to 10 units. Total fixed cost (*TFC*) is listed in column (2) for each level of output; note that by definition this cost does not vary. Column (3) presents the total variable cost (*TVC*) for each level of output. The total variable cost is derived by multiplying the amount of the variable resource employed by its price. When no output is produced, total variable cost equals 0.

If the only variable cost is for labor and if the prevailing wage rate is $10 per hour, then the $100 in variable cost for the first unit of output implies that 10 hours of labor are required to produce that first unit of output. Adding the total fixed cost and the total variable cost yields the total cost of production (*TFC* + *TVC* = *TC*), which is presented in column (4). Note that at 0 units of output, variable cost is 0, so total cost equals total fixed cost.

Marginal cost is the change in total cost when output changes by one unit.

Marginal Cost   Thus far we have considered the total cost of output. Another important question is how total cost changes as output changes. More specifically, what is the **marginal cost** of producing another unit? The marginal cost of production listed in column (5) is simply the amount by

EXHIBIT 4
HYPOTHETICAL COST DATA FOR A FIRM
IN THE SHORT RUN

Total Output (Q)	Total Fixed Costs (TFC)	Total Variable Cost (TVC)	Total Cost TC = TFC + TVC	Marginal Cost $MC = \frac{\Delta TC}{\Delta Q}$	Average Fixed Cost $AFC = \frac{TFC}{Q}$	Average Variable Cost $AVC = \frac{TVC}{Q}$	Average Total Cost $ATC = \frac{TC}{Q}$
(1)	(2)	(3)	(4)	(5)	(6)	(7)	(8)
0	$100	$ 0	$100	—	∞	—	∞
1	100	100	200	$100	$100.00	$100.00	$200.00
2	100	160	260	60	50.00	80.00	130.00
3	100	200	300	40	33.33	66.67	100.00
4	100	260	360	60	25.00	65.00	90.00
5	100	340	440	80	20.00	68.00	88.00
6	100	440	540	100	16.67	73.33	90.00
7	100	560	660	120	14.29	80.00	94.28
8	100	700	800	140	12.50	87.50	100.00
9	100	860	960	160	11.11	95.55	106.67
10	100	1040	1140	180	10.00	104.00	114.00

which total cost increases as output is increased by 1 unit. For example, the marginal cost of the second unit is the total cost of producing 2 units minus the total cost of producing 1 unit, which equals $260 − $200, or $60. The marginal cost of the third unit is the total cost of 3 units minus the total cost of 2 units, which equals $300 − $260, or $40.

Notice from column (5) that marginal cost first decreases, then increases. Changes in marginal cost reflect the productivity of the variable resource employed. Recall from the McDonald's example that the first few units of labor employed showed increasing marginal returns, with each additional worker producing more output than the last. Likewise, the firm described in Exhibit 4 is experiencing increasing marginal returns, which results in a falling marginal cost of production. Marginal cost falls because the marginal physical product of the variable resource is rising. Eventually, however, the marginal physical product of the variable resource declines as the firm experiences diminishing marginal returns. When the firm experiences diminishing marginal returns, the marginal cost of output increases.

Thus, the marginal cost in Exhibit 4 first falls, then rises because the variable resource experiences first increasing marginal returns, then diminishing marginal returns. Specifically, the variable resource employed by this hypothetical firm shows increasing marginal returns during the production of the first 3 units of output and decreasing marginal returns thereafter.

Total and Marginal Cost Curves   The total cost curves and the marginal cost curve are presented in Exhibit 5. Since the total fixed cost does not vary with output, it is drawn as a horizontal line at the $100 level in panel (a). Total variable cost is 0 when output is 0, so the total variable cost curve starts from the origin. Total variable cost increases slowly at first as output increases because of increasing marginal returns experienced by the variable resource. As soon as the variable resource experiences diminishing marginal returns, however, total variable cost begins to climb more rapidly as output expands. Overall, the total variable cost curve has a backward **S** shape.

To get total cost, we sum *vertically* total variable cost and total fixed cost. Because total cost adds the constant amount of fixed cost to total variable cost, total cost reflects a vertical shift of the total variable cost curve by the amount of fixed cost.

We have already discussed the reasons behind the behavior of marginal cost. In panel (b) marginal cost at first declines and then increases, reflecting increasing and then diminishing marginal returns to the variable resource.

There is a clear geometric relationship between panels (a) and (b) because the change in total cost resulting from a 1-unit change in production equals the marginal cost. With each successive unit of output, the total cost increases by the marginal cost of that unit. For example, from data in Exhibit 4 you will find that the fourth unit of output is produced at a marginal cost of $60, which is the amount by which total cost increases in going from 3 to 4 units of output. Because total cost increases by $60 when output increases by 1 unit, the slope of the total cost curve between output levels 3 and 4 is 60 (recall from the appendix to Chapter 1 that the slope equals the "rise," in this case 60,

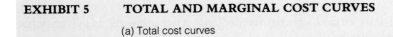

EXHIBIT 5   **TOTAL AND MARGINAL COST CURVES**

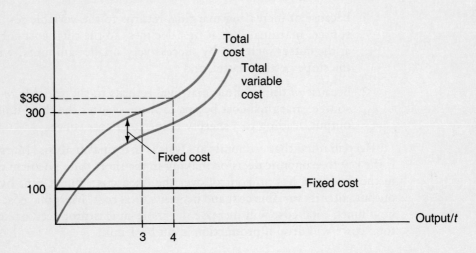

(a) Total cost curves

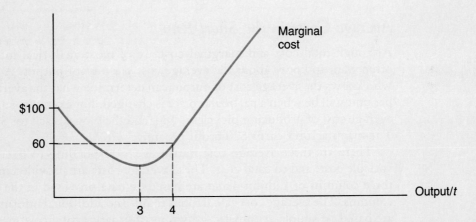

(b) Marginal cost

In panel (a) total fixed cost is constant at all levels of output. Total variable cost starts from the origin and increases slowly at first as output increases. When the variable resources experience diminishing marginal returns, total variable cost begins to increase more rapidly. Total cost is the vertical sum of total fixed cost and total variable cost. In panel (b) marginal cost first declines, reflecting increasing marginal returns, then increases, reflecting diminishing marginal returns.

divided by the "run," in this case 1, or 60/1 = 60). Thus, the slope of the total cost curve at any level of output equals the marginal cost of that unit of output.

The total cost curves can be divided into two sections based on what happens to marginal cost:

1. because of increasing marginal returns to the variable resource, marginal cost at first declines, so the total cost curve at the outset increases by successively smaller amounts, with the slope getting flatter, and

2. because of diminishing marginal returns to the variable resource, marginal cost begins to increase after the third unit of output, leading to a sharply rising total cost curve.

Keep in mind that economic analysis is marginal analysis. Marginal cost is the key to economic decision making in the short run. The firm operating in the short run has no control over the fixed cost, but it can, by varying output, alter its variable cost and hence its total cost. Marginal cost indicates how much total cost will increase if 1 more unit is produced or how much total costs will drop if production is cut by 1 unit.

Average Costs in the Short Run

Although total cost and marginal cost are of most analytical interest, we often want to know about the average cost per unit of output. A producer who knows the average cost of output can determine what the average profit per unit will be when a particular price is changed. For example, suppose the average cost of producing bicycles is $80, and the bicycles sell for $100 each. The manufacturer earns $20 profit per unit.

There are three average cost measures, corresponding to fixed cost, to variable cost, and to total cost. These average costs are provided in the final three columns of Exhibit 4 and are based on data provided in the first four columns. The average cost calculations require no additional information and are based on simple arithmetic—dividing alternative total cost measures by the quantity produced.

Calculating Average Cost   Let's begin with the easiest of the three cost relationships, the **average fixed cost**, which equals the fixed cost divided by the level of output. As the data presented in column (6) of Exhibit 4 indicate, the average fixed cost declines steadily as output increases because the same fixed cost is averaged over more and more units of output. Column (7) lists

Average fixed cost *is total fixed cost divided by output;* **average variable cost** *is total variable cost divided by output;* **average total cost** *is total cost divided by output—the sum of average fixed cost plus average variable cost.*

the **average variable cost**, which is total variable cost divided by the output. Total cost divided by output yields the **average total cost**, presented in the final column of Exhibit 4. The figures in the last two columns at first decrease and then increase, reflecting the underlying fall and rise in marginal cost. The relationship between the marginal and average costs is an important one in microeconomics, as we now see.

Average and Marginal Cost Curves   The average cost data in Exhibit 4 are presented as average cost curves in Exhibit 6, along with the marginal cost curve introduced in Exhibit 5. The average fixed cost curve falls as output expands. The average variable and average total cost curves at first fall, then reach a low point, and then rise; overall, they reflect a U shape. The shape of the average variable cost is determined by the shape of the marginal cost curve. At low levels of output the marginal cost curve declines as output expands because of increasing marginal returns. This falling marginal cost lowers average variable cost as output expands.

Marginal cost eventually starts to rise, however, because of diminishing marginal returns. Yet even after marginal cost starts to rise, marginal cost is still below average variable cost, so average variable cost will continue to fall. As long as marginal cost is below average variable cost, average variable cost will decline. The two curves intersect where marginal cost equals average variable cost. Once marginal cost exceeds average variable cost, the average variable cost curve starts to rise as output expands—higher marginal cost begins to pull up the average. Thus, the marginal cost curve explains why the average variable cost curve has a U shape.

The average total cost curve is the vertical sum of the average fixed cost and the average variable cost curves. Thus, the shape of the average total cost curve reflects the shapes of the underlying average cost curves. Note that as output increases, the average variable cost and average total cost curves grow closer and closer together because average fixed cost, which is the vertical difference between the two, becomes smaller.

The marginal cost curve has the same relationship to the average total cost curve as to the average variable cost curve, and for the same reasons. When marginal cost is below average total cost, average total cost declines as output expands, and when marginal cost is above average total cost, average total cost increases as output expands. Thus, there is a consistent relationship between the marginal cost curve and the average variable and average total cost curves. As long as marginal cost is below average cost, average cost declines as output increases. But when marginal cost exceeds average cost, average cost increases as output increases. Because of these relationships, the marginal cost curve intersects the average cost curves when the average cost curves are at their lowest point. Perhaps the following example will help you better understand the relationship between marginal and average cost curves.

EXHIBIT 6   AVERAGE AND MARGINAL COST CURVES

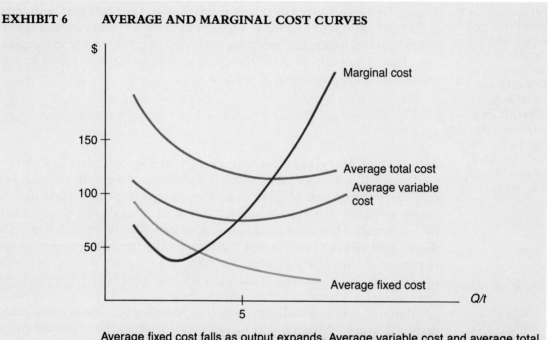

Average fixed cost falls as output expands. Average variable cost and average total cost fall, reach low points, and then rise; overall, they reflect U shapes. When marginal cost is below average variable cost, average variable cost is falling. When marginal cost equals average variable cost, average variable cost is at its minimum value. When marginal cost is above average variable cost, average variable cost is increasing. The same relationship holds between marginal cost and average total cost.

Semester Grades and Your Cumulative Grade Point Average
Consider your own experience with grades from semester to semester. Your average grades are reflected in your cumulative grade point average, and your marginal grades are reflected in your performance this semester. If your grades this semester are above your cumulative average, they will pull up your average, so your cumulative average will rise. If you do worse this semester than your cumulative average, your marginal grades will be below your average grades, pulling down your average grades, so your cumulative grade point will fall. Thus, whether we are talking about your grades or the firm's short-run cost curves, when the marginal is below the average, the average will fall, and when the marginal is above the average, the average will rise. When the marginal and average costs are equal, the average will be neither rising nor falling.

Summary of Short-Run Cost Curves

The level of the firm's fixed cost, the price of variable inputs, and the law of diminishing marginal returns determine the shape of all the short-run cost curves. The shape of the marginal physical product curve discussed earlier in the chapter determines the shape of the marginal cost curve. When the marginal physical product increases, the marginal cost of output must fall (given constant prices of variable inputs). Conversely, as diminishing marginal returns set in, the marginal cost of output must rise. Thus, the marginal cost curve first falls, then rises. And the marginal cost curve dictates the shapes of the average variable cost and average total cost curves. When marginal cost is less than average cost, average cost is falling; when marginal cost is above average cost, average cost is rising. In short, the shape of short-run cost curves is determined by the increasing and diminishing marginal returns to the variable resource.

COSTS IN THE LONG RUN

Thus far the analysis has focused on how costs vary as the rate of output expands in the short run for a firm of a given size. In the long run, however, all inputs that are under the firm's control can be varied, so there are no fixed costs. In the long run the firm is free to select any input combination that appears appropriate. The long run is best thought of as a planning horizon that is valid only for the firm that has not yet acted on its plans. Once the size of the firm is selected and resources are committed, the firm has fixed costs and is once again back in a short-run situation. We turn now to the long-run cost curves.

Long-Run Average Cost Curves

Suppose that, because of the special nature of the technology, the scale of the plant is confined to one of only three possible sizes—small, medium, or large. Exhibit 7 presents this simple case. The short-run average total cost curves are identified for the three plant sizes as SS', MM', and LL'. Which size plant should the firm build to minimize the average cost of production? The choice of the appropriate scale of the firm depends on how much the firm wants to produce. For example, if Q is the desired production rate in the long run, the average cost per unit will be lowest using the small plant size. If the desired output level is Q', the medium plant size ensures the lowest average cost.

More generally, for any output less than Q_a, the average cost of output is lowest when the small plant size is used. For output levels between points Q_a and Q_b, average cost is lowest when the medium plant size is used. And for output levels that exceed Q_b, average cost is lowest when the large plant size is used. Thus, the long-run average cost curve for this firm will be made up by connecting the lowest-cost portions of the three short-run average cost curves, which in Exhibit 7 consists of line segments connecting $SABL'$.

We argued at the outset that in the long run all resources are variable, so we now drop the assumption that there are only three plant sizes. Imagine an extremely large number of possible plant sizes, with a different plant size for each level of output. Although we cannot draw such a large number of short-run average cost curves, Exhibit 8 presents a sample of possible short-run

EXHIBIT 7   SHORT-RUN AVERAGE COST CURVES AND THE LONG-RUN PLANNING CURVE

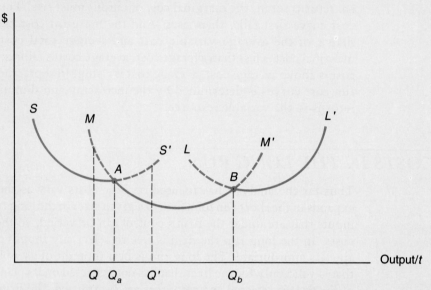

Curves *SS'*, *MM'*, and *LL'* show short-run average total costs for small, medium, and large plant sizes. For output less than Q_a, average cost is lowest when the small plant size is chosen. Between Q_a and Q_b, cost is lowest with a medium-size plant. If output exceeds Q_b, the large plant size is best. The long-run average cost curve is *SABL'*.

average cost curves. The long-run average cost curve consists of an *envelope* made up of the lowest-cost portions of each short-run average cost curve. Each of the short-run cost curves is tangent to the long-run planning curve, or envelope curve. If we could draw enough plant sizes, we would have a different plant size for each level of output. These points of tangency represent the least-cost way of producing that particular level of output, given the technology and resource prices. For example, the short-run average cost curve ATC_1 is tangent to the planning curve at point *a*, indicating that the least-cost way of producing output level Q is with plant size ATC_1.

No other firm size would produce output level Q at as low a cost per unit. Note, however, that at other output levels along ATC_1 the average cost of production is lower. In fact, for output level Q' at point *b* the average cost per unit is only $10 per unit, compared to an average cost per unit of $11 for producing Q at point *a*. Point *b* depicts the lowest average cost along ATC_1. Thus, even though ATC_1 is tangent to the long-run planning curve at point *a*, reflecting a cost of $11 per unit for producing output level Q, other points along ATC_1 produce other levels of output at a lower average cost. So while the point of tangency represents the least-cost way of producing a particular level of output, other levels of output along that same short-run average cost curve can be produced at a lower average cost.

EXHIBIT 8 **FAMILY OF MANY SHORT-RUN COST CURVES FORMING A FIRM'S LONG-RUN PLANNING CURVE**

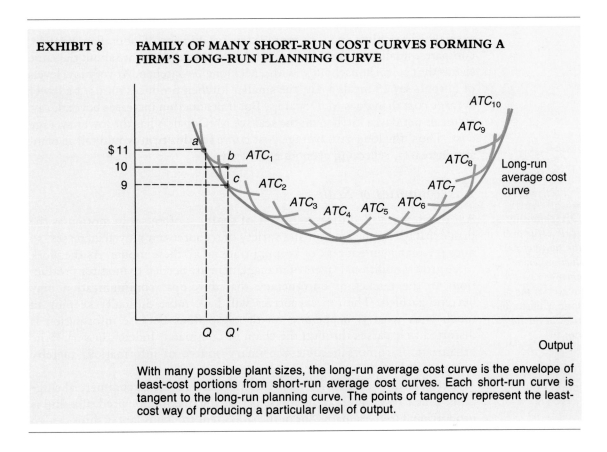

With many possible plant sizes, the long-run average cost curve is the envelope of least-cost portions from short-run average cost curves. Each short-run curve is tangent to the long-run planning curve. The points of tangency represent the least-cost way of producing a particular level of output.

If the firm decides to produce output level Q', which size plant should it choose to build to minimize the average cost of production? Output level Q' could be produced at point b, which represents the minimum average cost along plant size ATC_1. Would the firm therefore select size ATC_1? No, because the firm could achieve a lower average cost with a larger-size plant. Specifically, if the firm built a plant of size ATC_2, the average cost of producing Q' would be minimized at point c. In short, points of tangency between the short-run average cost curves and the long-run planning curve represent the least-cost way of producing each particular level of output, even though other levels of output along any given short-run average cost curve can usually be produced at a lower average cost.

Economies of scale occur over the range of production where reductions in average cost are made possible by increasing the scale of operations in the long run.

Economies of Scale

You cannot help noticing that the long-run average cost curve appears to be U-shaped like short-run average cost curves. Recall that the shape of the short-run average cost curve is determined primarily by the law of diminishing marginal returns. A different, though similar, principle molds the shape of the long-run cost curve. **Economies of scale** result in a decrease in long-run average cost as the plant size increases. Consider some sources of economies of scale. Larger plant size often allows for larger and more specialized machines and for a more extensive division of labor. For example, compare a small restaurant (whose kitchen and equipment are about the same size as the typical household's) with a McDonald's kitchen. At very low levels of output, say 15 meals a day, the smaller kitchen produces meals at a lower average cost than does McDonald's. But if production increases beyond, say, 50 meals per day, a kitchen on the scale of McDonald's has the lower average cost. Thus, the long-run average cost curve for this firm would fall as plant size increases, reflecting economies of scale.

Diseconomies of Scale

Diseconomies of scale occur over the range of production where average cost increases as the scale of operations rises in the long run.

Another force, called **diseconomies of scale**, is often set in motion as the firm expands. As the amount and variety of resources employed increases, so does the management task of keeping track of all these inputs. As the work force grows, additional layers of management are needed to monitor production. In the thicket of bureaucracy that develops, communication may become garbled. The top executives will have more difficulty keeping in touch with what is happening on the shop floor because information is distorted as it passes through the chain of command. Indeed, in very large organizations rumors become a primary source of information, thereby reducing the efficiency of the organization.

Let's consider economies and diseconomies of scale in commercial shipping. One rule of naval architecture is that the maximum speed of a ship is proportional to the square root of the ship's length. Thus larger ships can go faster. Larger ships also carry much more cargo. The cargo-carrying capacity of a ship increases more than in proportion to the cost of building and operating the ship. The economies of scale observed in ocean vessels are also found in trucks. For example, the cost of hiring a driver for a 50-foot truck is little more than for a 25-foot truck. Beyond some size of ships or trucks, however, diseconomies of scale dominate. Ocean-going vessels may become so large that few ports can handle them. Trucks may become so large that they cannot negotiate some roads. (Some trucking companies are able to take advantage of economies of scale by operating tandem trucks on highways and smaller trucks on urban streets.)

We assumed at the outset that in the long run the firm could vary all the inputs under its control. Some inputs, however, are not under the firm's control, and the inability to vary these inputs may be a source of diseconomies of scale, as we will see in the following case study, which describes both economies and diseconomies of scale.

CASE STUDY

At The Movies

Consider economies of scale at the movies. Even if a movie theater has only one screen, it still needs a manager, someone to sell tickets, another person to take tickets at the door, someone to operate the concession stand, another person to operate the projector, and perhaps an usher. If the owners add another screen, they do not need to double the work force. Many of the tasks can be performed for both screens by the same individual. Thus, the ticket taker becomes more productive because tickets are taken for both screens. And construction costs per screen can be saved because only one lobby and one set of restrooms are required. This is why we observe theater owners adding more and more screens at the same location; they are taking advantage of economies of scale.

Economies of scale clearly result from clustering screens together. But why stop at, say, 8 screens? Why not 10 or 14, particularly in densely populated urban areas, where sufficient demand would warrant such a high level of output? One problem with the expanded number is that the public roads leading to the theaters are not a resource that the theater owners can vary. The congestion around the theater grows with the number of screens at that location. You may have been bothered by the traffic at your nearby Cinema 1-2-3-4-5-6-7-8. Scheduling becomes more and more difficult because the manager must space out starting and ending times to avoid the arrival and departure of too many customers at once. Therefore, the average cost of production increases when the number of screens increases.

Also, the supply of potentially profitable films may not be great enough at any one time to keep the additional theaters filled. Finally, time itself is a resource that the firm cannot easily control. Only certain hours are popular with moviegoers. Theater owners can cluster showings during these hours, but they cannot create additional "prime time." Thus, the size of public roads, the supply of films, and the hours in the day are inputs over which the theater has little control, and this lack of control may contribute to diseconomies of scale.

Constant Returns to Scale

Constant returns to scale occur over the range of production where average cost does not change as the scale of operations changes in the long run.

It could be that long-run costs neither increase nor decrease with changes in the firm size. If neither economies of scale nor diseconomies of scale are apparent in the production process, the firm is said to exhibit **constant returns to scale**. It could be that some elements of both economies and diseconomies of scale exist simultaneously but have offsetting effects, so constant returns to scale are observed.

Exhibit 9 presents the firm's long-run cost curve, which is divided into segments of economies of scale, constant returns to scale, and diseconomies of scale. The rate of production would have to reach point *A* for the firm to achieve the **minimum efficient scale**, which is the lowest rate of output at which the firm takes full advantage of economies of scale. Thus, the firm experiences economies of scale until production level *A* is achieved. From output level *A* to level *B*, average cost reflects constant returns to scale. Beyond point *B* decreasing returns to scale dominate average cost.

The **minimum efficient scale** is the lowest rate of output at which the firm takes full advantage of economies of scale.

The discussion thus far has referred primarily to a particular plant—the local McDonald's or a nearby cinema—as opposed to the firm more generally. It is useful, however, to distinguish between economies and dis-

EXHIBIT 9   A FIRM'S LONG-RUN AVERAGE COST CURVE

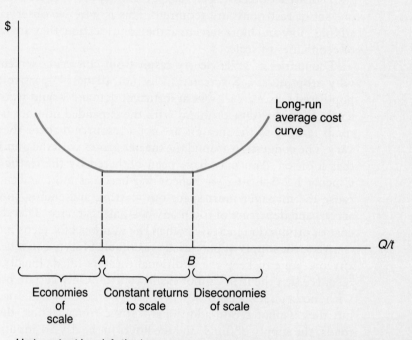

Up to output level *A*, the long-run average cost curve has a negative slope; the firm is experiencing economies of scale. Point *A* is the minimum efficient scale—the lowest rate of output at which the firm takes full advantage of economies of scale. Between *A* and *B* constant returns to scale prevail. Beyond output level *B* the long-run average cost curve is upward sloping, reflecting decreasing returns to scale.

economies of scale at the *plant level*—that is, at a particular location—versus at the *firm level*. We examine economies and diseconomies of scale at the firm level in the following case study.

CASE STUDY

Burgers By The Billions

McDonald's experiences economies of scale at the plant level because of its specialization of people and machines, but the company also benefits from economies of scale at the firm level. Operating many separate locations gives the company the ability to standardize menus and operating procedures, to centralize its management training program at Hamburger University, and to spread the cost of its advertising over its more than 6200 individual "plants."

The menu at a local fast-food outlet is not something taken lightly. Every step in the food-preparation procedure is timed and evaluated. Each of the major chains spends a great deal of time figuring out how long it takes employees to do everything from flipping burgers to putting pickles on buns.

Before any new product is introduced, labor requirements are monitored closely. For example, before Burger King decided to switch from one soft drink to another, they spent more than two years on market research. They reportedly sent undercover researchers to Jack-in-the-Box franchises to keep track of the time wasted informing customers who had asked for Coke that the chain served Pepsi instead.

Some diseconomies also arise in such large-scale operations. The fact that the menu must be uniform around the country means that if any part of the country does not like a product, it does not get on the menu regardless of how popular it is elsewhere. McDonald's McRib sandwich never quite caught on in some parts of the country and had to be dropped. Wendy's plans for a gourmet hamburger had to be canceled because most customers in two states were not familiar with such upscale ingredients as alfalfa sprouts and guacamole.

Another problem with a uniform national menu is that the ingredients must be available around the country and cannot be subject to droughts or sharp swings in price. One chain decided not to add bacon strips as an option on its burgers because the price of pork bellies was so unstable. Thus, when a firm expands the number of plants, it experiences both economies of scale and diseconomies of scale.

Source: John Koten, "Fast-Food Firms' New Items Undergo Exhaustive Testing," *The Wall Street Journal*, 5 January 1984.

A variety of studies has attempted to determine the shape of the long-run average cost curve for firms in different industries. Many of these studies have examined the relationship between cost and inputs over time. One finding turned up with enough consistency to deserve mention here. The long-run cost curve in many industries appears to be L-shaped, not U-shaped. There is little evidence that diseconomies of scale increase the long-run average cost as output expands. We should note, however, that this finding may be due to the limited range of the data observed. Perhaps few firms were found to be operating in the diseconomies-of-scale range because firms had determined that they were less competitive if their costs on average were higher than those of smaller firms. Put another way, the long-run average cost curve may still turn up for firms in most industries, but because firms choose not to become that large, we do not observe empirical evidence of diseconomies of scale.

CONCLUSIONS

Despite what may appear to be a tangle of short-run and long-run cost curves, only two relationships between resources and outputs underlie all the curves. In the short run it is increasing and diminishing returns to the variable resource. In the long run it is economies and diseconomies of scale. If you understand the sources of these two phenomena, you have mastered the central ideas of this chapter.

In the previous chapters we developed a theory of consumer behavior based on utility maximization. We then showed how the downward-sloping demand curve was derived from our theory of consumer choice. In this chapter, by considering the relationship between production and cost, we have developed the foundations of the theory of firm behavior. In the appendix we present an alternative way of determining a firm's most efficient combination of resources. Our examination of the relationship between resource use and the quantity of output produced in both the short run and the long run forms the basis for deriving an upward-sloping supply curve in the next chapter.

SUMMARY

1. The firm's objective is to earn a profit, but the definition of profit differs between accountants and economists. Accounting profit equals revenue minus explicit costs, which are costs that take the form of payments to resources not owned by the firm. Economic profit equals revenue minus both explicit and implicit costs. Implicit costs are the opportunity costs of using resources owned by the firm or provided by the firm's owners. A firm is said to be earning a normal profit if revenue just covers all implicit and explicit costs.

2. Resources such as labor are called variable resources because they can be easily varied to increase or decrease the output level. Other resources, such as capital, are called fixed resources because changing their employment level requires more time. In the short run only the variable inputs can be adjusted; at least one resource cannot be varied in the short run. In the long run all resources can be varied.

3. Short-run increases in the variable resource at first produce increasing marginal returns because the additional variable inputs can more efficiently utilize the fixed resources, taking advantage of both comparative advantage and the specialization of labor. As additional quantities of the variable resource are combined with a given amount of the fixed resource, however, the law of diminishing marginal returns indicates that a point is eventually reached where these additional units of the variable resource yield a smaller and smaller marginal product.

4. The law of diminishing marginal returns is the most important feature of firm production in the short run and is the reason why the marginal cost curve eventually becomes upward sloping as output expands. The law of diminishing marginal returns also explains the upside-down S shape of the total cost curve and the U shape of the average variable and average total cost curve.

5. In the long run all inputs under the firm's control are variable, so there are no fixed costs. The firm's long-run average cost curve is an envelope formed by a series of short-run average total cost curves. The long run is best thought of as a planning horizon. The firm selects the most efficient size based on the desired level of output. Once the size of the firm is selected and resources are committed, some resources become fixed, so the firm is back in the short run. Thus, the firm plans based on a long-run perspective but operates in the short run.

6. The long average cost curve, like the short-run average cost curve, is U shaped. As output expands, average costs at first decline due to economies of scale—a larger plant size allows for more specialized machinery and a more extensive division of labor. Eventually, average costs stop falling, and constant returns to scale may characterize output over some range. As output expands still further, the plant may experience diseconomies of scale as the cost of coordinating resources grows. But evidence of diseconomies of scale has been hard to find in empirical research.

QUESTIONS AND PROBLEMS _____

1. (Explicit versus Implicit Costs) Old MacDonald is currently raising corn on his 100-acre farm. He can make an accounting profit of $100 per acre. However, if he raises soybeans, he can make $200 per acre. Is the farmer currently earning an economic profit? Why or why not?

2. (Opportunity Costs) Corporate executives often take jobs with the government for much smaller salaries. What are their opportunity costs? Does your answer depend on whether you take a long-run or short-run view?

3. (Normal Profits) Why is it reasonable to think of normal profits as a type of cost to the firm?

4. (Diminishing Returns) All commercial jets have a pilot and a copilot. How would you interpret the marginal product of the copilot? Why not have a third or fourth pilot for the same flight?

5. (Diminishing Returns) Suppose that you have some farmland. During the year you must decide how many times you will grow your crops. Also, you must decide how to space each plant (or seedling). Will diminishing returns be a factor in your decision making? Relate your answer to Exhibit 3 in this chapter.

6. (Marginal Cost) Explain why marginal cost must intersect average cost and average variable cost at their minimum points.

7. (Average Cost and Average Variable Cost) Why must average total cost and average variable cost approach each other as output increases? Will this be true for all cost curves?

8. (Short-Run Costs) Which of the following would shift the short-run marginal cost curve? In which direction might marginal cost shift?
   a. an increase in wage rates
   b. a decrease in property taxes
   c. a rise in the purchase price of new capital
   d. a rise in oil prices (or energy prices)
   e. a sudden change in technology

9. (Long-Run Average Costs) What factors would shift the long-run average cost curve? Would these changes also affect the short-run average cost curves? Why or why not?

10. (Long Run versus Short Run) What will determine the length of the short run? Will this be different for different types of industries?

APPENDIX

A Closer Look at Production and Costs

The act of production can be viewed as a process that transforms resources into goods and services. The amount of goods and services that can be produced with a given amount of resources depends on the existing state of technology, which is the prevailing knowledge of how resources can be combined. Thus, resources coupled with technology yield output. In this appendix we develop the analysis to determine how a profit-maximizing firm will combine resources to produce particular amounts of output. We begin by considering the technological possibilities available to the firm.

The Production Function and Efficiency

The way resources can be combined to produce output is summarized by a firm's production function. The **production function** identifies the maximum quantity of a particular good or service that can be produced per time period by specific combinations of resources, using the best technology available. The production function can be presented as an equation, as a graph, or as a table.

The production function summarized in Exhibit 10 reflects, for a hypothetical firm, the relationship between resource use and the level of output. This firm uses only two resources, capital and labor. The amount of capital used is listed along the left-hand margin of the table, and the amount of labor employed is listed across the top. The table provides the output resulting from particular combinations of capital and labor. For example, if 1 unit of capital is combined with 7 units of labor, the firm can produce 350 units of output.

Since we assume that the production function combines resources efficiently, 350 units is the most that can be produced with that combination of resources. Thus, we say that production is *technologically efficient*. The

production function indicates the maximum amount of output that can be produced with alternative combinations of resources. We assume that the firm is aware of the production function and that the firm produces the maximum possible output given the combination of resources employed.

The assumption that firms are efficient is linked to our earlier assumption that firms maximize profit. If firms fail to use the best technology available or otherwise do not produce efficiently, they would be producing less than they could with a given amount of resources. If they produce less, their total revenue will be less than it could be. Since the cost of a given amount of resources is the same whether or not the resources are employed efficiently, the firm's profit—total revenue minus total cost—will be lower if it fails to produce efficiently. Inefficiency therefore implies that the firm does not maximize profits, but such behavior is ruled out by the assumption of profit maximization. So the assumption of profit maximization implies that firms produce efficiently.

Let's return now to the tabular presentation of the production function. You will recall that the marginal physical product equals the extra output resulting from increasing resource use by 1 unit, other things equal. In the chapter we examined the effects of adding additional labor to an existing amount of capital. We can perform that same experiment in Exhibit 10 by starting with some level of capital use and reading across the table. For example, when 1 unit of capital and 1 unit of labor are employed, the firm produces 100 units of output per year. If the amount of labor is increased by 1 unit, holding the amount of capital employed constant, output increases to 150 units, so the marginal physical product of labor is 50 units. If the amount of labor employed increases by 1 unit from 2 to 3 units, other things constant, output goes to 210 units, yielding a marginal physical product of 60 units. By reading across the table at a specific level of capital use, you will discover that the marginal

EXHIBIT 10
A FIRM'S TABULAR PRODUCTION
FUNCTION USING LABOR AND CAPITAL

PRODUCTION PER PERIOD

Units of Capital Employed per Period	Units of Labor Employed per Period						
	1	2	3	4	5	6	7
1	100	150	210	260	300	330	350
2	150	200	260	320	350	375	390
3	210	255	320	370	405	430	440
4	260	310	370	410	445	475	500
5	300	350	405	445	480	515	545
6	330	380	435	475	510	540	565
7	350	400	455	495	530	555	575

physical product first rises, showing increasing marginal returns to the variable resource, labor, and then decreases, showing diminishing marginal returns.

Changes in the quantity of labor at a specific level of capital use reflect short-run adjustments in the level of production. By considering the effect of changes in the amount of capital, we can consider long-run adjustments in the level of production. For example, by holding the amount of labor employed constant, we can follow a column down to find the marginal physical product of additional units of capital. Capital typically varies only in the long run, not in the short run, so movements down the columns of the production function require a long-run adjustment. Incidentally, notice that capital exhibits first increasing, then diminishing marginal returns as its use expands, given the level of labor employed.

Isoquants

The information provided in Exhibit 10 can be presented more clearly and concisely in graphical form. In Exhibit 11 the quantity of labor employed is measured along the hori-zontal axis, and the quantity of capital, along the vertical axis, Notice from the tabular presentation of the production function in Exhibit 10 that different combinations of resources may yield the same level of output. For example, several combinations of labor and capital yield 350 units of output. The combinations that yield 350 units of output are presented in Exhibit 11 as points *a*, *b*, *c*, and *d*. These points can be connected to form an isoquant curve, Q_1, which shows all the possible combinations of the two resources that will produce 350 units of output.

More generally, an **isoquant** is a curve that shows all the technologically efficient combinations of two resources, such as labor and capital, that can produce a certain amount of output. Along a particular iso-quant, the amount of output produced remains the same, but the combinations of resources vary. Isoquants provide the same information as a table such as Exhibit 10, but in a clearer way.

Thus, to produce a particular level of output, the firm can use either much capital and little labor or much labor and little capi-tal. For example, a paving contractor can put in a new driveway with 10 workers using

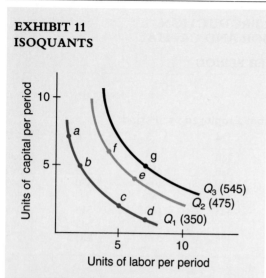

EXHIBIT 11
ISOQUANTS

Isoquant Q_1 shows all technically efficient combinations of labor and capital that can be used to produce 350 units of output. Isoquant Q_2 is drawn for 475 units, and Q_3, for 545 units. Each isoquant has a negative slope and is convex to the origin.

ference curves, we can highlight some properties of isoquants.

Isoquants Farther from the Origin Represent Higher Output Levels As you can see, isoquants farther from the origin indicate higher levels of output. Although we have included only three isoquants in Exhibit 11, there is an isoquant for every quantity of output depicted in Exhibit 10. Indeed, there is an isoquant for every output level the firm could possibly produce.

Isoquants Slope Down to the Right Isoquants slope down to the right as long as both resources have a positive marginal physical product—that is, as long as both resources contribute to production. If we increase the quantity of labor employed while holding the amount of output produced constant, then we must reduce the amount of capital employed. Hence, along a given isoquant, the quantity of labor employed is inversely related to the quantity of capital employed, so isoquants are negatively sloped.

Isoquants Do Not Intersect Since each isoquant refers to a specific level of output, no two isoquants intersect, for such an intersection would indicate that the same combination of resources could with equal efficiency produce two different amounts of output.

Isoquants Are Usually Convex to the Origin Finally, isoquants are usually convex to the origin, meaning that the slope of the isoquant gets flatter as we move down along the curve. To understand why, keep in mind that the slope of the isoquant measures the ability of additional units of labor to substitute in production for capital. When the quantity of labor increases as we move down the isoquant, by how much must capital be reduced to keep the output level constant?

shovels and hand rollers or can do the same job with only 2 workers, a road grader, and a paving machine. A Saturday afternoon charity car wash (to send the high school band to Disney World) is labor-intensive, involving perhaps a dozen workers per car. In contrast, the professional car wash is fully automated, requiring only 1 person to turn on the machine and collect the money.

Isoquants Q_1, Q_2, and Q_3 have been drawn for 350 units, 475 units, and 545 units of output. (The colors of the isoquants are coded to match the entries in the production function table in Exhibit 10.) By now you probably see the similarity between isoquants and indifference curves. Recall that indifference curves showed the alternative combinations of goods that offered the consumer the same level of utility. Similarly, isoquants show the alternative combinations of resources that produce the same level of output. Drawing on our knowledge of indif-

When much capital and little labor are used, the marginal productivity of labor is relatively great, and the productivity of capital is relatively small, so additional labor will substitute for a relatively large amount of capital. For example, in moving from point *a* to *b* in Exhibit 11, 1 unit of labor substitutes for 2 units of capital, so the slope of the isoquant between points *a* and *b* equals − 2. But as more units of labor and less of capital are employed, the marginal product of labor declines, and the marginal product of capital increases, so it takes more labor to make up for a reduction in capital. For example, in moving from point *c* to *d* along the isoquant in Exhibit 11, 2 units of labor substitute for 1 unit of capital; hence, the slope of the isoquant between points *c* and *d* equals − 1/2.

If labor and capital were perfect substitutes in production, the rate at which labor would substitute for capital would remain fixed along the isoquant, so the isoquant would be a downward-sloping straight line. Since most resources are not perfect substitutes, however, the rate at which one substitutes for another changes along an isoquant. In moving down along an isoquant, more labor is required to offset a decline in capital, so the slope of the isoquant gets flatter, yielding an isoquant that is convex to the origin.

The (negative of the) slope of the isoquant between any two points is the marginal rate of substitution, or *MRS*, which equals (minus) the ratio of the marginal physical products between the two points. Thus, we can say that

$$\textbf{Slope of isoquant} = MRS$$
$$= -\frac{MPP_l}{MPP_c}$$

We ignore the minus sign and focus on the absolute value of the slope. The slope of the isoquant measures the marginal rate of substitution between labor and capital, or the *MRS*, which indicates the amount by which capital can be reduced without affecting output when the amount of labor employed

increases. Between points *a* and *b*, the *MRS* is 2 units of capital per unit of labor, which also equals the absolute value of the slope between the two points. Isoquants are convex to the origin because the marginal rate of substitution diminishes as we move down the isoquant.

Conclusion   Isoquants are like indifference curves in that (1) isoquants farther from the origin represent greater levels of output, just as indifference curves farther from the origin represent higher levels of utility; (2) both isoquants and indifference curves are downward sloping; (3) neither intersects; and (4) both are bowed toward the origin. One notable difference between isoquants and indifference curves is that while there is no objective way of attaching a numerical value to a particular level of utility, the output level can be objectively measured. The parallel between consumption and production continues in the next section, as we consider firm costs.

Isocost Lines

Isoquants illustrate graphically a firm's production function for all quantities of output the firm could possibly produce. Given these isoquants, how much should the firm produce? More specifically, what is the firm's profit-maximizing level of output? The answer depends on the cost of resources and the amount of money the firm plans to spend.

Suppose a unit of labor costs the firm $15,000 per year, and the rental price for each unit of capital is $25,000 per year. The total cost (*TC*) of production is

$$TC = W \times L + R \times C$$
$$= \$15,000L + \$25,000C$$

where *W* is the wage rate, *L* is the quantity of labor employed, *R* is the rental price of capital, and *C* is the quantity of capital employed. Using an isocost line, we depict the possible combination of resources that the firm can purchase with a given amount of money. An **isocost line** identifies all combinations of capital and labor the firm can purchase for a given total cost. In Exhibit 12, for example, if the firm's total cost equals $150,000 per year, the line $TC = \$150,000$ identifies all combinations of labor and capital that cost the firm a total of $150,000. If the firm spent the entire $150,000 on capital, it could rent 6 units per year; if the firm spent the money on labor, it could hire 10 workers per year; or the firm could employ any combination on the isocost line.

The slope of the isocost line is determined by the relative prices of resources. Specifically, the slope equals (minus) the price of labor divided by the price of capital, or $-W/R$, which indicates the relative price of the inputs. In our example,

$$\text{Slope of isocost line} = -\frac{W}{R}$$
$$= -\frac{\$15,000}{\$25,000}$$
$$= -0.6$$

The wage rate of labor is 0.6 of the rental rate of capital, so hiring 1 more unit of labor, without incurring any additional cost, implies that the firm must rent 0.6 fewer units of capital.

Again, there is a close parallel between the firm's isocost line and the consumer's budget line. One notable difference, however, is that a consumer can spend no more than a particular budget, but a firm is not confined to a particular isocost line. A firm can expand resource use, financing additional resources through the sale of the addi-

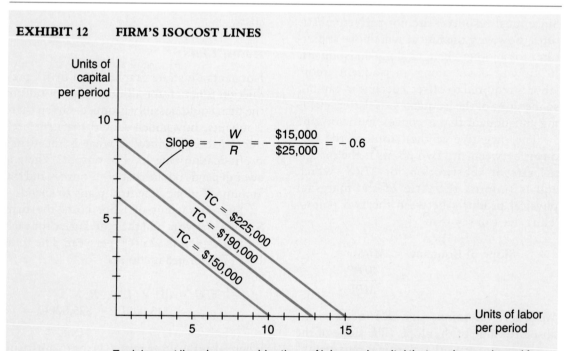

EXHIBIT 12   FIRM'S ISOCOST LINES

Each isocost line shows combinations of labor and capital that can by purchased for a fixed amount of total cost. Each one's slope is equal to (minus) the wage rate divided by the rental rate of capital. Higher levels of total cost are represented by isocost lines farther from the origin.

tional output. Thus, a firm's total cost is not constant but varies with the amount it chooses to produce. This is why in Exhibit 12 we include three isocost lines, not just one, with each corresponding to a different level of total cost. In fact, there is an isocost line for every possible level of cost. These isocost lines are parallel because they reflect the same relative price of resources to the firm. Resource prices in this model are assumed to be constant no matter how many resources the firm employs.

The Choice of Input Combinations

We bring the isoquants and the isocost lines together in Exhibit 13. Suppose the firm plans to spend $190,000 to purchase resources, so the firm can employ any combi-

nation of resources that falls along that line. The profit-maximizing firm will want to hire that combination of resources that yields the greatest output. The firm could hire combination *a*, where 7 units of capital totaling $175,000 and 1 unit of labor at $15,000 exhaust the budget of $190,000. At point *a*, however, only 350 units of the output would be produced. By moving to point *e* the firm produces 475 units of output for the same total cost. At point *e* the firm employs 4 units of capital, for a total of $100,000, and 6 units of labor, for a total of $90,000, so the total budget of $190,000 is exhausted.

This is the maximum output that could be produced for a total cost of $190,000. Higher isoquants lie completely above the isocost line and are thus unattainable for the given total cost. The firm maximizes output

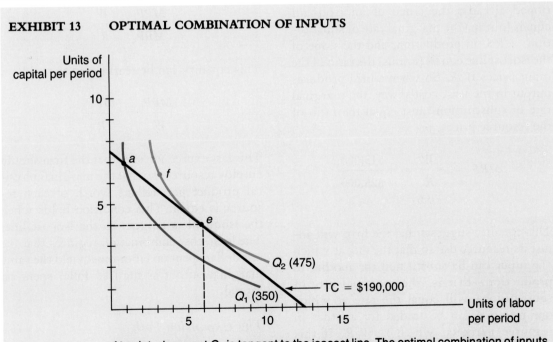

EXHIBIT 13   OPTIMAL COMBINATION OF INPUTS

At point *e* isoquant Q_2 is tangent to the isocost line. The optimal combination of inputs is 6 units of labor and 4 units of capital. The maximum output that can be produced for $190,000 is 475 units. Alternatively, point *e* determines the minimum-cost way of producing 475 units of output.

for a given total cost by choosing that combination of resources where the isocost line is tangent to the highest attainable isoquant.

We have shown that the combination at e is the maximum output that can be produced for $190,000. We could approach the problem differently. Suppose the firm decides to produce 475 units of output and wants to minimize its total cost. The firm could select point f, which employs 6 units of capital with 4 units of labor. This combination, however, would cost $210,000 at prevailing prices. Since the profit-maximizing firm wants to produce at the minimum cost, the firm tries to find the isocost line closest to the origin that still touches the isoquant. So the point of tangency between the isocost line and the isoquant shows the maximum output attainable for a given cost as well as the minimum cost required to produce that output.

Consider what is going on at the point of tangency. At point e the isoquant and the isocost line have the same slope. As mentioned already, the slope of an isoquant equals (minus) the marginal rate of substitution, MRS, in production, and the slope of the isocost line equals (minus) the ratio of the input prices W/R. So when a firm produces output in the least costly way, the marginal rate of substitution must equal the ratio of the resource prices, or

$$MRS = -\frac{W}{R} = -\frac{\$15,000}{\$25,000}$$
$$= -0.6$$

This equality suggests that the firm will adjust its resource use so that the rate at which one input can be substituted for another in production—that is, the marginal rate of substitution—will equal the rate at which one resource can be traded for another in resource markets, which is W/R. If this equality does not hold, it means that the firm, by adjusting its input mix, can produce the same output for a lower cost or produce more output for the same cost.

Consider why in equilibrium the marginal rate of substitution in production equals the ratio of resource prices. If the two are not equal, then the slope of the isoquant does not equal the slope of the isocost line at the point of intersection. For example, at a point a in Exhibit 13, the slope of the isoquant, the marginal rate of substitution, exceeds the slope of the budget line, the ratio of resource prices. You can see that whenever the isoquant intersects the isocost line at a point where the two slopes are not equal, there must be a higher isoquant that will be tangent to the given isocost line. Thus, a different combination of resources will yield more output at no additional cost. But once point e is achieved, no change in resources could yield as much output for the given cost.

Recall that the marginal rate of substitution equals the ratio of the marginal physical products of the resources. Therefore, we can rewrite the equilibrium condition as

$$\frac{MPP_l}{MPP_c} = \frac{W}{R}$$

This equality can be rearranged to yield

$$\frac{MPP_l}{W_c} = \frac{MPP_c}{R}$$

This last expression says that the firm should employ resources so that the marginal physical product per dollar's worth of each resource is equal. This condition holds when the isoquant is tangent to the isocost line. The least-cost combination requires that the last dollar spent on labor must yield the same marginal output as the last dollar spent on capital.

The Expansion Path

Imagine an isoquant representing each possible level of output. Given the cost of resources, we could determine the optimal combination of resources required to produce each level of output. The points of tangency in Exhibit 14 show the least costly way of producing several output levels. For example, output level Q_2 can be produced most cheaply using C units of capital and L units of labor. The line formed by connecting these tangency points is the firm's **expansion path**. If the goods are capital and labor, we often refer to this path as the long-run expansion path. The long-run expansion path identifies the least costly input combinations for each rate of output. It will generally slope upward, implying that firms will expand the use of both resources in the long run as output increases. Note that we have assumed that the prices of inputs remain constant as the firm varies output along the expansion path, so the slopes of the isocost lines are equal.

The expansion path is closely linked to the firm's long-run average cost curve. The expansion path indicates the lowest long-run total cost for which each level of output can be produced. For example, the firm can produce output level Q_2 for TC_2, output level Q_3 for TC_3, and so on. Similarly, the firm's long-run average cost curve conveys, at each level of output, the total cost divided by the level of output. The firm's expansion path and the firm's long-run average cost curve represent alternate ways of portraying costs in the long run, given resource prices.

One final point. If the relative price of resources changes, the least-cost combination of those resources will also change, so the firm's expansion path will change. For example, if the price of labor doubles, capital becomes cheaper relative to labor. The firm

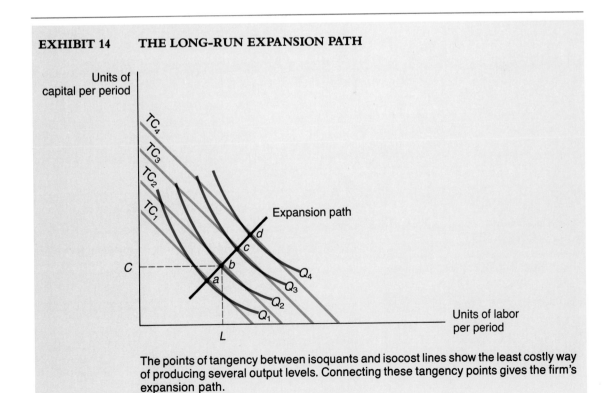

EXHIBIT 14   THE LONG-RUN EXPANSION PATH

The points of tangency between isoquants and isocost lines show the least costly way of producing several output levels. Connecting these tangency points gives the firm's expansion path.

will find that for each level of output, the least-cost combination of resources involves more capital and less labor.

Summary

A firm's production function specifies the relationship between resource use and output. The technologically feasible combinations of resources can be conveyed in mathematical form, in tabular form, or in graphical form. An isoquant is a curve that relates the possible combinations of resources that will produce a particular level of output. An isocost line presents the combinations of resources the firm can employ, given resource prices and the amount of money the firm plans to spend.

Given the amount of money the firm plans to spend—that is, given the isocost line—the firm maximizes output by finding the highest attainable isoquant that just touches, or is tangent to, the isocost line. Alternatively, for a given level of output—that is, for a given isoquant—the firm minimizes its total cost by choosing the lowest isocost line that just touches, or is tangent to, the isoquant. The least-cost combination of resources will depend on the relative cost of resources. So whether the firm minimizes cost for a given level of output or maximizes output for a given level of cost, the profit-maximizing equilibrium is found where an isocost line is tangent to the highest attainable isoquant. In equilibrium the last dollar spent on each resource yields the same marginal product.

PART
THREE

Market Structure, Pricing, and Government Regulation

PERFECT
COMPETITION

In the previous chapter we examined the cost curves of individual firms in both the short run and the long run. We discussed how a firm can minimize the total cost of producing a given level of output. We now must understand the relationship between a firm's cost curves and its supply curve. As we will see, the relationship between firm cost and firm supply will depend on the firm's economic environment.

Two questions we have not yet confronted are how much will a firm produce and what price will be charged? A firm will produce the amount that maximizes profit, but how much is that? In this chapter we find that, given the firm's cost curves, the amount a firm produces and the price of the good will depend on the demand for its output. We bring together supply and demand to determine the profit-maximizing level of price and output. In the next few chapters we will examine how firms respond to their economic environment—the decisions of what to produce, in what quantities, and at what price. Topics and terms discussed in this chapter include:

- Market structure
- Price takers
- Golden rule of profit maximization
- Loss minimization
- Competition and efficiency

AN INTRODUCTION TO
PERFECT COMPETITION

The kinds of decisions a firm faces depend on the structure of the market in which the firm is operating. **Market structure** describes the important features of the market, such as the number of firms (are there many or few?), the type of product (do all firms in the market produce identical products or are there differences?), the ease or difficulty of entering the market (is it easy to break into the industry or do patents or high capital costs block market

Market structure *describes the important features of a market, such as the number of firms, type of product, ease of entry, and forms of competition.*

entry?), and the forms of competition among firms (do firms compete by trying to offer lower prices than other producers or are advertising and product differentiation features of competition as well?). The various features of market structure will become clearer as we examine each type of market structure in the next few chapters. A word about terminology: an industry consists of all firms that supply output to a particular market. The terms *industry* and *market* are used interchangeably throughout the chapter.

Perfectly Competitive Market Structure

Perfect competition *is the market structure involving large numbers of fully informed buyers and sellers of a homogeneous product. There are no obstacles to entry or exit of firms.*

We begin with a perfectly competitive market, the simplest kind of market structure. **Perfectly competitive** markets are characterized by the following features: (1) a large number of buyers and sellers, each of whom buys or sells only a tiny fraction of the total amount bought and sold in the market; (2) a standardized, or *homogeneous*, product, meaning that the product of one firm is identical to that of others in the market; (3) all participants in the market are fully informed about the price and availability of all inputs, outputs, and production processes; and (4) freely mobile firms and resources, with no obstacles, such as patents or licenses, to prevent new firms from entering or existing firms from leaving the industry. In addition, no individual firm will devote resources to product improvement because, with free information, competitors could immediately copy any improvement. Nor will an individual firm advertise its product because in the consumer's eyes one firm's product is identical to that offered by other firms in the market.

A **price taker** *is any firm whose actions have no effect on the market price.*

If all these conditions are present in a market, firms in that market are said to be **price takers**. That is, individual firms have no control over the price; price is determined by market supply and demand. Once this market price is determined, individual firms can supply all they want at that price. Since each firm can sell all it produces at the market price, firms have no desire to charge less than the market price. Nor will a firm charge more than the market price. If a firm tried to charge a higher price than its competitors, customers would buy from competitors since the products are identical. Thus, firms in perfectly competitive markets, as price takers, must offer their product for sale at whatever price is established by the market. As we will see, perfectly competitive firms have only one decision to make: how much output should be produced?

The perfectly competitive market structure, where firms are price takers, is used as a benchmark for evaluating the efficiency of markets. Although it is an abstraction that is not usually observed in the real world, the perfectly competitive model is useful for analyzing markets in much the same way as a perfect vacuum is useful in physics or a utopian society is useful in philosophy.

Demand Under Perfect Competition

Exhibit 1 presents the relationship between the market supply and demand curves in panel (b) and the demand curve confronting the perfectly competitive firm in panel (a). The market price of $5 is determined in panel (b) by the

**EXHIBIT 1   THE FIRM'S DEMAND CURVE AND MARKET EQUILIBRIUM
IN PERFECT COMPETITION**

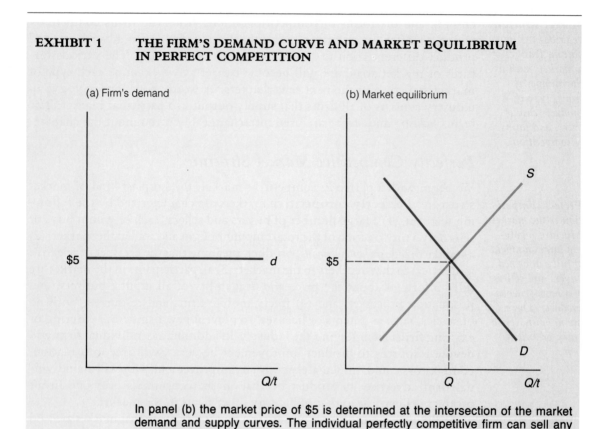

(a) Firm's demand

(b) Market equilibrium

In panel (b) the market price of $5 is determined at the intersection of the market
demand and supply curves. The individual perfectly competitive firm can sell any
amount at that price. The demand curve facing the competitive firm is horizontal at the
market price, as shown by demand curve *d* in panel (a).

intersection of the market demand curve, *D*, with the market supply curve,
S. Once the price is established in the market, any firm can sell all it wants at
that market price. The demand curve confronted by an individual firm is
therefore a horizontal line drawn at the market price. In our example a firm's
demand curve is drawn at the market price of $5 per unit, identified as *d* in
panel (a). The firm's demand curve indicates that the firm can sell all it wants
at the market price.

As we have said, each firm is a price taker because its output is so small
relative to market supply that each firm has no impact on the market price.
Also, because all firms are producing identical goods, no firm can charge
more than the market price. If a firm charged $5.50 per unit, customers in this
market would simply turn to other suppliers. A firm is free to charge less
than the market price, but why lower the price when the firm can already sell
all it wants at the market price?

Someone once remarked, "In perfect competition there is no competition." There is an irony that two neighboring wheat farmers in perfect
competition are not really competing in the sense of being rivals. The amount
that one farmer grows will have no effect on the price the other will receive

per bushel. They both must sell their output at the price determined in the wheat market. We now consider how farmers and other perfectly competitive producers will maximize profits in the short run, then in the long run.

SHORT-RUN PROFIT MAXIMIZATION

The assumption used here and throughout this text is that the firm's objective is to maximize economic profit. The firm's economic profit is equal to its total revenue minus its total cost, where total cost includes both explicit and implicit costs. Implicit cost, you will recall, is the opportunity cost of resources owned by the firm and includes a normal profit. So economic profit is any profit above normal profit.

The question is, How do firms maximize profit? As we have said, in perfect competition the demand curve encountered by each firm is a horizontal line drawn at the market-determined price. If the perfectly competitive firm has no control over price, what does it control? The firm controls its level of output. The question then becomes, What level of output will maximize profit? Now we can consider how the firm goes about maximizing profit in the short run.

Total Revenue Minus Total Cost

The firm has two ways of determining the profit-maximizing output. The first is to calculate total revenue minus total cost for each possible level of output, then to choose the level of output that maximizes the difference between the two—that is, that maximizes profit. Columns (3) and (4) in Exhibit 2 list the firm's total revenue and total cost for each level of output. The total cost column should look familiar since it was introduced in the previous chapter. Remember that total cost includes implicit cost, so it already includes a normal profit.

Although Exhibit 2 does not distinguish between total fixed cost and total variable cost, total fixed cost must equal $15 since this is total cost when output is 0. Since the firm incurs fixed cost, at least one resource must be fixed, so the firm is in the short run.

The total revenue for a firm facing a perfectly elastic demand curve is easily determined. Since the firm can sell all it chooses at the market price, the firm's total revenue equals its output multiplied by that market price. The total revenue column is simply the price of $5 times the level of output. Column (3) minus column (4) yields the economic profit, which is presented in the last column, column (7). As you can see, at very low and very high levels of output, total cost exceeds total revenue, so profit is negative. Between 7 units and 14 units of output, total revenue exceeds total cost, so profit is positive. Profit is maximized (at $12) when output is 12 units per period. All other levels of output yield less profit.

EXHIBIT 2
SHORT-RUN COSTS AND REVENUES FOR A PERFECTLY COMPETITIVE FIRM

Quantity of Output (Q)	Marginal Revenue (price) (P)	Total Revenue (TR) (1) × (2)	Total Cost (TC)	Marginal Cost (MC)	Average Total Cost (ATC) (4) ÷ (1)	Economic Profit or Loss (4) − (3)
(1)	(2)	(3)	(4)	(5)	(6)	(7)
0	—	$0	$15.00	—	—	− $15.00
1	$5	5	19.50	$4.50	$19.50	− 14.50
2	5	10	23.50	4.00	11.75	− 13.50
3	5	15	26.50	3.00	8.83	− 11.50
4	5	20	29.00	2.50	7.25	− 9.00
5	5	25	31.00	2.00	6.20	− 6.00
6	5	30	32.50	1.50	5.42	− 2.50
7	5	35	33.75	1.25	4.82	1.25
8	5	40	35.25	1.50	4.41	4.75
9	5	45	37.25	2.00	4.14	7.75
10	5	50	40.00	2.75	4.00	10.00
11	5	55	43.25	3.25	3.93	11.75
12	5	60	48.00	4.75	4.00	12.00
13	5	65	54.50	6.50	4.19	10.50
14	5	70	64.00	9.50	4.57	6.00
15	5	75	77.50	13.50	5.17	− 2.50
16	5	80	96.00	18.50	6.00	− 16.00

A graphical derivation of the same result is presented as panel (a) in Exhibit 3, where the total cost and total revenue curves are drawn. As output increases by 1 unit, total revenue increases by $5. Therefore, the total revenue curve is a straight line emanating from the origin, with a slope of 5. The short-run total cost curve was discussed in the previous chapter. Its backward **S** shape reflects first increasing marginal returns, then diminishing marginal returns to changes in variable resources. Total cost therefore increases first at a decreasing rate and then at an increasing rate.

At levels of output of less than 7 units or greater than 14 units, total cost exceeds total revenue, resulting in losses measured by the vertical distance between the two curves. Only when total revenue exceeds total cost does the firm earn a profit. Between output rates of 7 units and 14 units the firm is making a profit. Profit is maximized at the level of output where total revenue exceeds total cost by the greatest amount. We already know that this distance is greatest when 12 units are produced.

Marginal Cost Equals Marginal Revenue in Equilibrium

Marginal reve-nue is the change in total revenue after a one-unit change in sales.

The first way to find the profit-maximizing level of output is by comparing total cost and total revenue. A second and more revealing way uses marginal revenue and marginal cost information. Column (2) of Exhibit 2 presents the firm's marginal revenue. **Marginal revenue** is the amount by which total

EXHIBIT 3   SHORT-RUN PROFIT MAXIMIZATION

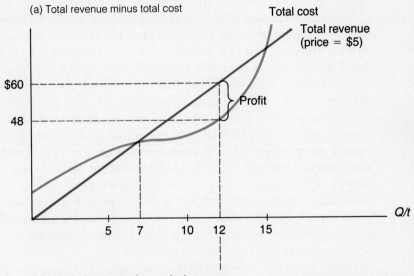

(a) Total revenue minus total cost

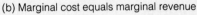

(b) Marginal cost equals marginal revenue

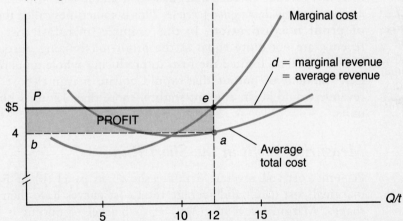

In panel (a) the total revenue curve for a competitive firm is a straight line with slope equal to the market price of $5. Total cost increases with output, first at a decreasing rate, then at an increasing rate. Profit is maximized at 12 units of output, where total revenue exceeds total cost by the greatest amount.

In panel (b) marginal revenue is a horizontal line at the market price of $5. Profit is maximized at 12 units of output, where marginal cost equals marginal revenue (point *a*). Profit is output (12 units) multiplied by the difference between price ($5) and average total cost ($4), or the area of rectangle *eabP*.

revenue changes if the firm sells 1 more unit. In perfect competition the firm is a price taker; if 1 more unit is sold, total revenue will increase by an amount equal to the market price. Thus, the marginal revenue in perfect competition equals the market price; in this example, the marginal revenue is $5.

Column (5) presents the firm's marginal cost, which is already familiar to you; it is the addition to total cost that results from a 1-unit increase in output. Marginal cost first declines, reflecting increasing marginal returns in the short run as more variable resources are employed. Marginal cost then increases, reflecting diminishing marginal returns. Average cost also initially declines with increased output, then eventually increases as output expands.

The firm will expand output as long as each additional unit sold adds more to total revenue than to total cost—that is, as long as marginal revenue exceeds marginal cost. Comparing columns (2) and (5) in Exhibit 2 indicates that marginal revenue exceeds marginal cost for each of the first 12 units of output. The marginal cost of unit 13, however, is $6.50, compared to a marginal revenue of $5. Producing the thirteenth unit would reduce total profit by $1.50. The change in total profit can be observed in the final column. Since we assume that the firm will maximize profit, the firm will limit its output rate to 12 units per period.

According to the **golden rule of profit maximiz-ation,** *the firm should produce the level of output where marginal cost equals marginal revenue.*

More generally, we can say that the firm will expand output as long as marginal revenue exceeds marginal cost, and it will stop expanding where *marginal cost equals marginal revenue.* This is sometimes called the **golden rule of profit maximization**. In this example, marginal cost and marginal revenue are not quite equal at the profit-maximizing output, but this is because we have limited the firm to producing whole units of output. The exact amount of output that would equate marginal cost and marginal revenue would be an amount slightly more than 12 units but less than 13 units.

Measuring Profit in the Short Run

Average revenue is total revenue divided by output.

Per-unit cost and revenue data are shown in panel (b) of Exhibit 3. The marginal cost (*MC*) and average total cost curves have their now-familiar shapes. Marginal revenue (*MR*) at each level of output is depicted as a horizontal line at the market price of $5, which also equals the competitive firm's demand curve. At any point along the demand curve marginal revenue equals the price. Marginal revenue for the competitive firm also equals the average revenue. The **average revenue** is the total revenue divided by the output. Thus, at any point along the demand curve faced by the competitive firm, the price equals both marginal revenue and average revenue. Regardless of the output, at all points on the competitive firm's demand curve the following equality holds:

Marginal revenue = Market price = Average revenue

The firm's task is to select the level of output that maximizes profit. The firm has a profit incentive to expand output as long as each additional unit adds more to total revenue than it does to total cost—that is, as long as marginal revenue exceeds marginal cost. The competitive firm will maximize profits by increasing output up to the point where marginal cost and marginal revenue are equal.

The marginal cost curve intersects the marginal revenue (and demand) curve at point *e*, where 12 units of output are produced. To the left of point *e* marginal revenue exceeds marginal cost, so the firm could increase profit by expanding output. To the right of point *e* marginal cost exceeds marginal revenue, so the firm could increase profit by reducing output.

Profit is identified by the shaded rectangle *eabP*. The height of that rectangle, *ea*, equals the price, $5, which also equals the marginal and average revenue, minus the average total cost, $4, at that level of output. This yields an average profit per unit of output of $1. Total profit equals the average profit per unit times the number of units produced, or $12. Thus, total profit is equal to the average profit per unit, denoted by *eb*, times the number of units produced.

Note that when total cost and total revenue curves are examined, profit is measured by the vertical distance between the two curves. But when per-unit curves are employed, profit is measured by an area—that is, by the two dimensions that result from multiplying the average profit per unit times the number of units sold.

MINIMIZING SHORT-RUN LOSSES

So far the firm has faced the pleasant problem of choosing the rate of output that maximizes short-run economic profit. But, alas, firms are not always so fortunate. Because firms in perfect competition are price takers, they have no control over the price they receive. Sometimes they find the price so low that no level of output will yield a profit. Faced with losses at all levels of output, the firm has two options: it can continue to produce at a loss or it can temporarily shut down.

Fixed Costs and Minimizing Losses

Your instincts probably tell you the firm should shut down rather than produce at a loss. Unfortunately, it is not that simple. Keep in mind that the firm has two kinds of cost in the short run: fixed cost, which must be paid even if the firm temporarily shuts down, and variable cost, which depends on the level of output. The short run is too short a period to allow new firms to enter or existing firms to leave the industry. Thus, even if the firm shuts down it must still pay property taxes on the building, fire insurance, and other overhead expenses incurred even when output is zero. In the long run the firm can go out of business altogether and thereby avoid fixed costs.

If the firm produces in the short run, it may continue to lose money. Under certain conditions, however, the loss the firm incurs by operating may be less than the loss suffered by shutting down. There may be some level of output greater than zero where the firm's revenue will not only meet its variable cost but will also cover some portion of its fixed cost. The firm's short-run objective is to find the level of output that minimizes the firm's loss.

Consider the cost data presented earlier in Exhibit 2, but now suppose the market price falls from $5 to $3. This new situation is depicted in Exhibit 4. At the lower price the revenue and profit columns have been changed. As you can see from column (8), the firm fails to earn a profit at any output level. If the firm produces nothing, its loss is the fixed cost of $15 it must still pay. If it produces between 1 and 5 units, the firm loses more than $15 because the $3 price is below average variable cost. Hence, the firm is not even covering variable costs. Output levels between 6 and 12 still generate losses, but the firm loses less than it would by shutting down. The firm will choose that level of output that minimizes its loss. From column (8) you can see that the loss is minimized at $10 when 10 units are produced.

Producing Where Total Cost Minus Total Revenue Is Minimized

Minimizing the short-run loss is presented in terms of the total cost and total revenue curves in panel (a) of Exhibit 5. Because the price has been lowered from $5 to $3 per unit, the slope of the total revenue curve changes from 5 to 3, so the total revenue curve is now flatter. Since only the price has changed, not the firm's costs, the total cost curve is the same as in Exhibit 3. Notice that the total cost curve now lies above the total revenue curve at all output levels. The vertical difference between the two curves measures the firm's loss at each level of output. If the firm produces nothing, the loss is $15. The distance between the two curves is minimized at an output level of 10 units, where the loss is $10. At any other level of output, the loss is greater.

Producing Where Marginal Cost Equals Marginal Revenue

Another way to derive the same result is to rely on marginal analysis. The per-unit data from Exhibit 4 are presented in panel (b) of Exhibit 5. The loss-minimizing level of output is found by choosing the level of output where marginal cost and marginal revenue are equal, provided that price exceeds average variable cost. The marginal cost and marginal revenue curves intersect at point *e*, where the price is $3 and the output level is 10 units per period.

The average total cost at this level of output is $4, and the average variable cost is $2.50. The difference of $1.50 is the average fixed cost. Since the price of $3 is higher than the average variable cost, the firm is able to cover all its variable cost and a portion of its fixed cost. Specifically, $2.50 of the price pays the average variable cost, and $0.50 covers a portion of average fixed cost. This leaves a loss of $1 per unit, which, when multiplied by 10 units, yields a total loss of $10. This loss is identified in panel (b) as the rectangle *aePc*. Again, the firm in the short run will produce 10 units per period at a loss of $10 because if it shuts down the loss will be $15 per period. Thus, 10 units

EXHIBIT 4
MINIMIZING LOSSES IN THE SHORT RUN

Quantity of Output (1)	Marginal Revenue (Price) (2)	Total Revenue (1) × (2) (3)	Total Cost (4)	Marginal Cost (5)	Average Total Cost (4) ÷ (1) (6)	Average Variable Cost (7)	Total Economic Profit or Loss (3) − (4) (8)
0	—	$0	$15.00	—	—	↓	−$15.00
1	$3	3	19.50	$4.50	$19.50	$4.50	− 16.50
2	3	6	23.50	4.00	11.75	4.25	− 17.50
3	3	9	26.50	3.00	8.83	3.83	− 17.50
4	3	12	29.00	2.50	7.25	3.50	− 17.00
5	3	15	31.00	2.00	6.20	3.20	− 16.00
6	3	18	32.50	1.50	5.42	2.92	− 14.50
7	3	21	33.75	1.25	4.82	2.68	− 12.75
8	3	24	35.25	1.50	4.41	2.53	− 11.25
9	3	27	37.25	2.00	4.14	2.47	− 10.25
10	3	30	40.00	2.75	4.00	2.50	− 10.00
11	3	33	43.25	3.25	3.93	2.57	− 10.25
12	3	36	48.00	4.75	4.00	2.75	− 12.00
13	3	39	54.50	6.50	4.19	3.04	− 15.50
14	3	42	64.00	9.50	4.57	3.50	− 22.00
15	3	45	77.50	13.50	5.17	4.17	− 32.50
16	3	48	96.00	18.50	6.00	5.06	− 48.00

EXHIBIT 5   **MINIMIZING SHORT-RUN LOSSES**

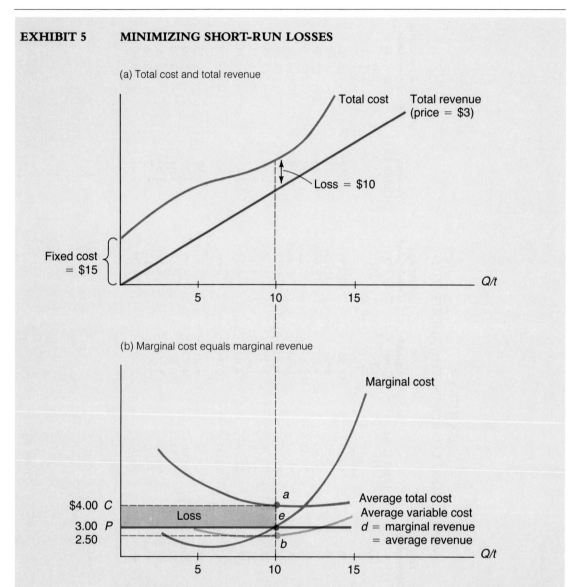

(a) Total cost and total revenue

Total cost

Total revenue
(price = $3)

Loss = $10

Fixed cost
= $15

Q/t

5   10   15

(b) Marginal cost equals marginal revenue

Marginal cost

$4.00 *C*

3.00 *P*

2.50

Loss

a

e

b

Average total cost

Average variable cost

d = marginal revenue
= average revenue

Q/t

5   10   15

Since total cost always exceeds total revenue in panel (a), the firm suffers a loss at every level of output. The loss is minimized at 10 units of output. Panel (b) shows that marginal cost equals marginal revenue at point *e*. The loss is equal to output (10) multiplied by the difference between average total cost ($4) and price ($3). Since price exceeds average variable cost, the firm will be better off continuing to produce in the short run.

is the firm's short-run equilibrium rate of output when the market price is $3 per unit.

Shutting Down in the Short Run

As long as the firm in the short run is able to cover all its variable cost and a portion of its fixed cost, it will produce rather than shut down. If, however, the price falls below the lowest point on its average variable cost curve, no level of output will allow the firm to cover even a portion of its variable cost, so the firm will shut down. After all, why should the firm produce if by doing so it only increases its loss? If the price falls to $2 per unit, you can see from column (7) in Exhibit 4 that at no output level does the average variable cost drop far enough to be covered by a price of $2.

The lowest price at which the firm would cover its average variable cost is $2.47, which is the average variable cost when output is 9 units. At this price the firm will actually be indifferent between producing and shutting down since either way its total loss will be the fixed cost of $15. Any price above $2.47 will allow the firm to cover a portion of its fixed cost by producing and thereby to reduce its loss.

The Firm and Industry Short-Run Supply Curves

As the price changes, the firm will vary its output to re-equate marginal cost with marginal revenue. The effects of various prices on the firm's output are summarized in Exhibit 6. Points a, b, c, d, and e are all intersections of the firm's marginal cost curve with different marginal revenue curves. (Recall that for perfectly competitive firms, the marginal revenue curve also equals the firm's demand curve and its average revenue curve.) At a price as low as P_1 the firm will shut down rather than produce where marginal cost equals marginal revenue because output level Q_1 does not permit the firm to cover even its average variable cost. Nor would any other level of output cover variable cost as long as the price is P_1. At a price of P_2 the firm will be indifferent between producing Q_2 and shutting down because either way the loss will equal its fixed cost. If the price is P_3, the firm will produce Q_3, but it will incur a loss because it cannot at that price cover its fixed cost. Although the firm will incur a loss at a price of P_3, that loss is less than what it would face by shutting down. At P_4 the firm will produce Q_4 and will just break even since its average total cost equals the price. When it breaks even, the firm earns a normal profit. If the price rises to P_5, the firm will earn an economic profit. To determine profit, subtract the average total cost from the price and multiply this difference by the output level, Q_5.

The Firm's Supply Curve   As long as the price is high enough to cover the firm's average variable cost, the firm will supply the quantity determined at the intersection of marginal cost and marginal revenue curves. Thus, that portion of the firm's marginal cost curve at or above the low point on its average variable cost curve becomes the firm's *short-run supply curve*. In Exhibit 6 it is the upward-sloping portion of the marginal cost curve,

EXHIBIT 6   SUMMARY OF SHORT-RUN OUTPUT DECISIONS

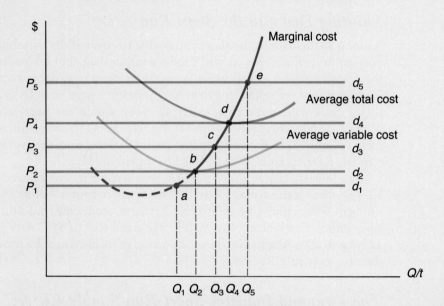

At price P_1, marginal cost equals marginal revenue at point *a*. The firm produces nothing because P_1 is less than average variable cost. At price P_2 the firm produces Q_2 units of output and suffers a loss equal to its fixed cost. At P_3 it produces Q_3 units and suffers a loss that is less than its fixed cost. At P_4 the firm produces Q_4 and just breaks even since P_4 equals average total cost. Finally, at P_5 it produces Q_5 and earns an economic profit. The firm's short-run supply curve is that portion of its marginal cost curve above the minimum point of average variable cost (point *b*).

beginning at point *b*. This supply curve indicates the quantity the firm is willing and able to supply in the short run at each alternative price. If the price is below P_2, quantity supplied will be zero. Quantity supplied when the price is P_2 or higher is determined by the intersection of the firm's demand curve and its marginal cost curve.

The Industry Supply Curve   As mentioned earlier, an industry consists of all firms that supply output to a particular market, so the market supply curve and the industry supply curve are the same thing. Exhibit 7 presents an example of how supply curves for just three firms with identical marginal cost curves are summed horizontally to form the industry, or market, supply curve. (In perfectly competitive industries there will be many more firms.) At a price below *P*, no output will be supplied. At a price of *P*, 10 units will be supplied by each of the three firms, for a market supply of 30 units. At a price above *P*, say, *P'*, each firm will supply 20 units, so the quantity supplied to the market equals 60 units.

EXHIBIT 7   **AGGREGATING INDIVIDUAL SUPPLY TO FORM MARKET SUPPLY**

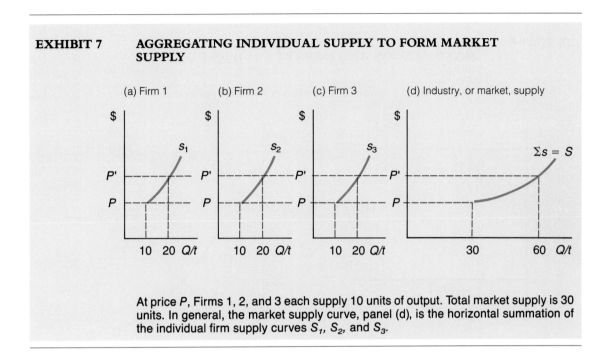

At price *P*, Firms 1, 2, and 3 each supply 10 units of output. Total market supply is 30 units. In general, the market supply curve, panel (d), is the horizontal summation of the individual firm supply curves S_1, S_2, and S_3.

Firm Supply and Industry Equilibrium   Exhibit 8 shows the relationship between the short-run profit-maximizing output of the individual firm and the market equilibrium price and quantity. The cost conditions of each firm are assumed to be identical and to reflect the hypothetical average and marginal costs used throughout this chapter. We assume that there are 1000 identical firms in this industry, and their individual supply curves (represented as the portion of the marginal cost curve above average variable cost) are summed horizontally to yield the market, or industry, supply curve. At a price of $5 per unit each firm will supply 12 units, for a market supply of 12,000 units. Each firm in the short run is making a profit, represented by the shaded rectangle.

In summary, firms in the short run can maximize profits or minimize losses by adjusting their variable resources. If it is confronted with a loss, the firm will either produce an output that minimizes its loss or will shut down temporarily. So far, so good. Next we will see what happens in the long run.

PERFECT COMPETITION IN THE LONG RUN

In the short run certain resources can be varied, but others, such as firm size, are fixed. In the long run, however, firms are free to come and go and to adjust their size—that is, to adjust their scale of operation. There is no distinction between fixed and variable costs because all resources are variable.

EXHIBIT 8   **RELATIONSHIP BETWEEN SHORT-RUN PROFIT**
                    MAXIMIZATION AND MARKET EQUILIBRIUM

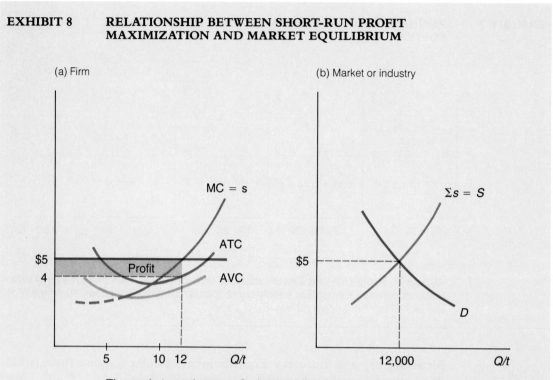

The market supply curve, *S**, in panel (b) is the horizontal sum of the supply curves of all firms in the industry. The intersection of *S** with the market demand curve, *D*, determines the market price, $5. That price, in turn, determines the height of the perfectly elastic demand curve facing the individual firm in panel (a). That firm produces 12 units (where marginal cost equals marginal revenue of $5) and earns an economic profit of $1 per unit, or $12 in total.

Economic profit will in the long run attract new entrants and may encourage existing firms to expand their scale. Sharp entrepreneurs will be attracted to profit opportunities like bears to honey. Economic profit attracts resources from industries where firms are earning only a normal profit or perhaps are losing money. Consequently, an industry earning short-run economic profits will attract other firms, and this additional output will expand market supply. This increase in market supply will lower the market price. Firms will continue to enter the market as long as economic profits are positive. Entry will cease only when the decrease in the price has driven economic profits to zero. In the long run, therefore, the entry of firms will eliminate economic profits.

A short-run loss will have the opposite effect. A loss will discourage new entry and will encourage existing firms to leave the industry or to reduce their scale of operation. This exit of firms will reduce market supply and increase market price. Departures will continue until the price increases enough to ensure that remaining firms make a normal profit—that is, make as much as they could in the next best alternative use of their resources.

Zero Economic Profits in the Long Run

This long-run tendency for firms to earn only a normal rate of return is fundamental to an understanding of the long-run production decision. Exhibit 9 shows what the individual firm and the market will look like in long-run equilibrium. In the long run, market supply will adjust through firm entry, firm exit, or adjustment in the scale of existing firms until the market-supply curve intersects the market demand curve at a price that equals the lowest point on each firm's long-run average cost curve. Because the long run is a time period during which all resources are variable, and because firms are driven to maximize profit, firms in the long run will adjust their size, or their scale of operation, until their average cost of production is minimized. Firms that fail to minimize costs will not survive in the long run.

Competition in the long run cuts economic profit to zero. At point *e* the firm is in equilibrium, producing *q* and earning a normal profit. At point *e* price, marginal cost, short-run average total cost, and long-run average cost are all equal. No firm will have any reason to alter its output, and no potential firm will have any incentive to enter this industry since each existing firm is

EXHIBIT 9 **LONG-RUN EQUILIBRIUM FOR THE FIRM AND THE INDUSTRY**

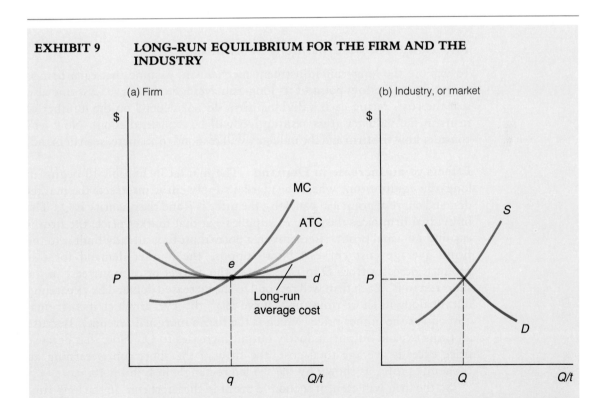

In long-run equilibrium the firm produces *q* units of output and earns a normal profit. At point *e* price, marginal cost, short-run average total cost, and long-run average cost are all equal. There is no reason for new firms to enter or for existing firms to leave. Thus, the market supply curve, *S*, in panel (b) will not shift. As long as market demand, *D*, is stable, the industry will continue to produce a total of *Q* units of output at price *P*.

earning normal, but not economic, profit. Any other price would cause adjustments in the market supply curve as firms attempted to increase profits or reduce losses. For example, a higher price would lead to economic profits and would therefore attract new entrants. A lower price would result in losses and cause some firms to leave the industry.

One way to understand the process of competition in the long run is to consider the evolution of a newly emerging industry. Video recorders are fast becoming standard equipment in the typical home. The wider availability of these recorders fueled household demand for videotapes of movies, and thus the videotape rental industry was born. The first rental outlets required customers to pay a membership fee, imposed a deposit on tapes, and rented tapes for as much as $5 per day. Those first entrants were often the only rental stores in the area, and they probably earned an economic profit in the short run. But in the long run this profit attracted many more competitors. The resulting increase in market supply reduced market prices. Competition from the proliferation of rental outlets eliminated membership fees and tape deposits and reduced the rental price to as low as $1 a day. Stores that could not compete dropped out of the industry. Over the long run rental stores that remain in business tend to earn just a normal profit.

The Long-Run Adjustment Mechanism

To explore the long-run adjustment mechanism, assume that each firm is operating on the low point of its long-run average cost curve. Assume also that the costs facing each individual firm do not depend on the number of firms in the industry (this assumption will be explained soon). Now let's consider how the firm and the industry will respond to an increase in demand.

Effects of an Increase in Demand   The market in Exhibit 10 begins in long-run equilibrium, where the market supply curve intersects the market demand curve at point a in panel (b); the price is P and the quantity is Q_a. The individual firm faces the price P, supplies q at that market price; the firm is earning a normal profit. (Remember, a normal profit is already built into the firm's average cost curves.) Now suppose the market demand for this product increases from D to D', causing the market price to increase in the short run to P'. Each firm will respond to the increased demand by expanding output along its short-run supply curve to q', the level at which its marginal cost equals the higher price (which is the firm's marginal revenue). Because all firms expand output, industry output increases to Q_b. Note that because price exceeds average total cost, the firm in the short run is earning an economic profit, as shown by the shaded rectangle in Exhibit 10(a).

So the firm will earn an economic profit in the short run. In the long run, however, resources will be attracted to this industry from markets where profits are just normal or where losses are incurred. Entry by new firms will increase supply, causing the market supply curve to shift out. As entry occurs and market supply expands, the market price falls. But as long as economic profit exists in this industry, entry will continue until the market supply curve shifts out to S', where supply intersects D' at point c, returning the

EXHIBIT 10   LONG-RUN ADJUSTMENT TO AN INCREASE IN DEMAND

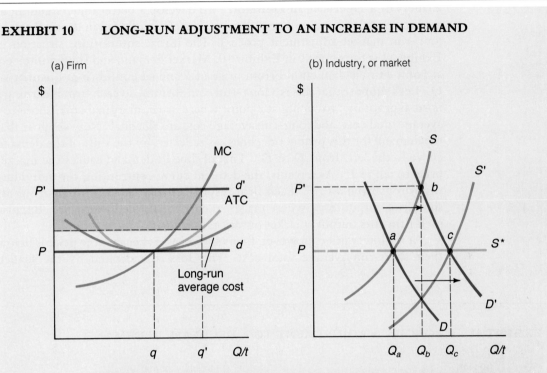

An increase in market demand from *D* to *D'* in panel (b) moves the equilibrium point from *a* to *b*. Output rises to Q_b, and price increases to *P'*. The rise in market price causes the demand curve facing the firm to rise from *d* to *d'* in panel (a). The firm responds by increasing output to *q'* and earns an economic profit.

With existing firms earning economic profits, new firms begin to enter the industry. Market supply shifts out to *S'* in panel (b). Output rises further, to Q_c, and price falls back to *P.* In panel (a) the demand curve shifts back to *d,* eliminating economic profits. Short-run adjustment is from point *a* to point *b* in panel (b), but long-run adjustment is from *a* to *c.*

price to its initial equilibrium level, *P*. Although the market price returns to where it was before the increase in demand, as a result of the entry of new firms, market quantity has increased to Q_c.

Because the market price falls, the demand curve facing the individual firm shifts back down from *d'* to *d*. As a result, each firm reduces output from *q'* back to *q* and each firm once again earns just a normal profit. Thus, the price of the good in the long run is determined at the minimum point on the firm's long-run average cost curve. Although the industry output increased from Q_a to Q_c, each firm's output returns to *q*. The additional output has been provided by the entry of new firms into the industry.

Because of the increase in demand, new firms are attracted to the industry by the resulting short-run economic profits. However, increased competition in the long run drives the profit of new and existing firms down to the normal level. In response to an increased demand, the short-run adjustment in Exhibit 10(b) is from point *a* to point *b*; in the long run the market equilibrium moves to point *c*.

Effects of a Decrease in Demand   To develop a better understanding of the logic involved, we will next consider the effect of a fall in demand on the long-run market adjustment process. The initial equilibrium situation in Exhibit 11 is the same as in Exhibit 10. Market demand and supply intersect at point *a* to yield an equilibrium price of *P* and an equilibrium quantity of Q_a. Let's suppose that this is a long-run equilibrium, so each firm is earning a normal profit by producing at a point where price, marginal cost, short-run average total cost, and long-run average cost are all equal. Now suppose that the demand for this product declines, as reflected by the shift of the demand curve to the left, from *D* to *D″*. This decline in demand causes the market price to fall to *P″*. As a result, the demand curve confronting the individual firm drops from *d* to *d″*. Each firm responds in the short run by cutting its short-run output to *q″*, where marginal cost equals the lower price. Because each firm cuts output, market output falls to Q_f.

At the lower price, however, firms suffer losses because the price is below their short-run average total cost. This loss in indicated by the shaded

EXHIBIT 11   LONG-RUN ADJUSTMENT TO A DECREASE IN DEMAND

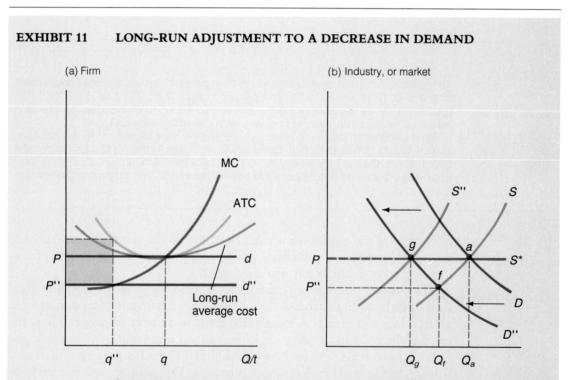

Starting from long-run equilibrium at point *a* in panel (b), a decrease in demand to *D″* drives price down to *P″*; output falls to Q_f. In panel (a) the firm's demand curve shifts down to *d″*. The firm reduces its output to *q″* and suffers a loss.

As firms leave the industry, the market supply curve shifts left to *S″*. Market price rises to *P* as output falls further, to Q_g. At price *P* the remaining firms once again earn zero economic profit. Thus, short-run adjustment is from point *a* to point *f* in panel (b); long-run adjustment is from *a* to *g*.

rectangle in Exhibit 11(a). Firms will produce at a loss in the short run. In the long run, however, some firms will leave the industry. As firms leave, market supply shifts to the left, so the market price increases. Exit will continue until the market supply curve shifts to S'', where supply intersects D'' at point g. Output has been reduced to Q_g, and price has returned to P. With the price back up to P, the firms still left in the industry can once again earn a normal profit. After the industry adjustment has occurred, firms remaining in the industry are producing the same amount as in their initial equilibrium, but market output has been reduced because some firms have left the industry.

THE LONG-RUN SUPPLY CURVE

Thus far we have shown the industry and firm response to changes in demand. This response could be broken down into a short-run adjustment and a long-run adjustment. In the short run firms respond to a shift in demand by moving up or down their marginal cost curve (that portion above average variable cost) until price equals marginal cost. The long-run adjustment, however, involves entry and exit of firms until the resulting shift in the short-run market supply curve generates an equilibrium price that provides firms with normal profit. For example, in Exhibits 10 and 11 we identified two long-run equilibrium points generated by the intersections of shifting demand and resulting short-run supply curves. In each case the price remained the same in the long run, but industry output changed from Q_a to Q_c in Exhibit 10(b) and from Q_a to Q_g in Exhibit 11(b). Connecting these equilibrium points yields the long-run market supply curve labeled S^* in Exhibits 10 and 11. In each case the long-run supply curve is horizontal, or perfectly elastic, reflecting unchanged industry costs in the long run.

Constant-Cost Industries

*A **constant-cost industry** can expand or contract without affecting the prices of the resources it employs.*

The industry we have depicted thus far is called a **constant-cost industry** because the cost curves did not shift as output changed. Resource prices and other production costs remain constant in the long run as industry output increases or decreases. Recall that at the outset of the discussion of the long run we assumed that the costs that each firm faced did not depend on the number of firms in the market. Therefore, industry output could change in the long run without changing production costs as firms enter or leave the industry. The long-run supply curve for a constant-cost industry is horizontal, as was depicted in Exhibits 10 and 11.

The constant-cost industry is most often characterized as one that hires only a small portion of the resources available in the resource market. That is, in a constant-cost industry the price of resources does not vary with a change in industry output. Firms need not increase the price paid for resources to draw them away from competing uses because firms in this industry hire only a small share of the resources available. For example, producers of pencils can expand industry production without having to worry about bidding up the price of wood, graphite, and synthetic rubber since the pencil industry uses such a small share of these resources.

Increasing-Cost Industries

*As an **increasing-cost industry** expands, it faces higher resource prices.*

Many industries encounter higher production costs as industry output expands in the long run. These so-called **increasing-cost industries** find that expanding output bids up the price of some resource, and this higher resource price causes an upward shift in each firm's cost curves. For example, an expansion of the oil industry will bid up the wages of petroleum engineers and geologists, raising the average and marginal cost for each oil exploration firm.

To show the equilibrium adjustment process for an increasing-cost industry, we again begin in long-run equilibrium in Exhibit 12(b), where the industry demand curve, D, intersects the short-run industry supply curve, S, at equilibrium point a to yield the price P_a and the quantity Q_a. When the price is P_a, the demand curve facing the firm is shown by d_a in panel (a). Recall that the firm's demand curve is also the firm's marginal revenue curve. The firm produces where marginal cost equals marginal revenue, which is at point a in panel (a). Since we begin in long-run equilibrium, at the equilibrium level of output the firm is at the low point of its average cost curve, so average cost equals the price. In the long run, firms earn no economic profit.

Now let's suppose that there is an increase in the demand for this product, as reflected by the shift to the right in the demand curve from D to D' in panel (b). The new demand curve intersects the short-run supply curve at point b, yielding the short-run equilibrium price P_b and quantity Q_b. With an increase in the equilibrium price, each firm's demand curve shifts from d_a up to d_b in panel (a). Each firm will expand output along its marginal cost curve to the point at which the marginal cost equals the new price level (or new marginal revenue). This new short-run equilibrium occurs at point b in panel (a), indicating that the firm produces output q_b. In the short run each firm earns an economic profit equal to q_b times the difference between the price and the average total cost at that level of output. So far the sequence of events is identical to that in the case of the constant-cost industry.

The economic profits earned by firms in the industry attract new entrants in the long run. The influx of new firms has two separate effects on the short-run industry supply curve. Because this is an increasing-cost industry, an expansion in the number of firms drives up the price of some of the industry's resources. These higher resource costs are reflected in an increase in each firm's marginal and average cost curves, which shift from ATC and MC up to ATC' and MC'. Because each firm's short-run supply curve is that portion of its marginal cost curve above the firm's average variable cost curve, a shift up in each firm's marginal cost curve means a shift up in each firm's supply curve, as reflected by the movement from MC up to MC'. So the first effect of new entry is to shift up each firm's short-run supply curve, reflecting higher firm costs. In effect each firm is less willing and able to offer goods for sale at each alternative price.

EXHIBIT 12   AN INCREASING-COST INDUSTRY

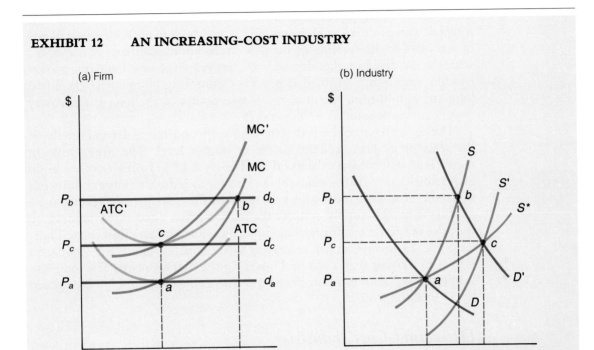

(a) Firm

(b) Industry

An increase in demand to *D'* in panel (b) disturbs the initial equilibrium at point *a*. Short-run equilibrium is established at point *b*, where *D'* intersects the short-run market supply curve, *S*. At the higher price, P_b, the firm's demand curve shifts up to d_b, and its output increases to q_b in panel (a). At point *b* the firm is earning an economic profit.

New firms enter to try to capture some of the profits. As they do so, input prices are bid up, so each firm's marginal and average cost curves rise. Consequently, each firm's supply curve shifts up from *MC* to *MC'*. In panel (b) market supply curve *S'* is the horizontal sum of the short-run supply curves of original and newly entering firms. The intersection of *S'* and *D'* determines the market price, P_c. At P_c, individual firms are earning zero economic profit.

Point *c* is a point of long-run equilibrium. By connecting long-run equilibrium points *a* and *c* in panel (b), the upward-sloping long-run market supply curve, *S**, is obtained for this increasing-cost industry.

But as long as economic profits exist in the industry, new firms will be drawn to the industry, and new entrants increase industry supply. New firms will enter the industry until the combination of expanded supply and higher firm costs drive economic profits to zero. This occurs when enough new firms have entered the market to shift the industry supply curve out to *S'*. Each firm's higher cost of production raises the price above the initial long-run equilibrium level.

Thus, two opposing forces are at work. The increase in resource costs raises each firm's marginal cost curve and thereby reduces each firm's supply curve, but the increase in the number of firms expands industry supply. Because higher production costs result from the increase in the number of firms, industry supply expands until a long-run equilibrium price of P_c is reached. This price is just high enough to provide all firms with a normal rate of return. The intersection of the new short-run market supply curve, S', with the increased market demand, D', provides the new long-run market equilibrium point, identified as point c. Connecting point c with the initial long-run equilibrium, point a, traces two points on the long-run industry supply curve, denoted as $S*$ in panel (b).

The key difference here is that the firm's costs no longer depend simply on the scale of its plant and its choice of output level. The firm's costs in increasing-cost industries depend on the level of industry output. In an increasing-cost industry long-run expansion in industry output eliminates short-run economic profits for two reasons. First, long-run expansion, by increasing market supply, reduces the market price. Second, by bidding up the price of certain resources, long-run expansion increases firm costs. Thus, long-run expansion in an increasing-cost industry eliminates short-run profits by raising firm costs and lowering the market price. The long-run supply curve for an increasing-cost industry is upward sloping, as depicted by $S*$ in Exhibit 12(b).

Decreasing-Cost Industries

*As a **decreasing-cost industry** expands, it faces lower resource prices.*

Some industries encounter lower production costs as output expands in the long run. Firms in these so-called **decreasing-cost industries** find that as industry output expands, the cost of production falls, causing a downward shift in each firm's cost curves. For example, in the coal mining industry a major cost is keeping water pumped out of the mine shafts. As more mines are operated in the same area, each mine pumps water. With all mines pumping water, the water table in the area is reduced, so it becomes easier to keep the water out of each mine shaft. The cost of production declines with an increase in the number of mines in the area. Decreasing-cost industries will have a long-run supply curve as depicted in Exhibit 13, where point a is the initial equilibrium, and point c is the long-run equilibrium adjustment to the increase in demand.

Decreasing costs could characterize an industry in the process of introducing a totally new product. When the product is initially produced, few resource owners specialize in its production, and firms must compete for the limited resources available. Over time, however, more resource owners offer specialized inputs to this market, so the cost of resources tends to decline. For example, microcomputers require a certain kind of processing chip. At the outset few suppliers produced that chip, and the cost to computer manufacturers was relatively high. But as the microcomputer industry expanded, many more firms began supplying chips to the industry, resulting in a lower price and wider availability. Whereas the long-run supply curve for most industries is either horizontal or upward sloping, decreasing-cost industries have a downward-sloping long-run supply curve.

Thus, firms in perfect competition can earn economic profit in the short run, but the entry or exit of firms drives long-run economic profit to zero. This is true whether the industry in question exhibits constant costs,

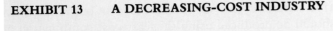

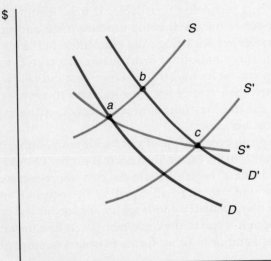

EXHIBIT 13   A DECREASING-COST INDUSTRY

Starting from point *a*, an increase in market demand moves the industry to short-run equilibrium at point *b*. With each firm earning an economic profit, new firms will begin to enter. If entry drives down input costs, long-run equilibrium will be reestablished at point *c*, with a lower price than at point *a*. Connecting long-run equilibrium points *a* and *c* yields the downward-sloping long-run market supply curve, *S**, for this decreasing-cost industry.

increasing costs, or decreasing costs. Notice also that the industry supply curve is less elastic in the short run than in the long run. In the long run firms can adjust all their resources, so they are better able to respond to changes in price.

We mentioned at the outset that perfect competition served the same function in economics as a vacuum in physics or a utopia in philosophy. We next examine the qualities of perfect competition that make it so special.

PERFECT COMPETITION AND EFFICIENCY

There are two concepts of efficiency. The first, called *productive efficiency*, refers to the notion of efficiency developed in the production possibilities curve, introduced in Chapter 2. The second, called *allocative efficiency*, emphasizes the choice of goods to be produced and the distribution of these goods among consumers.

Productive Efficiency

Productive efficiency is achieved when output is produced with the least-cost combination of inputs and using the best available technology.

The idea of **productive efficiency** is that whatever level of output the firm decides to produce should be produced using the least-cost combination of inputs and the best technology available. If firms could produce the same output using fewer resources or could produce more output using the same resources, resources are not being used efficiently. In the long run in perfect competition, the entry and exit of firms ensure that each firm is producing at the minimum point on its long-run average cost curve. Firms that are not must either adjust their size or leave the industry to avoid continued losses. Thus, the long-run industry output in perfect competition is produced at the least possible cost per unit.

In the long run an economic profit or loss is not possible because entry or exit will occur until firms earn only a normal profit. Output in the long run will be produced where the firm's marginal cost, short-run average total cost, and long-run average cost are all equal to the equilibrium price. In the perfectly competitive industry goods are homogeneous and *price* competition is the only factor of interest to the consumer. Therefore, resources will not be used up in advertising or in other forms of *nonprice* competition.

Allocative Efficiency

Allocative efficiency is achieved when firms produce the output that is most preferred by consumers.

Simply because the goods are produced at the least possible cost does not mean that this is the most efficient allocation of resources. It could be that the goods being produced are not the goods that consumers most prefer. This situation is akin to that of the airline pilot who informs the passengers that there is some good news and some bad news: "The bad news is we are lost; the good news is we are making record time!" Firms could be producing goods efficiently yet producing the wrong goods. **Allocative efficiency** occurs when firms produce the output that is most preferred by consumers.

How do we know that perfect competition guarantees that the goods produced are those most preferred by consumers? The answer lies with the demand and supply curves. Recall that the demand curve reflects the valuation that consumers attach to each unit they consume, so the price is the amount of money that people are willing to pay for the final unit they consume. We also know that, whether in the short run or the long run, the equilibrium price in perfect competition equals the marginal cost of supplying the last unit sold. Marginal cost measures the opportunity cost of using those resources in their best alternative use. Thus, supply and demand intersect at the combination of price and quantity where the opportunity cost of the resources employed to produce the last unit of output just equals the marginal value that consumers attach to that unit of output.

As long as marginal cost equals marginal benefit, the last unit produced is valued as much or more than any other good that could have been produced using those same resources. There is no way to reallocate resources to increase the value of output. Thus, there is no way to reallocate resources to increase the total utility or total benefit consumers enjoy from output. When the marginal cost of each good equals the marginal valuation that consumers derive from that good, the economy is said to pass the test of allocative efficiency.

Reviewing the Assumptions of Perfectly Competitive Markets

Let's reconsider the features that characterize the perfectly competitive market and see how they relate to conclusions developed in this chapter. *First*, there must be a large number of buyers and sellers. This is necessary so that no individual buyer or seller is large enough to influence price by its buying or selling. *Second*, firms must produce a homogeneous product. If consumers could distinguish among the output of different producers, then consumers might prefer the output of one firm even at a higher price, so different producers could sell at different prices. Therefore, each firm would no longer be a price taker—that is, the firm's demand curve would no longer be horizontal. *Third*, all market participants must have full information about all prices and all production processes. Otherwise, some producers could charge more than the market price, and some uninformed consumers would pay the higher price. Also, firms might, through ignorance, use the wrong technology or fail to recognize the opportunity for short-run economic profits. *Fourth*, all resources must be mobile in the long run, and no obstacles should prevent new firms from moving into profitable markets. Otherwise, some firms could earn economic profits in the long run.

Perfect competition is not the most common form of market observed in the real world. The markets for agricultural products, stocks, commodities such as gold and silver, and international currencies come close to being perfect. But even if no single example of perfect competition could be found, the model would be a useful tool for analyzing market behavior. As we will see in the next few chapters, perfect competition provides a valuable benchmark for evaluating the efficiency of other kinds of market structures.

SUMMARY ———————————————

1. Market structure describes important features of the economic environment in which the firm is operating. These features include the number of competing firms, the ease or difficulty of entering the market, the similarities or differences in the output produced by each firm, and the forms of competition among firms. There are several types of market structures. This chapter examined perfectly competitive markets.

2. Perfectly competitive markets are characterized by (1) a large number of buyers and sellers, (2) production of a homogeneous product, (3) full information about the availability and price of all resources and goods, and (4) free and complete mobility of resources. Firms in such markets are said to be price takers because no individual firm has control over price. The firm can vary only the amount it chooses to produce at the market price.

3. The market price in perfect competition is determined by the intersection of the market supply and market demand curves. Each firm then faces a demand curve that is a horizontal line drawn at the market price. Because this demand curve is horizontal, it represents the

average revenue and the marginal revenue the firm receives at each level of output.

4. In the short run the price-taking firm maximizes profits or minimizes losses by producing that output determined by the intersection of the demand, or marginal revenue, curve with that portion of the marginal cost curve at or above the minimum point on the average variable cost curve. For short, we say that the firm chooses that level of output where marginal cost equals marginal revenue.

5. That portion of the firm's marginal cost curve at or above the average variable cost curve becomes the firm's short-run supply curve. And the horizontal addition of all firms' supply curves becomes the market supply curve.

6. Because new firms are not free to enter the market in the short run, economic profits are possible. In the long run, however, firms will enter or leave the market until economic profits are driven to zero. In the long run each firm will be producing at the low point of its long-run average cost curve. At this level of output the price, marginal cost, and average

cost will all be equal. Firms that fail to produce at this least-cost combination will not survive in the long run.

7. In the short run firms will respond to a change in demand by moving up or down their marginal cost curve. The long-run adjustment to a change in demand involves the entry or exit of firms until the remaining firms in the industry earn just a normal rate of return. As the industry expands in the long run, the industry supply curve reflects either (1) increasing costs, meaning that each firm's costs rise as the industry output expands; (2) constant costs, meaning that firm costs do not change, or (3) decreasing costs, meaning that firm costs fall as the industry output expands.

8. Perfectly competitive markets are said to reflect (1) productive efficiency, because output is produced using the most efficient combination of resources available, and (2) allocative efficiency, because the goods produced are those most valued by consumers. In equilibrium, perfectly competitive markets allocate goods so that the marginal cost of the last unit produced equals the marginal valuation that consumers attach to that last unit consumed.

QUESTIONS AND PROBLEMS

1. (Perfect Competition) Some economists have argued that the U.S. stock market is competitive. Discuss the merits of and flaws in this view. Consider each assumption involved in perfect competition.

2. (Perfect Competition) Do patents and copyrights hinder competition? Should patents be allowed if they do hinder competition? Why or why not?

3. (Perfect Competition) Some people have claimed that there is strong competition in the U.S. auto market. What reasons would you give for denying that this market is perfectly competitive?

4. (Normal versus Economic Profits) Company A is making millions of dollars in accounting profits. Yet the same company has decided to quit producing its current product. How is this possible?

5. (Competition) Consider Exhibit 3 in this chapter. Explain why the total revenue curve is a straight line from the origin, while the total cost curve has a changing slope.

6. (Profit Maximization) Consider Exhibit 3 in this chapter. Why doesn't the firm choose the output that maximizes average profits (i.e., the output where average cost is the lowest)?

7. (Price and Marginal Revenue) Explain why price and marginal revenue are identical in the perfectly competitive model.

8. (Minimizing Losses) Consider Exhibit 5 in this chapter. The company portrayed is not able to cover its fixed costs by selling its product. However, it is able to cover its variable costs. How might the firm avoid default on its fixed obligations in the short run?

9. (Entry and Exit of Firms) Why is it reasonable that in the short-run competitive model, entry and exit of firms is impossible? Is entry into an industry intrinsically more difficult than exit from an industry?

10. (Long-Run Industry Supply) Why is the long-run industry supply curve in an increasing-cost industry upward sloping? What causes the increasing costs in an increasing-cost industry?

MONOPOLY

Monopoly is a Greek word meaning "one seller." Electricity, postage stamps, and meals along the turnpike are some of the goods and services sold by monopolies. You have heard much about the evils of monopoly. You may even have played the Parker Brothers game Monopoly on a rainy day. Now we will sort out fact from fiction. Pure monopoly, like perfect competition, is not as common as other market structures in the real world. Yet your study of the sources of monopoly power and the effects of monopoly on the allocation of resources will help you understand not only this market structure but also market structures that lie between pure monopoly and perfect competition. This chapter will examine pure monopoly in the same way the previous chapter considered perfect competition. Topics and terms discussed include:

- Barriers to entry

- Price elasticity and marginal revenue

- Welfare cost of monopoly

- Price discrimination

BARRIERS TO ENTRY

*A **barrier to en-
try** is an impedi-
ment that prevents
new firms from
competing on an
equal basis with
existing firms in
an industry.*

Perhaps the single most important feature of monopoly is that new firms cannot enter the market in the long run. Let's consider what factors prevent competitors from entering the monopolist's market. Three kinds of **barriers to entry** will be examined here: legal restrictions, economies of scale, and the monopolist's control of an essential resource.

Legal Restrictions

One way to create a barrier to entry is to make it illegal for new firms to enter the market. One such restriction results from exclusive patents awarded to the developers of new products. In the United State *patents* extend the rewards of invention to the patent holder for 17 years. During that time no other firm can produce the good unless authorized by the holder of the patent, so inventors are given a temporary monopoly over the use of their inventions.

Patents and Invention Incentives   The patent laws have remained essentially intact since the original patent act of 1790. These laws have been supported as an incentive for inventors to undertake the time and expense required to develop an invention. Moreover, these laws give firms the stimulus to make the outlays necessary to bring an invention to market. Turning an invention into a marketable product is called *innovation*. This process takes money and time and is carried out in an uncertain economic climate. If other firms could simply copy successful products, there would be less incentive for any one firm to incur the up-front costs of developing new products and bringing them to the market.

Licenses and Other Entry Restrictions   Federal agencies award certain firms a license to broadcast radio and TV signals. States license professional groups such as physicians and barbers. Those without a license cannot practice. More generally, governments often promote monopoly by awarding a single firm the exclusive right to provide certain goods and services. Governments confer monopoly rights to such activities as operating restaurants along the turnpike, selling hot dogs at the civic center, collecting garbage, driving buses and cabs in and out of town, and supplying services ranging from electricity to cable TV. The government itself may claim the right to provide certain products by outlawing competitors. For example, the U.S. Postal Service has the exclusive right to deliver a broad class of mail and many states sell liquor and lottery tickets.

Economies of Scale

Monopoly sometimes emerges when a firm experiences declining average costs over the full range of output that consumers will buy. When this is the case, a single firm can satisfy the market demand at a lower cost per unit than could two or more firms operating at smaller levels of output. Thus, a single firm will emerge from the competitive process as the sole seller in the market. For example, cable TV is an industry that exhibits economies of scale. Once the cable is strung throughout the community—that is, once the fixed cost has been incurred—the marginal cost of hooking up each household is relatively small. Consequently, the average cost per household declines as more and more households are tied into the system. You can see that the costs per household would be greater if two or more competing companies each ran their own wires throughout the community.

   Because such a monopolist would emerge from the natural forces of competition, it is called a *natural monopoly*, as compared with the artificial monopolies created by government patents, licenses, and other official decrees. Once the natural monopoly is operating, a new entrant will be unable to sell enough to experience the economies of scale enjoyed by the established firm; hence, entry will be blocked. In the real world it is often difficult to distinguish between natural monopolies and government-sanctioned monopolies because governments typically regulate natural monopolies. More will be said about the regulation of natural monopolies in a later chapter, when we examine the government regulation of markets.

Control of Essential Resources

Sometimes the source of monopoly power is a firm's control over some resource that is critical to production. Prior to World War II, for example, Alcoa controlled the world's supply of bauxite, the key raw material used in producing aluminum. Control of bauxite made Alcoa a monopolist in aluminum production. The world's diamond trade is operated primarily by the DeBeers Company, which controls the world's diamond mines. Professional sports leagues try to block the formation of competing leagues by signing the best players to long-term contracts and by seeking exclusive use of sports stadiums and arenas. Celebrities have a monopoly over the essential input to their success—themselves. Consequently, the most successful stars carefully control their public appearances to avoid overexposure (this, incidentally, is one reason why the biggest stars seldom appear on TV).

Despite the various barriers to entry, pure monopolies—where one firm sells a good for which there are no close substitutes—are rare because the possibility of economic profits provides other firms with a powerful incentive to produce close substitutes. Now that we have some idea of the source of monopoly power, we will examine the revenue picture the monopolist faces.

REVENUE FOR
THE MONOPOLIST

Because the monopoly firm supplies the entire market, the demand curve confronted by the monopolist is the market demand curve. The demand curve for goods and services produced by a monopolist is the same as any other market demand curve; it is downward sloping, reflecting the inverse relationship between price and quantity demanded.

Demand and Marginal Revenue

Exhibit 1 presents a typical downward-sloping market demand curve that confronts a monopolist. The price the monopolist can charge will clearly depend on how much the monopolist wants to sell; the price and the quantity of the monopolist's output demanded are inversely related. For example, 4 units are demanded at a price of $6; if the price drops to $5.50, quantity demanded increases to 5 units.

When the price is $6 per unit, the monopolist can sell 4 units, for a total revenue of $24. The average revenue per unit when the price is $6 is $6. Recall that average revenue equals the total revenue divided by quantity. When the price is $5.50, the monopolist can sell 5 units, for a total revenue of $27.50, or an average revenue of $5.50. Thus, for the monopolist, the average revenue equals the price, and both can be obtained from the demand curve for any level of output. Therefore, the demand curve is also the monopolist's average revenue curve, just as the perfectly competitive firm's demand curve is also that firm's average revenue curve.

The tricky part is understanding the relationship between price and marginal revenue. Recall that for the perfectly competitive firm, marginal revenue was always equal to the market price because each firm could sell as much as it chose at that price. Consider now the marginal revenue received by the monopolist from selling a fifth unit of the good. When the price drops from $6 to $5.50, total revenue goes from ($6 × 4 =) $24 to ($5.50 × 5 =) $27.50. Thus, marginal revenue, which is the change in total revenue resulting from selling one more unit, is only $3.50. The marginal revenue is therefore less than the price.

A closer look at Exhibit 1 will reveal why the marginal revenue will always be less than the price (except for the first unit sold). By selling one more unit of the good, the monopolist gains $5.50, which is identified by the vertical column marked Gain. But to sell the fifth unit for $5.50, the monopolist must lower the price of the first four units from $6 to $5.50. This results in a loss of ($0.50 × 4 =) $2, which is identified as the rectangular area marked Loss. The net change in total revenue from selling the fifth unit—that is, the marginal revenue from the fifth unit—equals the gain minus the loss, which equals ($5.50 − $2.00 =) $3.50. This analysis assumes that all

EXHIBIT 1   **MONOPOLY DEMAND: LOSS AND GAINS IN TOTAL REVENUE FROM SELLING ONE MORE UNIT**

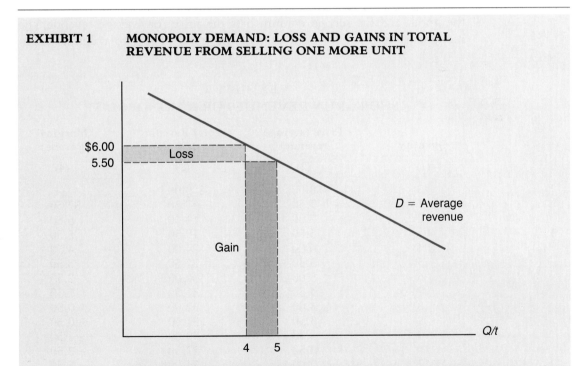

If a monopolist increases production from 4 units to 5, it gains $5.50, the revenue on the fifth unit sold. However, it loses $2 since each of the first 4 units now must be priced at $5.50 rather than $6. Marginal revenue equals Gain − Loss, or $5.50 − $2.00 = $3.50. Hence, marginal revenue is less than the price ($5.50).

units of the good are sold for the same price — that is, when the price is $5.50, all 5 units must be sold for $5.50 each. Although most markets appear to operate this way, later in this chapter we will consider some cases where monopolists may be able to charge different prices for different units of the same good.

To calculate the marginal revenue of selling one more unit of output, we must subtract from the amount received for that additional unit the loss resulting from having to sell all units — not just the marginal unit — at the lower price. When you look at the demand curve, perhaps you can see that when the price is relatively high, the amount gained by selling one more unit exceeds the amount forgone by selling all units at a lower price. At the high end of the demand curve, little revenue is forgone by lowering the price because not many units were sold at the higher price. But as you move down the demand curve two things happen: (1) the gain from selling another unit is less (since the price level is lower), and (2) the revenue forgone by selling all units at this lower price is greater (since the number of units that could have been sold for the higher price is greater). This means that the marginal revenue falls as the price falls, a feature that will become clearer as we continue.

The numbers behind the demand curve in Exhibit 1 are presented in the first two columns of Exhibit 2. The first column lists alternative quantities of the good, and the second column lists the price, or average revenue, the monopolist receives for each unit of the good. The two columns taken

EXHIBIT 2
SHORT-RUN REVENUE FOR A MONOPOLIST

Quantity	Price (average revenue)	Total Revenue (1) × (2)	Marginal Revenue
(1)	(2)	(3)	(4)
0	$8.00	$ 0.00	—
1	7.50	7.50	$7.50
2	7.00	14.00	6.50
3	6.50	19.50	5.50
4	6.00	24.00	4.50
5	5.50	27.50	3.50
6	5.00	30.00	2.50
7	4.50	31.50	1.50
8	4.00	32.00	0.50
9	3.50	31.50	− 0.50
10	3.00	30.00	− 1.50
11	2.50	27.50	− 2.50
12	2.00	24.00	− 3.50
13	1.50	19.50	− 4.50
14	1.00	14.00	− 5.50
15	0.50	7.50	− 6.50
16	0.00	0.00	− 7.50

together present the market demand schedule for the good—that is, the relationship between price and quantity demanded at that price. The monopolist's total revenue, which equals price times quantity, is presented in column (3). The marginal revenue, the net change in total revenue as a result of selling one more unit, is listed in column (4).

Note that for the first unit of output, the marginal revenue and price are equal. For additional units of output, however, marginal revenue is always below the price, and the difference between the two grows larger as the price declines. Marginal revenue becomes negative at a price at or below $3.50. This means that the revenue gained from selling one more unit is less than the revenue lost from selling all previous units at the lower price; therefore, the net change in revenue is negative.

Revenue Curves

The data in Exhibit 2 are depicted in Exhibit 3, with demand and marginal revenue curves in panel (a) and the total revenue curve in panel (b). Of importance are the relationships among the demand, marginal revenue, and total revenue curves. Notice in particular that the marginal revenue curve is below the demand curve, and that the total revenue curve is at a maximum when marginal revenue is 0. Take a minute to study these relations before continuing.

Earlier we learned that if demand is elastic—that is, if the price elasticity of demand is greater than 1—a decrease in the price will increase total revenue. This relationship holds because the percentage increase in quantity demanded will be greater than the percentage decrease in price. On the other hand, an inelastic demand indicates that total revenue will decline if the price falls because the percentage increase in quantity demanded is less than the percentage decrease in price.

We also learned that the elasticity for a straight-line demand curve decreases as we move down the curve. Therefore, when the demand curve is elastic, marginal revenue is positive, and total revenue increases. From Exhibit 2 you can see that marginal revenue becomes negative if the price drops below $4, indicating an inelastic demand at price levels below $4. At the price of $4 marginal revenue is 0, and total revenue is at a maximum. Demand is of unitary elasticity at that point. An understanding of elasticity will be of help later in determining the price and output combination that maximizes the monopolist's profit. We now turn to profit maximization.

FIRM COSTS AND SHORT-RUN PROFIT MAXIMIZATION

Given the demand curve, the important question is how the monopolist will choose among its price-quantity alternatives. We assume at the outset that the objective of the monopolist, like that of the perfect competitor, is to maximize economic profit. In the case of perfect competition the firm needed to choose the profit-maximizing quantity because the price was given to the firm. The monopolist's task is to search for the quantity that will maximize profits (or minimize losses). Given the demand curve, the quantity will then dictate the price at which that output can be sold.

Price and Output if Costs Are Zero

To give you an intuitive feel for the analysis before introducing complicated cost curves, suppose that there are no costs of production (you might imagine, for example, the monopolist as the sole supplier of drinking water on an island, with the water coming from a natural spring). Look again at Exhibit 3, which reflects the revenue data from Exhibit 2, and consider what would be the profit-maximizing price if output is produced at zero cost.

As with the perfectly competitive solution, there are two ways to approach the problem: the first is to search for the quantity where total revenue exceeds total cost by the greatest amount, and the second is to find the quantity where marginal cost equals marginal revenue.

Total Revenue Minus Total Cost   First, let's consider total revenue minus total cost. Since by assumption the total cost is zero at all levels of output, the total cost curve in Exhibit 3(b) is identical to the horizontal axis. Since the total cost is zero, the total revenue curve reflects the firm's profit at each level of output. Thus, profit is maximized where total revenue is maximized. From panel (b) of Exhibit 3 you can see that total revenue is at a maximum where 8 units of output are produced. The price shown by the demand curve in panel (a) is $4 per unit, yielding a total profit of $32.

Marginal Cost Equals Marginal Revenue   Another way to find the profit-maximizing level of output is to use the golden rule of profit maximization, which is to expand output as long as marginal revenue exceeds marginal cost and to stop expanding ouput when marginal revenue equals marginal cost. Since marginal cost is zero, the marginal cost curve is identical to the horizontal axis in Exhibit 3(a). The profit-maximizing output is therefore found where the marginal revenue curve crosses the horizontal axis, which is, not surprisingly, also at 8 units of output. Again, the price charged for this level of output is found on the demand curve to be $4; total profit equals price minus average cost multiplied by the level of output.

Since the average cost is zero, the average profit per unit is $4 and the total profit is $32 ($4 × 8). You can see the logic in the golden rule: the monopolist will lower the price and expand output only as long as the marginal revenue from selling additional units exceeds the marginal cost. Thus, even if the product costs nothing to produce, the monopolist will *never* voluntarily choose an output level where marginal revenue is negative or where demand is inelastic.

Profit Maximization with Only Fixed Cost   Examining the case where total cost is zero is useful, for it shows that the monopolist will never produce in the inelastic range of demand. But, of course, production usually does

EXHIBIT 3   **MONOPOLY DEMAND AND MARGINAL AND TOTAL REVENUE**

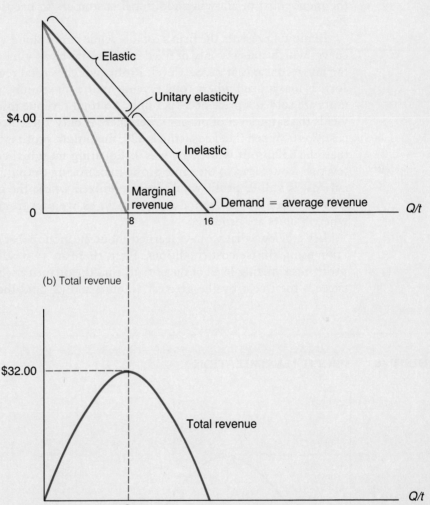

(a) Demand and marginal revenue

(b) Total revenue

If total cost is zero at every level of output, then the total cost curve is identical to the horizontal axis in panel (b). Profit is maximized where total revenue is maximized—at 8 units of output.

When total cost is zero at every level of output, the marginal cost curve is identical to the horizontal axis in panel (a). Profit is maximized where marginal cost equals marginal revenue, or where the marginal revenue curve cuts the horizontal axis, at 8 units of output.

involve a cost. A slightly more involved example would be the case where the only cost of production is a fixed cost. For example, you could think of a satellite communications company whose only cost is placing the satellite in orbit. Once the satellite is operating, the firm can sell the rights to bounce signals off the satellite. Because the variable cost is zero, the marginal cost to the monopolist of allowing additional customers to use the satellite is also zero.

Exhibit 4 presents the firm's total revenue curve along with the total cost curve, which consists only of fixed cost, presented as a line drawn parallel to the horizontal axis at the $20 level. Profit, which is total revenue minus total cost, is maximized where total revenue is at a maximum, which is where 8 units are sold at a price of $4 per unit. So total revenue minus the total cost yields the same level of output when there is only a fixed cost as when total cost was 0. When fixed cost equals $20, maximum profit is $12, which is less than the $32 profit when cost was 0. Equating marginal cost and marginal revenue would lead to the same profit-maximizing output. Since the marginal cost is still 0, profit would be maximized where the marginal revenue curve crosses the horizontal axis, which, as we saw from Exhibit 3(a), is where 8 units are produced.

Let's review what we have learned about the monopolist's profit maximization using simple cost conditions. First, there are two ways to identify the profit-maximizing level of output: (1) find the quantity where total revenue exceeds total cost by the greatest amount and (2) find the quantity where

EXHIBIT 4   PROFIT MAXIMIZATION

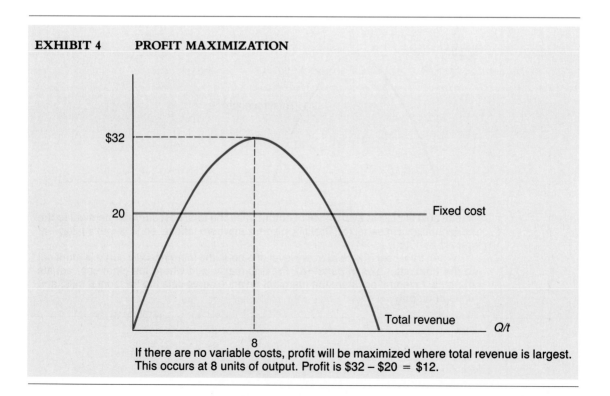

If there are no variable costs, profit will be maximized where total revenue is largest. This occurs at 8 units of output. Profit is $32 − $20 = $12.

marginal cost is equal to marginal revenue. These are the same profit-maximizing rules followed under perfect competition. A second point is that the monopolist will never produce in the range where demand is inelastic, which is another way of saying that the monopolist will never voluntarily produce where the marginal revenue is negative.

Profit Maximization Using Ordinary Cost Curves

What are the profit-maximizing price and output under ordinary cost conditions? Exhibit 5 repeats the revenue data from Exhibit 2 but also includes hypothetical cost data for this firm in columns (5), (6), and (7). In terms of the cost of production, the monopolist looks like any other firm. For example, since total cost equals $8 when output is 0, fixed cost must equal $8. Given the cost and revenue data, you know by now two ways to find the price and quantity that maximize profit.

Total Revenue Minus Total Cost The profit-maximizing monopolist will employ the same decision rule as the competitive firm. The monopolist will produce additional output as long as it adds more to total revenue than to total cost. The monopolist must find the level of output where the total revenue exceeds total cost by the greatest amount. This economic profit is presented in the final column of Exhibit 5. As you can see, profit is maximized at $7, when output equals 7 units and the price equals $4.50. At that level of output total revenue is $31.50, and total cost is $24.50.

Marginal Cost Equals Marginal Revenue The monopolist will maximize profit by expanding output as long as marginal revenue exceeds marginal cost but must stop before marginal cost exceeds marginal revenue. Profit is maximized by producing 7 units; the marginal revenue for unit 7 is $1.50, and the marginal cost is $1.25. (Because we are not allowing the firm to produce fractions of units, this is as close to equality between marginal cost and marginal revenue as we can get, based on our hypothetical cost and revenue data.) Expanding output beyond 7 units would lower profits because additional units add more to cost than they do to revenue. Unit 8, for example, adds $1.50 to cost but only $0.50 to revenue, so if the monopolist produced 8 units, profits would fall from $7 to $6.

Graphical Solution The cost and revenue data in Exhibit 5 are plotted in Exhibit 6, with per-unit cost and revenue curves in panel (a) at the top, and total cost and revenue curves in panel (b) at the bottom. Profits will be maximized where marginal cost equals marginal revenue. The intersection of the two marginal curves at point *e* in panel (a) indicates that profits will be maximized when 7 units are sold. At that level of output we move up to the demand curve to find the profit-maximizing price of $4.50 per unit.

Profit per unit equals the price, or average revenue, minus the average total cost. When output equals 7 units, the price equals $4.50, as identified by point *a*, and the average total cost is $3.50, as identified by point *b*. The average profit per unit sold is therefore $4.50 − $3.50, or $1. Total profit,

EXHIBIT 5

SHORT-RUN COSTS AND REVENUE FOR A MONOPOLIST

Quantity	Price (average revenue)	Total Revenue (1) × (2)	Marginal Revenue	Total Cost	Marginal Cost	Average Total Cost	Total Profit or Loss
(1)	(2)	(3)	(4)	(5)	(6)	(7)	(8)
0	$8.00	$ 0.00	—	$ 8.00	—	—	$ −8.00
1	7.50	7.50	$7.50	13.00	$5.00	$13.00	−5.50
2	7.00	14.00	6.50	16.75	3.75	8.37	−2.75
3	6.50	19.50	5.50	19.25	2.50	6.42	0.25
4	6.00	24.00	4.50	21.00	1.75	5.25	3.00
5	5.50	27.50	3.50	22.25	1.25	4.45	5.25
6	5.00	30.00	2.50	23.25	1.00	3.88	6.75
7	4.50	31.50	1.50	24.50	1.25	3.50	7.00
8	4.00	32.00	0.50	26.00	1.50	3.25	6.00
9	3.50	31.50	−0.50	28.00	2.00	3.11	3.50
10	3.00	30.00	−1.50	30.75	2.75	3.08	−0.75
11	2.50	27.50	−2.50	34.25	3.50	3.11	−6.75
12	2.00	24.00	−3.50	39.00	4.75	3.25	−15.00
13	1.50	19.50	−4.50	45.25	6.25	3.48	−25.75
14	1.00	14.00	−5.50	54.35	9.00	3.88	−40.25
15	0.50	7.50	−6.50	68.25	13.00	4.55	−60.75

EXHIBIT 6   MONOPOLY COSTS AND REVENUE

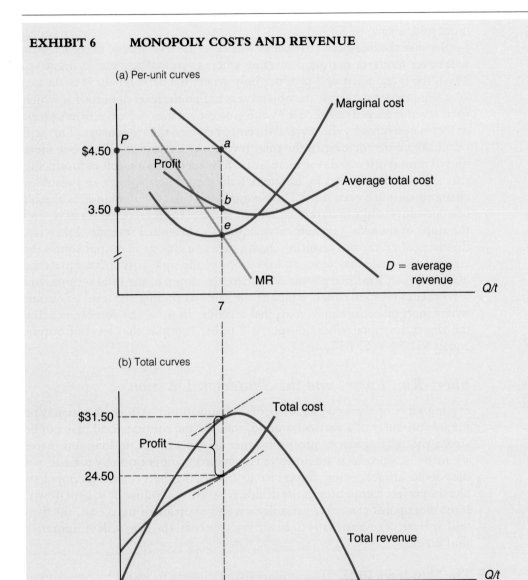

Like other firms, the monopolist maximizes profit where marginal cost equals marginal revenue—point *e* in panel (a). The monopolist produces 7 units of output and charges a price of $4.50, which is read off the demand curve at point *a*. Average profit per unit is price minus average total cost, or $4.50 − $3.50 = $1 per unit. Total profit, the area of rectangle *abcP*, is $7, the profit per unit multiplied by the number of units sold.

In panel (b) profit is maximized where marginal revenue (the slope of the total revenue curve) equals marginal cost (the slope of the marginal cost curve) at 7 units of output. Profit is total revenue ($31.50) minus total cost ($24.50), or $7.

measured by the rectangle *abcP*, is the profit per unit ($1) multiplied by the 7 units sold, a total of $7.

Because the marginal cost curve will never be less than 0, marginal cost will never intersect marginal revenue where marginal revenue is negative. Thus, the monopolist will produce only where the demand curve is elastic.

Using the total curves, the objective is to find the level of output at which total revenue exceeds total cost by the greatest amount since the firm's profit or loss is measured by the vertical distance between the two curves. This will occur where the increase in the total revenue as a result of selling one more unit of output just equals the increase in the total cost as a result of producing that additional unit. But by how much do these totals change as a result of changing output by one unit? The change in the total revenue curve as a result of a one-unit change in output equals the slope of the total revenue curve, and the slope of the total revenue curve equals the marginal revenue. Likewise, the change in total cost resulting from a one-unit change in output equals the slope of the total cost curve, and the slope of the total cost curve equals the marginal cost. Profit is maximized where the slopes of the total revenue and total cost curves are equal, which is the same as finding the level of output where marginal cost equals marginal revenue. In panel (b) you can see that the slopes are equal where output is 7 units. Profit at that level of output equals $31.50 − $24.50, or $7.

Short-Run Losses and the Shutdown Decision

Having a monopoly is no guarantee of economic profit. Although you may be the sole producer of a particular good, the demand for that good may not be strong enough to generate profits in either the short run or the long run. After all, many new products are protected from direct competition by patents, yet they do not attract enough buyers to survive. In the short run the monopolist, like the perfect competitor, must decide whether to produce or to shut down. If the monopolist can cover variable cost and a portion of fixed cost, the firm will operate. If revenue fails to cover variable cost, the firm will temporarily shut down.

The Shutdown Rule   The monopolist minimizes its losses by first setting marginal cost equal to marginal revenue and then checking to see whether the price at that level of output is above or below the average variable cost. If the price is above average variable cost, the firm, by producing that level of output, is able to cover its variable cost and at least a portion of its fixed cost. If the price is below average variable cost, however, the firm will only increase its loss by producing, so it will temporarily shut down. Thus, the shutdown rule for the monopolist, like that of the perfectly competitive firm, states that the firm will not produce unless the price, or average revenue, is equal to or greater than its average variable cost.

Loss minimization is demonstrated graphically in Exhibit 7, where the marginal cost curve intersects the marginal revenue curve at point *e*. At the equilibrium level of output, *Q*, the price, *P*, is above average variable cost, denoted at point *d*, but below average total cost, denoted at point *a*. Since the firm is able to cover its variable cost and make some contribution to fixed cost, it loses less by producing Q than by shutting down. The firm's loss per unit is *ab*, which is the average total cost minus the average revenue, or price. The total loss, identified by the area *abPc*, is the average loss per unit, *ab*, times the number of units sold, Q.

No Monopolist Supply Curve   For the perfectly competitive firm, that portion of the marginal cost curve that is above the average variable cost curve is called the supply curve because it reflects the quantity the firm is willing and able to supply at each price. The monopolist, however, identifies the profit-maximizing (or loss-minimizing) level of output by finding where marginal cost equals marginal revenue. The price at that profit-maximizing (or loss-minimizing) level of output is then found on the demand curve, not on the marginal cost curve. So the marginal cost curve does not show a relationship between price and quantity demanded, as was the case for perfectly competitive firms. Given the monopolist's cost curves, the profit-maximizing level of supply will vary, depending on the demand and marginal revenue curves. So there is no supply curve for the monopolist—no single curve that reflects the amount the monopolist will supply at alternative prices.

EXHIBIT 7   **THE MONOPOLIST MINIMIZES LOSSES IN THE SHORT RUN**

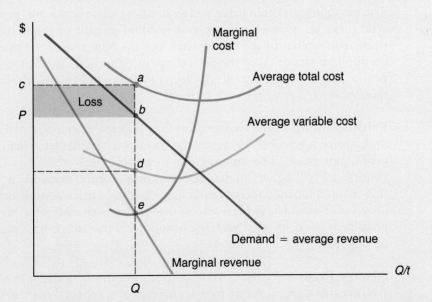

Marginal cost equals marginal revenue at point *e*. At quantity *Q*, price *P* (at point *b*) is less than average total cost *C* (at point *a*), so the monopolist is suffering a loss. The monopolist will continue to produce in the short run because price is greater than average variable cost (at point *d*).

Long-Run Profit Maximization

With perfectly competitive firms, the distinction between the short run and the long run is important. In the short run the number of firms in a competitive industry is fixed, and these firms may earn economic profits or losses, depending on the demand for the product. In the long run all resources can vary, so the firms will enter or leave the industry until each one is earning just a normal profit, which means zero economic profit. In the case of the monopolist, the distinction between the short run and the long run has less significance because new entry is by definition blocked. Hence, there is no tendency for economic profit to be eliminated in the long run by the entry of new firms. Likewise, there is no tendency for economic loss to disappear over time by exit of firms. So economic profit can persist in the long run under monopoly.

In the long run the monopolist, like the perfectly competitive firm, will produce where marginal cost equals marginal revenue. The monopolist's objective in the long run is to find the scale of firm that maximizes profit. Even a monopolist that earns economic profit in the short run may find that profits can be increased in the long run by adjusting the size of the firm. A monopolist that incurs losses in the long run may have to go out of business unless some change in the scale of the firm's operation can be found where price covers average cost.

Myths About Monopolies

The monopolist is often perceived as an obese, cigar-smoking, profit gouger who picks on widows and orphans in blind pursuit of the dollar. Perhaps some monopolists fit the description, but the objective of the monopolist is no different from that of the perfect competitor: both attempt to maximize profit. The following two myths keep cropping up in popular discussions of monopoly; let's examine each of them.

Price Gouging   One common myth is that the monopolist will charge as high a price as possible. However, the monopolist is interested in maximizing profit, not price. The amount the monopolist can charge is limited by consumers' willingness to demand the good. For the demand curve used in this chapter, the monopolist could have charged a price as high as $7.50, but only 1 unit would have been sold at that price, so charging the highest price possible is not consistent with the output level that maximizes profit for the monopolist.

Always Earns a Profit   Another common myth is that the monopolist always earns a profit. As we have seen, if the average total cost curve is above the demand curve, no combination of price and output can yield a profit. The fact that a firm is the only producer of a product does not guarantee that demand will be strong enough to allow the firm to earn even a normal profit. After all, only a tiny fraction of the millions of products that have received U.S. patents have ever earned their inventors a profit.

MONOPOLY AND THE ALLOCATION OF RESOURCES

If monopolists are no more greedy than competitive firms, if monopolists cannot set price wherever they want, and if monopolists are not guaranteed a profit, then why is the public concerned about the ills of monopoly? For reasons that will become obvious, the monopolist does not ensure the same efficient use of resources as does the perfectly competitive firm. The clearest way to understand the problems that arise from monopoly is to compare a monopoly to that benchmark established in the previous chapter, the perfectly competitive industry.

Price and Output Under Perfect Competition

Let's consider first the long-run equilibrium price and output for the perfectly competitive firm and industry. Assume we are looking at a constant-cost industry, so the long-run industry supply curve is a horizontal line. The long-run supply curve for the perfectly competitive industry is identified as line *PS* in Exhibit 8. There are many competitive firms, each with cost curves *ATC* and *MC*. Each firm produces *q*, resulting in an industry output of *Q*. The perfectly competitive industry is in long-run equilibrium at point *e*, with quantity *Q* and price *P*. At this combination of price and output all firms in the industry are in long-run equilibrium and thus earning a normal profit.

At the equilibrium combination of price and output the marginal cost to society of producing the final unit of output is just equal to the marginal benefit consumers attach to that unit of the good. Because consumers are able to purchase *Q* units at price *P*, they enjoy a consumer surplus that is measured by the triangle *aeP*. You will recall that consumer surplus represents the dollar value of the net benefits consumers enjoy from purchasing all units of the good at the market price of *P*.

Price and Output Under Monopoly

If there is only one firm in the industry, and if that firm could produce with constant returns to scale in the long run, then the monopoly firm, though much larger than the competitive firm, can produce output for the same minimum average cost. The monopoly will maximize profit in the long run by choosing a firm size depicted by the cost curves *ATC'* and *MC'*. Why? Because the industry demand curve becomes the monopolist's demand curve, and the price the monopolist can charge will depend on how much is sold. As a consequence, the monopolist will choose to produce output *Q'* at a price of *P'*, where marginal cost equals marginal revenue at point *b*.

At the price-quantity combination depicted by point *c*, the marginal cost of the resources used to produce the final unit of output is less than the marginal benefit consumers attach to that unit. Recall that the demand curve indicates consumers' marginal benefit from each level of output. In Exhibit 8 the price, or marginal benefit, which is at point *c*, exceeds the marginal cost, which is at point *b*. Thus, the value consumers place on an extra unit exceeds

EXHIBIT 8   **PERFECT COMPETITION AND MONOPOLY**

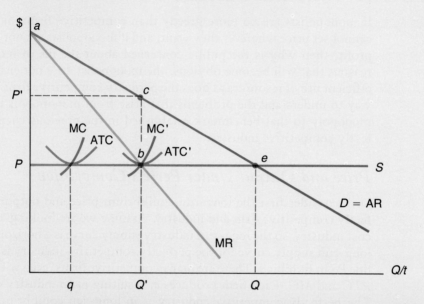

A perfectly competitive industry would produce output *Q*, determined at the intersection of market demand curve *D* and supply curve *S*. The price would be *P*.

A monopoly that could produce output at the same minimum average cost would produce output *Q'*, determined at point *b*, where marginal cost and marginal revenue intersect. It would charge price *P'*. Hence, output is lower and price is higher under monopoly than under perfect competition.

the cost of producing it. Society would be better off if output were expanded beyond *Q'* because the marginal value consumers attach to additional units exceeds the marginal cost of producing those additional units. In the next section we will examine more specifically the inefficiency arising from monopoly.

Allocative and Distributive Effects

Let's consider now the allocative and distributive effects of monopoly versus perfect competition. Output is lower and price higher under monopoly than under perfect competition. The monopolist's reduced output and higher price generates economic profit equal to the rectangle *cbPP'*. By contrasting the monopoly solution with the perfectly competitive solution, we see that monopoly profit comes entirely out of consumer surplus, which has been reduced under monopoly from the triangle *aeP* to the triangle *acP'*.

Notice, however, that consumer surplus has been reduced by more than the gain in monopoly profit. Consumers have lost more than *cbPP'*; they have also lost the triangle *ceb* as well, which had been part of the consumer surplus under perfect competition. Whereas monopoly profit represents a transfer from consumers to the monopolist, the triangle *ceb* is called the **deadweight**

*The **deadweight loss** of monopoly is the loss of consumer surplus (that goes to no one) following monopolization of an industry.*

loss, or *welfare loss*, of monopoly because it is a loss to consumers but a gain to no one. Thus, if the monopolist can produce output at the same minimum average cost as the competitive firm, the triangle *ceb* measures the welfare loss arising from the higher price and reduced output of the monopolist.

PROBLEMS WITH ESTIMATING THE WELFARE COST OF MONOPOLY

Forces at work in the economy could make the actual cost of monopoly less than or greater than the welfare loss described in the previous section. We will first consider reasons why monopoly might create less of a welfare loss and then examine why the welfare loss might be even greater than measured in Exhibit 8.

Why the Welfare Loss of Monopoly Might Be Lower

The welfare loss of monopoly may not be as great in the real world as presented here for two reasons.

Fear of Potential Rivals First, the monopolist may keep the price below what would be the profit-maximizing level because high profits are a powerful economic signal to potential rivals. If the monopolist does not have ironclad protection against the possibility of new firms entering the industry, then the monopolist may try to reduce the chances of attracting new competitors. For example, we mentioned earlier that before World War II Alcoa was the only manufacturer of aluminum in the United States. Some observers of the company claim that it kept prices low enough to discourage potential rivals.

Fear of Public Intervention A second reason why the welfare loss estimated above could overstate the true cost of monopoly is that monopolists may, in response to public scrutiny and political pressure, keep prices below what the market would bear. We are not talking here about monopolies that are regulated by government—they will be examined in a later chapter. We are talking about monopolies that curb their profit to avoid public scrutiny and criticism.

Although monopolists would like to earn as great a profit as possible, even "obscene" profits, whatever those are, the monopolist realizes that if the public outcry over high profit grows loud enough, some sort of government intervention might reduce profits. Because of the increase in oil prices during the middle and late 1970s, Congress increased the taxes on oil companies to capture as taxes part of the higher resulting profits. The "windfall" profits tax on oil producers is the type of government reaction to profits that firms want to avoid.

Why the Welfare Loss of Monopoly Might Be Higher

Other reasons, however, suggest that the welfare loss of monopoly may, in fact, be greater than estimated in our simple diagram.

Monopolists Grow Fat and Lazy   The first reason is that the monopolist, insulated from the rigors of competition in the marketplace, may grow fat and lazy—may become inefficient. Consequently, the assumption that the firm produces output using the least-cost combination of resources may not be realistic. Since some monopolies will still earn economic profit even if output is not produced at the least possible cost, corporate executives may employ resources in a way that creates a more comfortable life for themselves. Long lunches, afternoon golf, Oriental carpets, and cordial employee relations may make company life more enjoyable. But these additional expenses also raise the cost of production above what it would be if the firm had used the least-cost combination of resources.

Monopolists have also been criticized for being slow to adopt the latest production techniques, reluctant to develop new products, and generally lacking in innovation. Because monopolists escape the rigors of competition, they may be content to rest on their oars. As the British economist J. R. Hicks remarked, "The best of all monopoly profits is a quiet life."

Not all economists agree with the idea that monopolists will manage their resources with any less vigilance than those running perfectly competitive firms, however. If a firm is eroding its monopoly profits through bloated payrolls, company perks, and the failure to be innovative, actual profits will be below their potential. With reduced profits, the value of the firm's stock will be lower than it could be if the firm were more efficient. Lower stock prices provide a strong incentive for outsiders to buy a controlling share of the firm's stock, shape up the operation, and watch profits as well as the value of the firm's stock grow. Some economists argue that this market for corporate control ensures that even monopolistic firms will not stray too far from the path of efficient production.

Monopolists Expend Resources Trying to Secure and Maintain Monopoly Power   Another reason why monopolies may involve more of a welfare loss than simple models suggest is that resources must often be devoted to securing and maintaining a monopoly position. For example, radio and TV broadcasting rights are valuable because they confer on the recipient the exclusive privilege of using a particular band of the scarce broadcast spectrum. These rights are given away by government agencies to applicants who are deemed most deserving. Because these rights are so valuable, applicants expend abundant resources on lawyers' fees, lobbying expenses, and other costs associated with making the most deserving case.

*Activities undertaken by individuals or firms to redistribute income to them are called **rent seeking**.*

These costs multiply because many applicants typically seek the same broadcast right. The costs devoted to securing and maintaining a monopoly position are largely a social waste because they use up scarce resources but add not one unit to output. Activities undertaken by individuals or firms to influence public policy in a way that will directly or indirectly redistribute income to them are called **rent seeking**.

MODELS OF PRICE DISCRIMINATION

The model of monopoly examined thus far is based on the implicit assumption that the monopolist charges all consumers the same price. Some interesting insights emerge when we admit that monopolists may charge different consumers different prices. Under certain conditions the monopolist can increase profits by practicing what is called **price discrimination**, which is the practice of selling output at different prices to different groups of consumers or charging the same consumer different prices for different units of the good. The idea is to charge a higher price to those consumers whose demand is less elastic than to those whose demand is more elastic.

Price discrimination is selling at different prices to different consumers or charging the same consumer different prices for different units of a good.

Preconditions for Price Discrimination

Before a firm can price discriminate, demand must satisfy certain conditions. First, the producer must face a downward-sloping demand curve for its product. This condition holds for the monopolist, and, as we will see in the next chapter, for some other market types as well. Only perfectly competitive firms fail to satisfy this condition. Second, there must be at least two readily identifiable classes of consumers whose price elasticities of demand differ. Third, the producer must be able, at little cost, to distinguish between the different classes of consumers. Finally, the monopolist must be able to prevent those buyers who face a lower price from reselling the product to buyers who face a higher price.

Examples of Price Discrimination

Let's consider some examples of price discrimination. Because businesses have a less elastic demand for travel and communication than do households, airlines and telephone utilities try to maximize profits by charging the two classes of customers different rates. Because the costs of travel and communication are paid by the company and are tax deductible, businesspeople tend to be less sensitive to differences in price than households. But how do firms discriminate between households and businesses?

Telephone companies have been able to sort out their customers by charging different rates based on the time of day. Long-distance charges are higher during normal *business* hours than during evenings and on weekends, when households, which presumably have a lower price elasticity of demand, make social calls. The airlines try to distinguish between their business customers and household customers based on the terms under which tickets are purchased. Consumers plan their vacations well in advance and stay for a week or more. They have more flexibility about when and where to travel and are more sensitive to price than business travelers. Business travel, on the other hand, is often more urgent and more spontaneous and seldom involves a weekend stay. The airlines separate business travelers from vacationers by requiring customers who benefit from "super-saver" fares to purchase tickets well in advance and to spend a weekend at their destination.

Many businesses, such as movies, golf courses, and sports teams, offer reduced prices to students and senior citizens because these groups presumably are more sensitive to price—that is, they have a more elastic demand. Some firms can discriminate among consumers based on the amount of the purchase. For example, industrial users of electricity usually pay lower rates than households.

A Model of Price Discrimination

Exhibit 9 shows the effects of price discrimination. Consumers are divided into two groups with identifiable differences in demand. Their demand and marginal revenue curves are presented, along with the producer's marginal cost curve. For simplicity, we assume that the monopolist produces at a constant marginal cost and that these costs are the same for supplying both groups. The consumers in panel (a) generally attach a higher marginal value to each unit of the good than do those in panel (b).

In each market the price is determined by finding the level of output that equates marginal cost and marginal revenue. The monopolist charges the two groups of consumers different prices—a higher price, P, for consumers in panel (a) and a lower price, P', for consumers in panel (b). The total output is Q plus Q'. Although it is difficult to see from the diagrams, the elasticities of demand at the prices charged by the monopolist differ between the two

EXHIBIT 9   **PRICE DISCRIMINATION WITH TWO GROUPS OF CONSUMERS**

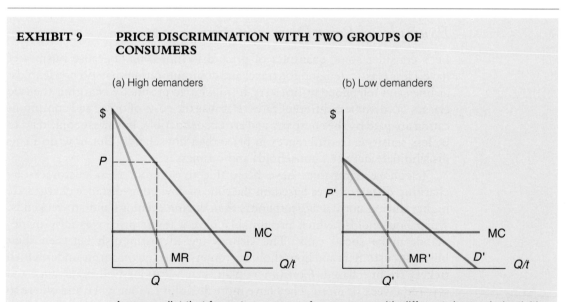

A monopolist that faces two groups of consumers with different demand elasticities may be able to practice price discrimination. With marginal cost the same in both markets, the firm sells Q units to the high-marginal-value consumers in panel (a) and charges them a price of P. It sells Q' units to the low-marginal-value consumers in panel (b) and charges them a price of P'.

groups. The price elasticity of consumers in panel (b) is greater than that of consumers in panel (a), so consumers in panel (a) are charged the higher price.

Perfect Price Discrimination: The Monopolist's Dream

The demand curve conveys the value consumers attach to each unit consumed. We know that consumers typically receive a consumer surplus when they are able to purchase all units of the good for a price equal to the marginal value of the last unit consumed. If the monopolist could charge a separate price for each unit consumed—a price equal to consumers' marginal value of each unit consumed—then the demand curve would become the firm's marginal revenue curve. The firm's marginal revenue from selling one more unit would equal the price of that unit. The discriminating monopolist would determine the profit-maximizing level of output by setting marginal cost equal to marginal revenue, as at point *e* in Exhibit 10. The firm's economic profit would be defined by the area *aecb*.

By charging a different price for each unit of output, the monopolist is able to convert every last dollar of consumer surplus into economic profit. Incidentally, while this outcome may appear unfair based on distributional grounds, it gets high marks based on allocative efficiency. The marginal cost of producing the last unit of output just equals the marginal benefit consumers attach to that unit. There is no way you could adjust the level of

EXHIBIT 10   PERFECT PRICE DISCRIMINATION

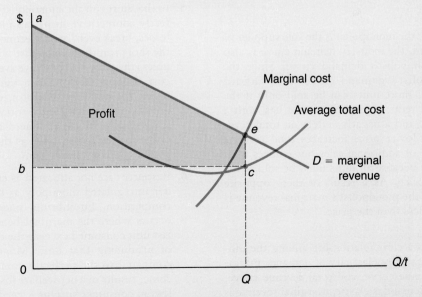

If a monopolist can charge a different price for each unit sold, it may be able to practice perfect price discrimination. By setting the price of each unit equal to the maximum amount consumers are willing to pay for that unit (shown by the height of the demand curve), the monopolist's profit equals the area *aecb*. Consumer surplus is zero.

output to make someone better off without harming someone else. And while consumers will no doubt miss the consumer surplus, the total benefits they receive from consuming the good just equal the total price they pay for the good.

Pure monopoly, like perfect competition, is seldom observed in the real world. Few firms earn economic profits over the long run by producing a product for which there are no close substitutes. Economic profit, as we have seen, provide a powerful signal for other firms to enter the market. Potential rivals will try to hurdle any barriers to entry. But even if pure monopoly is rare in the long run, our examination of pure monopoly and perfect competition has developed a framework that will be helpful for viewing market structures that lie between the two extremes. While pure monopoly may be rare, it is common for firms to have some amount of monopoly power—that is, to face a downward-sloping demand curve. In the next chapter we will consider two market structures in which firms have some monopoly power.

SUMMARY

1. Under pure monopoly there is one seller of a product with no close substitutes. Monopoly can persist in the long run only if the entry of new firms is somehow prevented. Three barriers to entry are (1) legal restrictions, such as patents and operating licenses, (2) economies of scale, which make it inefficient to have more than one firm produce the good; and (3) control over an essential resource used in producing the good.

2. Because the monopolist is the sole supplier of the good, the industry demand curve is also the monopolist's demand curve. Since the monopolist's demand curve is downward sloping, more units can be sold only if the price is reduced. A lower price has both a positive and a negative effect on total revenue. A lower price increases total revenue because of additional sales but reduces total revenue because all units must be sold at the lower price. As a result of these opposite effects, the monopolist's marginal revenue is always less than the price.

3. There is a clear relationship among the monopolist's price elasticity of demand, marginal revenue curve, and total revenue curve. When demand is elastic, marginal revenue is positive, and total revenue increases as output increases. When demand is inelastic, marginal revenue is negative, and total revenue decreases.

4. The monopolist maximizes profits or minimizes losses by searching for the price that equates marginal cost with marginal revenue. Because marginal cost is never less than zero, the monopolist never willingly produces where marginal revenue is negative. Put another way, the monopolist never produces where demand is inelastic, or where total revenue is declining.

5. In the short run the monopolist, like the perfectly competitive firm, can incur economic losses, break even, or earn economic profit. In the short run the monopolist will shut down unless the price is at or above average variable cost. But in the long run the monopolist, unlike the perfect competitor, can earn economic profits as long as the entry of new firms is somehow blocked. There is no supply curve for the monopolist, as there is for the perfectly competitive firm.

6. Resources are not allocated as efficiently under unregulated monopoly as under perfect competition. Equilibrium under monopoly occurs where the marginal benefit from the last unit consumed exceeds the marginal cost of producing that unit. Monopoly, when compared to the perfectly competitive outcome, results in a net welfare loss because the loss in consumer surplus exceeds the gain in monopoly profits. Thus, we say there is a deadweight loss of monopoly. Social welfare could be increased by forcing the monopolist to expand output to the point at which margi-

nal cost equals marginal benefit. Marginal benefit is measured along the demand curve.

7. A monopolist who is able to charge different types of consumers different prices for the same good or to charge the same consumer different prices for different units of the good can increase profits. To profitably price dis-

criminate the monopolist (1) must have at least two identifiable types of consumers with differing elasticities of demand, (2) must be able to charge different types of consumers different prices, and (3) must be able to prevent those consumers who pay the higher price from reselling to those who pay the lower price.

QUESTIONS AND PROBLEMS

1. (Barriers to Entry) What are some barriers to entry in the professional sports industry? For example, why aren't there more professional baseball teams?

2. (Barriers to Entry) In South Korea ginseng and tobacco distribution are state-owned monopolies. What might motivate a government to impose such barriers to entry?

3. (Monopoly) Are such wonders of the world as the Grand Canyon and the Great Wall of China monopolies because they are one of a kind? Are there substitutes for such places?

4. (Revenue Maximization) Suppose a UFO crashes in your backyard. Ignoring any costs that may be involved, what price would you charge people to come and view the site? Would you allow photographs? Why or why not?

5. (Monopoly) Only one airline company makes flights to and from some of the South Seas islands. Would this company qualify as a monopoly? How would such a company price its flights to the islands to maximize profits?

Would it price its cargo and mail at the same rate per pound? Why or why not?

6. (Demand and Marginal Revenue) Suppose that at a price of $3 per unit, the quantity demanded is 10 units. Explain why, when marginal revenue is equal to $3, quantity must be (roughly) equal to 5 units.

7. (Monopoly) Why is it impossible for a profit-maximizing monopolist to choose any price *and* any quantity it wishes?

8. (Monopoly and Welfare) Why is society worse off under monopoly than under perfect competition?

9. (Price Discrimination) Explain how it may be profitable for Koreans to sell newly produced autos at a cheaper price in the United States than in Korea, even including transportation costs.

10. (Perfect Price Discrimination) Why is the demand curve above marginal cost equal to the marginal revenue curve for the perfectly discriminating monopolist?

BETWEEN PERFECT COMPETITION *and* MONOPOLY

Perfect competition and monopoly represent the two extremes of market structure. Perfect competition is characterized by a homogeneous commodity produced by a large number of sellers that in the long run enter and leave the industry with ease. Monopoly involves only one seller of a product with no close substitutes; competitors are blocked from entering this market by natural or artificial barriers to entry. These polar market structures are logically appealing and are useful in describing the workings of some markets observed in the economy.

These models have limitations, however. A major shortcoming is that many markets are not well described by either model. Some markets involve many sellers producing goods that vary slightly across producers, such as the many radio stations that vie for your attention or convenience stores that blanket metropolitan areas. Other markets consist of a small number of sellers who in some cases produce identical goods, such as oil and steel, and in other cases produce differentiated goods, such as automobiles and breakfast cereal. In this chapter two additional models will be introduced to explain market structures that conform with neither perfect competition nor monopoly. Topics and terms discussed include:

- Monopolistic competition

- Differentiated product

- Excess capacity

- Oligopoly

- Competing models of oligopoly

MONOPOLISTIC COMPETITION

Economists during the 1920s and 1930s became dissatisfied with the limitations of perfect competition and monopoly as analytical tools. The problem was that many industries seemed to fit neither model. Because necessity is the

*Monopolistic
competition is
the market struc-
ture characterized
by a large number
of firms selling
products that are
close substitutes.*

mother of invention, economists in this country and abroad began developing models to fit between the two extremes. The fruits of this research were two separately developed models of **monopolistic competition**. At Harvard University Edward Chamberlin published *The Theory of Monopolistic Competition* in 1933. Across the Atlantic that same year, Cambridge University's Joan Robinson published *The Economics of Imperfect Competition*. Although the theories differed in some respects, their underlying principles were similar. In this section we will discuss Chamberlin's approach.

Characteristics of Monopolistic Competition

The expression *monopolistic competition* seems self-contradictory because monopoly and perfect competition have been described as opposites. But the expression is meant to suggest that the market contains elements of both competition and monopoly. Chamberlin used the term *monopolistic competition* to describe the structure of a market characterized by a large number of producers offering products that are not viewed as identical by consumers but are considered close substitutes. For example, the burgers sold by McDonald's, Burger King, Wendy's, and Roy Rogers can be distinguished from one another, but they are close enough substitutes that doubling the price of one brand will cause many consumers to switch to other brands.

There are not as many sellers under monopolistic competition as under perfect competition—rather than hundreds of sellers there may be only 25 or 50. There are enough sellers, however, so they behave very competitively. Also, there are enough sellers so that each firm's share of the market is too small to have much individual effect on the market price. Finally, there are enough sellers so that each firm feels lost in the crowd—that is, each firm feels so insignificant relative to the market that its price and output policies will be largely ignored by other firms. Hence, an individual firm can act independently; it need not be concerned about how competitors will react to any change in its price or output. You will understand the significance of this independent behavior later in the chapter.

Product Differentiation

Under monopolistic competition products differ somewhat across producers. At least, there is more variation than under perfect competition, where the product is viewed as homogeneous across producers. Sellers can differentiate their products in four basic ways.

Location The number and variety of locations where the product is available represents one dimension of the product's characteristic. Some products seem to be available everywhere, while others require some search and travel to locate. If you live in a metropolitan area, you may be surprised by the large number of convenience stores that seem to be all around you. Each wants to be closest to you when you need that half gallon of milk—hence, a proliferation of stores. These mini grocery stores are selling conve-

Joan Robinson
(1903–1983)

Peter Lofts Photography

In the history of economics, as in the history of most other sciences, a "multiple discovery" sometimes occurs: two or more people, working independently, publish a new and important idea at nearly the same time. What makes these episodes especially intriguing is that, when we look more closely at the discoveries and the discoverers, we usually find as much difference as similarity.

A good case in point is the invention of "monopolistic competition" in the early 1930s by Edward H. Chamberlin and Joan Robinson. Both writers set forth the analytics of a market in which there were many firms (each too small to affect the behavior of other firms) but in which each firm nonetheless retained some of the characteristics of a monopolist. There the similarity ends. Chamberlin began with the idea of product differentiation and deduced from this the result that firms must produce at higher-than-minimum average cost. Robinson started with the idea that firms produce where costs are still declining and then tacked on the idea that such firms must also face downward-sloping demand curves. Chamberlin viewed a "monopolistically competitive" market as a good thing, arguing that the diversity offered by such a market more than made up for any higher-than-minimum costs. Robinson saw the same market structure as unequivocally bad, arguing that the proliferation of monopolistic competitors amounted to social waste.

Most modern-day economists consider Chamberlin's version of the theory to be the more interesting and well developed of the two. But from a larger perspective, it is clear that Joan Robinson was the more interesting and important economist. In fact, it is a bit ironic that her name is linked so closely to the idea of monopolistic competition, for this piece of work is but a small part of her lifelong contribution. Many equally important contributions came in the theory of economic growth and distribution. Robinson was an early and enthusiastic supporter of Keyensian ideas. She saw in Keynes a clear message that the economic system cannot be trusted to work properly without interference, and she went on to help develop a school of thought that is now called "post-Keynesian" economics.

Joan Robinson was born in Camberley, Surrey, England. She spent her entire academic career at Cambridge University, progressing from student to Lecturer to Reader to Professor. Although her "heretical" views (as she herself called them) may have prevented her from receiving the Nobel Prize, she is widely seen as one of the foremost economists of her age.

Richard Langlois

nience. Their prices are higher and their selection more limited than regular grocery stores, but they are often nearer and stay open later.

Services A second way producers differentiate their product is by the extent of the services that accompany the product. Consider the personal computer. Some retail stores offer elaborate demonstrations by a well-trained sales staff, and the computer comes with an extensive warranty. Other stores are essentially self-service. The computers in these "no-frills" discount houses are stacked in crates and are sold with little more than a smile.

Quality Differentials The most obvious way products are differentiated is by their physical qualities. The ways that products can differ are seemingly endless—size, weight, taste, texture, and so on. For example, shampoo differs in color, scent, thickness, and lathering ability.

Product Image A final way products differ is in the image the producer suggests to the consumer. Whether or not the perception is based on real differences among products does not matter. For example, a clothing manufacturer may try to convince you that its jeans are special because some celebrity's name is on the back pocket. Some brands of facial cream sell for $35 a jar, but they contain virtually the same ingredients as other brands selling for less than one-tenth that price. Particular products may suggest high quality by the way they are promoted, the form of packaging, or the kinds of stores in which they are sold. Producers try to find a particular niche in the consumer's mind through product promotion and advertising.

Price and Output Under Monopolistic Competition

Monopolistic competition is a market structure with many firms selling products that are close, but not perfect, substitutes. Because the monopolistic competitor produces a product that is somewhat differentiated from those produced by others, the demand curve for its product is downward sloping.

The demand curve faced by a firm in monopolistic competition is highly, though not perfectly, elastic. Since many firms are producing goods that are close substitutes, any firm that raises its price can expect to lose some customers to rivals. In contrast, a firm in perfect competition can expect to lose all its customers if it raises its price since it is producing a product that is identical to those of its competitors. At the other extreme, the monopolist's demand curve is less elastic than a monopolistic competitor's because, by definition, the monopolist faces no competition for its output.

The degree of elasticity of the monopolistically competitive firm's demand curve depends on the number of rival firms that produce a similar product and the firm's ability to differentiate its product from those of its rivals. The firm's demand curve will be more elastic the greater the number of competing firms and the less differentiated the firm's product. We now examine the price and output behavior of firms in monopolistic competition.

Marginal Cost Equals Marginal Revenue   As we said, because the firm is selling a product that is somewhat different from those sold by competitors, its demand curve is downward-sloping, as shown in Exhibit 1. From our analysis of monopoly, we know that a downward-sloping demand curve means that the firm's marginal revenue curve is also downward sloping and that it lies below the demand curve. The profit-maximizing level of output is determined by the intersection of the marginal cost and marginal revenue curves, and the profit-maximizing price is found on the demand curve at that level of output. The two panels in Exhibit 1 identify the price and output combinations that maximize short-run profits, as in panel (a), or minimize short-run losses, as in panel (b). The intersection of marginal cost and marginal revenue is identified as e, the level of output is Q, the price is P, and the average total cost is measured on the vertical axis as c.

Maximizing Profits or Minimizing Losses in the Short Run   You will recall that the short run is a period that is too short to allow firms to enter and leave the market. Thus, firms in monopolistically competitive markets can earn economic profits in the short run. The demand and cost conditions depicted in Exhibit 1(a) indicate that this firm will earn a profit in the short run. At the firm's profit-maximizing level of output, the firm's average total cost is below the price. As noted earlier, the difference between the two is the firm's profit per unit, and profit per unit multiplied by the number of units

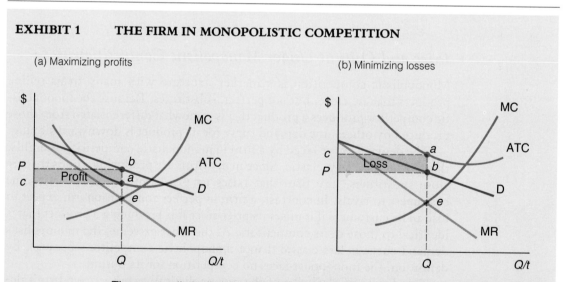

EXHIBIT 1   THE FIRM IN MONOPOLISTIC COMPETITION

(a) Maximizing profits

(b) Minimizing losses

The monopolistically competitive firm produces the level of output determined where marginal cost equals marginal revenue (point e) and charges a price read off the downward-sloping demand curve (at point b).

In panel (a) the firm produces Q units, sells them at price P, and earns a short-run profit equal to (P − c) multiplied by Q. In panel (b) average total cost exceeds price at the optimal level of output. Thus, the firm suffers a short-run loss equal to (c − P) multiplied by Q.

sold yields the total profit, as shown by the shaded rectangle in panel (a). The firm can earn a profit in the short run, but, as we will see, in the long run the lure of economic profit will attract new entrants into the industry until this profit is eliminated.

The monopolistically competitive firm, like other firms, has no guarantee of profit in the short run. The firm's demand and cost curves could be as depicted in Exhibit 1(b), where the firm's average total cost curve lies above the demand curve, so no level of output would allow the firm to break even. In such a situation the firm must decide whether to produce or to shut down temporarily. The decision rule here is the same as with perfect competition and monopoly: as long as the price is above average variable cost (not shown in Exhibit 1), the firm should produce and thereby cover at least a portion of its fixed cost. If price fails to cover average variable cost, the firm should shut down, at least temporarily. Recall that halting production may be only temporary; shutting down is not necessarily the same as going out of business. Firms that expect losses to persist will leave the industry but will still incur short-run losses.

Zero Economic Profit in the Long Run

In the long run the monopolistically competitive firm is in the same profit situation as the perfectly competitive firm. Because there are no barriers to entry, economic profit will attract new entrants into the industry. Because new entrants offer a product that is very similar to that offered by existing firms, new entrants draw many of their customers from existing firms, thereby reducing the demand facing each firm. Eventually, all firms reach the point where no economic profit is earned; there is then no incentive for further entry. Thus, monopolistically competitive firms will in the long run earn no economic profits.

If the firm incurs short-run losses, as in Exhibit 1(b), some firms will leave the industry in the long run, redirecting their resources to activities that are expected to earn at least a normal profit. As firms leave the industry, their customers will shift to the remaining firms, increasing the demand for each firm's product. Firms continue to leave until the remaining firms have enough customers to earn a normal profit, meaning no economic profit.

Exhibit 2 shows the long-run equilibrium for a typical monopolistically competitive firm. In the long run entry and exit will ensure that the typical firm earns just a normal profit. In the long run the monopolistically competitive firm, like the perfectly competitive firm and the monopolist, maximizes profit by equating marginal cost with marginal revenue. In panel (a) of Exhibit 2 marginal cost equals marginal revenue at the level of output where the firm's average total cost curve is tangent to the firm's demand curve. Since the average cost equals the price, the firm earns no economic profit.

We observe the same outcome in a different way in panel (b). In the long run the entry of new firms attracted by economic profit will reduce the demand faced by existing firms. The total revenue curve for each firm will rotate downward until it is tangent to the total cost curve, as shown by point *c* in panel (b). How can we be sure of such a tangency in the long run? If the

EXHIBIT 2   **LONG-RUN EQUILIBRIUM IN MONOPOLISTIC COMPETITION**

(a) Per-unit cost and revenue

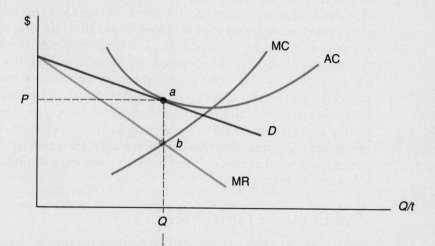

(b) Total cost and total revenue

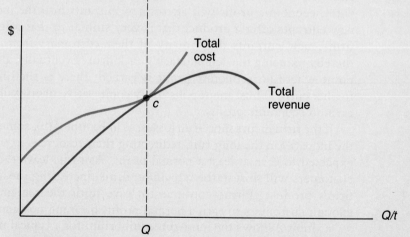

If existing firms are earning positive economic profits, new firms will enter the industry. The entry of such firms reduces the demand facing each firm. In panel (a) demand has been reduced far enough so that at output Q the demand curve is tangent to the average cost curve (point a), and marginal revenue equals marginal cost (point c). In panel (b) total cost equals total revenue at point c. Profit is zero at output Q. With zero profit, no new firms enter, so the industry is in long-run equilibrium.

total cost curve was everywhere above the total revenue curve, economic losses would result. We know, however, that firms will not endure losses in the long run because resource owners have better alternatives. If the total cost and total revenue curves touched at more than one point, this would imply that there is a range of output where total revenue exceeds total cost. Such economic profit, however, would attract new firms in the long run until economic profit falls to zero. Thus, the total cost and total revenue curves in the long run must be tangent at the equilibrium level of output.

Why is the average cost curve in Exhibit 2 (a) tangent to the demand curve at exactly the same level of output where marginal cost equals marginal revenue? The explanation lies with the total cost and total revenue curves as shown in panel (b). We have already established that in the long run the total cost and total revenue curves are tangent. Recall that the slope of the total cost curve equals the firm's marginal cost, and the slope of the total revenue curve equals the firm's marginal revenue. At the level of output where the total cost and total revenue curves are tangent, then it must also be true that the marginal cost equals the marginal revenue, as is shown in panel (a) by the intersection at point *b*.

What about the equality between price and average cost? The price equals the total revenue divided by the level of output, and the average cost equals the total cost divided by the level of output. Since total cost equals total revenue at output level Q, these totals divided by Q must also be equal. So at output level Q, price equals average cost. Therefore, it is no coincidence that price equals average cost at the same level of output where marginal revenue equals marginal cost.

Thus, if entry is easy and if all firms are selling goods that are close, though not perfect, substitutes, then economic profit will draw new entrants into the industry until that profit disappears. Economic losses will cause some firms to leave the industry in the long run until remaining firms earn just a normal profit.

Comparing Perfect Competition and Monopolistic Competition

How does monopolistic competition compare with perfect competition in terms of efficiency? In the long run firms are unable to earn economic profit in either situation, so what is the difference? The difference lies in the shape of the demand curve facing firms in each of the two market structures. Recall that the demand curve for the perfectly competitive firm is horizontal, or perfectly elastic, but the firm in a monopolistically competitive market faces a downward-sloping demand curve.

Exhibit 3 presents the long-run equilibrium price and quantity for firms in each of the two market structures. In each case the average cost curve is tangent to the demand curve faced by the firm, but because the firm in panel (a) is in a perfectly competitive industry, it faces a horizontal, or perfectly elastic, demand curve. Since the good produced by a perfectly competitive firm is exactly like those produced by other firms in the industry, no firm can

EXHIBIT 3   **MONOPOLISTIC COMPETITION VERSUS PERFECT COMPETITION**

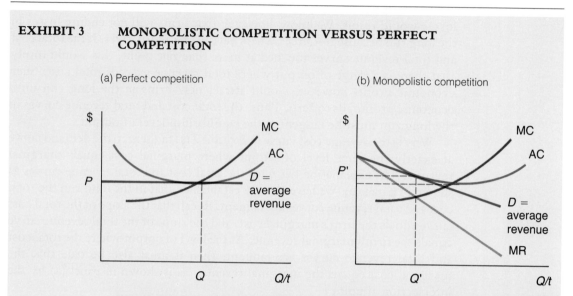

The perfectly competitive firm of panel (a) faces a demand curve that is horizontal at market price *P.* Long-run equilibrium occurs at output *Q,* where the demand (average revenue) curve is tangent to the average cost curve at its lowest point.

The monopolistically competitive firm of panel (b) is in long-run equilibrium at output *Q',* where demand is tangent to average cost. However, since the demand curve is downward sloping, the tangency does not occur at the minimum point of average cost. Hence, the monopolistically competitive firm produces less output at a higher price than does a perfectly competitive firm facing the same cost conditions.

charge more than the market price without losing all its customers. So each firm's demand curve is a horizontal line drawn at the market price, indicating that each firm can sell all it wants at the market price but none at a higher price. In the long run entry and exit ensure that economic profit equals zero. The firm's average cost curve is tangent to its demand curve at the low point of the average cost curve. Thus, output is produced at the lowest possible average cost.

In panel (b) the firm in monopolistic competition faces a downward-sloping demand curve because this firm's product is not exactly the same as those produced by other firms. For example, Chicken McNuggets differ slightly from Chicken Tenders and from Kentucky Nuggets. Because the monopolistically competitive firm's demand curve is downward sloping, the average cost curve and demand curve in the long run are tangent at a point that is not on the lowest portion of the average cost curve. The monopolistic competitor produces at an equilibrium rate of output that lies to the left of the minimum point on its average cost curve. The firm under monopolistic competition therefore tends to produce less and to charge a higher price than a firm under perfect competition.

Some economists argue that monopolistic competition results in a waste of resources because each firm fails to produce where average cost is at a minimum. For example, consider a crossroads with a gas station on each corner—more than enough to service the demands of passing motorists. Although each station earns a normal profit in the long run, the gas pumps are often idle. Or consider the excess capacity in the funeral home business. Industry analysts argue that the nation's 22,000 funeral homes could easily handle 4 million funerals a year, but only half that number of people die. Thus, the industry on average operates at only 50 percent of capacity, resulting in higher costs per funeral.

Earlier we reviewed the ways that firms in monopolistic competition try to differentiate their products. Firms in such industries will spend more on advertising and other selling expenses than firms in perfect competition. Whether consumers benefit from the greater diversity offered remains a debated question. Some economists argue that monopolistic competition results in too many brands, too much promotional effort, and product differentiation that is often artificial.

Edward Chamberlin, one of the developers of the theory of monopolistic competition, argued that the higher cost per unit resulting from excess capacity is the price consumers willingly pay for having a greater selection. According to this view, resources are not wasted because consumers are given a wider choice among gas stations, funeral homes, fast-food outlets, convenience stores, clothing stores, drugstores, computer software, and many other goods and services. We close our discussion by considering a familiar example of monopolistic competition, computer software and computer magazines.

CASE STUDY

Personal Computer Products

The introduction of the personal computer has given rise to many complementary activities, such as software production and personal computer magazines. In 1986 about 3000 software companies were producing some 20,000 different programs. The computer software industry closely approximates monopolistic competition. There are numerous participants. The product is heterogeneous across producers of close substitutes—one computer program is viewed as somewhat different from the others but not so different that its price can be increased without losing some customers to competing software producers. Entry is relatively easy; there are few legal restrictions and no heavy initial start-up costs. A computer whiz can develop a new program using little more than imagination.

In the early days of the industry producers relied on word of mouth to spread the good news to software buyers. As the use of personal computers grew and the number of software producers increased, more money had to be spent on advertising to differentiate each program. Program producers began hiring Madison Avenue advertising firms, who used multi-million-dollar budgets to reach a growing market. This growth in advertising supported the mushrooming growth of computer magazines. Depending on how you define them, there are now between 150 and 400 computer magazines on the market. Each tries to find its own niche. For example, a dozen magazines are devoted to the IBM PC; others specialize in the Apple

Macintosh. Thus these magazines are slightly differentiated but so numerous as to comprise a monopolistically competitive industry.

Sources: Theresa Engstrom, "Personal Computers Inspire a Rash of Magazines, but Shakeout Is Seen," *The Wall Street Journal*, 9 April 1984, "The Shakeout in Software: It's Already Here," *BusinessWeek* (20 August 1984): 102–104.

AN INTRODUCTION TO OLIGOPOLY

Oligopoly is the market structure where there is a small number of firms whose decisions are interdependent.

Another market structure that is very important in the economic order of things is oligopoly. **Oligopoly** is a market structure dominated by a few sellers. When we think of "big business," we should think of oligopoly. Many industries, including steel, automobiles, oil, breakfast cereal, and tobacco, are oligopolistic. Perfectly competitive firms and monopolistically competitive firms are so numerous that they need not be concerned about the effect of their own actions on the behavior of other firms in the industry. Because there are few firms in an oligopolistic market, however, each firm must weigh the effect its own policies will have on rivals' behavior. Consequently, oligopoly involves a few sellers who are interdependent.

Varieties of Oligopoly

In some oligopolistic industries, such as steel and oil, the product sold is homogeneous; in other industries, such as automobiles and tobacco, the product sold is differentiated. Where the goods sold are identical, there is greater interdependence among the few dominant firms in the industry because slight price changes by one firm have greater effects on others. For example, producers of steel ingots must be more sensitive to one another's pricing policies than the producers of autos because steel ingots are essentially identical, whereas autos differ across producers. A small rise in the price of an ingot will send customers to a rival supplier. Make no mistake, however; auto producers must still be sensitive to one another's pricing. They just are not as sensitive as steel producers.

Because of this interdependence among firms in the industry, it is more difficult to analyze the behavior of each firm. Each firm will react to other firms' changes in price, output, product quality, and advertising. Each firm knows that any changes in its own policies will produce a reaction from its rivals. Whereas the firm in perfect competition can be likened to a player on the professional golf tour, where each player is striving for a personal best, oligopoly is more like tennis, where one player's actions depend very much on how and where the opponent hits the ball.

Why have some industries evolved into an oligopolistic market structure, comprising only a few firms, while other industries have not? Although the reasons are not always clear, an oligopolistic market structure can often be traced to some form of barrier to entry, such as economies of scale, legal restrictions, or control over an essential resource. The number of firms is small because new firms find it difficult to break into the industry. In the previous chapter we examined barriers to entry as they applied to monopoly. The same principles apply to oligopoly. Perhaps the most significant barrier to entry is economies of scale, which we will now examine in greater detail.

Economies of Scale

If the production process in certain industries requires a relatively large output before low production costs can be achieved, only a few firms are necessary to produce the total output demanded in the market. Perhaps the best example of this is the auto industry. Recall that the minimum efficient scale is the lowest rate of output at which the firm takes full advantage of economies of scale. Research shows that an automobile plant of minimum efficient scale can produce enough cars to supply nearly 10 percent of the U.S. market demand. If there were 100 auto manufacturers, each would supply such a tiny portion of the market that the average cost per car would be higher than if only 10 producers manufactured autos.

The automobile industry is an industry where economies of scale can serve as a barrier to entry. Any potential entrant into this industry would have to sell enough cars to reach a scale of operation that would reduce the average cost per car to the low level enjoyed by those firms already in the industry. This situation is illustrated in Exhibit 4, which presents the long-run average cost curve for a typical firm in the industry. A new entrant might sell only enough cars to produce the quantity S; the average cost per unit for this new entrant is much higher than it is for firms that have reached the minimum efficient size, reflected here by output level M. So if autos sell for less than C_a, the average cost facing a potential entrant, potential entrants will expect to lose money.

Cost of Product Differentiation

There is another aspect to the problem. Often the cost of reaching that minimum efficient size is great. It could be that the cost of machinery to build a plant of minimum efficient size is extremely high. Or perhaps the cost of promoting a product enough to compete with established brands requires an enormous initial outlay. High start-up costs and the existence of established name brands would not be barriers to entry if information about future events were perfect. With perfect information, those new entrants that were going to be successful would have little difficulty borrowing the funds required to get the business up and running. In the real world, however, the future is uncertain; the chance of losing money on an unsuccessful attempt at securing a place in the market turns away many potential entrants. Consider, for example, the cost required to challenge Coke and Pepsi in the soft drink market.

EXHIBIT 4   ECONOMICS OF SCALE IN THE AUTO INDUSTRY

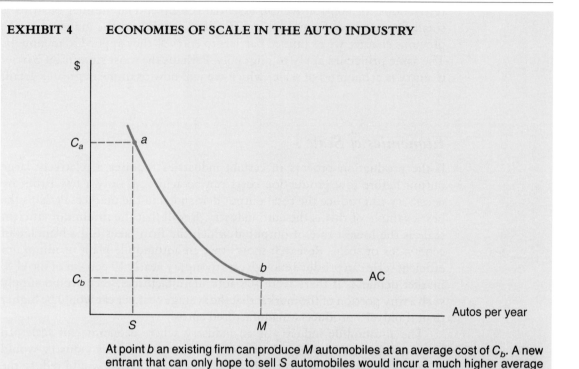

At point *b* an existing firm can produce *M* automobiles at an average cost of C_b. A new entrant that can only hope to sell *S* automobiles would incur a much higher average cost of C_a at point *a*. If cars sell for less than C_a, new entrants will suffer a loss. In this case economies of scale serve as a barrier to entry, protecting the existing firms.

Under perfect competition all firms sell identical products. There is no incentive to advertise or to promote a particular product since all products are alike. Moreover, since producers can sell all they want at the prevailing market price, there is no point in trying to sell more through product promotion. Under oligopoly, however, firms often pour resources into differentiating their product. Some of this cost has the beneficial effects of providing valuable information to consumers and offering consumers a wider array of products.

But some forms of product differentiation may be of little value. Some advertising may be primarily puffery rather than information, with the efforts of one producer largely canceling out the efforts of another. Little information is conveyed when consumers are told that Coke is "it" (which Coke is "it"—Classic Coke or the new Coke?) or that Pepsi is "the drink of a new generation," yet these companies spend millions on such messages. Much of the effort may be aimed at creating an artificial distinction in the consumer's mind between various brands of essentially identical products. Promotional efforts could thus result in a higher cost of production under oligopoly than under perfect competition. The following case study explores the costs associated with product differentiation in the auto industry.

*CASE
STUDY*

**The Cost
of Variety**

In the early days of auto manufacturing cars were very similar. Henry Ford's Model Ts were all the same—same style, same color. Since those days, however, car manufacturers have made an effort to follow Alfred Sloan's motto. Sloan, the head of General Motors from 1937 to 1956, wanted to build a car "for every purse and purpose." In recent years the number of choices has proliferated. Considering the possible combinations of engines, transmissions, colors, and other options, there are more than 32,000 versions of the Chevrolet Citation. You want more choice? The Ford Thunderbird comes in more than 69,000 possible varieties.

Engineers note that allowing for such variety adds tremendously to the cost of the car. For example, additional costs are necessary to support the sophisticated ordering system and the more complicated factories needed to produce a different car each minute. One study concludes that if the Ford Mustang were introduced today, the price would have to be 25 percent higher just to cover the added costs associated with providing a wider variety of that model.

Because Japanese producers must ship cars halfway around the world, they had difficulty responding to custom orders. Instead, they concentrate on providing only those features consumers appear to desire the most. The Honda Accord, for example, was offered in only 32 varieties, including all the combinations of engine, transmission, and color. Some industry analysts argue that this policy has given Japanese manufacturers a significant cost advantage and has allowed them to focus more on the quality of their cars. Now that Japanese companies have established plants in the United States, it remains to be seen whether they will continue to limit the number of options offered or will follow an American tradition.

The point is that while consumers like to select cars that most nearly match their own tastes and preferences, this wider selection increases the average car costs. Many items cost more when they are customized to particular tastes. A tailor-made suit, for example, is more expensive than one off the rack. A home built to the buyer's specifications costs more than a house built like others in a development. So the wider variety offered by oligopolists is both good and bad. It is good if consumers value the wider choice and are willing to pay the extra cost of variety; it is bad if efforts at product differentiation are costly yet amount to no difference that is valuable to customers.

Source: John Koten, "Giving Buyers Wide Choices May Be Hurting Auto Makers," *The Wall Street Journal,* 15 December 1983.

MODELS OF OLIGOPOLY

Because oligopolists are interdependent, the behavior of individual producers becomes more complicated. When the actions of one firm depend on the behavior of its rivals, almost anything can happen. If firms in the industry are able to coordinate their activities well enough, they can behave like a monopolist. But oligopolists may become so fiercely competitive that price wars erupt. Dozens of theories have been developed to explain oligopoly pricing behavior. Some of these are mathematically elaborate, and others are more intuitive. We will examine four of the better-known models: (1) the kinked demand curve, (2) cartels, (3) price leadership, and (4) cost-plus pricing. Each was developed to explain a different type of behavior observed in the oligopolistic market. As we will see, each model has some relevance, though none is entirely satisfactory as a general theory of oligopoly behavior.

The Kinked Demand Curve

Prices in some oligopolistic industries appear to be stable even during periods when altered market forces suggest a price change is expected. An often-cited case of price stability occurred in the sulfur industry, where the price remained at $18 per ton for a dozen consecutive years despite major shifts in demand and in the cost of production. One oligopoly model sheds light on this apparent price stability. That model is based on the simple idea that if a firm cuts its price, other firms will cut theirs as well to avoid losing customers to the price cutter. If a firm raises its price, however, other firms will stand pat, hoping to attract customers away from the price raiser. Such expected behavior by competitors leads to a special demand relationship, termed the *kinked demand curve*. This demand curve is actually made up of portions of two demand curves — one based on an assumption that rivals will follow price reductions and the other based on the assumption that rivals will not follow price increases.

To develop the kinked demand curve model, we must first derive the oligopolist's demand curve and then its marginal revenue curve. Suppose we start at point E in Exhibit 5, with the firm producing Q units at price P. The firm's demand curve based on the assumption that rivals will not follow any change in price is depicted as DD. The firm's demand curve based on the assumption that rivals will match any change in price is depicted as $D'D'$. As you can see, DD is flatter, or more elastic, than $D'D'$. To see why, suppose that General Motors (GM) raises its prices, but Ford and Chrysler do not. In this situation GM would lose far more sales than if other producers also raised their prices. Likewise, if GM cuts prices but Ford and Chrysler do not, GM will pick up more sales than if all producers cut prices. Thus, if rivals do not follow price changes, any price increase will lose more customers and any price decrease gain more customers than if rivals follow price changes. Therefore, each oligopolist's demand curve is more elastic when rivals do not follow price changes than when they do.

If we assume that rivals will follow a firm's price decreases but will not follow price increases, then we can draw the oligopolist's demand curve as DED'. Beginning with a price of P in Exhibit 5, you can see that an increase in the price will result in many lost sales because if rivals do not also increase their prices, the demand curve will be the portion of DED' above point E. On

EXHIBIT 5   **THE KINKED-DEMAND MODEL OF OLIGOPOLY**

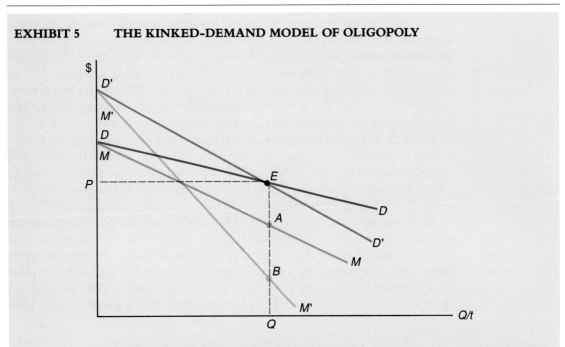

In the initial situation an oligopolist is at point *E,* selling *Q* units at price *P.* The firm's demand curve looks like *DD* if its competitors do not match its price changes; the demand curve looks like *D'D'* if competitors do match price changes.

On the assumption that this firm's rivals will match price cuts but not price increases, the relevant demand curve is *DED',* with a kink at quantity *Q. MABM'* is the associated marginal revenue curve, with a discontinuous jump at quantity *Q.*

the other hand, if the firm pictured in Exhibit 5 drops its price below *P,* the quantity demanded will not increase significantly because the oligopolist's rivals will follow suit along *ED'.* Since its rivals will match any price decrease, this firm is unable to attract competitors' customers by lowering price. Thus, that portion of the demand curve reflecting a price increase, *DE,* is less elastic than that portion of the demand curve reflecting a price decrease, *ED'.* Because the behavior of rivals differs between a price increase and a price decrease, this oligopolist's demand curve has a kink at point *E.*

Marginal Revenue   To find the marginal revenue curve for the kinked demand curve, we simply piece together the relevant portions of the underlying marginal revenue curves. Segment *MA* is the marginal revenue curve that is applicable to portion *DE* of the kinked demand curve. The *BM'* segment is the marginal revenue curve that is associated with the *ED'* portion of the kinked demand curve. The marginal revenue curve is thus *MABM'.* Because there is a kink in the demand curve, the marginal revenue curve is not a single line but rather has a discontinuous jump at the quantity corresponding to the kink in the demand curve.

Price Rigidity Within the discontinuous portion of the marginal revenue curve, *AB*, the firm will not respond to changes in marginal cost. Exhibit 6 is drawn to strip away portions of the demand and marginal revenue curves made irrelevant by kinked demand theory. Suppose *MC* is the initial marginal cost curve. This firm maximizes profits by equating marginal cost to marginal revenue, which occurs at point *f*, where *MC* crosses the discontinuous range, *AB*. That intersection yields equilibrium quantity *Q* and price *P*. If output were less than *Q*, the marginal revenue curve (*MA*) would be above the marginal cost curve, so the firm could increase profit (or reduce losses) by expanding output. If output exceeded *Q*, marginal cost would exceed marginal revenue (*BM'*), so the firm could increase profit (or reduce losses) by reducing output. Thus, the oligopolist maximizes profit or minimizes losses by selecting output level *Q*.

If the marginal cost curve drops to *MC'*, what will happen to equilibrium price and quantity? Nothing will happen because the new marginal cost curve will still intersect the marginal revenue curve within the discontinuous range, *AB*. The oligopolist can do no better than to offer quantity *Q* at price *P*. The same holds if marginal cost were to increase to *MC''*—again, no change in the equilibrium conditions. It would take a greater shift in the

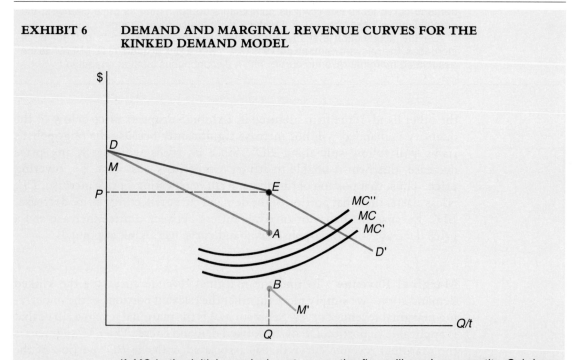

EXHIBIT 6   **DEMAND AND MARGINAL REVENUE CURVES FOR THE
KINKED DEMAND MODEL**

If *MC* is the initial marginal cost curve, the firm will produce quantity *Q* (where marginal cost equals marginal revenue) at price *P*. Marginal cost could fall to *MC'* or increase to *MC''* without affecting the quantity produced. Likewise, price *P* will be rigid if marginal cost varies between *MC'* and *MC''*.

marginal cost curve to produce a change in equilibrium price and quantity. Specifically, the intersection of the marginal cost curve with the marginal revenue curve would have to occur above point *A* or below point *B* to change the equilibrium price and quantity. Because the marginal cost curve can fluctuate within the discontinuous range of the marginal revenue curve without affecting equilibrium price, prices tend to be rigid in oligopolistic industries if firms behave in the manner described by the kinked demand curve.

An Assessment of the Kinked Demand Curve The kinked demand curve yields two primary predictions: (1) oligopolistic firms will not cut prices to attract customers because they expect that their rivals will follow, and (2) oligopoly prices will tend to be rigid. Both predictions are consistent with evidence based on oligopoly behavior. Interviews with business executives suggest that the primary deterrent to price cutting is the belief that price cuts will be matched. Earlier we introduced evidence that oligopoly prices adjust less frequently than prices in more competitive industries.

The kinked demand theory is an interesting way to explain price rigidity, but it is not without critics. Two basic criticisms have been leveled at the kinked demand theory. First, the theory provides no explanation of how the equilibrium price and quantity are initially determined. The theory simply explains why price, once established, will be less likely to change in oligopolistic industries. Second, even though there is some evidence supporting price rigidity, other evidence suggests that prices are not as rigid as the theory implies, particularly when it comes to price increases. During the inflationary periods of the 1970s and early 1980s, industries characterized as oligopolistic increased prices frequently. Other evidence comparing the frequency of price changes in oligopolies versus monopolies suggests that oligopolies changed prices more often than monopolies did, even though the kinked demand theory would imply just the opposite. Despite these limitations, the kinked demand theory is one explanation of those price rigidities that have been observed over the years.

Collusion and Cartels

Because there are few firms in an oligopolistic market setting, firms can collude, or get together to determine price and output decisions as a cartel. A **cartel** is an agreement among independent firms to coordinate their production and pricing decisions so each member of the cartel will earn monopoly profits. Cartels can result in many benefits to firms—increased profits, greater certainty about the behavior of "competitors," and an organized effort to block new entry.

*A **cartel** is an agreement among firms to coordinate their production and pricing decisions.*

Collusion and cartels are illegal in this country. When compared to a more competitive situation, colluding firms usually reduce output, increase price, and block the entry of new firms. Thus, consumers suffer because the price is higher, and potential entrants suffer because free enterprise is restricted. Despite the illegality of collusion, however, the rewards can be so tempting that firms sometimes break the law. For example, during the 1950s there was evidence of extensive collusion among electrical equipment producers, and some executives went to jail for their participation in the scheme. In many European countries formal collusion among firms through cartels is not only legal but is sometimes promoted by government. Some cartels are world-wide in scope, such as the now-familiar Organization of Petroleum Export-ing Countries (OPEC). Cartels can operate worldwide (even though they are outlawed in some countries) because there are no international laws to stop them.

Suppose that the firms in an industry establish a cartel. The industry demand curve is presented as *D* in Exhibit 7. What price will be charged to maximize the industry's profits and how will industry output be divided among participating firms? The cartel acts as if it were a monopolist operat-ing many plants, and like the monopolist, the cartel is interested in the marginal revenue curve. The marginal revenue curve is also presented in Exhibit 7. Given the demand and marginal revenue curves, the cartel, like the monopolist, maximizes profit by equating marginal cost with marginal revenue.

The first task of the cartel is to determine the marginal cost of production for the cartel as a whole. The marginal cost curve in Exhibit 7 represents the horizontal sum of the individual marginal cost curves for the firms in the cartel. The price and total output are determined by the intersection of the aggregate marginal cost curve and the marginal revenue curve. This intersec-tion yields price *P* and industry output *Q*.

The cartel has thus determined the price and total quantity. So far, so good. Collecting all the information required to arrive at price and quantity is no easy task, but it is relatively easier than determining how output is to be allocated among members of the cartel. The profit-maximizing solution for the cartel requires output to be allocated among firms to minimize the average cost of production. If all firms have identical cost curves, there is no problem in allocating output—each gets an equal share.

The fruits of collusion are tempting, indeed, for participating firms. After all, few firms find head-on competition attractive, particularly when matters can be settled in the back room. However, there are problems with establishing and maintaining an effective cartel, even where cartels are legal.

Number of Firms in the Cartel   The greater the number of firms in the industry, the more difficult it is to negotiate an acceptable allocation of output. Consensus is harder to achieve as the cartel size grows because the chances that at least one member will be dissatisfied increase.

Differences in Cost   If all firms have identical costs, output and profit are more easily allocated across firms, but if costs differ, problems arise. The greater the differences in average cost across firms, the more delicate will be the balancing act to ensure that each firm earns an acceptable share of the profits. For example, a high-cost firm would need to sell more than a low-cost firm to earn the same total profit, yet the maximization of total industry profit calls for allowing low-cost firms to sell more. Thus, there is a basic

EXHIBIT 7   CARTEL MODEL WHERE FIRMS ACT AS A MONOPOLIST

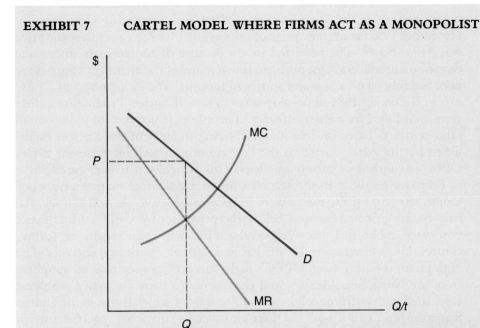

A cartel acts like a monopolist. Here *D* is the market demand curve, *MR* the associated marginal revenue curve, and *MC* the horizontal sum of the marginal cost curves of cartel members. Cartel profits are maximized by producing quantity *Q* and charging price *P*.

conflict between maximizing the total profits of the cartel and equalizing profits among the participants. If firms that experience higher costs are allocated too little output, they could drop out of the cartel, thereby undermining it.

In reality, the allocation of output is typically the result of haggling among cartel members. Firms that are more influential or more adept at bargaining will get a larger share of output. Allocation schemes are sometimes based simply on the historical division of output among firms, or cartel members may divide up the market along geographical lines.

Cheating   Perhaps a more fundamental problem in keeping the cartel running is that each oligopolist faces a strong temptation to cheat on the agreement. By lowering price slightly below the established price, a firm can usually increase its sales and profit. The urge to cheat is strong, especially during economic slumps.

New Entry into the Industry   A successful cartel sets the stage for its own demise. If the cartel cannot block the entry of new firms, new entry will over time force the price back down to where all firms earn only a normal rate of return. Thus, the profits of the cartel attract entry, entry increases market supply, and increased supply forces down the price. A successful cartel must therefore be able to block the entry of new firms.

Problems of establishing and maintaining a cartel are reflected in the spotty history of the Organization of Petroleum Exporting Countries. In December 1985 the average price of oil was $28 a barrel; a year later the price was $15 a barrel. The price fell partly because of competition among the world's oil producers. One problem is that many of the member countries are poor and rely on oil as a major source of revenue. The 13 members of OPEC met in December 1986 to develop ways to raise the price. Production quotas were established for each member, and members also agreed to phase out all sales contracts based on free market pricing in favor of fixed prices established by the cartel. Listed in the first column of Exhibit 8 are the prices OPEC established for various qualities of oil, which were to become effective in February of 1987. In the second column are the free market prices one month after the OPEC prices were to become effective. As you can see, the free market prices were well below the prices set by OPEC. Most cartel observers doubt that once-powerful OPEC will ever regain its former control. Like other cartels, OPEC has had difficulty with new entrants. The high prices resulting from OPEC's early success attracted new oil suppliers from the North Sea, Mexico, and elsewhere. So there are many problems associated with outright collusion, not the least of which is that in the United States the practice is illegal. Yet there are other, less obvious, ways for firms in an industry to act in unison without formalizing a collusive relationship, as we will see next.

EXHIBIT 8
COMPARISON OF PRICES SET
BY OPEC
WITH FREE MARKET
PRICES, FEBRUARY 1987

	Price per Barrel	
Grade of Oil	**Set by OPEC**	**Free Market Price**
Arab light	$17.52	13.47
Arab heavy	16.27	13.22
Iran light	17.50	16.80
Bonny light	18.92	13.47

Source: Youssef Ibrahim, "OPEC Begins New Strategy to Take Control," *The Wall Street Journal*, 22 December 1986; "Oil Prices," *The Wall Street Journal*, 2 March 1987.

Price Leadership

*A **price leader** is a firm whose prices are followed by the rest of the industry.*

Some industries contain **price leaders**, who set the price for the rest of the industry. A single dominant firm or a few firms establish the market price, and other firms in the industry follow that lead. Any changes in the price are initiated by the price-leading firm. By implicitly settling on a single price, firms in an industry hope to avoid price competition and thereby to increase profits. Let's consider the price leadership in the steel and cigarette industries.

The Steel Industry Historically, the steel industry has been a good example of the price-leadership form of oligopoly. USX (formerly U.S. Steel), the largest firm in the industry, typically would set the price for various products, and other firms would follow. Congressional investigations of the pricing policy in this industry indicate that smaller steel producers relied on the price schedules of USX. Public pressure on USX to avoid price increases forced the price leadership role onto smaller steel producers, resulting in a rotation of the leadership function among firms. Although the rotational form of price leadership produced less that perfect conformity among firms in the industry, particularly during the 1970s, close observers of this industry argue that price levels prevailing in the industry were higher than they would have been with no price leadership. As F. M. Scherer has noted, "It seems undeniable that in the absence of what leadership there was, steel prices in the United States, instead of rising, would have fallen sharply between 1974 and 1978, as they did elsewhere in depressed steel markets."[1]

The Cigarette Industry Three major cigarette producers account for over three-fourths of all sales. During the decades of the 1920s and 1930s these firms took turns as price leaders, a practice that resulted in nearly identical prices and above-normal profits for firms in the industry. Even though there was no evidence that the firms actually met and discussed prices, circumstantial evidence of prices moving in concert was enough to convince a jury that these firms were breaking the law. In 1946 the "tacit collusion" exercised by the three major cigarette producers was found to be a violation of the Sherman Antitrust Act, the law that prohibited such behavior. (Antitrust laws will be discussed more extensively in the next chapter.)

Problems of Price Leadership Like other forms of collusion, price leadership is subject to a variety of obstacles. First, as we have seen, the practice often violates antitrust laws. Second, there is no guarantee that other firms will follow the leader, which can be a real problem with price increases. If other firms in the industry do not follow a price increase, the leading firm must either roll back prices or suffer a loss in sales to lower-priced competitors (recall the results from the kinked demand curve model). Third, even if all firms officially follow the price leader, some producers may still cheat on the official price by offering extra services, rebates, or some other deal that lowers the actual price. The incentives to cut prices to gain more sales will be particularly strong when the industry is depressed and firms are operating well below capacity. When production is low, so is the marginal cost of producing more output.

Finally, if the product is not homogeneous across producers, then each producer has greater latitude in its pricing policy and is able to depart from an industry-wide price schedule. For example, at one time products in the

---

[1]F. M. Scherer, *Industrial Market Structure and Economic Performance*, 2d ed. (Chicago: Rand McNally College Publishing Co., 1980), 180.

ready-to-eat cereal industry were viewed by consumers as essentially the same, so producers needed to match one another's prices quite closely to avoid losing sales. The proliferation of new, more specialized cereals, however, gave producers some freedom in setting price without having to fear changes in sales volume. Firms were able to act with greater independence. Thus, the greater the product differentiation across producers, the less effective will be price leadership as a means of organizing oligopolists.

Cost-Plus Pricing

*Under **cost-plus pricing** the price is determined by adding a markup to average cost.*

A final model of oligopoly behavior is based on observations that many oligopolists employ **cost-plus pricing** strategies. Simply put, the firms establish price by calculating the average cost per unit and then adding a percentage, called a markup, to determine price. This approach largely ignores the demand curve since price is determined as a function of cost, not demand.

Cost-plus pricing appears attractive to producers for several reasons. First, it provides a way of coping with the uncertainty of not knowing the exact shape and elasticity of the demand curve. Second, the very effort of calculating appropriate prices based on marginal analysis is costly, particularly if the firm produces a variety of products. Adopting a simple markup rule greatly simplifies the pricing process. Third, if firms in the industry have similar costs, their use of the same mark-up percentage will yield uniform prices across the industry, representing an implicit form of price collusion.

Choosing the Target Level of Output and the Markup   Because the average cost per unit varies with the level of output, the firm must assume some target level of output, which is typically an amount less than the firm's capacity. For example, the firm may assume that its level of output will be 75 percent of its capacity. The markup policy is usually based on some percent of the firm's average cost. For example, a 50 percent markup on an item with an average cost of $80 results in a retail price of $120. This markup is designed to cover those elements of cost that are not reflected in the average cost calculations, including fixed costs that cannot be charged against a particular product.

Some producers build into the price a target rate of profit they anticipate earning. For example, General Motors has employed a markup policy aimed at earning a 15 percent after-tax rate of return on its investment. Since GM does not know how many cars it will sell, it does not know what the average cost per unit will be. GM therefore estimates that its output will be 80 percent of its capacity. The price is then calculated by adding to the average cost per unit enough profit to yield the firm a 15 percent after-tax rate of profit.

An Assessment of Cost-Plus Pricing   Cost-plus pricing has an appealing simplicity, and it grows more attractive with an increase in the variety of products sold by the firm. A firm such as General Electric produces hundreds of different products, and GE is hard-pressed to attribute such costs as basic research and overhead to particular products. Or consider the problems of your favorite grocery store in trying to assign its various costs of doing business to each of the thousands of products it sells. The store finds it easier to assign a percentage markup to determine the price of each product. There is abundant evidence that markup pricing is used extensively, particularly in retailing. Incidentally, firms do not have to be oligopolistic to adopt a cost-plus pricing policy—competitive firms and monopolistically competitive firms may employ the policy as well.

The problem for economists with cost-plus pricing is that this policy does not seem to use marginal analysis. To the extent that these policies focus on average cost rather than marginal cost, and to the extent that these policies ignore marginal revenue, there seems to be no equating of marginal cost with marginal revenue, so firms are not maximizing profits. Another problem with cost-plus pricing from an analytical viewpoint is that it remains unclear how the actual markup is determined. Obviously, the firm wants to charge "what the market will bear," but how is the percentage actually determined? No doubt demand plays a part in the calculations, though its exact role remains unclear. And what about the entry of new firms? Should the markup be set low enough so entrants are not attracted to this market?

Although cost-plus pricing appears at first to be inconsistent with the use of marginal analysis, some observers argue that the cost-plus approach is, in fact, a profit-maximizing response to complicated and uncertain market conditions. Executives who were interviewed said they did not believe profits could be increased by any change in pricing procedures, suggesting that these executives believed they were charging the prices that maximized profits. Moreover, a closer scrutiny of actual policies indicates the firms do not apply the same markup to all their products but vary the markup with the price elasticity of demand for the product. The greater the elasticity of demand, the lower the markup. This finding suggests that firms do take demand into account and do employ the markup rule in a way that is consistent with profit maximization.

Comparison of Oligopoly and Perfect Competition

We have seen that there is no single model of oligopoly behavior but rather several models. We discussed kinked demand curves, cartels, price leadership, and cost-plus pricing, and we could have produced a longer list. Each of the four models was developed to help explain certain observed phenomena in oligopolistic markets. Each model, however, has limitations, and at this point none is thought to be a valid depiction of all oligopoly behavior.

Therefore, it is difficult to compare the properties of an "oligopoly" model with those of the competitive model. We might, however, imagine an experiment where we took the hundreds of firms that populate a competitive industry and, through a series of giant mergers, combined them to form a half dozen firms. We thereby transform the industry from perfect competition to oligopoly. How would the behavior of firms in this industry differ before and after the massive mergers?

Price Is Usually Higher Under Oligopoly　With fewer competitors, these firms become more interdependent. Each of the oligopoly models presented in this chapter implies that firms could conceivably act in concert in their pricing policies. Even cost-plus pricing could be a tool for tacit price collusion if firms face similar costs and adopt similar markup rules. If some sort of implicit or explicit collusion allows oligopolists to set a profit-maximizing price, industry output will be smaller and price will be higher under oligopoly than under perfect competition.

Higher Profits Under Oligopoly　In the long run easy entry prevents firms in a perfectly competitive industry from earning more than a normal profit. Presumably with oligopoly, however, there are barriers to entry that allow firms in such an industry to earn long-run economic profits. In the real world the barrier to entry might be brand name identification built up over years of advertising by the firms in the industry. Or the barrier might be economies of scale in production. Such barriers might be insurmountable for a new entrant. Therefore, we should expect profit rates to be higher with oligopoly than with perfect competition.

Profit rates appear to be positively correlated with the proportion of industry sales made by the largest firms. Some economists view these higher profit rates as a matter of concern for public policy, but not all economists share this view. Harold Demsetz, for example, argues that since it is the largest firms in oligopolistic industries that tend to earn the highest rates of return, higher profit rates in oligopolistic industries stem from the greater efficiency arising from economies of scale in these large firms.[2] Many of these issues will be examined in the next chapter as we explore government's role in regulating the marketplace.

Mergers and Oligopoly

*In a **horizontal merger** one firm combines with another firm that produces the same product.*

Because large firms are potentially more profitable than small ones, some firms have pursued the fast track to growth by merging with other firms. In some industries the merging, or joining together, of two firms has contributed to the movement toward oligopoly. Over the last century there have been three major merger waves in this country. The first occurred between 1887 and 1904. Some of today's largest firms, including USX and Standard Oil, were formed during this first merger movement. These tended to be **horizontal mergers**, meaning that the merging firms produced the same products. For example, the firm that is today USX was formed in 1901 through a billion-dollar merger that involved many individual producers and two-thirds of the industry's productive capacity.

*In a **vertical merger** one firm combines with another from which it purchases inputs or to which it sells output.*

The second merger wave took place between 1916 and 1929, when vertical mergers were more common. A **vertical merger** is the merging of

---

[2]"Industry Structure, Market Rivalry, and Public Policy," *Journal of Law and Economics* 16 (April 1973): 1–10.

one firm with either a firm from which it purchases inputs or a firm to which it sells output. Thus, it is the merging of firms at different stages of the production process. For example, a steel firm might merge with a firm that mines iron ore. **Conglomerate mergers**, which join firms producing in different industries, were also common during the second merger wave. The third merger wave occurred during the 25 years following World War II. In that period many large firms were absorbed by other, usually larger, firms. More than 200 of the 1000 largest firms in 1950 had disappeared by 1963 as a result of mergers. In recent years corporate takeovers have become more common, but it is too soon to say whether this activity forms the basis of a fourth merger wave.

*A **conglomerate** merger involves the combination of firms producing in different industries.*

SUMMARY

1. In monopolistically competitive industries there are many firms selling somewhat differentiated products. Whereas the monopolist produces output that has no close substitutes, the firm in monopolistic competition must contend with many competitors that offer close substitutes. Because there are some differences among the products offered by different firms, each firm faces a demand curve that has some slope to it.

2. Sellers in monopolistic competition differentiate their products in a variety of ways, including (1) the locations where the product is available, (2) the services provided with the product, (3) physical qualities, and (4) the subjective image of the product in the consumer's mind.

3. In the short run monopolistically competitive firms maximize profits or minimize losses by producing where marginal cost equals marginal revenue. In the long run free entry and exit of firms ensures that monopolistically competitive firms earn only normal profits. In long-run equilibrium each firm produces where marginal cost equals marginal revenue and where the average cost curve is tangent to the downward-sloping demand curve.

4. Oligopoly is a market dominated by a few sellers, some of which are large enough relative to the entire market to influence market price. In some oligopolistic industries, such as steel, the product is homogeneous; in other oligopolistic industries, such as automobiles and tobacco, the product is differentiated.

5. Because there are few firms in oligopolistic market structures, each firm will react to other firms' changes in price, output, product quality, and advertising. Because of this interdependence among oligopolists, the behavior of producers is more difficult to analyze. No single model of behavior characterizes oligopolistic markets.

6. In this chapter we observed four possible models of oligopoly behavior: (1) the kinked demand curve, which assumes that rivals will follow price decreases but not price increases; (2) the cartel, which assumes that firms collude to behave like a monopolist; (3) price leadership, which assumes that one firm sets the price for the industry and other firms follow the leader; and (4) cost-plus pricing, which assumes that firms determine the price to charge by estimating their cost per unit and adding a percentage to cover the desired profit.

QUESTIONS AND PROBLEMS

1. (Monopolistic Competition) Why would the production of Hollywood movies be an example of a monopolistically competitive industry? What are some of the major firms and how do they differentiate their products?

2. (Monopolistically Competitive Demands) Why is the monopolistically competitive firm's demand downward sloping in the long run, even after the entry of firms?

3. (Oligopoly and Technology) How might changes in technology affect whether an industry remains oligopolistic? That is, might some barriers to entry be affected by technical change?

4. (Kinked Demand) How might a kinked demand curve change if there were a greater degree of product differentiation within the oligopoly? What can you say about the degree of price rigidity before and after greater product differentiation?

5. (Oligopoly) Consider again the kinked demand curve. Will oligopolists always experience economic profits, or could they have short-run losses?

6. (Oligopoly) If the United Auto Workers bargains for higher wages at Ford, then Ford will simply pass on the additional costs to consumers in the form of higher prices. Must this statement be true? Why or why not?

7. (Cartels) Why would each of the following induce some members of OPEC to cheat on their cartel agreements?

a. The Gulf War continues.
b. Underdevelopment of some members continues.
c. Some members are of small size.
d. International debts of some members grow.
e. Expectations grow that some members will cheat.

8. (Price Leadership) Is it reasonable to assume that a price leader will always be the largest producer (that is, the firm with the largest scale)?

9. (Cost-Plus Pricing) How might a firm decide if its markup is too high or too low? Is this search governed by market conditions? What is the difference between such sequential markups and profit maximization, or *is* there any difference?

10. (Horizontal Mergers) Why do horizontal mergers seem most likely to occur in those industries that have substantial economies of scale but have not yet achieved such economies?

REGULATION, DEREGULATION, and ANTITRUST

It has been said that businesspeople praise competition but love monopoly. They praise competition because it harnesses the diverse and often conflicting objectives of various market participants and channels them into the efficient production of goods and services. And it does this as if by an invisible hand. Businesspeople love monopoly because it provides the surest path to economic profit in the long run—and after all, profit is the firm's objective. The fruits of monopoly are so great they can tempt firms to try to eliminate, or collude with, competitors. As Adam Smith remarked more than two hundred years ago, "People of the same trade seldom meet together, even for merriment or diversion, but the conversation ends in a conspiracy against the public, or in some contrivance to raise prices."

Thus, the tendency of firms to seek monopolistic advantage is understandable, but it cannot be allowed in an economy that seeks to ensure the most efficient use of its scarce resources. Public policy plays a role by promoting competition in those markets where competition seems desirable and by reducing the harmful consequences of monopoly in those markets where the output can be most efficiently produced by one or a few firms. This chapter discusses the ways in which government regulates business activity. As you will see, there is some disagreement about what government is doing and what it should be doing. Topics and terms discussed include:

- Market power
- Economic regulation and deregulation
- Social regulation
- Antitrust laws
- Competitive trends of the economy

BUSINESS BEHAVIOR AND
PUBLIC POLICY

We have devoted a chapter to monopoly, and in the previous chapter we examined monopolistic competition and oligopoly. We noted that a single supplier of a product with no close substitutes can charge a higher price than would prevail if the market were competitive. When a few firms account for most of the sales, those firms are sometimes able to coordinate their actions, either explicitly or implicitly, to approximate the behavior of a monopolist. The ability of one or more firms to maintain a price that is above the competitive level is termed **market power**. The presumption is that a monopoly or firms acting together as a monopoly will use this market power to restrict output and charge a higher price than competitive firms. Monopoly power thereby creates a misallocation of resources and shifts wealth from consumers to producers. Other distortions have also been associated with monopolies. Because monopolies are insulated from competition, many critics argue that they are not as innovative as an aggressive competitor would be. Moreover, because of their size, monopolies have been said to exert a disproportionate influence in the political system.

Market power is the ability of one or more firms to maintain a price that is above the competitive level.

Market Structure, Conduct, and Performance

Economists have developed a branch of economic analysis called *industrial organization* to trace the relationship between the structure of a market and the performance of firms in that market. The *structure* of a particular market, such as the market for steel or personal computers, can be measured by observable characteristics such as the number and size of firms, the extent of product differentiation, and the effectiveness of barriers to entry. Market structure affects the *conduct* of firms in the market—that is, market structure affects how firms behave in such areas as pricing, research and development activity, advertising strategy, and investment policy. And the conduct of firms, in turn, affects their *performance* in the market. Market performance can be measured by the level of profit, the efficiency of production, and innovative activity in the industry.

In this three-part sequence, therefore, the causation runs from market structure to market conduct to market performance. Thus, market structure and market conduct are critical factors in determining market performance. The focus of industrial organization as it relates to market structure and market conduct is how to select public policies that will lead to the most desirable market performance. More specifically, how can public policy enhance social welfare by promoting competition where competition is feasible and by harnessing the benefits of economies of scale where production by only one or a few firms seems most efficient?

At present there is much interest in the field of industrial organization. This interest arises from several sources, including the current wave of deregulation of industry, changes in the interpretation and enforcement of laws that regulate competition, firms acquiring other firms through take-overs, and government efforts to encourage innovation and technological progress through various incentive programs.

Government Control of Business

Social regulation includes government measures designed to improve health and safety. Economic regulation is aimed at controlling price, output, entry, exit, and quality in conditions where monopoly is inevitable or desirable.

Antitrust activity is aimed at preventing monopoly and fostering competition.

There are essentially three kinds of government policy designed to alter or control the market structure and market conduct of firms: social regulation, economic regulation, and antitrust activity. **Social regulation** is government measures that address unsafe working conditions, dangerous products, damage to the environment, and other undesirable side effects, or externalities, of production and consumption. These concerns have brewed up an alphabet soup of regulatory agencies formed to control everything from the permissible level of auto emissions to health warnings on packages of cigarettes. Social regulation stems from a growing concern about the health and safety of workers and consumers.

Economic regulation is concerned with controlling the price, the output, the entry and exit into the market, and the quality of service in industries where monopoly appears inevitable or even desirable. The regulation of natural monopolies, such as electrical utilities, is an example of this type of regulation. Several other industries, such as land and air transportation and communication, have also been regulated for reasons that will be discussed later in this chapter.

Antitrust activity refers to efforts to prevent monopoly and foster competition by prohibiting firm behavior aimed at monopolizing or cartelizing a market. Whereas economic regulation involves policies aimed at controlling and in some cases even promoting monopoly, antitrust activity involves policies that attempt to curb monopoly and promote competition. Economic regulation is carried out by various regulatory bodies at the federal, state, and local levels; antitrust activity is pursued in court by federal government attorneys and by individual firms that charge other firms with violations of antitrust laws. Both economic regulation and antitrust activity will be examined in this chapter. We begin in the next section with the regulation of natural monopoly.

PUBLIC REGULATION OF NATURAL MONOPOLY

Recall that because of economies of scale, natural monopolies have a downward-sloping average cost curve throughout the entire range of market demand, which means that the lowest costs are achieved if one firm serves the entire market. As mentioned earlier, cable television is an example of a natural monopoly. The cost per household is lowest when a single company "wires" the community for signal reception. If four cable companies all strung their own wires throughout the community, the average cost per household would be higher.

Exhibit 1 shows the demand and cost conditions of a natural monopoly. A large fixed cost is usually associated with a natural monopoly, such as the cost of stringing the wires to transmit electricity, telephone, and cable TV signals, laying the tracks for a railroad, putting a satellite in orbit, building a nuclear power plant, or installing a natural gas transmission line. Because of the heavy fixed cost, the average cost curve is downward sloping where it intersects the demand curve. In this situation the cost of production is minimized by having only one producer.

From our knowledge of monopoly behavior, we know that a monopolist, if unregulated, will set price and quantity to maximize profit. In Exhibit 1 the firm sets marginal cost equal to marginal revenue, thereby selecting price P and quantity Q. However, the monopolist's choice of price and output is inefficient from society's point of view: consumers pay a price that is higher than the marginal cost of producing the good. Because price exceeds marginal cost, there is an underallocation of resources to the production of this good. The question arises, What can the government do to correct this misallocation?

EXHIBIT 1   PROFIT MAXIMIZATION FOR THE NATURAL MONOPOLY

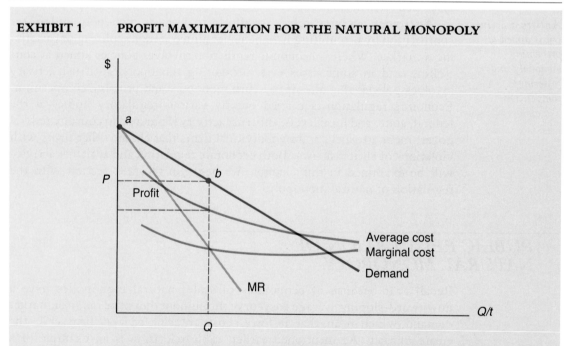

In a natural monopoly the average cost curve is downward sloping at its point of intersection with the market demand curve. The firm produces output Q (where marginal cost equals marginal revenue) and charges price P. This situation is inefficient because price exceeds marginal cost.

Regulation of Natural Monopolies

What is the appropriate public policy for an industry identified as a natural monopoly? The government has essentially three choices for dealing with natural monopolies. First, government can do nothing. If left alone, the monopolist would maximize profits, as in Exhibit 1. Second, the government can own and operate the monopoly, as is the case with the U.S. Postal Service, the Tennessee Valley Authority, municipal-owned electric utilities, and many urban transit systems. Third, the government can regulate the monopoly, as is the case with most electrical utilities and local phone services. Regulated industries have come to be known as *public utilities*.

Thus, the government must decide whether the industry will be regulated, and, if so, how. The focus here will be on government regulation rather than government ownership. Many facets of these industries have been regulated, including the quality of service and the entry of new firms. But the element of regulation that has captured the most attention has been the rates, or prices, these utilities can charge.

Setting Price Equal to Marginal Cost   Let's assume that the government regulators decide to make the monopolist act like a perfect competitor—that is, to produce the efficient level of output, where price equals marginal cost. This outcome is depicted in Exhibit 2, where the demand curve intersects the marginal cost curve at point e, yielding price P' and quantity Q'. Consumers will clearly prefer this outcome over the profit-maximizing solution because the price is lower and the quantity supplied is greater. The consumer surplus, a measure of the consumers' net gains, increases from the triangle abP in Exhibit 1 to the triangle aeP' in Exhibit 2.

Notice, however, that the monopolist now has a problem. At output level Q' the regulated price, P', is below the average cost per unit at that output level, identified as point c on the firm's average cost curve. The monopolist, rather than earning a profit, now suffers the loss identified by the shaded rectangle. Forcing the natural monopolist to price as a perfect competitor—that is, setting the marginal cost of the good equal to price, which is consumers' marginal valuation of output—results in an economic loss. Clearly, the monopolist would go out of business rather than suffer such losses in the long run.

Subsidizing the Natural Monopolist   How could the regulators encourage the monopolist to stay in business, yet still produce where the marginal cost equals price? One way is for the government to cover the monopolist's losses—to *subsidize* the firm's operation so that it will break even. The government could pay the firm an amount equal to the shaded area in Exhibit 2. The subsidy per unit of output would be the difference between the average cost per unit and the price. With this subsidy, the firm would earn a normal profit, which is as much as the subsidized firm's resources could earn in their best alternative use. Commuter transportation service often is regulated and subsidized based on this principle. The bus or subway fare is

EXHIBIT 2   REGULATING THE NATURAL MONOPOLY

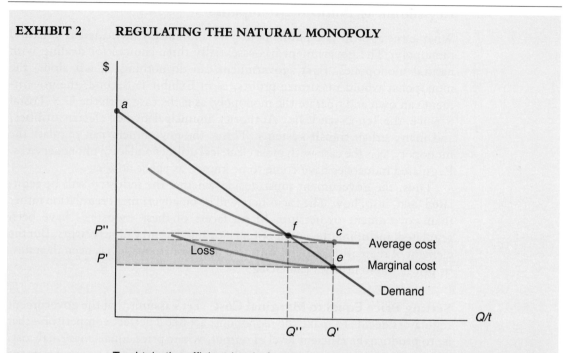

To obtain the efficient level of output, government could regulate the monopolist's price. At price P' the monopoly would produce output Q'—an efficient solution. However, at that price and quantity, the firm would suffer a loss and require a subsidy.

As an alternative, the government could set a price of P". The monopoly would produce output Q"—an inefficient level. Since P" equals average cost, the firm earns a normal profit, and no subsidy is required.

typically below the average cost of providing the service, with the difference made up through a subsidy. For example, the Washington, D.C., subway system receives over $200 million per year in subsidies. One problem with the subsidy solution is that to provide the subsidy, the government must raise taxes or forgo spending in some other area.

Setting Price Equal to Average Cost   Although some public utilities are subsidized, most are not. The regulatory commission attempts to establish a price that will provide the monopolist with a "fair return." Recall that the average cost curve includes a normal profit. Thus, when regulators set the *price equal to average cost*, this provides a normal, or "fair," profit for the monopolist. In Exhibit 2 the demand curve and the average cost curve intersect at point *f*, yielding a price of P" and a quantity of Q". The monopolist would rather earn an economic profit, as in Exhibit 1, but will settle for a normal profit since that is what could be earned if these resources were redirected to their best alternative use.

The Regulatory Dilemma   The difference between setting price equal to marginal cost, which would require a subsidy, and setting price equal to average cost, which would ensure a normal profit, underscores the dilemma confronted by regulatory authorities. When price is set equal to marginal cost, this yields the *socially optimal* allocation of resources because the marginal cost of producing the last unit sold equals the consumers' marginal value of that last unit. Under this pricing rule, however, the monopolist will face recurring losses unless a subsidy is provided. These losses disappear when price is set equal to average cost, thereby ensuring a normal, or fair, profit to the monopolist. But this solution only partially corrects the monopolist's tendency to restrict output; output is still less than would be socially optimal.

Thus, the dilemma facing regulators is whether to subsidize the firm and have the monopolist charge the socially optimal price or whether to have the monopolist set a price that is higher than is socially optimal but that allows for a normal profit. There is no right answer. When compared to the profit-maximizing solution, either outcome reduces price, increases output, increases consumer surplus, and eliminates the economic profit of the monopolist.

THEORIES OF ECONOMIC REGULATION

Why does government regulate certain markets? Why not allow market forces to allocate resources? There are two views of the rationale for government regulation. The first view has been implicit in the discussion thus far—namely, economic regulation is in the public interest. The public interest is often considered the same as the consumer interest. Regulation is designed to promote social welfare by controlling natural monopolies and by promoting competition where it is economically desirable.

A second view of regulation argues that regulation is not in the public, or consumer, interest but rather is in the special interest of producers. According to this view, well-organized producer groups expect to profit from regulation and are able to convince public officials to impose the desired restriction, such as limiting entry into the industry or preventing competition among existing firms. Producers have more to gain or lose from regulation than do consumers; producers typically are also more organized than consumers and are therefore better able to bring about regulations that are favorable to them.

To understand why producer interests could influence public regulation, consider the last time you had your hair cut. Whoever cut your hair probably cuts hair as a profession. Most states regulate the training and licensing of professionals. If any new regulation crops up that affects their profession, such as entry restrictions or license requirements, who has more interest in the outcome of that legislation, you or the person who cuts hair for a living? Producers have a special interest in matters that affect their livelihood, so they play a disproportionately large role in trying to influence such legislation.

As a consumer, however, you do not specialize in getting haircuts. You purchase haircuts, movies, toothpaste, notebooks, and thousands of other goods and services. You have no *special* interest in legislation affecting hair cutting. Because of this basic asymmetry in the interests of producers and consumers, some critics argue that business regulations often favor producer interests rather than consumer interests. Producer groups, as squeaky wheels in the legislative system, receive the most grease in the form of favorable regulations.

Legislation favoring producer groups is usually introduced under the guise of the consumer interest. Producer groups may argue that unbridled competition in their industry would lead to results that are undesirable for consumers. For example, the alleged problem of "cutthroat" competition among taxi drivers has led to regulations fixing rates and limiting the number of taxis in most large metropolitan areas. Or regulation may appear in the guise of quality control, as with the case of state control of professional groups such as doctors and lawyers, where regulations are viewed as necessary to keep unlicensed "quacks" out of the profession.

Another way the special-interest theory works is that the initial intent of the legislation may have been clearly in the consumer interest. Over time, however, the regulatory machinery begins to act more in accord with producer interests. Producers, because of their political power and strong stake in the regulatory outcome, are, in effect, able to "capture" the regulating agency and force it to serve producer interests. This "capture" theory of regulation was best explained by George Stigler of the University of Chicago, who argued that "as a general rule, regulation is acquired by the industry and is designed and operated for its benefit."[1]

A more complex variant of the "capture" theory has recently emphasized the idea that not all industry members may be of one mind regarding the most favorable kind of regulation. For example, small retail stores may support measures that would be opposed by large retail stores; major trucking companies may choose different regulations than smaller, independent truckers. Competing interest groups jockey with one another for the most favorable regulations. Thus, it is not simply a question of consumer interests versus producer interests but rather of one producer interest versus another producer interest.[2]

Perhaps it would be useful at this point to discuss in some detail the direction that regulation has taken in particular industries. First, we will examine the role of the Interstate Commerce Commission as a regulator of

---

[1] "The Theory of Economic Regulation," *The Bell Journal of Economics and Management Science* (Spring 1971): 3.

[2] But just as producer groups may not represent a single interest, consumer groups may not either. For example, major users of electricity prefer rates that decline with usage, whereas smaller users do not because they expect that rates for smaller users might be higher on average with a declining rate structure. Residents of small, rural communities view train service differently from residents in major metropolitan areas.

the railroads and trucking, referred to as the ground transportation industry. Then we will consider the Civil Aeronautics Board in its regulation of interstate airline passenger service. Both industries have been undergoing deregulation during the last decade.

Rail and Truck Regulation and Deregulation

The Interstate Commerce Commission (ICC), established in 1887 to regulate the railroads, was the first federal regulatory agency in this country. Because of the heavy fixed costs associated with laying tracks, the railroads had declining average cost curves and appeared to be a natural monopoly. The major railroads supported the establishment of the ICC to stabilize rates and to allocate business among the different railroad shippers. More generally, the ICC was established to reduce "cutthroat" competition among competing railroads and to ensure that even small towns would receive railroad service. Thus, at the outset regulation had several objectives, and it was unclear whether these regulations were in the consumer interest or more in the producer interest.

The railroads ran relatively smoothly under regulation until the 1930s, when they began to face vigorous competition from the emerging trucking industry. The railroads wanted to avoid competition with trucks, and in 1935 Congress extended control of the ICC to trucking. The intent of the regulation was to equalize the price to shippers of the two kinds of transportation, so the two did not directly compete on the basis of price.

In a variety of ways the ICC was able to control the structure of what has come to be called the ground transportation industry. Most important were regulations about new entry, price competition, and shipping conditions. With regard to entry, no carrier could operate without a license, and the ICC would not issue new licenses unless the applicant could show that such entry was "necessary for the public convenience." Existing shippers, however, had a strong interest in presenting evidence to the contrary, so few new licenses were granted. Recall that the ability to exclude new entrants is a prerequisite, though not a guarantee, of long-run economic profit.

Ability to Fix Prices   The ICC had control over shipping rates, but much of this power was relegated to rate-setting bureaus consisting of members drawn from the rail and trucking industries. Consequently, industry members could fix prices legally. Any competitor who wished to charge a lower price had to receive ICC permission. Because such rulings required hearings and often took up to a year to settle, the system discouraged price competition. The ICC also regulated the conditions of service, including the kind of products that could be hauled, the routes that could be taken, and even the number of cities that could be served along the way. The idea was to take away the versatility of trucks by treating them as if they ran on tracks, thereby reducing any advantage trucks had over the railroads.

Regulating Operating Conditions   As you might imagine, much inefficiency resulted from forcing trucks to operate like trains. Routes operated on the "gateway" system, similar to railroad junction points. For example, a carrier with a license to ship between points *A* and *B* and between *C* and *D* could haul from *A* to *C* only if it passed through point *B* first. Other rules allowed trucks to haul from *A* to *B* but not from *B* to *A*. So a truck could haul a load from St. Louis to Chicago but could not carry a return load. Such restrictions often required trucks to go hundreds of miles out of their way or to travel empty part of the time. Of course, all this added to the cost of transportation. Despite the higher cost of shipping created by regulation, however, the ability of truckers to fix their prices and restrict entry generally ensured their profitability because transportation services were much in demand, and there were no close substitutes. In fact, "shipping rights," or the authority to haul particular goods between cities, became valuable commodities, and an active market was created for buying and selling these rights.

Scholars who examined the issue concluded that regulation kept trucking rates higher than the competitive level. However, because regulation increased the cost of operation, not all of the higher rates translated into higher profits. As we have seen, some of the higher rates resulted from the inefficiency caused by the regulations. And a portion of higher rates was captured by those supplying resources to the industry—namely, truck drivers, in the form of higher wages, particularly to the members of the truckers' union, the International Brotherhood of Teamsters. Because regulation strictly limited the entry of new firms and prohibited price competition between particular locations, trucking firms could comply with union demands for higher wages without fear of losing business to nonunion competitors.

Deregulation   The Motor Carriers Act of 1980 began the deregulation of trucking. Not only was new entry allowed but the restrictions on routes, commodities, and the like were also reduced. The elimination of "gateways," one-way shipping, and other vestiges of a system aimed at treating trucks as if they were trains reduced duplication and waste. During the first three years of the deregulated environment, an estimated 10,000 small, new trucking firms entered the industry. During the same interval, trucking rates dropped substantially in many categories. For example, the average rate per mile for a full truckload of machinery dropped from $1.55 to $1.11, a 28 percent decline. And these drops were all the more dramatic because they came at a time when the cost of fuel was rising.

Although consumers gained from the increased competition and falling prices, deregulation also created some losers. More than 300 trucking firms, some of them very large, went bankrupt, and nearly one-third of the nation's 300,000 unionized truck drivers lost their jobs. In the wake of deregulation, Teamsters union members were often forced to accept labor contracts that called for wage cuts. Another predictable effect of the deregulation was a decline in the value of shipping rights. When shipping certificates were closely regulated, these rights had an estimated aggregate value of $750 million. When entry restrictions were eliminated, however, their value disappeared almost overnight.

Winners and Losers   Despite the clear efficiency gains of deregulation, the concentrated allocation of the losses to well-identified groups ensured that the path to full deregulation would not be smooth. Losers (existing shippers, truck drivers) are a concentrated group who know who they are, while winners (consumers) are widely dispersed and often do not even know they are winners. As a result, there has been growing resistance to deregulation. The ICC has been slow to deregulate the railroads, and pressure has been building to "reregulate" trucking. In fact, there was so much internal strife on the ICC that the commission did not meet at all in 1983. The chairman, supported by the Teamsters union, was slow to push deregulation.

The spirit of deregulation has also been slow to reach the ICC's sprawling bureaucracy. According to one report,[3] the ICC field staff continued to block those seeking an operating license and continued to pursue price cutters, even though Congress, the Reagan Administration, and the ICC were on record as favoring greater competition. But despite foot-dragging by the ICC bureaucracy and some ambivalence on the part of the commission, the efficiency gains of deregulation have been impressive.

The Railroads and Cross-Subsidization   Deregulation may have promoted thriving competition in trucking, but the railroads seemed beyond help, despite the setting of minimum rates, control of competition along rail routes, subsidies, the promotion of mergers among railroads, and other measures designed to prop up this ailing industry. Regulations required railroads to provide service to remote and rural locations that would not warrant service based on market demand. The railroads were not allowed to drop unprofitable routes or services. The result was that revenue from profitable routes was used to subsidize operations on unprofitable routes, a policy called **cross-subsidization**. This cross-subsidy from profitable to unprofitable routes contributed to the bankruptcy of some lines. After several railroads in the Northeast went bankrupt, deregulatory measures were introduced to promote efficiency and stability in the industry. One effect of deregulation was to allow for the abandonment of unprofitable routes.

Much of the experience with ground transportation regulation and deregulation is also reflected in the case of the airlines, as we will see in the next section.

*Under **cross-subsidization** revenues from profitable activities are used to subsidize unprofitable activities.*

---

[3]See Christopher Conte, "ICC Nears Paralysis as Its Members Feud Bitterly About Deregulation," *The Wall Street Journal,* 18 July 1984.

Airline Regulation and Deregulation

Throughout most of the history of aviation, the airline business was closely regulated by the Civil Aeronautics Board (CAB), established by the Civil Aeronautics Act of 1938. This regulatory body essentially prevented new entry into the airline industry and, by fixing prices, prevented price competition as well. Any carrier that was interested in serving an interstate route had to convince the CAB that the route needed another airline, a task that proved to be impossible. During the 40 years prior to deregulation, more than 150 applications for long-distance routes were submitted by potential entrants, but no new entry was allowed. The CAB also forced strict compliance with regulated prices. A request to lower prices on any route would result in a rate hearing, where scrutiny was given not only by the CAB but also by competitors.

Although the CAB, in effect, prohibited price competition in the industry, nonprice competition was abundant. Airlines competed in such ways as the frequency of flights, the quality of meals, even the friendliness of the staff. These nonprice forms of competition, particularly the frequency of flights, increased operating costs. High flight frequency meant that more seats were empty; before deregulation nearly half the seats in the air were flying without passengers. Thus, the price was fixed and entry was blocked, but there was no restriction on the quantity supplied. Firms in the industry expanded the number of flights they offered and spent more on promotion, trying to lure new customers, all of which raised the average cost of providing airline service. Costs rose until the firms in the industry earned only a normal rate of return. Thus, air fares set above competitive levels plus entry restrictions are no guarantee of economic profit as long as there are no restrictions on nonprice competition or on the number of flights each airline could offer.

Deregulation

In the late 1970s, under the direction of economist Alfred Kahn, the CAB began to deregulate. In 1978 Congress passed the Airline Deregulation Act, which reduced restrictions on price competition and on new entry. During the first year of deregulation the average fare fell by 20 percent. However, perhaps the biggest change was in the number of new entrants: between 1978 and 1983, 14 new airlines entered the industry. At the same time, some major airlines, such as Braniff, went bankrupt.

The insulation from price competition had allowed firms to pay higher wages than would have prevailed in a more competitive industry. The Air Line Pilots Association, the union that represented pilots for all the major airlines prior to deregulation, had been able over the years to negotiate extremely attractive wages for its members. A senior pilot, who typically worked less than two weeks a month, earned as much as $150,000 a year in

1983.[4] Just how attractive the pilot's position was became apparent after deregulation. America West Airlines, a nonunion employer that sprouted from deregulation, paid its pilots only $32,000 a year and required them to work 40 hours a week, performing dispatch and marketing tasks when they were not flying. Yet America West received some 4000 applications for its 29 pilot vacancies.

Problems with Deregulation

As we have noted, deregulation creates winners and losers. The winners, airline passengers, often fail to make the connection between deregulation and lower air fares. Few airline passengers are likely to write Congress and thank them for the lower fares. But the losers certainly can make the connection, and they express their concerns to Congress. For example, the Air Line Pilots Association pushed for a return to rate regulation and supported a bill proposed to add "stability" to air fares.

Other possible problems have been raised as a consequence of deregulation in the trucking and airline industries. Since one of the original rationales for regulation was to provide service even to smaller towns, there has been a concern that deregulation would strip these smaller communities of their services. Another concern is that the government will lose the control it had under regulation over the quality and safety of airline service. Although it is too early for definitive answers, there is little evidence to indicate that these fears have materialized. For example, despite the demise of the CAB, the Federal Aviation Administration still regulates the safety and quality of air service.

The course of regulation and deregulation raises some interesting questions about the true objective of regulation. Recall that there are competing views of regulation: one view holds that regulation is in the public, or consumer, interest; the second view holds that regulation is in the special, or producer, interest. The record of regulation and deregulation of ground and air transportation supports both views. Although regulation in these industries appeared more in accord with producer interest, the original movement toward deregulation probably sprang from a government policy to promote consumer interests.

At the outset we noted the confusion and ambiguity that often surrounds the relationship between government and business. The regulation of industry, for example, can appear aimed at reducing competition and promoting monopoly. Another set of government controls, called antitrust laws, attempts to promote competition and reduce monopoly. The history and development of these laws will be examined next.

---

[4]For an interesting account of life as a top pilot, see Victor F. Zohana, "End of Glamorous Life Looms for U.S. Pilots As Competition Grows," *The Wall Street Journal,* 2 November 1983.

ANTITRUST LAWS

Although competition typically ensures the most efficient use of the nation's resources, we have noted that an individual firm would prefer to operate in a business climate that is more akin to monopoly. And, if left alone, some firms would attempt to create a monopolistic environment by driving competitors out of business, merging with other firms, or colluding with competitors. In the United States *antitrust laws* attempt to curb these anticompetitive practices. Antitrust policy works in two ways. First, it tries to promote the sort of market structure that will lead to greater competition. Second, it tries to control market conduct to reduce or eliminate anticompetitive behavior. Thus, antitrust laws attempt to shape market structure and control market conduct in ways that will promote socially desirable market performance. In this section we examine the history and the record of antitrust policy in the United States. We then consider the future direction of this form of business regulation.

Origins of Antitrust Policy

Within a span of 25 years at the end of the nineteenth century and the beginning of the twentieth century, the essential features of U.S. antitrust laws were put into place. The key laws were the *Sherman Act* of 1890, the *Clayton Act* of 1914, and the *Federal Trade Commission Act* of 1914. What happened in this country to precipitate legislation that was virtually the first of its kind in the world?

The Business Climate   A variety of economic events occurred in the last half of the nineteenth century to create the political movement for antitrust legislation. Perhaps the two most important factors were (1) technological breakthroughs that led to more extensive use of capital, resulting in a larger optimal plant size in many manufacturing industries, and (2) the rapid growth of the railroads, which lowered the cost of transporting manufactured goods. Economies of scale in production and cheaper transportation extended the geographical boundaries of markets, allowing firms from outside a geographical area to penetrate what before had been only regional markets. So firms grew larger and reached a wider market.

Depressions in 1873 and 1883, however, caused a near panic among these large manufacturers, who were now committed to the heavy fixed cost associated with large-scale production. Their defensive reaction was to lower prices in an attempt to stimulate sales. Price cutting created economic turmoil, as might be expected, and firms began looking for ways to stabilize their markets. One solution was for competing firms to form a **trust** by either merging to form a single enterprise or simply agreeing on a uniform pricing policy. Early trusts were formed in sugar, tobacco, and oil. Although the history of early trust activity remains clouded, these trusts allegedly pursued anticompetitive practices to develop and maintain a dominant market position.

*A **trust** is a merger or collusive agreement among competing firms.*

These practices provoked widespread criticism and earned promoters of trusts the derisive title of "robber barons." Public sentiment lay on the side of the smaller competitors. Farmers, especially, resented the higher prices of manufactured goods, which resulted from the trusts' activity, particularly since the prices farmers were receiving for their own products were declining through the late 1800s. Public dissatisfaction with trusts led 18 states in the 1880s to enact antitrust laws, which prohibited the formation of trusts. State laws, however, were largely ineffective because the trusts could move to avoid them.

Sherman Antitrust Act of 1890   In 1888 the major political parties put antitrust planks in their platforms, which culminated in the Sherman Antitrust Act of 1890. The law contained two main sections:

> Section 1: Every contract, combination in the form of trust or otherwise, or conspiracy, in restraint of trade or commerce among the several states or with foreign nations, is hereby declared illegal.

> Section 2: Every person who shall monopolize, or conspire with any other person or persons to monopolize any part of the trade or commerce among the several states, or with foreign nations, shall be guilty of a misdemeanor.

Penalties for violations included fines of up to $5000 (this has since risen to over $1 million) plus a possible jail term.

During the first 10 years the enforcement of the law was hampered by a lack of funds and the absence of a forceful attorney general. Not until Theodore Roosevelt took office in 1901 was a special antitrust division established in the Department of Justice to prosecute offenders. The laws on the books were stiffened in 1914 by additional legislation.

The Clayton Act of 1914   It was apparent after more than 20 years of attempts to "bust" trusts that the Sherman Act let much anticompetitive activity slip between the cracks. President Woodrow Wilson was the force behind the Clayton Act of 1914, which was designed to outlaw certain practices not prohibited by the Sherman Act. Section 2 of the Clayton Act prohibited price discrimination where this practice tended to create a monopoly. Recall that price discrimination is charging different customers different prices for the same good or the same customer different prices for different quantities of the good.

*Under a **tying contract** a seller of one good requires buyers to purchase other goods as well.*

Section 3 of the Clayton Act prohibited tying contracts and exclusive dealing. **Tying contracts** occur when the seller of one good requires buyers to purchase another good as well. For example, a seller of a patented machine might require customers to purchase unpatented supplies. **Exclusive dealing** occurs when a producer sells a product only if the buyer agrees not to purchase from other manufacturers. For example, a computer chip maker sells chips to a computer maker only if the computer maker agrees not to

***Exclusive dealing** occurs when a producer requires a buyer not to purchase from other sellers.*

*In an **interlock-ing directorate** the same individ-ual serves on the boards of directors of competing firms.*

purchase chips elsewhere. Other sections of the law prohibited **interlocking directorates**, where the same individual serves on the boards of directors of competing firms.

Federal Trade Commission Act of 1914   In the course of early attempts to enforce antitrust laws, the government needed a group with a particular knowledge of business dealings to investigate and enforce these laws. To that end the *Federal Trade Commission* (FTC) was established in 1914. It consisted of five full-time commissioners appointed by the President for seven-year terms; the commissioners were assisted by a professional staff. As part of the supporting legislation, "unfair methods of competition" were prohibited. Originally, the FTC had the authority to determine exactly what was "unfair," but not for long. A 1919 Supreme Court decision ruled that only the courts could interpret the laws to determine what practices were fair and unfair. This ruling limited the role of the FTC, but in 1938 the *Wheeler-Lea Act* gave the FTC the added responsibility of prohibiting "deceptive acts or practices in commerce." Thus, the FTC took on the role of policing untrue and deceptive advertising.

The Sherman, Clayton, and FTC acts provided the basic framework for antitrust enforcement, a framework that has been clarified and embellished by subsequent amendments. Specifically, in 1936 the *Robinson-Patman Act* prohibited firms from selling "at unreasonably low prices" when the intent was to reduce competition. This law, however, proved difficult to enforce. Another loophole in existing legislation was closed in 1950 with the passage of the *Celler-Kefauver Anti-Merger Act*, which prevented one firm from buy-ing the assets of another firm if the effect was to reduce competition. This law prohibited both horizontal mergers and vertical mergers where these mergers tended to reduce competition in a particular industry. For example, a merger of Coke and Pepsi would probably be prohibited.

Antitrust Law Enforcement

Congress makes the laws, but the courts enforce them. Any law's effective-ness depends on the vigor and vigilance of enforcement. The pattern of enforcement goes something like this: a firm or group of firms is charged with breaking the law by the Antitrust Division of the Justice Department or the Federal Trade Commission. These government agencies are often acting on a complaint by a customer or a competitor. At that point those charged with the wrongdoing may be able, without any admission of guilt, to sign a *consent decree*, whereby they agree not to continue doing whatever they had been charged with. If the charges are contested, evidence from both sides is presented in a court trial, and a decision is rendered by a judge. Certain decisions may be appealed all the way to the Supreme Court, and in such cases the high court may render new interpretations of existing law.

Since these cases often start with the Justice Department, antitrust law enforcement can change with the Attorney General's inclination to file charges and with the judicial spirit of interpreting the laws. The vigor of this enforcement has varied with the political party in power and with the judicial climate. In the earliest days of antitrust legislation, the Attorney General had little interest in enforcing antitrust laws. The establishment of an Antitrust Division in the Justice Department added punch to the antitrust laws. But not until after World War II were these laws most aggressively enforced.

Those parties who can show injury by firms that have violated antitrust laws can sue the offending company and recover three times the amount of the damages sustained. These so-called treble damage suits increased after World War II; more than 1000 cases are initiated each year. Courts have been relatively generous to those claiming to have been wronged. The potential cost of being liable for treble damages makes firms more wary of violating antitrust laws.

Per Se Illegality and the Rule of Reason

The courts have interpreted the antitrust laws in essentially two ways. One set of practices has been declared illegal *per se*—that is, without regard to their economic rationale or their consequences. For example, under the Sherman Act all agreements among competing firms to fix prices, restrict output, or otherwise restrain the forces of competition are viewed as illegal *per se*. Under a *per se* rule, in order to find the defendant guilty, the government need only show that the offending practice took place; thus, the government need only examine the firm's *conduct*.

Another set of practices falls under the *rule of reason*. Here the courts consider a broader inquiry into the facts surrounding the particular offense— namely, the reasons why the offending practices were adopted and the effect of these practices on competition. The rule of reason was first set forth in 1911, when the Supreme Court held that the Standard Oil Company had illegally monopolized the petroleum refining industry. Standard Oil allegedly had come to dominate 90 percent of the market by acquiring more than 120 former rivals and by implementing predatory pricing tactics to drive remaining rivals out of business. In finding Standard Oil guilty, the court focused on both its market conduct and the market structure that resulted from Standard Oil's activity, and the court found that Standard Oil had behaved unreasonably.

This two-edged sword of the rule of reason allowed U.S. Steel in 1920 to be found not guilty because it had tried but failed to monopolize the steel industry. In this case the court ruled that not every contract or combination in restraint of trade was illegal. Only those that "unreasonably" restrain trade violate antitrust laws. The court said that mere size was not an offense. Although U.S. Steel clearly possessed monopoly power, the company was not in violation of antitrust laws because it had not unreasonably used that power. The courts changed that view 25 years later in reviewing the charges against the Aluminum Company of America (Alcoa). In a 1945 decision, the Supreme Court held that though a firm's conduct might be reasonable and legal, the mere possession of monopoly power—Alcoa controlled 90 percent of the aluminum ingot market—violated the antitrust laws. Here the court was using market *structure* rather than market *conduct* as the appropriate test of legality.

Problems with Antitrust

There is growing doubt about the economic value of some of the lengthy antitrust cases pursued in the past. For example, a government case against IBM began in 1969, when the Antitrust Division sued IBM under Section 2 of the Sherman Act, charging that the company, with nearly 70 percent of domestic sales of electronic data processing equipment, had a monopoly. IBM was also charged with introducing the 360 line of computers to eliminate competition in 1965. IBM responded that its large market share was based on its innovative products and on its economies of scale. The trial began in 1975, and the government took nearly three years to present its case. Litigation persisted for years. In the meantime many other computer manufacturers emerged both in this country and abroad to challenge IBM's dominance. Evidently, the threat of monopoly had diminished enough so that in 1982 the Reagan Administration dropped the case, noting that it was "without merit."

Too Much Emphasis on the Competitive Model   Joseph Schumpeter argued a half century ago that competition should be viewed as a dynamic process. Firms are constantly in flux, introducing new products, shedding old products, trying to compete for the consumer's dollar in a variety of ways. In light of this, antitrust policy should not necessarily be aimed at increasing the number of firms in each industry. In some cases firms will grow large because they are more efficient than rivals at offering what consumers want. Accordingly, firm size should not be the primary concern.

Role of International Markets   One yardstick for measuring the market power of a firm is its share of the market. With the growth of international trade, however, the local or even the national market share becomes less relevant. General Motors may dominate U.S. auto manufacturing, accounting for over half of domestic sales by U.S. firms in 1986. But when sales by Japanese and European producers are included, GM's share falls well below half. GM's share of world production has declined steadily since the mid-1950s. Where markets are open to foreign competition, domestic antitrust enforcement makes less economic sense.

Mergers and Public Policy

The Justice Department has been sensitive to some of its critics and in 1982 issued long-awaited guidelines on mergers. Perhaps the most significant feature of the new guidelines is the redefinition of market share. In determining the possible harm that a merger might have on competition, one important factor is the effect on the level of concentration in that market. The

*A **concentration ratio** measures the market share of the largest firms in an industry.*

measure of concentration employed until 1982 by the Justice Department was the four-firm **concentration ratio**, which is the sum of the percentage market shares of the top four firms in the market. Suppose a market consists of 44 firms. The top four firms represent 23 percent, 18 percent, 13 percent, and 6 percent, respectively, of the total share of market sales, and the remaining 40 firms have 1 percent each. The four-firm concentration ratio is the sum of the top four firms, which in this case is 60 percent.

One problem with the concentration ratio is that it says nothing about the distribution of market share among the four firms. For example, we would derive a four-firm concentration ratio of 60 percent if the top four firms each had 15 percent of the market share or if one firm had 57 percent of the market and the next three had 1 percent each. Yet clearly an industry in which one firm captures over half the market is likely to exhibit more market power than an industry with four firms of identical size.

*The **Herfindahl index** is the sum of squared percentage market shares of all firms in a market.*

To correct for this lack of precision, the Justice Department's new merger guidelines called for the use of the **Herfindahl index**, which is calculated by squaring the percentage market share of each firm in the market and then adding those squares. This measure provides more information than the four-firm concentration ratio because it places greater weight on firms with a larger market share. In Exhibit 3 we calculate the Herfindahl index for each of the three previous examples. Although each example has the same four-firm concentration ratio, they yield different Herfindahl index measures. Note that the index in Industry III is nearly triple that for the two other industries.

The new guidelines also sort all mergers into two bins: horizontal mergers, which involve firms in the same market, and nonhorizontal mergers, which include all others. Of most interest for antitrust purposes are horizontal mergers, such as a merger between competing oil companies. In evaluating whether to challenge an impending merger, the Justice Department examines not only what the level of market concentration would be after the merger (using the Herfindahl index) but also the ease of entry by other firms into the market, plus other factors affecting the profitability and ease of collusion in the market.

Perhaps the ultimate test of effectiveness of antitrust public policy is to examine the level and trend in competitiveness of the U.S. economy. To that topic we now turn.

COMPETITIVE TRENDS IN THE ECONOMY

For years there has been concern about the sheer size of some firms because of the real or potential power these firms might exercise in both the economic and the political arenas. One way to measure the power of the largest corporations has been to calculate the share of corporate assets controlled by the 100 largest firms. What percentage of the nation's assets do the top 100 manufacturing companies own, and how has this share changed over time?

EXHIBIT 3
COMPUTATION OF THE HERFINDAHL INDEX
BASED ON MARKET SHARE IN
THREE HYPOTHETICAL INDUSTRIES

Firm	Industry I		Industry II		Industry III	
	Market Share (percent)	Market Share Squared	Market Share (percent)	Market Share Squared	Market Share (percent)	Market Share Squared
A	23	529	15	225	57	3249
B	18	324	15	225	1	1
C	13	169	15	225	1	1
D	6	36	15	225	1	1
Remaining 40 firms (at 1 percent each)	1 each	40	1 each	40	1 each	40
4-Firm Concentration Ratio	60%		60%		60%	
Herfindahl Index		1098		940		3292

The largest 100 firms now control about half of all manufacturing assets in the United States, up from a 40 percent share after World War II. Thus, the largest firms have increased their share of the country's manufacturing assets. We should recognize, however, that size alone is not synonymous with market power; a very big firm, such as a large oil company, may face stiff competition, while the only movie theater in an isolated community may be able to raise its price with little concern about competition.

Market Competition over Time

More important than the size of the largest firms in the nation is the market structure in each industry. A variety of studies has examined the level and change in industry structure over the years. All used some variation of the concentration ratio as a point of departure, sometimes supplementing this measure with data from the specific industry about barriers to entry and other evidence suggesting whether the largest firms can control prices. Among the most comprehensive of these studies is the research of William Shepherd, who relied on many sources to determine the competitiveness of each industry in the U.S. economy.[5]

Shepherd sorted industries into four groups: (1) pure monopoly, in which a single firm controlled the entire market and was able to block entry; (2) dominant firm, in which a single firm had over half the market share and had no close rival, (3) tight oligopoly, in which the top four firms had more than 60 percent of the market, with stable market shares and evidence of cooperation; and (4) effective competition, in which firms in the industry exhibited low concentration, low entry barriers, and little or no collusion.

Exhibit 4 presents Shepherd's breakdown of all U.S. industries into each of the four categories in 1939, 1958, and 1980. The table shows a modest trend toward increased competition between 1939 and 1958, with those industries rated as "effectively competitive" growing from 52.4 percent to 56.3 percent of all industries. Between 1958 and 1980, however, there was a clear gain in the economy's competitiveness, with the share rated as effectively competitive jumping from 56.3 percent to 76.7 percent.

Exhibit 5 provides greater detail about Shepherd's findings based on eight broad industrial sectors. The first column lists the sector. To provide some idea of the relative importance of each sector, the second column lists the income generated by that sector. The remaining columns list the percentage of the industries in each sector that are rated "effectively competitive." The table shows a modest but widespread increase between 1939 and 1958 in competition, with increases in seven of the eight industrial sectors. Between

---

[5]William G. Shepherd, "Causes of Increased Competition in the U.S. Ecomony, 1939–1980," *Review of Economics and Statistics* 64 (November 1982).

EXHIBIT 4
TRENDS OF COMPETITION IN THE U.S. ECONOMY,
1939–1980

Competitive Group	Percentage Income Share of Each Category		
	1939	**1958**	**1980**
Pure monopoly	6.2	3.1	2.5
Dominant firm	5.0	5.0	2.8
Tight oligopoly	36.4	35.6	18.0
Effectively competitive	52.4	56.3	76.7
	100.0	100.0	100.0

Source: William G. Shepherd, "Causes of Increased Competition in the U.S. Economy, 1939–1980," *Review of Economics and Statistics* 64 (November 1982): 618, Table 2. The income share is the percentage of national income made up of industries in each competitive group.

EXHIBIT 5
COMPETITIVE TRENDS IN THE U.S. ECONOMY,
1939–1980, BY INDUSTRY SECTOR

Sectors of Economy	National Income Arising from Each Sector in 1978 ($ billions)	Percentage of Each Sector Rated as Effectively Competitive		
		1939	**1958**	**1980**
Agriculture, forestry, and fishing	54.7	91.6	85.0	86.4
Mining	24.5	87.1	92.2	95.8
Construction	87.6	27.9	55.9	80.2
Manu- facturing	459.5	51.5	55.9	69.0
Transportation and public utilities	162.3	8.7	26.1	39.1
Wholesale and retail	261.8	57.8	60.5	93.4
Finance, insurance, and real estate	210.7	61.5	63.8	94.1
Services	245.3	53.9	54.3	77.9
Totals	1512.4	52.4	56.4	76.7

Source: William G. Shepherd, *op. cit.*, 618, Table 2.

1958 and 1980, according to Shepherd, there were solid gains in the economy's competitiveness, with all sectors showing greater competition.[6]

Reasons for the Growth of Competition: 1958 to 1980

According to Shepherd, the growth in competition from 1958 to 1980 can be traced to three primary causes: imports, deregulation, and antitrust. Foreign imports between 1958 and 1980 resulted in increased competition in 13 major industries, including autos, tires, and steel. Imports were attractive to consumers because of their superior technology and lower price. Because they were competing with U.S. producers, who often had been tightly-knit domestic oligopolies, foreign competitors found these markets relatively easy to penetrate. At a cost and technological disadvantage, domestic producers' initial response was to seek trade barriers, such as quotas and tariffs, to reduce the foreign competition. According to Shepherd, the growth in imports accounted for one-sixth of the increase in competition.

A second reason for the growth in competition between 1958 and 1980 was the deregulation of several industries, including trucking, the airlines, and banking. We have already discussed some of the effects of this deregulation, particularly in reducing barriers to entry and in eliminating uniform pricing schedules. According to Shepherd's study, the deregulation movement has accounted for one-fifth of the increase in competition.

Although it is difficult to attribute an increase in competition to specific antitrust activity, Shepherd concludes that about two-fifths of the increase in competition between 1958 and 1980 can be credited to the effects of antitrust. He argues that although imports and deregulation were also important, their benefits could be quickly reversed by a shift toward protectionism and a return to regulation. In contrast, the effects of antitrust legislation are more permanent, and a reversal would require a much greater movement in both legislation and judicial opinion.

Thus, if we look at all large corporations, the share of corporate assets controlled by the largest firm has been increasing over time, but if we focus on particular industries, the overall degree of competition in the U.S. economy appears to be increasing. How is this paradox resolved? Many mergers in the years since World War II have been of the conglomerate variety, which joins firms operating in unrelated markets. If two giant firms from different industries merge, the assets held by the top 100 firms increase, yet there is no effect on the competitiveness of particular industries.

---

[6]He notes, however, that though competition has blossomed, market power remained high in many manufacturing industries, such as computers, drugs, and soups, as well as among utilities.

SUMMARY

1. Three types of government regulation of business are (1) social regulation, which attempts to foster a healthful environment, safety in the workplace, and consumer protection; (2) economic regulation, such as the regulation of natural monopolies; and (3) antitrust activity, which promotes competition and prohibits efforts to cartelize or monopolize an industry. This chapter examined economic regulation and antitrust activity.

2. Natural monopolies are regulated by government so that output is greater and price lower than would be the case if the monopolist were allowed to maximize profits. One problem with regulation is that the price that maximizes social welfare requires the government to subsidize the firm, whereas the price that allows the firm to earn normal profits does not maximize social welfare.

3. There are two views of economic regulation. The first is that economic regulation is in the public interest because it controls natural monopolies where monopoly is most efficient and promotes competition where competition is most efficient. A second view is that regulation is not in the public, or consumer, interest, but is in the special interest of producers.

4. Both the ground transportation and airlines industries were regulated for much of this century. Regulation had the effect of restricting entry and fixing prices. Both industries underwent deregulation in the early 1980s. Deregulation increased the number of firms in each industry but forced some existing firms into bankruptcy.

5. The Sherman, Clayton, and FTC acts provided the basic framework for antitrust enforcement, a framework that has been clarified and embellished by subsequent amendments. Antitrust laws are aimed at promoting competition and prohibiting efforts to cartelize or monopolize an industry.

6. Research indicates that while the percentage of all assests owned by the 100 largest firms has been increasing, the competition in U.S. industries has also been increasing since World War II. Three reasons for the growth in competition are foreign trade, deregulation, and antitrust activity.

QUESTIONS AND PROBLEMS

1. (Government Control of Business) Which of the three types of regulation of business— social, economic, or antitrust regulation—is the motivation for the following:
   a. marginal cost pricing
   b. liquor licensing
   c. building codes
   d. Clayton Act of 1914
   e. the establishment of the Small Business Administration

2. (Regulation) Why do most states require a doctor's prescription to obtain antibiotics? Such regulations do not exist in countries such as Mexico and Taiwan. Should all countries have such laws?

3. (Social Regulation) Recently the disease AIDS has brought into sharp focus the role of the drug regulatory agency known as the FDA. Why would AIDS patients feel resentment toward this agency? How might they circumvent FDA regulations?

4. (Trucking Regulations) The trucking industry has an unfair advantage (over other transportation, such as trains) since it uses the public highways, which were not built exclusively by the trucking companies. Therefore, the trucking industry should be regulated. Comment on this assertion.

5. (Regulation) Why might some industries prefer to be regulated rather than face an unregulated environment?

6. (Utility Regulation) It has often been noted that utility stocks tend to go up more slowly than the market and fall more slowly than the market. Is the stability of the utility stocks a result of the regulation of the industry? Why or why not?

7. (Antitrust) Why might a company plead guilty to anticompetitive behavior even though it knows such charges are unjustified? Will this plea depend on how large the company is?

8. (Antitrust) Since there are only three or four big auto manufacturers in the United States, this is prima facie evidence that an anticompetitive market structure exists and that antitrust laws therefore are being broken. Evaluate this assertion.

9. (Antitrust) Why might the Herfindahl index indicate the relative success of certain firms in an industry rather than measuring the anticompetitive structure of the industry?

PART
FOUR

Resource Markets

RESOURCE MARKETS

Why does Larry Bird earn more than Big Bird? Supply and demand. Why does prime Iowa corn acreage cost more than scrubland in the Texas panhandle? Supply and demand. Why are the buildings in Chicago taller than those in Bismarck, North Dakota? Supply and demand. Why do M.D.s earn more than Ph.D.s? Supply and demand. You say you have been through supply and demand already. True. But the earlier discussion focused on the product market—that is, the market for final goods and services. These goods and services, however, are produced by resources—land, labor, capital, and entrepreneurial ability. Resources are supplied by households and are demanded by firms. The payments resource owners receive are determined in resource markets. The supply and demand for these resources determine the distribution of income throughout the economy.

Because your income will depend upon the value of your resources in the market, the discussion of resource markets should be of particular interest to you. Certainly one key element in your career decision is the expected earnings associated with alternative careers. For example, after college should you become a regional sales representative or go on to law school? This chapter and the following few chapters will provide the framework to show how resource supply and demand interact to establish market prices for various resources. Topics and terms discussed include:

- Resource markets
- Resource demand
- Resource supply
- Economic rent
- Elasticity of resource demand

THE DEMAND AND SUPPLY OF RESOURCES

Without knowing any more about resource use than you know right now, see if you can answer the following questions about the demand for resources. Consider first the use of land. Old MacDonald had a farm. A neighbor offers him the opportunity of leasing an additional plot of farmland. MacDonald figures that farming the extra land will increase total revenue by $600 per year, but it will increase total production costs by $900 per year. Should Old MacDonald farm the extra land? What do you think? Since the additional cost of farming that land exceeds the additional revenue, the answer is no.

Next, consider labor. A firm's manager knows that hiring one more worker will increase the firm's total cost by $400 per week, but the firm's total revenue as a result of hiring the extra worker will increase by $500 per week. Should the profit-maximizing firm hire that additional worker? Sure. The firm can increase its profit by $100 per week by hiring the additional worker. As long as the additional revenue resulting from employing another worker exceeds the additional cost, the firm should hire that worker.

What about capital? Suppose that you cut lawns during the summer, earning an average of $10 per lawn. With your push-type mower, you cut about 15 lawns a week, for total earnings of $150. You are content until you read about a larger, faster mower—called the Lawn Monster—that will cut your time in half, allowing you to double the number of lawns you mow per week with the same effort. The Lawn Monster will double your total revenue to $300 per week, but will cost an extra $100 per week to use. Should you switch to the larger mower? Well, since your total cost increases by $100 per week but total revenue increases by $150 per week, your net revenue increases by $50 per week, so you should move up to the Monster.

A resource will be demanded as long as its marginal revenue exceeds its marginal cost. The previous examples involve the demand for resources. The same intuition can be used to examine the decision to *supply* resources. Consider the following choices. You are contemplating two jobs that you view as identical with one exception: one job pays more than the other. Is there any question about which job you will take? The simple point is that when other things are held constant, resource owners will supply their resources to the highest-paying alternative.

Now turn the example around to consider the case where you must choose between two jobs that are identical in all ways (including pay) except one: one job requires you to report for work at 5 A.M., a time of day when your body tends to reject conscious activity. The other job requires normal hours. Which job will you choose? Most of us will choose the job that is more in accord with our natural body rhythms. As a resource owner, you supply resources to maximize your utility. Usually this means that you choose the highest-paying job, though this is not always the case. You may, for example, be willing to accept less pay for the job with normal hours rather than start at 5 A.M.

Although you may as yet have no formal experience with resource markets, you should understand the economic logic behind resource supply. Resource owners will supply their resources to the highest-paying alternative, other things constant. Since other things are not always held constant, however, resource owners must often be paid more to supply their resources to certain uses. Households, as resource owners, will supply additional resources as long as doing so increases their utility. In the case of labor, the household's utility includes both pay and other, nonmonetary, aspects of the job. Jobs that are dirty, dangerous, exhausting, and of low status are generally less attractive than jobs that are clean, safe, stimulating, and of high status.

The firm demands resources from the household to maximize profits. The household supplies resources to firms to maximize utility. Differences between the profit-maximizing objectives of firms and the utility-maximizing objectives of households are reconciled through voluntary exchange in resource markets. We will now examine the workings of these markets.

The Demand and Supply of Resources

The easiest way to understand the resource market is to draw upon what you already know about the market for final goods and services. In the market for goods and services—that is, in the product market—households are demanders, and firms are suppliers. In resource markets, however, the supply and demand roles are reversed: firms are demanders, and households are suppliers. Whereas in the product market households demand that bundle of goods and services that maximizes utility, in resource markets firms demand that combination of resources that maximizes profit. The goal of profit maximization ensures that the firm will choose the most efficient production process and the least costly combination of resources available.

You should feel comfortable with the market for resources because the supply and demand curves have the same familiar shape. Exhibit 1 presents the market for a particular resource, in this case the labor market for economists. This market is characterized by an upward-sloping supply curve and a downward-sloping demand curve. This market will converge to the equilibrium wage rate, or the market price for this type of labor. The reasons behind the shape of the curves in resource markets are in some ways the same as the reasons for the curves in product markets. Like the supply and demand for final goods and services, the supply and demand for resources depend on the *willingness* and the *ability* of market participants to supply and demand these resources.

The Market Demand Curve   Why does a firm employ resources? Resources are used to produce goods and services, which a firm tries to sell for a profit. The firm does not value the resource itself; what the firm values is the resource's ability to produce goods and services. Because the value of any resource depends on the value of what it produces, the demand for a resource is a **derived demand**—derived from the value of the final product. Resource owners have an abiding interest in selling their resources in the market where the demand for the product of that resource is the greatest. Talented stage actors flock to New York City rather than Kansas City, for instance.

The market demand for a resource is the sum of the demands for that resource in all its various uses. For example, the market demand for economists will be made up of all the various demands for this type of labor in

*The demand for a resource is a **derived demand** — derived from the demand for the product the resource helps to produce.*

EXHIBIT 1   **RESOURCE MARKET FOR ECONOMISTS**

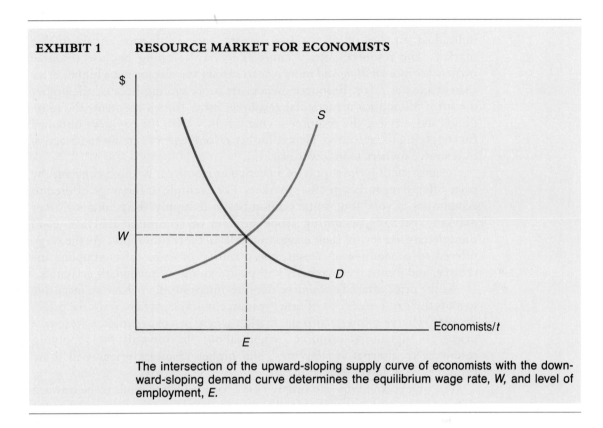

The intersection of the upward-sloping supply curve of economists with the down-ward-sloping demand curve determines the equilibrium wage rate, *W,* and level of employment, *E.*

higher education, industry, finance, and government. Similarly, the market demand for timber will consist of its demand in housing construction, paper products, railway ties, toothpicks, pencils, and so on. The demand curve for a resource, like the demand curve for the goods produced by that resource, is downward sloping, as depicted in Exhibit 1. As the price of a resource falls, producers are more *willing* and more *able* to employ that resource.

Consider first the producer's greater willingness to hire resources as the price falls. In constructing the demand curve for a particular resource, the prices of other resources are assumed to be constant. Consequently, if the price of this particular resource falls, it becomes relatively cheaper compared to other resources the firm could use to produce the same output. Hence, as the price of a resource declines, firms are more willing to hire this resource rather than other, now relatively more costly, resources. Thus, we observe *substitution in production,* such as economists for business administrators, coal for oil, or plastic tubing for copper tubing.

A lower price for a resource also increases a producer's *ability* to hire that resource. At a lower price firms can purchase more resources for the same total cost. If the price of a resource drops by half, a producer can buy twice the amount for the same total cost. This does not mean that the firm *would* buy twice the amount, only that because price has fallen, the firm *could* buy twice the amount.

The Market Supply Curve   The market supply of a resource is the sum of individual supplies of all resource owners, such as all economists, to that market. The resource supply curve is upward sloping because resource owners are more *willing* and more *able* to supply the resource at a higher price than at a lower price. Resource owners are more willing because the higher the price offered for a particular resource, other things constant, the more goods and services the resource owner can buy with the payment obtained for supplying the resource. Hence, higher resource prices are more attractive to resource owners than lower prices.

In constructing the supply of a particular resource, we hold constant the price offered resources in other markets. For example, if the wage offered to economists is very low, some economists will supply their labor to other markets, perhaps becoming stock brokers or computer analysts, even though they use few of their economic skills in these other jobs. As the wage offered to economists increases, the quantity of economists supplied increases, and existing economists will be drawn out of secondary activities.

As the price offered a resource rises, resource suppliers have an incentive to shift their resources out of other resource markets, where resource prices are now relatively lower, into the market where prices are higher. Resource prices are signals to resource owners about the rewards for supplying resources to alternative activities, and higher resource prices will draw resources from lower-valued uses.

The first reason why the supply curve for a resource tends to be upward sloping is the resource owners' *willingness* to supply more of the good as the price goes up. The second reason is the resource owners' increased *ability* to supply more of the resource at a higher price. For example, as the price of oil increased, more oil exploration became economically feasible in less accessible locations, such as the remote jungles of the Amazon or the stormy waters of the North Sea. It is the higher price offered for the resource that enables resource suppliers to support a higher cost of supply.

Equilibrium and Resource Price Differences

We have sketched only one resource market, but there are as many resource markets as there are resources—markets for farmhands and farmland. Resource markets operate so that the price paid to identical resources should, over time, tend toward equality. This should be true even if these resources are supplied to different uses. For instance, consider the wages earned by a group of identical workers supplying their labor services to different uses. Assume that the nonmonetary benefits of these jobs, such as the social status of each job, are identical across the jobs under consideration, so we need to be concerned only with pay. Under these conditions, the wage offered identical workers should tend toward equality for the different uses. Otherwise, if wages differed across uses, workers would move from lower-wage uses into higher-wage uses, reducing the supply in the lower-wage occupations and increasing the supply in the higher-wage occupations. Such shifts would continue until wages equalized, and nobody had an incentive to move. Likewise, firms paying the higher price would try to hire the lower-priced resources, and this too would drive prices for identical resources toward equality. Differences in the price offered to identical resources provide a stimulus for firms and resource owners to adjust until these resources earn the same in each alternative use.

We often observe earnings differentials. On average, corporate economists earn more than academic economists, land in the city rents for more than rural land, brain surgeons earn more than tree surgeons, and good pickers of corporate stocks earn more than good pickers of navel oranges. As we will see, these differences can be traced to the workings of supply and demand and can be described as either disequilibrium differentials or equilibrium differentials.

Disequilibrium Differentials   Resource markets are often in the transitory state of groping toward equilibrium. Wage differentials can sometimes be observed for workers who appear equally qualified. Often these differentials reflect the vagaries of the marketplace, in which certain industries emerge and others decline. As we have noted, however, the mere presence of differences in the price of similar resources will encourage resource owners and firms to adjust supply and demand until the prices of identical resources are equal.

For example, the computer explosion has increased the demand for programmers. As a result, college graduates majoring in computer science expect to earn more than equally talented graduates with other majors. Over time, however, the signal of higher earnings in the computer field will draw more and more students into that field, increasing the supply and lowering the relative earnings. Meanwhile, the supply of graduates to other fields requiring similar aptitude will fall, increasing the relative earnings in those fields. Over time the increased supply of computer programmers and the decreased supply in fields such as mathematics and engineering will tend to equalize earnings in these different fields. The process could take years, but

Disequilibrium differentials are wage differences that trigger resource reallocation and wage adjustments.

when resource markets are free to adjust, **disequilibrium differentials** trigger the reallocation of resources, which equalizes payments for similar resources. Just as nature abhors a vacuum, markets abhor disequilibrium. Differentials in the prices of similar resources will set into motion equilibrating forces.

Equilibrium Differentials   Not all resource price differences will cause a reallocation of resources. For example, land along New York's Fifth Avenue sells for as much as $36,000 a square yard; for that amount you could buy many acres of farmland in upstate New York. Yet such a differential does not prompt any land owners in upstate New York to supply their land to New York City. This, of course, is impossible because land is immobile. Resource price differentials that do not precipitate the shift of resources among uses are called **equilibrium differentials**.

Equilibrium differentials are wage differences that do not precipitate resource reallocation.

Farmland itself sells for widely varying prices per acre, typically reflecting differences in the land's fertility. Such differences do not trigger forces to generate equality. Certain wage differentials stem from different costs of the underlying education and training required to perform particular tasks. This difference explains the differential in earnings between the brain surgeon and the tree surgeon. Other earnings differentials reflect differences in the nonmonetary aspects of similar jobs. For example, most people must be paid more to work in a grimy factory than in a pleasant office. Similarly, academic economists earn less than corporate economists because academic economists typically have greater freedom in their daily schedule and in their choice of research topics.

Whereas disequilibrium differentials spur resource movements away from lower-paid uses toward higher-paid uses, equilibrium differentials cause no such reallocations. Equilibrium differentials are explained by lack of resource mobility (urban land versus rural land), differences in the inherent quality of the resource (fertile land versus scrubland), differences in the time and money involved in developing the necessary skills (file clerk versus certified public accountant), and differences in the nonmonetary rewards of the job (lifeguard at Malibu Beach versus prison guard at San Quentin).

Transfer Earnings and Economic Rents

Larry Bird makes more than $1 million a year playing professional basketball. But he would likely be willing to play for less. The question is, how much less? How much does Mr. Bird have to be paid to play basketball rather than do something else? What is his next best alternative? Suppose his next best alternative is earning $25,000 as a high school basketball coach. And assume that, aside from the pay differences, Mr. Bird is indifferent between playing professional basketball and high school coaching. Thus, he must earn at least $25,000 playing basketball to keep him in the profession. This amount represents his **transfer earnings**, the amount he must be paid to "transfer," or to supply his talents, to professional basketball. His transfer earnings are what he could earn in the best alternative use of his resources. Transfer earnings can be thought of as the resource's opportunity cost.

Transfer earnings are what a resource could earn in its best alternative use.

Economic rent is the portion of a resource's total earnings in excess of transfer earnings.

The amount Larry Bird earns in excess of his transfer earnings is called **economic rent**. Economic rent is that portion of a resource's total earnings that is not necessary to keep the resource in its present use; it is, as they say, pure gravy. Economic rent may be thought of as a surplus over transfer earnings. The division of resource earnings between economic rent and transfer earnings depends on the resource owner's elasticity of supply. In general, the less elastic the resource supply is, the greater will be economic rents as a proportion of total earnings. As a way to develop a feel for the differences between economic rents and transfer earnings, consider the following three cases.

Case 1: All Earnings Are Economic Rent When a resource has no alternative use, the supply of a resource to a particular market is perfectly inelastic. Hence, there are no transfer earnings, and all returns are in the form of economic rents. Examples include the supply of a machine so specialized that it has only one particular use, and the supply of forest land so remote that it has no use other than as a source of timber. The supply of such a resource is presented by the vertical curve in panel (a) of Exhibit 2. The supply curve

EXHIBIT 2   TRANSFER EARNINGS AND ECONOMIC RENT

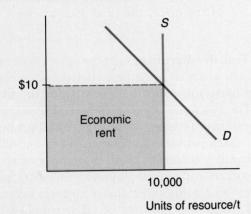

(a) All resource returns
are economic rent

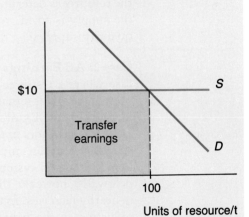

(b) All resource returns
are transfer earnings

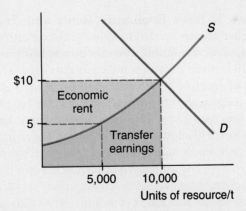

(c) Resource returns divided between
economic rent and transfer earnings

In panel (a) the labor supply curve is vertical, indicating that the resource has no alternative use. The wage rate is demand-determined, and all earnings are in the form of economic rent. In panel (b) the supply curve is horizontal, indicating that the resource can earn as much in its best alternative use. Employment is demand-determined, and all earnings are transfer earnings.

Panel (c) shows an upward-sloping supply curve. At the equilibrium price of $10, resource earnings are partly transfer earnings and partly economic rent. Both supply and demand determine the equilibrium price and quantity.

indicates that the 10,000 units of the resource have no alternative use. When the equilibrium price of the resource is $10 per unit, the economic rent is depicted by the shaded red area—an amount totaling $100,000. In this case the resource earns no transfer earnings; all earnings are economic rent. Because the value of this resource in its best alternative use is 0, the price of the resource is determined exclusively by the demand for the resource. Since the supply is fixed, regardless of the price, the price has no effect on the quantity supplied.

Case 2: All Earnings Are Transfer Earnings   At the other extreme is the case where a resource can earn as much in its best alternative use as in its present use. This situation is illustrated by the perfectly elastic supply curve in panel (b) of Exhibit 2. For example, suppose Exhibit 2(b) depicts the market for janitors in the local school system. At a wage of $10 per hour the school system can employ as many janitors as it chooses. At a wage of $10 an hour, the school system demands 100 units of labor. If the wage offered falls below $10, however, these workers will find employment elsewhere, perhaps in nearby factories. In this case all earnings are transfer earnings because any reduction in the wage will reduce the quantity of labor supplied to this particular use to 0. The next best alternative for these resources also pays a wage of $10 per hour. Here the demand curve determines the equilibrium quantity hired but not the equilibrium wage; the equilibrium wage is determined exclusively by the supply curve.

Case 3: Both Economic Rents and Transfer Earnings   Whenever a higher price is needed to increase the quantity of a resource supplied—that is, whenever the supply curve is upward sloping—resource owners will collect both transfer earnings and economic rent. This situation is presented in panel (c) of Exhibit 2, where economic rent is the shaded red area and transfer earnings is the blue area. A rising resource price attracts additional resources to this use. Since some resource owners had been willing to supply their resources at a lower price, however, the rising price creates economic rent for these resource suppliers. For example, if the price of a resource increases from $5 to $10, the quantity supplied increases by 5000 units. For those resource suppliers who had been offering their services at a price of $5, the difference between $5 and $10 is economic rent. This group did not require the higher price to supply their services, but they certainly are not going to turn it down. In the case of an upward-sloping supply curve and a downward-sloping demand curve, both supply and demand determine the equilibrium price and quantity. Note that when resources are very specialized, they tend to earn a higher proportion of economic rent than do resources with many alternative uses. Thus, Larry Bird earns a greater *proportion* of his income as rent than do economists.

To review, when a resource supply curve is vertical (perfectly inelastic), all resource earnings are in the form of economic rent. When resource supply is horizontal (perfectly elastic), all resource earnings are called transfer earnings. And when supply is upward sloping (an elasticity greater than zero but less than infinity), earnings are divided between transfer earnings and economic rent. When the supply of a resource is perfectly inelastic, supply determines the equilibrium quantity, but demand determines the equilibrium price. That is, if a resource is in fixed supply, the demand for the resource will dictate the price. When resource supply is perfectly elastic, demand determines the equilibrium quantity, but supply determines the equilibrium price. When supply is upward sloping, both supply and demand determine equilibrium price and quantity.

This completes our introduction to resource supply. In the balance of this chapter we take a closer look at the demand side of resource markets. As it turns out, the determinants of the demand for a resource are largely the same whether we are talking about land, labor, or capital. Thus, the demand for resources can be examined more generally. The supply of different resources, however, has certain peculiarities for each resource, so the supply of specific resources will be taken up in the next three chapters.

A CLOSER LOOK AT RESOURCE DEMAND

What resources are demanded and in what quantities? These are the fundamental questions for the firm making decisions in resource markets. In Chapter 2 we learned that the art of economic reasoning involves marginal reasoning—that is, focusing on adjustments to the status quo. Although we know that production usually involves the cooperation of many inputs, to cut the analysis down to size, we will focus primarily on the use of a single resource under the assumption that the quantities of all other resources are held constant. We will then generalize the analysis to show its relevance to all resources. As in the past, we assume that the firm's objective is to maximize profit.

Demand for One Resource

You may recall that when we introduced the firm's cost, we considered an example where labor was the only variable resource. By varying the amount of labor employed, we examined the relationship between the quantity of labor employed and the amount of output produced per day. The same idea is captured for the firm depicted in Exhibit 3, where all but one of the inputs are held constant. By increasing the amount of the variable resource, we can observe what happens to output. The first column presents units of the variable resource, in this case labor. The second column presents the total output, or total physical product, and the third column, the marginal physical product. The marginal physical product of labor shows how much additional output is produced by each additional unit of labor. The first unit of labor has a marginal physical product of 10 units, the second unit has a marginal physical product of 9 units, and so on.

The marginal physical product declines as more labor is used, reflecting the law of diminishing marginal returns. Recall that the law of diminishing marginal returns states that as additional units of the variable resource are combined with a given amount of other resources, a point is eventually reached where these additional units yield a smaller and smaller marginal physical product. In Exhibit 3 diminishing marginal returns set in immediately—that is, right after the first unit of output.

Note that although labor is used here as the variable resource, we could examine the marginal physical product of any resource by holding the quantities of other resources constant. For example, we could consider how many lawns you could cut per week if you vary the quantity of capital. You might start off with very little capital—imagine cutting the grass with a pair of scissors—and eventually move up to the Lawn Monster and beyond. By holding labor constant and varying the quantity of capital, we could compute the marginal physical product of capital. Likewise, we could compute the marginal physical product of land by examining crop production for varying amounts of land, holding other inputs, such as the amount of farm labor and capital, constant. The point is that although we focus on labor in this example, the analysis applies to other resources as well.

Marginal Revenue Product

Marginal revenue product is the change in total revenue when an additional unit of a resource is hired.

The first three columns of Exhibit 3 show what happens to the firm's output as the quantity of labor is varied. The important question for the profit-maximizing firm, however, is what happens to the firm's revenue as a result of hiring additional labor? What the firm wants to determine is the **marginal revenue product** of labor, which is how total revenue changes when an additional unit of labor is hired. Given that the quantities of other resources are held constant, a resource's marginal revenue product will depend on two things: (1) the amount of additional output produced and (2) the price of that output. As we will see next, if the firm sells its output in competitive markets, it can sell each additional unit of output at the prevailing market price because the firm faces a horizontal demand curve. If the firm has some monopoly power, however, the price must fall if the monopolist is to sell that additional output because the monopolist faces a downward-sloping demand curve.

Sales in Competitive Markets   The calculation of the marginal revenue product (*MRP*) is simplest when the firm sells its output in perfectly competitive markets, which is the assumption in Exhibit 3. Since the individual firm in perfect competition cannot affect the market price of its product regardless of how much it sells, the firm's selling price does not vary with output. The marginal revenue product, listed in column (6), is the change in total revenue that results from changing input by 1 unit. For the competitive firm the marginal revenue product is simply the price, in this case $2, multiplied by the marginal physical product, or $MRP = P \times MPP$. The marginal revenue product[1] indicates how much more revenue each

---

[1]For the competitive firm, the marginal revenue product is sometimes also called the value of the marginal product.

EXHIBIT 3
THE MARGINAL REVENUE PRODUCT WHEN A FIRM SELLS
IN A COMPETITIVE MARKET

(1)	(2)	(3)	(4)	(5)	(6)	(7)
Units of Variable Resource	Total Physical Product (TPP)	Marginal Physical Product (MPP)	Product Price	Total Revenue (TPP × Price)	Marginal Revenue Product (MRP)	Marginal Resource Cost (MRC)
0	0	—	$2	$0	—	$10
1	10	10	2	20	$20	10
2	19	9	2	38	18	10
3	27	8	2	54	16	10
4	34	7	2	68	14	10
5	40	6	2	80	12	10
6	45	5	2	90	10	10
7	49	4	2	98	8	10
8	52	3	2	104	6	10
9	54	2	2	108	4	10
10	55	1	2	110	2	10
11	55	0	2	110	0	10
12	53	−2	2	106	−4	10

additional unit of labor will generate. You could think of the marginal revenue product as the firm's "marginal benefit" from hiring 1 more unit of the resource. Because of diminishing returns, the marginal revenue product falls steadily as additional units of the input are employed.

Sales as a Monopolist If the firm has some monopoly power in the product market, the demand curve that firm faces is downward sloping, so to sell more output, the firm must lower its price. Exhibit 4 repeats the first two columns of Exhibit 3, but the remaining columns differ to reflect the revenue of a firm selling as a monopolist.[2] Column (2) lists total output for each level of labor employed. Column (3) presents the price at which consumers will demand that quantity of total output. Together, columns (2) and (3) represent the demand schedule for the good because they list the price at which consumers will demand each level of output. Total output multiplied by the price at which that output can be sold yields the firm's total revenue, which is presented in column (4).

The marginal revenue product of labor, which is the change in total revenue resulting from a 1-unit change in the quantity of labor employed, is listed in column (5). For example, the 10 units produced by the first unit of labor can be sold for $4 each, yielding total revenue of $40. The second unit of labor adds 9 units to total product, but in order to sell these additional units, the price for all output must be lowered from $4 to $3.52. If the 9 additional units could have been sold for $4 each, total revenue would have increased by

---

[2]Note that the marginal physical product schedule has been omitted because it is not directly used in the calculations.

EXHIBIT 4
THE MARGINAL REVENUE PRODUCT WHEN A FIRM SELLS AS A MONOPOLIST

(1) Units of Variable Resource	(2) Total Physical Product (TPP)	(3) Product Price	(4) Total Revenue (TPP × Price)	(5) Marginal Revenue Product (MRP)
0	0	—	—	—
1	10	$4.00	$40.00	$40.00
2	19	3.52	66.88	26.88
3	27	3.14	84.78	17.90
4	34	2.78	94.52	9.74
5	40	2.50	100.00	5.48
6	45	2.25	101.25	1.25
7	49	2.05	100.45	−0.80
8	52	1.90	98.80	−1.65
9	54	1.80	97.20	−1.60
10	55	1.75	96.25	−0.95
11	55	1.75	96.25	0.00

$36. Since we assume that this monopolist cannot price discriminate, however, *all* units must be sold for $3.52, so total revenue increased by less than $36. In this case total revenue increases by $26.88, which is the marginal revenue product for the second unit of labor. The marginal revenue product for a firm with monopoly power is most easily determined by computing the change in total revenue resulting from a 1-unit change in the input.

Recall that for firms selling in competitive markets, the marginal revenue product equals the marginal physical product times the price. For firms with some monopoly power, however, this direct calculation is not possible because the price must fall to sell the additional output. The marginal revenue product for competitive firms declined only because of diminishing marginal returns. Under monopoly, however, it declines both because of diminishing returns and because the selling price of the good must fall in order to sell increased output.

Resource Demand   The marginal revenue product schedule for the competitive firm depicted in Exhibit 3 is plotted as the firm's demand for the resource in Exhibit 5. The marginal revenue product curve indicates the additional revenue, or the "marginal benefit" to the firm, as a result of employing more labor. The profit-maximizing firm should be willing to pay as much as the marginal revenue product for an additional unit of labor. Thus, the marginal revenue product curve can be viewed as the firm's demand curve for that resource. To develop a better understanding of resource markets, we must consider the cost of hiring the resource.

Marginal Resource Cost

Given the firm's marginal revenue product curve—its demand curve for the input—can you tell how much labor the firm should employ to maximize

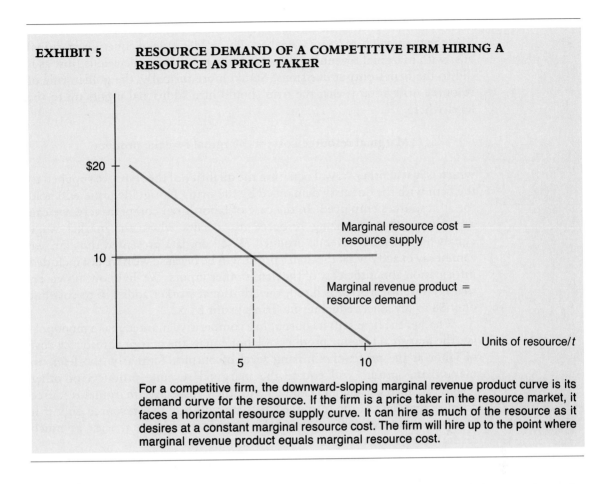

EXHIBIT 5

RESOURCE DEMAND OF A COMPETITIVE FIRM HIRING A RESOURCE AS PRICE TAKER

For a competitive firm, the downward-sloping marginal revenue product curve is its demand curve for the resource. If the firm is a price taker in the resource market, it faces a horizontal resource supply curve. It can hire as much of the resource as it desires at a constant marginal resource cost. The firm will hire up to the point where marginal revenue product equals marginal resource cost.

Marginal resource cost is the change in total cost when an additional unit of a resource is hired.

profits? Not yet, because you know only one side of the equation—the demand side. What you need to know is how much this resource costs the firm. Specifically, what is the **marginal resource cost**—that is, what is the marginal cost to the firm of employing one more unit of the resource? The simplest example of marginal resource cost occurs when the firm is a *price taker* in the resource market. A price taker hires such a tiny fraction of the available resource that the firm's actions have no effect on the price. Thus, the price taker faces a given market price of the resource and decides only on the quantity to be hired at that price.

Let's consider the case where the firm is a price taker for the input. If the market wage for factory workers is $10 per hour, the firm can hire as much labor as it wants without influencing that wage. Therefore, the marginal resource cost of labor is $10 per hour regardless of how much is employed. A marginal resource cost of $10 is listed back in column (7) of Exhibit 3 and is presented as the flat line drawn at the $10 level in Exhibit 5. The marginal resource cost curve is the supply curve faced by the price taker.

Given a marginal resource cost of $10 per hour, how much labor will the profit-maximizing firm purchase? The firm will hire more labor as long as doing so adds more to revenue than to cost—that is, as long as the marginal revenue product exceeds the marginal resource cost. The firm will stop hiring labor only when the two are equal. If the marginal resource cost equals $10, the firm will hire 6 units of labor. The golden rule of equating marginal cost with marginal revenue applies to all the firm's input decisions, just as it did to the firm's output decisions. Stated more formally, the golden rule of resource utilization is that the firm should hire additional inputs up to the level where

Marginal resource cost = Marginal revenue product

which is just another way of equating the quantity of the resource supplied to the firm with the quantity demanded by the firm. This golden rule will hold for all resources employed. In the case of labor hired competitively, we can say that profit-maximizing resource use occurs where the market wage equals the marginal revenue product. Based on data presented thus far, we cannot say exactly what the firm's profit will be because we have not included information about the cost of the firm's other inputs. We do know, however, that if a seventh worker is hired, the additional worker adds $10 to cost but only $8 to revenue, reducing the firm's profit by $2.

Whether the firm sells its output in a competitive market or as a monopolist, the marginal revenue product of labor equals the marginal resource cost of labor at the profit-maximizing level of output. Similarly, the firm, in maximizing profit, will equate the marginal revenue products of other resources, such as land and capital, with their respective marginal resource costs. Regardless of the resource, the firm will hire that resource only if it "pulls its own weight"—only if the resource produces at least as much revenue as it costs the firm.

Hiring Resources as a Monopsonist

The profit-maximizing resource use for the firm that is a price taker in the resource market is quite straightforward. A more complicated case involves the situation where the price the firm pays for a resource depends in part on how much of the resource the firm employs. A **monopsonist** is the only purchaser of a particular resource, just as a monopolist is the only seller of a product. But even if a firm is not literally the only buyer of a particular resource, we say a firm has monopsony power if it faces an upward-sloping resource supply curve.

*A **monopsonist** is the sole purchaser of a particular resource.*

Suppose the firm is an aircraft designer that employs such a large proportion of the total supply of aeronautical engineers in the market that the amount of this kind of labor supplied to the firm depends on the wage the firm offers. This firm is clearly not a price taker in the resource market. The supply curve of these engineers to the firm will be upward sloping, as reflected in Exhibit 6. The first column in Exhibit 6(a) lists the quantity of labor hired, and the second column shows the wage the firm must pay to attract that quantity of labor to the firm. Together the first two columns represent the supply of labor schedule faced by the monopsonist. This schedule is presented as the supply curve in Exhibit 6(b). To avoid having to

EXHIBIT 6 **RESOURCE DEMAND FOR A FIRM HIRING A RESOURCE AS A MONOPSONIST**

(a) MRC and MRP schedules

(1)	(2)	(3)	(4)	(5)
Units of Variable Resource	Wage	Total Cost (TRC)	Marginal Cost (MRC)	Marginal Revenue Product (MRP)
0	—	0	—	—
1	$8	$8	$8	$20
2	9	18	10	18
3	10	30	12	16
4	11	44	14	14
5	12	60	16	12
6	13	78	18	10
7	14	98	20	8
8	15	120	22	6

(b) MRC and MRP curves

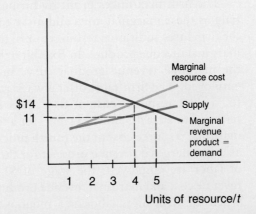

A monopsonist faces an upward-sloping resource supply curve. Marginal factor cost lies above that supply curve. The firm will hire the resource up to the point where marginal revenue product equals marginal resource cost (4 units) and will pay a wage read off the resource supply curve ($11).

calculate a new marginal revenue product schedule, we simply borrow the one from Exhibit 3 and list it as the final column in Exhibit 6(a). This marginal revenue product schedule is then plotted as the firm's demand curve in Exhibit 6(b).

Given the firm's supply and demand for labor, the temptation is to conclude that the firm will hire 5 units of labor because that is where the labor supply and labor demand curves intersect. But wait a minute. If the firm wants to hire additional units of engineering labor, it must raise the wage paid to all the engineers it employs. Consequently, the marginal resource cost exceeds the wage required to attract the marginal unit of labor. For example, according to the supply schedule, the firm must pay $9 to attract a second unit of labor. But if the firm pays $9 for a second unit, it must also pay $9 for the first unit. If the firm hires two units of labor, it cannot pay the second unit more than the first. Hence, the total cost must increase by $10 when 2 units rather than 1 unit of labor are hired ($9 for the second unit plus $1 more for the first unit). Thus, the $10 marginal resource cost for the second unit exceeds the wage of $9 required to attract that second unit.

Likewise, if the firm decides it needs 3 units of labor, it must pay $10 per unit to attract 3 units to the firm, for a total labor cost of $30. The labor cost for hiring 3 units is $12 more than the $18 cost of hiring 2 units, so the marginal resource cost of the third unit is $12. Compare columns (2) and (4) in Exhibit 6 and you can see that after the first unit of labor is hired, the marginal resource cost exceeds the wage, and the difference grows as more labor is employed. This growing difference is reflected most clearly by comparing the labor supply curve and the marginal resource cost curve in Exhibit 6(b).

The firm maximizes profit by hiring additional units of the resource as long as these marginal units add more to revenue than to cost. Specifically, the firm hires additional resources until the marginal resource cost equals the marginal revenue product. In Exhibit 6 the marginal resource cost curve and the marginal revenue product curve intersect where 4 units of labor are employed. The firm must offer a wage rate of $11 to attract 4 units of labor, for a total resource cost of $44. This compares with the $10 wage rate required to attract 3 units of labor, for a total resource cost of $30. Thus, the marginal resource cost of the fourth unit of labor is $14 ($44 − 30), which is also the marginal revenue product for the fourth unit of labor. When 4 units of labor are employed, the wage of $11 per hour is below the marginal revenue cost and marginal revenue product of the fourth unit of labor. Thus, when the firm hires labor as a monopsonist, in equilibrium the marginal revenue product of labor exceeds the wage rate.

Summarizing Four Market Possibilities

Let's review the market conditions examined thus far. On the product side of the market, a firm can sell its output in a competitive market, where the firm is a price taker, or the firm may have some degree of monopoly power and can sell more output only if the product price is reduced. On the resource side of the market, a firm either hires resources as a price taker or as a monopsonist.

The monopsonist can hire more of a resource only if the resource price is increased.

Thus there are two possibilities in the product market and two in the resource market. These possibilities are summarized in the matrix presented in Exhibit 7. Across the top are listed the two alternative markets the firm may face in hiring resources. The firm either hires resources in perfectly competitive markets and is therefore a price taker, or the firm hires resources as a monopsonist. The firm as a price taker is shown in Exhibits 7(a) and (c),

EXHIBIT 7   **RESOURCE MARKET EQUILIBRIUM UNDER ALTERNATIVE MARKET CONDITIONS**

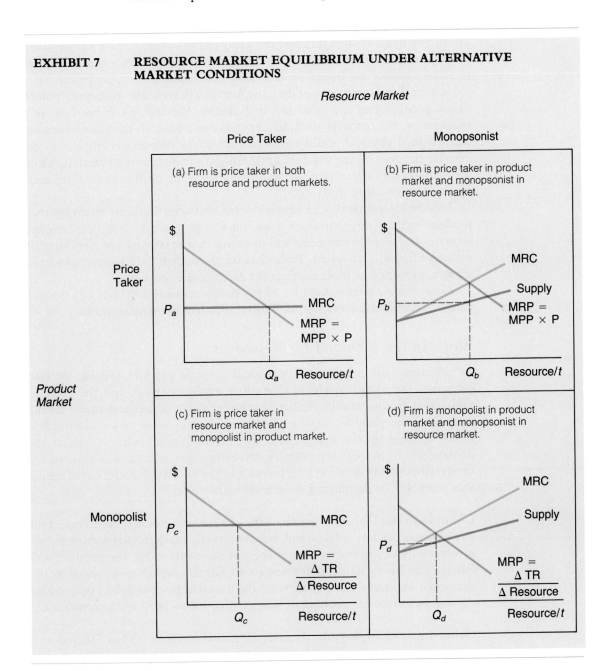

Resource Market

Price Taker   Monopsonist

(a) Firm is price taker in both resource and product markets.

(b) Firm is price taker in product market and monopsonist in resource market.

(c) Firm is price taker in resource market and monopolist in product market.

(d) Firm is monopolist in product market and monopsonist in resource market.

Product Market

Price Taker

Monopolist

where the marginal resource cost is a horizontal line drawn at the market-determined resource price. The firm as a monopsonist is shown in Exhibits 7 (b) and (d), where the marginal resource cost is an upward-sloping line drawn above the resource supply curve. Recall that the monopsonist's marginal resource cost curve exceeds the resource supply curve because the firm, in order to attract more resources, must pay all units of the resource the higher supply price.

Along the left-hand side of Exhibit 7 are listed the two possible product markets the firm could face. The firm may sell its output in a perfectly competitive market, in which case the firm would be a price taker in the product market, as shown in Exhibits 7(a) and (b). If the firm is a price taker in the product market, its resource demand is simply the resource's marginal physical product multiplied by the market-determined product price.

Rather than being a price taker, the firm may have some monopoly power in the product market, as shown in Exhibits 7(c) and (d). If the firm is a monopolist, the resource demand curve is downward sloping both because the marginal physical product falls as more of the resource is employed and because the price of the product must fall if more output is to be sold. Thus the demand for each unit of the resource reflects the change in total revenue resulting from using that unit.

Exhibit 7 presents the four possible combinations that arise when the two product market structures are combined with the two resource market structures. The resource price and quantity that maximize the firm's profit are identified in each panel. Note that when the firm is a monosponist the marginal revenue product exceeds the price of the resource.

Now that we have some idea of the profit-maximizing level of resource use, let's consider factors that will cause resource demand to shift.

Shifts in the Demand for Resources

As we have said, a resource's marginal revenue product consists of two elements, the marginal physical product of the resource and the price at which that product is sold. A change in either will change the demand for the resource. The previous section discussed the derivation of an individual firm's demand for resources. As a way of confirming what is behind the demand curve, we should examine the forces that will cause a shift in the firm's demand for resources. An increase in the demand for a resource means that more will be demanded at each resource price.

Changes in the Demand for the Final Product   Because the demand for any resource is a derived demand, based as it is on the demand for the product produced by the resource, any change in the demand for the product will change the firm's demand for resource. For example, an increase in the demand for automobiles will increase their market price and thereby increase the marginal revenue product of labor employed to produce automobiles.

Other Inputs Employed   Although the analysis thus far has focused on a single input, resources are used in conjunction with one another. The marginal physical product of any resource depends on the quantity and quality of other resources used in the production process. Sometimes the resources are *complements*, such as a truck driver and a truck. If the relationship is complementary, a reduction in the price of one resource will increase the demand for the other. If the price of bigger and better trucks falls, bigger and better trucks will be purchased. This increase in capital will increase the marginal productivity of labor because labor has more to work with. A driver behind the wheel of rig with a capacity of many tons will be able to haul more goods than a driver behind the wheel of a pickup truck. An increase in the quantity and quality of trucks increases the marginal revenue product of truck drivers, so the demand for truck drivers shifts to the right.

One big reason why the typical truck driver in the United States earns over $15 an hour and a rickshaw driver in the Far East earns more like $0.15 an hour is the truck. The rickshaw driver pulls a cart that may be valued at less than $100, whereas the truck driver is behind the wheel of a rig that may have cost more than $100,000. The truck makes the driver more productive. More generally, the greater the quantity and quality of complementary resources used in production, the greater will be the marginal productivity of the resource in question, and the greater will be its demand.

Changes in Technology and Training   Technological improvements can also enhance the productivity of any resource. The development of fuel-efficient cars has increased the miles that can be squeezed out of a gallon of gasoline, so the productivity of gasoline has increased. An improved word processing program increases the productivity of an author or typist. A training program that teaches workers how to operate machinery will obviously increase their productivity. (Imagine someone who has driven only the family car trying to operate a road grader.) Thus, any technological improvement or training program that affects the quality of the resource will increase its marginal productivity and will consequently increase the demand for that resource.

Price Elasticity of Demand

The flatter the demand curve for a resource, the more elastic that demand will be at a given price. The more elastic the demand for a resource, the greater will be the change in quantity demanded in response to a given change in price. A variety of forces influence the elasticity of demand for a resource. Some of these relate to the fact that the demand for a resource is a derived demand; others relate to the productivity of the resource itself.

Ease of Substitution   In the previous section we mentioned that some resources are complements. Sometimes, however, resources are *substitutes*. If resources are substitutes, a reduction in the price of one will reduce the demand for the other. The more abundant and the closer the substitutes are in production, the more elastic will be the demand for the resource. For example, to the baker, white eggs and brown eggs are virtually identical, and an increase in the price of white eggs will increase the demand for brown eggs. The demand for white eggs is price elastic, as is the demand for brown eggs. On the other hand, there are no close substitutes for jet fuel in providing airline transportation, and an increase in the price of this fuel will not cause airlines to switch to other forms of energy, at least not in the short run. So the demand for jet fuel will be relatively inelastic.

The Resource's Share of Production Cost   The greater the resource's cost as a fraction of the total product cost, the more elastic will be the demand for that resource, other things constant. For example, because the cost of lumber represents a relatively large share of housing costs, an increase in the price of lumber raises the cost of a new house, thereby reducing the quantity of housing demanded, and, in turn, reducing the quantity of lumber demanded. On the other hand, the cost of electrical wire makes up only a tiny fraction of the cost of new housing. Therefore, a rise in the price of electrical wire will have little impact on the quantity of housing demanded and will consequently have little effect on the quantity of wire demanded in the construction of housing.

Time   Finally, as with consumer demand, the longer the time period under consideration, the greater will be the elasticity of demand for the resource. For example, if the price of steel increases, auto manufacturers cannot quickly switch to substitutes. Over time, however, they can change production processes and perhaps redesign cars so that the quantity of steel required for auto production declines. Or consider the experience with oil. The price increases in the 1970s precipitated substitution away from oil. In addition to the increased fuel economy of cars have come more fuel-efficient airplanes, the substitution of coal for oil in electricity production, and the "reinvention" of the coal-fired locomotive to replace the diesel locomotive.

Optimal Resource Use

The discussion thus far has focused on only one resource, other things constant. The firm in fact employs several resources. When several resources are used, how does the firm decide how much of each to employ so as to maximize profit? What determines optimal resource use? For simplicity, let's suppose there are just two resources and that both are purchased in competitive markets. The same results could be derived for any number of resources and could be extended to the case where the firm hires resources as a monopsonist.

As long as the marginal resource cost is less than the marginal revenue product, the firm will increase profit by employing more of the resource. The firm will increase resource use until the marginal resource cost just equals the marginal revenue product. If the resource is labor and labor is hired in competitive markets, the marginal cost of labor equals the price of labor, P_L, which is the wage rate. The firm will hire labor up to the point where the price of labor equals the marginal revenue product of labor, MRP_L, or $P_L = MRP_L$.

This same policy applies if there are two or more resources. The firm that is a price taker in resource markets will increase profit by expanding output as long as the marginal revenue product exceeds the price of the resource. If the firm hires two resources, labor and capital, it will maximize profit by employing that amount of each resource such that

$$MRP_L = P_L \quad \text{and} \quad MRP_C = P_C$$

Another way of writing each expression is

$$\frac{MRP_L}{P_L} = 1 \quad \text{and} \quad \frac{MRP_C}{P_C} = 1$$

or

$$\frac{MRP_L}{P_L} = \frac{MRP_C}{P_C} = 1$$

Therefore, to maximize profit the firm should employ resources so that the last dollar spent on each resource yields one dollar's worth of marginal revenue product. In other words, the last dollar spent on each resource yields the same marginal revenue product.

At the beginning of the chapter we asked why the buildings at the center of the city are taller than those farther out. One rule of optimal resource use is that the firm will combine resources in a way that conserves the use of the scarcest resource. Land is more expensive at the center of the city because of the convenience of the location. Land and capital are to a large extent substitutes in the production of building space. When land is more expensive, builders substitute additional capital for land, building up instead of out. Hence, buildings are taller when they are closer to the center of the city and are tallest in cities where the land is relatively more expensive. Buildings in Chicago and New York are taller than buildings in Bismarck and Tucson, for example.

The high price of land in metropolitan areas has other implications for the efficient employment of resources. For example, in New York City, as in most large cities, vending carts on street corners specialize in everything from hot dogs to doughnuts. Why are there so many carts? Consider the resources used to supply hot dogs: land, labor, capital, entrepreneurial ability, plus hot dogs, buns, and other ingredients. Which of these do you suppose is most expensive in New York City? As we have noted, space is very costly. Retail space along Fifth Avenue rents for as much as $400 a year per square foot. Since a hot dog cart requires about three square yards to operate, it could cost more than $10,000 a year to rent the necessary space. Aside from the necessary public permits, however, space on the public sidewalk is free. Profit-maximizing street vendors substitute free public sidewalk space for costly commercial rental space. No wonder vending carts proliferate.

The framework we developed focuses on marginal analysis of resource use to determine the equilibrium resource price. Resources cooperate to produce output, much like the musicians in an orchestra combine to produce music. The firm uses each resource up to the point where the marginal revenue product of that resource equals its marginal resource cost. The objective of profit maximization ensures that firms will produce using the least-cost combination of resources. Thus, the least-cost combination of resource use implies that the last dollar spent on each resource yields a marginal revenue product of one dollar. If this were not so, firms could lower their cost by adjusting their resource mix.

SUMMARY

1. The firm demands resources to maximize profits. Households supply resources to maximize utility. Any differences between the profit-maximizing goals of firms and the utility-maximizing goals of households are reconciled through voluntary exchange in resource markets.

2. Because the value of any resource depends on the value of what it produces, the demand for a resource is a derived demand—derived from the value of the final product. A resource demand curve is downward sloping because firms are more willing and able to increase the quantity demanded as the price of a resource declines. A resource supply curve tends to be upward sloping because resource owners are more willing and able to increase the quantity supplied as their reward for supplying the resource increases.

3. Differentials in the market prices of similar resources stem from a variety of sources, but we can classify them into two broad categories. Price differentials that do not precipitate a shift in resources among uses are called equilibrium differentials. Price differentials that trigger the reallocation of resources to equalize prices for similar resources are called disequilibrium differentials.

4. Resource earnings can be divided into (1) transfer earnings, the amount that must be paid a resource owner to supply resources to a particular use, and (2) economic rent, that portion of a resource's total earnings that is not necessary to keep the resource in its present use. If a resource has no alternative use, earnings consist only of economic rent; if a resource has many alternative uses, transfer earnings predominate.

5. A firm's resource demand curve is based on the marginal revenue product of that resource. If a firm sells its output in a perfectly competitive market, the marginal revenue product equals the marginal physical product of the resource times the price of the product. If a firm has some monopoly power in the product market, it must take into account both changes in the marginal physical product of resources and reductions in the price necessary to sell additional output. As a result, the demand for resources by firms with monopoly power tends to fall more quickly than the demand for resources by firms selling in competitive markets.

6. The marginal resource cost is the marginal cost to the firm of employing one more unit of the resource. If a firm hires resources in competitive markets, the firm is a price taker and has no control over resource prices. If the price a firm pays for a resource depends on the quantity of the resource it employs, the firm is a monopsonist. A monopsonist, like a price taker in the resource market, maximizes profit by employing each resource to the point where the marginal revenue product equals the marginal resource cost. The marginal resource cost to the monopsonist, however, exceeds the supply price.

7. The demand for a resource will increase if there is an increase in its marginal physical product or in the price of the product produced with the resource. Increases in the use of complementary resources will increase a resource's marginal productivity.

QUESTIONS AND PROBLEMS _____

1. (Resource Demands) How might the elasticity of demand for a resource depend on the substitutability among resources in the production process?

2. (Supply of Resources) Suppose that individual *A* speaks only German, while individual *B* speaks only English; otherwise they are identical in their skills. Consider the relative elasticities of supply for their labor in:
   a. the Federal Republic of Germany
   b. the United States
   c. all other places

3. (Resource Demand) Suppose that good *A* has a perfectly inelastic demand. What would we expect the elasticity of demand for the resources used to produce good *A* to be? Must they also be perfectly inelastic? Why or why not?

4. (Transfer Earnings versus Economic Rent) If the supply of a resource has unitary elasticity, then transfer earnings will be equal to economic rent—at every resource price. Evaluate this assertion.

5. (Diminishing Returns) To have diminishing returns, one must add a variable resource to a set of fixed resources. Why must we assume that some fixed resources are present?

6. (Competitive Marginal Revenue Product) If a competitive firm hires another worker full-time, then total output will increase from 100 units to 110 units per month. Suppose the wage is $200 per week. What is the market price that allows the additional worker to be hired?

7. (Competitive Resource Market) Explain why a competitive resource market requires the resource price (that is, the wage rate) to be equal to the marginal resource cost to the firm.

8. (Monopsony) Explain why a monopolist need not be a monopsonist. Are all monopsonists also monopolists by necessity? Why or why not?

9. (Monopsony) Why is it true that for a monopsonist to hire an additional worker, it must pay a higher wage to all of its workers?

10. (Complements in Production) Many countries are predominately agrarian. How would the amount of fertilizer available affect the marginal product, and thus the income, of the farmers in such societies?

LABOR MARKETS
and WAGE
DETERMINATION

According to an annual survey of 230 major U.S. companies, the starting salaries for 1986 college graduates with degrees in economics and finance averaged $22,284—about $1000 more than those with degrees in accounting but about $7000 less than those with degrees in engineering.[1] In 1986, 88 athletes earned more than a million dollars; 58 of them played baseball and none played hockey.[2] Why did those with degrees in economics and finance earn more than those in accounting but less that those in engineering? Why did baseball players earn more than hockey players? Will this same pattern be observed in 1996? What determines the pattern of wages in the economy?

These and related questions will be examined in this chapter. You can be sure of one thing: supply and demand play a central role in the answers. We have already examined what determines the demand for labor or any other resource. Demand depends on the resource's marginal revenue product. In this chapter we focus on the market supply of labor, then bring supply and demand together to arrive at the market wage. Topics and terms discussed include:

- Theory of time allocation

- The backward-bending supply curve for labor

- Nonmonetary factors and labor supply

- Why wages differ

- The functional distribution of income

---

[1]See "Dollars for Diplomas," *The New York Times*, 13 April 1986.
[2]See "Who Makes What in Sports," *Sport* (June 1986): 21–31.

INDIVIDUAL LABOR SUPPLY

So far we have discussed how markets direct resources to their highest-valued use. We noted that a firm's demand for a resource depends on the marginal productivity of the resource. In the previous chapter more attention was given to labor than to other resources, but the discussion was intended to convey a general understanding of the demand for any resource. In this section we look in greater detail at the supply of labor.

Perhaps the easiest way to consider labor supply is to introduce it in the context of something you already understand—consumer demand. Recall that as a consumer, you have demand curves for all kinds of products. Your demand for a product—that is, the relationship between price and the quantity you demand—is based on your willingness and ability to purchase that product at each alternative price. Your demand could shift in response to changes in several factors, including your income, the prices of related goods, and your tastes.

You, as a consumer, have demand curves for each of the many products available; similarly, you, as a resource supplier, have labor supply curves for each of the many possible uses of your labor. To some markets your quantity supplied is zero over the realistic range of wages. (We say "over the realistic range" because if the wage were high enough, say $1 million per hour, there may be no activity to which you would not supply labor.) In those instances where your quantity supplied is zero over the realistic range of wages, this may be because you are *willing* but *unable* to perform certain jobs (for example, airline pilot, professional tennis player, novelist); or it may be because you are *able* but *unwilling* to do so (for example, soldier of fortune, gym teacher, economist).

Therefore, you have as many supply curves as there are labor markets, just as you have demand curves for the markets in goods and services. In fact, because information is costly, you may not have even heard of some of these labor markets. (Similarly, on the demand side, there are many products that you may not know about.) Your labor supply to each market depends on the opportunity cost of your time in other activities. Each supply curve is developed under the assumption that the wages offered in other markets are held constant, just as each demand curve is developed under the assumption that prices of related goods are held constant.

Labor Supply and Utility Maximization

Recall the definition of economics: it is the study of how individuals choose to utilize their scarce resources to produce, exchange, and consume products in an attempt to satisfy their unlimited wants. More to the point, we say that individuals attempt to use their limited resources to maximize their utility. Two sources of utility are of interest to us, the consumption of goods and services and the enjoyment of leisure. The utility derived from consuming goods and services is obvious and has served as the foundation of consumer demand. Leisure time spent relaxing, sleeping, eating, and in recreational activities also represents a valuable source of utility. Leisure can be viewed as a normal good that, like other goods, is subject to the law of diminishing marginal utility. Thus, the more leisure time you have, the less you value each additional unit. Sometimes you may have so much leisure that you are "just killing time." As that well-known economist/cat Garfield once lamented, "Spare time would be more fun if I had less to spare."

Thus, the consumption of goods and services and the enjoyment of leisure are the primary sources of utility. Individuals employ their limited resources in an attempt to maximize their utility. Typically, we sort resources into land, labor, capital, and entrepreneurial ability. The resource of greatest interest in this chapter is labor. Labor, however, is created out of an even more fundamental resource: time. Probably the most important resource you own at this stage in your economic development is your time. Time is perhaps the ultimate raw material of life. Without it, you can accomplish nothing; with it, much is possible. There are essentially three uses of time: market work, household work, and leisure.

Three Uses of Time   Consider the three uses of your time. First, you can undertake **market work**, selling your time in the labor market in return for money. When you offer yourself for employment, you surrender to the employer the direction over the use of your time in return for a wage. Second, you can undertake what we will call **household work**, using time to produce your own goods and services. Household work includes the time you spend doing your laundry, preparing your meals, or typing a term paper. Household work also includes the time spent not in direct production but in acquiring skills and education to enhance the value of your time in the future. Although the time you spend attending class, reading, and studying course material provides no instant payoff, you are betting that the skills and perspective you will gain will be rewarding later. Third, you can convert time directly into leisure. (Some of you may specialize in this use of time.)

Market work is the sale of labor in return for a money wage.

Household work is time spent producing goods and services in the home.

Work and Utility   Unless you are one of the fortunate few, work is not a direct source of utility. Rather, time spent working is often associated with irritation, discomfort, or aggravation; in short, time spent working is a source of *disutility*—the opposite of utility. You work nonetheless, despite this disutility, because of the goods and services you can consume as a result of working. You expect the utility generated by the goods and services made possible through working will exceed the disutility of work. Thus, the net utility of work—the utility of the consumption made possible through work minus the disutility of the work itself—is what makes work an attractive use of your time. In the case of market work, you earn wages, which are used to buy goods and services. In the case of household work, you either make goods and services directly, as in making yourself an egg salad sandwich, or you increase your future ability to consume goods and services, for example, by studying to be an accountant.

Utility Maximization   Within the limits of a 24-hour day, 7 days a week, you balance the competing uses of your time among market work, household work, and leisure to maximize utility. As a rational consumer, you attempt to maximize utility by allocating your time so that the expected marginal utility of the last unit of time spent in each activity is identical. Thus, in the course of a week the marginal utility of the last hour of leisure equals the net marginal utility of the last hour of market work, which equals the net marginal utility of the last hour spent on household work. In the case of time spent acquiring skills, you must consider the marginal utility expected from the future increase in earnings that will result from your enhanced productivity.[3]

Perhaps at this point you are saying, "Wait a minute. I don't allocate my time with that sort of precision or logic. I just sort of bump along, doing what feels good." We do not claim that you are even aware of making such marginal calculations. But as a rational decision maker, you allocate your scarce time to satisfy your wishes, or to maximize utility. And utility maximization, or "doing what feels good," implies that you act "as if" at the margin you use time to derive the same utility from the last unit of time spent in each alternative use.

You probably have settled into a rough plan (for meals, entertainment, study, sleep, and so on.) that accords with your overall objectives and appears reasonably rational. This plan is probably in constant flux as you make expected and unexpected adjustments in the use of your time. For example, this morning you may have slept later than you planned; last weekend you failed to crack a book, despite good intentions. Over a week or a month, however, your use of time is roughly in line with an allocation that maximizes utility as you perceive it. Put another way, given your various resource constraints of time, money, energy, and the like, if you could change your use of time to increase your utility, you would do so. Who's stopping you?

Thus, this time-allocation process will ensure that at the margin the utility from the last unit of time spent in each activity is equal. Because information is costly and because the future is uncertain, you sometimes make mistakes in allocating time; you do not always get what you expect. Some mistakes are minor, such as the movie that proved to be a waste of time. But other mistakes can be costly. For example, you may now be preparing for a field of study that will be too crowded by the time you graduate, or the skills you are now acquiring could become obsolete because of changing technology. Some skills could be displaced by a new piece of technology no bigger than this word: *chip*.

Implications   The model of time allocation as it has been described thus far yields several implications about individual choice. First, consider the choice between market work and household work. The higher your market wage, other things equal, the greater will be the opportunity cost of household production in terms of forgone earnings. Hence, individuals with a high market wage will produce less for themselves, other things equal. Surgeons

---

[3]We will develop a way of analyzing choices involving future production and consumption when we consider human capital more explicitly in a later chapter.

are less likely to mow their own lawns than are butchers. By the same logic, the higher the expected earnings right out of high school, other things equal, the less inclined the individual will be to go on to college.

Alternatively, the more productive people are in household work, other things equal, the less labor they will supply to the market. People who are proficient at preparing meals or handy around the house will do more of this for themselves and hire fewer of these services in the market. Conversely, those who find boiling water difficult will eat out more frequently, and those who are all thumbs around the house will hire various services; both will be more inclined to supply their labor to market work rather than to household work. With regard to the production of human capital, those who find education useful and productive are more inclined to spend time in school than those who find it "a waste of time." In summary, utility maximization in the use of time implies that individuals will use household work to produce those goods they can provide more cheaply than the market can.

How Will You Spend Your Summer Vacation?

To breathe life into the time-allocation problem, consider your choices for next summer. You can take the summer off, spending it entirely on leisure, as perhaps a fitting reward for a rough academic year. You can do what has been referred to as household work by producing goods and services for yourself, such as painting the family house or attending summer school. Or you can supply your time to market work. As a rational decision maker, you will select that combination of leisure, home work, and market work that you expect will maximize your utility. And the optimal combination is likely to involve allocating some time to each activity. For example, even if you plan to be a "full-time" student next summer, you might still consider a part-time job. After all, many students hold down part-time jobs during the academic year.

Suppose that the only job you are qualified for next summer is some form of unskilled labor, such as working at a car wash or in a nearby fast-food restaurant. For simplicity, let's assume that you view all the jobs for which you qualify to be equally attractive (or unattractive) in terms of their nonmonetary aspects. (These nonmonetary aspects will be discussed in the next section.) Since in your view there is no difference among these unskilled jobs, the most important question for you in deciding how much labor to supply is, What is the market wage?

Suppose the wage is $3 per hour—not even the minimum wage. At a wage that low, you may decide to paint the family house, attend summer school full-time, spend the summer as a beach bum, take a long nap, or perhaps some combination of these. In any event, you decide to supply no labor at such a low wage. The market wage must rise to $4 per hour before you find it attractive enough to supply any labor. Suppose that at a wage of $4 per hour you supply 20 hours per week, perhaps reducing time devoted to summer school and cutting back your beach time.

What if the wage increases to $5 per hour, holding everything else constant? The higher wage raises the opportunity cost of the time you spend in other activities, so you substitute market work for other uses of your time. You decide to work 30 hours per week, earning a total of $150 a week. At $6 per hour you are willing to cut more into studying or surfing, increasing your quantity of labor supplied to 40 hours per week, for a weekly total of $240. At $7 per hour you increase your weekly labor supply even more, to 48 hours, earning $336 per week, and at $8 per hour you increase your quantity supplied to 55 hours, or $440 per week. At a wage of $9 you go to 60 hours per week; you are starting to earn serious money — $540 per week.

Finally, what if the wage offered is $10 per hour — a wage you consider to be very attractive indeed? You decide to cut back to 55 hours per week and you earn $550 per week — more than you did when the wage was $9 per hour. The additional income provided by a higher wage allows you to reduce your market work to spend more time on other activities, particularly leisure. Since leisure is a normal good, the higher income resulting from the higher wage will tend to increase your demand for it; the higher wage also makes leisure more costly. What has been going on at the different wage rates will now be described in greater detail.

Substitution and Income Effects   As the wage rate rises, it affects the choice between market work and other uses of your time in two ways. First, at a higher wage each hour of work buys more goods and services, so a higher wage provides you with an incentive to work more — to substitute work for other activities. This is referred to as the *substitution effect* of a wage increase; this effect encourages you to supply more time to market work. Something else also happens as the wage rate increases, however. A higher wage means a higher income, and a higher income means that you demand more of all normal goods. Since leisure is a normal good, a higher income increases your demand for leisure time, thereby reducing your supply of time to market work. The higher wage rate therefore has an *income effect*, which tends to reduce the quantity of labor supplied.

These opposite effects occur as the wage goes up — the substitution effect causing you to supply more time to market work, and the income effect causing you to supply less time to market work and to demand more leisure time. In the previous example the substitution effect dominates the income effect for wage increases up to $9 per hour, resulting in a greater quantity of labor supplied as the wage rises to $9. When the wage hits $10 per hour, however, the income effect exceeds the substitution effect, causing a net reduction in the quantity of labor supplied to market work.

Backward-Bending Labor Supply Curve   Your hypothetical labor supply curve, as it has been described, is presented as Exhibit 1. As you can see, this supply curve is upward sloping until a wage of $9 per hour is reached, and then the supply curve begins to bend backward. The *backward-bending supply curve* gets its shape because the income effect of a higher wage eventually outweighs the substitution effect, so the quantity of labor supplied at some point declines with an increase in the wage. We often see evidence of a backward-bending supply curve, particularly among high-wage individuals, who reduce their work and consume more leisure. For example, doctors often play golf on a weekday afternoon. Entertainers typically perform less as they become more successful. Unknown bands play for hours for peanuts; name bands play less for more.

Flexibility of Hours Worked   This model assumes that workers have some control over the number of hours worked per week. At first blush this assumption appears to conflict with the practice of a standard work week of, say, 40 hours. The ability to vary the hours worked seems to be a reasonable assumption, however, particularly in view of the opportunity to work overtime or to work part-time in different jobs. In this way workers can bundle together their most preferred quantity of hours (for instance, 40 hours in the restaurant and 15 hours at the car wash). In addition to the amount of overtime and the number of jobs, workers have some control over the timing and length of their vacations. More generally, individuals can control the length of time they stay in school, when and to what extent they enter the work force, and when they choose to retire. Thus, the worker actually has more control over the number of hours worked than you might think if you focus on the standard work week.

EXHIBIT 1   INDIVIDUAL LABOR SUPPLY CURVE

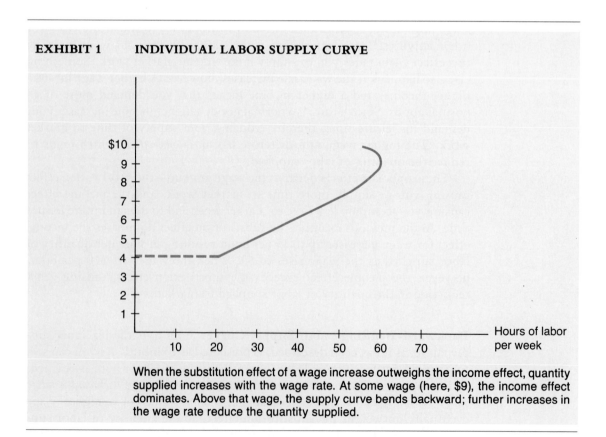

When the substitution effect of a wage increase outweighs the income effect, quantity supplied increases with the wage rate. At some wage (here, $9), the income effect dominates. Above that wage, the supply curve bends backward; further increases in the wage rate reduce the quantity supplied.

Nonwage Determinants of Labor Supply

The quantity of labor supplied depends on a variety of factors other than the wage rate, just as the quantity of a good demanded depends on factors other than the price. What are the nonwage factors that go into a decision about your supply of labor to the market next summer?

Other Sources of Income While some jobs are rewarding in a variety of nonmonetary ways, the primary reason people work is to earn money to buy goods and services. If your family income is relatively high, you may have less need for additional income; consequently, you will have less reason to work next summer. Thus, your willingness and ability to supply your time to the labor market depends on your income from other sources, including savings, borrowing, and family support. Perhaps your parents set up a trust to fund your education in the manner to which you have grown accustomed. Your other sources of income do not necessarily have to be money income: maybe you receive "in-kind" income. For example, you may live at home, where your parents provide your room and board, or you may drive one of the family cars. The greater these other sources of income, the less inclined you are to supply your time to market work, other things constant.

Nonmonetary Factors in General Labor is a special kind of resource. Unlike capital and land, which can be provided regardless of the whereabouts of the resource owners, time supplied to market work requires the seller of that time to be on the job. Because the individual must be present to deliver labor, such *nonmonetary factors* as the difficulty of the job and the quality of the work environment are important considerations in labor supply. The labor supply curve shows the relationship between the wage rate and the quantity of labor you are willing and able to supply, other things constant. Among the other things held constant are these nonmonetary factors. Thus far we have been able to ignore the role of nonmonetary factors by assuming no difference in them among the unskilled jobs from which you could choose. Now we look more realistically at these nonmonetary factors.

Job Amenities Jobs have many nonmonetary qualities. Indeed, the ways that jobs can differ seem as endless as the variety of jobs that exist. If you want to see a small sample of the number of different jobs involved in producing just one good, at the end of your next movie notice the credits as they roll by. In addition to the actors, there are dozens of people who make movies—everything from wardrobe assistants to a "gaffer" (lighting electrician).

Consider the ways job amenities might differ. For a student, a library job that allows you to study much of the time is more attractive than a job that affords no study time. A job in the college cafeteria may allow you to eat all you want at no extra charge; you may find this feature attractive or negative. Some jobs allow you to work flexible hours; others impose a rigid work schedule. Is the workplace air-conditioned or do you have to sweat it out? The more attractive these on-the-job amenities are to you, the greater will be your supply of labor to that particular market, other things constant.

The Value of Job Experience   As a student, you are more inclined to take a job that provides what employers will view as valuable experience: serving as the assistant treasurer for a nearby business looks better than serving hash at the college cafeteria. Some students are willing to accept relatively low wages now because of the promise of higher wages later. Such positions enhance the worker's human capital. For example, new lawyers are eager to fill clerkships for judges, though the pay is low, because these positions provide experience that is valued by future employers. Some individuals are willing to accept relatively low pay to work for certain government agencies because the experience and the personal contacts developed will be valuable later in the private sector, especially by those private-sector employers who deal with that particular government agency. Thus, the greater the investment value of a position is in terms of enhancing your future earning possibilities, the greater will be your supply of labor to that market, other things constant.

Discretion in the Use of Time   One job quality that is generally valued is latitude in the use of time on the job. As we said earlier, when you sell your labor in the resource market, you surrender the use of your time to the direction of a manager or entrepreneur. The amount and the intensity of this direction depends on the kind of job. If you are like most people, the more closely you are monitored and directed, other things constant, the less willing you are to supply labor to that market.

For example, workers on an assembly line typically have little choice in how their time is spent. Closely directed workers must be paid more than those in jobs that allow more personal discretion. College professors typically earn less than those in private industry with a similar education. This is partly because professors are subject to less direction in the classroom and in their research interests. Thus, professors pay for their "academic freedom" by earning a lower salary than they could earn in more closely directed positions. If you value personal discretion in the use of your market labor time, your supply of labor will be greater to such job markets, other things constant.

Taste for Work   Some jobs are mentally or physically exhausting; others are easy. Some are interesting; others are boring. Some jobs may be easy but boring, such as checking books out at the library or collecting highway tolls. Others may be difficult but interesting, such as directing movies or splicing genes. Of course, whether a job is exhausting, interesting, or easy will depend to some extent on your individual capacity and taste for work. Just as the tastes for goods and services differ across consumers, the tastes for doing certain kinds of work also differ across labor suppliers. Some people like physical labor and avoid any job that would keep them desk-bound. Some can't stand the sight of blood; others choose to be surgeons. Some fear flying; others want to be pilots. Often writers and artists stick with their profession even if the pay is low and employment is not always available. Apparently, the satisfaction gained from the creative process offsets the low expected pay. In fact, some people evidently have such a strong preference for certain kinds of work that they are sometimes willing to perform those duties free, such as people who serve as auxiliary police officers or as volunteer fire fighters.

As with the taste for goods and services, we do not attempt to explain the taste for work. We simply argue that people will tend to match themselves with jobs they prefer based on their tastes and preferences. Put another way, your supply of labor will be greater to those jobs that are more in accord with your job preferences. Perhaps a particular job provides an opportunity to meet other people. If this is important to you, then you should supply more labor to a job that offers high visibility—as a lifeguard perhaps. Someone with an urge to travel will more likely join the navy or run guided tours rather than become a librarian.

Voluntary sorting based on tastes allocates workers among different jobs in a way that tends to minimize the disutility associated with work. This is not to say that everyone will be perfectly matched to their most preferred occupation. The cost of information about jobs and the cost of changing jobs may prevent some matchups that might otherwise seem desirable, but people will tend to find jobs that suit them. We are not likely, for example, to observe airline pilots who are afraid of heights or zoo keepers who are allergic to animals.

Market Supply

In the previous section we considered those factors, both monetary and nonmonetary, that influence individual supply. The market supply of labor to particular markets is the horizontal sum of each individual's supply curve. If an individual supply curve of labor is backward bending, does this mean that the market supply of labor is also backward bending? Not necessarily. Since different individuals have different opportunity costs and different tastes for work, the bend in the supply curve occurs at different points for different individuals—in some instance at lower wages and some at higher wages. Exhibit 2 shows how just three individual labor supply curves can be summed to yield a market supply curve that is upward sloping over the realistic range of wages.

The market supply curve combines with the market demand curve for labor to yield the equilibrium wage and the equilibrium level of employment in the market. Why do wages differ across markets?

WHY WAGES DIFFER

In the previous chapter we discussed the elements that influence the demand for resources and examined labor in particular. In brief, a firm is willing to hire labor up to the point where labor's marginal revenue product equals its marginal resource cost—that is, where the last unit employed earns the firm just enough to cover its cost. Since we have already discussed the factors that enhance the productivity of labor, we consider in this section primarily those

---

EXHIBIT 2   **DERIVING THE MARKET LABOR SUPPLY CURVE**

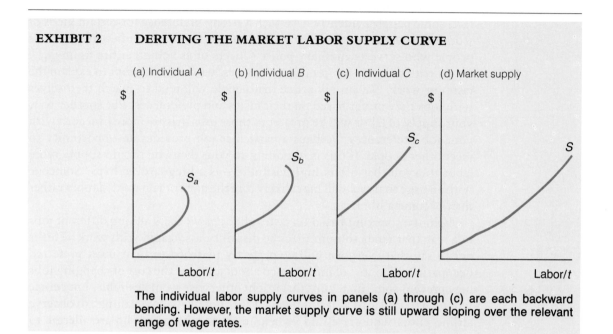

The individual labor supply curves in panels (a) through (c) are each backward bending. However, the market supply curve is still upward sloping over the relevant range of wage rates.

---

forces that affect market supply. In the previous section the market supply of labor was shown to be the sum of each individual's supply. The market wage rate is determined by the intersection of market supply and market demand for labor. Just as both blades of a pair of scissors contribute equally to cutting cloth, both the supply and the demand for labor determine the market wage rate.

As a reminder of the joint contribution of supply and demand, let's consider the market for orange pickers in Florida, as presented in Exhibit 3. The demand for orange pickers is presented as D, and the supply of pickers as S. We begin with an equilibrium wage of $0.75 per box of oranges picked and an equilibrium level of employment of E. In December 1983 frost hit the orange groves of Florida, damaging trees on 250,000 acres in the state's "citrus belt." As a consequence, there were fewer fruit-bearing trees the following year. The decline in the number of trees reduced the demand for orange pickers, reflected by the shift to the left in their demand curve, from D to D'. With no change in the supply curve, the resulting price paid per box of oranges picked declined from $0.75 to $0.50.

Tastes and Wage Differentials

Because of differences among individuals in their taste for work, there may be little relationship between jobs that you find attractive and the market wage for those jobs. There may be certain jobs you would not take regardless of the wage. If, however, enough workers find these jobs attractive, the market wage may be relatively low. What determines the market wage is both market

EXHIBIT 3   LABOR MARKET FOR ORANGE PICKERS IN FLORIDA

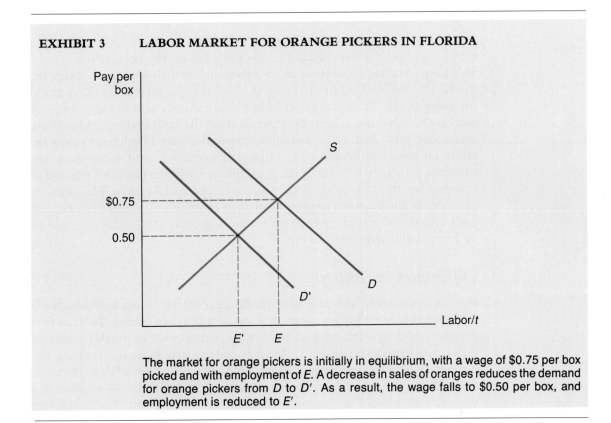

The market for orange pickers is initially in equilibrium, with a wage of $0.75 per box picked and with employment of *E*. A decrease in sales of oranges reduces the demand for orange pickers from *D* to *D'*. As a result, the wage falls to $0.50 per box, and employment is reduced to *E'*.

supply and market demand. Your individual labor supply typically represents such a small share of the market supply that your particular tastes have virtually no effect on the market wage.

Some job characteristics are so generally disliked, however, that the equilibrium wage must be higher to draw enough labor into this market. The simple fact is that, other things equal, employers generally must pay more for work that is dirty, smelly, noisy, dangerous, boring, irregular, or of low social status. This does not mean that jobs of low social status must pay more than other jobs. After all, a computer programmer earns more than a janitor. What it means is that, *other things constant*, jobs of lower status must pay more than jobs of higher social status that require the same skills. The requirement of higher pay for jobs of low social status is reflected by remarks made some 200 years ago by Adam Smith, who argued that the wages of actors and singers were necessarily high because of the "discredit" of performing in public. Smith likened acting and singing to "a sort of public prostitution." How times have changed. Few people would argue today that entertainers are paid so much because they must embarrass themselves by performing in public.

Differences in Training and Education Requirements

Some jobs pay more than others because they require a long and costly training period. Costly training reduces market supply because fewer individuals are willing to incur such an expense. But the training increases the productivity of each additional unit of labor, thereby increasing the demand for these skills. Thus, longer training requirements reduce the supply of workers to more specialized jobs but increase the market demand for those specialized jobs. Reduced supply but increased demand both have a positive effect on the equilibrium wage. Brain surgeons are paid more than tree surgeons primarily because of the great difference in the time and expense of training for the two jobs. Tree surgeons need little formal education to practice. Brain surgeons require more than ten years of preparation beyond high school, so a high expected income is necessary to induce people to undergo such extensive training.

Differences in Ability

Even when training and education levels are identical, some individuals are paid more because they are more able and talented than others. Two lawyers may have had identical educations, but one earns twice as much because of differences in underlying ability. Most executives have extensive training and business experience, but only a few become chief executives of large corporations. We need not dwell on the source of this differing ability — whether it is the result of "nature" or "nurture," heredity or environment. The simple fact is that even with identical training and experience, certain individuals will prove more talented and able than others, and their pay will typically reflect these differing abilities.

Differences in Risk

There are differences across jobs in the risk of work-related injury or death. If enough workers are not concerned about such risks, employers need not pay a wage premium over jobs that are less risky. Substantial research devoted to uncovering wage differences based on the risk of a job, however, indicates that jobs with a higher probability of injury or death pay a higher wage. Hence, workers are paid more for jobs that are dangerous. Workers are also paid more, other things equal, in fields where the risk of being unemployed are greater.

Problems of Labor Mobility

Identical individuals may earn different wages because one is able to sell in a market where their particular talents are more valued. Wages in rural areas are often lower than in metropolitan areas in part because there are fewer employers in rural areas and therefore less demand for labor. This difference in wages creates incentives to migrate to high-wage areas. But some workers fail to migrate, perhaps because they are unaware of the higher-paying alternatives or they are reluctant to leave the community in which they were raised. Generally, however, individuals have a strong incentive to sell their resources in the market where these resources are valued the most, as discussed in the following examples.

Did you ever notice that place kickers in professional football have names that are difficult to pronounce? Consider the job prospects for someone with a special talent for kicking a ball. The rewards for ball kicking in the small country where he lives amount to a paltry wage as chief kicker for the Grog City Grapplers. This kicker has a strong incentive to offer ball-kicking services in the market where these services are most valued. If he is lucky, he will end up as a place kicker in the National Football League.

Consider another example. Physicians are paid relatively more in the United States than in any other country in the world. Consequently, foreign-trained physicians have a strong incentive to practice medicine in the United States. Indeed, every year more than 10,000 physicians migrate to the United States.

Those people who seek high pay, however, do not always migrate to the United States. Talented basketball players who are not quite good enough to play for the National Basketball Association migrate to Europe, where their skills are better rewarded than they would be among the minor leagues in this country.

Job Discrimination

Sometimes individuals with skills that are identical to the skills of other people may be paid different wages because of racial or sexual discrimination in the job market. Although such discrimination is illegal, history shows that certain groups have systematically earned less than others of apparently equal ability. While racial discrimination has long been a matter of public concern, only recently has there been interest in the reasons underlying the differences in average earnings between males and females, as discussed in the following case study.

CASE STUDY

Comparable Worth

Comparable worth calls for pay to be determined by job characteristics rather than by supply and demand.

Despite laws in this country requiring affirmative action and equal pay for equal work, women on average still earn only about 65 percent as much as men earn. After adjusting for several factors, such as the tendency of women to interrupt their careers for child rearing, the differential between the sexes shrinks but does not disappear. One explanation for this pay gap is that women have crowded into certain occupations, such as secretarial work and nursing, and the increased supply of labor to these markets has lowered the prevailing wage. Another view is that the pay difference between the sexes is the result of sexual discrimination by employers.

Some advocates of women's rights have promoted a notion called **comparable worth** as a way of addressing pay differences. The comparable worth approach calls for each job to be evaluated based on that job's requirements—

the training necessary, previous experience needed, and so on. Pay should then be determined based on this evaluation. Proponents of comparable worth believe that such a system would eliminate situations in which men working in low-skilled jobs are paid more than women working in higher-skilled occupations.

For example, pay differences were dramatized in a 1984 strike of clerical and technical workers against Yale University. The predominantly female labor union noted that administrative assistants, who were mostly female and whose pay averaged $13,424 per year, perform work that required, in the union's view, at least as much training and experience as the work performed by the university's truck drivers, who were mostly men and whose pay averaged $18,470.

Comparable pay laws have been adopted in several states. Indeed, female workers in Washington state won a discrimination suit that could cost the state government nearly $1 billion. Legislation has been proposed to have the federal government reevaluate all of its jobs, with the idea of raising the pay for jobs held mainly by women.

Will basing pay on some standard of comparable worth reduce pay differentials between males and females? And what other effects will it have on the economy? Put aside for the present any consideration of the administrative cost of setting up the bureaucracy to establish and police such a system, and assume that such a group can accurately calculate and assess the skills associated with each position. The effect of such laws depends on how efficiently the market for labor was operating before the law's implementation. If the lower pay for women in certain professions was the result of employer discrimination, the laws would likely reduce the wage gap and enhance the efficiency of the economy.

If, however, wages in some professions are lower because of crowding, and if pay is based on comparable worth in a way that pays these crowded occupations more than they now receive, the job market will play a reduced role in allocating labor. In this case more women will attempt to crowd into certain fields because the wage will be relatively more attractive. To the extent that employers base their hiring on the marginal productivity of labor, they will cut back on the quantity demanded in these fields. Thus, fewer will be employed in these historically female professions, but those who keep jobs will earn more than before.

Information Problems of Measuring Marginal Product

In our market analysis of the supply and demand for particular kinds of labor, we typically assume that workers are identical. In equilibrium, each worker in the market is assumed to be paid the same wage, which is equal to the marginal revenue product of labor. Problems arising from differences in the quality of workers have been downplayed in our formal analysis.

Differences in the quality of workers would present no particular problem as long the effect of these differences on the worker's productivity could be readily observed. If the productivity of each particular worker is easily measured, such as the quantity of oranges picked, the number of shoes stitched, or the number of papers typed, that measure itself can and does serve as the basis of pay. But because production usually takes place through the coordinated effort of several workers, it is often easier simply to pay workers by the hour rather than attempt to keep detailed account of each worker's contribution to total output.

Often the pay will be some combination of an hourly rate and an additional incentive linked to a measure of productivity. A sales representative typically receives a base salary plus a commission tied to the quantity sold. At times the task of evaluating marginal product is better left to the consumer rather than the firm. Those workers who provide personal services, such as waiters and waitresses, have a pay structure based heavily on tips. Since this service is by definition "personal," customers are considered to be in the best position to judge the quality of service and to tip accordingly.

Adverse selection occurs when unobservable labor skills are misvalued in the market.

Adverse Selection Problem   An **adverse selection** problem occurs in the labor market when labor suppliers have much better information about their productivities than employers do. Because the abilities of workers are not observable before employment, a given wage tends to attract the least productive workers available in the labor pool. The most productive workers consider that the given wage is below their marginal productivity.

For example, let's assume that the employer wants to hire a program coordinator for a new project, a job that calls for imagination, organizational skills, and an ability to work independently. The employer would like to attract the most qualified person, but because the qualities demanded are not directly observable, the employer must rely on proxy information, such as education and previous employment history. The pay level advertised for the position is not the marginal product of the best person in the market but is more like the expected, or average, marginal product of all those in the market. Individual workers have a good idea of their own intelligence, creativity, and the like and are able to evaluate this wage in view of their own abilities and opportunity cost. The really talented person will find that the salary offered by the employer is below his or her true abilities and will be less inclined to apply for the job. Less talented individuals, however, particularly those who otherwise meet all the proxy qualifications (that is, they "look good on paper"), will find that the offered wage exceeds their true marginal productivity, and thus they are more likely to pursue the job. The recruiting task will suffer from this adverse selection because the pool of applicants will be of below-average ability.

A signal is a proxy for unobservable characteristics.

Signaling   Adverse selection gives rise to signaling. Because the true requirements for many positions are unobservable, the employer must rely on proxy measures, such as educational attainment. The proxy measure is called a **signal**. The signal serves as a useful way of screening applicants as long as it is a true indicator of the unobservable quality of interest. The effectiveness of any signal depends on how easily less productive workers can acquire the same signal. A signal that is acquired with equal ease or difficulty by all workers, regardless of their productivity, does not provide the employer with a way of identifying the best workers.

If, however, it takes less productive individuals significantly more effort to acquire the signal, then the signal does serve as a useful way of screening applicants. For example, if more productive workers find it easier to succeed in college (getting accepted, earning good grades, surrendering leisure time) than do less productive individuals, then productive workers will find a good college record to be a signal worth acquiring to distinguish themselves from less productive workers. In this case education may be efficient not so much because it enhances worker productivity, but rather because it enables employers to distinguish between more productive and less productive workers. Thus, a college education may serve as a good signal for more productive workers and a good screen for employers who are trying to identify the best workers.

Principal-Agent Problems   One case in which people on one side of the market have better information than those on the other side is in the principal-agent model. This expression is used to describe a relationship where one party, known as the **principal**, makes a contractual agreement with another party, known as the **agent**, in the expectation that the agent will act on behalf of the principal. You could confront a principal-agent problem when you deal with an insurance agent, a stock broker, a lawyer, or a garage mechanic, to name a few. In each case you, the principal, are hiring an agent who has more expertise than you to provide a service. More generally, any employer-employee relationship is a principal-agent relationship as well.

*In the principal-agent relationship, the **principal** makes an agreement with an **agent** in the expectation that the agent will act in the principal's behalf.*

In an age of specialization there are many tasks we do not do for ourselves because someone else either does the task better or has a lower opportunity cost of time. Suppose that you want your car repaired. Although you know where the gas goes, what if you know little more? Your objective is to have your car repaired. The mechanic, however, may have other objectives, such as maximizing on-the-job leisure or maximizing the garage's revenue. Suppose that your car has only a loose wire, but the mechanic inflates the bill by charging you for service you do not really need. You, as principal, are poorly served by the mechanic, your agent. Principal-agent problems arise when the agent is better informed or has easier access to information than the principal.

There are ways of reducing the consequences of the principal-agent problem. An incentive structure, or an information-revealing system, can be developed to reduce the problems associated with the lopsided availability of information. In the case of the auto mechanic, for example, some garages provide written estimates before the work and, when the job is done, return the defective parts to the customer as evidence of the necessity of the repair.

These are just a few of the information problems that arise in the market for labor. Hiring and paying workers based on their marginal product is often more easily said than done. But the marginal productivity theory of resource use is a good first approximation of how resource markets work. In the next section we change gears to consider the actual distribution of earnings across different types of resources.

FUNCTIONAL DISTRIBUTION OF INCOME

One way to develop an overview of resource markets and labor's role in particular is to consider the distribution of resource earnings in the economy. Of special interest is how income is distributed among resource owners as a result of the workings of resource markets. Specifically, after the dust settles, what share of the income goes to suppliers of labor and what share goes to suppliers of each of the other resources? In this final section we examine how the income of the nation as a whole is divided among resource owners.

Exhibit 4 shows the proportion of national income that goes for (1) wages and salaries, (2) proprietors' income, (3) corporate profits, (4) interest, and (5) rent. As you can see, over time wages and salaries have claimed by far the largest share of national income, most recently earning about three-fourths of the total. This understates the proportion going to labor, however, because a portion of proprietors' income consists of wages as well: the proprietor of the corner store typically works long hours, and much of those earnings should be considered compensation for the proprietor's labor.

Exhibit 4 also shows the sharp decline over time in the share of national income received by proprietors. A portion of the shift is due to the growing dominance of the corporation as the most prevalent organizational form. A generation ago the income received by Mom and Pop from their corner store was counted as proprietors' income; the people who ring up your Pepsi today are more typically earning salaries and wages as employees of a corporate chain of convenience stores, such as 7-Eleven.

EXHIBIT 4
FUNCTIONAL DISTRIBUTION OF INCOME:
PERCENTAGE SHARE OF EACH SOURCE OF INCOME

Time Period	(1) Wages and Salaries	(2) Proprietors' Income	(3) Corporate Profits	(4) Interest	(5) Rent
1900–1909	55.0	23.7	6.8	5.5	9.0
1910–1919	53.6	23.8	9.1	5.4	8.1
1920–1929	60.0	17.5	7.8	6.2	7.7
1930–1939	67.5	14.8	4.0	8.7	5.0
1940–1948	64.6	17.2	11.9	3.1	3.3
1949–1958	67.3	13.9	12.5	2.9	3.4
1959–1963	69.9	11.9	11.2	4.0	3.0
1964–1970	71.6	9.6	12.1	3.5	3.2
1971–1979	74.6	7.4	9.8	6.3	1.9
1980–1984	75.0	4.9	8.2	10.1	1.8

Sources: Irving Kravis, "Income Distribution: Functional Shares," *International Encyclopedia of Social Sciences*, vol. 7 (New York: Macmillan Co. and Free Press, 1968), p 134; *The Annual Report of the Council of Economic Advisers*, 1985, Table B-21. Figures after 1963 are not fully consistent with prior figures, but they convey a reasonably accurate picture of income trends.

The major problem with Exhibit 4 is that the categories and definitions do not really match the tidy definitions we have used. We already noted that proprietors' income includes labor income. Additionally, the columns listing Corporate Profits, Interest, and Rent do not correspond closely to the terms *economic profit*, *interest*, and *economic rent* as they are used in this book. Yet the definitions in Exhibit 4 bear enough similarity to the way economists view the world to make the table of interest to us. The most important conclusion is that labor's share of total income is relatively large and has grown during this century. This conclusion still holds even if the definitions of each income category are changed somewhat.

SUMMARY

1. The supply of labor shows the relationship between the wage rate and the quantity of labor people are willing and able to supply. The demand for labor shows the relationship between the wage rate and the quantity of labor firms are willing and able to demand. The intersection of supply and demand determines the equilibrium wage rate.

2. People use their time to maximize their utility. There are three uses of time: market work, household work, and leisure. A higher market wage means that each hour of work yields more in terms of the goods and services that can be purchased, so a higher wage provides an incentive to substitute market work for other uses of time. But the higher the wage, the higher the income, and as income increases, people consume more of all normal goods including leisure. The net effect of a higher wage on an individual's quantity of labor supplied depends on both the substitution effect and the income effect.

3. The quantity of labor supplied depends on a variety of factors other than the wage, including (1) other sources of income, (2) job amenities, (3) the future value of job experience, (4) the amount of discretion allowed in the use of time while working, and (5) taste for the work.

4. Market wages differ because of (1) differences in the training and education requirements, (2) differences in the skill and ability of workers, (3) differences in the riskiness of the work, both in the workers' safety and in the chances of getting laid off, (4) problems of labor mobility, and (5) racial and sexual discrimination.

5. Although wage determination is based on the marginal productivity of workers, problems arise if differences in worker productivity cannot be readily determined by employers. Adverse selection occurs because workers are more familiar with their own productivity than employers are. When the productivity of workers is not directly observable, employers sometime try to hire workers based on some signal related to productivity, such as education or personal appearance. This system of screening applicants is effective as long as more productive workers find it easier to send the correct signal than less productive workers do.

6. The principal-agent model describes a relationship in which one party, known as the principal, makes a contractual agreement with another party, known as the agent, in the expectation that the agent will act on behalf of the principal. Principal-agent problems arise when the agent is better informed or has easier access to information than the principal does.

7. During this century wages and salaries have grown as a source of total resource income, and they now account for about three-quarters of the total. Proprietors' income and rent have fallen as a percentage of the total.

QUESTIONS AND PROBLEMS

1. (Utility Maximization) Explain how the consumption of goods, the supplying of labor, and the consumption of leisure each affects utility and each other.

2. (Labor Supply) Suppose that the substitution effect of an increase in the wage rate exactly offsets the income effect for all wage levels. What would the supply of labor look like in this case? Why?

3. (Labor Supply) Many U.S. companies have a problem of worker absenteeism. How is this problem related to labor supply and, in particular, to the level of wages? What other considerations are there?

4. (Equilibrium Differentials) Suppose that two jobs are exactly the same except that one provides an air-conditioned workplace. How might an economist measure the value workers place on such a job amenity?

5. (Labor Supply) What education and general skills are important to improve the productivity of the labor force? Do you believe that high schools and colleges provide such an education? Why or why not?

6. (Risk and Labor Supply) Suppose that you have a choice between a job that, with great certainty, results in the loss of one life in a hundred and another job that bears no such risk. If the no-risk job pays $20,000 per year, what income would be necessary to induce you to take the risky job?

7. (Adverse Selection and Signaling) Suppose that you were charged with the responsibility of recruiting for a major corporation. What signals would you use to reduce the problem of adverse selection? How might these signals be faulty indicators of productivity?

8. (Principal-Agent) Export management companies help firms market their products in foreign countries. Are such export management companies principals or agents? What skills must the agent possess to be successful?

9. (Distribution of Income) How might technological advances affect the distribution of income in an economy?

10. (Distribution of Income) Why was land reform essential to provide a more equitable distribution of income in some countries? What dangers exist for countries with very unbalanced distributions?

UNIONS and COLLECTIVE BARGAINING

Perhaps no aspect of the labor market is more in the news than the activities of labor unions. Labor contract negotiations, strikes, picket lines, confrontations between workers and employers—all these fit neatly into TV's "action news" format. Each September, for example, brings football and news of a teacher's strike somewhere in the country. This drama may cause you to miss the true economic significance of unions. Also, you may have developed the mistaken impression that the majority of workers belong to unions and that many hours are lost to strikes. In this chapter we will step back from the charged rhetoric typically used to discuss union-employer relationships to review the history of the union movement in the United States, examine more carefully the economic effects of unions, and discuss recent trends in the union employment. Topics and terms discussed include:

- Craft unions

- Industrial unions

- Collective bargaining

- Tradeoff between wages and employment

- Union objectives

A BRIEF HISTORY OF THE LABOR MOVEMENT

We will begin by setting the union movement in its historical context. First, we will describe working conditions before labor unions achieved national prominence. In 1860, 60 percent of the labor force was employed in agriculture. The work day for nonfarm employees averaged about 11 hours, and people normally worked a 6-day week. Those who were employed in steel mills, paper mills, and breweries typically worked 12 hours a day, 7 days a week.

Not only were the hours long but the pay was low, and the working conditions were often frightful. Insurance company estimates show that at the turn of the century 25,000 to 35,000 deaths per year and more than 2 million serious injuries resulted from accidents on the job. About 1 of 15 workers was seriously injured each year. Mining and metal processing were particularly dangerous.

To win compensation for injuries, a worker had to sue the employer. Not only did the employer's negligence have to be proven but no award would result if the employer could show that the employee was aware of the hazardous nature of the work or that the accident stemmed from the employee's negligence or the negligence of a coworker. Most workers did not know how to sue their employers.

Child labor was also common. In 1880 a million children between the ages of 10 and 15 were in the work force; this number doubled to 2 million by 1910, when one-fifth of those between 10 and 15 held full-time jobs. Thus, the hours were long, the pay was low, working conditions were hazardous, and child labor was common. Moreover, immigration during the period sent millions of new workers streaming into the work force, competing for jobs and keeping wages relatively low. Employers were therefore assured of a ready pool of workers despite working conditions.

Early Labor Organizations

While there was a strong tradition of organized labor in Europe, particularly among the craft guilds, the first effort at unions in the United States dates back to the early days of national independence, when employees in various crafts, such as carpenters, masons, shoemakers, and printers, formed local groups to seek higher wages and shorter hours. In the 1850s, because improved transportation systems extended markets beyond the locality, unions in the same trade began widening their membership to regional and even national levels. The National Typographical Union, formed in 1852, was soon followed by several other national craft unions.

Knights of Labor The first major national labor organization in the United States was the Knights of Labor, formed in 1869. Its objectives were generally more political than economic, but the Knights sought an 8-hour workday and the abolition of child labor. Within 20 years the union had over 750,000 members. But the union's pursuit of socialism and lack of progress toward specific labor objectives evidently disenchanted many of its members, who left the union. Another major problem was that the Knights of Labor tried to include as members both skilled and unskilled labor, a combination that proved difficult to organize.

American Federation of Labor The Knights of Labor did not appeal to the various craft unions that had developed during the nineteenth century.

Consequently, these craft unions formed their own national organization, called the American Federation of Labor (AFL). The AFL was founded in 1886 under the direction of Samuel Gompers, a cigar maker, and from the outset the focus was on economic issues, not social or political issues, as with the Knights of Labor. The AFL accepted the existing political system but tried to make economic changes that would help its members. It was not a union but rather an organization of national unions, with each member union retaining its autonomy.

By the beginning of World War I the AFL, still under the direction of Gompers, was viewed as the voice of labor. Because of favorable government legislation, membership jumped during World War I, increasing from less than 1 million at the turn of the century to about 4 million by 1920, about 13 percent of the nonfarm labor force. The next decade, however, was a period of stagnation and decline for organized labor. After the war, government retreated from its support of union efforts, and employers in some cases failed to recognize labor unions. As a result, the union movement foundered, with membership falling by half between 1920 and 1933.

A New Deal for Labor

By the 1930s unions had become creatures of government legislation. But the worst economic disaster in the history of the country—the Great Depression—set the stage for a new era of the labor movement. The unemployment rate reached 25 percent, prices dropped, and output fell by more than 33 percent between 1929 and 1933. President Franklin D. Roosevelt naturally viewed this pattern of events with alarm and believed that higher prices and wages were necessary to pull the economy out of its disastrous slump. Government support for organized labor was, he thought, a way to boost wages. The *Norris–La Guardia Act* of 1932 provided this support by sharply limiting the courts' ability to stop strikes. The act also failed to uphold *yellow-dog contracts*, under which workers had to agree not to join a union as a condition of employment.

Wagner Act Another important law passed during this period was the *Wagner Act* of 1935, which was based on the view that big business had been holding the upper hand in its match with labor. This act made it an unfair labor practice for employers to fail to bargain with unions that represented the majority of the workers. The act also made it illegal for employers to interfere with their employees' right to unionize. To investigate unfair labor practices and to oversee union elections, the law established the *National Labor Relations Board*. Because the Wagner Act laid the legal foundation for unions to negotiate on an equal footing with employers, the act has come to be known as the Magna Carta of the American labor movement.

The Congress of Industrial Organizations The nutrient supplied by favorable legislation stimulated the growth of a new kind of union, organized not along craft lines, as was the AFL, but along industry lines. The Congress of Industrial Organizations (CIO) was established in 1935 to serve as a national organization of unions in mass-production industries, such as autos and steel. Whereas the AFL had organized along craft lines, such as plumbers and carpenters, the CIO was made up of unions whose members included all workers in a particular industry. This industry-wide approach proved successful, and in 1937 the steel workers union joined the CIO, bringing into the organization more than 200,000 members. In 1938 the charismatic leader of the United Mine Workers, John L. Lewis, became president of the CIO. Workers in autos and rubber were able to organize through the use of sit-down strikes, in which workers occupied the plants but did not work, thereby paralyzing operations.

The Labor Movement After World War II

The period from the mid-1930s to 1960 can be thought of as the golden years of union organization and growth. Both the CIO and the AFL flourished; in fact, their rivalry appeared to stimulate union growth. Total union membership grew from less than 4 million, or about 7 percent of the labor force, in 1930 to more than 18 million, or about 25 percent of the labor force, in 1960. Yet during this period of increasing union membership, the labor movement had growing pains.

The Taft-Hartley Act of 1947   After World War II economic conditions and public sentiment appeared to turn against unions. Postwar inflation seemed to be aggravated by a series of strikes. In November 1946 the United Mine Workers defied a court order to return to work after a long and bitter strike. In response, Congress in 1947 passed the *Taft-Hartley Act*, which reversed the direction of labor legislation. The act attempted to limit strikes that would affect the public's safety and welfare. The President could obtain a court order to stop or prevent a strike for 80 days, during which time the parties could continue to negotiate.

Also, under provisions of the Taft-Hartley Act, the *closed shop*, which required workers to join a union before they could be hired, was prohibited. Moreover, individual states could pass **right-to-work** laws, which said that workers did not have to join the union as a condition of continued employment. Thus, states could outlaw the **union shop**, which usually required workers to join the union once they were hired. About 20 states eventually outlawed union shops in favor of **open shops**, which allowed employers to hire both union and nonunion workers. With an open shop, the nonunion employees, once hired, did not have to join the union.

*Workers must join the union after being hired by a **union shop**. Such shops are outlawed in **right-to-work** states, where **open shops** hire both union and nonunion workers.*

All this shop talk can become confusing, so let's summarize. There were three types of shops: (1) closed shops, which required workers to join the union before they could be hired, were outlawed by the Taft-Hartley Act; (2) union shops, which usually required workers to join the union once employed, were legal in states that allowed them; and (3) open shops, which did not require union membership, were the only kind of union shops allowed in the 20 "right-to-work" states.

The 1955 Merger of the AFL and CIO   A strong rivalry existed between the craft union approach of the AFL and the industry union approach of the CIO. A new generation of labor leaders saw the advantages of merging the country's two major labor organizations to present a united labor front and to provide labor with greater political clout, which would attract new members. The AFL and CIO merged in 1955, bringing together the national craft unions and the national industrial unions. The merger did not put to rest rivalries among national union leaders. Differences between George Meany, the new AFL-CIO president, and Walter Reuther, the head of the United Auto Workers (UAW), led to Reuther pulling his UAW out of the AFL-CIO in 1968. The 1.5 million UAW members joined a union of the same size, the International Brotherhood of Teamsters, then headed by Jimmy Hoffa, to form the Alliance for Labor Action.

The Landrum-Griffin Act of 1959   During the 1950s organized labor also suffered from allegations of corruption and misconduct by union leaders. Congressional investigations into the internal workings of several unions uncovered questionable practices and raised public concern about union operations. As a consequence, union officials became more tightly regulated by the *Landrum-Griffin Act*, passed in 1959, which was designed to protect the rights of rank-and-file union members against abuses by union leaders. Among its provisions, the act regulated union elections, required union officials to file financial reports, and made theft of union funds a federal offense. This act has been called the Bill of Rights for union members because it attempted to guarantee each member's right to open elections and honest union leadership.

Collective Bargaining and Other Tools of Unionism

Now that you have some idea of the labor movement's history, it is time to introduce the mechanics of unionism. We begin with a discussion of collective bargaining.

Collective bargaining is the process by which union and management negotiate a mutually agreeable contract.

Collective bargaining is the process by which union and management negotiate a mutually agreeable contract specifying wages, fringe benefits, and working conditions. Wage-related issues include not only the pay for each type of labor but also overtime provisions, the length of the work week, job security issues, and seniority pay privileges. Fringe benefits cover pensions, health insurance, vacations, and other benefit programs. Working conditions can involve issues as broad as the employee's right to question management practices and as narrow as the size of the locker provided for each worker. The labor contract is worked out between representatives of the union and representatives of the employer. The actual contract can run to many pages of fine print written in language only a lawyer could understand. Once an agreement is reached, union representatives must carry it back to the membership for a vote. If it is rejected, the union can vote to strike or to continue negotiations.

*In **mediation** an impartial observer attempts to resolve differences between union and management. Under **arbitration** both parties agree to respect the arbitrator's decision.*

Mediation and Arbitration   If negotiations for a contract reach an impasse and if the public interest is involved, government officials may ask an independent **mediator** to step in. A mediator is an impartial observer with no actual power who listens to both sides separately and makes suggestions about how each side could adjust its position to resolve differences. If a resolution appears possible, the mediator will bring the parties together to iron out a contract.

If negotiations have stalled but both sides want to avoid a strike, the parties can agree to appoint an **arbitrator**, who is an outsider empowered to resolve differences to get a contract. In certain critical sectors, such as police and fire protection, where a strike would seriously harm the public interest, an impasse in negotiations must sometimes be settled through *compulsory arbitration*. Because each side ends up delegating some power to an arbitrator, arbitration is typically a last resort short of a strike. Some disputes skip the mediation and arbitration steps altogether, going directly from impasse to strike.

*A **strike** is a union's attempt to withhold labor from a firm.*

The Strike   A major source of union power in the bargaining relationship is the threat of a **strike**, which is the union's attempt to withhold labor from the firm. The purpose of a strike is to disrupt production and thereby to impose costs on an employer to force acceptance of the union's position. At the same time, however, a strike imposes significant costs on union members because they must go without pay or fringe benefits for the duration of the strike. Union funds and other sources can provide some support during a strike, but the typical striker's income falls substantially.

Thus, strikes can be very costly for both sides. In 1985, for example, British coal miners went back to work after losing a strike that lasted a year. The threat of a strike hangs over labor negotiations and can serve as a real spur to reach an accord. Although usually neither party wants a strike, both sides must act as if they could endure a strike rather than concede on key points.

The union's success in any strike depends on its ability to make the strike as costly as possible for the employer. To this end, unions usually picket the targeted employer to prevent or discourage so-called strike-breakers, or "scabs," from working. Since the success of the strike depends on blocking the supply of labor to the firm, it is not surprising that in confrontations between striking and nonstriking workers, violence occasionally erupts. Although reports of strikes are often in the news, most bargaining agreements—over 95 percent—are resolved without a strike.

THE ECONOMIC EFFECT OF UNIONS

Samuel Gompers, the long-time president of the AFL, was once asked what unions want. "More!" he said. Union members, like everyone else, have unlimited wants, but no union can regularly get more of everything it desires. Because resources are scarce, choices must be made. One could prepare a menu of union desires: higher wages, more fringe benefits, more jobs, greater job security, better working conditions, and so on. To keep the analysis manageable, we consider first a single objective: higher wages. Given the market for labor, how can the union alter the supply or the demand for labor to raise the price of labor? We will examine three possible ways of increasing wages: (1) inclusive, or industrial, unionism, (2) exclusive, or craft, unionism, and (3) increasing the demand for union labor.

Inclusive, or Industrial, Unions

Let's consider first the market for labor in the absence of union intervention. In Exhibit 1(a) the market supply and demand for a particular type of labor are presented as *S* and *D*. The equilibrium wage is *W*, and the equilibrium employment level is *E*. At the market wage each individual employer faces a horizontal, or perfectly elastic, supply of labor, as reflected in Exhibit 1(b). Thus, each firm as a price taker can hire as much as it wants at the market wage of *W*. The firm hires labor up to the point where the marginal revenue

EXHIBIT 1   EFFECT OF A UNION'S WAGE FLOOR

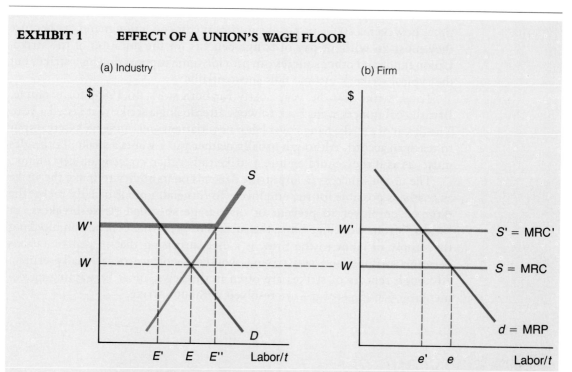

In panel (a) the equilibrium wage rate is *W*. At that wage the individual firm of panel (b) hires labor up to the point where the marginal revenue product equals *W*. Each firm hires quantity *e*; total employment is *E*.

If a union can negotiate a wage *W'* above the equilibrium level, the supply curve facing the firm shifts up to *S'*. The firm hires fewer workers, *e'*, and total employment falls to *E'*. At wage *W'* there is excess supply of labor equal to *E'' − E'*.

product, or demand, equals the marginal resource cost, or supply; this amount is shown by quantity e in Exhibit 1(b). In equilibrium each worker hired is paid an amount just equal to what the marginal worker earns for the firm.

Suppose that the union, by negotiating with employers in this industry, is able to establish a minimum wage in this industry of W'. Evidence suggests that union wages in the United States are on average about 15 to 20 percent higher than nonunion wages. Once this wage is established in the market, each individual firm, as a price taker, faces a horizontal supply curve for labor at the collectively bargained wage, W'. Because of the law of demand, as the price of labor goes up, each employer demands less labor, as reflected in the drop in employment by the individual firm from e to e' in Exhibit 1(b). Consequently, higher wages lead to a reduction in total employment; the quantity demanded by the industry drops from E to E' in Exhibit 1(a). Assuming that the union wage is higher than the market-clearing wage, there will now be an excess supply of labor. At wage W' the amount of labor supplied, E'', exceeds the amount demanded, E'. Ordinarily, this "surplus" of labor would cause unemployed workers to lower their asking wage, but since union members bargained *collectively* for the wage floor of W', workers cannot individually offer to work for less, nor can employers hire them at a lower wage.

Because of this excess supply of labor, the union must develop some mechanism to ration the available jobs among its members. Rationing devices include selecting workers based on seniority and attempting to spread the available work over more members through shorter work weeks and by rotating workers among available jobs. Thus, even if the union is able to set the wage above the market-clearing level, it must still deal with the worker frustration that arises from excess supply. This model characterizes strong industrial unions, such as autos and steel, which attempt to set the industry-wide wage for each class of labor. The union sets the wage even though all who would like to work at that wage cannot be hired. Wage gains come at the expense of reduced total employment.

Those who cannot find union employment will look for jobs in the nonunion sector, increasing the supply of labor there. Because of this greater supply of labor, the equilibrium wage in the nonunion sector will fall below the level that would prevail in the absence of unions. So wages are higher in the union sector first because unions bargain for a wage rate that exceeds the market clearing level and second because those unable to find employment in the union sector supply their labor to the nonunion sector. This increased supply of labor to the nonunion sector reduces the nonunion wage.

Exclusive, or Craft, Unions

One way to increase wages while avoiding the instability and frustration created by the industrial-union approach is for the union to somehow shift the supply curve to the left, as shown in Exhibit 2, thereby increasing the market wage from W to W'. Successful supply restrictions of this type require that two conditions be met. First, the union must be able to restrict its

EXHIBIT 2   EFFECT OF LABOR SUPPLY RESTRICTIONS

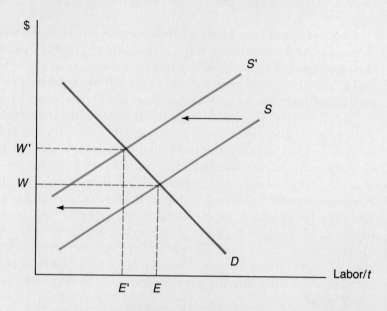

If a union can restrict labor supply to an industry, the supply curve shifts left from *S* to *S'*. The wage rate rises from *W* to *W'* but at the cost of a reduction in employment from *E* to *E'*.

membership, and second, the union must be able to force employers to hire only union members. The union can restrict membership by high initiation fees, long apprenticeship periods, difficult qualification exams, and other devices designed to slow down or discourage new membership.

Whereas wage setting is more typical of the industrial unions, restricting supply is more characteristic of craft unions, such as carpenters, plumbers, and bricklayers. Professional groups such as doctors, lawyers, and accountants also impose entry restrictions through education and examination standards. Such restrictions, though usually justified on grounds of protecting the public, may often be no more than self-serving attempts to increase earnings by reducing supply.

Increase Demand for Union Labor

A third way to increase the wage is to increase the demand for union labor. This is shown in Exhibit 3 as an outward shift of the labor demand curve from *D* to *D'*. This approach is an attractive alternative because it increases both wages *and* employment, so there is no need to ration jobs or to restrict union membership.

Increase Demand for Union-Made Goods One way to increase the demand for union labor is a direct appeal to consumers to buy only union-made products (such as in the familiar refrain, "Look for the union label"). Because the demand for labor is a derived demand, an increase in the demand for union-made products will increase the demand for union labor.

Restrict Sales of Non-Union-Made Goods   Another way to increase the demand for union labor is to restrict the supply of products that compete with union-made products. Again, this relies on the derived nature of labor demand. For example, United Auto Workers have over the years supported restrictions on imported cars. Fewer imported cars means a greater demand for cars produced by U.S. workers, who are mostly union members.

Increase Productivity   Another theory is that unions increase the demand for union labor because unions represent an efficient way to organize and monitor the labor-management relationship. According to this argument, unions increase worker productivity by minimizing conflicts, resolving differences, and at times even straightening out workers who are goofing off. Under this view, the union serves as a source of information and communication, promoting harmonious relationships in the firm and serving as a buffer to cushion labor-management relations. In the absence of a union, an individual worker may be reluctant to complain to the employer about some unsatisfactory element of the job. Instead, the really dissatisfied worker may simply look for another job, thereby causing job turnover, which is costly to

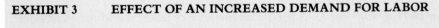

EXHIBIT 3   EFFECT OF AN INCREASED DEMAND FOR LABOR

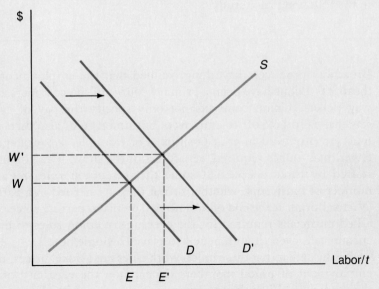

An increase in labor demand from *D* to *D'* raises both the wage and the level of employment.

the firm. With a union, however, each worker can feel more comfortable complaining through union channels, and a negotiated response to such a complaint will reduce the employee's urge to leave the firm. If unions increase the productivity of workers in this way, the demand for union labor would increase. An outward shift in the demand for union labor, as reflected in Exhibit 3, will increase both the wage rate and the employment level.

Featherbedding   Still another way unions attempt to increase the demand for labor is by trying to limit the output per worker to increase the number of workers required to perform a particular task. This practice, called *featherbedding*, tries to ensure that more labor is hired than producers would prefer. Such measures are sometimes part of the union's response to the introduction of labor-saving technology. For example, when the diesel engine replaced the coal-fired engine, locomotives no longer needed someone to shovel coal. For years after the adoption of the diesel engine, however, the railroad unions required such a crew member. Similarly, some newspaper typesetter unions required any ready-to-use advertising layouts to be reset by hand; court transcribers refuse to permit tape recordings of legal proceedings; and painters unions often prohibit the use of spray guns, limiting members to paintbrushes.

Featherbedding is not a true increase in demand, in the sense of shifting the demand curve to the right; instead, it is more like an attempt to force firms to hire a quantity to the right of their demand curve. The union tries to say either hire a certain number of workers or you can hire none. Thus, the union attempts to dictate not only the wage but also the quantity that must be hired at that wage, thereby moving the employers off and to the right of their demand for labor curve. A particular instance of featherbedding is considered in the following case study.

CASE STUDY

Featherbedding on Broadway

Broadway producers have long claimed that the employment rules of the theatrical unions have been a primary source of the cost increases of Broadway tickets. Union contracts not only specify the pay of everyone from stagehands to box-office employees but union rules also dictate how many must be employed in each position. For example, a backstage crew of no fewer than four is required, regardless of the show. The box office must be staffed by three people. At some theaters union rules require a certain number of musicians, whether or not they are needed in a particular show. (Victor Borge, at the end of his one-person piano performance on Broadway, asked musicians required for the evening by union rules to line up for the curtain call, even though none had played a single note.)

To the extent that these union work rules raise ticket prices, the continued employment of union members depends on the elasticity of demand for theater tickets. With the top price per ticket over $50, there is evidence that the price elasticity of demand has been responsive enough to put many theater employees out of work. Only 19 shows were playing during the 1986–87 theater season, down from 27 shows a decade earlier. Less than half the theaters were operating. With theaters shut down, many union members are unemployed. Featherbedding rules have required each theater to hire a specified number of employees, but these same rules cannot dictate that theaters stay in business.

With the cost of putting on a new show approaching $1 million, producers have grown more resistant to union rules and have attempted to seek compromises. The 14 unions involved have agreed to a wage freeze during the first year of a three-year agreement. Because union staffing requirements are based on the number of seats in the theater, producers have been moving off Broadway to smaller theaters. Shows are shifted to the larger Broadway theaters only after their success seems assured. Producers have also reduced staffing requirements by simply reducing the number of seats that can be sold; blocking off the balcony has been one way to do this.

Sources: "Unions Are Losing Their Star Billing On Broadway," *Business Week* (26 November 1984); Robert Lenzner; "Economics Is Dimming the Lights of Broadway," *The Boston Globe*, 1 February 1987.

Conclusion   We have examined three ways that unions can attempt to raise members' wages: (1) by negotiating a floor wage above the equilibrium wage for the industry and somehow rationing the limited jobs among union members, (2) by restricting the supply of labor, and (3) by increasing the demand for union labor. Using this last approach, unions can attempt to increase the demand for union labor in four ways: (1) through a direct public appeal to buy only union-made products, (2) by restricting the supply of products made by nonunion labor, (3) by increasing productivity through reducing misunderstandings and other sources of conflict between labor and management, and (4) by forcing employers to employ more workers than they would prefer through featherbedding.

Bargaining in a Monopsonistic Labor Market

A union sells labor as a monopolist. Thus far we have assumed that the wage was determined through negotiations between the labor union and the entire industry. Because each firm hired labor as a price taker in the market for labor, each firm was free to hire as much labor as it chose at the negotiated price. The model of a union bargaining with the entire industry captures much of what is observed in labor markets.

At times, however, the negotiations are between a union and the only employer of that kind of labor. The employer in this case is a monopsonist. When we first introduced resource markets, we noted that because the monopsonist is the sole employer of a particular type of labor, the supply of labor appears to the monopsonist as upward sloping. For simplicity, we begin by examining the monopsonist in the absence of a union, as depicted in Exhibit 4(a). The supply curve represents the average resource cost the firm must pay for each unit of labor; the marginal resource cost curve for labor is above the labor supply curve. In the absence of a union, the profit-maximizing firm will hire labor up to the point where labor's marginal resource cost equals its marginal revenue product, as reflected by its demand curve for labor. Thus, in Exhibit 4(a) the profit-maximizing level of employment is E, and the profit-maximizing wage as found on the supply curve is W.

Thus, a profit-maximizing monopsonist pays nonunionized labor a wage below labor's marginal revenue product. In the absence of a union, workers have little power in dealing with the employer. A worker's only decision is whether or not to work for the firm at the wage offered by the employer. Those workers whose opportunity cost is at or below W will work for the firm; those with a higher opportunity cost will not.

EXHIBIT 4   MONOPSONIST HIRING LABOR IN NONUNIONIZED AND UNIONIZED LABOR MARKETS

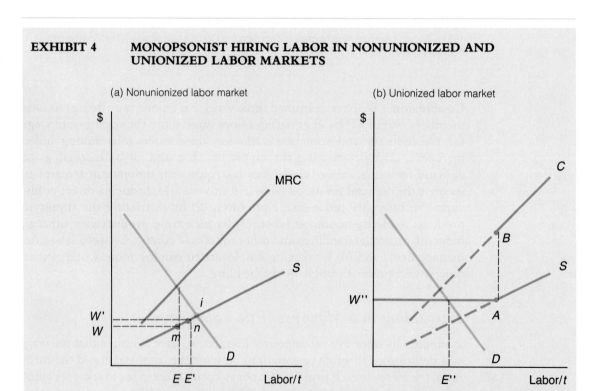

(a) Nonunionized labor market   (b) Unionized labor market

In panel (a) a monopsonist faces a nonunionized work force. Employment is E, and the wage rate is W. If a union is able to organize the workers, it would negotiate a higher wage rate, such as W'. In this case the movement up the supply curve from point m to point n leads also to higher employment (E'). Between points m and i employment and the wage rate rise together.

In panel (b) the union has negotiated a wage floor at W''. The labor supply curve is $W''AS$, and marginal resource cost is $W''ABC$. The intersection of the demand for labor and marginal resource cost curves yields a wage of W'' and employment of E''—both higher than in the nonunion situation.

The introduction of a union changes the terms of the bargain. Instead of accepting the wage offered, the union, as a monopoly supplier of labor to the firm, has some power to negotiate the wage. The union's power rests on its willingness and ability to withhold *all* labor—to strike—if the employer does not comply. Thus, both sides have some economic power—the firm as the only employer of this type of labor, and the union as the only supplier of this type of labor. The union will try to push wages up, and the firm will try to keep wages down. **Bilateral monopoly** describes the situation where a union bargains with a monopsonist. Since both sides have some power, the wage will depend on the relative bargaining skills of each side. Economic theory alone cannot predict what the bargained wage will be.

Bilateral monopoly is the situation where a union bargains with a monopsonist.

Of special significance in this bargaining model is that the union, by pushing up wages, can initially increase both wages *and* employment. Notice in Exhibit 4(a) that without unions, workers are initially at point *m* on their supply curve. If workers unionize and are able to negotiate a higher wage, these workers will move up the supply curve from point *m* to point *n*. The wage will rise from W to W', and employment will expand from E to E'. Thus, the union can increase both wages and employment. This will be true for movements up the supply curve to point *i*; wage demands exceeding the level at point *i* will cause employers to begin cutting back employment as employers move up their demand curve.

Suppose that the union is able to negotiate a wage floor of W'' in Exhibit 4(b), meaning that no labor will be supplied at a lower wage, but that any amount desired by the firm, up to quantity identified at point A, will be supplied at the floor wage. In effect, the supply of union labor is perfectly elastic at the union wage up to point A. If more than A is demanded, the floor wage no longer comes into play; the upward-sloping portion, AS, becomes the relevant part of the labor supply curve. For a firm facing a floor wage of W'', the entire labor supply curve is $W''AS$, which has a kink where the floor wage joins the upward-sloping supply curve.

Given this kinked supply curve, the monopsonist's marginal resource cost curve for labor consists of two separate segments. For quantities less than A, the marginal resource cost curve is given by the horizontal segment, $W''A$, which is the floor wage. Within this range of employment, the firm can hire more labor at the floor wage, so the marginal cost is constant and equal to that wage. For employment levels greater than A, the labor supply curve is upward sloping, so hiring another unit of labor means paying a higher wage to *all* workers. Thus, for labor quantities greater than A, that portion of the marginal resource cost above the supply curve becomes the relevant segment. The marginal resource cost curve is therefore traced out by the line segments $W''ABC$. The kink in the labor supply curve has divided the firm's marginal resource cost curve in two (just as a kink in the oligopolist's demand curve broke the marginal revenue curve in two).

In Exhibit 4(b) the intersection of the firm's marginal resource cost curve for labor and its demand curve for labor yields a wage of W'' and a quantity of E''. In this example both the wage and the quantity are greater than when there was no union. As we have said, the actual wage rate and quantity hired will depend on the relative bargaining strengths of the two parties. The union will recognize that there is a tradeoff between the number employed and the negotiated wage.

Union Objectives

Thus far we have assumed that unions attempt to maximize wages. While this appears to be a reasonable first approximation, union behavior at times seems to suggest other possible objectives. In this section we explore those other objectives. Keep in mind during this discussion, however, that unions may adopt a variety of goals, depending on the circumstances, so no simple model can capture all the variation.

Let's return to the market for labor of a particular type, in this case workers skilled in the production of widgets. In Exhibit 5 the demand curve is labeled D, and the supply curve is labeled S. Without a union, the competitive market wage is W, and the equilibrium quantity of labor is E. Now suppose that the workers in the widget industry form a union called the Worldwide Widget Workers (3W). Consider the alternative wage and employment policies the union could adopt.

Maximize Employment   The union could attempt to maximize the number of workers employed in the industry. Look at the market for widget workers in Exhibit 5, and see what wage rate will maximize the quantity of labor hired. Employment is maximized when the competitive wage is selected. Any wage higher than W lowers employment since quantity demanded will be reduced, and any wage below W lowers employment since quantity supplied will be reduced. Thus, at wage rates above W, the demand curve dominates the employment decision, and at wage rates below W, supply dominates the employment decision. We have thickened these segments of supply and demand to highlight the dominance of what is called the "short side" of this market. Thus, the competitive wage rate maximizes employment, but, of course, the workers do not need a union to achieve this objective.

*Employment multiplied by the wage rate is the **total wage bill**.*

Maximize the Wage Bill   Another possible objective for the union is to maximize the **total wage bill**, which is employment multiplied by the wage rate. To maximize the total amount paid to workers in this industry, consider the union as a monopoly seller of labor. The demand for labor faced by the union is like the demand for any other item sold by a monopolist. To induce firms to hire additional labor, the union must lower the wage. But as the union lowers the wage, the wage earned by those workers who had already been employed in the industry must also fall. As a result, the union's marginal revenue will always be less than the wage identified by the market demand curve for labor.

To better understand the relationship between demand and marginal revenue, let's consider the following example. Assume that 100 workers are hired when the wage floor is $20 per hour, for a total wage bill of $2000. To get 1 more worker hired, the union must lower the wage floor to $19.90 per

---

EXHIBIT 5   **MAXIMIZING EMPLOYMENT**

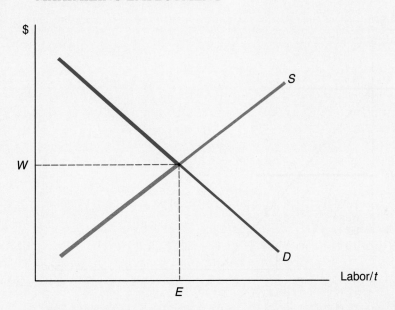

W is the equilibrium wage. At any other wage, employment is the lesser of quantity demanded and quantity supplied. Employment is maximized at *E* when the wage rate is at equilibrium.

---

hour. That is, getting the 101st worker hired means accepting lower wages for the original 100 workers; their wage must drop by $0.10 per hour, from $20 to $19.90, for a drop of $10 in total earnings. As a result of the lower wage, however, an additional worker is hired, who earns the new wage of $19.90. The net change in the total wage bill, which we will call the union's marginal revenue, is the new worker's earnings of $19.90 minus the loss of $10 in wages to existing employees, which equals $9.90. A simpler way of computing marginal revenue is to compute the total wage bill before and after the drop in the wage, then examine the difference. The total wage bill before the wage drop was $2000; after the drop it is $2009.90 ($=$19.90 \times$ 101). Thus, the union's marginal revenue of $9.90 is below the wage of $19.90.

The union's marginal revenue curve is drawn in Exhibit 6. This curve shows by how much the total wage bill changes for each 1-unit change in employment. The total wage bill is maximized where marginal revenue is equal to 0. Thus, if the union negotiates a wage floor of W^*, the industry will employ the number of workers E^*; W^* will maximize the total wage bill. A higher or a lower wage will reduce the wage bill.

Another way to arrive at this same outcome is by reference to the elasticity of demand for labor. By calculating the elasticity of labor demand, we can determine where that elasticity is equal to 1.0 and thereby identify the wage

EXHIBIT 6   MAXIMIZING THE TOTAL WAGE BILL

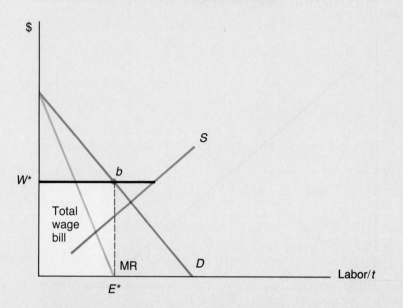

A union that is interested in maximizing the total wage bill paid to its members should negotiate wage *W**. With employment at *E**, the union's marginal revenue is zero. Further increases in employment will cause the wage bill to decrease. Wage *W** is read off the labor demand curve at point *b*. There is excess labor supply at that wage.

that will maximize the total wage bill. Not surprisingly, the elasticity is equal to 1.0 at point *b* on the demand curve. Notice in this example, however, that at the wage where the total wage bill is maximized, there is an excess supply of workers willing to work at that wage, so jobs must somehow be rationed among the many eager widget workers.

Maximize Economic Rent   Yet another possibility for the union is to maximize the economic rent earned by its members. This approach takes each member's opportunity cost explicitly into account. Recall that the total earnings of any resource can be divided between the amount necessary to attract the resource to a particular use, called transfer earnings, and any payment over and above transfer earnings, called economic rent. The labor supply curve represents the amount workers must be paid to "transfer," or to supply each additional unit of labor to the production of widgets. The height of the supply curve at each level of employment represents workers' opportunity cost of providing that marginal unit of employment. For example, at a wage of $5 per hour, only 10,000 hours of labor will be supplied because most workers have higher-paying alternatives. If the wage is raised to $7.50 per hour, however, an additional 10,000 hours is supplied by workers whose opportunity cost was greater than $5 but less than $7.50.

EXHIBIT 7   MAXIMIZING ECONOMIC RENT

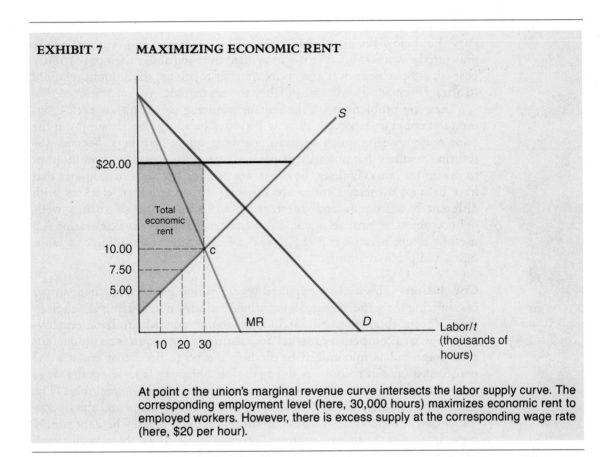

At point *c* the union's marginal revenue curve intersects the labor supply curve. The corresponding employment level (here, 30,000 hours) maximizes economic rent to employed workers. However, there is excess supply at the corresponding wage rate (here, $20 per hour).

Given this notion of transfer earnings and economic rent, some observers have suggested that the union should attempt to maximize the difference between what workers receive in this market and the value of their time in its next best alternative—that is, unions should maximize the economic rent their members can earn. To do this, the union should expand employment until the marginal revenue from supplying additional units of labor equals the opportunity cost of supplying those additional units of labor.

In Exhibit 7 the union's marginal revenue curve and the labor supply curve intersect at point *c*, where the opportunity cost of time, or transfer earnings, as identified on the labor supply curve is $10 per hour, and the quantity supplied is 30,000 hours. To determine the wage rate that maximizes economic rent, at the rent-maximizing level of employment we move up to the labor demand curve to identify the most employers will pay for 30,000 units of labor. The labor demand curve indicates that employers are willing and able to pay a wage of $20 per hour. If the labor unions can negotiate a floor wage of $20 per hour, the economic rent earned on the last unit of labor employed is $20, the wage rate, minus $10, the opportunity cost of the last unit hired. So at a floor wage of $20 per hour, each employed worker earns at least $10 per hour in economic rent.

The total economic rent is reflected by the shaded area above the supply curve but below the floor wage of $20. This economic rent represents pure gravy to the workers because it is a payment over and above their opportunity cost—it is a payment over and above transfer earnings, the amount required to attract each additional unit of labor to this market.

There are problems with the rent-maximizing solution, however. First, even if it could be achieved, there will always be a large excess supply at the floor wage, causing much frustration among union members. Second, the solution assumes that unions are operated by leaders who somehow attempt to maximize rents. Unions, however, are not like business monopolies that have definite owners. Unions are made up of a variety of workers with different backgrounds and different opportunity costs, so such a well-defined objective probably would not emerge. Still, rent maximization is a useful concept because it is the closest we can come to thinking of a labor union as a profit-maximizing monopolist.

Conclusion   This section explored several union goals other than simply maximizing the wage. The goals examined included maximizing (1) employment, (2) the total wage bill, and (3) economic rent. Maximizing employment is what a competitive market does naturally—it requires no union. The total wage bill is maximized by finding the wage floor that equates the marginal wage bill to zero. A third possible objective is to select the wage floor that will maximize the economic rent received by union members. The idea is to maximize the difference between the floor wage and the opportunity cost of supplying labor. Economic rent is maximized where the supply curve intersects the union's marginal revenue curve. Both the maximization of the total wage bill and the maximization of rents will likely create excess supply, requiring the union to ration jobs. As we said at the outset, unions probably have no rigid objective, and, consequently, they may adopt a variety of goals, depending on the circumstances.

RECENT TRENDS IN UNION MEMBERSHIP

Picture, if you will, a typical union member at work. You probably imagine a blue-collar worker with a hard hat, tending a steel furnace or perhaps working on an assembly line. This conception may have been typical at one time, but the image is no longer accurate. Only one in three union workers is in the goods-producing sector, and even fewer union members are in the heavy industries, such as autos and steel. A more typical union member these days is a schoolteacher.

Union membership remained relatively stable through the 1960s and much of the 1970s, rose in the late 1970s, and has been on the decline since 1980, as reflected in Exhibit 8. The union participation rate is highest among government employees, where more than a third are unionized. The lowest rate of unionization is among service workers in the private sector, where

EXHIBIT 8
RECENT TRENDS IN UNION MEMBERSHIP

	1980		1984	
	Union Members (millions)	Union Members as Percent of Total Employed	Union Members (millions)	Union Members as Percent of Total Employed
All wage and salary workers	20.1	23.0%	17.3	18.8%
All private workers	14.3	20.1	11.6	15.3
Private goods workers	8.4	30.5	6.5	24.0
Private services workers	5.9	13.5	5.2	10.5
Government workers	5.8	35.9	5.7	35.7

Source: Bureau of Labor Statistics.

only 10 percent belong to unions. The most dramatic drop since 1980 has been among those in the private goods-producing sector.

Compared with European countries, the United States has a relatively low level of union participation. Nearly 50 percent of the work force in both Britain and Italy are unionized, and the rate is about 35 percent in Holland and West Germany. Only France, with a rate of 20 percent, has as low a rate as the United States. Membership patterns in both Europe and the United States reflect the same trend of declining membership in recent years.

In this section we explore recent developments that have contributed to current trends in unionization.

Public Employee Unions

The rising star of the union movement since 1970 has been the growing membership among public employees, where membership nearly doubled during the decade of the 1970s. Along with public union membership, however, has come the ticklish problem of strikes by such groups. Whereas some consumers would suffer modest inconveniences if, say, household appliance workers went on strike, a strike called by police personnel or fire fighters could jeopardize public safety. Laws have been passed in most states to restrict strikes by public employees, but these laws are sometimes ignored.

The issue of public employee strikes was dramatized in 1981, when the Professional Air Traffic Controllers Organization (PATCO) called a strike. As federal employees, their strike was against the law. Public sympathy appeared to support President Reagan's decision to fire the striking controllers. This firing was virtually unprecedented, and it sent a strong signal to other public employee unions. Indeed, public employee membership, which had grown so vigorously during the 1970s, has remained flat during the 1980s. Although other factors are also responsible, strike activity throughout organized labor has also been relatively quiet since the controller firings. The following case study indicates why the PATCO strike was so very costly to those fired controllers.

CASE STUDY

PATCO's Billion Dollar Gamble

On August 3, 1981, PATCO struck for higher wages and better working conditions. The rest is history. PATCO's strike was a big gamble because, by undertaking an illegal strike, they put at risk secure jobs that at the time paid an average of $35,000 per year (which amounts to about $44,000 in 1988 dollars). PATCO made three major demands: a $10,000 across-the-board raise for all controllers, a 32-hour work week, and retirement after 20 years of service at 75 percent of the highest pay. President Reagan warned the controllers that unless they returned to work by August 5, they would be fired. True to his word, the President fired the 11,345 controllers who ignored the back-to-work ultimatum.

Exhibit 9 presents a model that crudely approximates the market for air traffic controllers. In the absence of a union, the equilibrium wage and employment level would be W and E. PATCO, however, was able to force the wage floor up to an average of $35,000 per year, quite an attractive salary for a

EXHIBIT 9   LABOR MARKET FOR AIR TRAFFIC CONTROLLERS

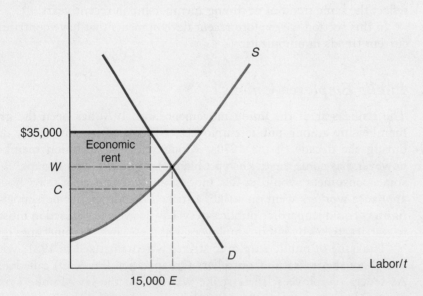

In the absence of a union, the equilibrium wage and employment level would be W and E. At the negotiated wage of $35,000 per year, 15,000 PATCO controllers were employed. The corresponding economic rent was about $170 million.

job that requires no college degree (this sum exceeded the average salary earned by full professors that year). At that wage 15,000 controllers were employed. As you can see, there was excess supply at that wage. Evidence of excess supply was the overwhelming number of applications received to replace the striking controllers (over 200,000 people applied for the 11,345 openings).

The supply curve represents the opportunity cost of offering labor services as an air traffic controller. The opportunity cost for the last worker hired, identified as C in Exhibit 9, was below the actual wage paid. Given the narrow nature of their job experience and the fact that most controllers had no college degree, their alternatives probably paid much less than a controller's salary. The shaded area is a rough approximation of the economic rent earned by air traffic controllers. Those who were fired lost this economic rent.

Fired workers paid a very high price for their strike. What was their next best alternative wage? A survey of 900 former controllers found that about 60 percent had annual household incomes of less than $25,000 three years after the strike. Thus, we can conservatively estimate that in 1981 the average alternative wage was about $20,000, implying average economic rent of $15,000 per ex-controller, for a total rent of $170 million. In the next chapter we will learn how to find the present value of an income stream; this stream of economic rent has a present value of $2 billion.

But there is more than money to the job. If the next best alternative was an easier, more pleasant job, the dollar difference in pay would have overstated the true economic rent of the job. But most air traffic controllers apparently enjoyed the tension and the prestige associated with the job. As one former controller lamented, "It's hard to get out of your blood. It's the most exciting thing that most of us will ever do." Many say that guiding traffic produced a deep sense of satisfaction. According to one researcher who has tracked many controllers since 1981, most have since found other work, "but they have suffered a substantial drop in income and prestige in occupation."

Source: Roger Lowenstein, "For Fired Air-Traffic Controllers, Life's OK, But Not Like Old Times," *The Wall Street Journal*, 1 August 1986.

Competition from Nonunion Suppliers

Since the Middle Ages craft unions have attempted to increase their wages by restricting output. Weavers from the city would sometimes make forays into the countryside to destroy looms and other weaving devices, thereby shutting off this competing source of labor. Many unions face similar competition today. While unions often can prevent their employers from hiring nonunion workers, they cannot prohibit new firms from hiring nonunion workers and then competing with the unionized firm. Nor can they easily block lower-cost foreign imports.

In competitive markets high-cost producers will not survive. For example, the building trades unions now claim only about 30 percent of the 4 million construction workers in the United States, down from about 65 percent during the 1970s. Many workers gave up their union card in the 1970s because they were unable to find union jobs. In the face of such competition, these unions have been forced to make concessions over wages and work rules to compete. In some parts of the country unions are permitting construction contractors to hire a larger proportion of apprentices, who are typically paid only half the union scale, and unions are allowing their members to work on the same job as nonunion members — which was unheard of a few years ago.

Industry Deregulation

For the last 20 years the Teamsters Union has negotiated union wages for truckers through a national contract. Trucking regulations that blocked new entry into the industry and prevented existing firms from competing on the basis of price provided an environment that was conducive to union demands. But the deregulation of several major industries, including trucking, has reduced the union's negotiating power in these industries.

Although the Teamsters Union can prevent unionized firms from hiring nonunion drivers, it cannot prevent other firms from entering the industry. The Motor Carrier Act of 1980 allows any existing or new trucking firm to operate on any route and to change rates on short notice. Deregulation of the trucking industry dropped the floor that had propped up the rates of all companies, both union and nonunion. The demise of regulation set off rate competition, leading to business failures and eliminating nearly one-third of the jobs controlled by the Teamsters. Since deregulation, more than 10,000 low-cost, nonunion operators have entered the industry, nearly doubling the number of nonunion carriers. In 1985 the union gave up its automatic cost-of-living adjustment and agreed to allow new employees to be paid only 70 percent of the regular wage. Similarly, deregulation has also diminished union power in the airlines, intercity bus lines, and telecommunications.

Unionization and Technological Change

With employment stagnant in the so-called smokestack industries, the union movement looked to emerging high-technology areas for growth. Unions made a special effort in the 1970s and early 1980s to organize that industry sector. These organizing drives have been largely unsuccessful, however. Aside from some gains among defense contractors, the electronics industry remains primarily nonunion.

The problems of unionizing such a group are many. Union organizers found it difficult to contend with the high job turnover created by the rapid entry and exit of firms in the high-technology industries. Moreover, progressive management styles in many high-tech firms encouraged worker participation and often provided lavish bonuses and perks. The workers in such firms were not good prospects for unionization.

The Urge to Merge

With their membership shrinking, unions have sought various routes to survival. One alternative has been to merge with other unions. Mergers can reduce costs per member by sharing staff and headquarters, and increased numbers can enhance the group's political clout. For example, the Chemical Workers Union had 260,000 members in 1970, but it was less than one-fourth that size in 1985. Like other unions with diminished membership, this union has been actively seeking a merger partner. Since 1980 more than 30 union mergers have taken place. Some unions have even resorted to unfriendly takeovers of rival membership.

One problem with the merger solution is that the interests of the resulting organization can be divided. For example, in 1976 the Pottery Workers Union merged with the Seafarers International Union—an unlikely marriage. The two interests turned out to be so different that they parted 18 months later. Mergers thus appear to be only a temporary solution to problems of declining membership.

CONCLUSIONS

When unions first appeared in our nation's history, working conditions were dreadful. The hours were long, the pay was low, and the workplace was hazardous—if not outright dangerous. A worker who was injured on the job had no recourse other than trying to sue the employer, but the deck was stacked against the injured worker. Child labor was common. And a steady flow of new immigrants continuously expanded the labor pool, ensuring employers of an abundant labor supply despite poor working conditions.

Improvements in the conditions of the average worker during the last century have been revolutionary. The average work week for some industries has been cut in half. Thanks to the growth of worker productivity, the real income of workers has increased many times over. The workplace is now monitored more closely for health and safety hazards. Workers injured on the job automatically receive compensation. And child labor has been outlawed for years.

We cannot credit all these improvements to the birth and development of organized labor. Some of the improvements resulted from competition among employers to attract qualified workers. But the labor movement clearly focused attention on the problems and helped develop the political consensus to introduce employee-oriented legislation. Although union members were always a minority of the work force, never exceeding 25 percent of total employment, the union presence in the workplace extended beyond these numbers. For example, firms that were not unionized probably treated their employees better to prevent unionization, so union benefits spilled over to nonunion firms.

The union battle has to a large extent been won. Many of the hazards and inequities of the workplace have been reduced either through market pressure or legislation. Union members are now among the worker elite, earning about 15 to 20 percent more than nonunion workers. At one time, because of government regulation or the lack of competition from nonunion firms, union firms were dominant in some markets. But deregulation and growing competition from nonunion firms both here and abroad have seriously challenged the union position in industries such as steel, autos, trucking, airlines, and construction. As markets grow more competitive, employers have a harder time passing higher wages along to consumers. Even where union producers still dominate, such as in Broadway theaters, union jobs and benefits are limited by the ability to pass these costs along to consumers. Unions to some extent have fallen victim to their own success.

SUMMARY

1. Labor unions in the United States were in part a response to long hours and poor working conditions in the nineteenth and early twentieth centuries. Early union success relied on government support. Unions received their greatest boost from government during the Great Depression, when several laws were passed providing unions with improved legal standing.

2. Unions and employers attempt to negotiate a mutually agreeable labor contract through collective bargaining. If negotiations break down, both sides can agree to the appointment of an arbitrator, who is an outsider empowered to resolve the disagreement. A major source of the unions' power is the threat of a strike, which is an attempt to withhold labor from the firm.

3. Inclusive, or industrial, unions attempt to establish a floor wage that exceeds the free market wage. Because there is an excess supply of labor when the wage is above the market-clearing level, the union must use some system to ration jobs to its members. Exclusive, or craft, unions try to raise the wage by reducing the supply of labor through long apprenticeship periods, difficult qualifying exams, and other measures aimed at restricting entry into the profession.

4. Another way to raise wages is to increase the demand for union labor. Unions attempt to do this by (1) appealing to consumers to buy only union-made goods, (2) restricting the supply of products made by nonunion labor,

(3) increasing the productivity of union workers by smoothing conflicts between labor and management, and (4) forcing employers to employ more workers than they prefer.

5. When a labor union negotiates with the only employer of that type of labor, the relationship is one of bilateral monopoly. The resulting wage will depend on the relative bargaining strength and skills of each side. When a labor union negotiates with a monopsonist, both the wage rate and the employment level can initially be increased over the level of wages and employment the monopsonist set with nonunion employees.

6. Unions may pursue goals other than maximizing the wage. The maximization of employment already occurs as a result of natural market forces and requires no union. Objectives requiring a union include maximizing the total wage bill paid to union members and maximizing the total economic rents of union members. No single goal describes all union behavior.

7. Union membership as a percentage of the labor force has been falling since union participation reached a high in 1960. Most recently only about one-sixth of the labor force was unionized, compared to one-fourth in 1960. Problems for unions have been competition from nonunion workers, competition from imports, industry deregulation, and technological change.

QUESTIONS AND PROBLEMS

1. (Labor History) What historical reasons can be given for the development of labor organizations?

2. (Unions and the Law) Why was the passage of federal laws rather than state or local laws more important to the large labor organizations, such as the AFL-CIO?

3. (Strikes) How might a large company protect itself against a protracted strike? Take coal mining as an example in your answer.

4. (Strikes) Why would strikes be most effective in industries where there are very high fixed costs?

5. (Unions and Fringe Benefits) Why have past tax laws encouraged unions to ask for higher fringe benefits rather than just higher wages?

6. (Bilateral Monopoly) What is the marginal resource cost curve for a monopsonist who faces collective bargaining with a union?

7. (Union Behavior) Do economic rents for union workers increase if unions are successful in raising the demand for the products the workers produce? Will transfer earnings also increase? Why or why not?

8. (Union Behavior) Show that maximizing the wage bill always leads to greater employment than maximizing economic rent.

9. (Unions and Business) Why might unions and business find it in their best interests to lobby together in Washington, D.C., to protect the industry from foreign competition? Who would oppose such lobbying?

CAPITAL, INTEREST, ENTREPRENEURIAL ABILITY, and PROFIT

So far the discussion of resources has focused primarily on labor. This emphasis is well aimed because labor income represents more than 75 percent of all resource income. As we have seen, however, the returns to labor depend largely on the amount and quality of the other resources employed. A farmer driving a huge tractor is more productive than one who scrapes the soil with a stick. In this chapter we discuss the returns to the remaining resources, particularly capital and entrepreneurial ability. As we will see, entrepreneurial ability is in many ways the most important of the resources for determining the wealth of nations, but it is also the most elusive.

One problem that could trouble us throughout the chapter is that economists sometimes use the same term to define different things or use the same term in slightly different ways. The term *return to labor* is unambiguous, but the description of other rewards may be confusing. For example, the term *interest* is used to mean both the amount earned for lending money and the return earned by capital as a resource. Another term that could be a source of confusion is *rent*. Earlier we distinguished between transfer earnings, which is the payment necessary to attract a resource to a particular use, and economic rent, which is a surplus over transfer earnings. Economic rent is not strictly required to keep a resource in a particular use. Often we refer to the return to land as rent because land is typically thought to be in fixed supply, and the return to a resource in fixed supply consists entirely of economic rent. Describing the return to land as rent is quite appropriate, but rent as the return to land will not receive special treatment in this chapter. Topics and terms discussed include:

- Time, consumption, and production
- Roundabout production
- Market for loans
- Present value and discounting
- Theories of profit

THE ROLE OF TIME IN CONSUMPTION AND PRODUCTION

Until now our discussions of consumption and production have not distinguished between the present and the future, largely ignoring the fact that time plays an important role in both production and consumption. In this section we first consider the effect of time on the production decision and show why firms are willing to pay for the use of household savings. Next we consider time in the consumption decision and show why households must be rewarded to defer consumption, or save. By bringing together the desires of borrowers and savers, we arrive at the equilibrium rate of interest.

Production, Saving, and Time

Suppose Old MacDonald is a primitive farmer. Isolated from any neighbors or markets, he literally scratches out a living on a plot of land, using only crude sticks as farm implements. He plants a crop in the spring, weeds the field, and otherwise attempts to grow the largest crop possible. While the crop is growing, none of it is available for present consumption. Old MacDonald would starve unless he had set aside, or saved, food from an earlier crop.

If the crop grew instantly, he would not need savings. Since production takes time, however, he must save food from a prior period's production to support him during the time required to grow the crop. The longer the production process lasts, the more savings will be required. Thus, even in this simple example, it is clear that production cannot occur without savings. As we will see, the role of savings becomes more critical when we add capital to the production process.

So far Old MacDonald's operation is primitive. With inputs consisting of land, labor, and some crude sticks, suppose he grows about 100 bushels of corn per year. He soon realizes that if he had a plow—something better than the sticks he now uses—his productivity would increase. Making the plow, however, is a major undertaking in such a crude setting, and that task will keep him away from the fields for a year. Thus, the plow has an opportunity cost of 100 bushels of corn. Old MacDonald will be unable to survive this temporary drop in production unless he has saved enough food from previous harvests to allow him to forgo an annual harvest.

During the time required to produce capital, Old MacDonald must live off his savings from prior production. By producing capital, the farmer is investing his time. The plow is called an investment good, or capital. The question is, Should Old MacDonald invest his time in the task of making the plow? The answer depends on how much the plow will increase crop production. He figures that the plow will allow him to grow 20 more bushels of corn per year. Thus, he must decide whether the benefit of increasing crop production by 20 bushels per year exceeds the opportunity cost of 100 bushels required to make the plow. The answer will depend on how strongly the farmer prefers present consumption to future consumption. If his family would starve without the annual harvest, the cost of capital in terms of forgone consumption would be prohibitive. If, however, the family has been able to save enough to survive the year, and if the farmer feels the benefit of increased production exceeds this opportunity cost, Old MacDonald will make the plow.

Roundabout production is the production of capital goods that can then be used to produce consumer goods.

If Old MacDonald makes the plow, he will engage in **roundabout production**. Rather than producing corn directly, he will be investing his time in the production of a plow, which is a capital good. This plow will then be used to help grow more corn. Roundabout production involves the production of capital goods rather than consumer goods. These capital goods are then used to increase the production of consumer goods. An increased amount of roundabout production in an economy means that more capital accumulates, and the more capital accumulation there is, the greater will be the economy's productivity. Advanced industrial economies are characterized by abundant capital accumulation.

We have yet to discuss production in an economy with money or even with markets. Nonetheless, we have demonstrated two reasons why production cannot occur without savings. Old MacDonald must save because both direct and roundabout production require time—time during which no food is available from current production.

Let's now modernize the example by introducing the ability to borrow. Many farmers visit the bank each spring to borrow enough "seed money" to support their families until the crop is produced and sold. More generally, businesses often borrow at least a portion of the start-up funds needed to get the business going. Thus, in the modern economy production need not rely on each producer's prior savings because a producer can borrow money from financial institutions such as banks. Notice, however, that someone else must save before producers can borrow. Because production typically takes time, it cannot occur unless someone saves. We now consider consumption and saving.

Consumption, Saving, and Time

Did you ever burn the roof of your mouth biting into a slice of pizza before it had sufficiently cooled? Have you done this more than once? Why does such self-mutilation persist? It persists because that bite of pizza is worth more to you now than the same bite five minutes from now. In fact, you are even willing to risk burning your mouth rather than wait until the pizza has lost its destructive properties. In a small way this phenomenon reflects the fact that you and other consumers value *present* consumption more than *future* consumption. Call it instant gratification, living in the present, or whatever, but the simple fact is that utility-generating activities are valued more the sooner they can be enjoyed.

A *positive rate of time preference* means that present consumption is more highly valued than future consumption.

We say that consumers have a **positive rate of time preference**, meaning that they value present consumption more than future consumption. Because present consumption is valued more than future consumption, you are often willing to pay a higher price to consume something now rather than wait.

And prices often reflect this greater willingness to pay. Consider the movies. You must pay more to see a movie at a first-run theater rather than waiting until it shows up at other theaters. (If you are very patient, you can wait to see it on TV.) The same is true for books. If you are willing to wait until a new book is available in paperback, you can usually buy it for less than one-third the hardback price. More generally, firms often compete to provide goods and services more quickly. Photo developers and dry cleaners tout the speed of their services, knowing that consumers are willing to pay more for this earlier availability, other things equal.

Because present consumption is valued more than future consumption, households must be rewarded to postpone consumption; in other words, saving must be rewarded. By saving their money in a financial institution such as a bank, households surrender a claim on present consumption in return for the promise of a greater ability to consume in the future. The **interest rate** is the reward offered to households to forgo present consumption. Specifically, interest is the amount of money earned by savers for giving up the use of $1 for a year. Thus, if the interest rate is 10 percent, a saver earns $0.10 per year for each dollar saved in a financial institution.

*The **interest rate** is the amount paid for the use of a dollar for one year.*

The greater the interest rate, other things constant, the more consumers are rewarded for saving, so the greater will be the opportunity cost of present consumption in terms of future consumption. The greater the interest rate offered for saving, therefore, the greater will be the household's willingness to save. For example, at an interest rate of 5 percent, a household can save $100 in an account earning 5 percent and end up with $105 a year from now. So $100 worth of consumption today has an opportunity cost of $105 in consumption a year from now. At an interest rate of 10 percent, $100 worth of consumption today has an opportunity cost of $110 in consumption a year from now.

Consequently, the quantity of money households are willing to save is directly related to the interest rate offered on savings, other things held constant. Banks are willing to pay interest on consumer savings because the banks can, in turn, lend these savings to those who need money, such as farmers. The banks play the role of financial intermediaries in what is known as the market for loans. The positive relationship between the supply of loans, which is the supply of savings, and the interest rate is shown by the upward-sloping supply curve in Exhibit 1.

Optimal Use of Capital

What happens when we introduce capital into the modern economy? In a market economy characterized by specialization and exchange, Old Mac-Donald no longer has to produce his own capital. In fact, he need not even buy capital; he can lease it. Suppose Old MacDonald is contemplating leasing a tractor. There are many sizes of tractors on the market, ranging from the garden variety to giants able to plow a swath 30 feet wide. Old MacDonald can choose from among several tractor sizes at his local U-Plow Leasing outlet. In column (1) of Exhibit 2(a) the tractor sizes available are listed in 40-

EXHIBIT 1   **SUPPLY OF LOANS**

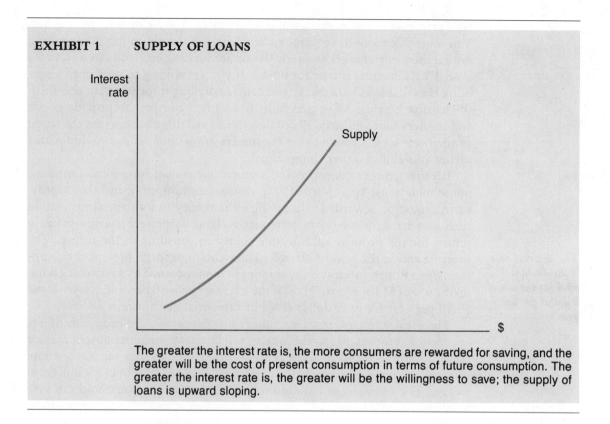

The greater the interest rate is, the more consumers are rewarded for saving, and the greater will be the cost of present consumption in terms of future consumption. The greater the interest rate is, the greater will be the willingness to save; the supply of loans is upward sloping.

horsepower increments from the smallest to the largest. The total and marginal physical products of each tractor are listed in columns (2) and (3). Note that we are holding other resources constant (in this case, the farmer's labor and land).

Without capital, Old MacDonald could grow 100 bushels of corn per year. Leasing the smallest tractor will allow the farmer to double his production, going from 100 to 200 bushels per year, reflecting a marginal physical product of the smallest size tractor of 100 bushels. With the next largest size, total output increases from 200 to 280, so the marginal physical product is 80 bushels. Note that diminishing marginal returns sets in after the smallest tractor is employed. The marginal physical product of using a larger tractor continues to fall with each successive increase in tractor size, reaching 0 for the 240-horsepower tractor. In fact, the marginal physical product becomes negative if the largest tractor is used. (You might imagine a tractor so large that it becomes difficult to maneuver on the farmer's relatively small plot.)

Suppose Old MacDonald sells corn in a perfectly competitive market, so he is a price taker in the market for corn. He can sell all he wants at the market price of $4 per bushel, the price listed in column (4) of Exhibit 2. This price is multiplied by the total physical product from column (2) to yield the farmer's total revenue in column (5). The change in total revenue resulting from increasing the tractor size by 40 horsepower is the marginal revenue product

EXHIBIT 2
MARGINAL PRODUCTIVITY OF CAPITAL

(a) Productivity schedule

(1) Tractor size (horsepower)	(2) Total Physical Product (bushels) (TPP)	(3) Marginal Physical Product (MPP)	(4) Price ($)	(5) Total Revenue (TPP × P)	(6) Marginal Revenue Product (MRP) (MPP × P)	(7) Total Resource Cost (TRC)	(8) Marginal Resource Cost (MRC)
0	100	—	$4	$400	—	$0	—
40	200	100	4	800	$400	80	$80
80	280	80	4	1120	320	160	80
120	340	60	4	1360	240	240	80
160	380	40	4	1520	160	320	80
200	400	20	4	1600	80	400	80
240	400	0	4	1600	0	480	80
280	380	−20	4	1520	−80	560	80

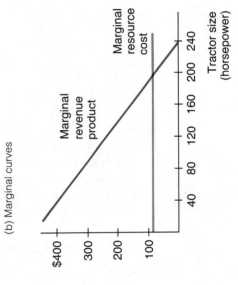

(b) Marginal curves

of that increase in tractor size. The marginal revenue product is listed in column (6). Since Old MacDonald is a price taker, the marginal revenue product can also be found by multiplying the price times the marginal physical product. The downward-sloping marginal revenue product curve is presented in Exhibit 2(b). Recall that the marginal revenue product curve shows the change in total revenue resulting from employing one more unit of the variable resource, in this case capital. The marginal revenue product curve is Old MacDonald's demand curve for capital.

Let's assume that tractors lease for a standard amount per 40-horsepower increment, so the marginal resource cost is constant. The rate is for the growing season and includes all operating expenses. Thus, an 80-horsepower tractor will lease for twice the rate of a 40-horsepower tractor. The question is, Should the farmer lease a tractor and, if so, what size? The answer will depend on the rate at which tractors can be leased. If this rate is more than $400 per 40-horsepower increment, the marginal revenue generated by even the smallest tractor would not cover its marginal cost, so Old MacDonald would lease none.

Suppose instead that tractors lease for $80 per 40 horsepower. Thus, there is a constant marginal resource cost of $80 per 40-horsepower increment, which is shown in column (8) of Exhibit 2(a) and is depicted as the horizontal line in Exhibit 2(b). The rules for the optimal use of capital are the same as those for other resources: additional capital should be employed up to the point where the marginal revenue product just equals the marginal resource cost. This equilibrium condition results in a tractor size of 200 horsepower, where the marginal physical product is 20 bushels, and the marginal revenue product is 20 times $4, or $80. Leasing a larger tractor than the optimal size would result in a smaller profit. Thus, the farmer should increase the tractor size until the marginal revenue product equals the marginal resource cost.

Purchasing Capital

So far the decision to employ capital is much like decisions involving any other input. How does the analysis change if the farmer must buy the tractor rather than lease it? To keep the problem simple, suppose the farmer has enough money saved to buy any size tractor, and his savings are in an account earning 10 percent interest. Let's assume also that tractor prices increase by $800 with each 40-horsepower increase in size, that tractors are so durable that they last indefinitely, that operating expenses are so negligible that they can be ignored, and that the price of corn is expected to remain at $4 per bushel in the future.

Again, tractors of different sizes are listed in Exhibit 3(a). Since the marginal productivity of tractors and the price of corn have not changed from the previous example, the marginal revenue product is identical to that derived in Exhibit 2(a). Rather than duplicate columns (2) through (6) from Exhibit 2(a), we simply list the marginal revenue product in column (2) of Exhibit 3(a). For example, the smallest tractor will increase the farmer's productivity by 100 bushels per year, which, if sold at the market price of $4 per bushel, yields an annual marginal revenue product of $400—the marginal revenue product of the smallest tractor as listed in column (2). Because we assumed that the price of corn will remain constant in the future, the marginal revenue product for that first unit of capital will remain at $400 per year indefinitely.

The purchase price of each tractor is listed in column (3). The smallest tractor sells for $800, the next largest for $1600, and so on, increasing by $800 with each 40-horsepower increase in tractor size. Thus, the marginal cost of buying a larger tractor is $800, as listed in column (4). Keep in mind that in

EXHIBIT 3
MARGINAL EFFICIENCY OF CAPITAL

(a) Schedule

(1)	(2)	(3)	(4)	(5)	(6)
Tractor Size (horse-power)	Marginal Revenue Product (MRP)	Total Resource Cost	Marginal Resource Cost (MRC)	Marginal Efficiency of Capital (MEC = MRP/MRC)	Market Rate of Interest
0	0	—	—	—	—
40	$400	$800	$800	50%	10%
80	320	1600	800	40	10
120	240	2400	800	30	10
160	160	3200	800	20	10
200	80	4000	800	10	10
240	0	4800	800	0	10
280	−80	5600	800	−10	10

(b) Curves

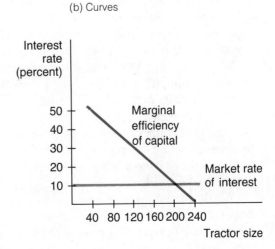

the earlier example the farmer was leasing the tractor, and now he is buying it. So before, the marginal resource cost was the increase in the leasing price as the tractor size increased. Here, however, the marginal resource cost is the increase in the purchase price of the larger tractor.

The first task is to compute the marginal rate of return that could be earned by investing in tractors of different sizes. The *marginal rate of return*, often referred to as the **marginal efficiency of capital**, is equal to the marginal revenue product of capital divided by the marginal cost of purchasing that capital. The smallest tractor yields a marginal revenue product of $400 per year and has a marginal purchase cost of $800. Thus, the smallest tractor yields a marginal efficiency of capital of $400/$800, or 50 percent per year, as shown in column (5) of Exhibit 3(a). This means that the smallest-size tractor earns an annual return equal to 50 percent of its purchase price. The next largest tractor has a marginal revenue product of $320 per year and has a one-time marginal cost of $800, so the marginal efficiency of capital equals $320/$800, or 40 percent per year. By dividing the marginal revenue product of capital in column (2) of Exhibit 3(a) by the marginal resource cost of that capital in column (4), we get the marginal efficiency of capital in column (5). increasing the tractor size by 40 horsepower is the marginal revenue product The data in column (5) are depicted as the downward-sloping marginal efficiency of capital curve drawn in Exhibit 3(b).

Should Old MacDonald buy a tractor, and, if so, what size? The tractor size selected will depend on the market rate of interest he can earn on his savings account. The interest forgone on his savings is Old MacDonald's opportunity cost of investing in a tractor. You can think of him as facing the choice of saving his money and earning the market rate of interest or investing his money in a tractor and earning a marginal rate of return equal to the marginal efficiency of capital.

Old MacDonald, as a profit maximizer, will increase the tractor size as long as the marginal efficiency of capital exceeds the interest rate he earns on his savings account. After all, if he can earn more than the market rate of interest by investing in a tractor, he should invest in a tractor. So Old MacDonald should increase the tractor size until the marginal efficiency of capital just equals the interest rate he earns on savings.

We have already said that the interest rate offered to savers is 10 percent, as listed in column (6) of Exhibit 3(a). The profit-maximizing tractor size can be seen in Exhibits 3(a) and 3(b) to be a 200-horsepower tractor since that is where the marginal efficiency of capital equals the market rate of interest. Because the farmer can always earn the market rate of interest paid for saving by simply leaving his money in the bank, he will not dip into those savings to buy a tractor that has a marginal efficiency of capital that is below the market rate of interest.

Would the example change if Old MacDonald had to borrow the money rather than draw from savings? Not as long as he can borrow at 10 percent interest. If 10 percent represents the marginal cost of borrowing, he would increase the amount borrowed as long as the marginal efficiency of capital exceeds 10 percent; he would stop when the marginal efficiency of capital was just equal to the marginal cost of borrowing.

*The **marginal efficiency of capital** is the marginal rate of return on capital.*

Note that Old MacDonald ends up with the same size tractor regardless of whether it is leased, purchased out of savings, or purchased out of borrowed funds. If the markets for capital and for loans are perfectly competitive and are working efficiently, it should make no difference whether Old Mac-Donald leases the tractor or buys it outright. Whoever was offering tractors for lease was earning the market rate of return of 10 percent on their capital.

The simplified version of the farm depicted here can be generalized to other firms. The major demanders of loans are firms that want to borrow to invest in capital goods, such as machines, trucks, and buildings. At any time the firm has a variety of possible investment opportunities. These opportunities can be arranged from highest to lowest based on their expected marginal efficiency of capital. Firms will finance those investments that are expected to earn a rate of return that exceeds the rate at which these firms can borrow. When other inputs are held constant, as they were on Old Mac-Donald's farm, the demand for capital is downward sloping, reflecting the declining marginal efficiency of capital. Recall that the marginal efficiency of capital declines because of the law of diminishing marginal returns.

Investing in Human Capital

The tractor has a substantial impact on the farmer's ability to produce. Similarly, education and training that improve Old MacDonald's knowledge of farming can also enhance productivity. Rather than invest in the tractor, he can invest in his own education—he can invest in human capital. The decision to invest in human capital involves all the issues of investing in physical capital. For example, suppose Old MacDonald realizes he is never too old to learn and by taking agricultural courses at a nearby college, he can increase his knowledge of plant science, fertilizers, soil drainage, agricultural economics, and other subjects that will make him a more productive farmer.

He reads through the course descriptions and estimates by how much each course will increase his total revenue. Some courses are obviously of more benefit than others. A course in pest-resistant corn plants is likely to increase his annual yield more than one on how to keep his farm looking neat. He then ranks courses based on the marginal increase in annual yield expected from each course. His increased productivity is expected to continue indefinitely. By multiplying the expected marginal crop yield by the market price of corn, Old MacDonald determines the marginal revenue product of each additional course.

Now consider the cost of acquiring this human capital. The cost per course consists of the tuition, books, and fees, plus Old MacDonald's opportunity cost of not tending his fields while in class or studying. Suppose he estimates these costs to be $1000 per course. (To avoid any problems associated with nonmonetary aspects of acquiring human capital, assume that he is indifferent between spending time on his studies and spending time farming.)

By dividing the marginal revenue product from each course by the marginal cost of acquiring that human capital, we can compute the marginal efficiency of capital. For example, the first course is expected to increase his total revenue by $400 per year, for a marginal efficiency of capital of 40 percent. The second course has a marginal revenue product of $300 per year, for a marginal efficiency of capital of 30 percent, and so on. The marginal efficiency of acquiring human capital is shown in Exhibit 4. This curve is downward sloping because the acquisition of human capital, like the acquisition of other resources, is subject to diminishing marginal returns.

The costs of acquiring human capital are incurred when the courses are taken, but the benefits will come in the future as he applies his newfound knowledge. How many courses should Old MacDonald take? The answer depends on the market rate of interest. If Old MacDonald has savings to pay the cost of education, his opportunity cost will be the forgone interest he loses on his savings. If he must borrow the funds, the annual cost, again, is equal to the market rate of interest. Old MacDonald should increase his course load as long as the marginal efficiency of human capital exceeds the market rate of interest.

The equilibrium number of courses occurs where the marginal efficiency of human capital just equals the market rate of interest, which in our example occurs when Old MacDonald takes four courses. Although we have greatly

EXHIBIT 4   OPTIMAL INVESTMENT IN HUMAN CAPITAL

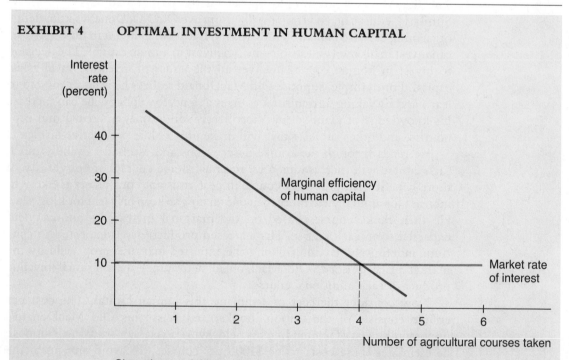

Since the acquisition of human capital is subject to diminishing marginal returns, the marginal efficiency of acquiring human capital is inversely related to the interest rate. Equilibrium investment occurs where marginal efficiency equals the market interest rate.

simplified matters, investing in human capital can be analyzed in the same manner as investing in physical capital.

Let's review the procedure used to determine the optimal amount of capital investment. First, compute the marginal physical product from each additional unit of capital. Second, if the product is sold in a competitive market, we can derive the marginal revenue product of capital by multiplying the marginal physical product times the market price.[1] Third, to determine the marginal efficiency of capital, divide its marginal revenue product by its price. The marginal efficiency of capital curve equals the firm's demand for capital—that is, it shows the amount of capital the firm will purchase at each alternative interest rate. Fourth, the marginal resource cost of capital is given by the market rate of interest because that is the opportunity cost of investing in capital. Fifth, the firm invests in additional capital as long as the marginal efficiency of capital exceeds the opportunity cost of capital.

The Market Demand for Loans

We have now examined why firms are willing to pay to borrow money—money gives firms a command over resources that makes roundabout production possible. For the economy as a whole, if the supply of other resources and the level of technology are fixed, the marginal efficiency of capital (which is the same as the market demand for capital) will be downward sloping. Each firm has a downward-sloping demand for loans, reflecting the declining marginal efficiency of capital. The demand for loans by each firm can be summed horizontally to yield the market demand for loans.

We should note at this point that firms are not the only demanders of loans. As we have seen, households value present consumption more than future consumption; they are often willing to pay extra to consume now rather than later. One way to ensure early availability of goods and services is to borrow money for present consumption. Mortgages, car loans, and other forms of consumer credit, including credit cards, are examples of household borrowing. The household's demand for loans, like the firm's demand, is downward sloping, indicating a greater ability and a greater willingness to borrow at lower interest rates, other things constant. The government sector is also a demander of loans. Thus, the market demand curve for loans, presented in Exhibit 5, is the total demand by firms, households, and governments.

By bringing the supply of loans and the demand for loans together, as in Exhibit 5, we can determine the market rate of interest. The equilibrium interest rate, r, is the only rate that will exactly match up the wishes of both borrowers and savers. Any change in the supply or demand for loans will

---

[1] If the product is sold in a market where the firm has some market power, the proper accounting of the marginal revenue product requires the firm to consider the impact of increased output on the product's price.

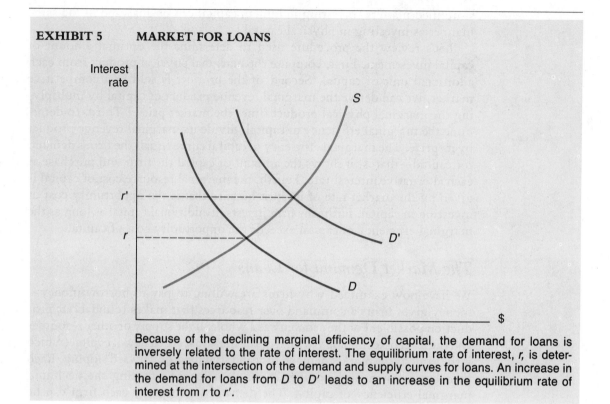

EXHIBIT 5   MARKET FOR LOANS

Because of the declining marginal efficiency of capital, the demand for loans is inversely related to the rate of interest. The equilibrium rate of interest, r, is determined at the intersection of the demand and supply curves for loans. An increase in the demand for loans from D to D' leads to an increase in the equilibrium rate of interest from r to r'.

change the equilibrium rate of interest. For example, some technological breakthrough could increase the productivity of capital, thereby increasing the marginal efficiency of capital, which would increase the demand for loans. The demand for loans will shift out to the right, as shown in the movement from D to D' in Exhibit 5; an increase in the demand for loans raises the equilibrium rate of interest from r to r'.

One final note about the demand for loans. When we listed the major resources, we did not include money. Strictly speaking, money is not a resource. If Old MacDonald wants to borrow money, it is not the money itself that is valued but the claim on resources that money represents. The demand for money is, in fact, the demand for the ability to buy productive resources. If money were a resource, then the poor countries of the world could become rich simply by printing more money. When economists talk about capital, they are usually referring to human or physical capital, whereas when businesspeople refer to capital, they are usually talking about money.

Real Versus Nominal Interest Rates

Up to this point we have implicitly assumed that there was no inflation in the economy—that is, the price level was assumed to be constant over time. Because the spending power of each dollar remained constant over time, inflation was not a factor in determining the supply and demand for loans. In a world without inflation the equilibrium rate of interest is called the *real rate of interest*. The use of the term *real* in this context means that each dollar repaid has the same spending power as each dollar borrowed — that is, each dollar can buy as much as before in the way of goods and services.

Let's consider now the significance of inflation in the market for loans. Once we introduce inflation, which is a general rise in the price level, savers are less willing to save because each dollar they are repaid buys less than the dollar they saved. Conversely, borrowers are more willing to borrow because each dollar they repay is worth less than the dollar they borrowed. Therefore, an increase in the anticipated rate of inflation, other things held constant, decreases the supply of savings and increases the demand for loans, thereby increasing the equilibrium rate of interest.

The *nominal rate of interest* measures the interest rate in terms of the actual dollars paid, even if these dollars have been eroded by inflation. The nominal rate of interest — the rate of interest that appears on the loan agreement — will be higher when the anticipated rate of inflation is higher. The nominal rate of interest is the interest rate usually discussed in the media.

The nominal rate of interest changes to reflect changes in expected inflation. If inflation is expected to be 6 percent, lenders must earn 6 percent interest just to maintain the same real purchasing power when the loan is repaid. Any interest above 6 percent equals the real rate of interest. For example, if the real rate of interest equals 4 percent and expected inflation is 6 percent, the nominal rate of interest will be 10 percent. Thus, the nominal rate equals the real rate plus expected inflation. If inflation is expected to be zero, the nominal rate and the real rate are identical. The real rate of interest measures interest not in terms of the actual dollars paid but in terms of the real purchasing power of those dollars. Economic behavior is based on the expected real rate of interest, not the nominal rate.

Why Interest Rates Differ

So far we have been talking as if only one interest rate prevails in the market for loans. At any particular time, however, a range of interest rates can be found in the market. Why? Let's consider some reasons.

*The **pure rate of interest** is the rate on a risk-free loan.*

Risk   Some borrowers are more likely to repay their loans than others. Differences in the risk associated with different borrowers are reflected in differences in the interest rate negotiated. As a point of reference, the **pure rate of interest** is the rate charged on a risk-free loan. In the United States the federal government is thought to be the most reliable borrower around, so the closest thing to a risk-free rate is the rate on funds loaned to the federal government. As loans become more risky, the interest rate on those loans rises, reflecting a higher risk. For example, a bank may charge more interest for a loan to a new video rental store than it would charge IBM.

Duration of the Loan   The future is uncertain, and the farther we go into the future, the more uncertain it is. One potential source of uncertainty about a loan that is fixed, say, in dollar terms, is the course of inflation. If the inflation rate increases beyond what was expected over the period of the loan, the purchasing power of repaid dollars is lower than expected. The longer the period of repayment is, then, the greater will be the risk of inflation, and thus, the greater will be the interest rate charged. The **term structure of interest rates** refers to the relationship between the duration of a loan and the interest rate charged. The term structure depends primarily on the supply and demand for loans of different maturity dates and on expectations about inflation.

*The **term structure of interest rates** is the relationship between the duration of a loan and the interest rate charged.*

Cost of Administration   The cost of executing the loan agreement, monitoring the conditions of the loan, and collecting the payments of a loan are called the administration costs of the loan. These costs as a proportion of the total cost of the loan decrease as the size of the loan increases. For example, the administrative costs on a $100,000 loan will be less than 10 times greater than these costs on a $10,000 loan. Consequently, that portion of the interest charge reflecting the cost of administering the loan will be smaller when the loan is larger. Thus, one reason interest rates differ is because administrative costs decrease relative to the size of the loan as loan size increases. So the larger the loan, other things constant, the lower the interest rate will be.

Tax Treatment   Differences in the tax treatment of different types of loans will also affect the market rate of interest. For example, the interest earned on funds loaned to state and local governments is not taxable as part of the federal income tax. Since lenders are interested in their after-tax rate of interest, state and local governments can pay lower interest rates than other borrowers yet still attract lenders.

PRESENT VALUE AND DISCOUNTING

Because present consumption is valued more than future consumption, future consumption cannot be directly compared to present consumption. A way of standardizing the discussion is to measure all consumption in terms of its **present value**. *Present value* is an expression used to convey the current value of a payment or payments that will be received in the future. For example, how much would you pay now to acquire the right to receive $100 one year from now? Put another way, what is the present value of receiving $100 one year from now?

Present value is the value today of a payment to be received in the future.

Present Value of Payment One Year Hence

Assume that the equilibrium interest rate is 10 percent, so you can either lend or borrow money at that rate. One way to determine how much you would pay for the right to receive $100 one year from now is to ask how much you would have to save, at the market rate of interest, to end up with $100 one year from now. You should not be willing to pay any more than that since you always have the option of depositing that amount in a savings account to yield a total of $100 in a year.

Here is the problem we are trying to solve: What amount of money, if saved at a rate of 10 percent, will accumulate to $100 one year from now? We have a way of calculating this by using a formula. If *PV* stands for the unknown present value, we can say $PV \times 1.10 = \$100$, or $PV = \$100/1.10 = \$90.90$. Thus, $90.90 is the present value of receiving $100 one year from now; it is the most you would be willing to pay today to receive $100 one year from now. If you were asked to pay more than $90.90, you could simply deposit your $90.90 at the market rate of interest and end up with $100 a year from now. The procedure of dividing the future payment by 1 plus the prevailing interest rate to express it in today's dollars is called *discounting*. The interest rate that is used to discount future payments is called the *discount rate*.

The present value of $100 to be received one year from now will obviously depend on the interest rate used to discount that payment. The higher the interest rate is, the more the future payment is discounted, and the lower the present value will be. In other words, the higher the interest rate is, the less you need to save now to yield a given amount in the future. For example, if the interest rate is 15 percent, the present value of receiving $100 one year from now is $100/1.15, which equals $86.96. Conversely, the lower the interest rate is, the less the future income is discounted, and the greater will be its present value. Thus, a lower interest rate means that you must save more now to yield a given amount in the future. As a general rule, we can say that the present value (*PV*) of receiving *M* dollars one year from now when the interest rate is *r* per year is

$$PV = \frac{M}{1 + r}$$

For example, when the interest rate is 5 percent, the present value of receiving $100 one year from now is

$$PV = \frac{\$100}{1 + 0.05} = \frac{\$100}{1.05} = \$95.24$$

Present Value for Payments in Later Years

Rather than finding the present value of receiving $100 one year from now, we can consider the present value of receiving that amount two years hence. The question is, What amount of money deposited at the market rate of interest of 5 percent will yield $100 two years from now? Again, let *PV* represent the unknown amount of money. At the end of the first year its value would be $PV \times (1.05)$, which would then earn the market rate of interest during the second year. At the end the second year the deposit would accumulate to $PV \times (1.05) \times (1.05)$. Thus, we have the equation

$$PV \times (1.05) \times (1.05) = \$100$$

Solving for PV yields

$$PV = \frac{\$100}{(1.05)(1.05)} = \frac{\$100}{1.1025} = \$90.70$$

If the $100 is to be received three years from now, we would discount the payment over three years. More generally, the present value formula for receiving M dollars in year t at interest rate r may be written as

$$PV = \frac{M}{(1 + r)^t}$$

Because $1 + r$ is greater than 1, the more times it is multiplied by itself, the greater the result in the denominator will be. Thus, the present value of a given payment will diminish the farther in the future that payment is to be received.

Present Value of an Income Stream

The previous analysis is used to compute the present value of a single sum paid at some time in the future. Most assets, however, yield a stream of payments over time. In the case where the payments are made over a period of years, the present value of such a stream is computed as the sum of the discounted stream of payments. The present value of each payment can be computed individually, and then the results can be summed to yield the present value of the entire payment stream. For example, the present value of receiving $100 next year and $150 the year after is simply the present value of the first year's payment plus the present value of the second year's payment.

Present Value of an Annuity

*An **annuity** is a given sum of money received each year for a specified number of years.*

A given sum of money received each year for a specified number of years is called an **annuity**. If this payment continues indefinitely into the future, it is called a perpetuity. For example, the tractor in the earlier example increased the farmer's productivity indefinitely. The present value of receiving a certain amount forever seems like a very large sum indeed. But because payments are valued less the farther in the future they are received, it turns out that the present value of receiving a particular amount forever is not much more than receiving it for, say, 20 years.

To determine the present value of receiving $100 each year forever, we need only ask how much money must be deposited in a savings account to yield $100 in interest per year. When the interest rate is 10 percent, a deposit of $1000 will earn $100 per year. Thus, the present value of receiving $100 a year indefinitely when the interest rate is 10 percent is $1000. More generally, we can use the formula $PV = M/r$, where M is the amount received each year. Recall that Old MacDonald in equilibrium expected to earn $80 more per year from the marginal increase in tractor size. The present value of a revenue stream of $80 when the discount rate is 10 percent is $80/0.10, or $800. It is no coincidence that $800 was also the marginal cost of buying the tractor of equilibrium size. Thus, the marginal cost of buying a tractor of a particular size equals the present value of the increase in revenue expected from that tractor size. To develop a better feel for present value and discounting, let's consider the following case study.

CASE STUDY

The Million-Dollar Lottery?

Since New Hampshire introduced the first state-run lottery in the early 1960s, many states have followed suit, and payoffs of a million dollars or more are now common. As a winner of a million-dollar lottery, you might expect to be handed a check for a million dollars. Instead, you would typically be paid in installments, such as $50,000 per year for 20 years. And though this adds up to a total of a million dollars, you now know that such a stream has a present value of less than the advertised million. To put this payment schedule in perspective, at a discount rate of 10 percent the $50,000 received in the twentieth year has a present value of only $7450. If today you deposited $7450 in an account earning 10 percent interest, you would wind up with $50,000 in 20 years.

At 10 percent the present value of a $50,000 annuity for the next 20 years is $425,700. Thus, the present value of the actual payment stream is less than half of the promised million, which is the reason lottery officials pay it out in installments. Incidentally, we might consider the present value of receiving $50,000 per year *forever*. Using the formula $PV = M/r$, where M equals $50,000 and r equals 10 percent, we have $PV = \$50,000/0.10 = \$500,000$. Since the present value of receiving the $50,000 for 20 years is $425,700, continuing the $50,000 annual payment indefinitely adds only $74,300 in present-value terms. This shows the dramatic effect of discounting on the present value of payments after year 20.

With this discussion of present value and discounting, we conclude our treatment of capital and interest. There remains only one more resource to discuss, a resource that in some respects is the most important—entrepreneurial ability. Entrepreneurial ability is the wellspring of economic vitality and the source of a rising standard of living. Yet as we will see, it is also the most elusive of resources and the most controversial.

ENTREPRENEURIAL ABILITY
AND PROFIT

It is difficult to teach, though some 160 business schools now offer courses in it. It is difficult to measure, though business publications try to track the success of rising stars. And it is difficult to analyze, though new books on the topic appear almost daily. What is it? Entrepreneurial ability. Perhaps no other economic resource is more widely discussed yet so poorly understood.

There is no market for entrepreneurial ability in the sense that we usually think of markets. In fact, the reason firms are formed is because entrepreneurs believe that their total expected utility from running their own firm exceeds the expected utility from selling their abilities to another firm. They are their own boss—that is, they hire themselves—because there is no formal market for their special kind of ability.

Role of the Entrepreneur

An *entrepreneur* is a profit-seeking decision maker who organizes an enterprise, assumes the risk of the enterprise, and claims any profit or loss that results. By bidding among themselves for resources, entrepreneurs establish equilibrium prices for other resources. The entrepreneur guarantees to pay other resource owners the market price in return for the right to direct or control these resources in the firm. The entrepreneur is responsible for paying resource owners regardless of how the firm performs.

Thus, entrepreneurs acquire the right to direct resources in the firm, assume responsibility for paying these resources, and claim any profit or loss that is left over after all other resources have been paid. This right to control resources does not necessarily mean that the entrepreneur must manage the firm. But the entrepreneur must have the power to hire and fire the manager; the entrepreneur must have the power to control the controller.

Recall that the firm's total revenue minus all the payments to resource owners other than to the entrepreneur can be considered "accounting" profit. Before arriving at economic profit, we should carefully remove from accounting profit that portion of the entrepreneur's income that is a return for supplying resources other than entrepreneurial ability. To the extent that the entrepreneur provides any resource other than entrepreneurial ability, an implicit return should be assigned to those inputs based on what those resources could earn in resource markets.

For example, economic profit should exclude any salary to the entrepreneur for managing the firm. Managers can be viewed as another form of labor, albeit a rather special kind, and the manager's salary should not be confused with profit. The services of managers, like those of janitors and steelworkers, are bought and sold in the labor market. Similarly, any capital owned by the entrepreneur should be assigned imputed interest equal to the market rate of interest paid on an investment involving a comparable degree of risk—what we have referred to as a normal profit. Economic profit is then the amount over and above all of these imputed payments for resources supplied by the entrepreneur other than entrepreneurial ability. The net result could also be an economic loss.

The Entrepreneur Can Supply Other Resources

The entrepreneur can supply a variety of resources to the firm in addition to entrepreneurial ability. To understand this, imagine that a posh, new restaurant called the Blue Beagle is opening in your community. Suppose initially that the founder of the Blue Beagle acts primarily as an entrepreneur, who borrows money from a bank to start the restaurant and selects a manager to hire all other employees (including a chef, maitre d', and other staff), and to lease or buy a building, furniture, and anything else the operation requires.

The entrepreneur promises to pay all these resource owners at least the market return for putting their resources under the manager's direction. Otherwise, these resources would go elsewhere. In the operation of the Blue Beagle the entrepreneur, by hiring the manager and agreeing to pay all resource suppliers, supplies no resources other than entrepreneurial ability. The entrepreneur nonetheless controls the restaurant and is liable for its success or failure.

Since all the resources except entrepreneurial ability are either rented or hired, who is the Blue Beagle's owner and what does the owner own? The firm's owner is the entrepreneur. The "firm" owned by the entrepreneur consists of a bundle of contracts or agreements between the entrepreneur and resource suppliers. The entrepreneur has acquired the right to direct and control these resources in return for a promise to pay their owners a specified amount. At the end of the year the entrepreneur can consider as economic profit whatever is left after paying all other resource suppliers.

The entrepreneur is what we have referred to earlier as the residual claimant—someone who receives the excess of revenues over costs. If revenues fail to cover contractual outlays, however, the entrepreneur is obliged to make up the difference. Thus, the entrepreneur owns the firm, the firm consists of a bundle of contracts obligating the entrepreneur to pay resources in return for the right to control these resources in the firm, and the entrepreneur is the residual claimant of any profits or losses resulting from the firm's operation.

It is not the management of resources that distinguishes the entrepreneur; it is the control in deciding who manages resources. Even if the entrepreneur decides to serve as the restaurant's manager, the entrepreneur as manager would likely still delegate to the chef many decisions about resource use—which assistant chefs to hire, what ingredients to purchase, how to combine these ingredients. In fact, the entrepreneur could serve as the chef, maitre d', cashier, or dishwasher or might serve in whatever capacity was most needed at the time. Therefore, do not think entrepreneurs have to manage (though they often do); entrepreneurs simply must have the power to appoint the manager and to claim the profit or loss that arises from the manager's decisions.

Why Entrepreneurs Often Invest in Capital

The entrepreneur rarely has the limited role described in the restaurant example. Entrepreneurs usually provide at least a portion of the capital required to start and maintain a business. In fact, aside from entrepreneurial ability, capital is the resource most commonly supplied by the entrepreneur. Since it is not strictly necessary for the entrepreneur to provide resources in addition to entrepreneurial ability, why do we observe entrepreneurs providing capital to the firm?

In our example the entrepreneur borrowed from the bank the funds necessary to finance the restaurant's operations. In reality a bank would be reluctant to lend all of the funds required to start a firm, especially for a business as risky as a new restaurant. Even though the entrepreneur promised to repay the bank, the restaurant could go bankrupt. And, as noted in Chapter 4, under the corporate business structure an entrepreneur's liability is limited to his or her own investment in the firm. Even if the firm is not incorporated, the entrepreneur, in the face of huge losses, could still file for personal bankruptcy.

Because of the possibility of bankruptcy and default, lenders typically want entrepreneurs to supply additional resources, usually capital, to the firm. The entrepreneur's supply of capital to the firm serves at least two functions for wary creditors. When the entrepreneur's own resources are tied up in the firm, the bank might expect that individual to exercise greater care and vigilance in shepherding all the firm's resources, including the bank's funds. Second, the entrepreneur's capital investment in the firm—called owner's equity—serves as a buffer, providing creditors and other resource suppliers some insulation against a default in the event that the firm's costs exceed its revenues in a particular year. Losses can be covered out of owner's equity rather than out of payments due to some other resource owner, such as the bank. So owner's equity gives the entrepreneur a greater incentive and a greater ability to repay the debt to the bank as well as to make good on guarantees made to other resource owners.

The entrepreneur as the firm's owner is essentially saying, "I will pay all other resource owners before I receive a cent, and if the firm operates at a loss, I will dig into my own investment in the firm to make good on my guarantees." The entrepreneur is last in line to be compensated and is the chief bag-holder should anyone be left holding the bag.

ENTREPRENEURSHIP AND THEORIES OF PROFIT

There is no single theory to explain the source of economic profit in the capitalist system. Rather, there are several theories of profit, each of which focuses on a different function played by the entrepreneur. Here we examine three functions of the entrepreneur that represent potential sources of economic profit.

Entrepreneur as Broker

Perhaps the simplest view of the entrepreneur is that of a broker whose aim is to "buy low and sell high." Entrepreneurs bid against one another for the available resources, and this bidding establishes market prices for the various resources. Entrepreneurs can be thought of as brokers who contract with resources and combine these resources to produce goods and services. The difference between what the entrepreneur pays for resources (including the opportunity cost of any other resources supplied by the entrepreneur) and the revenue received from sales equals the entrepreneur's economic profit. Thus, entrepreneurs earn an economic profit by selling output for more than it costs to produce.

At the first sign of economic profit, however, other entrepreneurs will emerge to enter this industry. If markets are perfectly competitive, economic profit will be driven to zero in the long run. If markets are perfectly competitive, entrepreneurs will earn just a normal rate of return on resources they supply the firm, and in the long run they will earn no economic profit for their entrepreneurial ability. In viewing the entrepreneur as broker, we are saying that the entrepreneur and the firm are one and the same.

Entrepreneur as Risk Bearer

Some economists think of the profit earned by entrepreneurs as arising from the risk associated with venturing into a world filled with uncertainty. According to this theory of profit, a portion of the return received by entrepreneurs is a payment for their willingness to bear that risk. But the consideration of risk bearing as a source of economic profit gives rise to a more general treatment of risk and return for various resource owners. We can speak of two sources of risk for resource owners: (1) the risk of not getting paid after providing the resource and (2) the risk of a fall in the market value of a resource.

Risk of Not Getting Paid Despite the entrepreneur's guarantees, resource suppliers, particularly suppliers of loans, often face the possibility of not being paid. If resource owners take a risk by turning the use of their resources over to the entrepreneur, they will require greater compensation than they would if their payment were assured. In this sense resource suppliers are risk bearers, and they are typically compensated for bearing risk. Consequently, if we define profit as a return for risk bearing, then the greater resource payment required for bearing risk can be considered profit. Resource suppliers who do not get paid obviously suffer an economic loss.

Think of the resource owners as standing in line waiting to receive the payment guaranteed them by the entrepreneur, not knowing when or if the cashier's window will close. Some owners try to put themselves first in line by requiring payment before their resource is supplied, by requiring payment before other resources are paid, or by requiring the entrepreneur to post collateral, which can be claimed by the resource owner should payment not be forthcoming. Labor suppliers typically are paid weekly or biweekly, so little labor is extended without compensation. Lenders, however, usually extend the entire amount up front and are repaid in installments; lenders thus often require collateral. If resource suppliers have doubts about getting paid, they will demand a higher return for their services. This additional payment can be considered a return for risk bearing.

Risk of a Decline in the Value of the Resource   The capitalist system is based on the private ownership of the resources and the right of resource owners to freely contract for the lease or sale of their resources. An important feature of capitalism is the right of a resource owner to the gain or the loss in the value of that resource. Thus, resource owners bear the risk associated with acquiring or developing resources. While we typically associate risk bearing with the acquisition of physical capital, investment in human capital is often no more certain.

For example, right now you are acquiring human capital that you hope will serve you a lifetime. Your decision to specialize in a particular area, such as accounting, chemistry, or engineering, involves some risk because you cannot know what return this investment will yield in the future. You can only guess how changes in tastes, technology, taxes, and the supply of resources will shape the future supply and demand for your particular resource.

Many college students are understandably tempted to train for that first job; the tendency is to acquire very specific skills. The more specific your human capital is, however, the more risk you assume in an uncertain world. Thus, there is a risk involved in the investment of human capital just as there is in investing in physical capital, and a portion of the return to human capital could be identified as an economic profit or an economic loss.

Entrepreneur as Innovator

A variation of the broker role is to view entrepreneurs as resource suppliers earning profits arising from successful innovations. For example, profits can be thought of as the rewards for "building a better mousetrap." If entrepreneurs can make an existing product more cheaply than competitors do or can introduce a new product demanded by consumers, they will be able to earn at least short-run economic profits. The possibility of economic profits serves as a powerful motive for productive innovations. Whether these profits continue in the long run will depend on the ability of other firms to imitate the cost-saving activity or the new product. If the entrepreneur is somehow able to acquire monopoly power, economic profit can be earned in the long run as well. For more about the entrepreneur as innovator, see the profile of Joseph Schumpeter in this chapter.

The entrepreneur as innovator comes closest to our earlier discussion linking economic profit to monopoly power. The entrepreneur may have patented an innovation that provides the firm with market power. We briefly mention some other sources of monopoly power here as well. The

Joseph A.
Schumpeter
(1883–1950)

Harvard University News Office

Businesspeople are not troubled by the concept of profit: they know it when they see it. But for economists, profit has long been a somewhat elusive—or at least controversial—concept. Some have seen profit as merely the wages of management; others have viewed it as a reward for bearing risk; and Marxian economists have always maintained that profit is extracted from laborers through exploitation. But one of the most brilliant and challenging formulations of the theory of profit arose from a somewhat unlikely source: an urbane, aristocratic Viennese named Joseph Schumpeter.

Profit, said Schumpeter, is neither a wage nor the fruits of exploitation; it is not even a reward for bearing risk. Profit, he argued, is a residual: it's what's left over after all the factors of production have been paid. In the ordinary course of things, there is no such profit. But an enterprising individual who creates a new technology or opens a new market generates profit--at least for a while, until imitators swarm in to copy the innovation and drive profit back to zero. These path-breaking entrepreneurs, as Schumpeter called them, are not only the source of profit. They are also the source of the momentum and drive of the entire economic system. Innovations are the wellspring of economic growth, and entrepreneurs are the fountainhead of innovation.

Capitalism, Schumpeter said in a famous phrase, is a "perennial gale of creative destruction."

In America of the 1980s this theory conjures up images of "cowboy capitalism" and the dynamism of Silicon Valley. But the author of the theory himself calls to mind a different picture. Joesph Schumpeter was a flamboyant and cultured European of the old school. He was born in Triesch in the Austro-Hungarian Empire, moving to Vienna as a lad when his widowed mother married an aristocrat. A star student at the University of Vienna, he published his first book at the age of 25. After a multifarious career (including positions as Austrian finance minister and as president of a failed bank), he settled into academia, ending up at Harvard University in the 1930s.

Schumpeter was one of the widest-ranging thinkers of his time. In a massive 1939 tome he traced depressions and recessions to cycles in entrepreneurship and to the "clustering" of innovations. His most famous work, a 1942 book called *Capitalism, Socialism, and Democracy,* presented a dark and ironic argument that capitalism must eventually fail—not because of its weaknesses but because its very *success* will undermine the attitudes and values that support it.

Richard Langlois

entrepreneur may be the sole owner of a key resource used in production. The entrepreneur may have secured a monopoly position through government regulation of the industry. Or economies of scale in production might provide monopoly power and yield economic profit in the long run.

Profit and the Supply of Entrepreneurs

The ranks of entrepreneurs are in constant flux, as some emerge from the labor market to form their own enterprises and others return to the labor market after failing with their own firm or after selling a successful firm. To be sure, the total supply of entrepreneurial ability is influenced by a variety of forces, such as the pace of technological change, the tax laws, and the market return to the other resources entrepreneurs could supply.

Evidence suggests that most new firms fail. According to the Small Business Administration, about 7 of every 10 new businesses fail during the first year of operation. What is it that encourages someone to take on such odds rather than settle for the predictable salary, vacation time, health benefits, and other amenities that typically come with serving as an employee rather than as an employer? Why do more than 10 million people in this country call themselves boss?

Are Entrepreneurs Overly Optimistic?   An entrepreneur is an optimist. Individuals who choose self-employment evidently feel that the net expected returns to this activity (including, no doubt, the satisfaction of being one's own boss) are greater than the rewards expected from putting their resources under the direction of someone else. Frank Knight argued nearly 70 years ago that most people "have an irrationally high confidence in their own good fortune," which "is doubly true when their personal prowess comes into the reckoning, when they are betting on themselves."[2]

Knight, in fact, argued that entrepreneurs, rather than requiring economic profit as a reward for taking risks, would be willing *to pay* to take risks because each feels able to beat the odds. Knight believed that because entrepreneurs are on average overly optimistic about their own abilities, economic profit—that is, the profit left after subtracting the entrepreneur's imputed earnings—is negative on the average. Knight's view is intriguing, and there is evidence of economic losses in some industries, such as during most of the first 50 years of the auto industry. Given the central role rationality plays in economic decision making, however, we should be reluctant to admit that entrepreneurs, those most important of the economy's decision makers, delude themselves.

Ability to Capitalize Expected Profits   One strong economic incentive for founding a firm is that any entrepreneur who can develop a profit-making

---

[2] *Risk, Uncertainty and Profit* (Chicago: University of Chicago Press, 1971), 366 (originally published in 1921).

operation can typically sell the firm for a price equal to the present value of the expected profit stream. For example, assume you put together a company that yields a net profit of $25,000 per year. Using a 10 percent discount rate, the present value of such a stream, if expected to continue indefinitely, is $25,000/0.10, or $250,000. The present value often exceeds this because profits are usually expected to grow in the future, and this growing stream of profits is what becomes capitalized into the value of the firm. Some entrepreneurs are motivated by the ability to capitalize on a successful firm. In closing our look at entrepreneurs, consider the following case study of the entrepreneur who developed Lotus 1-2-3.

CASE STUDY

Feasting In The Land Of Lotus

Milton Kapor's job background hardly seemed to qualify him to become such a successful producer of computer software. He had held various jobs, ranging from disk jockey to instructor of transcendental meditation. One day he traded his stereo for an Apple II computer, and therein lies the tale. He was enraptured by the machine and soon developed his programming skills to the point where he reportedly took only two months to write two business applications programs that he sold for more than a million dollars!

With these funds and with additional support, both financial and entrepreneurial, from a venture capital firm, he founded the Lotus Development Corporation in 1982. In less than a year Lotus 1-2-3 became the industry's best-selling business program, with sales of $50 million the first year. In October 1983 the company made its first public offering of stock. At that time Kapor's stock in the company was worth $70 million. In a few short years Lotus grew out of his basement to become a firm with 1200 employees and annual sales exceeding $250 million.

The other side of this success story is the venture capital firm that in 1982 invested $2.1 million in Kapor's company. Venture capitalists shop around, investing in promising new firms. Such investors could be considered entrepreneurs in that, by becoming part owners, they share the responsibility of guaranteeing the payments of the other resources, they share in the control of these resources, and they are residual claimants of any profit or loss. When Lotus made its public offering in 1983, the stock held by the venture capital firm was also worth $70 million, or about 33 times the original investment.

In July 1986 Kapor resigned as chairman of Lotus. He evidently did not find the job of managing people and payroll as attractive as founding an empire. Since Kapor was viewed as the imaginative force behind Lotus, the day after he resigned the share price dropped by $2.25, an amount that at the time represented about 10 percent of the stock's value. The stock market evidently felt that Kapor's special skills could not easily be replaced.

Source: "A Software Whiz Logs Off," *Newsweek* (21 July 1986): 32.

SUMMARY

1. Production cannot occur unless there is saving because both direct production and roundabout production require time—time during which the resources required for production must be paid. Because present consumption is valued more than future consumption, consumers must be rewarded to defer consumption. The interest rate is the reward paid to savers for forgoing present consumption and the cost charged to borrowers to ensure early availability.

2. The marginal physical product of employing additional units of capital declines as more capital is employed, other things constant, because of the law of diminishing marginal returns. For the competitive firm the marginal revenue product of capital equals the marginal physical product times the price of the product. The marginal efficiency of capital equals the marginal revenue product divided by the cost of capital.

3. The profit-maximizing firm hires capital up to the point where the marginal efficiency of capital equals the market rate of interest, which is the opportunity cost of borrowing the money to buy the capital.

4. In a world without inflation the rate of interest is called the real rate of interest. The nominal rate of interest measures the interest rate in terms of the actual dollars paid, even if dollars have lost purchasing power because of inflation. The nominal rate of interest equals the real rate of interest plus the expected inflation rate.

5. Interest rates differ in the real world because (1) some borrowers are less likely than others to repay their loan, so higher-risk borrowers are charged higher interest; (2) some loans are extended for longer periods than others; (3) smaller loans have higher administrative costs as a percentage of the loan than do larger loans; and (4) different kinds of loans have different tax treatments.

6. An entrepreneur is a profit-seeking decision maker who guarantees payment for the other resources in return for the right to direct these resources in the firm. The entrepreneur is also the residual claimant of any profits or losses in the firm. The entrepreneur need not supply any resource other than entrepreneurial ability, though resources such as capital and managerial ability are usually also supplied by the entrepreneur.

7. There is no single theory explaining the profit earned by entrepreneurs. Entrepreneurs have been viewed as brokers who earn a profit by buying resources for less than they sell the product of those resources. They have been viewed as risk bearers who earn a profit by taking chances. And they have been viewed as innovators who earn a profit by producing existing products for less or by developing new products.

QUESTIONS AND PROBLEMS

1. (Capital in Production) Consider the example of Old MacDonald of the chapter. Why would seed also be considered as part of saving? Should seed be considered part of the capital stock? Why or why not?

2. (Marginal Efficiency of Capital) Consider Exhibit 3 in this chapter. If the marginal resource cost rises to $2400, what will be the optimum stock of capital? If the interest rate then rises to 16.6 percent, what will be the optimum stock of capital?

3. (Human Capital) Why are banks more willing to lend to medical students than to graduate students in education? Is the level of interest rates the only consideration in the accumulation of human capital? What other variables affect the ability to accumulate such capital?

4. (Real Interest Rates) Is it possible for the real rate of interest to be negative? If so, what would cause this?

5. (Taxes and Investment) How does the tax deductability of mortgage interest payments affect the demand for housing and building construction?

6. (Present Value) How would the present value of an investment project change if interest rates rise?

7. (Bond Prices) Why is $10,000 a reasonably close approximation for the price of a bond paying $1000 each year for 30 years at 10 percent interest?

8. (Entrepreneurs) The success and value of entrepreneurship is easier to identify in small, self-owned businesses. How would you identify the effects or value of entrepreneurship in large corporations? Give some examples of such entrepeneurs.

9. (Valuing Entrepreneurship) *The Concise Oxford Dictionary* defines the business term *goodwill* as a "privilege granted by seller of an established business, of trading as recognized successor; amount paid for this." How might a company's goodwill be a measure of previous entrepreneurship?

10. (Profits) Some people claim that profits are bad or can be excessive. Does this claim seem justified in light of the discussion of the chapter?

POVERTY and INCOME DISTRIBUTION

Income in a market economy depends primarily on the marginal productivity of the household's resources. The problem with allocating income according to marginal productivity is that some people have difficulty earning income. Those born with mental or physical disabilities may be unable to earn a living. Others may face limited job choices and reduced wages because of a poor education or discrimination in the marketplace. Still others may be unable to work because they must care for small children.

In his first budget message President Reagan said he wanted to reform welfare programs "to eliminate unintended benefits," while at the same time preserving a "social safety net." In this chapter we begin by examining the distribution of income in the United States, with special attention to the extent of poverty in recent years. We then discuss and evaluate the "social safety net"—public policies aimed at helping the poor. We consider the impact of the changing family structure on the incidence of poverty, focusing in particular on the age, race, and gender of the head of the household. We also explore the effects of discrimination on the distribution of income. Topics and terms discussed include:

- Personal distribution of income
- Lorenz curve
- Official poverty level
- The feminization of poverty
- Negative income tax

THE PERSONAL DISTRIBUTION OF INCOME

We begin by examining the distribution of income in the United States. The best way to consider the distribution of income is to focus on the family as the appropriate economic unit.

Distribution of Household Income

By dividing the total number of families into five groups of equal size according to income, we can examine what percentage of income is received by each group. Such a division is presented in Exhibit 1. Notice that in 1929, families in the lowest, or poorest, fifth of the population received only 3.5 percent of the income, while families in the highest, or richest, fifth received 54.4 percent of the income. Thus, the richest 20 percent of the families received over half the income.

EXHIBIT 1
THE DISTRIBUTION OF MONEY INCOME
AMONG FAMILIES FOR SELECTED YEARS,
1947–1985

	Percentage Share					
Year	Lowest Fifth	Second Fifth	Middle Fifth	Fourth Fifth	Highest Fifth	Top 5 Percent
1929	3.5%	9.0%	13.8%	19.3%	54.4%	30.0%
1947	5.0	11.9	17.0	23.1	43.0	17.5
1957	5.1	12.7	18.1	23.8	40.4	15.6
1967	5.5	12.4	17.9	23.9	40.4	15.2
1977	5.2	11.6	17.5	24.2	41.5	15.7
1985	4.6	10.9	16.9	24.2	43.5	16.7

Source: U.S. Bureau of the Census, *Current Population Reports*, series no. P-60, no. 137; 145 (Washington, D.C.: U.S. Government Printing Office, 1986).

Notice also that the share going to the richest group dropped from 54.4 percent in 1929 to 43.0 percent in 1947. What caused the amount going to the top group to fall? The Great Depression erased many personal fortunes and the income that flowed from those fortunes. World War II also brought more people into the labor force and increased the average wage. Labor unions may have also boosted the pay of the average worker.

Beginning in 1947 the data display a remarkable stability, with the share going to the lowest fifth hovering around 5 percent, and the share to the highest fifth ranging between 40 and 43 percent. Since the lowest 20 percent of the families receive only 5 percent of the income, there is much inequality in the distribution of income. The reasons for this will be examined shortly, but first let's take a picture of distribution of income.

*The **Lorenz curve** shows the percentage of total income received by a given percentage of recipients when incomes are arranged from smallest to largest.*

The Lorenz Curve

We have just examined the distribution of income with a table. The Lorenz curve is another way of picturing the distribution of income in an economy. As shown in Exhibit 2, the cumulative percentage of families arranged from lowest income to highest income is measured along the horizontal axis, and the cumulative percentage of income is measured along the vertical axis. The **Lorenz curve** shows the percentage of total income received by any given percentage of recipients when incomes are arrayed from smallest to largest.

Any given distribution of income can be compared to an even distribution of income among families. If all families received the same income, it would make little sense to order the families based on income. Nonetheless, we can say that if income were evenly distributed, the poorest 20 percent of the population would receive 20 percent of the total income; the next poorest 20 percent of the population would receive 20 percent of the income, and so on. The Lorenz curve in this case would be a straight line with a slope equal to 1.0, as shown in Exhibit 2.

As the distribution becomes more unequal, the Lorenz curve is pulled down and to the right, away from the line of equal distribution. The Lorenz curves in Exhibit 2 were calculated for 1929 and 1985, based on the data in Exhibit 1. As a point of reference, point *a* on the 1929 Lorenz curve indicates that the bottom 80 percent of families had 45.6 percent of the income, while the top 20 percent had 54.4 percent of the income. Point *b* on the 1985 Lorenz curve shows that the bottom 80 percent now have 56.5 percent of the income; the income share of the top 20 percent is down to 43.5 percent. Because the Lorenz curve for 1985 is closer to the center, the shift since 1929 indicates an equalizing in the distribution of income among families.

Households receive income from two primary sources, resource earnings and transfers from the government. Exhibits 1 and 2 measure money income after cash transfers but before taxes. Thus, the distribution in Exhibits 1 and 2 omits the effects of taxes and of in-kind transfers, such as food stamps and free medical care to poor families. The tax system as a whole tends to be

EXHIBIT 2   LORENZ CURVES, 1929 AND 1985

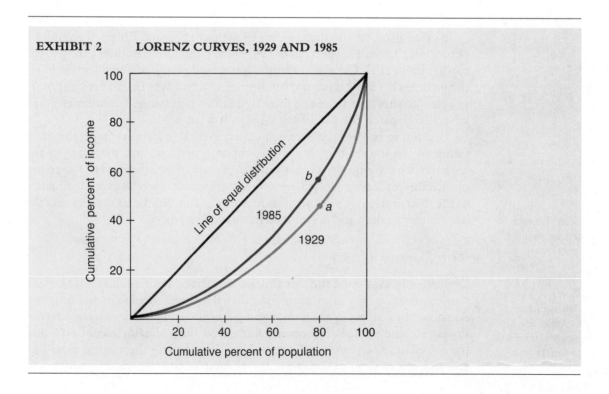

mildly progressive, so families with a higher income pay a larger fraction of income in taxes. In-kind transfers tend to benefit the lowest-income groups the most. If we included the effect of taxes and the value of in-kind transfers when we computed the distribution of income, the share of income going to the lower groups would increase, and the share going to the higher group would decrease, so income would be more evenly distributed.

Why Do Family Incomes Differ?

A major reason incomes differ across families is because of differences in the number of family members who are working. Households where both the husband and wife work typically earn more than households with only one working spouse. In the poorest households nobody is employed. Since most income comes from selling labor, differences in family income arise for all the reasons labor income differs—namely, differences in ability, training, education, tastes, job amenities, and possibly racial or sexual discrimination.

*The **median** is the middle number in a series of numbers that are arranged from smallest to largest.*

Perhaps the clearest difference can be seen from education. Exhibit 3 shows the **median** family income based on the education of the family head. As you can see, the median income in households where the head attended elementary school was $15,370 in 1985; that same year the median income of households where the head had 5 or more years of college was $50,525—more than triple the income of the least educated families.

EXHIBIT 3
MEDIAN FAMILY INCOME BASED ON EDUCATION OF FAMILY HEAD, 1985

Education	Money Income
Elementary	$15,370
High school	27,472
College	
1–3 years	32,177
4 years	43,187
5 or more years	50,525

Source: U.S. Bureau of the Census, *Current Population Reports*, Series P-60, no. 151 (Washington, D.C.: U.S. Government Printing Office, 1986).

The age of the family head also has an important effect on income. Those just entering the work force tend to be at the bottom of the scale. As workers get older, they develop job experience, are promoted, and earn more. Thus, income tends to increase with age. Differences in earnings based on age reflect the normal life-cycle pattern of income and are not matters of public concern. In fact, most income differences across households reflect the normal workings of resource markets, where workers are rewarded according to their productivity. When incomes are very low, however, they become a matter of public concern, as we will see in the next section.

More generally, high-income households tend to have a middle-aged head who is well educated, and two people from the household are working. Low-income households tend to have a single parent who is young, poorly educated, and not working.

POVERTY AND THE POOR

Before examining poverty in the United States we should develop a wider perspective on wealth and poverty. Poverty is a relative term. If we studied the distribution of income across the countries of the world, we would find huge gaps between rich and poor nations. For example, in 1984 GNP per person in the United States was more than twenty-five times greater than GNP per person for three-fourths of the world's population.[1] Also, an income at the U.S. poverty level today provides a standard of living that would be considered attractive to many people who lived in the United States at the turn of the century. At that time only 15 percent of families had flush toilets, only 3 percent had electricity, and only 1 percent had central heating.

Since poverty is such a relative concept, how do we measure it objectively and how do we ensure that our measure can be applied with equal relevance over time? In 1955 the federal government developed the calculations to define an official poverty level; this level has since become the benchmark for poverty analysis in this country.

Official Poverty Level

To derive the official poverty level, the Department of Agriculture first estimated the cost of minimum food consumption requirements for a family of four. Then, by assuming that the poor spent about one-third of their income on food, the official poverty level was calculated by multiplying these food costs by three. Adjustments were made for family size and for inflation.

For example, the official poverty level of income for a family of four was $11,203 in 1986; families of four at or below that income level would be regarded as living in poverty. Each year the Census Bureau conducts a survey to determine the extent and composition of poverty. The Census Bureau compares a family's annual cash income to the annual poverty threshhold that is applicable to that family.

The percentage of the population classified as below the official poverty line is shown in Exhibit 4. As you can see, the biggest decline in the rate of poverty came prior to 1970; the rate dropped from 22.4 percent in 1959 to 12.1 percent in 1969. During that period the number of poor people as measured by the official government definition dropped from about 40

---

[1]See The World Bank, *World Development Report 1986* (New York: Oxford University Press, 1986), Table 1.

EXHIBIT 4   **PERCENTAGE OF POPULATION BELOW THE OFFICIAL POVERTY LEVEL, 1960–1985**

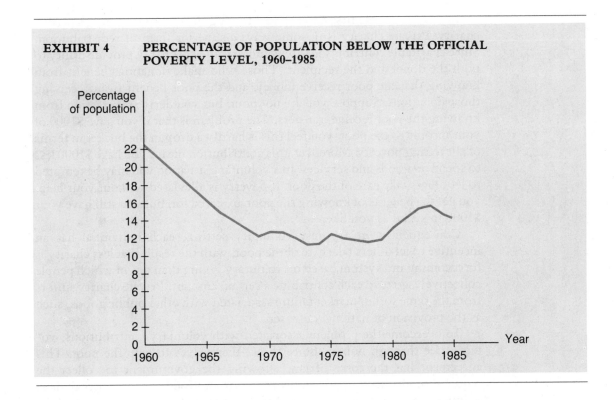

---

million to 24 million. Although the poverty rate bounced around during the 1970s, there was no significant reduction in the poverty rate during that decade. The rate began to rise after 1979, reaching 15.3 percent in 1983 before falling back to 14.0 percent in 1985. In 1985 there were about 8 million more poor people than in 1970.

Public Policy and Poverty

What should the government response to poverty be? Families where the head of the household has a job are much more likely to escape poverty than families without employment. Thus, the government's first line of defense in fighting poverty is to promote a healthy economy and to provide job opportunities. Education and training programs can enhance job opportunities.

Yet some people may remain poor because they lack marketable skills, must care for small children, or face discrimination in the labor market. The government has several alternatives when confronted with the problems of poverty: (1) it can do nothing, relying on private charity and support from relatives to help the poor; (2) it can intervene in private markets with the intent of helping the poor, such as with rent controls, minimum wage legislation, or affirmative action employment policies; or (3) it can wait until private markets have cleared and then tax the income of those with higher incomes to provide transfers to the poor.

Let's consider the first alternative—leaving the care of the poor to private charity. Private charity is in some ways a superior form of redistribution. Since charitable contributions are voluntary, they probably provide utility to both the donor and the recipient. Those who make donations benefit from knowing that the poor receive money, and the poor benefit from receiving those donations. Suppose you are not poor, but you derive satisfaction from knowing the poor receive transfers. The problem is that if you gave $1000 of your income to the poor, you feel this is hardly a drop in the bucket in terms of alleviating poverty. Moreover, this contribution means you have $1000 less to spend on goods and services. In a voluntary situation you may be tempted to let others take care of the poor. If poverty is alleviated without your help, you get the benefits of knowing the poor are cared for, but you still have your $1000 to spend as you like.

Consequently, in a purely voluntary setting, each individual has an incentive to let others take care of the poor, with the result that less charity is forthcoming in a system based on voluntary giving than one in which people collectively agree to each contribute a certain amount. Private charity suffers from the same sort of market failure associated with other public goods, such as the provision of national defense.

To overcome the problem associated with voluntary contributions, voters agree through public choice to tax themselves to help the poor. This agreement has the force of law, allowing the government to collect the required funds. Such public choices result in more aid to the poor than does voluntary giving through private charity. You may be more willing to aid the poor if you are assured that others will contribute as well.

If you think we are being overly pessimistic about the prospects for voluntary giving, consider your own experience. How much of your income or time did you contribute to charity this past year? If you contributed as much as 5 percent, you are exceptional. What have you done lately for the poor of the world? Consider the following case study.

CASE STUDY ***Live Aid***	In 1985 a devastating drought swept across Africa, leaving hunger and misery in its wake. Rock musicians on both sides of the Atlantic supported the famine relief effort by staging two 16-hour "Live Aid" concerts on the same day in London and in Philadelphia. The concerts were broadcast on television and were reportedly viewed by a quarter of the world's population. The concerts raised about $50 million from ticket sales, broadcast rights, and pledges from a worldwide telethon. The Live Aid concert thus appears to be an overwhelming response to the problem of poverty, and it suggests that voluntary giving may indeed be an effective solution. But let's take a closer look.

The broadcast was interspersed with tragic pictures of starving children, and appeals for support were made by rock stars and other celebrities. If ever there was a time when people would be moved to charity, this would be it. How much charity did these dramatic appeals elicit? We cannot credit much charitable behavior to those who paid even the top price of $35 per ticket to attend the concerts. Since many people are willing to camp out for days to buy tickets to see just one of these performers, there seems to be little room left for charity in purchasing a ticket to see dozens of top performers. Similarly, we cannot credit to charity those advertisers who purchased air time during the broadcast. Perhaps we can credit the performers themselves with the charitable giving of their time, but public relations probably played no small part in such a heralded act of charity.

If we subtract earnings from ticket sales and broadcast rights, we have the amount raised through pledges, which was about $35 million. This is an impressive sum indeed, but how does it compare with the size of the viewing audience? If we divide the $35 million contributed by the 1.2 billion people who reportedly viewed the concert, the average contribution works out to be about three cents per viewer. If we assume that the average donation was $10, only 1 viewer in 330 contributed. Although Live Aid was called "the biggest charity extravaganza ever," the quality of mercy reflected by the contributions seems to be a bit thin.

Source: "Rock Around the World," *Newsweek*, (22 July 1985): 56.

Programs to Help the Poor

Although some government programs to help the poor involve some direct market intervention, the most important programs result from redistributing income after the market has provided an initial distribution. The administrations of Presidents Johnson, Nixon, and Ford led the expansion of social welfare spending in this country. Between 1965 and 1976 social welfare expenditures at all levels of government increased dramatically. We can divide social welfare programs into two major categories: social insurance and income assistance.

Social Insurance   The social insurance system is designed to protect those who retire or who are unable to work because of total disability, unemployment, or work injury. By far the major social insurance program is Social Security, which provides retirement income to those with a work history and a record of contributing to the program. Medicare pays for short-term medical care for those aged 65 and older, regardless of income. Other social insurance programs include Unemployment Insurance and Worker's Compensation, where benefits again depend on a prior record of employment. Benefits under the social insurance system are based on an income test but in a way that provides higher benefits to those with higher earnings before retirement, disability, or unemployment. These programs do protect some families from poverty, but they are aimed more at middle-income families.

Income Assistance   Income-assistance programs—what we usually call "welfare"—provide money and in-kind assistance to the poor. Unlike social insurance programs, income-assistance programs do not require the recipient to have worked or to have contributed to the program. People who satisfy the criteria are *entitled* to the program; hence, they are sometimes called entitlement programs. The two primary cash transfer programs are Aid to Families with Dependent Children (AFDC), which provides cash to poor, single-parent households, and Supplementary Security Income (SSI), which provides cash to the indigent elderly and the totally disabled. Cash transfers vary inversely with household income from other sources.

AFDC began with the 1935 Social Security legislation and was originally aimed at providing support for widows with small children. The cost is divided between the state and federal governments. Because benefit levels are set by each state, they can vary widely. For example, in 1985 a family of four with no other income could receive $120 per month in Mississippi but $660 per month in California. In the median state the transfer was $340. Some states also offer AFDC benefits to two-parent families, but these payments account for only 5 percent of the total AFDC program.

The Supplemental Security Income program provides a minimum income guarantee for about 4 million elderly poor. A uniform level is provided by the federal government, but this amount can be supplemented by the states. Most states also offer modest General Assistance aid to those who are poor but do not qualify for one of the other programs.

Finally, a variety of in-kind benefit programs provide health care (through Medicaid), food stamps, and housing assistance to the poor. Medicaid is by far the biggest income-assistance program, costing more than all cash transfer programs combined. Medicaid pays for medical care for all who have income below a certain level, who are aged, blind, disabled, or in families with dependent children. The qualifying level of income is set by each state.

Food stamps are vouchers that can be used like money to purchase food. The program is aimed at reducing hunger and providing for proper nutrition in poor households. In 1965 the program covered fewer than half a million persons; by 1985 the program reached over 20 million people and provided about $60 per person per month for food. Food stamps have been one of the fastest-growing transfer programs; the cost is paid for by the federal government, so benefits are uniform across states. Housing-assistance programs include direct assistance for rental payments and subsidized low-income housing. There are also minor in-kind programs, such as energy assistance and school lunches.

Expenditures and the Rate of Poverty

Social insurance programs and income-assistance programs at all levels of government totaled about $400 billion in 1986, or about 10 percent of the GNP. More than three-quarters of the total went to the social insurance programs, and only one-quarter to those programs aimed more specifically at the poor. Thus, income-support programs—what we typically think of as welfare programs—amounted to only about 2.5 percent of GNP.

Exhibit 5 indicates what happened between 1960 and 1986 to federal expenditures specifically aimed at assisting poor people. Expenditures are measured in billions of 1986 dollars, so outlays are in real terms, or inflation-adjusted dollars. As you can see, the most rapid growth occurred between 1970 and 1981, when real expenditures increased from $26 billion to $71.4 billion, for a growth rate of 9.6 percent per year.

If you compare Exhibit 5 with Exhibit 4, which presented the poverty rate during the same period, you will notice that the war against poverty seemed to fizzle just when the federal outlays for the poor showed their greatest increase. What was going on? Were efforts to eradicate poverty facing diminishing returns? First, we should say that while transfer programs grew greatly during the 1970s, programs for the poor still amounted most recently to only about 2.5 percent of the GNP. Thus, poverty programs could not be called massive.

Effect of the Economy   One explanation for the rise in poverty in recent years requires a look beyond the possible effects of federal programs to the health of the underlying economy. "A rising tide lifts all the boats"—so goes the old axiom about the relationship between a thriving economy and rising individual fortunes. Between 1959 and 1969, the period during which poverty dropped the most, the economy showed the strongest growth; real output per capita increased by 3.1 percent per year, and median family income, measured in constant dollars, grew by 34 percent during the period.

Between 1969 and 1979, however, the economy was relatively flat, with median family income, adjusted for inflation, hardly changed. As it turns

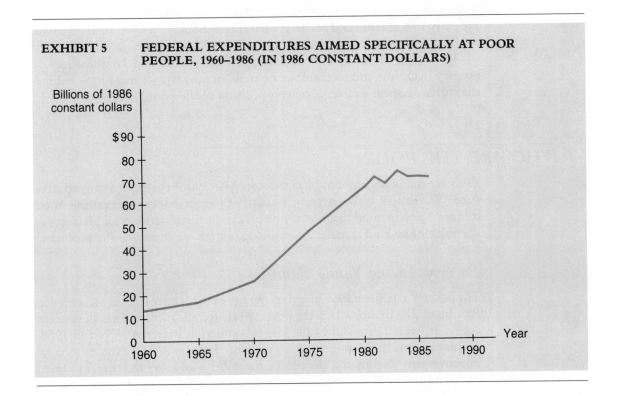

EXHIBIT 5   **FEDERAL EXPENDITURES AIMED SPECIFICALLY AT POOR PEOPLE, 1960–1986 (IN 1986 CONSTANT DOLLARS)**

out, a healthy economy can reduce poverty more than all but the largest increases in government assistance. As we saw at the outset, the bottom fifth of the population receives about 5 percent of the income, a figure that has changed little in the last 40 years. A 10 percent income increase throughout the economy would have raised the income of this lowest group by about $17 billion in 1986, which is more than was spent on AFDC that year.

The economy after 1969 was less robust than it was before, and this in part contributed to the problems of the poor. The effect of the growth in transfer spending during the 1970s may have been to compensate in part for a weak economy, with the result that poverty rates remained relatively unchanged. But between 1979 and 1985 poverty increased, reflecting the double trouble of a relatively flat economy and cutbacks in the real level of transfer spending.

Exclusion of In-Kind Transfers   Another reason official poverty statistics seem so unresponsive to what appear to be large increases in the level of transfers is that the Census Bureau includes only money transfers in the definition of income. It ignores the value of in-kind transfer programs, such as food stamps, housing assistance, and Medicaid. Yet in-kind programs experienced the greatest growth during the 1970s.

When poverty figures are reestimated to include the value of in-kind transfers, this revised poverty rate is below the official estimate, as expected. For example, while the official rate in 1984 was 14.4 percent, the Census Bureau reestimated the rate to include most in-kind transfers and found it to be 9.7 percent. Still, the overall trend in poverty using this expanded definition is similar to the official estimates: the poverty rate declined until the early 1970s, remained relatively flat throughout the 1970s, then began to rise in 1979.

To develop a fuller understanding of the extent and composition of poverty over time and to examine the trend in poverty, we must look behind the totals. We next examine the composition of the poor.

WHO ARE THE POOR?

Who are the poor, and how has the composition of the poor changed over time? We will slice the poverty statistics in several ways to examine their texture. Keep in mind that we rely on official poverty statistics, which ignore the value of in-kind transfers, so to some extent we overstate the problem.

Poverty Among Young Families

The poverty rate since 1959 based on the age of the family head is presented in Exhibit 6. The first row lists the poverty rate for all families regardless of the age. The overall rate shows the largest reduction between 1959 and 1968, declining from 18.5 percent to 10.0 percent. There was, however, no general improvement during the decade of the 1970s, and the rate has increased slightly since 1980.

EXHIBIT 6
OFFICIAL POVERTY RATE OF FAMILIES
BY AGE OF HOUSEHOLD HEAD FOR
SELECTED YEARS, 1959–1985

Age of Household Head	Year					
	1959	**1968**	**1970**	**1975**	**1980**	**1985**
All families	18.5%	10.0%	10.1%	9.7%	10.3%	11.4%
Under 25	26.9	13.2	15.5	21.0	21.8	30.2
25–44	16.5	9.3	9.5	10.3	11.8	13.2
45–54	15.0	7.0	6.6	6.6	7.6	7.9
65 and over	30.0	17.0	16.5	8.9	9.1	7.0

Source: U.S. Bureau of the Census, *Estimates of Poverty Including the Value of Noncash Benefits* (Washington, D.C.: U.S. Government Printing Office, 1986).

Poverty is highest in families where the head of the household is under 25 years old. Older heads of households have a lower poverty rate, especially in more recent years. Higher poverty rates among younger households reflect the fact that earnings tend to be the lowest for those just entering the labor market. The data, however, show more than simply an age-wage effect because the poverty rates among young families have grown relatively worse over time. In 1968, for example, poverty rates for families headed by someone under 25 were only one-third greater than the rate for all families, but by 1985 these younger families had a poverty rate that was nearly three times the average.

The most dramatic reversal of poverty has occurred among those families where the head of the household is 65 and over. In 1959 the elderly group was the poorest, with a poverty rate of 30 percent. By 1985 the poverty rate for the elderly group had dropped to 7.0 percent, a lower rate than for any other age group. In fact, those 65 and over were the only ones to have a lower rate in 1985 than in any previous year. Compared to other groups, particularly those under 25, where the poverty rate nearly doubled between 1970 and 1985, the rate reduction among the elderly has been remarkable.

Credit this reduction in poverty to a tremendous growth in Social Security transfers, which grew from $39 billion in 1959 to $280 billion in 1986, measured in 1986 dollars. More was spent on Social Security in 1986 than on national defense. Social Security outlays were also more than three times the amount spent on income-assistance programs. The average retired couple received $822 per month in 1986, which puts them above the poverty level. And many elderly people have other sources of income. Social Security, though not strictly an antipoverty program, has done wonders for poverty among the elderly.

Poverty and Gender

The data in Exhibit 7 distinguish between poor families headed by a female with no husband present and all other poor families. The poverty rate is presented in parentheses below the number of poor in each group. As we know, poverty declined the most between 1959 and 1969. We can now see, however, that this decline was confined mostly to those living in male-headed families. Among male-headed families both the poverty rate and the numbers of poor declined substantially between 1959 and 1969. Among female-headed families the poverty rate declined somewhat. The number of female-headed families in the entire population was growing faster than the number of male-headed families.

The sharp decline in poverty in male-headed families suggests the strong role played by a surging economy during the 1960s. Male-headed households were in the best position to gain from this economic vitality because they typically had one more potential wage earner than female-headed households did.

EXHIBIT 7
POVERTY OF FAMILIES BY GENDER
OF HOUSEHOLD HEAD, 1959–1985
(Millions of Poor and the Poverty Rate in Parentheses)

Gender of Household Head	Year			
	1959	1969	1979	1985
Families with female household head and no husband present	7.0 (49.4%)	6.9 (38.2%)	9.4 (34.9%)	11.6 (37.6%)
Primarily male-headed families	27.5 (18.2%)	12.3 (7.4%)	10.6 (6.3%)	14.1 (8.2%)

Source: U.S. Bureau of the Census, *Current Population Reports*, series P-60, no. 137 (Washington, D.C.: U.S. Government Printing Office, 1986).

Between 1969 and 1979 the poverty *rate* declined for both groups, but because the total number of female-headed households increased sharply, the number of poor in female-headed families actually increased by 2.5 million. Between 1979 and 1985 both the rate and the number of poor increased for both groups, probably because of a sagging economy during the period and a leveling off in transfer programs. The percentage of all the poor who were in families headed by a female increased from 20 percent in 1959 to 45 percent in 1985.

Poverty has become increasingly feminized, in part because female-headed households have become more common in the population as a whole. In 1960 only 1 family in 14 was headed by a female; by 1985, 1 family in 5 was. Female-headed households are more vulnerable to poverty because they typically have fewer potential wage earners than do households headed by males, and the one adult in the household has child-care responsibilities.

Poverty and Race

Next, let's consider poverty based on race. Exhibit 8 presents the differences over time between white and black poverty rates.[2] For both groups there was a sharp decline from 1959 to 1969, a relatively flat rate between 1969 and 1979, and an increase by 1985. Even more striking, of course, is the difference in poverty rates between the two groups. Despite movements in the levels, the black poverty rate has remained nearly three times the white poverty rate. About 3 of 10 blacks were poor in 1985 compared to about 1 in 10 whites. For blacks the poverty rate was slightly lower in 1985 than in 1969; for whites the rate was higher in 1985.

EXHIBIT 8
POVERTY BY RACE,
1959–1985
(Millions of Poor and the Poverty Rate in Parentheses)

Race of Family	Year			
	1959	**1969**	**1979**	**1985**
Black	9.9 (55.1%)	7.1 (32.2%)	8.1 (31.0%)	8.9 (31.3%)
White	28.5 (18.1%)	16.7 (9.5%)	17.2 (9.0%)	22.9 (11.4%)

Source: U.S. Bureau of the Census, *Current Population Reports*, series P-60, no. 137 (Washington, D.C.: U.S. Government Printing Office, 1986).

We have looked at poverty by race and by the gender of the household head. In Exhibit 9 we break out the separate effects of race and gender on the poverty rate since 1959. For each group the poverty rate, presented in parentheses, declined between 1959 and 1979. The rate remained about the same for black families between 1979 and 1985 but increased among white families during that period.

Among white families in 1959 there were about five times as many poor people in male-headed families as there were in female-headed families. By 1985, however, there were fewer than twice as many poor in male-headed families as in female-headed families. Among black families in 1959 there were nearly three times as many poor people in male-headed families as in female-headed families. Between 1959 and 1985, however, the number of poor in female-headed families more than doubled, while the number of poor in male-headed families dropped by two-thirds. As a result, by 1985 there were more than twice as many poor blacks in female-headed families as in male-headed families.

---

[2]The experience of other ethnic and racial groups would be of interest as well, but census data over the full period are available only for whites and blacks. Only in recent years have figures for persons of Hispanic origin been collected.

EXHIBIT 9
POVERTY IN FAMILIES BY GENDER
AND RACE, 1959–1985
(Millions of Poor and the Poverty Rate in Parentheses)

Race and Gender	Year			
	1959	**1969**	**1979**	**1985**
Black female-headed households	2.4 (70.6%)	3.2 (58.2%)	4.8 (53.1%)	5.3 (53.2%)
Black male-headed households	6.7 (50.9%)	3.0 (20.6%)	2.0 (14.6%)	2.2 (14.8%)
White female-headed households	4.2 (40.2%)	3.6 (29.1%)	4.4 (25.2%)	6.0 (29.8%)
White male-headed households	20.2 (14.7%)	9.0 (6.0%)	8.1 (5.4%)	11.1 (7.3%)

Source: U.S. Bureau of the Census, *Current Population Reports*, series P-60, no. 137 (Washington, D.C.: U.S. Government Printing Office, 1986).

Among both black and white families poverty has become feminized, but the change has been more dramatic among black families. In 1985, 35 percent of poor whites and 71 percent of poor blacks were in families headed by females.

Conclusions

We have just plowed through a pile of data examining the course of poverty since 1959. The overall poverty rate declined among all groupings of age, gender, and race between 1959 and 1969, probably because of the strong growth in the economy during the 1960s. During the decade of the 1970s the economy was flat, and despite the growth in outlays for income assistance, reductions in the poverty rate were modest. The number of female-headed households grew sharply during the 1970s, and since these households tend to be poorer than male-headed households, the number of poor in female-headed households increased. Between 1979 and 1985 poverty rates have remained constant among black families but have increased among whites, perhaps because there has been little real growth in the median family income or in income-assistance programs.

The high poverty rate in female-headed households and in black households raises the question of whether this higher poverty rate arises from discrimination in the job market or in the availability of transfers. Poverty in female-headed households is greater in part because the mother is the only potential breadwinner in these households, but she often has child-care responsibilities that limit her employment opportunities. In an earlier chapter we considered discrimination against women and examined the issue of comparable worth. In the next section we consider discrimination against blacks.

POVERTY AND DISCRIMINATION

We have seen that poverty rates among blacks are about three times higher than among whites. Family income comes from two primary sources: resource earnings—typically labor—and transfer income. The question we ask is this: Is the lower family income and greater incidence of poverty among blacks the result of discrimination in job markets or discrimination in the availability of transfer programs or are there other explanations?

We should note that discrimination can occur in many ways: in school admissions, in school funding, in housing, in employment, in career advancement. Also, discrimination in one area can affect opportunities in another. For example, housing discrimination may reduce job opportunities because the black family cannot move within commuting distance of the best employers.

The legacy of discrimination can affect career choices long after discrimination has ceased. A black man whose father and grandfather found job avenues blocked may be less inclined to pursue an education or to accept a job that requires a long training program. Thus, discrimination is a complex topic and one we cannot do justice to in this brief section.

Discrimination in the Job Market

Job market discrimination can take many forms. An employer may not hire a black job applicant because the applicant lacks training, but this lack of training may arise from discrimination in the schools, in union apprenticeship programs, or in training programs run by employers. Job market discrimination can occur not only in the hiring decision but also in the amount of training the employer provides for the worker. For example, evidence suggests that black workers receive less on-the-job training than otherwise similar white workers.

We first consider the ratio of nonwhite to white earnings for full-time workers. In 1939 nonwhite workers earned less than half of what white workers earned. The earnings gap based on race has been reduced, especially since 1965. By 1980, among full-time workers, nonwhite males earned 71 percent of what white males earned, and nonwhite females earned 95 percent of what white females earned. Such data are very crude, of course, since they fail to account for differences in education, job experience, or other characteristics that can affect productivity and pay.

What happens when we adjust for education? Exhibit 10 compares median family incomes between blacks and whites. For each group, family income increases with education as expected, but at each level of education the income of whites is about one-third higher than the income of blacks. Exhibit 10 does not control for other factors that affect family income, however, such as the number of earners in the household or their job experience. For example, the lower family income among blacks may be reflecting the fact that a larger percentage of black households are headed by a female and thus tend to have one fewer wage earner.

EXHIBIT 10
MEDIAN MONEY INCOME OF FAMILIES
BY EDUCATION AND RACE, 1984

Education	Race	
	Black	White
Elementary school		
Less than 8 years	$11,321	$14,501
8 years	12,164	17,002
High School		
1–3 years	14,041	19,894
4 years	18,427	26,541
College		
1–3 years	21,700	30,215
4 years	29,373	40,531
5 or more years	35,643	47,486

Source: U.S. Bureau of the Census, *Current Population Reports*, series P-60, no. 142 (Washington, D.C.: U.S. Government Printing Office, 1986).

We attempt to adjust for more variables in Exhibit 11, which presents the ratio of standardized hourly wage rates for white and black males. These data not only account for education and age but also adjust for marital status, geographic location, veteran status, and the probability of employment in the public sector. The idea was to adjust for those factors that could contribute to the worker's productivity. Among workers who only finished high school, the results indicate that blacks earned less than otherwise identical whites at all age levels. Among recent college graduates, however, blacks earned more than whites. Only for workers 42 years and older did blacks earn markedly less than whites. Thus, there may be job discrimination

EXHIBIT 11
THE RATIO OF BLACK TO WHITE WAGE
RATES FOR MALES AS OF 1980

Age	Years of Schooling	
	12	16
22	0.90	1.18
27	0.83	1.10
32	0.84	0.99
37	0.94	0.98
42	0.90	0.94
47	0.86	0.89
52	0.82	0.86

Source: Computed based on data reported in Daniel S. Hamermesh and Albert Rees, *The Economics of Work and Pay*, 3d ed. (New York: Harper & Row, 1984), Table 13.3, 319.

against older and less educated blacks, but there is no evidence of discrimination against blacks who have graduated from college since 1970.

Could other explanations besides discrimination account for the differentials found in Exhibit 11? Even though the data adjust for the *years* of schooling, some research suggests that black workers received a lower *quality* of schooling than white workers.[3] This quality difference could account for at least a portion of the remaining difference in standardized wages, particularly among those with only a high school education. But we hasten to add that if blacks receive a poorer quality of education, this may reflect discrimination in the funding of schools.

Finally, even though Exhibit 11 accounts for the age of workers, there is evidence that black and white workers of the same age have not acquired the same amount of job experience. Black males who worked full-time in 1980 were less likely than white workers to have worked full-time their entire working lives. This implies that for any given age group, black workers are likely to have less job experience than white workers, and, again, this difference in experience could account for some of the difference in wages between the two groups. Differences in job experience, however, may reflect past discrimination in hiring or a greater reluctance of employers to provide training programs for black workers.

Affirmative Action

The Equal Employment Opportunity Commission, established by the Civil Rights Act of 1964, monitors cases involving unequal pay for equal work and unequal access to promotion. Executive Order 11246, signed by President Lyndon Johnson, required all companies doing business with the federal government to set numerical hiring, promotion, and training goals. The objective was to ensure that these firms did not discriminate in hiring on the basis of race, sex, religion, or national origin. Today that executive order governs employment practices in 73,000 firms employing nearly 35 million workers. At the state level as well greater attention has been focused on hiring practices and equality of opportunity.

The federal focus on employment practices appears to have improved employment opportunities for blacks. One study, for example, found that black male employment increased sharply in those firms required to file affirmative action plans.[4] Black participation in white-collar jobs increased from 16.5 percent in 1960 to 40.5 percent in 1981 (though it remains unclear how much credit affirmative action deserves for this increase.)

---

[3]See Finis Welch, "Black-White Differences in Returns to Schooling," *American Economic Review* 63 (September 1973): 893–907.

[4]James Heckman and Kenneth Wolpin, "Does the Contract Compliance Program Work?" *Industrial and Labor Relations Review* 29 (1976): 544–564.

Discrimination in Transfer Programs?

Market-related earnings represent only one source of income; the other major source is government transfers. Is the lower family income and the higher incidence of poverty among blacks linked to an unequal treatment of blacks in the transfer system? For whatever reason, are blacks more likely than whites to fall through the safety net provided by social service programs? For example, blacks living in rural areas of the South must often travel to the county seat to apply for welfare; does this affect their participation rate?

Exhibit 12 presents by race the percent of families and unrelated individuals reached by federal cash transfers. There is also a separate breakdown for those below the poverty line. No matter which group is examined, there is no evidence that blacks participate any less than whites in the transfer system.

EXHIBIT 12
PERCENTAGE OF FAMILIES AND
UNRELATED INDIVIDUALS WHO
RECEIVED CASH TRANSFERS
IN 1982

	Families		Unrelated Individuals	
	Black	White	Black	White
All income levels	56.0%	42.5%	45.5%	43.9%
Below the poverty level	75.3	57.5	63.5	53.5

Source: U.S. Bureau of the Census, *Statistical Abstract of the United States* (Washington, D.C.: U.S. Government Printing Office, 1984), Table No. 766, 459.

In summary, evidence presented in this section suggests that older black men and less-educated black men appear to earn less for comparable jobs than do whites. To the extent that blacks earn less than whites, part of this difference may reflect differences in the quality of education and differences in job experience. But differences in the quality of education and in job experience could themselves be the product of past discrimination. With regard to the availability of government transfers, there is no evidence that blacks have less access to transfer programs. We should note that black families are not a homogeneous group. In fact, the distribution of income among black families is more uneven than among the population as a whole.

SOME UNINTENDED CONSEQUENCES OF INCOME ASSISTANCE

On the plus side, antipoverty programs increase the consumption possibilities of poor families, and this is good, especially since children are the largest poverty group. There may be arguments about the level of assistance because the benefits are not great enough to move the family above the poverty line, but most poor families receive assistance. In addition, few families received unnecessary aid. But programs to assist the poor may have secondary effects that limit their ability to reduce poverty. In the next section we consider some secondary effects.

Work Disincentives

Society tries to provide families with an adequate standard of living but also wants to ensure that only the most needy receive benefits. This results in a system that reduces benefits sharply as earned income increases. Efforts to reduce benefits as earned income increases in effect impose a high marginal tax rate on that earned income. This high marginal tax rate could discourage employment and self-sufficiency.

As we have seen, income assistance consists of a bundle of cash and in-kind programs. Because these programs are designed to help the poor and only the poor, the level of benefits is inversely related to income from other sources. For example, a family of four with no earned income received $240 per month in food stamps in 1986. Food stamp benefits were reduced by $30 per month for each $100 of outside income. Thus, the marginal tax rate on earned income (as reflected by the reductions in benefits) was 30 percent under this program. This tax rate alone appears reasonable, particularly since the program is for the poor. But since most welfare programs are linked to earned income, any increase in earnings will cause a decline in benefits received from food stamps, AFDC, housing allowance, Medicaid, energy assistance, and other programs.

With a bite taken from each program as earned income increases, working may result in little or no increase in total income. In fact, over certain income ranges the welfare recipient may lose well over $1 in benefits for each $1 in earnings. Thus, the marginal tax rate can exceed 100 percent! When you consider that holding even a part-time job involves additional expenses, such as transportation and child care, such a system of incentives can frustrate those who would like to work their way off welfare.

Until 1981 the marginal tax rate in the AFDC program was 67 percent— that is, benefits were reduced by $0.67 for every extra dollar earned by the family on AFDC. In 1981 the marginal tax rate was increased to 100 percent, meaning that benefits are reduced by $1 for each extra $1 earned. Just how much the higher marginal tax rates reduce the incentive to work remains unclear. We do know that only about 1 of every 20 of those receiving AFDC is employed. Twice as many welfare recipients worked in the mid-1970s.

What if the high marginal tax rates discourage recipients from working? The longer people are out of the labor force, the more their job skills deteriorate, so when they do seek employment, their marginal product and their pay is lower than when they were last employed. This lowers their expected wage and makes work less attractive. Some economists argue that in this way welfare benefits can lead to long-term dependency. We consider that possibility next.

Does Welfare Cause Dependency?

Does the system of incentives created by high marginal tax rates create a dependency among welfare recipients? How could we examine such a question? High turnover among welfare recipients would be evidence of little dependency. If, however, the same families are poor year after year, this would be a matter of concern.

To explore the possibility of welfare dependency in the United States, a recent University of Michigan study tracked 5000 families over a number of years, paying particular attention to economic mobility both from year to year and from one generation to the next.[5] The study found that there were two major groups of welfare recipients: one group had a constantly changing membership from year to year, and the other group would be on welfare for at least eight years. Thus, for most recipients welfare was of short duration, but there were some long-term recipients. Despite a core of long-term recipients, there is no evidence that welfare encourages young women to have children.

The first question involved poverty from year to year, or dependency within a generation. A second and more serious concern is, Do the children of the poor end up in poverty as well? Is there a cycle of poverty? To answer this question the Michigan study examined the relationship between the income of one generation and that of the next generation. The results indicate that only a minority of those who grew up in heavily welfare dependent homes become heavily dependent on welfare. For white women there was a modest link between the welfare dependence of parent and child. For black women there was no link.

Another way to look at the cycle-of-poverty question more generally is to examine how much mobility there is in the income distribution from one generation to the next. Parents were divided into five equal groups based on income. Their grown children were also placed in five groups according to income to see if the children of poor parents also tended to be poor. Exhibit 13

EXHIBIT 13
INTERGENERATIONAL MOBILITY

Parents	Young Adults Forming Households				
	Poorest Fifth	Second Fifth	Middle Fifth	Fourth Fifth	Highest Fifth
Poorest fifth	44%	27%	18%	9%	2%
Second fifth	23	24	19	19	15
Middle fifth	11	23	23	26	17
Fourth fifth	10	17	22	26	25
Highest fifth	9	13	19	23	36

Source: Computed based on Greg J. Duncan, Richard D. Coe, and others, *Years of Poverty, Years of Plenty* (Ann Arbor, Mich.: University of Michigan Press, 1984).

[5]Greg. J. Duncan, Richard D. Coe, and others, *Years of Poverty, Years of Plenty,* University of Michigan, 1984.

presents the mobility between generations for the sample tracked by the University of Michigan study. Parents are ranked from poorest to richest into five groups, indicated down the left-hand column; children are ranked based on their income from poorest to richest into five groups across the top.

Before addressing the numbers, we might reflect on how much mobility would be considered desirable? Perhaps we would like to see the children of all income groups have an equal opportunity of joining the highest group, which would also mean that the children of the rich would be just as likely to end up poor as rich.

To give you an idea of how to interpret the table, the first row indicates how the children of the poorest parents were distributed among the succeeding generation, based on income. For example, 44 percent of the children of the poorest parents were themselves among the poorest fifth of their generation; 27 percent moved up to the next highest fifth, 18 percent jumped to the middle fifth, and so on. In contrast, among children of the wealthiest parents, only 9 percent found themselves among the poorest fifth, 13 percent in the next poorest, and so on. While having poor parents does not doom you to being poor, your chances were nearly 5 times more likely of being in the bottom group if your parents were in the poorest group than if your parents were in the wealthiest group. Conversely, your chances of ending up in the wealthiest group are 18 times greater if your parents were in that group than if they came from the poorest group.

Poverty and Public Choice

In a democratic country such as ours, public policies depend very much on the political power of the interest groups represented. In recent years the elderly have become a strong political force. Unlike most interest groups, the elderly are a group we all expect to join one day. The elderly are actually represented by four constituencies: (1) the elderly themselves, (2) those under 65 who are concerned about the benefits to their parents or other elderly relatives, (3) those under 65 who are concerned about their own benefits in the future, and (4) those, such as doctors and nursing home operators, who earn their living by caring for the elderly.

Moreover, the voter participation rate of those 65 and over tends to be higher than that of other age groups. Specifically, those between 65 and 74 vote at more than twice the rate of those under 34. The political muscle of the elderly has been flexed whenever a question of Social Security benefits comes up. In 1985, for example, at a time when Congress was seeking ways to address a $200 billion federal deficit, a proposal to delay the cost-of-living increase in Social Security benefits was defeated, with much posturing about how the country could not solve the deficit at the expense of the elderly. Yet as we have seen, the poverty rate among the elderly is now lower than that of any other group, including households headed by white males. Congress had less difficulty trimming programs specifically targeted at low-income people.

We close this section by considering a group with perhaps the most urgent needs of any group yet with little political power—the homeless.

Some appear to be in touch with a distant galaxy. They are the bag ladies, the derelicts, the street people wandering our cities. Just how many there are is unclear. One government estimate puts the number between 250,000 and 350,000; other estimates exceed a million.

Many homeless people appear to have serious mental problems. Most studies report that between one-fifth and one-third of the homeless are deinstitutionalized mental patients. In the mid-1950s the development of drugs that were effective in treating mental illness led the nation's mental hospitals to begin releasing patients on a large scale. In theory, the miracle drugs would follow these patients into society, helping them lead productive lives. In the last 30 years the population of state mental institutions dropped from 560,000 to 125,000.

It seemed like a good idea at the time, but now most experts believe that the plan has failed. Some former patients survived the transition, but many ended up homeless and on the street. Fewer than one-fourth of those discharged are in any kind of mental health program. Moreover, most of the homeless who are mentally ill are young, but because of deinstitutionalization, they have never been hospitalized. The median age of the homeless in a Boston study was 34.

Since most street people have no permanent address, they have problems registering for the few welfare programs for which they qualify. It is difficult for someone who may call a dumpster home to receive public assistance. The homeless have lost track of their families, so they must depend on the kindness of strangers. There is episodic support, most of it in-kind from shelters, soup kitchens, and emergency rooms, but coverage varies widely across regions. Massachusetts has developed an ambitious program to provide shelters for the homeless and now has more than a dozen community shelters. Arizona, on the other hand, discourages support for people they feel are attracted to the state because of the warmer climate.

Surprisingly, about 20 percent of the nation's homeless consist of families, many of whom stay in temporary shelters. A Massachusetts survey indicates that homeless families consist mainly of young, single women with two or three children who were receiving AFDC and had received it longer than other welfare families. The problem of the homeless suggests that there is a major tear in the social service safety net.

Sources: Ellen L. Bassuk, "The Homeless Problem," *Scientific American*, 251 (July 1984): 42; Ellen L. Bassuk, "Mental Health Needs of Homeless Persons," *The Harvard Medical School Mental Health Letter*, 3, no. 7 (January 1987): 4–6; "Fighting Back," *Newsweek* (2 January 1984): 47.

WELFARE REFORM

There is much dissatisfaction with the current welfare system, both from those who pay for the programs and from those who receive the benefits. A variety of welfare reforms have been suggested in recent years. The most drastic suggestion has been to dismantle many of our existing transfer programs, leaving the care of the poor to local governments and to private charity. Another suggestion is to centralize benefits at the federal level to ensure greater uniformity in eligibility and more equality across states in the level of support. Specific reforms have already been implemented by some states. One possible reform, the so-called negative income tax, has been subject to a massive social experiment. In this section we consider measures implemented by the states and review the results from the negative income tax experiment.

State Reforms

One advantage of a federal system of government is that it allows for innovation and experimentation by the states. Two measures that have been adopted by some states are programs to encourage those on welfare to work and efforts to collect child support from absent fathers.

Workfare   Few women on welfare hold jobs. One approach to reducing poverty has been to provide job skills for welfare recipients and to find jobs for those who are able to work. As a condition of receiving AFDC, the head of the household must agree to search for work, participate in education and training programs, or take some form of paid or unpaid position. The idea is to acquaint those on welfare with the job market so they need not depend on welfare. Over 35 states have now introduced some sort of "workfare" component for welfare recipients. Evidence from these programs suggests that mandatory job search, short-term unpaid work, and training programs can be operated at low cost and can affect employment.

Child Support from Absent Fathers   Another possibility is to have mothers collect child support from absent fathers. This has met with some success in Wisconsin. In 1975 Congress passed the Child Support Enforcement Program, which requires each state to develop a system to establish paternity, locate absent fathers, and enforce child support obligations. One problem is that half of the children receiving AFDC had parents who were not married, and in many cases the whereabouts of the father is unknown. Also, since AFDC aid is reduced dollar for dollar by child support payments, the mother has no economic incentive to identify the father for support.

One suggestion that has received serious consideration over the last 20 years is the negative income tax. We will now examine that alternative more closely.

*The **negative income tax** is a cash transfer program in which benefits are reduced as earnings rise.*

Negative Income Tax

A **negative income tax** (NIT) gives cash transfers to poor families, providing them with a guaranteed minimum income and allowing them to keep a portion of any earnings. It is called a negative income tax because the cash transfer is reduced as the family's earnings rise. Let's see how an NIT works.

Suppose that the program guarantees a family of four at least $8000 regardless of the family's earnings. If the family has no earnings, it will receive $8000 in transfers. The cash transfer falls as the family's earned income increases; the amount by which transfers are reduced depends on the negative income tax rate. For example, if the negative income tax rate is 40 percent, transfers will be cut by $0.40 for each $1 in income the family earns. If the family earns $6000, its $8000 cash transfer will be reduced by $6000 × 0.40, or $2400. Thus, the family's total income will be $6000 in earnings plus $5600 in transfers, for a total of $11,600.

As the family's earned income increases, the tax rate (or benefit reduction rate) on these earnings will reduce the family's net cash transfer. If the family earns $20,000, its negative income tax of $8000 would reduce the transfer to zero. Such a family would be at the *break-even point*, where the tax and subsidy cancel out. Thus, we can specify three components to the negative income tax: the guaranteed minimum, G, the negative tax rate, r, and the break-even point, B. They are related as follows: $B = G/r$. If you know the value of any two variables, you can solve for the third.

In structuring the negative income tax, providing a higher guaranteed minimum and providing incentives to earn are expensive. A higher guaranteed minimum ensures that a family's living standard will not fall below a certain level, but providing all families with such a level is costly. Also, allowing the family to keep a fraction of their earnings provides incentives to work, but it means that families will continue to receive transfers even after their income exceeds what is viewed as the basic minimum.

The NIT is aimed at poor people, not at members of some favored group, such as farmers or the elderly. The NIT could be substituted for a variety of specific programs now in effect. In fact, existing programs are variants of an NIT. Transfers under an NIT are made in cash, the form most valued by the recipients. Like other transfer programs, the NIT might reduce work incentives, but it does not eliminate these incentives altogether. As long as the tax rate is less than 100 percent, an extra dollar earned always means more income. Administrative costs of existing programs could be reduced because the NIT could fit into the existing tax system rather than requiring its own bureaucracy.

Experts in the Office of Economic Opportunity, the agency set up in the 1960s to fight the war on poverty, believed that some sort of NIT was the best solution to the problem of poverty. One shortcoming with such a program that critics raised was the question of incentives. Some argued that providing people with a guaranteed income would reduce their incentives to work. The Office of Economic Opportunity set up an extensive economic experiment to explore the issue. The experiment began in 1968 and lasted 10 years, eventually involving 8700 people. The intent was to observe the effects of providing a guaranteed minimum income on work incentives and on family stability.

The test ran for different intervals in different parts of the country. The most extensive experiments ran from 1971 to 1978 in Seattle and Denver. The important question for the researchers was whether the guaranteed minimum reduced work effort. The results suggest that it did. In the Seattle and Denver experiments the desired hours of work fell on average by 9 percent for husbands and by 20 percent for wives. The greatest effect appeared to be among young males not yet heading households, who reduced their work effort by 43 percent. This latter outcome is troubling because young males are considered most in need of developing the work skills and job discipline required to establish themselves in the work force.

Another concern of the experiment was the effect of the NIT on the stability of the family. There is some evidence that a guaranteed income had a destablilizing effect on the family. In the Seattle–Denver experiments, families in the experimental group broke up at a rate that was about 40 percent higher than those in the control group (that is, those who received no special treatment). The results concerning work effort and family stability have been given varying interpretations by different researchers, but the net result has been to drain some of the enthusiasm for a negative income tax as a solution to the problem of poverty.

CONCLUSIONS

In 1987 Congress began deliberating an overhauling of the core welfare program, AFDC. Senator Daniel Patrick Moynihan, chairman of the Finance Committee's Subcommittee on Social Security and Family Policy, outlined three guidelines for developing a new system. First, the primary responsibility of child support rests with the child's parents. Second, the able-bodied mother of a child also has the responsibility to support her child by working, at least part-time. And third, the government should provide time-limited child support to the extent that parental support is inadequate.[6] In Moynihan's view, therefore, public assistance should be viewed as a short-term supplement to family income.

Absent fathers create special pressures on home economics. In 1960 only 5.3 percent of all births were to unmarried mothers; by 1980 this rate had climbed to 18.4 percent. Since the father in such cases typically assumes little financial responsibility for the support of the child, the rate at which children are born outside marriage has a very real impact on the resources available to the child.

Because of the rising divorce rate, even those children born in marriage face a higher prospect of living in a one-parent household before they grow up. Divorce usually reduces the resources available for the children. Thus, the rising instability of the family, both because of the increasing percentage of births to unmarried women and the rising divorce rate, means that the family has fewer resources available to care for its children.

---

[6]Maureen Dowd, "Moynihan Opens Major Drive to Replace Welfare Program," *The New York Times,* 24 January 1987.

Most of the income transfer that takes place in society occurs within the family, from parents to children. The traditional father-mother family is the chief source of support for most children. Consequently, any change in a family's capacity to earn income has serious consequences for dependent children. Children have been the innocent victims of the changing family structure. One fifth of children in America live in poverty—13 million in all. Any reform of the welfare system must be sensitive to the needs of children and to the effect that any reform could have on the family structure.

SUMMARY

1. Money income in the United States became more evenly distributed across households between 1929 and 1947, but this distribution has changed little since 1947. The Lorenz curve pictures the distribution of income by showing the percentage of total income received by any given percentage of recipients when families are arrayed by incomes from the poorest to the richest.

2. The Census Bureau estimates the poverty level each year, using the cost of food as the basic building block. During the 1960s the economy boomed, and poverty fell. Between 1969 and 1979 poverty fluctuated but showed no substantial decline. Since 1979 the poverty rate has drifted up.

3. Since 1959 poverty rates have dropped the most among the elderly and among families headed by black males. Households where the head was under 25 were the only group to experience an increase in the poverty rate since 1959. A major contributor to poverty was the increase in female-headed households.

4. Black men who are older and who have a high school rather than a college education appear to earn less for comparable jobs than do white men. Affirmative action provisions appear to have increased employment opportunities among blacks. There is no evidence that blacks have less access to transfer programs.

5. Among unintended effects of income assistance is a high marginal tax rate on earned income. This high tax rate is said to discourage employment and may create welfare dependency. While some families may depend on welfare for long periods, there is little evidence of a cycle of poverty from one generation to the next.

6. Several measures are under consideration to reform the existing welfare system. Some reforms have already been implemented by the states, such as efforts to provide job training and job placement for mothers on welfare and efforts to force absent fathers to support their children. One of the largest social experiments in history examined the effects of a negative income tax. The results suggest that simply providing families with cash transfers could affect the incentives to work.

QUESTIONS AND PROBLEMS

1. (Depressions and the Rich) The only people who benefit from a depression are the rich, who can adequately protect themselves. Evaluate this statement in light of Exhibit 1 in the chapter.

2. (Lorenz Curve) Construct a Lorenz curve using the following hypothetical income data for a country with only 5 households: H1, $10,000; H2, $4000; H3, $3000; H4, $2000; H5, $1000.

3. (Poverty in America) Consider Exhibit 4 in the chapter. How would you explain the fall in the percentage of population below the

official poverty level? Why did the percentage rise after 1980? Are these statistics deceptive?

4. (Poverty in America) Should the U.S. government attempt to completely eliminate poverty in America? Why or why not?

5. (Economic Growth and Poverty) Economic growth is more effective than welfare programs in reducing poverty in the United States. Evaluate this statement.

6. (Poverty and Age) Why has poverty been rising dramatically for younger households and falling dramatically for elderly households?

7. (Poverty and Gender) Why are female-headed households more vulnerable to poverty than male-headed households are?

8. (Discrimination and Earnings) What types of discrimination can drive a wedge between what whites earn and what nonwhites earn? Consider discrimination in schooling, for example. How could you detect such discrimination?

9. (Welfare and the Underground Economy) How might the implicit tax on earned income due to the loss of benefits from the government assistance programs affect the underground economy? Is it possible for some people to avoid the implicit tax? How?

10. (Negative Income Tax) What are some reasons why the experiment on the negative income tax, as discussed in the chapter, led to a reduction in work effort? How could adjustments be made to reduce this loss of incentives?

PART
FIVE

An Inside Look at Economic Institutions

INSIDE the HOUSEHOLD

Nearly everything about the family is changing, and changing fast. In 1950 only one woman in eight with children under six years of age was in the labor force; today more than half are. Since 1960 the birth rate has fallen by nearly half, and the divorce rate has doubled. The post–World War II baby boom has given way to a baby bust, sending ripples through the schools, the housing market, and the job market.

These and other developments in the family that affect the way we live and the quality of our lives will be examined in this chapter, using the tools of economic analysis. Economics does not have all the answers to questions about the changing role of the family, but it does provide some special insights into these important events. Topics and terms discussed include:

- Economics of marriage
- Allocating time between market work and household work
- Economics of children
- Women in the labor force
- Demography

INTRODUCTION

Not many years ago the economic study of the household stopped at the front door. The household was viewed as a single decision unit using its limited resources to maximize utility. Decisions about marriage, divorce, children and the like were viewed as internal family matters, perhaps better left to the sociologist or the theologian. Then a small group of economists began applying the tools of their trade to family decisions, and the fruitfulness of the economic approach became apparent. Their belief was that if economics has validity, its theories should apply not only to market decisions but also to decisions involving the market less directly, such as family choices. After all, decisions in both the market and the household involve choice in the face of scarcity. In fact, the original meaning of the word *economic* relates to household management.

You should be warned, however, that some people still have reservations about stepping through the front door to examine the economics of the household. Some of you no doubt will find it strange or perhaps even somewhat offensive to examine issues such as the economics of marriage and the demand for children. How could such special events in one's life be compared to buying a new car or a new home, you might ask? Perhaps the following case study, a look at the demand for a family pet, can serve as an appropriate bridge to more serious matters.

---

*CASE
STUDY*

**The
Family's
Best
Friend?**

Do you think economic criteria are relevant in the decisions about the family dog? Consider the dilemma pet owners in New York faced in 1979 when the city passed a dog-litter law requiring owners to clean up after their pets. People had to follow their pets around the city's sidewalks with scoopers and plastic bags or whatever else would do the job. The law increased the cost of owning a dog because that cost now included what had been a negative externality imposed by dog owners on the rest of society. This externality is an unpriced by-product of pet ownership that reduces the utility of those using the city's streets and sidewalks. Because the cost of owning a dog increased, we should expect a decline in the quantity of dogs demanded as pets.

The new law appeared to have curbed the willingness to own a dog in New York City. After the law went into effect, the number of dogs turned in to the New York chapter of the American Society for the Prevention of Cruelty to Animals (ASPCA) doubled. Many other dogs were simply abandoned by their owners, raising the number of strays in the city to over 400,000 in late 1979, according to ASPCA estimates. Dog owners were behaving in a way that could have been predicted by economic theory.

Source: "Department of Unintended Consequences," *Policy Analysis* (Winter 1979).

When we think of the family, the nuclear group of Mom, Dad, and the kids comes to mind, but this is by no means a long-standing or universal model. Old Testament figures, such as Abraham, Isaac, and Jacob, were nomadic chieftains with several wives and concubines. In Roman times the husband was limited to one wife, but the household was more an extended family in which the father, or patriarch, had absolute power—power even to kill his own sons. The sons would marry and live in the father's home as long as the father was alive. Patriarchy in a less dominant form continued during the Middle Ages. European peasants up to the modern era followed many of the cultural dictates established during Roman times.

In some parts of the world today the central unit is not the nuclear family but rather the extended family, clan, or tribe. This chapter will focus primarily on the economics of the modern family, but comparisons will be made with the more traditional family. We begin with a discussion of the central relationship in the family—marriage.

THE ECONOMICS OF MARRIAGE

Marriage is an ancient institution serving many objectives, only some of which relate directly to economics as narrowly defined. Yet all these objectives relate to the central goal of maximizing utility. Payments such as dowries are sometimes associated with a marriage, but the exchange of marriage vows is more often a barter agreement, where each partner agrees to "love, honor, and serve" the other. Although the terms of the marriage contract are usually vague, this barter agreement nonetheless has the force of law. This section takes a closer look at marriage as an economic institution. We will analyze the marriage market by considering you as a participant in this market. We realize that many people are not necessarily looking for a marriage partner, at least not yet. Since only about 1 person in 20 never marries, however, the discussion of the marriage market is likely to apply to you some day.

The Marriage Market

The marriage market is characterized by much uncertainty on both sides. You, as a supplier, are unsure of just exactly how you are perceived by the opposite sex. Thus, you are uncertain about who from the pool of eligible candidates might be interested in you. You are both a supplier and a demander, but you do not know for certain the perceived quality of the product you offer (that is, yourself) or the quality of others in the market. Because marriage is such an important step and because the penalties of a bad choice can be great, however, you have a strong interest in exploring this market and are willing to spend time and money trying to gather useful information.

The marriage relationship is characterized by the couple's joint sharing of a variety of goods and activities, such as a home, mutual affection, children, friends, leisure activities, furniture, meals, even toothpaste. Because of this joint consumption, it is more efficient to marry someone with similar tastes and preferences. The less a couple has in common, the more difficult it will be to find goods and activities that are mutually satisfying.

For example, meal preparation will take more time if you have quite different tastes in food. If you enjoy movies but your spouse loves professional wrestling, spending your leisure time together will be less fun than if you both are interested in the same activities. If you want two children and would like them to grow up to be doctors but your spouse wants eight and would like them all to join the circus, you know the marriage will face some problems. In short, whether we are talking about the consumption of goods and services, spending leisure time with one another, or sharing common interests, the more compatible two people are, the lower the cost of this joint activity will be.

Gathering Information

In the identification of possible marriage partners, traits that are directly observable, such as appearance, tend to be weighted more heavily, at least initially. As a supplier, you are willing to devote resources to these obvious qualities. As a demander, if physical appearance is most important to you, you may start your search where such information is most easily provided and acquired, such as at the beach, pool, or health spa. If intelligence matters more to you, cultural activities may be the most appropriate source of contacts.

Some traits are difficult to evaluate, so a proxy is often employed as a signal. For example, potential earnings of a partner may be a consideration to some people, but this is not always easy to predict. Thus, the level of education achieved can be used as a signal of potential earnings.

More generally, when you seek a compatible marriage partner, you tend to go where you are most likely to find an individual with tastes like your own. For some of you, this might be the "right" college, an upscale singles apartment, or the "in" nightspot. For others, a Bruce Springsteen concert, a square dance, or a meeting of the local motorcycle gang may be more appropriate. Some of you may rely on blind dates, dating services, or even classified advertisements in the local tabloid, though many people feel uncomfortable leaving matters of the heart to such impersonal channels.

Once you have identified a prospect, you both spend time and money trying to get to know one another better. When you buy a new car, you may kick the tires and take it for a test drive. The process of dating is more subtle, but the intent is not so different. In the marriage market, as in the market for a new car, your bargaining position is weakened if you appear anxious or desperate. It is usually better to express little interest in marriage, at least during the early stages of a relationship. Eventually, however, the couple may begin to explore mutual compatibility on issues such as personal preferences, children, the division of household responsibilities, finances, and so on.

All of this social interaction is aimed at gathering the necessary information to identify a suitable marriage partner. Such prior knowledge becomes especially important because the legal responsibilities contained in the marriage contract are vague. The greater the cost of a poor decision—for example, the greater the economic, social, or religious stigma of divorce—the greater will be your willingness to devote resources to searching for the best possible mate.

Love and Marriage

What is love? The poets, philosophers, and psychologists all have their own definitions. For our purposes, love is defined as an abiding concern for the welfare of the other individual, even to the point of caring as much for the other's welfare as for one's own. As noted earlier, most marriage contracts are not well specified, leaving the door open for all kinds of behavior. Because of this lack of precision, one side could take advantage of the other. If there is little love in the marriage or if the love is one-sided, there is the very real possibility of selfish or opportunistic behavior. One partner could contribute little to the relationship or could even be psychologically or physically abusive.

Of course, there is always divorce as an escape, and this option will be examined later. Often the presence of small children or of other joint investments, however, may make the situation not quite bad enough for that solution. Since love has been defined here as a genuine concern for the other individual's welfare, opportunistic behavior is less likely to occur where there is love in the marriage. Therefore, love ensures that one partner does not take advantage of the other.

Love and Externalities   A loving relationship also means that externalities that arise in marriage will not create the inefficiencies typically associated with them in the market. Because of the close physical proximity of the couple in marriage, externalities are more likely to arise. Recall that externalities are unpriced by-products of production or consumption that affect another individual's utility.

For example, the cost to one individual of smoking a cigarette does not include the cost imposed on other people from residual smoke. Normally, externalities imply some social inefficiency because the private choice leads to too much activity involving negative externalities and too little activity involving positive externalities. If a couple is in love, however, then each will have more concern for the other's welfare, or utility. If your spouse is sensitive to cigarette smoke, you are less inclined to smoke when you two are together. Therefore, you are less likely to impose negative externalities on your spouse. Because positive externalities confer benefits on your spouse, you are more inclined to undertake such activities when you have a loving relationship. For example, you may shower more frequently. In short, you will be more thoughtful about the effects of your activities on the welfare of your spouse.

Love and Marriage in More Traditional Cultures   Certain cultures over time have viewed marriage in much more economic terms than is the case in most developed countries today. Love as we understand it has not always been a prerequisite. In earlier times and in many developing countries today, marriage was and is an important event in the welfare of the extended family.

The economy has been primarily agricultural in more traditional cultures. Life on the farm was fraught with uncertainty. The vagaries of weather and disease could sometimes kill a crop or wipe out a herd of cattle. When disaster struck, there was no insurance settlement, no government disaster loan, no unemployment compensation, and no welfare payments because in these societies insurance markets were not well developed and government's role was limited. Ties of the tribe, the clan, or the extended family formed a safety net for sharing difficulties during hard times. That is why bringing outsiders into the traditional family through marriage was such an important event.

Because partner selection has a very direct bearing on the economic and social status of the whole family, this selection was carefully arranged to ensure the economic viability of the family. In traditional cultures the welfare of the family is considered more important than the individual's welfare; thus, the personal preferences of the bride and groom are secondary to the priorities of the family.

In India, for example, some couples do not see one another until the day they are irrevocably married. In certain cultures the bride is promised while still a young child, or even before birth. In Western cultures these calculated arrangements seem devoid of emotion and love. Defenders of the arranged marriage argue, however, that because it is difficult to distinguish between lasting love and temporary infatuation, less weight should be given to love as a prerequisite for marriage.

Once the couple marries, they must make decisions about the division of labor in the household. We now turn to the time-allocation decision, but be forewarned that the presentation becomes less narrative and more analytical.

ALLOCATING TIME BETWEEN MARKET WORK AND HOUSEHOLD WORK

Once married, the couple lives together in one household and must decide on their division of labor between household work and market work. To begin our discussion, let's consider the marginal productivity of household work. Each spouse's marginal product of time spent in the household depends on a variety of factors, such as the skills of the individual, the size of the home, the family size, access to labor-saving technology such as vacuum cleaners and washing machines, and the amount of household work provided by the other spouse.

Household Work Versus Market Work

Let's assume for now that the other spouse devotes no time to household work. Holding everything else constant, consider what the marginal product of time spent per week on household work by one spouse would be. The first hour spent on household work is devoted to the most critical needs and is therefore the most productive. In an hour the individual could sweep the floor, load the washer, empty the trash, and do whatever other short tasks were most essential. The marginal product of that first hour is the dollar value the household attaches to having those tasks done.

With only one hour of household work, the family would not have time to cook, so they would either have to eat out or buy a bucket of chicken on the way home from work. If another hour is devoted to household work, there might be time to cook some frozen meals in the microwave oven. Each additional hour is spent doing tasks that are valued less and less by the family. For example, the eightieth hour of household work might involve ironing permanent-press sheets or arranging the canned goods according to size — activities that have a lower marginal value than those first undertaken.

The marginal value product curve for time spent in household work is depicted as downward sloping in Exhibit 1. This curve shows the relationship between time spent in the household and the dollar value the family attaches to the activities performed during that hour. The marginal value product curve is downward sloping, indicating that the dollar value of the services provided decreases as the time devoted to household tasks increases. Simply put, those tasks first undertaken are more critical to the household's performance and are therefore more highly valued by the family than subsequent tasks. Again, this curve is drawn assuming that the amount of household work provided by the other spouse is constant (and in this case equal to zero). If the time spent on household work by the other spouse increases, the marginal product curve depicted in Exhibit 1 would decrease, or shift to the left, because fewer household chores would need to be performed.

The Market Wage, Household Work, and Market Work

The question is, How much time will this spouse spend on household work and how much on market work? Before we proceed, recall that there is another use of time — leisure. Even though decisions about the time devoted to leisure are very much related to the decisions about household work and market work, suppose that L hours per week are devoted to leisure, leaving the balance to be allocated between household work and market work. Since there are 168 hours in a week and since L equals the time spent on leisure, then 168 minus L is the time this person spends working, either in the home or in the market.

The horizontal axis in Exhibit 1 indicates the total amount of time available per week for market work and household work. The total time available is N, which is 168 hours minus leisure time, L. How much of the total time will this individual devote to household work and how much to market work? That depends on the market wage. Suppose that the market wage is W, as indicated by the horizontal line drawn at the wage level W. This line indicates that the individual can supply any amount from zero to N and earn the market wage for each hour worked. The market wage is the opportunity cost of time spent on household work.[1]

This person will undertake household work as long as the marginal value product of time so spent exceeds the market wage. The optimal, or utility-

---

[1]The wage rate is also the opportunity cost of time spent on leisure. For simplicity, we have assumed that the amount of leisure time equals L, but L is in fact determined simultaneously with the decision about household work and leisure work.

EXHIBIT 1 **ALLOCATING TIME BETWEEN HOUSEHOLD AND MARKET WORK**

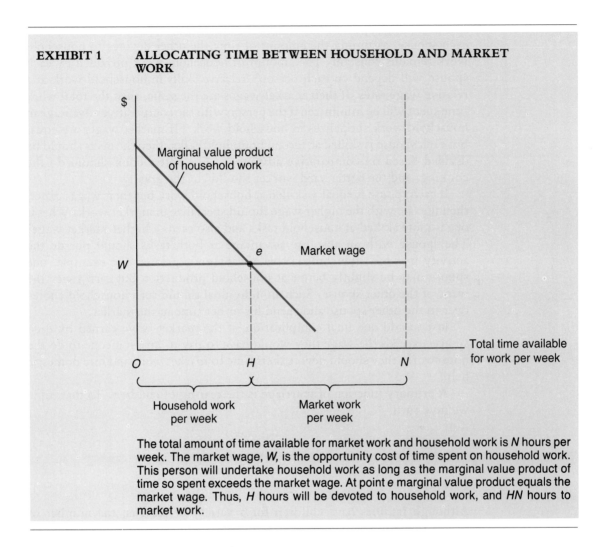

The total amount of time available for market work and household work is *N* hours per week. The market wage, *W,* is the opportunity cost of time spent on household work. This person will undertake household work as long as the marginal value product of time so spent exceeds the market wage. At point *e* marginal value product equals the market wage. Thus, *H* hours will be devoted to household work, and *HN* hours to market work.

maximizing, allocation of time occurs where the marginal value product of time spent on household work equals the market wage. This equilibrium occurs at point *e* in Exhibit 1, indicating that *H* hours will be spent in household work, and the balance of the time, *HN*, will be spent in market work.

If the market wage increases, the wage rate line will shift up, so at the new equilibrium allocation more time will be spent in market work. The opposite occurs if the market wage declines. If the amount of household work provided by the other spouse increases, this will reduce the marginal value product of time devoted to household work by the individual depicted in Exhibit 1, reducing the time that individual spends in household work and increasing the time spent in market work. Thus, any increase in the market wage or any decrease in the marginal value product of time spent in household work, other things equal, will reduce household work and increase market work.

Deciding Who Does What

The preceding approach can be used to analyze the time allocation decision of each spouse, assuming the amount of time the other devotes to household work remains constant. The amount of household work provided by each spouse will depend on each person's relative skills in household work and relative wage rates. If their market wages are the same, then the total work time spent will be minimized if the person with the comparative advantage in household work specializes in household work.[2] If market wages are equal but each spouse is skilled at certain household tasks, then the tasks should be divided based on comparative advantage. The better cook should do the cooking, and the better yard worker should cut the grass.

If each spouse is equally skilled at household work but their wages differ, then the one with the higher wage should specialize in market work. What if one is more skilled at household tasks and also earns a higher market wage? The spouse with an absolute advantage at both tasks should pursue the activity in which the comparative advantage is greater. For example, one spouse may be slightly better at household production but earn twice the wage of the other spouse. Such an individual should turn household chores over to the other spouse and spend his or her time in the market.

Just to add one final complication, if the market wage earned by each spouse exceeds the wage they would have to pay to hire someone to do the housework, they should devote their time to market work and hire domestic help.

A primary function of marriage is the rearing of children. To that topic we now turn.

THE ECONOMICS OF CHILDREN

Although families have children for a variety of reasons, the number of children a family has and the resources devoted to each child will depend on their expected costs and benefits. The household is both the supplier and the demander of children. An increase in the cost of rearing children or a decrease in the benefit will reduce the number of children the family has.

The Supply and Demand for Children

Children are reared by the household using market goods and services plus household work provided by family members. If children are like other goods, the quantity of children demanded will depend on their relative price and on household income. Because the opportunity cost of time differs

---

[2]For a review of comparative advantage, see Chapter 2.

**Gary S. Becker
(b. 1930)**

The University of Chicago

What is economics? In the nineteenth century the classical writers saw their subject as restricted to purely "economic" activities—to business, finance, material well-being. By the 1930s, however, economists had begun to see their task quite differently. Today economics deals not with a particular sphere of human activity but with a particular aspect of *all* human activity: the aspect that involves allocating scarce resources—whatever those resources are.

There is no better example of this transformation in economics than the work of Gary Becker. From racial discrimination to education to crime to the intimate decisions within the family, Becker has pioneered the application of economic perspectives to areas of human life previously considered "noneconomic." Largely thanks to him, economic ideas have now spread so widely into subjects once the domain of other disciplines that angry cries of "economic imperialism!" routinely reverberate from the walls of sociology, philosophy, history, and other university departments.

This entire chapter bears the stamp of Becker's thought. But to see his approach more clearly, consider another area he has written about: the economics of crime and punishment. Crime, Becker argues, is from the economist's point of view an occupation like any other. The decision to engage in criminal activity—as in any activity—will hinge on the costs and benefits involved. The higher the punishment if the criminal is caught—and the higher the probability of getting caught—the less criminal activity there will be, other things constant. Conversely, the more lucrative the criminal opportunities are relative to other opportunities (the lower the opportunity cost of engaging in crime), the more crime there will be, other things constant. Also, since crime is an extremely risky business, it is likely to attract people with a taste for taking chances, just as low-risk occupations (like being an economist?) are likely to attract people who are averse to risk.

Gary Becker was born in Pottstown, Pennsylvania. He received his undergraduate degree from Princeton University and his Ph.D. from the University of Chicago. He taught at Columbia University, where he became a full professor at age 30, only 5 years after leaving school. Since 1970 he has been a professor at the University of Chicago.

Richard Langlois

among households, the cost of rearing children will differ as well. A decrease in the relative price of children will increase the quantity demanded, and an increase in household income will increase the demand.

A family's supply and demand for children are depicted as *S* and *D* in Exhibit 2. The demand for children is downward sloping, indicating that the marginal benefit associated with each additional child declines as the number increases. Put another way, the quantity of children demanded increases as the price of rearing children declines.

What about the shape of the supply curve? Supply reflects the marginal cost of each child. The marginal cost probably declines, at least initially. The production of children involves fixed costs, such as the cost of the baby clothes, cribs, strollers, and the time required to develop child-care skills. Once these costs have been incurred for the first child, they are largely available for others. The second child can wear hand-me-downs, sleep in the crib, and ride in the same stroller as the first.

Perhaps the greatest cost of children is the opportunity cost of the time required for their care. There may be economies as the number of children increases. Looking after two children does not require twice the time as looking after one, though the work may be more intensive. Cooking for two children should not take twice the time as cooking for one. If the couple has

EXHIBIT 2   SUPPLY AND DEMAND FOR CHILDREN

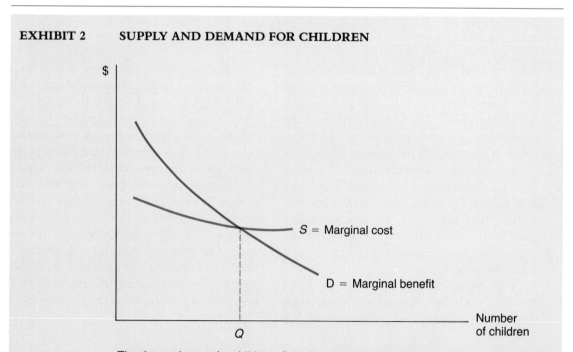

The demand curve for children, *D,* is downward sloping because the marginal benefit of children declines as their number increases. The supply curve, *S,* reflects the marginal cost of each child; it probably declines, at least initially. *Q* is the number of children—determined at the point where marginal cost equals marginal benefit.

several children, at some point the older ones can assist in caring for the younger ones.

Thus, the marginal cost of children may decline, at least over the first few children. The supply curve, or marginal cost curve, for children is depicted in Exhibit 2 as downward sloping over the relevant range. At some point the marginal cost will probably increase, if for no other reason than there is a biological limit on the number of children a family can produce. The shape of the supply curve is not critical to our discussion, and for simplicity we could have assumed it to be horizontal. What is important is to understand that the decision about the number of children can be viewed from the perspective of supply and demand.

Even if all couples have identical supply curves for children—that is, if all couples face the same opportunity cost of children—family size would still differ if the demand for children differs. Some couples might want a houseful of children; other couples prefer a smaller family or perhaps no children at all. Conversely, even if the demand for children were identical across households, family size would still differ if the opportunity cost of rearing children differs across households—that is, if the supply of children differs.

To breathe more life into the discussion, let's consider the supply and demand for children from a historical perspective.

The Farm Family

Prior to the nineteenth century the household could be thought of as a tiny factory taking advantage of the law of comparative advantage. The roles for individual family members reflected the division of labor and specialization of tasks on the farm. Each household member performed specific tasks, based on the person's size and skill. This household was a much more self-contained economic unit than is the modern household—food, clothing, and shelter could be produced primarily within the household. Government played little or no role.

Consider the benefits of children on the farm. In addition to any religious and social reasons for rearing a family, children served as a valuable source of labor. In fact, the school year was scheduled around the crop cycles, with the long vacation coming in the summer and early fall when the farm work load was greatest. Moreover, because financial institutions such as banks were not well developed and because there were no government programs to provide for old age, it was difficult for a couple to save for retirement. In this setting children represented a comforting insurance policy against poverty in old age. The more children a couple had, the more likely it became that the parents would be cared for in later years. This same rationale contributes to family size in less developed countries today.

How about the opportunity cost of rearing children? The nature of farm work required the couple to stay around the farm much of the time to care for the crops and farm animals. Thus, child care did not require either of the parents to give up a well-paying job to stay home with the kids. Child care could be blended with farm work, so the opportunity cost of rearing children on the farm was relatively low. The cost of food was also relatively low on the farm, keeping the marginal cost of children low.

In short, because the costs of rearing children on the farm were relatively low and the benefits were relatively high, we would expect families to be large, and farm families have traditionally been large.

Inheritance and Industrialization

The course of economic development depended very much on how farmland was passed on from generation to generation. In parts of Europe, including France, children inherited equal shares of the farm. These children tended to marry and remain in the farming village, working the farm together or cultivating only their share. However, the earnings from their inherited land were often so modest that to support a family, many had to work on other farms or in some small domestic industry. Thus, industrialization, to the extent that it occurred in rural areas, remained on a small scale.

In other European countries, such as England, the eldest son typically inherited the farm under a legal practice called *primogeniture*. His younger brothers and unmarried sisters could remain on the farm, but the younger brothers usually did not marry unless they were able to develop an independent source of income. This system of keeping the family farm in the hands of the eldest son meant that younger members of the family had less reason to stay in the community. Consequently, they tended to migrate to the emerging industrial centers, where they grew independent from family ties and customs. This new class of industrial worker felt free to marry and to have children, and these children became the pool of workers to support the Industrial Revolution. To some extent the Industrial Revolution required a breakdown of the extended family. Where family ties were strong, low-wage, large-scale industry in the city could not attract workers away from the family farm and from the small domestic industries in rural areas.

The Move to the City

As families moved from the farm to the city, one benefit of children—their ability to work at farm chores—disappeared. Children could still do chores around the house, but in the early years of this century child labor laws restricted them from working in formal labor markets. Another benefit of children in the earlier setting, security against old age, also became less necessary as economic development took place. The growth of reliable financial institutions made it possible to save for old age. More recently, the growing role of government provided income in old age through programs such as Medicare and Social Security.

Increased Costs of Children   Rearing children in the city was more costly than rearing them on the farm because many goods that had been readily available on the farm, such as food, now had to be purchased. The opportunity cost of caring for children also increased with the greater participation of married women in the work force, especially since 1950. The higher real wages and the greater availability of jobs made employment more attractive than staying home with children. When the alternative to having children is a well-paid and satisfying career, we might expect women to be less inclined to have children. The evidence tends to support this view. Research shows that after adjusting for other factors, the number of children a family has is inversely related to the wife's opportunity cost—that is, to her expected wage rate in the market.

Decreased Cost of Family Planning Changes in technology and in attitudes have reduced the cost of planning the desired family size. The development of reliable birth control measures and the legalization of abortion have reduced the cost of avoiding an unwanted pregnancy. Experience has shown that these factors do affect the number of births. For example, in 1967 Romania outlawed abortion because of official concern that the population growth was too low to support a healthy economy. The following year the birth rate nearly doubled. Over time, however, the rate gradually dropped as families adopted other birth control measures.

In those parts of the world where the economic benefits of children remain attractive relative to the costs, family size has not declined despite the availability of inexpensive and reliable birth control devices. The poor in India and some African countries, for example, continue to have among the largest families in the world despite aggressive government efforts to reduce population growth.

Smaller Family Size Although many factors contribute to the decision about the size of the family, the economic costs and benefits of children play an important role. With rising costs but reduced economic benefits of rearing children, plus a greater ability to plan family size, we should expect the average family size to decline. In fact, average family size has been falling since the beginning of the nineteenth century. The most accurate way of measuring the number of children born is the fertility rate, which is the number of births per thousand women aged 15–44. Between 1800 and 1960 this rate dropped by more than half in the United States. Just since 1960, however, the fertility rate has fallen by nearly half again. So women today are having on average only about half as many children as in 1960 and only one-fourth the number of children that women were having at the beginning of the last century.

The farm family's supply and demand for children are presented in panel (a) of Exhibit 3 to be contrasted with the urban family's supply and demand for children in panel (b). Note that in the urban setting the marginal cost, or supply, is higher, and the marginal benefit, or demand, is lower. Thus, the equilibrium family size is smaller in the city than on the farm. Although the graphs greatly simplify matters, they do explain in a clear way the economic forces leading to the decline in the average family size.

This same framework could be used to analyze the urban family size under various conditions. For example, if the government provides free day-

**EXHIBIT 3   SUPPLY AND DEMAND FOR CHILDREN FOR A FARM
FAMILY AND AN URBAN FAMILY**

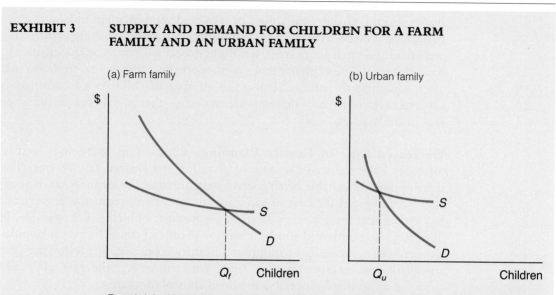

(a) Farm family

(b) Urban family

Panel (a) shows the supply and demand for children in a farm setting; Q_f is the equilibrium number of children. Panel (b) shows supply and demand in the city. In urban areas the marginal cost, or supply, of children is higher, and the marginal benefit, or demand, is lower. Hence, the equilibrium number of children for an urban family, Q_u, is lower than for a farm family.

care services, this would lower the cost of having children, which should increase the family size. If child-care costs become deductible in computing the family's personal income taxes, this would lower the cost of children and increase the family size. More generally, any government program that changes the cost of children could affect family size.

Other implications flow from the economics of children. For example, since children are more productive on the farm than in the city, we should expect farm parents to take their children out of school earlier than other parents do.

Quantity and Quality of Children

The number of children is certainly an important consideration for the household, but so is the amount of resources a household devotes to each child. The resources spent on each child has a critical impact in shaping the child's future. Does the child receive proper nutrition, essential medical care, a good education? Do the parents spend time developing the young child's mind or does the television become the primary baby sitter?

The demand for children has two dimensions: quantity and quality. To some extent these two dimensions are substitutes. Families can have fewer children and spend more per child or they can have more children and spend less per child. Gary Becker of the University of Chicago has shown that when birth rates declined, more was spent on education, suggesting that quality has been substituted for quantity.[3]

An extreme example of many children but few resources per child was related by Adam Smith more than 200 years ago: "It is not uncommon, I have been frequently told, in the Highlands of Scotland for a mother who has borne twenty children not to have two alive. . . . This great mortality, however, will everywhere be found chiefly among the children of the common people, who cannot afford to tend them with the same care as those of better station."[4]

Economists do not claim that economic considerations are the only determinants of family size, only an important element. Indeed, the systematic evidence examining the economics of children has led one researcher to conclude: "In modern society the decision to have a baby is frequently as deliberate and as calculated as the decision to attend graduate school, buy a house, or move to a new state."[5]

We have not drawn attention to a "price" for children because there is no legal market for children. Developments in reproduction technology, however, have created a market of sorts. For example, in the last several years hundreds of women have served as surrogate mothers, bearing children for other couples. Perhaps you have heard of the first such agreement to be contested in court, the case of "Baby M," where a New Jersey women who was paid $10,000 plus expenses felt she could not surrender the baby.

Evidence about the "price" of a child can also be uncovered by examining the cost of adopting a child. Some lawyers specialize in adoption services and for a fee serve as a go-between between couples who wish to adopt and women who want a better home for their infants. International adoption is also becoming more common. For additional evidence on the economics of children, read the following case study, which discusses one troubling effect of population-control policies implemented in Communist China.

CASE STUDY **Children In China**	In recent years the Peoples' Republic of China, with over 1 billion people, has been trying to bring its population growth under control. In 1982 the government made the practice of birth control a civic responsibility. To provide incentives, couples who pledged to have only one child are granted monthly bonuses, priority in school enrollments, jobs, and housing. Those who had more than one child, however, receive stiff fines, have their paychecks cut, lose benefits, and can be subject to sterilization.

---

[3]*A Treatise on the Family* (Cambridge, Mass.: Harvard University Press, 1981), 110.

[4]*The Wealth of Nations*, edited by Andrew Skinner (New York: Penguin Books, 1977), 182.

[5]Victor R. Fuchs, *How We Live* (Cambridge, Mass.: Harvard University Press, 1983), 17.

Overall, the plan has reduced birth rates in China and has worked best in the cities. In the countryside it met with much opposition. The plan ran counter to new agricultural policies that allowed peasants to keep more of what they produced, thus making larger families more profitable. In addition, China has no national retirement system, so Chinese peasants must rely on their children for support in their later years. Sons, in particular, represent old age insurance because daughters traditionally take care of their husbands' families.

Couples felt that if they were to be restricted to only one child, they wanted a son. Limiting couples to one child meant that the opportunity cost of having a daughter was never having a son. This increased opportunity cost resulted in what has become an ugly side effect of the attempts to control the population—female infanticide. Although there are understandably no official statistics on the extent of the practice, Chinese newspapers report that in some rural areas the ratio of male to female children is five to one, suggesting that many female babies are being killed. Indeed, China's Premier publicly condemned female infanticide in 1982.

Source: "An Unwanted Baby Boom," *Newsweek* (30 April 1984), 47.

THE CHANGING AMERICAN FAMILY

We observed that as the family moved from a rural-agricultural setting to an urban-industrial setting, specialization and market exchange displaced household production. Households produced less of what they consumed and consumed less of what they produced. Families then faced the choice of how much to work in the home and how much of their time to sell in formal labor markets. Next we look at some important developments in the family that have affected the choices about the division of labor in the household.

Women in the Work Force

Perhaps the most important development in the evolution of the family over the last half century has been the increasing participation of married women in the work force. For women with children under 6 years of age, the participation rate went from about 10 percent just after World War II to about 50 percent today. The average participation rate for women with children aged 6 to 17 went from about 25 percent to over 60 percent.

A variety of explanations has been put forth for this growing participation rate, including the women's liberation movement and government-backed affirmative action programs. But the trend was well under way by the 1960s when these other movements began. Economists who have studied the phenomenon argue that higher real wages and the increased demand for services were the primary reasons for the rising tide of married women in the work force. The service sector has traditionally provided employment to women. Women entered the work force when their expected wage exceeded the marginal value product of time spent in household work.

The increase in two-earner households means that there is less time spent in household work, resulting in smaller families and in a greater reliance on market-produced goods and services. The industries serving the two-earner home have been a source of growth in recent years. Just in the last decade the number of restaurants in the United States increased by 25 percent. McDonald's now has more employees than General Motors. If you have any doubt about the variety of family-related services available, just let your fingers do the walking through any metropolitan phone book. Services are available to help get a date, arrange a wedding, plan a family, adopt a child, take care of a child, do the shopping, clean the house, cut the lawn, reconcile a marriage, or file for divorce.

Because less is produced in the household, the gains arising from comparative advantage and the specialization of labor are reduced. Thus, marriage as an economic unit becomes less attractive. At least tentative support for the declining economic advantage of marriage can be drawn from the growing divorce statistics. Between 1965 and 1975 the divorce rate doubled, and since then it has remained at a high level. Divorce, however, has many possible causes, as we will see in the next section.

We should not be too quick to predict the demise of marriage as an economic and social institution, however. The divorce rate has leveled off after the rise from 1965 to 1975. Many forces are having an effect. For example, the growing incidence of sexually transmitted diseases raises the cost of casual relations, making the relative safety of marriage more attractive. Also, consider the following passage: "The family with its home was a domestic institution, a factory, and a well integrated social institution. . . . Many of the activities connected with consumption, such as the refining of food and the making of furniture and clothing, have left the home."[6] This quotation captures the spirit of much of the present thinking about the economic evolution of the household, but these words were written more than 50 years ago.

Divorce

Because information about potential mates is costly and because the marriage contract is vague, marriages do not always work out. There is a quick accumulation of new information about one's spouse during the first few years of marriage. To the extent that this information does not conform to expectations, problems arise. In this section we view the economics of divorce and look at the role of information and marriage-specific capital in the divorce decision.

---

[6]C. C. Zimmerman and M. E. Frampton, *Family and Society* (New York: Van Nostrand, 1935), 8.

Divorce rates are highest during the first five years of marriage, in part because of the effect of fresh information the parties have about one another. For example, the working wife could grow dissatisfied because the actual division of household responsibilities in her two-earner household does not conform to her expectations.

We would expect divorce rates to be higher where the couple has poorer information about one another prior to marriage and where the couple's tastes are less compatible. Evidence appears to support this. Research on the predictors of divorce indicate that, other things constant, the probability of divorce is higher if the mates do not know each other well before marriage and if they come from different backgrounds.

As years go by the couple has more invested in the relationship. Children are the prime example. The couple has also invested time adjusting to one another's idiosyncrasies. They have developed a common set of friends and have purchased and furnished a home to their tastes. These investments have the most value when the couple stays together. Thus, the cost of divorce, in both money and psychic terms, increases with the length of the marriage.

Research shows that several years before a divorce occurs, women increase their market work, perhaps to gain job skills and to develop market connections that will serve them when they are on their own.[7] There is no evidence that the increase in market work increases the likelihood of divorce. Women increase their time spent in market work still more after the divorce, but men reduce their market work, probably because divorced men must devote more time to household work.

The Rise of the One-Parent Household

In 1970 one in eight families with children had only one parent; by 1986 one in four families with children had only a single parent. In 86 percent of the cases the single-parent family is headed by a woman. The primary causes of single-parent families have been an increase in the divorce rate and a growing number of births to unmarried women. Why have both divorce rates and rates of births to unmarried women increased? What has changed to explain such a shift? First, as noted previously, job opportunities for women expanded after World War II, which has provided women with greater economic security. Second, the government has expanded its provision of social services. Programs such as Aid to Families with Dependent Children, food stamps, and Medicaid make it easier for women to rear children without a husband. These changes have given women greater independence. Hence, they rely less on the economic security of marriage and are more willing to avoid or to escape from a bad marriage.

---

[7]See William R. Johnson and Jonathan Skinner, "Labor Supply and Marital Separation," *American Economic Review* 76 (June 1986) 455–469.

Although we have raised possible economic explanations of why women are more frequently choosing to rear children without a husband, we should not too hastily contemplate the demise of the family as an institution. Even if the economics of single parenting are more attractive than they used to be, households consisting of women rearing children alone are still more likely to be poor than are two-parent households.

Until now we have considered the effects of family choices on the size and composition of the household. Also of interest is the collective effect of these individual choices on one another. The reasons why a family has fewer children are important, but what if 10 million other families make the same choice? We can view individual choice in the household as microeconomic analysis; an examination of what happens if millions of families are making choices is closer to macroeconomic analysis. We take this approach in the our closing section.

DEMOGRAPHY

Demography is the study of the size, density, and distribution of human populations.

Demography is the study of human populations, especially the size, density, and distribution of these populations. The number of babies born in any time period is called the *cohort size*. Because resources in the economy are relatively scarce, a large cohort size means that these resources must be spread over a large number of people during the childhood years of the cohort. Greater numbers also put pressure on the educational system. As the group matures and is absorbed into the labor force, however, production increases. Thus, the quality of your life depends very much on how many others were born when you were. We will consider in this section the demographic effects of family choices in recent years.

The Baby Boom

The Depression and World War II combined to keep birth rates very low in the 1930s and the first half of the 1940s, resulting in a small cohort size born during that period. This group appeared to benefit from its smaller size. Schools and colleges had abundant space for them, and when they entered the labor market in the 1950s, employers were eager to hire them. This group settled down in the suburbs and had many babies, setting off what has come to be known as the baby boom.

Because the growth in the cohort size exceeded the growth in the economy's resources, there were fewer resources per child. Baby boomers had to contend with crowded classrooms throughout their education; college admissions became more competitive. As this cohort matured and entered the job market in the 1970s and 1980s, competition for jobs increased. Between 1970 and 1986, the number of 25- to 39-year-olds in the labor force nearly doubled. Pressure for jobs was most severe among blue-collar workers, where foreign competition and increased automation reduced the number of high-paying production jobs in industries such as steel and autos.

As the economy shifted away from manufacturing, however, many new jobs were found in the service sector. Growth industries during the 1970s and early 1980s included health care and financial services. The growth of the professional ranks during this period was impressive, particularly since the labor force as a whole grew by only one-third. Since 1970 the number of lawyers, accountants, bankers, health administrators, and nurses more than doubled, and the number of computer specialists more than tripled. The country now has more lawyers than Alaska, Wyoming, or Vermont has people.

Baby boomers formed their own households at record rates, bidding up the price for new homes and apartments. Since 1970 the number of households has grown twice as fast as the population.

The Baby Bust

Between 1980 and 1990 the number of people in the age group most of you are in, aged 15 to 24, will decline by 15 percent. If you are in this "baby-bust" cohort, the group that followed in the wake of the baby boom, you have already been the beneficiary of the changing demographics. You went through primary and secondary school at a time when class size was shrinking, so you were accorded more individual attention. Admission to most colleges was also a bit easier because of the declining pool of applicants. And when you enter the job market, you will probably receive a warmer reception than those who preceded you.

A shrinking cohort size also generates other benefits. Since most crime is committed by young people (more than half of those arrested are under 24 years of age), crime rates, which have already begun to fall, will probably continue to drop for the next decade. With a smaller family size, a larger proportion of those in this cohort have had the advantage of being born first. For example, if the average family had three children, only one-third of these children will be born first; but with an average of two children per family, half will be born first. Researchers who have studied the issue argue that firstborn children receive better care because they do not have to share parental time and resources with brothers and sisters, especially during the early years. This advantage is reflected in greater success of the firstborn child in school and in later life.

Following the Sun

Migration has played an important role in the economic development of this country. This nation of immigrants has long shown a willingness to move on to greener pastures. Although people migrate for a variety of reasons—to seek a warmer climate, to be closer to some people or farther away from others—economic considerations are often at the heart of the move. As resource suppliers, households attempt to maximize the value of their labor: they go where their particular skills are most valued. As demanders of public and private goods and services, households seek the most attractive combination of price and quantity. They may be drawn to an area where the cost of living is lower, where the public school system is better, or where the level of public assistance is adequate in the event that they do not find a job. All we are saying is that households attempt to allocate their limited resources to maximize their utility, and migration is one way to do that.

Mobility and Education   The willingness to migrate increases sharply with an individual's education. This is easy to understand on economic grounds. The costs of migration are similar regardless of the education level, but the benefits usually will increase with the level of education. For example, suppose that wage levels in one state are about 20 percent higher than those in another state. The absolute difference for a college graduate earning $30,000 per year is $6000, whereas it is only $3000 for the high school graduate earning $15,000. Since the cost of moving should be no higher for the college graduate than the high school graduate, the net benefits of moving are greater for the college graduate. This difference in moving patterns can be seen in Exhibit 4, which shows the relationship between education and mobility for three age groups. Specifically, it measures by age and education the percentage of the population in 1980 that had moved from one state to another during the previous five years.

The data in Exhibit 4 show a strong positive relationship between mobility and the level of educational attainment. Note, for example, that people in every age group with at least one year beyond college were three times more likely to have moved than those with only an elementary school education. Also notice that for a given level of education, mobility decreases with age. We should expect this in part because as people get older the net gains from any move will be available for a shorter period.

Recent Population Shifts   In recent years major migrations of young and old from the Northeast and the North Central regions to the South and the West have caused a shift in the country's economic and political base. Four of the last five of the country's presidents have come from the South or the West.

EXHIBIT 4
EDUCATION AND MOBILITY: THE PERCENTAGE
OF POPULATION WHO MADE INTERSTATE
MOVES BETWEEN 1975 AND 1980

Highest Education Attained	Age		
	25–29	30–34	35–40
Eighth grade or less	9	7	5
High school	13	10	7
College	24	18	13
At least one year beyond college	31	24	16
All levels	17	14	9

Source: Adapted from Victor Fuchs, *How We Live* (Cambridge, Mass.: Harvard University Press, 1983), Table 5.3.

Particularly fast growing have been states such as Alaska, Arizona, Nevada, and Wyoming. Thirty percent of the residents of these states in 1980 had moved there in the previous five years. In contrast, only 5 percent of the 1980 population of New York, Pennsylvania, and Michigan had moved into those states during the previous five years.

As we have said, migration may be influenced by a variety of factors, including the weather, but people move primarily to seek out better economic opportunities. Workers are drawn to states with more job opportunities and higher prevailing wages than the states they leave. Over time this pattern of migration will reduce the wages in the high-wage areas and raise the wages in low-wage areas until job opportunities and wage levels are equalized across states. In fact, over the last forty years, wages in the South have moved up toward the average and wages in the Northeast have dropped toward the average.

SUMMARY

1. Because the selection of a marriage partner is such an important decision, people are willing to devote time and resources to the task of searching for the best possible mate. A marriage involves the couple's joint sharing of many goods and activities. Because of joint consumption, marrying someone with tastes and preferences similar to your own is more efficient.

2. To maximize the family's utility, each spouse will devote time to household work and market work based on the laws of comparative advantage. If the market wages of each spouse are identical, the one who is more productive in household work should spend time in that work. If both are equally productive in household chores and if wage rates differ, then the individual with the lower market wage should spend time in household work. If both earn more than they would have to pay to hire household help, they should hire the help.

3. One function of marriage is the rearing of children. The greater the benefits of children, other things constant, the larger the average family size will be. The greater the costs of children, other things constant, the smaller the family size will be. On the farm the benefits of children are relatively greater, and the cost is relatively smaller than in the city. So, other things constant, farm families tend to be larger than urban families.

4. Over the last half century the participation rate of married women in the work force has increased because of a higher real wage offered to women and an increased demand for labor in the service sector, the sector that typically employs women. An increase in the market wage offered married women has raised the opportunity cost of household work.

5. Greater job opportunities for women and expanded government programs for single mothers have provided women with greater economic security outside of marriage. Hence, women are more willing to avoid or escape an unhappy marriage. One reflection of this greater economic independence is a higher divorce rate and a growing number of births to unmarried women. As a result, more children are are being reared in single-parent households.

6. After World War II families started having more children, following a drop because of the Depression and the War. Baby boomers moved through the schools and into the job market, swelling many professional ranks and increasing the demand for housing. The baby boom has since given way to a baby bust.

7. Although people move for a variety of reasons, economic factors are among the most important. As labor suppliers, people move to those markets where their labor is most valued. Those with the greatest education

tend to be the most mobile because, while the costs of moving varies little with educa-

tion, the potential benefits increase with education.

QUESTIONS AND PROBLEMS

1. (Arranged Marriages) What economic arguments can be made for the old Chinese practice of arranged marriages, where parents conducted searches and arranged betrothals for the children?

2. (Early and Late Marriage) Some people marry at an early age, while others marry late. How might choice in this matter be related to the concept of the rate of time preference?

3. (Marginal Value Product of Household Work) How might you go about measuring the marginal value product of household work (at least conceptually)?

4. (Household Work) Some households that are building homes decide to finish the work on the house themselves. Discuss the economic reasoning behind this decision. How much finishing should one do?

5. (Household Work) If both spouses earn the same wages, should they do equal household work? Why or why not?

6. (Marginal Cost of Children) Why might the marginal cost of an additional child be higher if the additional child is of the other sex?

7. (Uncertainty and Family Size) Would greater uncertainty over infant and child mortality lead to larger families on average? Why or why not?

8. (Primogeniture) Consider a predominantly agricultural economy that practices primogeniture. Would such a cultural practice be related to agricultural economies of scale? What would happen to farm output if land were equally divided among all of the children for each generation?

9. (Demography and Social Security) Why is demography especially important to the proper functioning of the U.S. Social Security system? What would happen to the system if a prolonged baby bust occurs?

INSIDE *the* FIRM

The features of firm behavior that have received attention thus far are the quantity of output and the price of that output. The firm has been viewed as a "black box" that hires resources in resource markets based on marginal products, combines these resources efficiently to produce the profit-maximizing level of output, and sells this output for the profit-maximizing price. We have assumed that the firm knows what resources to employ and in what quantities. The firm is also aware of the latest technology, the price, quality, and availability of all resources, and the demand for its product.

We have said little about the internal structure of the firm. But this emphasis has been appropriate because our objective was to understand how the price system coordinates the use of resources, not to understand the internal workings of the firm. In this chapter we step inside the factory gate to consider some of the assumptions about the firm and its behavior. Specifically, we examine these three assumptions: (1) all participants in the market are fully informed about the price and availability of all inputs, outputs, and production processes; (2) in the perfectly competitive model there is a large number of buyers and sellers, each of whom buys or sells only a tiny fraction of the total amount bought and sold in the market; and (3) firms attempt to maximize profits.

In some cases we point out limitations of the idealized model of the firm. In other cases we show that the model's usefulness does not necessarily rely on a particular assumption. In still other instances we extend the model of the firm to add greater realism. Overall, this chapter should help you develop a deeper understanding of the firm's role in the economy. Topics and terms discussed include:

- Transaction costs
- Vertical integration
- Shirking
- Contestability
- The separation of ownership from control
- The market for corporate control

THE RATIONALE FOR THE FIRM AND THE SCOPE OF ITS OPERATION

The first assumption about firm behavior we wish to explore is that all participants in the market are fully informed about the price and availability of all inputs, outputs, and production processes. Such an assumption slights the role of the entrepreneur. Because neoclassical models of the firm assume that everyone has easy access to all the information they require to make decisions, there is little need for entrepreneurs. The firm is assumed to be headed by a brilliant decision maker with a computerlike ability to calculate all the marginal productivities. These individuals have no problems knowing everything they need to know to solve complex production and pricing problems.

The irony is that if the black box characterization of the firm were accurate—that is, if the marginal products of all inputs could be easily measured, and if prices for all inputs could be determined without cost—then there would be little reason for production to take place in firms. In a world characterized by perfect competition, perfect information, and frictionless exchange, the consumer could bypass the firm, purchase inputs in the appropriate amounts and pay each resource owner accordingly. Someone who wanted a table could buy timber, have it milled, contract with the carpenter, contract with the painter, and end up with a finished product. The consumer would carry out transactions directly with each resource supplier. By assembling a bundle of contracts with resource suppliers, the consumer in this case would operate as a firm.

In this section we explore two theories of why production is carried out within the firm. The first argues that the firm is a response to the transaction costs of using the market directly. The second focuses on the role of the entrepreneur as a monitor of "shirking" that arises when output is produced by a team of resource suppliers. As you will see, these are not so much competing theories of the firm as rationales that emphasize different functions of the firm.

The Firm Reduces Transaction Costs

Fifty years ago, in a classic article titled "The Nature of the Firm," Ronald Coase asked the fundamental question: "Why do firms exist?" [1] Why do people organize in the hierarchical structure of the firm and coordinate their decisions through a central authority, the entrepreneur, rather than rely simply on market exchange? Coase's answer would not be surprising to

---

[1] *Economica* 4 (November 1937): 386–405.

today's students of economics: the hierarchy of the firm is often more efficient than market exchange because production requires the coordination of many transactions among many resource owners. The costs of transacting this business through market relationships are, according to Coase, often higher than undertaking the same activities within the firm.

Coase's insight into the firm comes down to the idea that economic activity is best understood in terms of the transaction costs involved in any system of exchange between individuals. The exchange relationships between individuals is contractual in nature; when you buy a product, you agree to pay a certain amount—a contract is implicit. With major purchases, such as homes or cars, you actually sign a contract. Many resource owners sign a contract specifying the terms of supply. Thus, contractual relations abound.

The firm itself is most easily understood in terms of a particular kind of contractual relation, the authority relationship. As noted earlier, the entrepreneur agrees to pay the resource owner a specified amount in return for the authority to direct the use of that resource in the firm. The owner therefore sells to the entrepreneur the right to control the resource.

In the market, resources are allocated by prices, but in the firm, resources are guided by the decisions of managers. Coase argues that firms emerge when the transaction costs involved in using the price system exceed the costs of organizing those same activities through direct managerial controls in a firm.

Consider again the example of the consumer purchasing the table by contracting directly with all the different resource suppliers involved, from the grower of timber to the individual who paints the table. Using resource markets directly involves (1) the cost of determining what inputs are needed and (2) the cost of negotiating a separate agreement with each worker for each specific contribution to production. Where inputs are easily identified, measured, priced, and hired, production can be carried out through markets rather than within the firm. For example, getting your house painted is a relatively simple production task; you can buy the paint and brushes and hire painters by the hour. In this case you, the consumer, have become your own painting contractor, hiring inputs in the market and combining these inputs to do the job.

Where the costs of determining inputs and negotiating contracts for each specific contribution are high, the consumer minimizes transaction costs by purchasing the product from a firm rather than hiring all the inputs directly through markets. For example, attempting to buy a car by contracting with the hundreds of resource suppliers required would be time-consuming and costly. Some inputs you could purchase with ease: four tires, car seats, a battery, headlights. The price and quantity of other inputs, however, would not be so easily discovered and negotiated: What type of skilled labor would you need to hire and at what wages? How much steel, aluminum, and other materials? How should the resources be combined and in what proportions? In what sequence should the resources be brought together? The task is impossible for someone who lacks special knowledge of car production.

Consequently, it is more efficient for cars to be produced through the firm rather than through market transactions.

At the margin there will be some activities that could go either way, with some consumers using firms and some hiring resources directly in the markets. The choice will depend on the skill and the opportunity cost of time for each consumer. For example, some people may not want to be troubled with hiring all the inputs to get their house painted; instead, they simply contract with a firm to do the entire job for an agreed-upon price—they hire a contractor.

As we will see next, two other economists have more recently developed a variation of the transaction costs theory to focus on the role of the entrepreneur in the firm.

Shirking and the Entrepreneur

Like Coase, Armen Alchian and Harold Demsetz contend that contractual arrangements typically associated with the capitalist firm are often more efficient than those contractual arrangements found exclusively in markets.[2] The very existence of firms, they argue, can be inferred from an analysis of rational behavior. In complex production, teams of resource suppliers can produce more in cooperation with one another than they can separately. Hence, they have an incentive to coordinate their actions. But a special problem arises with team production—the tendency of team members to shirk.

Because of the complex interdependence of inputs, and because the contribution of each input typically cannot be observed directly as part of the final product, the marginal products of resources are difficult to determine. If there is no way of keeping track of each worker's contribution, there is no way of dividing revenues among the team members based on their respective contributions. Consequently, some other kind of allocation scheme is needed to divide the revenue arising from team production, such as an equal sharing of revenues. Since each worker's earnings are unrelated to that supplier's actual contribution, these sharing schemes give rise to an additional problem—shirking. **Shirking** is the tendency to goof off or otherwise take it easy on the job.

Shirking is the tendency not to work as hard as required.

The problem of shirking arises because whereas individual workers bear the full cost of their effort, each receives only a portion of what that effort produces. If a particular worker takes it easy, this reduction in effort is enjoyed exclusively by that "shirker," while the resulting diminished productivity is divided among all members of the group and is thus largely borne by others.

Thus, equal sharing of the fruits of production involves a fundamental asymmetry in incentives: the product of any individual's effort must be

---

[2]"Production, Information Costs, and Economic Organization," *American Economic Review* 62 (December 1972): 777–795.

shared with all other members of the group, whereas the benefits of shirking are enjoyed exclusively by the shirker. Since each member will find it attractive to shirk, the group's total product will fall. As a result, each member may be worse off than if no shirking had occurred.

Even if some group members identify the problem, it is not easily solved. Workers are confronted with the same problem that makes the provision of a public good difficult in the absence of government. Each worker's contribution to total product is a public good to be shared by all. Similarly, if one person shirks, the cost of this reduction in output is also shared by all.

Alchian and Demsetz contend that the usual market mechanism, whereby outsiders can offer to replace shirkers, will not work because an outsider cannot identify the shirkers. Moreover, how can new members be prevented from shirking once they join the team? If the marginal products of team members could be monitored somehow so that shirking could be identified, this would resolve the problem.

The question that Alchian and Demsetz address is, How can this monitoring be carried out most efficiently? One possibility is to rotate jobs so that members of the team take turns serving as monitor. This, however, surrenders the benefits arising from specialization of the monitoring task. Moreover, the monitor has the incentive to shirk at that task since monitoring costs are borne solely by the monitor, whereas the benefits are shared by all. Thus, who will monitor the monitor?

Because of the critical role of the monitor, the incentives must be structured to elicit the efficient amount of monitoring. Alchian and Demsetz argue that the best way to do this is to establish the monitor as the central contracting authority with each of the team's members and to give the monitor the right to all the output in excess of contractual payments to other team members. Each member would be paid based on the estimated marginal product, according to a contract between the monitor and each team member. The monitor would then get to keep any difference between total revenues and contractual costs. In these circumstances there are clear incentives for the monitor to police shirking up to the point where the marginal cost of policing just equals the monitor's expected marginal gains from reducing that shirking.

The monitor now has the incentive and the authority to adjust the contract in accordance with the observed marginal productivities of each resource. Rational team members should support such a move because these contracts are entered into voluntarily, and team members would be paid their marginal products. Moreover, team members need not be concerned about shirking by other team members. The result is a hierarchical relationship based on voluntary contracting. Workers surrender control over their resources to the monitor in return for a contractual guarantee of payment.

What we end up with is a description of the firm, where the monitor is the entrepreneur who guarantees payment in return for control. The firm emerges as the dominant form of organization whenever the net value of team production exceeds the net value of carrying out production through market arrangements—that is, whenever production is more efficiently organized within a firm rather than through market exchange.

The Scope of the Firm

Vertical integration is the expansion of a firm into earlier or later stages of production.

We now have explained why firms exist: firms minimize both the transaction and the production costs of economic activity. Next we ask, What is the efficient scope of the firm? The theory of the firm described in earlier chapters has been largely silent on questions about the boundaries of the firm—that is, on the appropriate degree of vertical integration. **Vertical integration** is the expansion of a firm into earlier or later stages of production. For example, a steel company may decide to mine its own ore or form its steel into various parts. A large manufacturer employs an amazing variety of production processes, but on average about half of the cost of production goes to purchasing various components, machines, special services, and raw materials from other firms.

What determines which activities the firm will undertake and which it will purchase from other firms? Should IBM manufacture its own computer chips or buy them from another firm? The answer depends on a comparison of the costs and benefits of internal production versus market purchases. The point bears repeating that internal production and markets are alternative ways of organizing transactions. The choice will depend on which form of organization is the more efficient way to carry out the transaction in question. Prices coordinate activities in markets, whereas managers coordinate activities in the firm. Markets coordinate resources without conscious direction, but firms coordinate resources through the conscious direction of the manager. Coordination through markets is often more efficient than coordination in firms because markets require less conscious activity.

Thus, the usual assumption is that transactions will be organized by markets unless market exchange presents problems. Sometimes, for example, markets are difficult to utilize because the item in question is not standardized or the exact performance requirements are hard to specify. Consider, for example, trying to contract with another firm to supply research and development services. The presence of uncertainty in such a purchase means that it becomes difficult to write, execute, and enforce contracts that cover all possible circumstances that could arise. Many contingencies cannot be addressed adequately during contract negotiations. Because exchange is often characterized by incomplete contracts, events not covered in the contract inevitably occur. Market participants do not like surprises, so incomplete contracts represent a potentially troublesome situation. Rather than purchase products such as research and development services from other firms, it is often more efficient for the firm to provide such activities itself. Thus, producing a particular component in the firm often involves a lower transaction cost than purchasing the component in the market. Coase's attention to transaction costs helps explain why the firm is often a more efficient way of carrying out production than are market transactions. His analysis also suggests the appropriate amount of vertical integration in the firm.

At this point it will be useful to discuss specific criteria the firm considers in deciding whether to purchase a particular component in the market or produce it internally.

Bounded Rationality of Managers   To direct and coordinate activity in a conscious way in the firm, the manager must comprehend how all the pieces of the puzzle fit together. As the firm takes on more and more activities, however, the manager starts losing track of things, so the quality of managerial decisions suffers. One limit to the extent of vertical integration is that the management has **bounded rationality**, meaning that the manager can comprehend only a limited amount of information about the firm's operation. When the firm takes on additional functions, it can experience diseconomies similar to those experienced when the firm expands output beyond the efficient scale of production. The limits of the manager's rationality limit the scope of the firm.

Bounded ratio-
nality means that
a manager can
comprehend only
a limited amount
of information.

Minimum Efficient Scale   In the long run the average cost of production is minimized when the firm achieves its minimum efficient scale. For example, suppose that scale economies in the production of dishwashers are exhausted when the production rate is 100,000 units per year, as shown by the average cost curve in Exhibit 1(a). Steel is an important component of household appliances, but suppose that scale economies in steel production are not exhausted until production achieves a rate of 1 million tons per year. The question is, Should the dishwasher manufacturer integrate backward into steel production? If each dishwasher requires 50 pounds of steel, the dishwasher manufacturer needs only 2500 tons of steel per year—a tiny fraction of the amount produced at minimum efficient scale. As you can see in Exhibit 1(b), if only 2500 tons of steel were produced per year, the cost per ton would be very high relative to the minimum costs that could be achieved at minimum efficient size. The dishwasher manufacturer therefore minimizes production costs by buying from a steel firm of optimal size rather than trying to produce its own steel. More generally, other things equal, firms should buy an input in the resource market when the cost is lower than if the input were internally produced.

Quality Easily Observed   When an input is well defined and when quality is easily determined at the time of purchase, that input is more apt to be purchased in the market rather than produced internally, other things equal. For example, a flour mill will typically buy its wheat in the market rather than grow its own. The quality of the wheat can be easily assessed upon inspection. In contrast, the quality of other inputs may be determined only during the production process. Firms whose reputations depend on the production of a key component are more likely to produce that component, especially if the quality of that component cannot be easily observed by inspection. For example, suppose that the manufacturer of a sensitive measuring instrument requires a crucial gauge. The quality of each gauge can be observed only as the gauge is being produced. If the firm produces the gauge itself, it can closely monitor quality.

Number of Suppliers   A firm wants an uninterrupted source of component parts. When there are many interchangeable suppliers of a particular input, a firm is more likely to purchase that input in the market rather than

EXHIBIT 1 **MINIMUM EFFICIENT SCALE AND VERTICAL INTEGRATION**

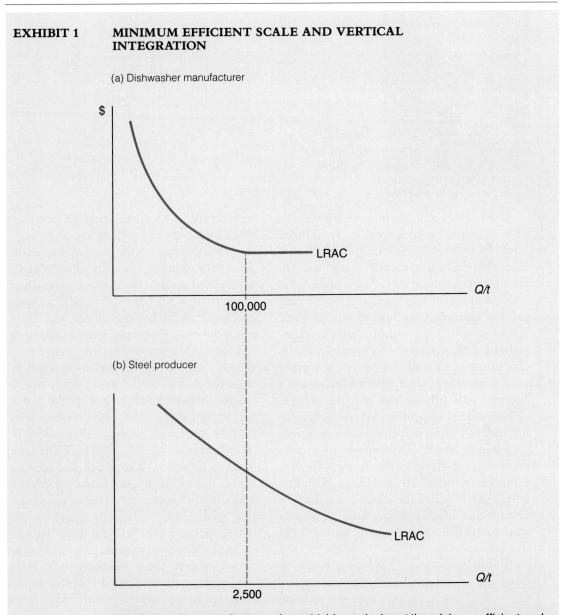

(a) Dishwasher manufacturer

(b) Steel producer

The dishwasher manufacturer of panel (a) is producing at the minimum efficient scale of 100,000 units per period. That level of production requires 2500 tons of steel. If the manufacturer produced its own steel, the cost would be much higher than if it purchased steel from a steel producer operating on a much larger scale. As panel (b) shows, at 2500 tons, scale economies in steel production are far from exhausted.

produce it internally, other things equal. The existence of many suppliers not only ensures a dependable source of components but also competition among the many suppliers keeps the component price down. If the resource market is so unstable that the firm cannot rely on consistent availability of the component, the firm may produce the item to insulate itself from the vagaries of that market.

Oliver E.
Williamson
(b. 1932)

Yale School of Organization
and Management

Individuals and businesses sometimes find it profitable to invest in specialized assets of various kinds—unique machines, for example, that are not easily sold or transferred to other uses. Most often, specialized assets of this sort create problems for the smooth functioning of markets. Someone who plays a unique part in a specialized and complex production process can threaten to pull out unless the other parties involved agree to transfer most of the gains of production to that person. (Think of the star professional athlete walking out of camp until management agrees on a higher salary.) This possibility creates friction in the marketplace. And, as we saw, a market works best when it is "contestable," that is, when there are no irreversible commitments or specialized assets to prevent competitors from quickly entering the market.

But the market also has ways of making good use of irreversible commitments and specialized assets. Sometimes, in fact, an irreversible commitment can help make contracts go through more smoothly. In order to convince you to use your specialized asset productively with my assets, I can agree to make an irreversible commitment of my own. My commitment becomes a kind of hostage insurance that I won't pull out of the contract because it would hurt me as much as you.

More generally, the market has a nifty device for reducing the difficulties posed by specialized assets. It's called a business firm. If one party—the firm—owns all the unique machines and other specialized assets used in production, there is no longer a threat of a holdout. One reason for the existence of firms, then, is that common ownership is sometimes less costly than contractual arrangements when there are specialized assets involved.

The author of many of these ideas is a Yale professor named Oliver Williamson. Born in Superior, Wisconsin, and educated at MIT, Stanford, and Carnegie-Mellon, Williamson has made a career of opening up the "black box" of the firm and looking inside. In the 1960s, he did pioneering work on the behavior of managers within corporations. Since then, he has developed an approach to theory called transaction-cost economics. This approach attempts to explain market behavior and organizational structure by recognizing that firms face not only normal costs of production but also various other, less visible, costs of transacting and exchanging. The difficulties of specialized assets, for example, are one source of such transaction costs.

Richard Langlois

CONTESTABILITY

*A market is **contestable** as long as firms can enter or leave at will — as long as there are no irreversible investments.*

Another assumption discussed at the outset is that perfect competition requires a large number of firms. Research suggests, however, that as long as firms can enter and leave the market with ease, existing firms will be unable to earn economic profit in the long run regardless of how many firms are in the market. Such markets are said to be **contestable**. Even though only one firm may now be serving the market, as long as there are no entry barriers, the opportunity of economic profits will attract other firms to enter and "contest" this market if the existing firm charges a price that provides economic profits. A contestable market is one in which the potential entrant can serve the same market and has access to the same technology as the existing firm.

Suppose that you cut grass in the neighborhood during the summer. All you need is the family lawn mower, some gasoline, and some time. If you are the only one in your neighborhood who offers these services, does this make you a monopolist? Well, you are a monopolist in the sense that you are the only seller of services in this particular market, but you are not necessarily a monopolist in the sense of having market power. Because no special skills are required and because most homes already have a lawn mower, entry into this business is easy. No irreversible investments need to be made. Investments are said to be *irreversible* if, once the investment is made, the asset is dedicated to the production of a particular good and cannot easily be redirected toward producing another good. Whenever irreversible investments must be made in human or physical capital to produce in a particular market, that market is not likely to be contestable. For example, auto manufacturers and cosmetic surgeons make irreversible investments in capital.

How high would the price you charge for cutting lawns have to rise to attract rivals? Since the mower in most households is underutilized, its opportunity cost is near zero. The gasoline is also a relatively minor expense. Hence, only the opportunity cost of time is important. Suppose the opportunity cost of your time is the same as that of potential competitors. If you charge a price that yields an economic profit — that is, that pays you more than the opportunity cost of your time — you will be undercut (or mowed down?) by new entry. Thus, this market is contestable because entry barriers are relatively low.

Let's consider contestability on a larger scale in another example. Perhaps only one airline offers passenger service between two cities. If other airlines can easily send planes into that market when profits arise, the market is contestable. In summary, a large number of firms is not necessary to ensure the competitive outcome as long as firms will be challenged whenever they earn more than a normal profit [3]

---

[3]For an extensive discussion of contestability, see Elizabeth E. Bailey and William J. Baumol, "Deregulation and the Theory of Contestable Markets," *Yale Journal on Regulation* 1, no. 2 (1984): 111–137.

CORPORATE OWNERSHIP
AND CONTROL

Up to this point we have assumed that firms attempt to maximize profit. Earlier we described the entrepreneur as the individual responsible for guaranteeing payment to the other resources in return for the opportunity to direct the use of these resources in the firm and the right to any profit or loss. We said it was not important that the entrepreneur actually manage the firm's resources as long as the entrepreneur had the power to hire and fire the manager—that is, as long as the entrepreneur controlled the manager. There was no concern that the hired manager would not, in fact, follow the wishes of the owner. After all, a manager who did not respond to the owner's desires could be replaced by one who would.

Managerial Behavior in Large Corporations

Separation of ownership from control *occurs when no single stockholder has the incentive or ability to control the management of a corporation.*

As the modern corporation has evolved, however, its ownership has become widely distributed among many stockholders, leaving no single stockholder with either the incentive or the ability to control the manager. Economists since the days of Adam Smith have been concerned with what has come to be known as the **separation of ownership from control** in the large corporation.

Some 200 years ago Smith warned against the popularity of the corporation because its managers used other people's money and were as a consequence given to "negligence and profusion." The issue was presented most dramatically more than 50 years ago in a famous book by Adolf Berle and Gardiner Means titled, *The Modern Corporation and Private Property*. Berle and Means documented the decline of the owner-entrepreneur and the rise of the "manager-controlled" firm. Where firms were controlled by managers, Berle and Means questioned whether there was any reason to believe that such managers would operate the firms in the best interests of the owners. These authors were raising a principal-agent problem in the modern firm's operation. Could the owners, in this case the principals, be assured that the managers, in this case the agents, would look out for the owners' best interests?

Because death and taxes have eroded the position of the owner-entrepreneur of old, the ownership of today's corporation is even more widely dispersed than it was in the days of Berle and Means. The following question consequently takes on even greater importance: What difference does the replacement of the owner-entrepreneur with a hired manager make in terms of a firm's performance? Various economists have formulated theoretical models suggesting that, when freed from the bonds of a dominant stockholding influence, managers will attempt to pursue their own selfish goals rather than those of the firm's owners.

The alternatives vary from model to model, but emphasis has focused on such goals as the firm's rate of growth and the perquisites and discretionary resources available to the managers, such as attractive surroundings, corporate jets, and other amenities. Managers may pursue firm growth because of the power, security, and status associated with a growing firm. As goals other than profit are pursued, so the argument goes, resources are used less efficiently in the firm, resulting in a lower level of profit. Thus, the stockholders—the owners of the firm—suffer because the manager is not representing their best interests.

Constraints on Managerial Discretion

To the extent that managers seek goals other than profit, what are the constraints on such behavior? After all, if there were no constraints, managers could simply take profits home in their briefcases while thumbing their noses at the stockholders. Analysts have identified a variety of constraints that can serve as possible checks on wayward management. The nature and effectiveness of each constraint will be examined next.

Economics of Natural Selection   One argument is that even if managers are freed from the control of a dominant stockholder, the rigors of competition in the product market will force managers to maximize profits to survive. The "economics of natural selection" ensures that only the most efficient firms will be able to stay in business. Other firms will simply not earn enough profit to attract and retain resources and so will go out of business sooner or later.

The problem with this argument is that while pressure to pursue profits may arise when firms sell their product in competitive markets, many large corporations are at least partially insulated from intense product competition. Because of either government regulations or some degree of market power, many managers have a certain amount of discretion in how they utilize the firm's resources. As a result, the managers in these large firms could divert corporate resources into activities reflecting their own interests yet still earn enough profit to ensure the firm's survival.

Managerial Incentives   Another approach has been to consider the manager's incentive structure. What is the manager paid to do? After all, if executive pay is linked more closely to the firm's profit than to its growth, the compensation scheme may encourage the manager to pursue profit rather than growth even in the absence of a dominant stockholder or competition in the product market. Empirical evidence suggests that at least a portion of the typical manager's compensation is tied to the firm's profitability through various types of bonus pay schemes and stock option plans, which are widely used.

Yet even if the manager's income is tied to profit, the manager will not necessarily attempt to maximize profit. The manager in a large corporation who diverts profit to other ends will simply forgo some income. This profit diversion, however, may still be "cheap" in view of the small fraction of the firm's shares typically owned by management. For example, if the manager owns 1 percent of the firm's shares and can divert $10,000 of potential profits to buy an expensive desk, this diversion will cost the manager only $100 in forgone pretax profits. After corporate taxes and personal income taxes, the cost is less than half that amount. The point is that existence of a link between executive pay and firm profit is not necessarily evidence that managers will attempt to maximize profit; this is only evidence that profit diversion will involve some personal cost, although that cost may be quite small.

Stockholder Voting   Each year stockholders have an opportunity to attend the company meeting and elect the board of directors. Couldn't the mass of stockholders join forces to oust the inefficient manager? What about that "corporate democracy" so often heralded on Wall Street?

The chances of an effective stockholder revolt appear to be slim. The average stockholder does not have the information, the resources, or the incentive to challenge the management. Most shareholders either ignore the voting altogether or dutifully pass their votes to the managers.

The dissatisfied stockholder, however, does have one very important alternative. The stockholder can "fire" the manager and the firm simply by selling shares in the corporation. Some economists contend that the possibility of a widespread vote of no confidence provides a check on managerial discretion that may ultimately lead to corporate reform. According to this argument, as stockholders sell their holdings, the share price will drop, and the firm will become more attractive as a target for a reform-minded capitalist. A so-called corporate raider can buy a controlling interest in the firm at a relatively low price, reform or replace the management, and then benefit from the improved profit prospects through an appreciation in the value of shares. The effects of this market discipline will be examined next.

The Market for Corporate Control

The market for corporate control has been championed by some economists as an efficient mechanism for allocating and reallocating corporate assets. If the firm's assets are undervalued in the stock market, then some entrepreneur has an incentive to "buy low and sell high"—that is, to buy firms that own undervalued resources and undertake measures to increase the value of these resources.

The effectiveness of this market in checking managerial abuses depends on the existence of someone with (1) the ability to identify firms that are performing below potential, (2) access to the resources necessary to carry off a successful takeover, and (3) the savvy to turn the situation around. Despite the general view among economists that the market for corporate control allocates corporate assets to those who value them most highly, there are a variety of reasons why this market may not operate perfectly.

A major problem with the market for corporate control is the difficulty for an outsider of determining whether a firm is run efficiently. When a firm performs poorly, it is often unclear whether the management is poor or the assets of the firm are not what they seem. Management is more likely to be better informed than a potential corporate raider. Yet some types of information are more public than others. For example, the value of oil reserves tends to be widely known in that industry. When an oil firm's market value falls significantly below the underlying value of the firm's assets, we expect some entrepreneur to attempt to buy the firm's assets at a discount.

Problems arise when an entrepreneur bids for the firm's assets. Once a likely takeover target has been identified, this information is hard to keep secret. Although the entrepreneur would prefer to quietly buy up a controlling interest in the firm, such major purchases would probably not go unnoticed in the stock market. Moreover, once ownership in a firm reaches 5 percent, this ownership becomes public knowledge because the stockholder must register with the Securities and Exchange Commission, the body that regulates the stock market.

*A **tender offer** is an attempt to attain a controlling interest in a firm by purchasing shares at a premium over the market price.*

The corporate raider typically attempts to acquire a controlling interest in the firm through a public **tender offer** for the firm's shares. The raider will offer shareholders a premium over the prevailing market price in hopes of acquiring a controlling interest in the firm. If enough shares are tendered by shareholders, these shares will be purchased by the raider, and the takeover will be successful. If too few shareholders agree to sell, however, the deal will fall through, and the tender offer will be withdrawn or amended. For example, a corporate raider may offer to pay $30 per share for stock trading at $20 per share before the takeover attempt is announced. If enough shareholders offer to sell their shares so that the corporate raider ends up with over half the shares, the takeover is a success.

Studies suggest that the stock market incorporates the effects of various events into the value of a firm's shares. What is the stock market's judgment about the effects of corporate takeovers? The evidence indicates that successful takeovers increase the wealth of stockholders in the company taken over. Estimates of the share appreciation vary from study to study, but the range appears to be between 16 and 34 percent. There is also evidence that the value of the acquiring company's shares increases as well, though by a smaller amount. Thus, stockholders appear to benefit from takeover activity.

A Glossary of Takeover Terms

The incumbent managers have access to all the firm's resources in defending themselves against an unwanted suitor. They are in a position to adopt strategies designed either to make the firm less attractive as a takeover target or to make a takeover more difficult. Defensive strategies range from costly legal actions to newspaper advertisements urging stockholders to reject the tender offer. The recent wave of takeover activity has created a colorful vocabulary to describe the offensive and defensive strategies of each side in a takeover. What follows is a brief glossary of these expressions.

Golden Parachutes   Provisions that provide lavish payments to incumbent managers if they are fired as a consequence of a takeover. These lucrative severance agreements have been criticized because they seem to protect managers' interests at the stockholders' expense. Defenders of the practice argue that these contracts give management the security necessary to be unbiased in negotiating with possible merger partners.

White Knight   Someone or some organization who comes to the rescue of the firm facing an unwanted takeover. The target firm, when confronted with the possibility of being swallowed up by an unsolicited takeover, often seeks out a "white knight" as a merger partner. For example, in 1982 Cities Service sold out to Occidental Petroleum Corporation rather than allow itself to be acquired by T. Boone Pickens of Mesa Petroleum. Incumbent managers presumably expect to receive kinder treatment from a white knight than from a hostile suitor.

Greenmail   A premium paid by the target company to buy back its own shares from a potential raider. The expression arises because management is forced to pay "greenmail" (that is, blackmail paid in green money) in the form of an inflated share price to avoid the takeover. As a defensive strategy, paying greenmail to one raider often attracts another. For example, after T. Boone Pickens was paid off by Phillips Petroleum, Carl Icahn, another feared corporate raider, made a similar effort to buy a controlling interest in Phillips. Supporters of greenmail say that to the extent that it makes attempts at takeovers less risky for would-be corporate raiders, these share repurchases stimulate the market for corporate control by increasing the number of attempted takeovers. Critics claim that the management is using the company's resources to prevent a takeover that may, in fact, be in the stockholders' best interests. Congress is considering measures to limit greenmail.

Junk Bonds   Debt securities issued by a corporate raider to help finance a takeover. Junk bonds are either not rated by the bond-rating companies or are rated among the poorest of risks. A typical takeover using junk bonds might proceed as follows. The corporate raider first visits major financial institutions, asking for an agreement to purchase bonds in the event that the tender offer elicits a sufficient number of shares. As collateral for these junk bonds, the raider pledges the assets and expected profits of the target company. Because these bonds offer a high interest rate, financial institutions often find them attractive. When the necessary commitments are lined up, a tender offer is made to the public. If enough shares are tendered, the raider sells the bonds to raise enough money to buy the shares. If too few shares are tendered, the deal falls through and no bonds are sold.

Poison Pills   Actions sometimes taken by the management of the target firm to make that firm less tempting (that is, poison) to potential raiders. These actions may include selling attractive assets, merging with another firm to create antitrust problems for potential raiders, or imposing heavy costs for replacing the existing management (that is, golden parachutes). Some oil companies, for example, sold their much-sought-after oil reserves.

The following case study demonstrates a variety of the offensive and defensive strategies employed in a play for corporate control.

CASE STUDY

Control of the Oil Patch

The fight for control between T. Boone Pickens and Unocal Oil was the longest and toughest of the attempted takeovers in the mid-1980s. Unocal, with assets of over $10 billion, ranked among the largest 25 industrial corporations in the country. The battle raged in courtrooms from coast to coast and called for the services of high-priced lawyers, investment bankers, and a passel of financial consultants.

When Pickens made a tender offer for Unocal's shares, he had already moved on several major oil companies, including Gulf, Phillips Petroleum, and Cities Service. All were forced to make some sort of defensive move, either finding a "white knight" or paying "greenmail" for the shares purchased by Pickens. In each case Pickens earned millions when his shares were repurchased.

Unocal started preparing its defenses long before the actual battle for control. In 1983 it enacted staggered terms for directors, which means that rather than having all the seats on the board of directors contested each election, only a fraction would be up for election each term. With elections held every two years and with only one-third of the seats at risk each election, it would take someone with a majority of shares six years to replace the board. Unocal also pushed for federal legislation to curb takeover activity.

Each side hired teams of high-priced lawyers and professionals whose job it was to solicit votes from the stockholders—something like campaign managers. As part of the legal proceedings, Unocal even sued its own bank because the bank was loaning money to Pickens. Pickens then sued Unocal, charging the company with conducting an "intimidation campaign" against banks lending to Pickens.

By the end of March 1985 Pickens had acquired 24 million shares, or 13.6 percent of the company, and he made a tender offer for enough shares to give him a majority. The tender offer of $54 was several dollars higher than the share price at the time, but the share price had already been bid up by speculation of a takeover. To counter the offer, Unocal offered to buy back 29 percent of its own shares at $72 per share. Unocal included in its offer a controversial provision saying it would not accept any shares owned by Pickens. If Pickens had been allowed to sell back his shares at the price Unocal was offering, he would have netted about $650 million.

Under the circumstances, Pickens faced the prospect of eventually acquiring a company that had accumulated a giant debt from buying back its own shares. The buy-back scheme had become a "poison pill" for Unocal. Pickens challenged in court the attempt to exclude his shares, claiming that such provisions violated the equal treatment of all shareholders. In May 1985 the Delaware Supreme Court upheld the Unocal exclusion.

Pickens lost about $100 million in his failed attempt to control Unocal. Meanwhile, Unocal stockholders could hardly be considered winners; to buy back the shares at such a premium, the company had to increase its debt from $1.2 billion to $5.3 billion. As a result, the company will be short of cash for years to come.

Sources: "How T. Boone Pickens Finally Met His Match: Unocal's Fred Hartley," *The Wall Street Journal*, 24 May 1985; "The Raiders," *Business Week*, (4 March 1985): 80–90.

CONCLUSIONS

In this chapter we reconsidered some of the simplifying assumptions made earlier about firm behavior. The first assumption we examined was that all participants in the market are fully informed about the price and availability of all inputs, outputs, and production processes. We argued that if this were true, there might be little need for the firm or the entrepreneur. Consumers could bypass the firm, contracting directly with resource suppliers to produce goods and services.

What this perfect knowledge and frictionless exchange assumption ignores is that in addition to production costs, there are transaction costs. Much of microeconomics focuses on production efficiency. In this chapter we addressed transaction efficiency. The central question we attempted to answer was, Why do firms exist? Why are economic transactions carried out under the authority relationship of the firm rather than through contracts in the market? Another question explored was the efficient scope of a given firm. To what extent should the firm substitute nonmarket administrative relations within the firm for cross-firm market relations? What activities should be brought inside the firm, and what activities should be handled by other firms? We found that transaction costs helped explain both the existence of firms and the optimal amount of vertical integration.

A second assumption scrutinized was whether competition requires a large number of buyers and sellers. We discovered that a large number of firms is not a prerequisite for competition. Indeed, a market may be competitive even with only one producer as long as that market is contestable—that is, as long as other firms can easily enter and leave the market.

Finally, we reconsidered the assumption that firms attempt to maximize profits. We asked whether such an assumption appeared reasonable in view of what has come to be known as the separation of ownership from control in the modern corporation. We considered other possible managerial objectives and reviewed the effectiveness of various incentives and constraints on managerial behavior. The most extensive coverage involved the market for corporate control, which appears to reallocate corporate assets to those who value them most highly.

The firm has evolved through a natural selection process as the form of organization that minimizes both transaction and production costs. According to this natural selection argument, those forms of organization that are most efficient will be selected by the economic system for survival. Those attributes that result in profits will be rewarded, and those that do not will fall by the wayside. The form of organization selected may not be optimal in the sense that it cannot be improved upon, but it is the most efficient form among those that have been tried. If a more efficient way to organize production than the firm remains, some entrepreneur will stumble upon it one day and be rewarded with greater profits. Thus, the improvement may not be the result of any conscious activity; once a more efficient way of organizing production is uncovered, others will imitate the successful innovation.

SUMMARY

1. According to Ronald Coase, firms exist because the hierarchy of the firm is often more efficient than transactions carried out through markets. Because production requires the extensive coordination of transactions among many resource owners, all this activity can be carried out under the direction of a manager in a firm rather than by specifying detailed performance contracts with many separate suppliers.

2. The extent to which a firm vertically integrates will depend on both the transaction and the production costs of economic activity. The firm is more likely to buy a component part rather produce it if, other things equal, (1) the item can be purchased for less than it would cost the firm to produce it, (2) the item is well defined and the quality is easily observable, or (3) there is a large number of interchangeable suppliers.

3. Alchian and Demsetz argue that in team production it is often difficult to observe each team member's marginal contribution in the finished product. Team members may therefore have an incentive to goof off, or "shirk."

This shirking can be reduced by appointing a monitor to police shirking in the firm. The monitor can contract with each resource supplier, then keep any difference between total revenues and contractual costs. The monitor, as residual claimant, therefore has a clear incentive to see that other resource suppliers do not shirk.

4. The ownership of the modern corporation is typically fragmented among many stockholders, with no stockholder owning a dominant share. There is some concern that managers in such firms will not behave in the best interests of the owners. Competition in the product markets may require managers to maximize profits to survive. Even where firms lack stiff competition in the product market, managers may still attempt to maximize profits if their pay is linked to profits. The market for corporate control is another way of keeping managers in line. The ability to buy an underachieving firm in the stock market at bargain prices, shape it up, and sell it at a profit is also said to keep management in accord with stockholders' interests.

QUESTIONS AND PROBLEMS

1. (Internal Production versus the Market) What economic factors will determine whether a firm has its own legal staff or retains an outside law firm to handle its litigation?

2. (Shirking) What is the difference between the shirkers in a group and the less-skilled employees? Can this difference always be observed and monitored?

3. (Monitoring) What problems may exist with the practical application of Alchian and Demsetz's "monitor system?"

4. (Internal Production versus the Market) Ashland Oil, Inc. is largely a refiner of oil that buys its crude oil in the marketplace. Larger oil companies, such as Texaco, have their own crude oil production facilities. How would you explain this situation?

5. (Contracting) Department stores, among other enterprises, often contract with a janitorial services firm to clean the store every night. Why doesn't the store simply hire its own janitors?

6. (Contestable Markets) What are the differences and similarities between contestable and competitive markets?

7. (Berle-Means Hypothesis) Why would separation of ownership from control possibily lead to lower profitability for the firm?

8. (Berle-Means Hypothesis) How might the objectives of stockholders and the objectives of a growth-oriented management conflict?

9. (Corporate Takeovers) Who stands to gain and who stands to lose in a corporate takeover? Is the economy helped by such takeovers?

10. (Corporate Indebtedness) Why do corporate takeovers frequently lead to a rise in corporate indebtedness? Does corporate indebtedness benefit the economy? Why or why not?

INSIDE the GOVERNMENT

In Chapter 4 we introduced the various roles government plays in the economy. Where private markets fail to provide those activities demanded by the electorate, the government often steps in. Government programs are intended to (1) protect private property and enforce contracts, (2) promote competition and regulate natural monopolies, (3) provide public goods and services, (4) encourage positive externalities and discourage negative externalities, (5) address inequalities in the distribution of earnings, and (6) promote full employment and price stability. The government tries to finance these programs with a revenue system that is efficient, equitable, simple, and easy to administer.

Until now we have assumed that government makes optimal decisions in response to shortcomings of the private market. When confronted with a failure in the private market, government adopts and implements the appropriate program to address the problem. But this is easier said than done. As we will see in this chapter, there are problems with public choice, just as there are with private choice. There are limitations to the effectiveness of government activity, just as there are limits to the effectiveness of private sector activity. Indeed, turning every instance of private market failure over to government is like awarding the talent prize to the second contestant after hearing only the first.

In this chapter we trace the government decision-making process to explore problems that arise with public choice. Beginning with the problem of majority rule in direct democracy, we proceed to complications that arise when public choices are delegated to elected representatives, who, in turn, delegate the implemetation of these choices to government bureaus. Topics and terms discussed include:

- Negative-sum games

- Median-voter model

- Representative democracy

- Rent seeking

- Bureaucratic behavior

THE ECONOMY AS A GAME

One useful way of understanding the role of government is to think of the economy as a game, which initially involves two major groups of players: consumers and producers. The players pursue their own self-interest—consumers attempt to maximize utility, and producers attempt to maximize profit. Economic coordination in a market economy hinges on the ability to secure the rights and obligations of property as well as the ability to enforce contracts. From time to time disagreements arise about property rights or the interpretations of contracts.

Players can either police themselves, as they do in card games, or hire an umpire or referee, as they do in most physical games. A market economy often requires some third party, government, to resolve disputes, protect the rights to resources, and enforce contracts. Also, a government may provide public goods and services and control activities that involve externalities in production or consumption. In short, to promote the efficient allocation of resources, the market economy often needs some authority to specify rules of behavior and to enforce these rules.

Fairness of the Game

The participants often attach a value to the fairness, or equity, of the game. Fairness can be viewed in two senses. First, are the rules of the game fair to all participants—that is, is the process fair? Where the stakes are high, players may have an incentive to cheat. The game may not be fair because the cards are marked, one player can see another's hand, or a group of players conspires against another player.

Fairness can also be viewed in terms of the results of the game. Is the outcome of the game fair? Suppose the game is over but a few skilled or lucky players seem to have won all the chips. The losers are often irked by their own lack of chips compared to the mounds of chips they see before the winners. Some players argue that if the rules are fair—that is, if the process is fair—then the outcome must by definition be fair, even if big winners and losers result. Others argue that even fair rules will not result in a fair outcome if the players are not on equal footing at the outset. For example, what if certain players begin the game with fewer chips than the others? Or what if some players lack the skill to become effective? Do these differences among players make the game less fair? If by fairness we mean that every player has an equal opportunity to win, do differences in the initial endowment of chips or in the ability to play the game make the outcome less fair? If fairness of result is valued by the players, the rules could be changed to bring about what is viewed as a fairer outcome.

Kinds of Games

By comparing the total amount of winnings and losses, we can classify the kinds of games that are played into three categories. We subtract the total losses from the total winnings to determine whether the net result is positive, zero, or negative. If the winnings exceed the losses, it is called a **positive-sum game**; if the winnings are just offset by the losses, it is called a **zero-sum game**; and if the losses exceed the winnings, it is called a **negative-sum game**. Poker is a zero-sum game because the total amount of the winnings just equals the total amount of the losses. Most gambling activities, such as horse racing, casinos, and state lotteries, are negative-sum games because the "house" and the government take a cut of the amount wagered.

*A game in which total winnings exceed total losses in a **positive-sum game**; if winnings just offset losses, it is a **zero-sum game**; if losses exceed winnings, it is a **negative-sum game**.*

Many people mistakenly think of market activity as a zero-sum game. Intuition suggests that the gains from one side of the market must come at the expense of the other side. But a key feature of market activity ensures that most exchanges will yield positive gains. Because market exchange is *voluntary*, participants expect to be at least as well off after engaging in market exchange as before. Consumers expect consumer surplus, and producers typically expect at least a normal profit. Thus, market exchange is usually a positive-sum game.

Just as we can classify games, so we can classify changes in the rules of the games. There are three categories of rule changes. In positive-sum changes the gains outweigh the losses. Especially prized in this category are **Pareto optimal** rule changes, where at least one player is made better off, and none is made worse off. In zero-sum changes, the losses just equal the gains conferred on the winners, and in the negative-sum changes the losses outweigh the gains.

*Any change to the status quo is **Pareto optimal** if it makes at least one person better off while making no one worse off.*

Rules and Behavior

Rules and rule changes can affect either the way the game is played or the distribution of winnings when the game is over. Laws such as those governing minimum wages, pollution controls, import restrictions, affirmative action, and farm price supports affect the conditions of market production and exchange. They influence what resources are used, in what quantities, and often at what price. These rules thereby have a direct effect on how the game is played.

Another set of rules redistributes the winnings when the game is over. Taxes and transfers redistribute earnings after production and exchange have taken place. The problem is that the way the winnings are reallocated can also influence the way the game is played. For example, what if all the winnings are divided equally among the players when the game is over? What effect do you suppose this would have on the intensity and quality of play? The probable effect would be that players would not accord the same attention to the game as when the game is "for keeps." Likewise, each individual's incentives to work, to invest, and to take risks will be affected by the redistribution of earnings.

Allowing for changes in the rules can introduce other distortions that can affect the efficiency and equity of the game. A player can either devote more resources toward winning under the existing rules (either sharpening game skills or playing with greater intensity) or spend time trying to change the rules to his or her advantage. Some rule changes can be of the positive-sum variety, actually helping players on net by making the game more efficient. The problem, however, is that changes in the rules that help one player or class of players often harm other players. In fact, rule changes may in the aggregate impose more harm on the losers than is gained by the winners; such changes thus have a negative sum.

As you can see, the introduction of rules and rule changes can affect the economy in a variety of ways. Choices about the rules of the game are typically public choices. We turn now to a closer examination of the public choice process.

PUBLIC CHOICE IN DIRECT DEMOCRACY

Government decisions about the supply of goods and services and the collection of revenues are public choices. In a democracy public choices usually require approval by a majority of the voters. As we will see, majority voting often amounts to surrendering the choice to the typical, or median, voter in the community. Consequently, it will be possible to explain the choice of the electorate by focusing on the preferences of the median voter.

Median-Voter Model

Here is the logic behind the median-voter framework. Suppose you and two roommates have just moved into an apartment, and the three of you must decide how it should be furnished. You all agree that the common costs will be divided equally among the three of you and that majority rule will prevail, with one vote per person. The issue at hand is whether to rent a TV and, if so, of what size? The problem is that you each have different preferences. The more studious of your roommates considers a TV to be an annoying distraction and would rather not have one around. Your other roommate, a real TV fan, prefers the 36-inch screens often seen in bars and other cultural centers. Although by no means a TV addict, you enjoy watching TV as a relief from the rigors of academe; you think a 19-inch screen would be just fine. What to do, what to do?

Exhibit 1 describes your preference and those of your roommates. The horizontal axis measures the size of the TV screen, and the vertical axis measures the order of preference each of you has for the different sizes. Your studious roommate is identified as S, the TV fan is F, and you are Y. We focus on three possibilities: no TV, a 19-inch TV, and a 36-inch TV. For example, your studious roommate, S, most prefers the option of no TV, has medium preference for the 19-inch TV and least prefers the 36-inch set. The preference orderings of the TV fan, F, are just the opposite. You, Y, most prefer the 19-inch screen but would rather have the 36-inch TV to no TV at all.

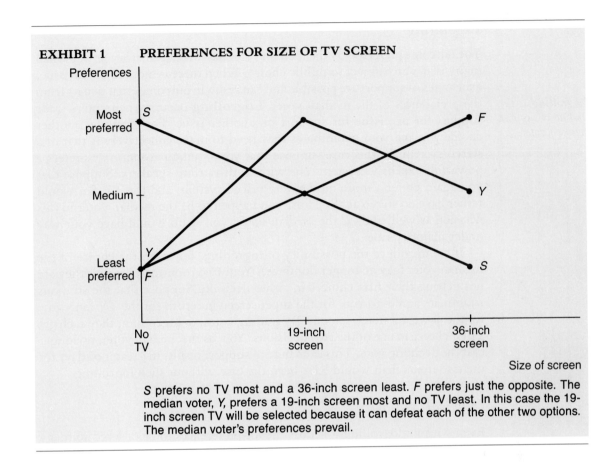

EXHIBIT 1   PREFERENCES FOR SIZE OF TV SCREEN

S prefers no TV most and a 36-inch screen least. F prefers just the opposite. The median voter, Y, prefers a 19-inch screen most and no TV least. In this case the 19-inch screen TV will be selected because it can defeat each of the other two options. The median voter's preferences prevail.

Since the three of you decided to be ruled by the majority, you all agree to make the decision by voting on two alternatives at a time, then pairing the winner against the remaining alternative until one choice dominates the others. When a motion for no TV is put forth against the motion to rent the 19-inch set, the 19-inch set gains majority support because this option gets your vote and the TV fan's vote, who prefers the 19-inch set to no TV. When a motion for the 36-inch screen is then paired against the 19-inch screen, the 19-inch screen wins a majority again, this time because your studious roommate sides with you rather than supporting the super screen.

As you can see, majority voting in effect delegates the public choice to the person whose preference is the median for the group. You, as the median voter in this case, can have your way; if you wanted a 12-inch screen, you could have received majority support for that size. Similarly, the median voter in an electorate often decides public choices.

Note that under majority rule, only the median voter actually receives his or her most preferred amount of the good. All other voters are required to buy either too much or too little of the good. In contrast, under voluntary exchange in private markets, each consumer can purchase the desired amount.

Logrolling

Logrolling *is the trading of support between voters.*

The outcome preferred by the median voter has less explanatory power when many issues are subject to public choice. When there is more than one issue, exchanges of support are possible and can result in outcomes that depart from the preferences of the median voter. **Logrolling** occurs when voters trade support for one issue for support on another issue. For example, another choice you and your roommates may need to make collectively is that of a stereo system. In this case suppose that your studious roommate prefers a powerful, expensive system, one with teeth-rattling speakers. Suppose that you again prefer a more moderately priced system, and the TV fan would rather have no stereo at all. Thus, you happen to be the median voter in this decision as well, and, as the median voter, you again would have your way under majority rule.

If we introduce the possibility of logrolling, however, the choice of the median voter may no longer dominate. Your two roommates realize they are not getting their first choices in either decision. Suppose that the studious roommate agrees to vote for the super screen in return for the TV fan's vote for the powerful stereo system. By trading votes, or logrolling, they each get a first choice in one of the two decisions. You, as the median voter, no longer cast the deciding vote. This exchange of support results in greater outlays for the two items than would have been the case without such logrolling.

Cyclical Majority

Even without logrolling it is possible for preferences to be ordered so that a clear majority choice does not exist. Suppose, for example, that the TV fan still prefers the super screen the most, but, as a purist, prefers no TV to any TV smaller than the super size. Such an ordering is shown for F in Exhibit 2; preferences for S and Y remain as before. If under these circumstances the 19-inch screen is up for a vote against the giant screen, the 19-inch screen wins a majority, as before. If a motion for the 19-inch screen is then paired with no TV, however, the no-TV alternative gains a majority, winning both the studious roommate's vote and the TV fan's vote. If the no-TV option is then paired with the 36-inch screen, the large screen wins your vote and the TV fan's vote, thereby gaining a majority.

There is no dominant winner in this case. For example, although the 19-inch option defeats the 36-inch option, the no-TV option defeats the 19-inch option, but then the 36-inch option defeats the no-TV option. No matter which alternative wins in a particular pairing, there is always another option that can beat that winner. Instead of having a clear majority, there is a *cyclical majority*, with the outcome depending on the order of voting. What causes this cycle is that the TV fan prefers no TV to any TV smaller than the giant screen.

Perhaps an application to public finance would be helpful. Let's consider the preferences for education in your town. Suppose that high-income families prefer that the public schools be first-rate. Those families of middle

EXHIBIT 2 **PREFERENCE PATTERN THAT CAUSES CYCLICAL MAJORITY**

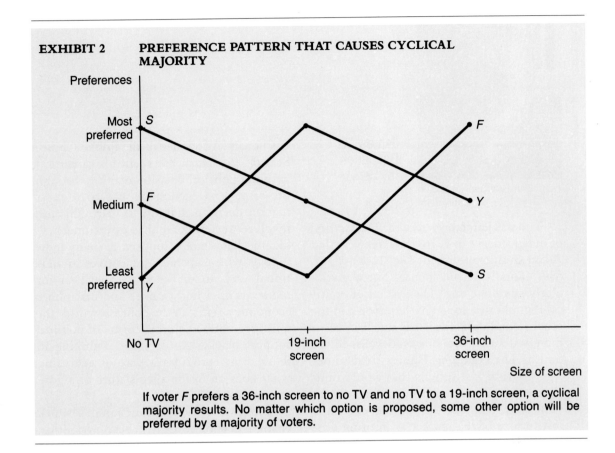

If voter *F* prefers a 36-inch screen to no TV and no TV to a 19-inch screen, a cyclical majority results. No matter which option is proposed, some other option will be preferred by a majority of voters.

income and below are not able to afford a Cadillac school system and prefer a moderate budget. High-income voters believe that if the schools are not going to be first-rate, then a private school becomes a more attractive option for their children. If high-income families send their children to private schools, they would no longer support public school spending and would prefer a low budget to a moderate budget. Thus, the most affluent families prefer the highest school budget, but if this fails, they prefer a low school budget to a moderate budget. This set of preferences will lead to a cyclical majority in public choices regarding the school budget.

You should remember several points from this discussion of majority rule. First, majority rule usually reflects the views of the typical, or median, voter. Second, under majority rule all but the median voter will usually be required to purchase either more of less of the public good than they would have preferred. Thus, majoritarian democracy means that there are likely to be many dissatisfied voters. Third, because of the possibility of logrolling, the preferences of the median voter may not dominate when many issues are decided. And fourth, because of the possibility of a cyclical majority, majority rule may result in no clear choice.

James M.
Buchanan
(b. 1919)

Carl Zitzmann/George Mason
University

Thomas Jefferson wrote the Declaration of Independence in 1776, the same year that Adam Smith published *The Wealth of Nations.* This is a coincidence, but a particularly symbolic one. The system of political thought developed by Jefferson and the other Founding Fathers has much in common with the economics developed by Smith. The Founding Fathers tried to design political institutions that would limit abuses of political power—in much the same way that Smith saw the economic institutions of the market as limiting economic power and channeling self-interest in beneficial directions. The separation of powers among the three branches of government is just one of the "checks and balances" that preoccupied political thought in the early republic.

The connection between economic and political thought grew weaker over the years. Economists concentrated on market phenomena; and, to the extent they mentioned the political process at all, they tended to assume that governments acted in an uncomplicated and disinterested manner to correct imperfections in the market. Recently, however, the gap between economics and politics has begun to close, and economists are returning to the insights of 200 years ago.

The most influential figure in this reunion of economics and politics is James Buchanan. A founder of the Public Choice School, Buchanan has spent his career examining political decision making through the same lens economists use to look at market decision making. In part, this has involved recognizing that governments—like markets—are composed of many individuals who respond to incentives in a rational way. In markets, competition for money profits both guides and disciplines economic agents; in the political world, the quest for votes and other forms of political support plays a similar role. Thinking in these terms provides a way of analyzing what goes on inside a legislature or a government bureau.

But not only has Buchanan's work brought economic ideas to bear on politics, it has also brought political concerns back into economics. Buchanan's writings have often centered on questions of constitutional design and political philosophy. Like the political writers of the early United States, he is concerned with setting up institutions that constrain abuses of political power and channel the interests of political agents in the same directions as those of the citizens they serve.

James Buchanan was born in Murfreesboro, Tennessee. He attended Middle Tennessee State, the University of Tennessee, and the University of Chicago, where he received the Ph.D. in 1948. Most of his career has been spent in Virginia, first at the University of Virginia, later at Virginia Polytechnic Institute, and now at George Mason University. Buchanan won the Nobel Prize in economics in 1986.

Richard Langlois

Thus far we have considered outcomes when individuals make public choices by voting directly on the issues. In practice, however, voters usually elect representatives, who, in turn, vote on specific issues. The effects of representation on public choice will be considered next.

REPRESENTATIVE DEMOCRACY

People vote directly on issues at a New England town meeting and at occasional referenda, but direct democracy is not the most common means of public choice. When you consider the thousands of public choices that must be made on behalf of the individual voters, direct democracy through referendum becomes unwieldy and impractical. Rather than make myriad decisions by direct referendum, voters typically elect a representative, who, in turn, makes public choices to reflect constituents' views.

In our federal system each voter helps choose representatives at a minimum of three levels of government: federal, state, and local. Many properties of public choice remain the same whether voting is direct or through representative democracy. For example, under certain conditions the public choice reflects the preferences of the median voter. The question of representation, however, raises a special set of issues that we will explore in this section.

Goals of the Participants

We assume that consumers maximize utility and firms maximize profit, but what about governments? As noted in Chapter 4, there is no common agreement about what governments maximize, or, more precisely, what objective elected officials maximize. One theory that appears to reflect the rational self-interest employed in private choices is that elected officials attempt to *maximize their political support*. Political support can take the form not only of votes but also of campaign contributions and in-kind support, such as campaign workers.

Producers have an intense interest in any program that affects their livelihood. However, because consumers do not specialize in the consumption of any particular product, each consumer has less of an interest in any of the thousands of special-interest proposals that come before elected officials. This conflict between the special and the common interests was underscored during our discussion of government regulations. You may recall that there remained some question about whether government regulation served the interests of consumers or those of producers. Since producers were found to have a much more intense interest in regulations affecting their industry than consumers, producers were thought to exert inordinate influence on the course of such regulations. The problem can be extended from the narrow issue of regulation to include all issues involving taxation and subsidies of particular groups of voters.

When representative democracy replaces direct democracy, a greater possibility arises that elected representatives will cater to the special interests rather than serve the interests of the majority. The problem arises because of the asymmetry between the special interest and the common interest or between producers and consumers.

Let's consider only one of the thousands of decisions that are made each year by elected representatives: an obscure federal program that subsidizes wool production in the United States. Under the wool-subsidy program, the federal government establishes and guarantees a floor price to be paid to sheep farmers for each pound of wool they produce. In 1983, for example, the guaranteed price was $1.53 per pound at a time when the world market price was $0.61 per pound, thereby providing wool producers with a subsidy of $0.92 per pound. During deliberations to renew the subsidy program, the only person to testify before Congress was a representative of the National Wool Growers Association, who noted how vital the subsidy was to the country's economic welfare.[1] This federal subsidy costs taxpayers about $75 million per year. Why had not a single representative of taxpayer interests testified against the subsidy? Why were sheep farmers able to pull the wool over the taxpayers' eyes?

Rational Ignorance

As we have said, households consume so many different public and private goods and services that they have neither the time nor the incentive to understand the effects of public choices on every one of these products. Voters realize that each has but a tiny possibility of influencing the outcome of public choices. Moreover, even if an individual voter is somehow able to affect the outcome, the impact of the policy on that voter is likely to be small. For example, even if a taxpayer could successfully stage a grass-roots campaign to eliminate the wool subsidy, that individual would probably save less than $1 per year in federal income taxes. Therefore, unless voters have concentrated interests, they adopt a policy of *rational ignorance*, which means that they remain largely oblivious to the cost and benefits of the thousands of proposals to come before legislative bodies. The costs of acquiring and acting on such information are typically less than any expected benefits.

In contrast, consumers have a greater incentive to gather and act upon information about decisions they make in private markets because they benefit directly from the knowledge acquired. In a world where information

---

[1]As noted by James Bovard, "A Subsidy Both Wooly-Headed and Mammoth." *The Wall Street Journal*, 17 April 1985.

and the time required to acquire and digest it are scarce, consumers concentrate on private choices rather than public choices because the payoff in making private choices is usually more immediate and more direct. The consumer in the market for a new car has an incentive to examine the performance record of different models rather than get stuck with a lemon. That consumer can then decide on the Ford versus the Buick. But the same individual has less incentive to examine the performance record of candidates for public office because that single voter has virtually no chance of deciding the election.

Distributions of Costs and Benefits

More generally, the possibility remains that in representative democracy an influential minority may be able to use the public sector to transfer wealth from the majority to itself. To facilitate the discussion and sharpen the focus, redistributional issues can be classified according to their underlying distributions of costs and benefits. The costs imposed by a particular legislative measure may be either narrowly borne or widely distributed over the population, depending on the issue. Likewise, the benefits can either be narrowly conferred on a small band of voters or affect much of the population.

Given the total amount of the transfer, or benefits, the more widespread the cost or benefits are, the less they will affect any individual. Alternatively, the more concentrated the costs or benefits are, the more important they become to those affected. The possible combinations of costs and benefits yield four alternative types of distributions: (1) widespread costs and widespread benefits, (2) widespread costs and concentrated benefits, (3) concentrated costs and concentrated benefits, and (4) concentrated costs and widespread benefits. These categories are displayed in Exhibit 3.

Issues of type 1 perhaps best characterize traditional public goods, such as national defense and a system of justice. Nearly everyone pays, and nearly everyone benefits from this category of distribution. The distribution of type 2 involves concentrated benefits but widespread costs, a distribution of benefits and costs typically associated with **special-interest legislation**. For example, if some special-interest group, such as wool producers, can get Congress to adopt legislation that takes just $1 from each taxpayer and transfers it to wool producers, this would yield that special interest over $85 million. Type 3 issues involve both concentrated costs and concentrated benefits, such as importers of shoes versus domestic manufacturers of shoes, or the Airline Pilots Association versus the airlines. Such measures can be thought of as **competing-interest legislation**.

The final type of issue imposes costs in a concentrated way to confer benefits widely. The special-interest group whose ox is being gored will cry foul and discourage the passage of such legislation. Meanwhile, the potential beneficiaries will remain rationally ignorant of the proposed legislation, so they will provide little political support for such a measure. For example,

Special-interest legislation *involves concentrated benefits but widespread costs.*

Competing-interest legislation *involves concentrated cost and concentrated benefits.*

EXHIBIT 3   **POSSIBLE DISTRIBUTIONS OF COSTS AND BENEFITS OF GOVERNMENT PROGRAMS**

Distribution of Benefits

	Widespread	Concentrated
Widespread	(1)	(2)
Concentrated	(4)	(3)

Distribution of Costs

whenever Congress considers imposing a tax on a particular industry, that industry floods Washington with lobbyists and mail, usually noting how the tax will lead to economic ruin, not to mention the decline of Western civilization as we know it today. Thus, legislation that imposes costs on a small group but confers benefits widely has little chance of being passed.

RENT SEEKING

An important feature of representative democracy is the incentive it offers participants to employ legislation to increase their wealth, either through direct transfers or through favorable public expenditures and regulations. The primary motive for such redistribution is that the recipients want it, and they have the political power to direct income toward themselves. Special-interest groups try to persuade elected officials to approve measures that provide the special interest with some market advantage or some outright transfer or subsidy. Such benefits are sometimes called *rents*, in yet another use of that term. The term *rents* in this context implies that the government transfer or subsidy constitutes a payment to the resource owner that is over and above the earnings necessary to call forth that resource. The activity that interest groups undertake to elicit these special favors from government is called **rent seeking**.

Rent seeking is the expenditure of resources to obtain favorable treatment from government.

Competition among groups to obtain rents has been of growing concern to scholars of public choice. As a firm's profitability becomes more and more dependent on decisions made in Washington, resources are diverted from productive activity to rent seeking, or lobbying. One firm may thrive because it secured some special advantage at a critical time, while another firm may fail because its managers were more concerned with productive efficiency than with rent seeking.

Let's consider, for example, the market depicted in Exhibit 4. Suppose that this good is produced in a constant-cost industry, so the long-run supply curve is horizontal. With no barriers to entry, firms will enter this industry until the market supply intersects the market demand at point *b*, where output equals *Q*, price equals *P*, and all firms earn a normal profit. Consumers enjoy the consumer surplus of *abP*.

Now suppose that the government for some reason decides that this good should be supplied by an unregulated monopolist and invites applications for the designation of monopoly supplier. As long as entry is restricted, an unregulated monopolist will reduce market output to *Q'*, raise the price to *P'*, and earn economic profit identified by the red-shaded rectangular area. The entry barrier could be import restrictions, a tariff on foreign goods, operating licenses, or some other device that effectively blocks entry.

EXHIBIT 4   MONOPOLY PROFIT, RENT SEEKING, AND WELFARE LOSS

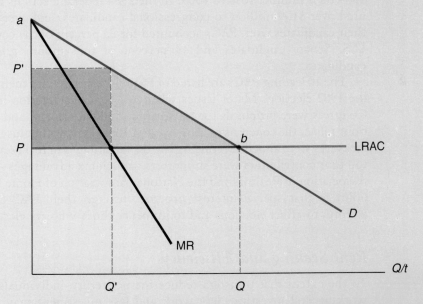

A competitive industry will produce at point *b*, with output *Q* and price *P*. All firms will earn a normal profit, and consumers will enjoy a consumer surplus equal to the area *abP*. If government decides to allow the industry to become monopolized, output will fall to *Q'*, and price will rise to *P'*. The monopolist will earn a profit shown by the red-shaded area.

The welfare loss to society includes the loss of consumer surplus, identified by the blue-shaded welfare triangle. In addition, potential monopolists will devote resources to rent seeking—an additional welfare loss.

Many would-be monopolists are understandably interested in securing this monopoly profit and will expend resources on campaign contributions, lobbyists, and other efforts to win the right to produce as a monopolist. We learned earlier that the welfare loss associated with monopoly includes the loss of consumer surplus, identified by the welfare triangle, designated in Exhibit 4 by the blue shading. But with many potential monopolists competing for the profits—with many who are rent seeking—the total cost of monopoly is now more than the simple welfare triangle. The welfare cost includes the resources devoted to rent seeking. These resources result in no output that is of social value. Firms competing for rents may be expected to spend in the aggregate an amount equal to the present value of the economic profits identified by the red-shaded rectangle. The government frequently bestows some special advantage on a producer or group of producers, and abundant resources are expended to secure these rights. In the next section we consider one type of such expenditures.

Political Action Committees

Special-interest groups can direct campaign contributions to favored candidates through *political action committees*, often referred to as PACs. In 1974, 608 such committees were registered with the Federal Election Commission; in 1984 their number rose to 4009. In the 1984 federal elections PACs contributed over $100 million to congressional candidates, and over 75 percent of their candidates won. PACs accounted for 23 percent of the contributions to U.S. Senate candidates and 44 percent of the amount given to House candidates.

The 10 leading PACs are listed in Exhibit 5, along with their growth since the 1982 election. Major issues scheduled for consideration in the ensuing Congress were proposals for budget cuts and tax reform, and the contributions reflect the concerns of interested groups. Perhaps because proposed tax measures were aimed at reducing the tax advantages in real estate, two of the top four contributers were supporters of such tax advantages—the National Association of Realtors and the National Association of Home Builders. The point is that special-interest groups, through their PAC contributions, attempt to affect elections and to influence those who are elected.

Rent Seeking and Efficiency

To the extent that transfers reduce the net return individuals expect from working and investing, less work and less investment may occur. If this happens, income will not simply be transferred but also potential income will go unearned. Moreover, if people choose between income-creating activity and income-transferring activity—rent seeking—they shift resources from productive activities to rent-seeking activities, such as lobbying, which focus on the transfer of income. Resources that are employed in an attempt to get government to redistribute income or wealth are largely unproductive because they do nothing to make the pie bigger and often end up making it

EXHIBIT 5
CONTRIBUTIONS OF POLITICAL ACTION
COMMITTEES (PACs)
TO CONGRESSIONAL CAMPAIGNS, 1984

PAC	1984 Contribution	Growth from 1982 Election (percent)
National Association of Rentors	$2,564,962	21
American Medical Association	2,043,644	18
National Education Association	1,911,147	62
National Association of Home Builders	1,750,557	74
United Auto Workers	1,689,348	4
Machinists Union	1,570,323	9
Letter Carriers Union	1,477,968	281
Seafarers Union	1,437,812	69
Food & Comm'l Workers Union	1,383,806	90
Association of Milk Producers	1,179,059	23

Source: Brooks Jackson, "PAC Money Talks Louder Now," *The Wall Street Journal*, 24 December 1984.

smaller. And often many firms compete for the same government advantage, thereby wasting still more resources.

As Mancur Olson notes, special-interest groups typically have little incentive to make the economy more efficient.[2] In fact, any special interest will usually support legislation transferring wealth to them even if the measure reduces the economy's overall efficiency. Thus, special-interest groups have incentives to support negative-sum transfers. For example, assume that lawyers are able to introduce a measure that has the effect of increasing their incomes by a total of $1 billion per year; this amounts to about $1400 per lawyer. Suppose that, as a result of this measure, litigation increases and insurance premiums go up, raising the total cost of production by $5 billion. Lawyers themselves will have to bear part of this higher cost, but since lawyers account for only about 1 percent of the spending in the economy, they bear only about 1 percent of the higher cost—a total of $50 million, or about $70 per lawyer. Thus, the legislation is a bargain for lawyers because it increases each lawyer's income by $1400 but increases each lawyer's costs by only $70.

Lawyers are only one of hundreds of special-interest groups. With many competing interest groups—farmers, physicians, lawyers, teachers, manu-

---

[2] *The Rise and Decline of Nations* (New Haven, Conn.: Yale University Press, 1982.)

facturers, barbers, and on and on—rent seeking, in Olson's words, is "like a china shop filled with wrestlers battling over the china, and breaking far more than they carry away."[3] Olson argues that most redistribution is not from the upper- and middle-income groups to the lower-income groups but from one middle-income group to another middle-income group, and from all income groups to certain high-income groups.

Olson, incidentally, is far less concerned about incentive problems associated with redistribution to the poor than he is about the major distortions that arise when special-interest groups get into the act. Since the poor are by definition contributing less to the economy's output, the incentive problems created by distorting the use of those resources are relatively modest compared to the loss that arises when the country's best minds are occupied with devising schemes to avoid taxes, developing and enforcing restrictive work rules, and other practices that transfer income to favored groups at the expense of market efficiency. For example, the pursuit of tax loopholes encourages some of the best and the brightest to become tax lawyers and accountants.

Since the division of earnings is often represented in pie charts, think of the economy's output in a particular period as depicted by a pie. Thus, the pie is the total value of goods and services produced. In deciding the "what," "how," and "for whom" questions, rule makers have three alternatives: (1) they can introduce changes that will yield a bigger pie (that is, positive-sum changes), (2) they can decide simply to carve up the existing pie differently (zero-sum changes), or (3) they can start fighting over the pie, so some of it ends up on the floor (negative-sum changes).

CASE STUDY

Farm Subsidies: The Negative-Sum Game

Let's trace the redistributive and efficiency effects of a specific example of rent-seeking legislation—farm subsidy programs. The Agricultural Marketing Agreement Act was introduced in 1937 to prevent what had been viewed as "ruinous competition" among farmers. Over the years the government has introduced a variety of policies to set floor prices for farm products ranging from milk to honey. For example, in 1984 the federal government paid nearly $100 million to buy more than half of all the honey produced in this country. A much more extensive and expensive program involves the price supports in the dairy industry. Let's consider the economic effects of that program.

Let's assume that the market price of milk in the absence of any government intervention is $1 per half gallon. This is depicted in Exhibit 6, where 100 million half-gallons are sold per week. Suppose that this represents the long-run equilibrium for the dairy industry in the absence of government intervention, so dairy farmers are earning just a normal rate of return. Consumers as a group earn the consumer surplus shown as the shaded area in

[3]Mancur Olson, "What We Lose When the Rich Go on the Dole," *The Washington Monthly* (January 1984): 49.

Exhibit 6. Recall that consumer surplus is the difference between the most that consumers would have been willing to pay for each unit of the good and the price actually paid.

EXHIBIT 6   **EFFECTS OF MILK PRICE SUPPORTS**

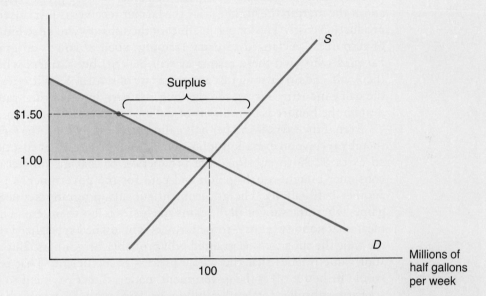

In the absence of government intervention, the market price of milk is $1 per half gallon and 100 million half gallons are sold per week. If Congress establishes a floor price of $1.50 per half gallon, then the quantity supplied will increase and the quantity demanded will decrease. To maintain the higher price, the government must buy up the surplus milk at $1.50 per half gallon.

Consumers are worse off as a result of this policy. The price has increased by $0.50. Also, they must pay for government purchases of surplus milk as well as for the cost of storing that milk. In the long run, farmers are no better off since the policy will drive up the prices of resources specialized to dairy farming.

Suppose, however, that farmers are able to convince Congress that such a price is too low. As a result, Congress introduces legislation establishing a floor price for milk of, say, $1.50 per half gallon. Farmers clearly have an incentive to increase the quantity supplied at the higher price, but consumers buy less. To make the higher price stick, the government must also agree to buy any "surplus" milk left over after consumer demand has been satisfied. Assume that at $1.50 per half gallon consumers buy only half of all the milk farmers produce, as indicated by Exhibit 6.

Consumers end up paying dearly to subsidize the farmers. First, the price per half gallon has increased by $0.50. Second, taxpayers must pay for government purchases of surplus milk. And third, taxpayers must then pay for storing all that surplus milk. Consider the price the typical consumer-taxpayer now pays for a half gallon of milk. The consumer must pay $1.50 for the half gallon; the consumer as an average taxpayer must also pay another $1.50 for the half gallon the government buys, plus, say, an extra $0.25 per half gallon to store that government purchase. Instead of paying just $1—the price in the absence of government price supports—the typical consumer-taxpayer is "milked" for a total outlay of $3.25 per half gallon, or an extra outlay of $2.25 per half gallon of milk consumed.

How do the farmers make out? Each farmer receives an extra $0.50 per half gallon over what would have prevailed in a free market. As farmers increase their output, however, the marginal cost of production increases, and at the margin the higher price the farmer receives is just offset by higher production costs. The long-run effect of the subsidy will be to bid up the cost of resources specialized to dairy farming, such as cows and grazing land. Farmers who own these resources will benefit, but farmers who purchase them will end up earning just a normal rate of return. So with free entry into the dairy industry, farmers in the long run earn just a normal rate of return despite the hundreds of millions of dollars spent on the program.

Even if the extra $0.50 per half gallon were pure profit, the farmer would thereby receive an extra $1 for producing each *gallon*. But it cost the taxpayer an extra $2.25 to subsidize the production of that gallon (recall that the consumer bought a half gallon and paid for the government's purchase of another half gallon). The government subsidy program is a negative-sum game, where the sum of all the gains and losses is less than zero. This does not mean that nobody gains—those farmers who owned specialized resources at the time the subsidy was granted will probably be winners. But a negative-sum game implies that the whole process is inefficient. That is, everyone would be better off if the government made a direct payment to farmers.

Farm subsidies totaled $25 billion in 1986, with dairy subsidies accounting for $2 billion of the total. Farm subsidies cost more in 1986 than Aid to Families with Dependent Children, the primary cash transfer program for the poor. A straight income transfer between taxpayers and dairy farmers that was not tied to milk production would be more efficient.

Although a direct transfer program is often more efficient, it is usually less acceptable politically because it is so obvious. Rent seeking is often pursued under the cover of some greater good, such as ensuring the national defense, promoting stability in the economy, saving domestic jobs, stabilizing farm prices, and the like. It is seldom couched in terms of seeking a particular program because it would transfer income from a majority of taxpayers to the special-interest group. Such a transparent special-interest proposal could attract the public's attention and be doomed. Whether it is milk or honey, when you subsidize a particular activity, you tend to get more of it. Conversely, when you tax it, you tend to get less of it, as we will now see.

The Underground Economy

Did you ever work as a waiter or waitress? Did you faithfully report all your tips to the Internal Revenue Service? To the extent that you did not, your unreported tips became part of the underground economy. The *underground economy* is a term used to represent all market activity that goes unreported to the government because the earners of that income are trying to evade taxes.

The introduction of a tax has two effects. First, if a tax reduces the net return expected from supplying a resource, often less of the resource will be supplied. Second, in an attempt to evade taxes, market participants divert their economic activity from the formal, reported economy to an underground, "off-the-books" economy. Thus, when the government taxes market exchange, or the income arising from that exchange, less formal market activity occurs.

Higher taxes lead to barter. For example, a plumber and an accountant may barter services to evade taxes. Although tax evasion is the primary reason why certain market exchanges go unreported, some types of economic activity are not reported because they are illegal. Thus, income arising in the underground economy ranges from the earnings of drug dealers to those of the "moonlighting" accountant.

We should take care to distinguish between tax avoidance and tax evasion. Tax avoidance is the legal attempt to arrange one's economic affairs so as to pay the least tax possible. For example, the loss of tax revenue in 1984 because individuals and corporations took advantage of legal tax loopholes amounted to $322 billion, more than enough to cover the federal deficit that year. This action is tax avoidance. Tax evasion is illegal and arises from either failing to file a tax return or filing a fraudulent return by understating income or overstating deductions.

While there are no official figures on the size of the underground economy, federal agencies have developed estimates using different approaches. The problem is that there is no common definition of what activities should be included in the underground economy. The Census Bureau estimates that the nation's underground economy was $222 billion in 1981, or 7.5 percent of the gross national product. The Internal Revenue Service conducted a survey that same year to estimate just how much revenue was lost through tax evasion and concluded that the government lost $90.5 billion. This figure was three times their estimate from a decade earlier, suggesting that the underground economy was growing faster than the economy as a whole.

One motive for lowering the rates on personal income taxes in the 1986 tax reform was to encourage those in the underground economy to join the mainstream of recorded economic activity. A lower marginal tax rate reduces the benefit of tax evasion. With a top marginal tax rate of 50 percent, the person who has gone underground evades $0.50 in taxes for each $1 earned. But with the highest marginal rate falling to 28 percent, as it did in the 1986 reform, the tax evader now saves only $0.28 in taxes.

Those who pursue rent-seeking activity and those involved in the underground economy view government from opposite perspectives. Rent seekers would like government to become actively involved in a way that will transfer wealth to them. But those in the underground economy want to evade any government contact. Subsidies and other advantages bestowed by government draw some groups closer to government; taxes encourage others to go underground.

BUREAUCRACY AND
REPRESENTATIVE DEMOCRACY

Elected representatives approve legislation, but the task of implementing that legislation is typically left to the various executive departments and agencies. The organizations charged with implementing legislation are usually referred to as *bureaus*, which are nonprofit agencies whose activities are financed by an appropriation from legislative bodies. Bureaus differ from firms primarily in the form of ownership and the method of financing, and as we will see, these differences influence the behavior and performance of bureaus.

Ownership and Funding of Bureaus

We can get a better feel for government bureaus by comparing them to corporations. Ownership of the corporation is based on the proportion of shares owned by each stockholder. Stockholders are the residual claimants of any profits or losses arising from the firm's operations. Ownership in the firm is also transferable; the shares can be sold in the stock market. In contrast, residents of each jurisdiction, by dint of their citizenship, are in a sense the "owners" of the government bureaus in that jurisdiction. If the bureau earns a "profit," taxes will be reduced; if the bureau operates at a "loss," as most do, this loss must be covered by taxes. Ownership in the bureau is surrendered if the taxpayer moves to another jurisdiction, but ownership of the bureau is not transferable—it cannot be bought and sold.

Whereas firms derive their revenue when customers voluntarily purchase their product, bureaus are typically financed by a budget appropriation from the legislature. Most of this budget comes from taxpayers. On occasion bureaus will earn revenue through the sale of output at specified user charges, but even here bureaus often receive supplementary assistance through budget appropriations. Because of these differences in the forms of ownership and the source of revenue, bureaus may have different incentives than for-profit firms do, so we might observe different behavior in the two organizations.

Ownership and Organizational Behavior

An underlying principle of economics is that people behave rationally and respond to economic incentives. To the extent that compensation is linked to individual incentives, people will behave more in accord with those incentives. If a letter carrier's pay is based on customer satisfaction, greater effort will be made to deliver mail promptly and intact.

The firm has a steady stream of consumer feedback because the product is sold in private markets. If the price is too high or too low to clear the market, the firm will know as the surpluses or shortages develop. Not only is there abundant consumer feedback but also the firm's owners have an incentive to act on that information in an attempt to satisfy consumer wants. The promise of profit also creates incentives to produce the output at minimum cost. Thus, the firm's owners stand to gain from any improvement in customer satisfaction or in production efficiency.

Problems arise, however, when the good is not sold. Bureaus receive their budget from the legislature and, in turn, supply public goods and services, which, once provided, are free to all. Since consumers do not usually purchase public goods and services directly, the system has little consumer feedback. There are no prices and no obvious shortages or surpluses. For example, how would you know whether there was a shortage or a surplus of police protection in your community? (Would gangs of police hanging around the doughnut shop indicate a surplus?)

Bureaucrats typically receive their marching orders through the legislative budget appropriation, which is based on the support for the bureau expressed by the voters. The formal means of communication between taxpayers and the legislature are the periodic elections. Elections, however, are relatively crude devices for communicating preferences about the output of a particular bureau.

Not only do bureaus receive little consumer feedback about the most desired quantity and quality of output, but they also have less incentive to act on the information available. Because any "profits" or "losses" arising in the bureau are spread among all taxpayers, and because there is no transferability of ownership, bureaus have less incentive to satisfy customers or to produce their output using the least-cost combination of resources. (Laws prevent bureaucrats from taking home any "profit" in brown paper bags.) Nor is there much incentive to return unspent funds to the legislature since this may well result in the bureau's budget being cut the next time around. Thus, because bureaucrats can neither take home nor return any money they save in the bureau's operation, they appear to have less incentive to minimize costs than managers in a firm have.

Some pressure for customer satisfaction and cost minimization may be communicated by voters to their elected representatives and thereby to the bureaus. This discipline, however, is likely to be less precise than that operating in the firm, particularly since any gains or losses in efficiency are diffused among all taxpayers. For example, suppose you are a citizen in a state with a million taxpayers and you become aware of some inefficiency costing taxpayers a million dollars a year. If you undertake measures that succeed in correcting the shortcoming, you save yourself about a dollar per year in taxes.

Because of differences between public and private organizations in the ability to transfer ownership and to appropriate profits, we expect bureaus to be less concerned with minimizing costs than private firms are. A variety of empirical studies have attempted to compare costs for products that are provided by both public bureaus and private firms. One of the best-known studies is by David Davies of Duke University, who compared the efficiency of two Australian airlines—one owned and operated by the government and the other privately owned and operated.[4] Even though the government regulated both airlines to make the conditions of operation as identical as possible, Davies found that when compared to the public airline, the private airline carried more passengers and freight per employee and had greater earnings per employee. Private firms have also been shown to be more efficient than public bureaus in the provision of other services, such as fire protection and garbage collection.

Bureaucratic Objectives

To the extent that bureaus are not simply at the beck and call of the legislature—that is, to the extent that bureaucrats have some autonomy—what sort of objectives will they pursue? One widely discussed theory of bureaucratic behavior has been put forth by William Niskanen, who argues that bureaus attempt to maximize their budget, for with the budget goes size, prestige, amenities, and staff, which are valued by bureaucrats.[5]

How do bureaucrats maximize the bureau's budget? Rather than sell units of output to the public for a price, bureaus are funded by the legislature. The bureau supplies its output to the legislature as a monopolist. Rather than charge a price per unit, bureaus attempt to offer the legislature the entire amount as a package deal in return for the requested appropriation. The legislature in this theory has little ability to dig into the budget and cut particular items. If cuts in the bureau's budget are proposed, the bureau will threaten to make those cuts that will be the most painful to the legislature and its constituents. For example, if town officials attempt to reduce the school budget, school bureaucrats may threaten to eliminate kindergarten or dissolve the high school football team. Similarly, any attempts by Congress to cut the defense budget may elicit threats by the Pentagon to close military installations located in the districts of key members of Congress. If such threats are effective in forcing the legislature to back off from any cuts, the government budget turns out to be larger than taxpayers would prefer.

Private Versus Public Production

Simply because public goods and services are financed by the government does not mean that they must also be produced by the government. For-profit firms have contracts to provide everything from fire protection to the operation of prisons. The mix of firms and bureaus varies across jurisdictions. At times elected officials can contract directly with private firms to produce the public output. For example, the city council can contract with a

---

[4]David G. Davies, "The Efficiency of Public Versus Private Firms: The Case Study of Australia's Two Airlines," *Journal of Law and Economics* 14 (April 1971): 149–165.

[5]William A. Niskanen, Jr., *Bureaucracy and Representative Government* (Chicago: Aldine-Atherton, 1971).

garbage collection firm to handle those services for the city. Elected officials may also use some combination of bureaus and firms to produce the desired output. For example, the Pentagon, a giant bureau, hires and trains military personnel, yet the government contracts with private firms to develop and produce various weapon systems. State governments typically hire contractors to build roads but use bureaus to maintain the roads.

When governments produce public goods and services, they are using the internal organization of the government—the bureaucracy—to supply the product. When governments contract with private firms to produce public goods and services, they are using the market to supply the good. Legislatures might prefer to deal with bureaus rather than with firms for two reasons. First, where it is difficult to specify a contract that clearly spells out all the possible contingencies, the internal organization of the bureau may be more responsive to the legislature's concerns than contractual agreements with firms. Second, to the extent that legislatures view bureaus as a source of political patronage and discretion, bureaus may provide legislators with more opportunities to reward friends and supporters with jobs than firms would.

Where services are not well defined, such as the guidance provided by a social worker, market competition might lead inevitably to poor service. A private firm that wins the contract might be tempted to shade on quality, particularly if the quality of the service can only be determined by direct observation when the service is provided. For example, suppose that government put social work out for bid, selected the lowest bidder, then attempted to monitor the quality of the service by direct observation. The government would find direct monitoring too costly. These services thus might be provided best by a government bureau. Because the bureau is less concerned with minimizing costs, it has less reason to lower quality to reduce cost.

CONCLUSION

This chapter examined how individual preferences are reflected in public choices. We began with direct voting based on majority rule, moved on to problems arising from representative democracy, and finally examined bureaus, the organizations that usually implement public choices.

We considered two forms of redistribution: direct transfers and indirect transfers. Direct transfers from one group to another now account for more the half of the federal budget (more is now spent on Social Security than on national defense). Indirect transfers arise because of changes in the rules governing economic activity in the private sector. Price supports, import restrictions, and other indirect transfers do not show up in the budget but often have a profound effect on the economy. Whenever governments become involved in the workings of the economy to favor one group over another, some resources will shift from productive activity to rent seeking—that is, efforts to persuade the government to confer benefits on certain groups. Individual incentives may also be distorted in a way that reduces total output.

Governments attempt to address failures in the private economy. But simply turning problems of perceived market failure over to government may not always be the best solution because government has failings of its own. Perhaps we should be more sensitive to government failure. Participation in markets is based on voluntary exchange. Governments, however, have the legal power to enforce public choices. We should employ at least as high a standard in judging the performance of government as we do in judging the private market, where decisions are based on voluntary exchange.

SUMMARY

1. Under certain conditions public choice under majority rule reflects the preferences of the median voter, implying that other voters must buy either more or less of the public good than they would prefer. When a cyclical majority arises, no clear public choice emerges. Logrolling allows voters to trade votes, resulting in public choices that may represent the preferences of a minority of voters rather than those of the median voter.

2. Producers have an abiding interest in the legislation that affects their livelihood. Consumers, however, purchase thousands of different products and have no special interest in legislation affecting the production and sale of any one good in particular. Consumers are said to adopt a posture of rational ignorance about producer-oriented legislation because the costs of keeping up with special-interest issues outweigh the benefits.

3. The intense interest that producer groups express for relevant legislation, coupled with the rational ignorance by the mass of voters on most issues, leaves government vulnerable to rent seeking by special interests. Elected officials who are interested in maximizing their political support may have a tendency to serve the producer interests rather than consumer interests--special interests rather than the public interest.

4. Special interests can lobby the government for direct transfers or for privileges that grant them some advantage in the marketplace. With government support, producers may be able to collude to raise prices or wages and thereby enhance their earnings or economic rents.

5. Much of the redistribution that occurs is not from rich to poor but from all taxpayers to some special-interest groups. These groups often inflict more harm on the economy than the benefits they reap, so it is not simply a case of transferring money from one group to another; it is not simply a zero-sum game.

6. Bureaus differ from firms in the amount of consumer feedback received, in their incentive to minimize costs, and in the transferability of ownership. Because of these differences, bureaus may not be as efficient and may not be as sensitive to consumer preferences as firms.

QUESTIONS AND PROBLEMS

1. (Median Voter) In a single issue vote, such as the television example in the chapter, will the median voter necessarily always get his most preferable outcome? If not, how would you alter the preferences in Exhibit 1 to show this?

2. (Majority Vote) We often hear that in the United States we are governed by the principle of majority rule. Is it true that majorities must always exist? Evaluate.

3. (Representative Government) What would guide the decision for a senator who must vote on an issue which does not directly affect his or her constituency? Is logrolling an important issue here? Why?

4. (Party Affiliation) Why might it be important to a person running for office to have a party affiliation? Does the existence of political parties reduce the transaction costs involved in voting?

5. (Consumer Interest Lobbies) Are there reasons why consumer interest groups in Washington are less effective than producer lobbies? If so, what reasons would you give?

6. (Voting) Why do less than 50% of the U.S. voting population consistently fail to vote? Is this failure related to the concept of rational ignorance?

7. (Logrolling) Is it possible for lobbies to also engage in a type of logrolling? How?

8. (Political Action Committees) How might the emergence of political action committees have contributed to the soaring costs of running a political campaign? Why are seats in the government, which pay so poorly, becoming so expensive to obtain?

9. (Subsidies) "To subsidize the price of milk or other agricultural products is not very expensive considering how many consumers there are in the United States. Therefore, there is little harmful effect from such subsidies." Evaluate.

10. (Underground Economy) How might the government control the growth of the underground economy? Why is it important to reduce the size of the underground economy?

PART
SIX

The International Setting

INTERNATIONAL TRADE

This morning you rolled out of bed, put on your Jordache jeans from Taiwan, laced up your Reebok shoes from Korea, and pulled on your Benetton sweater from Italy. After a breakfast that included ham from Poland and coffee from Brazil, you climbed into your Japanese Toyota fueled by petroleum from Saudi Arabia and headed for a lecture by a visiting professor from Yugoslavia.

Americans buy Japanese cars, French wine, Swiss clocks, and thousands of other goods from around the globe. Foreigners buy U.S. wheat, personal computers, aircraft, and thousands of other American products. The world is a giant shopping mall, and Americans are big spenders. In this chapter we examine the economics of international trade.

The family from Georgia that sits down to a meal of Kansas prime rib and Idaho potatoes has been involved in interstate trade. We have little difficulty understanding why the residents in one state trade with those in another. Comparative advantage, specialization, and trade allow people to use their scarce resources most efficiently to satisfy their unlimited wants. Residents of one country trade with those of another for the same reasons. International trade arises from voluntary exchange among buyers and sellers pursuing their self-interest. International trade is trade not between countries but between individuals in different countries. In this chapter we examine the gains from trade and the effects of trade restrictions. Topics discussed include:

- World prices

- Tariffs

- Quotas

- Arguments for trade restrictions

- General Agreement on Tariffs and Trade

THE GAINS FROM TRADE

Back in Chapter 2 we introduced the gains arising from specialization and exchange. You may recall how you and your roommate each specialized to reduce the time required to do daily chores. Just as no household is self-sufficient, no nation is naturally self-sufficient. To enjoy the gains that arise from specialized production, countries engage in international trade. With trade, each country can concentrate on producing those goods and services that it produces most efficiently.

Reasons for International Specialization

How can two countries both be better off as a result of exchange? And how do we know what each country should produce and what goods should be traded? There is no mystery about trade. Countries trade with one another—or more precisely, people in one country trade with those in another—because each side expects to gain from the exchange. Because exchange is voluntary, people do not trade unless they expect trade to be to their advantage. What are some reasons why exchange can benefit those involved?

Differences in Resource Endowments   Trade is often prompted by differences in resource endowments. Let's consider agriculture. Some countries have fertile land in abundance and a favorable growing season. The United States, for example, has been called the breadbasket of the world because of its rich farmland. Honduras has the ideal climate for growing bananas. Coffee is grown best in the climate and elevation of Columbia, Brazil, and Jamaica. Thus, the United States exports wheat and imports coffee and bananas.

Mineral resources are also distributed unevenly around the globe and are often concentrated in particular countries: oil in Saudi Arabia, bauxite in Jamaica, diamonds in South Africa, coal in the United States. The United States also has oil reserves, but not enough to satisfy domestic demand. Thus, the United States exports coal and imports oil, bauxite, and diamonds. More generally, countries export those products that they produce more cheaply in return for those that are unavailable or are more costly to produce than in other countries.

Differences in Tastes   Even if all countries had identical resource endowments and combined those resources with equal efficiency, each country would still gain from trade as long as tastes and preferences differed among countries. And consumption patterns do appear to differ, perhaps based on custom or religion. For example, the per capita consumption of beer in Germany is triple that in Norway and Spain. People in Italy and France drink eight times more wine than residents of Sweden and the Soviet Union. The English like tea; Americans, coffee.

A Profile of Imports and Exports

Some nations are more involved in international trade than others, just as some states are more involved with interstate trade than others. For example, international trade accounts for about half the GNP in the Netherlands and about a quarter of the GNP in Canada, West Germany, and the United Kingdom. Despite the perception that Japan has a giant export sector, only about 14 percent of Japanese production is involved in international trade.

America's foreign trade, though small relative to GNP, plays a vital role in the economy. Looked at by broad groupings, about half of our imports are manufactured goods, such as automobiles from Japan and color TVs from Taiwan. About 20 percent of our imports are petroleum and related products. About 10 percent of imports are agricultural products, such as cocoa, coffee, sugar, and bananas. The United States also depends on imports for some key inputs. Nearly all the bauxite used to produce aluminum is imported, and most of the platinum and chromium and all of the manganese, mica, diamonds, and nickel are also imported. The two main export groups are (1) high-technology manufactured products, such as computers, aircraft, and telecommunication equipment, and (2) agricultural products, such as corn, wheat, and soybeans.

The primary shift over the last two decades has been a growth in machinery exports; the biggest change in imports has been the fourfold increase since 1970 in the share of petroleum as a percentage of imports. The United States trades most with Canada, followed by Japan. Other important trading partners include Mexico, West Germany, Great Britain, South Korea, France, Hong Kong, Italy, and Brazil.

Absolute and Comparative Advantage

The rationale behind some international trade is obvious. The United States should not try to mine bauxite because the mineral is unavailable here; likewise, a country without coal deposits should not try to mine that mineral. However, the gains from trade are best explored where the cost advantage is not quite so obvious. Suppose that just two goods are produced and consumed—food and clothing—and there are only two countries in the world: the United States, with a labor force of 100 million workers, and Izodia, with 200 million workers. The conclusions we derive from our simple model will have general relevance to the pattern of international trade.

Based on the size of the labor force and the productivity of workers in each country, each country's production possibilities in the absence of trade are presented in Exhibit 1. Since no trade occurs between countries, Exhibit 1 presents each country's consumption possibilities as well. Suppose that each worker in the United States can produce either 6 units of food or 3 units of clothing per day. If all 100 million U.S. workers produce food, 600 units could be produced per day, as reflected by combination C_1 in Exhibit 1(a). If all workers produce clothing, the United States could produce 300 units per day, as reflected by combination C_6. Combinations in between represent possible output mixes of food and clothing.

Because an American worker can produce either 6 units of food or 3 units of clothing, the opportunity cost of producing 1 more unit of clothing is 2 units of food. Note from the combinations in panel (a) that each additional 60 million units of clothing reduces food production by 120 million units.

In Izodia workers are less educated, less capital is available per worker, and land is less fertile, so each worker can produce either 1 unit of food or 2 units of clothing per day. If all 200 million Izodian workers specialize in food production, the country can produce 200 million units of food per day, as reflected by combination I_1 in Exhibit 1(b). If all Izodian workers are involved in clothing production, 400 million units of clothing can be produced per day, as reflected by combination I_6. Some other production possibilities are also listed.

Since each worker can produce either 1 unit of food or 2 units of clothing per day, the opportunity cost in Izodia of producing 1 more unit of clothing is 0.5 unit of food. Note from the combinations in panel (b) that each additional 80 million units of clothing reduces food production by 40 million units.

Thus, American workers can produce 6 units of food per day compared to only 1 for the Izodian workers. Also, American workers can produce 3 units of clothing per day compared to only 2 units for Izodian workers. Because of

EXHIBIT 1
PRODUCTION POSSIBILITIES TABLES
FOR THE UNITED STATES AND IZODIA

(a) United States

	Units Produced per Worker per Day	Production Possibilities at Full Employment of 100 Million Workers (millions of units per day)					
		C_1	C_2	C_3	C_4	C_5	C_6
Food	6	600	480	360	240	120	0
Clothing	3	0	60	120	180	240	300

(b) Izodia

	Units Produced per Worker per Day	Production Possibilities at Full Employment of 200 Million Workers (millions of units per day)					
		I_1	I_2	I_3	I_4	I_5	I_6
Food	1	200	160	120	80	40	0
Clothing	2	0	80	160	240	320	400

natural endowments, education, and training, each worker in the United States can produce both more food and more clothing per day than can a worker in Izodia. American workers have an absolute advantage in the production of both goods because each good can be produced in less time.

Since the United States has an absolute advantage in the production of both commodities, should the United States be self-sufficient, producing both food and clothing, or can the U.S. gain from trade? We learned the answer in Chapter 2, when we observed the gains from trade between you and your roommate. In that example, even though you were better at both typing and ironing than your roommate, you each benefited from specializing in the activity in which you had a comparative advantage.

As long as the *relative* production costs of the two goods differ between the United States and Izodia, there are gains from specialization and trade. The opportunity cost of producing 1 more unit of clothing is 2 units of food in the United States, compared to only 0.5 unit of food in Izodia. Since the relative production cost of clothing is higher in the United States than in Izodia, both countries will gain if Izodia concentrates on producing clothing and exports it to the United States, and the United States concentrates on producing food and exports it to Izodia. Let's explore these gains from trade further.

Production Possibilities Frontiers

Gains from trade can be best underscored if we convert the tables in Exhibit 1 to production possibilities frontiers for each country, shown in Exhibit 2. In each diagram the amount of clothing produced is measured on the horizontal axis, and the amount of food on the vertical axis. Production combinations for the United States are reflected in panel (a) by C_1, C_2, and so on. Production combinations in Izodia are reflected in panel (b) by I_1, I_2, and so on.[1]

With no trade between these two countries, Exhibit 2 illustrates the possible combinations of food and clothing that residents of each country could produce and consume, given that all resources are fully employed. Suppose that American producers maximize profit and American consumers maximize utility with the combination of 240 units of food and 180 units of clothing, which is combination C_4. Suppose also that Izodians maximize profit and utility by consuming 120 units of food and 160 units of clothing, which is combination I_3. We next introduce trade and consider the gains that can result.

---

[1]Notice that because each production possibility curve is a straight line, we implicitly assume that in each country resources are perfectly adaptable to the production of each commodity. Thus, for simplicity we have temporarily repealed the law of increasing opportunity costs, described in Chapter 2. We could give each curve the usual bowed-out shape, but this complication would not alter the important conclusions of the analysis.

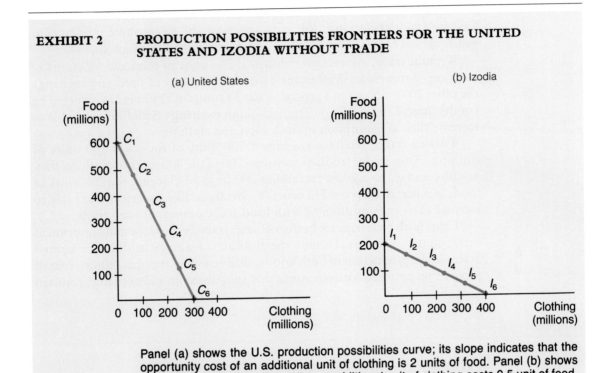

EXHIBIT 2   **PRODUCTION POSSIBILITIES FRONTIERS FOR THE UNITED STATES AND IZODIA WITHOUT TRADE**

(a) United States

(b) Izodia

Panel (a) shows the U.S. production possibilities curve; its slope indicates that the opportunity cost of an additional unit of clothing is 2 units of food. Panel (b) shows production possibilities in Izodia; an additional unit of clothing costs 0.5 unit of food. Clothing is cheaper to produce in Izodia.

The Gains from Trade

Since the opportunity cost of producing goods differs between the two countries, there will be mutual gains from trade. As we said, the opportunity cost of producing 1 more unit of clothing is 2 units of food in the United States but only 0.5 unit of food in Izodia. Thus, clothing has a lower opportunity cost in Izodia. From Chapter 2 we learned the law of comparative advantage, which says that the producer should specialize in the good with the lowest opportunity cost. Both countries can gain if the United States specializes in food and Izodia specializes in clothing.

Here is why. One unit of clothing costs 2 units of food in the United States but only 0.5 unit of food in Izodia. If the two countries can agree on an exchange rate where the United States can buy clothing for less than 2 units of food and Izodia can sell clothing for more than 0.5 unit of food, both countries will be better off with trade.

Suppose that the two countries agree on an exchange ratio where 1 unit of clothing trades for 1 unit of food. At this ratio the United States sacrifices less food by trading with Izodia for clothing than by producing clothing, so American workers specialize in the production of food. Similarly, Izodia sacrifices less clothing by trading with the United States for food than by producing food themselves, so Izodian workers specialize in the production of clothing. Exhibit 3 shows that with the exchange rate equal to 1 unit of food for 1 unit of clothing, Americans are now able to consume at point *C* in panel (a), and Izodians are able to consume at point *I* in panel (b).

Without trade, Americans consumed 240 units of food and 180 units of clothing. After trade, Americans consume 400 units of food and exchange the other 200 units of food produced for 200 units of clothing, as reflected by combination *C* in panel (a). Thus, through exchange Americans are able to increase their consumption of both food and clothing.

Without trade, Izodians consumed 120 units of food and 160 units of clothing. After trade, Izodians consume 200 of the 400 units of clothing they produce and exchange the remaining 200 units of clothing for 200 units of food, as reflected by point *I* in panel (b). Izodians, like Americans, are able to increase their consumption of both food and clothing through trade.

Thus, both countries are better off after trade because the consumption in each country increases. Despite the absolute advantage held by the United States in the production of both goods, differences in the opportunity cost of production between nations ensure that specialization and exchange result in

EXHIBIT 3   **PRODUCTION (AND CONSUMPTION) POSSIBILITIES FRONTIERS WITH TRADE**

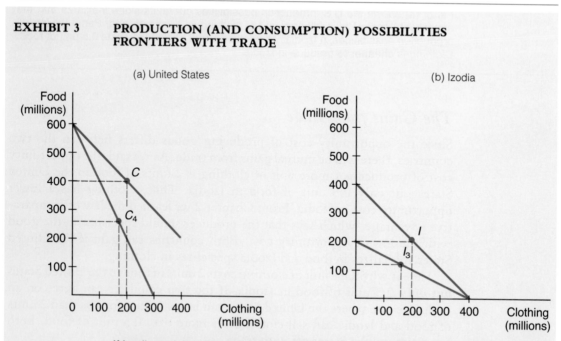

If Izodia and the U.S. can trade at the rate of 1 unit of clothing for 1 unit of food, both can benefit. At that exchange rate consumption possibilities are shown by the blue lines. The U.S. was previously producing and consuming combination C_4. By trading with Izodia, it can produce only food and still consume combination C—a combination that contains more food and more clothing than combination C_4 does. Likewise, Izodia can attain the preferred combination *I* by trading its clothing for U.S. food. Both countries are better off as a result of international trade.

mutual gains. Remember that comparative advantage, not absolute advantage, is the source of gains from trade.

The only constraint on trade is that, for each good, the total world production must equal total world consumption. We simplified trade relations in our example to highlight the gains from specialization and exchange. We assumed that each country would specialize in producing a particular good, that resources were equally adaptable to the production of either good, that the costs of transporting the goods from one country to another were inconsequential, and that there were no problems in arriving at an exchange rate.

So far we have observed the case where each country specializes in the production of a particular good. How does international trade affect prices and output in domestic markets when both countries produce a certain good? In the next section we rely on supply and demand analysis to develop an understanding of international markets.

TRADING ON THE WORLD MARKET

*The **world price** is the price determined by the world supply and world demand for a product.*

We now broaden our perspective to consider the world market for a product. The **world price** is the price determined by the world supply and demand for a product. This is the price at which any supplier can sell output on the world market and at which any demander can purchase output on the world market. If there are enough buyers and sellers throughout the world, no country's supply or demand for the good can affect the world price. Thus, the world price faced by each country is similar to the market price faced by each firm in perfect competition. Let's consider the market for a particular product — steel.

World Price Is Above the Domestic Equilibrium Price

Exhibit 4(a) shows the long-run supply and demand for steel in the United States. The world price of steel per ton is measured on the vertical axis. The U.S. demand curve for steel intersects the U.S. producers' supply curve at a price of $150 per ton. If the world price of steel is $150 per ton, the world price would equal the market-clearing price in the United States, so the world price of steel is the same as the price prevailing in the United States without international trade. As long as the world price of steel is $150, there is no need for international trade. U.S. demanders are willing to buy all that is produced by U.S. producers at that price. To develop a rationale for international trade, suppose that the world price of steel differs from what would be an equilibrium price based on domestic supply and demand.

What if the world price of steel is $200 per ton — above the $150 price that would prevail in the United States in the absence of trade? If international trade were prohibited, the world price would be irrelevant, and only the price determined in the United States would matter. But if U.S. producers can easily export steel to the rest of the world, they will increase their quantity supplied when the world price rises above $150 per ton. You can see from the supply curve in panel (a) that U.S. suppliers increase the quantity supplied from 100 to 130 million tons. Because of the higher price, U.S. demanders reduce their quantity demanded to 70 million tons.

The amount by which the quantity supplied by U.S. producers exceeds the quantity demanded in the United States equals the amount of steel exported by U.S. producers. Thus, when the world price equals $200, 60 million tons of steel are exported from the United States. U.S. exports relative to the world price are identified more explicitly in panel (b) of Exhibit 4. The vertical axis still presents the world price of steel, but the horizontal axis measures the amount of steel that is imported or exported based on the world price. As a point of reference, steel is neither imported nor exported if the world price equals $150 because the quantity supplied in the United States equals the quantity demanded in the United States. The point on the horizontal axis of panel (b) where the world price is $150 per ton and imports and exports equal 0 is identified as point *e*.

EXHIBIT 4   **THE DOMESTIC U.S. MARKET AND THE WORLD MARKET FOR STEEL**

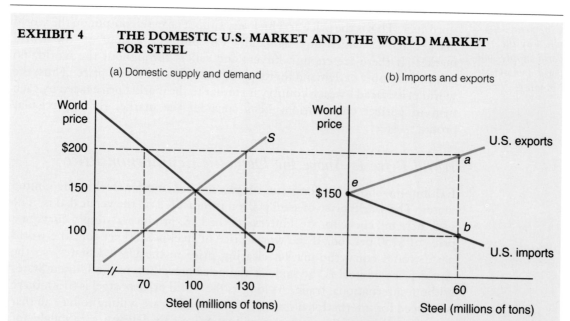

Panel (a) shows the domestic supply and demand for steel in the United States. At a world price of $150 per ton, U.S. consumers demand all that U.S. producers supply. Panel (b) shows that no U.S. steel is exported or imported at that price.

For world prices above $150 per ton, U.S. producers supply more than enough to satisfy domestic demand. The excess is exported. The U.S. exports curve of panel (b) shows the volume of exports at prices above $150. If the world price is below $150, domestic demand exceeds domestic supply. The difference is made up by imports.

When the world price is $200, exports equal 60 million tons of steel, a combination identified as point *a* in panel (b). By connecting points *e* and *a*, we form an upward-sloping export line in panel (b). This export line shows that at prices above $150 the quantity exported by the United States equals the difference between the U.S. quantity supplied and the quantity demanded, as shown in panel (a).

World Price Is Below the Domestic Equilibrium Price

What if the world price is below $100 per ton? If U.S. steel buyers cannot buy from abroad, the world price of steel would be irrelevant. If, however, U.S. buyers can purchase foreign output at the world price, the United States will become an importer of steel when the world price falls below $150 per ton. If the world price is below $150, the quantity demanded in the United States exceeds the quantity supplied by U.S. producers, so the excess demand in U.S. markets is satisfied by purchases from foreign producers. For example, suppose the world price is $100 per ton. In Exhibit 4(a) you can see that when the price is $100 per ton, the amount producers are willing to supply drops to 70 million tons, and the quantity demanded increases to 130 million tons. At that price, 60 million tons of steel are purchased on the world market.

The quantity of steel imported by the United States is shown by point *b* in panel (b). We could find the quantity of imports at other prices below $150 as the excess quantity demanded in panel (a) and could thereby construct the import curve in panel (b), which starts at a price of $150 (point *e*) and slopes down to the right.

Thus, when the world price of steel is $150 per ton, the quantity of steel demanded in the United States equals the quantity supplied by U.S. producers, so steel is neither imported nor exported. When the world price is above $150, the quantity of steel supplied by U.S. producers exceeds the quantity demanded by U.S. buyers, so steel is exported. And when the world price of steel is below $150, the quantity demanded by U.S. buyers exceeds the quantity supplied by U.S. producers, so steel is imported. The lower the world price falls below what would be the equilibrium price in the United States in the absence of trade, the greater will be the quantity of imports, as indicated by the downward-sloping U.S. imports curve in panel (b). Thus, the world price determines whether the United States will be an importer or an exporter.

The Rest of the World

Although we have been talking about the world price of steel, suppose there is just one other country in the "rest of the world"—Japan, a major producer and user of steel. To keep the accounting simple, we convert all Japanese prices into U.S. dollars.

Just as the United States has a domestic supply and demand for the good, so does Japan. Japan's supply and demand for steel, along with its supply of exports and demand for imports, are presented in Exhibit 5. As you can see

EXHIBIT 5   **THE DOMESTIC JAPANESE MARKET AND THE WORLD MARKET FOR STEEL**

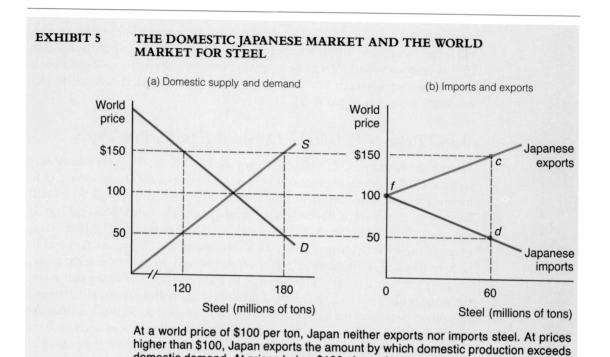

(a) Domestic supply and demand   (b) Imports and exports

At a world price of $100 per ton, Japan neither exports nor imports steel. At prices higher than $100, Japan exports the amount by which domestic production exceeds domestic demand. At prices below $100, Japan imports steel.

from panel (a), when the world price of steel is $100 per ton, the amount supplied by Japanese producers just equals the quantity demanded in Japan. In panel (b) there is no need to import or export when the world price is $100 per ton. But at a world price above $100 per ton, Japanese producers supply more steel than is demanded in Japan, so the difference will be exported to the world market, as shown in panel (b). The reverse is true for prices below $100. The quantity demanded in Japan will exceed the quantity Japanese producers want to supply, with the difference amounting to Japan's imports, as shown in panel (b).

Determining the World Price

To determine the world price for steel and to understand which country exports and which imports, we bring together the export and import curves from Exhibits 4 and 5. Panel (a) of Exhibit 6 again reflects the supply and demand for steel in the United States, and panel (c) presents the same information for Japan. Information about imports and exports for both countries is presented in panel (b).

The world price of steel is determined by international supply and demand. Panel (b) focuses on the exports and imports for each country. In our simplified model the world price is found where the exports of one country equal the imports of the other country. To begin with, you can see that U.S. producers would like to export at prices above $150, but Japanese buyers would like to import at prices below $100. Since the lowest price at which American producers would like to export exceeds the highest price at which Japanese buyers would like to import, U.S. exporters and Japanese importers will do no business.

But at a price above $100 per ton Japanese producers are willing to export, and at a price below $150 per ton American buyers are willing to import. Specifically, the intersection of the Japanese exports curve with the U.S. imports curve yields the world equilibrium price of steel, assuming that the world market consists only of these two countries. Given the supply and demand for steel in the two countries, the equilibrium price will be $125 per ton. At that price Japan will export 30 million tons of steel to the United States.

The Gains from Trade Again

Let's consider the gains from trade in each country. At a price of $125 per ton in panel (a) of Exhibit 6, 85 million tons are supplied by U.S. producers, and 30 million tons are imported from Japan. In the United States prices are lower and the quantity is greater than would be the case without trade. The blue areas in panel (a) reflect the gain in consumer surplus. The lightly shaded gain

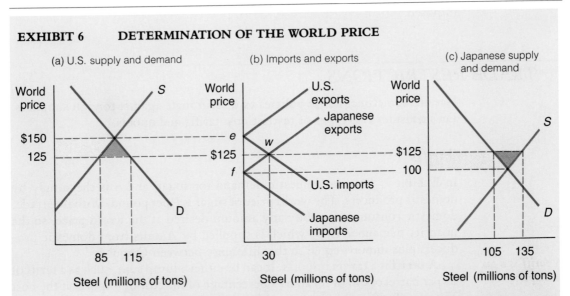

EXHIBIT 6   DETERMINATION OF THE WORLD PRICE

In panel (b) the intersection of the Japanese exports and U.S. imports curves determines the nature of trade between the two countries. At a world price of $125 per ton Japan exports 30 million tons of steel to the United States.

In the United States prices are lower and the quantity is greater as a result of trade. The blue areas reflect the gain in consumer surplus. In Japan, too, prices are higher and quantity is greater. The red areas indicate the gain in producer surplus. The net gains in the two countries are shown by the darkly shaded triangles in panels (a) and (c).

in consumer surplus results from a lower price received by domestic producers, so this gain is merely a transfer from domestic steel producers to domestic consumers of steel. But the darkly shaded gain in consumer surplus is a net gain in social welfare in the United States. Thus, the gain in consumer welfare resulting from the lower price in the United States more than offsets the loss to domestic producers.

Japan reflects the other side of the coin, as shown in panel (c). At a world price of $125 per ton, Japan produces 105 million tons for its domestic market and exports the other 30 million tons to the United States. Japanese producers are better off with international trade because they get to sell more output for a higher price than they could if they were limited to their domestic market. The red areas represent the gain to Japanese producers, who can sell steel for a world price of $125 per ton instead of the $100 price prevailing in Japan without international trade. The lightly shaded producer gain in panel (c) comes at the expense of forgone consumer surplus because of the higher price resulting from trade. But the darkly shaded gain in producer surplus represents a net gain in social welfare in Japan. Again, the gain to Japanese producers of steel because of a higher market price more than offsets the loss to Japanese consumers of steel.

Despite the benefits of international trade, nearly all countries at one time or another erect barriers to impede or block free trade among nations. In the next section we consider the effects of restrictions and the reasons they are imposed.

TRADE RESTRICTIONS

Nations sometimes adopt policies to discriminate against foreign suppliers. Let's consider two types of restrictions: tariffs and quotas.

Tariffs

In Exhibit 7, D is the domestic demand for sugar, and S is the supply by domestic producers. The world price of sugar is P per pound. With free trade, domestic consumers can buy any amount desired at the world price, so the quantity demanded is Q, which is supplied by A units from domestic producers plus imports equal to the difference between Q and A.

*A **tariff** is a tax on imports.*

A **tariff** is a tax on imports. It can be either a lump sum, such as a tariff of $5 per barrel of oil, or it can be a percentage of the cost of imports at the port of entry. Tariffs raise the price of imported goods to domestic purchasers. With the price higher, the quantity supplied by domestic producers expands. Suppose a lump-sum tariff of T is imposed on each pound of sugar imported, raising the price of imported sugar from P to $P + T$.

The only reason domestic producers could charge no more than price P in the first place was because domestic buyers could purchase sugar in the world market for price P. Now that consumers must pay $P + T$ on the world market, domestic producers can raise their price to $P + T$ as well without

EXHIBIT 7   **EFFECT OF A TARIFF**

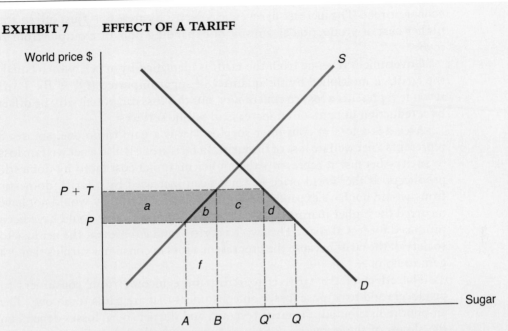

At world price *P,* domestic consumers demand *Q* units and domestic producers supply *A* units; the difference, *Q − A,* is imported. With the imposition of a tariff, the domestic price rises to *P + T,* domestic suppliers increase production to *B* units, and domestic consumers cut back to *Q'.* Imports fall to *Q' − B.*

At the higher domestic price, consumers are worse off; their loss of consumer surplus is the sum of areas *a, b, c,* and *d.* Area *a* is an increase in economic rent—a transfer from consumers to producers. Areas *b* plus *f* are revenues to producers that are just offset by the higher production costs of expanding output from *A* to *B.* Area *c* is government revenue from the tariff. The net welfare loss to society is the sum of area *d,* a loss of consumer surplus that is a gain to no one, plus area *b,* which reflects the higher marginal cost of producing output that could have been more cheaply produced abroad.

loss of sales to imports. Because of the higher price, the quantity supplied by domestic producers increases from *A* to *B,* while the quantity demanded by domestic consumers declines from *Q* to *Q'.* Imports continue to make up the difference between the quantity demanded in the domestic market and the quantity supplied by domestic producers. But because the quantity demanded has declined and the quantity supplied by domestic producers has increased, imports decline from *Q − A* to *Q' − B.*

Because the price is higher after the tariff, consumers are worse off. The loss in consumer surplus can be identified in Exhibit 7 by the area under the demand curve between the initial price and the price after the tariff. More specifically, we can identify the loss as the sum of areas *a, b, c,* and *d.* Because the domestic price has increased, the quantity of sugar supplied by domestic producers has increased as well. The total revenue received by domestic producers increases by the areas *a + b + f.* Area *a* represents a clear increase in net income to domestic producers—an increase in what we earlier called economic rent. The increase in revenue reflected by areas $b + f$ just offsets the higher cost of production as a result of expanding domestic output from A to B.

Government revenue from the tariff is identified by area c, which equals the tariff, T, multiplied by the quantity of sugar imported ($Q' - B$). Tariff revenue represents a loss to consumers, but this loss can potentially be offset by a reduction in taxes or an increase in public services.

Area d is a loss in consumer surplus that is a gain to no one, so area d represents a net welfare loss of the tariff. In fact, area b is also a net welfare loss to society because it represents the higher marginal cost faced by domestic producers. If the world price had not been increased by a tariff, domestic firms would not have expanded output from A to B, so they would not have incurred the higher marginal cost of producing output that could have been produced for less abroad. The two triangles b and d represent the net loss to society of the tariff because they represent a loss in consumer surplus that is a gain to no one.

The effect of the tariff is to redistribute income from consumers to producers and to impose losses on consumers that are gains to no one. The amount redistributed, the tariff revenue, and the net social losses depend on the slopes of the domestic supply and demand schedules. The steeper the supply curve is, the less will be the net social loss resulting from a higher cost of production. The steeper the demand curve is, the less will be the net social loss resulting from a reduction in quantity demanded. And for a given tariff, the steeper the supply and the demand curves are, the greater will be the government's tariff revenue.

The level of tariffs in the United States has fluctuated over the years. After a sharp jump in tariffs during the 1930s, tariff levels fell sharply between the late 1930s and the late 1940s. After World War II the United States invited trading partners to negotiate lower trade restrictions. The result was the General Agreement on Tariffs and Trade (GATT), adopted in 1947. Originally 23 countries signed the agreement; the number of signers has since grown to 92. International trade increased in the 1950s and 1960s, partly in response to a lowering of the trade barriers. GATT has become a permanent international organization. There have been a series of reductions in trade barriers, including the Kennedy round of tariff negotiations and the Tokyo round in the 1970s.

Quotas

*A **quota** is a legal limit on the quantity of a particular commodity that can be imported per year.*

Tariffs are the most common form of trade restrictions, but quotas are also used to limit imports. A **quota** is a legal limit on the quantity of a particular commodity that can be imported per year. Quotas are often targeted at exports from certain countries. For example, a quota may limit the number of autos that can be imported from Japan or the amount of steel that can be imported from Poland.

To have an impact on the market, a quota must limit imports to less than would be imported under free trade. For example, suppose that with no restrictions 2.5 million autos would be imported from Japan each year. A quota of 3 million cars would not affect imports from Japan. When a quota effectively limits imports, it reduces the supply of the good to the domestic market and thereby raises the domestic price. As we will see, tariffs and quotas have similar effects.

Let's consider the effect of a quota on the domestic market for sugar. In Exhibit 8 the domestic supply of sugar is S, and the domestic demand is D. Suppose that the world price of sugar is P. Under free trade P is the price that would prevail in the domestic market, and 70 million pounds would be the quantity demanded at that price. Domestic suppliers would provide 20 million pounds, and importers, 50 million pounds. A quota of 50 million pounds or more would have no impact on the domestic price or quantity

EXHIBIT 8   EFFECT OF A QUOTA

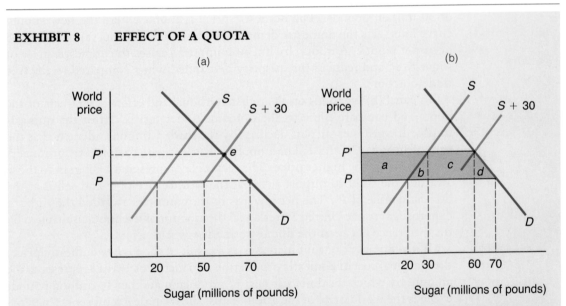

In panel (a) *D* is the domestic demand curve and *S* is the domestic supply curve. Following imposition of a quota of 30 million pounds per year, the supply curve becomes horizontal at the world price, *P*, until 50 million pounds is reached. For prices above *P*, the supply curve equals the horizontal sum of the domestic supply curve, *S*, plus the quota. The new domestic price, *P'*, is determined by the intersection of the new supply curve, *S* + 30, with the domestic demand curve, *D*.

Panel (b) shows the welfare effect of the quota. As a result of the higher domestic price, consumer surplus is reduced by the shaded area. Area *a* is a transfer from domestic consumers to domestic producers. Rectangle *c* represents a gain to those who can import sugar at the world price and sell it at the higher domestic price. Triangle *b* is a net loss; it represents the amount by which the cost of producing an extra 10 million pounds of output in the United States exceeds the cost of producing abroad. Area *d* is also a net loss—a reduction in consumer surplus that is a gain to no one.

demanded. Any smaller quota, however, would restrict the supply of imports, which, as we will see, would raise the domestic price.

For example, suppose that an import quota of 30 million pounds is declared. As long as the price in the U.S. market is at or above the world price of P, foreign producers supply 30 million pounds to the U.S. market. So the supply of sugar to the domestic market is found by adding 30 million pounds of sugar to the supply by domestic producers for price levels at or above P. At the world price of P domestic producers are willing to supply 20 million pounds, and importers provide the limit of 30 million pounds, for a quantity supplied of 50 million pounds. Domestic producers will never sell their output below P because they can always sell it on the world market for P. At prices above P importers cannot expand their quantity supplied because of the quota, but domestic producers can and do expand their quantity supplied.

Thus, the domestic supply curve is horizontal at the world price P until 50 million pounds is reached. For price above P, the supply curve equals the horizontal sum of the supply curve of domestic producers, S, plus the quota of 30 million pounds. The domestic price is found where the new supply curve intersects the domestic demand curve, which in panel (a) of Exhibit 8 occurs at point e. A quota, by limiting imports, raises the domestic price of sugar to P' and reduces the quantity demanded when compared to the free trade outcome.

In panel (b) we focus on the redistributional and efficiency effects of the quota and compare these to the outcome under tariffs. After the quota is imposed, consumer surplus declines by the shaded amount, identified as the sum of areas a, b, c, and d. The amount a is a clear gain to domestic producers resulting from the higher price. The rectangle c represents a net gain to those awarded the right to import sugar at the world price of P and sell it at the domestic price of P'. The net rewards to the countries awarded the right to export sugar to the United States equal the amount of the quota multiplied by the difference between the domestic and the world prices.

When domestic output increases as a result of the higher domestic price, the marginal cost of domestic production also increases. Area b represents the amount by which the domestic cost of producing another 10 million pounds exceeds the world price of the good. Thus, the triangle b represents a net loss in social welfare because domestic resources could have been used more efficiently in the production of other goods. Area d is also a net welfare loss because it represents a reduction in consumer surplus with no offsetting gain to anyone.

Comparison of Tariffs and Quotas

Consider the similarities and differences between this quota and a tariff that raises the domestic price by an identical amount. If the tariff and quota had identical effects on the price, they would also result in the same quantity demanded. The tariff and quota also involve the same net social loss. In both cases domestic producers would gain the same amount of economic rent. And domestic consumers would suffer the same loss in consumer surplus.

The only difference between the two restrictive policies is that under a tariff the U.S. government would collect the amount equal to imports times the tariff. But under quotas those with the right to export sugar to the United States will earn the premium over the world price. Consumers, as taxpayers, could do better under a tariff than under a quota because tariff revenues could be used to reduce taxes or increase public expenditures. Under quotas, whoever is given the right to export sugar to the United States can earn the difference between the world price and the U.S. price on each pound of sugar sold. As you might expect, the rights to export goods to the United States are much valued, and lobbyists for foreign exporters work the halls of Congress trying to secure these rights.

Currently the United States grants export quotas to specific countries. These countries, in turn, award these rights to their exporters through a variety of means. The value of these export rights has been estimated to exceed $7 billion in 1987, with more than half of this due to quotas on textiles and apparel.[2] By rewarding both domestic producers with higher prices and foreign producers with export quotas, the current system creates two groups intent on perpetuating the existing system. With such strong producer support and with consumers remaining rationally ignorant, we should not be surprised to learn that the quota system has lasted for decades. Steel quotas have been in effect for over 20 years; apparel quotas, over 30 years; and sugar quotas, over 50 years.

Some economists have argued that if quotas are to be used, the United States should auction off import quotas to foreign producers, thereby capturing the difference between the world price and the U.S. price. Auctioning off these quotas would not only increase federal revenue but would also reduce foreign enthusiasm for quotas.

ARGUMENTS FOR TRADE RESTRICTIONS

Considering the distributional effects and net social loss of tariffs and quotas, they often appear to be little more than welfare programs for the affected domestic industries. Because of the deadweight loss of these restrictions, it would be more efficient simply to transfer money from consumers to producers. But, of course, such a bald transfer would probably be too obvious to gain political favor. Arguments for tariffs are couched in terms of rationales other than a direct transfer to domestic producers. Some of these arguments have more validity than others. Here are some of the more common ones.

---

[2]See C. Fred Bergsten, "Reform Trade Policy with Auction Quotas," *Challenge* (May/June 1987): 5.

National Defense Argument

Certain industries are said to be in need of protection from import competition because they produce output that becomes vital in time of war. Because of their strategic importance, industries such as weapons manufacturing must be kept alive and flourishing. Thus, national defense considerations outweigh concerns about efficiency and equity.

How valid is this argument? Trade restrictions may shelter the defense industry, but other methods may be more efficient. For example, basic military hardware can be stockpiled, so maintaining productive capacity becomes less essential. Also, since nearly all industries could make some claim to be needed for defense, such trade restrictions can get out of hand. For example, one reason domestic wool producers benefit from protective policies is that wool is said to be critical in military uniforms.

Infant Industry Argument

In the late eighteenth and early nineteenth centuries the infant-industry argument was formulated as a rationale for protecting emerging domestic industry from foreign competition. The idea is that in cases where production exhibits economies of scale, new firms must be protected from foreign competition until they reach sufficient size to be competitive. The firms must be insulated from the rigors of international competition during this growth period or they will not survive. Trade restrictions are thus viewed as temporary devices to allow the industry time to secure a place in the market, thereby making the economy less dependent on foreign producers.

When does an infant industry become old enough to look after itself? The very existence of protection may foster production inefficiencies that firms may not be able to outgrow. The short-run cost of such restrictions is the net social loss from higher domestic prices. A possible cost in the long run is that the industry may never realize the expected economies of scale, so the industry may never become competitive. As with the national defense argument, policymakers should be careful in adopting restrictions based on the infant-industry argument, which is more valid for developing economies than for mature ones.

Antidumping Argument

Dumping is the sale of a commodity abroad for less than its price in the domestic market.

Dumping is the sale of a commodity abroad for less than its price in the domestic market. Exporters may be able to sell the good for less overseas because of subsidies provided by the exporting country, subsidies aimed at fostering exports. Or firms may simply find it profitable to practice price discrimination by charging lower prices in foreign markets than they charge at home.

What is the problem with foreign producers selling goods for less in the United States than in their own country? Why should U.S. consumers be prevented from buying the product for as little as possible even if these low prices are the result of an export subsidy? Dumping can drive out established firms, particularly if they are small firms with less capital than the dumping firm. Predatory dumping attempts to kill off competition. Dumping may also be a way to discourage the development of domestic production of the good. Domestic firms would not find entry into this industry attractive because of the low prevailing price that results from dumping. By driving out established firms or by discouraging domestic entry, the dumpers may place themselves in a position to monopolize the market. The trouble with these arguments is that monopoly profits would still attract entry. Also, it would be difficult to block entry around the world.

Sometimes the dumping may be sporadic, as firms try to unload excess inventories or attempt to disrupt domestic markets. Sporadic dumping could be unsettling for domestic industry. Dumping is prohibited by the Trade Agreement Act of 1979, which calls for the imposition of tariffs when the good is sold for less in the United States than in its home market.

Protecting Jobs and Labor Income

One rationale for trade restrictions that is pervasive today is the protection of American jobs and wage levels. Using trade restrictions to protect domestic jobs is a strategy that dates back to the mercantilists, who considered a favorable balance of trade to be the path to domestic prosperity. The problem with this policy is that other countries will probably retaliate to restrict their imports to save their jobs, so trade is reduced, along with the gains from trade.

Wages, especially those in developing countries, are often a small fraction of wages in the United States. American workers are understandably troubled when threatened by foreign competition from millions of low-paid workers. Looking simply at differences in the wage rate narrows the focus too much, however. Wages represent just one component of total cost and may not necessarily be the most important component. Employers are interested not only in the wage rate but also in the labor cost per unit of output. The labor cost per unit of output depends on both the wage rate and labor productivity.

The high wage rate in the United States is based on labor's high marginal productivity, which can be traced to education and training and the abundant machines and other physical capital that assist workers and make them more productive. American workers also benefit from the negotiating power of labor unions and a business climate that is relatively stable and that provides appropriate incentives to produce. How about the lower wages in many competing countries? These low wages can often be linked to a lack of education and training, a meager amount of physical capital accompanying each worker, and a business climate that is less stable and that offers fewer productive incentives. Thus, wages tend to be higher in the United States because American workers are better trained and benefit from superior technology and more capital.

Once multinational firms build plants and provide technological know-how in developing countries, however, American workers lose some of their competitive edge, and their relatively high wages could price American products out of the world market. Wage differentials across countries will decline over time, much as wage differentials between northern states and southern states have fallen. As technology and physical capital spread, U.S. workers cannot expect to maintain their wages at levels far above wages in other countries.

Domestic producers do not like to compete with lower-priced foreign producers and often push for some sort of trade restrictions. But if restrictions eliminate any cost advantage a foreign producer might have, this repeals the law of comparative advantage and denies domestic consumers access to the lower-priced goods.

Declining Industry Protection

Economic theory predicts that profit-maximizing firms attempt to produce output at the lowest possible cost even if this involves establishing plants in developing countries. As developing countries acquire technology and capital, these countries will grow more competitive. Also, developing countries tend to be well endowed with labor.

Where an established domestic industry is in jeopardy of being displaced by lower-priced imports, there could be a rationale for temporary restrictions to slow the demise of the domestic industry. After all, domestic producers have much industry-specific capital—both specialized machines and specialized labor. This physical and human capital is worth much less in its next best alternative use. By forestalling the extinction of the domestic industry through trade restrictions, specialized machines can be allowed to wear out naturally, and specialized workers can retire voluntarily or gradually pursue more promising careers.

Thus, in the case of declining domestic industries, trade protection is viewed as a temporary measure to help absorb the shock and allow for a normal transition. But the protection offered should not be so generous as to encourage continued investment in the industry. Protection should be of specific duration and should be phased out over that period.

Let's consider what happens to the workers in the declining industry. Workers with skills that are unique to that particular industry will have difficulty finding another job that pays as well, particularly since many such workers will be in the job market at the same time. The result could be more temporary unemployment. Older workers may be particularly hard pressed to pursue new careers. Since foreign trade can disrupt domestic labor markets in this way, the federal government provides assistance to workers who can demonstrate that foreign competition was responsible for their layoffs.

Shoe production is an example of a declining U.S. industry. Shoe manufacturing requires much labor and relatively little capital, so shoes need not be produced on a large scale. Brazil, South Korea, and Taiwan are now among the world's leading producers of low-priced shoes. In 1980 imports accounted for about half of all shoes sold in the United States. Despite tariffs, by 1985 imports were up to 75 percent of the market. Import restrictions proposed by

Congress in 1985 were estimated to save 33,000 American jobs at an annual cost of $68,000 per job.[3] The proposed restrictions were not approved mostly because the cost of the legislation became embarrassing, but there remains a complicated set of tariffs on imported shoes, affecting everything from thong sandals to ski boots and requiring several pages of tariff schedules.

Problems with Protection

While particular workers suffer in the short run as imports displace workers, many more jobs have been created by private enterprise than have been destroyed by imports. This does not deny the problems facing those workers who are displaced by imports. Perhaps a list of problems associated with protection would summarize our treatment of trade restrictions.

Protecting one stage of production often requires protecting downstream stages of production. If the government protects domestic textile manufacturers, it must also protect the domestic garment industry. Otherwise, foreign garment manufacturers will fashion lower-priced foreign textiles into exports to the United States, where they will sell for less than U.S.-made garments made from higher-priced American textiles. Thus, protecting the U.S. textile industry from foreign competition raises the cost of cloth to U.S. clothing manufacturers, reducing their competitiveness.

The cost of protection includes not only the deadweight loss arising from the higher domestic price but also the resources used by domestic producers and groups to secure the favored protection. The cost of rent seeking—lobbying fees, propaganda, legal actions—can amount to as much as or more than the direct deadweight loss of restrictions.

A final problem with restrictions is policing and enforcing the myriad quotas, tariffs, and other restrictions. Consider the following case study.

CASE STUDY

Enforcing Trade Restrictions

America is the richest, most attractive market in the world. Trade restrictions often make American markets even more attractive to foreign producers because the U.S. price exceeds the world price. Thus, we should not be surprised when some importers try to skirt trade restrictions, either by avoiding tariffs or by illegally importing goods that are controlled by quotas. Fraudulent imports include a diverse array of goods, such as clothing, sugar, coffee, gems, and steel pipes. Illegal imports have been estimated at more than 10 percent of all imports.

Restrictions affect not only the quantity of imports but also the quality. For example, restrictions limit the polyester content of men's suits. Nearly all

---

[3]Rather than trying to save jobs at such an expense, it would be more efficient to allow domestic shoe workers to lose their jobs through international competition, then provide them with cash transfers of up to $68,000.

the schemes to import clothing illegally involve fraudulent documents to misrepresent the clothing so that it fits into some quota or pays a lower tariff. Sometimes the garments are altered to evade detection. For example, imports of men's running shorts are controlled by a quota. A shipment of these shorts reportedly had a flimsy inner lining basted in so they would pass for swimming trunks, which face no quotas.

Because the United States allows some countries more generous quotas than others, exporters in countries under tight control sometimes ship their goods through a country with a liberal ceiling. For example, Japan typically makes so little clothing for export that the United States has no clothing quota for imports from Japan. As a result, clothing made in Korea is often shipped through Japan to evade quotas on Korean goods. Similarly, Nepal has no clothing quota but India does, so India ships clothing through Nepal.

Tariffs are often imposed to tax lower-priced goods relatively more. Foreign steel companies have been accused of falsely inflating the price of steel to avoid import duties on low-priced steel. The higher prices paid by importers were secretly rebated to the steel producers through a variety of schemes. Other steel has been mislabeled and falsely weighed to avoid certain restrictions.

Some foreign producers and U.S. importers are said to engage in "port shopping," or testing various ports to see where inspections are most lax. Documents are often forged. U.S. Customs inspectors are responsible for policing all this activity. These inspectors have their work cut out for them in view of the thousands of tariffs, quotas, and other trade restrictions in effect.

Source: Anthony De Stefano, "Customs Agents Fight Often Losing Battle Against Illegal Imports," *The Wall Street Journal*, 26 January 1986.

Winners and Losers

Who are the losers from trade restrictions? For now let's ignore welfare losses in the exporting country and focus only on losses in the United States. The consumers who must pay higher prices for the protected goods are losers, as are the domestic producers who use imported intermediate goods. The domestic economy may be less productive because the protected industry is less innovative than is the industry on the cutting edge of competition. Over the long run this lack of innovation reduces employment and income. Also losers are U.S. exporters, who face higher barriers in trading with foreign countries because these countries have retaliated by introducing their own trade restrictions. Some of these losers may go out of business; other firms may never start producing. To the extent that protected industries expand and thereby drive up resource prices, other producers using these same resources are losers.

Trade restrictions are often imposed gradually over a period of years. Because the domestic adjustments to them are slow, the losers often fail to attribute their losses to the offending restriction. Thus, the losers are spread throughout the economy, often they do not know they are losers, or they fail to connect their troubles with trade policy.

The winners are the domestic producers who are able to sell their output for a higher price because of the restrictions. Under a system of quotas, the winners' circle includes those who have secured the right to import the good at the world price and sell it at the domestic price. The winners from trade restrictions are usually a well-defined group who can clearly identify the source of their gains. One reason restrictions exist is that most losers do not know they are losers, whereas winners know what is at stake. Producers have an abiding interest in trade legislation, but consumers remain rationally ignorant. Congress tends to support the group that makes the most noise, so trade restrictions are often imposed.

Although our emphasis has been on tariffs and quotas, domestic producers can fight imports in a variety of ways as reflected in the following case study.

CASE STUDY

Pistachio Wars

Consider the nutty trade war involving pistachios, which have annual sales in the United States exceeding $100 million. Most U.S.-grown pistachios are from California. Imports are primarily from Iran, which accounts for nearly half of the U.S. market.

California growers have used a variety of weapons to fight Iranian imports. They petitioned the U.S. International Trade Commission (ITC) and the Commerce Department, accusing Iran of dumping its pistachios at below-market prices. In November 1985 the ITC ruled that the California growers had been injured by the influx of Iranian nuts.

California growers in December 1985 saw that legislation requiring the country of origin to be reported on the package was approved. With sentiments against Iran running high, the growers evidently hoped that consumers might refuse to buy nuts from Iran. In patriotic fervor, California growers asked the President to ban imports from Iran because the country supports international terrorism. The growers also sought import duties on Iranian nuts.

Finally, California growers have raised questions about the quality of the Iranian pistachios. For example, they claim that Iranian nuts are dyed red to hide blemishes and imperfections that arise because the nuts fall on the ground, where they are left to dry. In contrast, California nuts are caught in nets and are mechanically dried, so they need no such camouflage. Assailing the quality of pistachios based on the color is a two-edged sword for California growers, however, because most consumers do not distinguish between imported and home-grown nuts. Moreover, consumers from the East Coast prefer the red nuts, so California growers dye pistachios headed for eastern markets.

Source: Albert Karr, "The Pistachio War: U.S. Growers Fight Imports from Iran," *The Wall Street Journal*, 6 November 1985.

SUMMARY

1. Even if one country has an absolute advantage in producing all goods, the country should specialize in the good where it has a comparative advantage—that is, where the opportunity cost of production is lowest. If each country specializes and trades according to the law of comparative advantage, all countries will be better off.

2. Despite the advantages of international trade, restrictions on trade date back hundreds of years. Two restrictions examined in this chapter are tariffs and quotas. Tariffs impose a tax on imports. By raising the price of imports, tariffs raise the price in domestic markets, redistributing some of the gains of exchange from consumers to producers.

3. For any given tariff, a quota can be devised to have the same effect on domestic price and quantity. The primary difference between a tariff and a quota is in the redistribution of the gains resulting from a higher domestic price. Tariff revenues go to the government and could be used to lower taxes; quotas confer benefits on those with the right to buy the good at the world price and sell it at the higher domestic price. Both tariffs and quotas impose net social costs because of a loss in consumer surplus that yields gains to no one.

4. Despite the gains from free trade and the net welfare losses arising from tariffs and quotas, trade restrictions have been a part of trade policy since the mercantilists. Arguments for trade restrictions include fostering national defense industries, giving infant industries time to grow, preventing foreign producers from dumping goods in domestic markets, protecting domestic jobs, and allowing declining industries time to phase out.

QUESTIONS AND PROBLEMS

1. (Resources and Trade) Malaysia exports tin and rubber. Why have these resources become increasingly less important to the world economy? Also, explain why these developments could hinder the growth of the Malaysian economy.

2. (U.S. Trade) What reasons would you give for the rise in importance of international trade to the U.S. economy? Will these reasons continue to have an influence in the future?

3. (Differences in Tastes and Trade) How might the Virgin Islands (U.S.) trade with the Bahamas (British) or Martinique (French)? Is trade possible among islands that are so much alike?

4. (Absolute and Comparative Advantage) Suppose each worker in the United States can produce 8 units of food or 2 units of clothing. Izodia, which has the same number of workers, can produce 7 units of food or 1 unit of clothing for each worker. Why does the United States have an absolute advantage in both goods? Which country enjoys a comparative advantage in food? Why?

5. (Specialization and Consumer Welfare) Why do economists believe that consumers are better off when countries specialize in the goods for which they have a comparative advantage and then trade with each other?

6. (World Equilibrium Price) Draw a domestic supply and demand diagram for steel and assume the world equilibrium price is the same as the domestic equilibrium price. If there is an increase in foreign supply, what will happen in the domestic market for steel?

7. (Tariffs) Very high tariffs usually cause black markets and smuggling. How is government revenue reduced by such activity? Relate your answer to the graph found in Exhibit 7 in this chapter. Does smuggling have any social benefits?

8. (Voluntary Quotas or Restraints) The United States tried to limit Japanese exports to the United States by way of voluntary restraints. Why did the U.S. government lose revenues by this approach rather than an approach using tariffs?

9. (Quotas) The Immigration Service in the United States allows only a certain number of individuals to apply each year for U.S. citizenship. Quotas are set for each country. How might the Immigration Service allocate such privileges among so many applicants?

The SOVIET ECONOMY

In Chapter 2 we considered the three questions that every economic system must answer: what to produce, how to produce it, and for whom to produce it. Laws regarding resource ownership and the role of government in resource allocation determine the "rules of the game"—the incentives and constraints that guide the behavior of individual decision makers. Under pure capitalism the rules of the game include the private ownership of resources and the coordination of economic activity by price signals generated by competitive markets; market coordination answers the three questions. Under a command economy the rules of the game include government ownership of resources and the direction of resources through central planning rather than through markets. No country exhibits either capitalism or a command economy in its pure form.

This book has focused on how market forces operate in a capitalist economy such as the United States. Although government has an important role in the U.S. economy, most other economies rely on government more extensively. Some countries carefully limit the private ownership of resources such as land and capital. Each country employs a slightly different system of resource ownership, resource allocation, and individual incentives to answer the three economic questions.

In this chapter we will examine the economic system in the Soviet Union, the second largest economy in the world. We will consider how the economy operates, and we will evaluate its performance. Topics and terms discussed include:

- Planned socialism

- Market socialism

- Bureaucratic coordination

- Material balance system

- The Soviet elite

INTRODUCTION TO ALTERNATIVE ECONOMIC SYSTEMS

An *economic system* is the set of mechanisms and institutions that resolve the what, how, and for whom questions. Several criteria are used to distinguish among economic systems: who owns the resources, what decision-making process is used to allocate resources, and what type of incentives guide activities.

Planned and Market Socialism

Capitalism means the private ownership of all resources; *socialism* means state ownership of all resources other than labor; *communism* means state ownership of all resources, including labor. Thus, under communism a worker has no claim to labor earnings. Workers provide their labor in service to the state. No economies practice communism in its pure form. The countries that are typically referred to as communist are, in fact, socialist.

*Under **planned socialism** the state owns resources other than labor and directs them through economic plans and central decision making.*

Under **planned socialism** the state owns the resources other than labor and directs these resources through economic plans and central decision making. The state attempts to motivate labor through both moral and economic incentives. Under **market socialism** the state owns the resources other than labor, but incentives are largely economic, planning is decentralized, and market forces are used to allocate economic resources.

*Under **market socialism** the state own resources other than labor, but market forces are used to allocate the resources.*

Just as capitalism and socialism represent polar cases not found in the real world, planned socialism and market socialism are also not found in their pure form. The Soviet Union can be described best as planned socialism because of public ownership of resources other than labor, resource allocation by plan, and centralized decision making. Yugoslavia is the best example of market socialism, but other countries, including Hungary and China, are experimenting with combinations of socialism and capitalism.

Kinds of Coordination

An economic system coordinates the activity and interaction of individuals and organizations. We distinguish between two polar types of coordination: market coordination and bureaucratic coordination.

In *market coordination* the relationship between buyers and sellers is horizontal—that is, from a legal perspective, buyers and sellers are on equal footing. Both are motivated by self-interest. Coordination occurs based on agreed-upon prices. Transactions take place because each party hopes to benefit, not because one side has the pressure to coerce the other. Exchange is voluntary.

In bureaucratic coordination control is exercised through a hierarchy. The relationship is vertical, from the higher level of the organization to the lower level. Administrative pressure and legal restraints force individuals and organizations to accept the orders and restrictions from above. The transactions among levels in the bureau need not necessarily involve money, but when they do, the lower level of the organization depends on the higher level for its finances. The decision makers in the bureacracy control the allocation of resources as well as the distribution of income.

In planned economies governments rely primarily on *central plans* rather than on market signals to answer the three economic questions. Bureaucratic coordination rather than market coordination determines the appropriate method of producing goods and services. Decisions about how to produce goods and services are based on historical experience and technological know-how. To ensure that the directions of the central planners are followed, the government relies on moral suasion, coercion, and a mix of economic incentives.

Why would a country want a planned economy? The leaders can establish whatever priorities they believe are appropriate and can pursue these objectives using the full authority of the state. The state can ensure that savings are sufficient to promote the capital formation required for growth. The problem of unemployment can be solved by creating enough enterprises to hire all those seeking employment.

Communism, Socialism, and the Soviet Union

Adam Smith provided the theoretical underpinnings and intellectual justification for capitalism, and Karl Marx provided the same support for socialism, which he considered a stage on the way to communism in economic development. As previously mentioned, under communism the means of production are owned by the community, and the income that results from production is shared by all citizens according to their needs.

According to communists, capitalism is doomed because of the tendency toward declining profits, increased unemployment, and successively more severe economic crises. Communists believe that modern industrial economies will eventually achieve communism, but only after a long period of socialism. During the socialist stage of evolution, the state will own and operate the means of production, distribution, and exchange, but workers will have a right to their labor, and each person will be paid based on the work performed. Over time, however, the state will wither away, and pure communism will arise. People will work according to their ability and receive according to their needs. Thus, socialism is a transitory economic system on the road to communism.

The writings of Marx inspired the Russian Revolution of 1917, which overthrew the czarist form of government. The Soviet Union was formed in 1922, and since 1928 it has been guided by a series of five-year plans. The Soviet Union is a country of about 280 million people. Its land area is 2½ times that of the United States and 60 times that of Japan. The country covers a large area of the map, including 11 of the world's 24 time zones. When a Moscow family sits down to dinner, fellow citizens of the Soviet Far East are greeting the next day's sunrise. The Soviet Union has the world's longest frontier and borders a dozen countries and a dozen seas belonging to three oceans.

Under a constitution adopted in 1977, the political foundation is formed by Soviets, or Councils, of People's Deputies. The Communist party is, according to the Soviet constitution, "the leading and guiding force of the Soviet society and the nucleus of its political system." The economy is based on "socialist ownership of the means of production."

Thus, the hallmark of the socialist state is public, or government, ownership of property. With limited exceptions, the central government in the Soviet Union owns all land, natural resources, and capital goods, nearly all businesses, and most urban housing. Land was declared to be public property at the time of the Russian Revolution. Virtually all of the industrial sector is owned by the state.

Central Planning

Leaders of the Communist party believe that central planning can direct resources better than market coordination can. Party leaders establish priorities and present them to the State Planning Agency, called Gosplan, which develops long-term economic and social plans and generally supervises their execution. Regional Gosplans take the plans and provide directives to regional ministries, which formulate orders to individual plant directors. These orders include the kinds and amounts of commodities that the industrial plant should produce, the wages to be paid, the prices to be charged, and the profit to be earned. Thus, Gosplan and others involved in the planning process translate the priorities established by the Communist party into specific directives for each enterprise.

Individual plants are the heart of the industrial sector in the Soviet Union. These plants are operated by a director, or plant manager, who is appointed by the government with the approval of the local Communist party. Although they are far from entrepreneurs, plant directors have some discretion over how to combine resources to meet the output objectives established by the planning hierarchy. As we will see later, often they must be creative to meet their production goals.

Household income in the Soviet Union consists almost exclusively of labor earnings—wages and salaries paid to employees of government enterprises and bureaus. Since the state owns nearly all resources except labor, any return to resources other than labor is income from state-owned enterprises. This nonlabor income is either turned over to the state to finance government activities or kept by the enterprise to support expansion. The state, not the enterprise, determines the share of profits the enterprise retains.

Karl Marx (1818–1883)

The Bettmann Archive, Inc.

On the whole, economics is not a profession from which one expects larger-than-life political figures to emerge. But there is one famous political economist whose name is synonymous with a political movement that governs more than half the world's population. His name, of course, is Karl Marx.

Marx was a British political economist in the classical tradition of David Ricardo (1772–1823), from whom he borrowed a number of key ideas. But Marx was also in part a German philosopher, influenced especially by the writings of G. W. F. Hegel (1770–1831). In Hegel's scheme of things, history moved according to predictable stages by a clash of contradictory opposites, what he called the process of *dialectic*. Marx adapted this philosophy to economics and sought to map out the stages of economic history and to analyze the "internal contradictions" of capitalism.

Capitalism emerged from the contradictions of an earlier stage of history—the feudalism of the Middle Ages. In contrast to feudalism, capitalism is a dynamic system that unleashed productive forces never before seen in history. But for Marx, the system also contains the seeds of its own destruction. Whereas Adam Smith looked at the economy of market prices and saw an invisible hand, Marx looked at the price system and saw chaos. Because capitalists mainly produce goods to be sold to others

(rather than producing for one's own immediate uses), there was, to Marx, no effective way of coordinating production and use. This problem would lead, he believed, to ever-deepening crises (depressions) followed by consolidation of capital ownership into fewer and fewer hands. Eventually, he predicted, exploited workers would rise up against the capitalists and take over the system the capitalists had created. The result would be communism, the final stage of history. About the details of this stage Marx was almost completely silent, and mystery, it now appears, is the soul of prophecy.

Karl Marx was a dark, intense, brooding figure. Born into an upper-class family in Trier, Germany, the young Marx studied philosophy at the University of Bonn. Unable to find an academic job, he edited a number of radical journals, fleeing from country to country as the authorities tried to suppress him. Eventually he settled in London with his wife, Jennie, the daughter of a German nobleman. There he lived in dire poverty, often dependent on handouts from his friend and coauthor Friedrich Engels (1820–1895). Marx toiled every day from 10 in the morning until 7 in the evening, always in the same seat in the library of the British Museum, to produce his prodigious four-volume tome *Capital,* one of the most famous and important books in the history of ideas.

Richard Langlois

Supply and Demand

*The **material balance system** was a system of central planning designed to ensure a balance of supply and demand for important types of industrial output.*

How can central planning coordinate hundreds of different resources in thousands of different enterprises? The system of central planning developed in the Soviet Union during the 1930s is called the **material balance system**, where central authorities control only the most important industrial output, leaving decisions about less important output to the lower levels of the planning hierarchy. For example, Gosplan in Moscow plans the production of steel, energy, motor vehicles, and machine tools. Lower-level planners guide the production of shoes, clothing, and household services. Items of still lower priority are not planned for at all and may be left to market coordination.

The planning machinery must achieve a material balance of supply and demand. For example, Gosplan sets a target for steel production based on past experience and technological know-how. Suppose the economy's productive capacity of steel is 100 million tons per year. The Soviet Union has already agreed to export 20 million tons, leaving a possible domestic supply of 80 million tons. Based on past experience, Gosplan knows how much steel will be demanded to meet output targets for automobiles, machine tools, construction, and other uses. Gosplan selects a target for steel production that will equate the quantity of steel supplied with the quantity demanded, thereby achieving a material balance through bureacratic coordination rather than through market coordination. Gosplan follows the same approach for each critical commodity, as well as for labor, machinery, and finance.

The plan for the economy is actually the result of bargaining among planning elements — Gosplan, Communist party officials, the various ministries, and the plant managers. After much haggling up and down the hierarchy, a final plan is prepared and submitted to the central government for final approval. Once approved, the economic plan becomes law and provides each enterprise with its marching orders about how many employees to hire, what resources can be expected through supply channels, and how much bank credit will be available. The plan is broken down by week, month, quarter, and year.

Capitalist economies equate quantity supplied with quantity demanded through the invisible hand of market coordination; centrally planned economies use the visible hand of bureaucratic coordination. If supply and demand are not in balance, something has to give. In capitalist systems what gives is the price. In centrally planned economies what usually gives is the plan itself. A common problem in centrally planned economies is that production often falls short of the plan. If the quantity supplied falls below the planned amount, Gosplan reduces the quantity each sector will receive — the quantity demanded. These cuts will not be across the board. Critical sectors, such as heavy industry and national defense, will be cut the least, and lower-priority sectors, such as consumer products, will be cut the most.

The Soviet approach to central planning is not the only alternative to capitalism but rather just one of many. The Chinese, for example, have used sample surveys to gauge public sentiment on policy questions. A study of economic planning over different countries or over different periods would uncover much diversity.

Labor Markets

Under socialism the state owns all resources other than labor. Except during times of war, Soviet workers have some discretion in their choice of occupations and place of work. Most workers are hired in an independent labor market. The enterprise manager also has some discretion over whom to hire.

Central planners set relative wages to reflect market realities, the plans of the state, and the nature of the work performed—its complexity, the responsibility involved, and other relevant features. Those involved in more arduous or unhealthy work are paid more, other things constant. For example, coal miners and metalworkers earn more than other industrial workers do. Thus, there is a Soviet labor market, and wage differentials are not very different from those observed in capitalist markets. As a way of providing production incentives, many industrial workers are paid by the amount produced rather than by the hour.

The choice of occupations allows workers to select jobs that more nearly suit their preferences, and this greater discretion enhances worker productivity. The government, however, has been concerned about the high job turnover that has resulted from worker discretion in employment and has attempted to restrict mobility in various ways. Wages, bonuses, housing availability, and other amenities have been tied explicitly to length of employment in a particular job. University graduates and others with specialized training receive administrative assignments to particular jobs and are expected to hold these jobs for several years. More generally, movement into large cities is restricted by a system of internal passports. Housing availability is also a limiting factor.

PERFORMANCE OF THE SOVIET ECONOMY

The Communist Party Congress meets every five years. In 1986 Mikhail Gorbachev addressed the Congress in a six-hour speech in which he called the economy a "mess." He identified three reasons for the demise of the Soviet economy: (1) bureaucracy had become so overburdened that it could no longer administer the economy, (2) technical progress was too slow, and (3) so many public officials were using their office for personal gain that corruption was a national scandal. In this section we will take a closer look at how the Soviet economy has performed, and in the process we will come to understand better the strengths and weaknesses of central planning.

Economic Growth

How has the Soviet system performed based on the standards typically used to evaluate an economic system? The Communist party began with a relatively undeveloped agrarian economy and created the world's second largest economy. Central planning has mobilized resources by forcing a high rate of capital formation and by shifting labor from agriculture to industry.

After adjusting official Soviet figures, experts say the Soviet economy grew at a rate of about 5 percent per year between 1930 and 1980, compared with a growth rate of only 3 percent in the United States. This impressive Soviet growth rate appeared to provide credibility to the economy and its leadership. Any inefficiencies arising from central planning could be papered over by the economy's access to cheap and plentiful resources, particularly labor. The Soviet Union, like other developing countries, could show dramatic growth simply because millions of workers were moving from the rural agricultural sector, where productivity was low, into the urban industrial sector, where productivity was high. Once all available workers had shifted out of agriculture, however, the era of abundant labor ended.

During the plan period 1981 to 1985, production increased at an annual rate of only 2 percent—only half the amount targeted in the Eleventh Five-Year Plan. The drop in the growth rate of the Soviet economy has been attributed to a shortage of labor, poor labor morale, little government credibility, and some loss of ideological fervor at the top. When a system depends on patriotic zeal to mobilize resources, a loss in that zeal affects productivity.

Prices, Shortages, and Consumer Satisfaction

Most prices in the Soviet system are not determined by market forces but rather are set by central planners. As a result, consumers have very little to say about what gets produced. Prices, once set, tend to be inflexible. In the spirit of equity, Soviet planners price many consumer goods below the market-clearing level, so shortages (or "interruptions" in supply, as the Soviets call them) are common. For example, the planning process may call for a certain amount of toothpaste to be produced per period and sold for a particular price. In Exhibit 1 the amount produced is identified as Q. The quantity supplied depends not on how much consumers would be willing to pay but on the priority that toothpaste holds in the larger scheme of the economy. Thus, the supply is fixed. Note that a price of P would equate quantity demanded and quantity supplied. In fact, the price of toothpaste and many other consumer goods is usually set below the market-clearing price. In Exhibit 1 a price of P' results in a shortage.

Housing, necessities such as electricity, and basic food are cheap, but because the price is set below the market-clearing level, these items are also in short supply. Probably the scarcest good in the Soviet Union over the years has been housing. Couples may wait years for a cooperative apartment.

Shortages are evident from long waiting lines at retail stores, empty store shelves, and the "tips" shop operators can expect for supplying scarce consumer goods. Scarce goods are also diverted to the black market, where they sell at a premium over set prices. Shortages are especially common in medicine, soap, toothbrushes, toothpaste, needles, thread, and diapers. Quality is also a problem because producers are trying to meet production

EXHIBIT 1 **SUPPLY AND DEMAND FOR TOOTHPASTE**

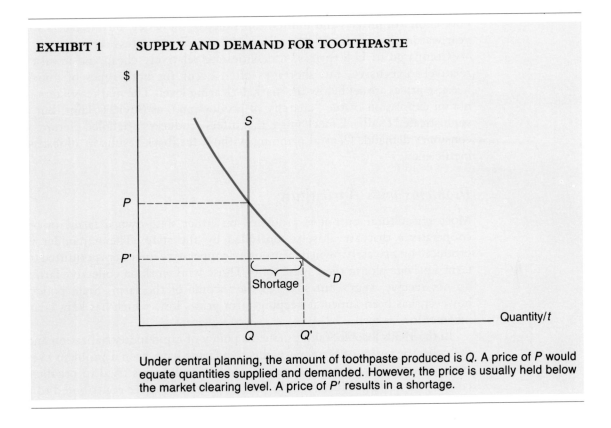

Under central planning, the amount of toothpaste produced is *Q*. A price of *P* would equate quantities supplied and demanded. However, the price is usually held below the market clearing level. A price of *P'* results in a shortage.

quotas rather than trying to satisfy consumers. Plant managers do not score extra bureaucratic points by producing a garment that is in style and in popular sizes. Tales of shoddy products abound.

Thus, necessities are scarce because the price is set below the market-clearing level. On the other hand, Soviet officials try to discourage the consumption of luxuries by allocating few of the economy's resources to their production. For example, automobiles are expensive and are of poor quality (by American standards). But because so few automobiles are produced, the prices are relatively high, and waiting lists are long. Even used cars are scarce. For example, a four-year old Lada, a compact car, costs about $12,000—one and a half times the typical yearly household income. In the United States this would be comparable to a four-year-old Plymouth Reliant selling for $50,000.

A pair of Soviet-made pantyhose costs about $10; a 21-inch color television costs about $1000. On the black market Japanese videocassette recorders (VCRs) were reportedly selling for up to $2450, and blank videotapes for $67. With such strong demand, the Russians began producing their own brand, the Electronika VM, which sold for $875 but which has no recording function (evidently because of the security problems recording ability posed). In 1986 there were only six tape rental stores in the entire country, and the pickings of titles were slim—mostly reruns from Russian TV. Despite the poor choice of movies and limited capability of the VCR, buyers face a 10-year waiting list for the Electronika VM, according to press reports.[1]

Compared to U.S. prices, necessities are relatively cheap and luxuries relatively expensive, but shortages often occur for both types of goods because prices are set below the market-clearing level. The market system is not an expression of the "anarchy of production," as Soviets claim, but a sophisticated feedback mechanism that offers producers a detailed picture of consumer demand. Central planning without feedback results in allocative inefficiency.

Problems with Agriculture

Most agricultural output is produced on either state-owned farms or on cooperatives that are closely controlled by the state. The remainder is produced on privately owned farms or by cooperative members permitted to farm a private plot in their spare time. Those who work on collective farms do not receive wages but share in the income of the farm. State policy, however, has been aimed at keeping farm prices low, which has kept farm incomes low as well.

In the 1930s Joseph Stalin pursued a policy of rapid industrialization and the collectivization of farmers. Collective farms have been a problem ever since peasants were forced to join them. Soviet planners tried to organize farming like other industries, but collectivization initially contributed to a famine, killing millions of peasants. A farm is not a factory that can be shut down for the holidays; farming requires constant care and attention. The care and feeding of plants and animals is no less urgent on weekends. Perhaps it is no coincidence that farms in most economic systems tend to be owner-operated. Even the Chinese have a system of incentives that rewards farmers who are especially productive.

Bureaucracies abound in the Soviet Union, and agriculture is no exception. For example, the details of how teams of farmers are to be rewarded are worked out by the Union-Republic Council of Ministers, the Ministry of Agriculture, the Ministry of Fruit and Vegetables, the State Committee for the Supply of Production Equipment to Agriculture, the Ministry of Procurement, the State Committee on Labor and Social Questions, and the All-Union Central Council of Trade Unions. Get the idea?

Agriculture in the Soviet Union has become increasingly mechanized over the last few decades and has therefore come to rely on inputs from the industrial sector. But the marriage of industry and agriculture has not been a happy one. For example, huge tractors are built but without the support equipment to take advantage of their size. Farm machinery is scrapped at a much higher rate in the Soviet Union than elsewhere because of the lack of spare parts and trained mechanics. Between 1976 and 1980, for example,

---

[1]"VCRs Are in a Sorry State in the U.S.S.R.," *The Hartford Courant,* 6 August 1986.

industry provided 1.8 million tractors to the agricultural sector, but the stock of tractors rose by only about 250,000. During that same period farmers received 539,000 grain combines, but the stock of combines rose by only 33,000.[2] Enough mechanics are trained, but Soviet planners have difficulty keeping them down on the farm because mechanics are paid much more in urban areas.

In summary, poor morale, low farm prices, unreliable equipment, and interrupted supplies of key inputs combine to reduce job incentives on the farm and reduce farm productivity. Industrial production also suffers from the limitations of central planning, as we will see in the following case study.

CASE STUDY

The Informal Economy

There are really three economies in the Soviet Union: (1) the official economy, where things are done by the book—according to the orders from on high; (2) the so-called second economy, the Soviet version of the underground economy, where individuals buy and sell to promote their self-interest, and (3) the "informal economy," where Soviet managers pursue official objectives by skirting the official rules. In this case study we will examine the informal economy.

The resource distribution system in the Soviet economy is not the well-oiled operation envisioned by the central planners. For example, enterprises often fail to receive critical resources and receive resources they can't use. Because of the chronic problem of inadequate and late resources, factory workers often have little to do. The pace of the work is therefore uneven, with workers idle for days only to frantically try to meet the month's production quota once the required supplies or replacement parts have arrived.

To alleviate these problems, managers often barter with other enterprises for critical resources or buy resources on the black market. More importantly, rather than depend on a sporadic supply system, the enterprise frequently manufactures key replacement parts. Thus, Soviet enterprises try to reduce the risk of interrupted supplies by bringing activities inside the firm. Plants of all sizes often design and produce equipment for their own use. For example, an automobile plant makes its own robots, a shoe plant makes its own machines and glue, and a computer center develops its own programs. If an enterprise wants to expand, it may use its own workers to put up the building. Some enterprises have even built their own power generators if electricity is frequently interrupted.

Soviet enterprises often produce their own replacement parts. For example, in the Soviet Union only about 4 percent of standard metalworking products are produced in specialized plants. The rest are produced by the

---

[2]These examples are found in Gale Johnson and K. M. Brooks, *Prospects for Soviet Agriculture in the 1980s* (Bloomington: Indiana University Press, 1984).

enterprises that use the product. In contrast, in the United States 70 percent of these products are produced by specialized firms.

Self-reliance is not confined to resources. Because many consumer goods are so scarce, enterprises also produce goods and services for employee consumption. That is, many industrial firms raise crops and livestock on the side, much like an American firm might provide day-care facilities for its employees with small children. The resources needed to produce these other products are siphoned from official channels, acquired through barter, or purchased on the black market.

Thus, self-service is the implicit motto of Soviet enterprise. Because the transaction costs of relying on the bureaucratic hierarchy as a source of supply are high, more and more activities are brought inside the enterprise. The informal economy reflects abundant entrepreneurial spirit by plant directors. Rather than serving as perfunctory underlings who carry out orders in the chain of command, they try to satisfy their production quotas while providing their employees with goods and services that are hard to get on the market.

But this intramural activity violates one of the basic axioms of efficiency: the division of labor. As an individual enterprise expands into more and more activities, workers are spread thinner, so they perform all jobs less efficiently. Each worker becomes a jack-of-all-trades but a master of none. The plant director's attention span is strained, and the coordination of resources becomes a problem. Many studies in the Soviet Union show that the cost of in-house production is higher than production in specialized plants. Soviet planning officials are understandably concerned about the loss of production as enterprises seek self-sufficiency.

Source: V. Kontorovich and V. Shlapentokh, "Soviet Industry Grows Its Own Potatoes," *The Wall Street Journal*, 1 January 1985.

Secondary Effects of Socialist Property

Because everyone owns state property, nobody in particular owns it. The lack of private property takes its toll on the way resources are managed. Since those who allocate and utilize resources do not immediately benefit from that use, resources are sometimes wasted. For example, an estimated 10 percent of all fertilizer is lost on its way from factory to fields because it is shipped in unsuitable freight cars or is improperly stored. At 600 railroad stations, fertilizer is just dumped on the open ground. Also, about one-third of the harvest reportedly deteriorates before it reaches consumers, and some food is allowed to spoil in stores.[3]

---

[3]These examples are provided in Vladimir Shlapentokh, "Soviet Ideas on Private Property Invite Abuse of Capital Stock," *The Wall Street Journal*, 20 March 1986.

Soviet workers are said to have little regard for equipment that belongs to the state. New trucks or tractors may be dismantled for parts or working equipment may be sent to a scrap plant. Pilfering of state-owned property is a high art and a favorite sport. The 1986 Program of the Communist party called for "the adoption of all measures for the defense of socialist property." The political elite has been trying to persuade Soviet citizens to regard themselves as the "masters of their enterprise."

In contrast, the Soviet people take better care of their personal property than do people in capitalist countries. For example, personal cars on average run for 20 years or more—doubling the official projected automobile life. The incentives of private ownership are also evident on the farm. Each farmer on the collectives is allowed to cultivate a small plot of land for personal consumption or for sale at prices determined in unregulated markets. Income earned by farmers from their private plots is taxed at rates that vary inversely with what the farmer produces on the collective. The tax rate is low, but it increases sharply if the farmer fails to achieve the established workday quota on the collective. This tax system tries to ensure that farmers do not neglect their collective work in favor of their private plots. Despite the small size of the plots and the taxes on earnings from these plots, farmers produce a disproportionate share of output on private plots. Privately farmed plots make up only 2 percent of the Soviet Union's farmland but supply 30 percent of all meat, milk, and vegetables, and 60 percent of all potatoes.

Soviet agriculture lacks an adequate refrigeration and transportation system to balance the distribution of fruits and vegetables throughout the country. This vacuum creates an opportunity for enterprising farmers in the warmer regions to fill suitcases with fresh produce and fly north to Moscow or Kiev, where this produce is sold at public markets.

In urban areas many mechanics, carpenters, plumbers, and tailors moonlight to provide a substantial share of the service sector. Everyday life would grind to a halt without these free spirits. Like grass growing between the bricks of a sidewalk, capitalism thrives unless it is trampled. The private sector in the Soviet Union is tiny but dynamic.

Innovation

Despite the emphasis on technical progress in Soviet planning, the technological gap between the Soviet Union and major capitalist countries is great and has not diminished in the last two decades. To supplement their own technological developments, Soviet officials buy, borrow, or steal technology from capitalist countries. Yet the problem in the Soviet Union is not so much the availability of the latest technology but the diffusion of technology throughout the economy. The reluctance of plant managers to develop or employ new technologies is described in the following case study of computers.

CASE STUDY

Computers in the Soviet Union

No major American corporation could be competitive without the aid of computers to provide data about payroll, inventories, production, sales, and other details that facilitate the coordination of resources in the firm. Computers become especially important for an economy that tries to coordinate resources through a hierarchy rather than through markets. Thus, computers were considered to be a natural tool of the centrally planned economy. The Ninth Five-Year Plan, introduced in 1971, established the goal of connecting all levels of the Soviet economy through a computer network. The various ministers could then serve as field marshalls, redeploying resources as needed. This objective has received continued support in subsequent five-year plans.

Although the Soviet Union has acquired Western computer technology, the Soviets have had difficulty producing modern computers and have not exploited the computer's tremendous capabilities. For example, only about one-third of plants with at least 500 employees had mainframe computers in 1984, compared with 100 percent coverage in the United States. Fewer than 10 percent of smaller firms use computers. The computers now commonly in use are copies of mainframes that IBM stopped making a decade ago.

The main problem with the acceptance and implementation of computers by plant directors springs from the role that information plays in the Soviet system. Central planners often present the enterprise with unrealistic production targets, creating chronic shortages of resources. When plant directors fall short of their targets, they tend to dress up the results. If by some chance they exceed targets, plant directors tend to downplay the results so their future targets will not be raised.

Plant directors also hoard key resources to avoid production delays, but these excess inventories must be concealed from the higher-ups; otherwise, the supply of resources will be reduced. Because Soviet managers frequently acquire resources through barter or on the black market, they need a slush fund to support these transactions. Supervisors might therefore pad the payroll to provide the necessary funds.

Information is a source of power, so plant directors are understandably wary of computers because an accurate accounting system would allow superiors to survey plant directors' performance. The director with anything to hide would be tripped up by a computer yielding accurate reports to the higher-ups. Information that fell into the wrong hands could prove incriminating. Because plant directors have an incentive to distort information, they view computers as tools of the hierarchy rather than as management tools.

Even the plant manager who wants to develop a computer system faces many obstacles. Any enterprise fortunate enough to acquire a computer confronts a bureaucratic maze to get the computer into operation. The service, training, and repair capabilities of the state employees who provide the computers leave much to be desired. Once installed, computers break down more frequently than would be accepted in the West. Moreover, Soviet telecommunications is of such poor quality that electronic data transmission is slow, and computer links are often interrupted, creating severe problems for computer operations.

Central planners have provided plant directors with incentives to use computers, but these incentives can have perverse effects. Some computer executives, for example, receive bonuses for the number of tasks performed by the computer system and the number of subsystems operating. Consequently, rather than developing a unified accounting system, managers introduce many subsystems, and the result is cumulative inefficiency.

The goal of a computerized economy seems impossible in the near future. Plant managers appear reluctant to accept the rope they think could be used to hang them. More generally, the growth of computers, particularly personal computers, has been hampered by the state control of information. In a country where typewriters and duplicating machines are considered potential tools of sedition, a word processor and printer pose a threat to Soviet leadership. Nearly all computers in the Soviet Union are in state-run institutions and are closely guarded. The state has a monopoly on ideas, and a personal computer represents a challenge to that monopoly.

Source: Daniel Seligman, "The Great Soviet Computer Screw-Up," *Fortune* (8 July 1985): 32–36.

SOVIET ELITE

Another way of evaluating an economic system is in terms of equity. How evenly are the fruits of production distributed among Soviet households?

Income Distribution

The average household income in 1984 was the equivalent of about $8000. Wages and salaries accounted for about 70 percent of income. Wage and salary inequality across households in the Soviet Union is roughly comparable to the inequality found in other industrial countries, as can be seen from Exhibit 2. Among urban households, a group that accounts for two-thirds of the population, the highest fifth of the population received 38.5 percent of the income share, and the lowest fifth received 8.7 percent of the income share. Income is more evenly distributed in the U.S.S.R. than in the United States, although the difference is not substantial.

Direct taxes tend to have a limited effect on redistribution in the Soviet Union. Most income consists of wages and salaries, and tax rates tend to be only mildly progressive on this income, rising to a maximum of 13 percent. Transfer income in the Soviet Union is not particularly redistributive by Western standards.

But the distribution of money income has less significance in the Soviet Union because many goods are in short supply and cannot be purchased without waiting in line or having an inside connection. The Soviet Union has a well-defined class structure, and not all people are created equal, as we will see next.

EXHIBIT 2
PERCENTAGE SHARE OF HOUSEHOLD INCOME
BY GROUPS OF HOUSEHOLDS FOR THE
U.S.S.R. AND WESTERN COUNTRIES

Country	Year	Lowest Fifth	Highest Fifth
Pretax Income			
U.S.S.R. (nonfarm household)	1967	10.4	33.8
Australia	1966–67	8.3	41.0
Norway	1970	8.2	39.0
U.K.	1973	8.3	39.9
France	1970	5.8	47.2
Canada	1969	6.2	43.6
U.S.	1972	5.5	44.4
Posttax Income			
U.S.S.R. (urban households)	1972–74	8.7	38.5
Sweden	1972	9.3	35.2

Source: Based on data presented in Abram Bergson, "Income Inequality Under Soviet Socialism," *Journal of Economic Literature* 22 (September 1984), Table 6.

Soviet Elite

To promote technological development, Stalin instituted a series of rewards that resulted in a class structure favoring the technical intelligentsia. The intelligentsia forms the artistic, social, technical, and political vanguard of the Soviet elite. Socialist dogma called for a "withering away" of the state as a classless communism emerged, but Stalin held that in the meantime special rewards were required to call forth productive capabilities. Thus, Stalin fostered social stratification, and the Soviet elite has flourished.

While there are no exact definitions or reliable statistics, the Soviet ruling class, or *nomenklatura*, comprises about 250,000 members. Counting family members, this ruling class makes up less than 1 percent of the population. Who are the elite? Exhibit 3 presents the percentage distribution of elite personnel across occupations. Note that 7.5 percent of the elite are enterprise directors. Actually, only a fraction of directors qualify for elite status. Salaries for the elite in academic and research positions average about four times that of the average worker. As we will see, rank has its privilege not only in pay but in virtually every aspect of Soviet life.

Consumption   Ordinary citizens of Moscow might spend hours in line trying to buy meat, but members of the Soviet elite can shop at the famous Kremlin canteen. This shop accepts payment only in *kemliovka* coupons, which purchase the best food available at the lowest prices anywhere. Members of the *nomenklatura* receive part of their pay in *kemliovka*. Similarly, the Central Committee building in Moscow has three dining rooms on different floors, each serving a different category of official. The food is said

EXHIBIT 3
ELITE PERSONNEL BY OCCUPATION
AS A PERCENT OF ALL ELITE
FOR THE 1970s

Occupation	Percent
Enterprise directors	7.5
Intelligentsia (Academicians, Artists, Editors)	17.6
Government and trade union officials	26.5
Military, police, and diplomats	13.2
Communist party officials	35.2

Source: Based on data presented in Abram Bergson, "Income Inequality Under Soviet Socialism," *Journal of Economic Literature* 22 (September 1984), Table 10.

to be as good as in the best restaurants, but the prices are considerably lower. The most select restaurant has a military guard at the door.

Housing Housing is heavily subsidized and in short supply, and it is allocated by bureaus rather than by markets. The Soviet elite is accorded the most spacious and the highest-quality housing. The discrimination based on one's status can be finely tuned. For example, in one research complex, a Soviet academy member—the cream of academe—merits a separate cottage. Next in line is a professor, who is provided with an apartment that has 97 square feet per family member plus an extra family allotment of 216 square feet. An engineer or junior scientific worker is given an apartment with 97 square feet per family member, and a construction or service worker is given an apartment with 77 square feet per family member.[4] This example conveys not only the clear distinctions based on rank but also how scarce housing is. A member of the academy belongs to the Soviet elite; a mere professor does not. A family of four headed by a professor would rate only 604 square feet of living space—about the size of an efficiency apartment. A service worker's family would have to make do with only half that space.

Intergenerational Mobility

In the United States wealth and power are passed from one generation to another through genes, education, and inheritance. These same transmission mechanisms operate in the Soviet Union. Since most resources are owned by the state, private wealth is limited primarily to savings deposits, government bonds, housing, and other personal possessions. Interest rates in the Soviet Union are fixed at a low level, but there is little or no inheritance tax, so large sums can be passed along to the next generation.

How does one join the elite? The surest way is to be born into the class. Children of the elite have a much better chance of acceptance to the right

---

[4]This example is found in Abram Bergson, "Income Inequality Under Soviet Socialism," *Journal of Economic Literature,* 22 (September 1984): 1059.

schools. The children of the elite also have a much greater probability of being among the elite themselves. Young men from elite families are routinely appointed to *nomenklatura* positions, and their sisters marry those who hold such positions. (Soviet women from elite families usually do not seek employment.) For an outsider, the best route is to join the Communist party and capture someone's attention.

Tales of bribery and abuse of official positions abound and are evidently so pervasive that Gorbachev felt obliged to express concern about the problem in his speech to the Communist Party Congress. Interviews with thousands of emigrants from the Soviet Union suggest the wide use of bribery to obtain first jobs and university positions. When bureaucratic coordination replaces market coordination, some nonmarket system of rationing must be used to deal with excess demand. Bribes replace long lines and may be more efficient, though not necessarily more equitable.

SOVIET REFORMS

The word *reform* means different things in different countries. In the United States reform often implies greater bureaucratic intervention because of a perceived market failure, such as reform of the way hazardous waste is handled or reform of corporate takeover activity. In the Soviet Union, however, reform is more a reaction to bureaucratic failure, and the solution is to introduce more market mechanisms into the resource allocation system.

Economic reform in the Soviet Union has had a checkered past over the last several decades. Most economic reforms have been aimed at changing policies adopted during the Stalin era. First introduced by Nikita Khrushchev in 1957, economic reform was halted by Leonid Brezhnev in 1965, revived by Yuri Andropov in 1983, and slowed by Konstantin Chernenko in 1984. Gorbachev introduced major reforms in 1986.

Industrial Reforms

Decentralization is a code word for introducing private incentives into the economy. Gorbachev's economic experiment is to allow enterprises to retain a majority of their profits. Plant managers are now given a freer hand in solving problems, so central planners have less direct control. For example, the number of targets a plant manager must meet has been reduced from 40 to 8. Factories are encouraged to compete with each other.

Reforms have created incentive funds. The first is for material incentives, which is a bonus the enterprise can receive based on how well it performs relative to its sales and profit targets. A production and development fund is designed to allow more internal financing for those enterprises that meet their profit targets and are efficiently managed. The idea is to promote an efficient use of capital resources, so that only the most efficient firms can expand. To deal with the question of quality, central planners have changed their pricing system to pay producers less for lower-quality goods and more—up to 30 percent more—for higher-quality goods.

According to the official Soviet news agency, Tass, under the Gorbachev reforms, work collectives would become "full-fledged masters of their enterprises and will independently decide practically all matters related to the production and social development of a mill or factory."[5] New regulations affecting thousands of factories and mills allow managers to "combine elements of centralized guidance and socialist self-management by the work collective." The new law is quite significant. The collective will pay salaries and research and development costs out of its profits. Another change in the law allows Soviet enterprises to develop ties with companies from capitalist countries to create joint enterprises and encourage technology transfer.

By 1991 Gorbachev's reforms call for sharp staff reductions at central ministries and further dismantling of the centralized pricing system. These efforts to decentralize decision making and to provide more incentives to meet targets, to produce high-quality goods, and to earn profits, move the Soviet industry away from planned socialism and toward market socialism.

Allowing for Private Enterprise

The first day of May—May Day—1987 marked a declaration of independence of sorts for private enterprise in the Soviet Union. On that day for the first time self-employed individuals could tailor a suit, change a spark plug, drive a taxi, or sand a floor. In all, 29 categories of services could be offered by private individuals. Two to three million people were affected. Those involved need a license and become liable for the income tax; they also must hold a full-time public sector job. In preparation for the new law, penalties were increased for receiving "unearned income." These self-employed workers can allow family members to assist in the business but cannot hire outsiders. The change in the law simply ratified what had been happening in the second economy anyway. This way the state can keep better track of these activities and can tax them.

Earlier we discussed the greater farm productivity on private plots. Although the country clearly benefits from the greater output, this shining example of capitalism has long irritated Communist officials. In 1961 the Party Congress called for the elimination of private plots by 1980, but the Soviets now seem to recognize the benefits of private incentives. Under a Gorbachev proposal, a fixed amount of the harvest from cooperatives would be turned over to the state. The balance could be sold at market prices for whatever the cooperatives and state farms could get. Soviets are looking for ways to reintroduce the incentives associated with private property as a spur to production.

Centralized planning is a comfortable habit for the Soviet elite. Private production represents competition to the state monopoly. The success of the Gorbachev reforms depends on the support of the Soviet elite. This group is powerful and has a clear interest in the status quo. A Communist party

---

[5]"Soviets Seek to Relax Controls on Economy," *The Hartford Courant,* 8 February 1987.

official's wife was quoted in *Pravda* as challenging Gorbachev: "We are the elite, and you will not pull us down. You don't have the strength. We'll rip the flimsy sails of your restructuring."[6]

CONCLUSIONS

Central planning and control have difficulty addressing the complexities of developing and operating a modern economy. Capitalism has outshone socialism in terms of technical progress and in matching production to market needs. The consumer reigns supreme under capitalism. From compact disc players to microwave popcorn, capitalism dominates socialism as a way to satisfy a variety of consumer wants. Capitalism thrives where it is permitted and even where it's prohibited.

Nevertheless, where capitalist markets fail, central planning may be able to correct this failure and thereby improve the efficiency and equity of the economy. There is no denying that in socialist economies full employment is a fact. Fluctuations occur at irregular intervals in planned economies, but no business cycle is experienced, as in the capitalist economy. The growth record of the Soviet Union between 1930 and 1980 exceeded that of the United States, although the Soviet Union had started from a much lower level of economic development and still lags behind the U.S. economy in terms of GNP per capita. Thus, socialist countries, like capitalist countries, have had their successes.

SUMMARY

1. We can distinguish between economic systems based on the ownership of resources, the way these resources are allocated to produce goods and services, and the incentives used to motivate people.

2. In capitalist systems resources are owned by individuals and are allocated by market coordination. People are motivated by self-interest. In socialist economies resources are owned by the state, and people are motivated by a combination of self-interest and patriotic interest in social welfare. Under planned socialism resources are directed by bureaucratic coordination. Under market socialism resources are directed by market coordination.

3. Gosplan is the state agency that develops the central plan for production targets in major

industrial sectors. Production decisions for less important commodities are relegated to a lower level of the planning bureaucracy or in some cases are left to the market. The objective is to arrive at a material balance between the quantity supplied and the quantity demanded; if these two are not in balance, something must give. Usually the quantity of resources demanded exceeds the the quantity supplied, and what gives is the amount obtained by the consumer products sector.

4. There are three economies in the Soviet Union: (1) the official economy as followed by the central plan, (2) the "second economy," the Soviet version of the underground economy, and (3) the "informal economy," where

---

[6]As reported in "Gorbachev's Opposition," *Newsweek* (18 May 1987): 48.

Soviet managers pursue official objectives by skirting the official rules. The second economy and the informal economy address shortcomings of the official economy.

5. Several reforms have been introduced in recent years to decentralize decision making, to provide greater production incentives to the workers, and to allow more room for private markets, particularly in the service sector.

QUESTIONS AND PROBLEMS

1. (Socialism) Is it reasonable to believe that socialist economies will have as much diversity in the production of goods as capitalist economies do? Does your answer depend on how much central planning is undertaken by the government?

2. (Capitalism) Many socialists stress the fact that in market economies there is much waste through the production of useless luxuries for the rich. Also, they claim consumers are often fooled into buying products they do not really want through advertising ploys. How would you respond to such claims?

3. (Ownership of Resources) Socialists argue that no person was responsible for creating the natural resources found in the country. Therefore, these resources should be publicly owned. What problems do you see with this line of reasoning? Consider also the efficiency of private ownership.

4. (Material Balance System) Would the Soviet method of material balance planning lead to a burdensome expansion of the bureaucracy? How might lags in decision making cause problems?

5. (Internal Passports) Why might the authorities in centrally planned economies attempt to prevent migration within a country through the use of internal passports?

6. (Soviet Reform) What has been Gorbachev's criticism of Soviet economic performance?

7. (China and Socialism) One of the best periods of Chinese economic growth was shortly after the communist revolution of 1949. How might you explain this short-term economic success of central planning?

8. (Specialization) Explain why central planning in the Soviet Union has led many companies to abandon specialization of production in favor of self-reliance and independence of production.

9. (Private Agriculture) Of what value to the Soviet economy is the private production of agricultural goods? How does the government tax such production? Should privatization be extended to other facets of the Soviet economy?

10. (Soviet Computerization) Why are managers in the Soviet Union wary of widespread computerization of companies and enterprises? Can such computerization reduce the amount of fraud and waste in the Soviet system?

GLOSSARY

Absolute advantage   the ability to produce something with fewer resources than other producers use.

Accounting profit   total revenue minus explicit costs.

Adverse selection   when unobservable labor skills are misvalued in the market due to a lack of information.

Agent   a person who acts on behalf of another person, the *principal*.

Allocative efficiency   the situation achieved when firms produce the output that is most preferred by consumers.

Annuity   a given sum of money received each year for a specified number of years.

Antitrust activity   activity aimed at preventing monopoly and fostering competition.

Arbitration   an agreement under which all parties to a dispute agree to respect the decision of an impartial observer.

Association-causation fallacy   the idea that if two variables are associated in time, one must *necessarily* cause the other.

Average fixed cost   total fixed cost divided by output.

Average revenue   total revenue divided by output.

Average total cost   total cost divided by output; the sum of average fixed cost plus average variable cost.

Average variable cost   total variable cost divided by output.

Barrier to entry   any impediment that prevents new firms from competing on an equal basis with existing firms in an industry.

Barter   the exchange of one good for another without the use of money.

Bilateral monopoly   the situation where a union bargains with a monopsonist.

Bounded rationality   a situation where a manager can comprehend only a limited amount of information.

Budget line   a line showing all combinations of two goods that can be purchased, at given prices, with a fixed amount of income.

Capital   manufactured equipment used in the production of goods and services.

Cartel   an agreement among firms to coordinate their production and pricing decisions.

Collective bargaining   the process by which union and management negotiate a mutually agreeable contract.

Collusion   the joint determination of price and output by two or more firms.

Comparable worth   a scheme where pay is determined by job characteristics rather than by supply and demand.

Comparative advantage   the ability to produce something at a lower opportunity cost than other producers face.

Competing-interest legislation   legislation that involves concentrated cost and concentrated benefits.

Complements   a pair of goods such that an increase in the price of one leads to a decrease in demand for the other.

Concentration ratio   a measure of the market share of the largest firms in an industry.

Conglomerate merger   a combination of firms producing in different industries.

Constant-cost industry   an industry that can expand or contract without affecting the prices of the resources it employs.

Constant returns to scale   the range of production where average cost does not change as the scale of operations changes in the long run.

Consumer surplus   the difference between what a consumer is willing to pay for a given quantity of a good and what is actually paid.

Contestable market   one that firms can enter or leave at will and in which there are no irreversible investments.

Corporation   a legal entity owned by stockholders whose liability is limited to the value of their stock.

Cost-plus pricing   a scheme where the price of a good is determined by adding a markup to average cost.

Cross-price elasticity of demand   the percentage change in the quantity demanded of one good divided by the percentage change in the price of another good.

Cross-subsidization   using revenues from profitable activities to subsidize unprofitable activities.

Deadweight loss   the loss of consumer surplus (that goes to no one) following monopolization of an industry.

Decreasing-cost industry   an industry that faces lower resource prices as it expands.

Demand   a schedule showing how much of a good a consumer is willing and able to buy at each possible price during a given period of time, other things constant.

Demand curve   a downward-sloping curve showing how much of a commodity is demanded at various possible prices.

Demography   the study of the size, density, and distribution of human populations.

Dependent variable   one whose value is affected by some other variable(s).

Derived demand   the demand for a resource is derived from the demand for the product the resource helps to produce.

Diseconomies of scale   the range of production where average cost increases as the scale of operations rises in the long run.

Disequilibrium differentials   wage differences that trigger resource reallocation and wage adjustments.

Division of labor   the organization of production into tasks in which people specialize.

Dumping   the sale of a commodity abroad for less than its price in the domestic market.

Economic profit   total revenue minus all (explicit and implicit) costs.

Economic regulation   government regulation aimed at controlling price, output, entry, exit, and quality in conditions where monopoly is inevitable or desirable.

Economic rent   the portion of a resource's total earnings above transfer earnings.

Economics   the study of how people choose to use scarce resources in an attempt to satisfy unlimited wants.

Economies of scale the range of production where reductions in average cost are made possible by increasing the scale of operations in the long run.

Efficiency the situation where there is no way resources can be reallocated to increase the production of one good without decreasing the production of another.

Entrepreneurial ability managerial and organizational skills and the willingness to take risks.

Equilibrium a situation in which the plans of buyers match the plans of sellers.

Equilibrium differentials wage differences that do not precipitate resource reallocation.

Exclusive dealing when a producer requires a buyer not to purchase from other sellers.

Expansion path a curve showing the least costly input combination for each rate of output.

Explicit costs opportunity costs taking the form of actual cash payments.

Externality an unpriced byproduct of consumption or production that harms or benefits individuals not involved in the transaction.

Fallacy of composition the belief that what is true for the individual or part must *necessarily* be true for the group or whole.

Fiscal policy the use of government spending, taxes, and borrowing to influence aggregate economic activity.

Fixed cost any cost that is independent of the rate of output.

Fixed resource any resource that cannot be easily varied to increase or decrease the level of output.

Golden rule of profit maximization the firm should produce the level of output where marginal cost equals marginal revenue.

Good anything that is scarce and valuable.

Herfindahl index the sum of squared percentage market shares of all firms in a market.

Horizontal merger a situation where one firm combines with another firm that produces the same product.

Household work time spent producing goods and services in the home.

Hypothesis a statement about relationships among variables.

Implicit costs opportunity costs of using resources owned by the firm or provided by its owners.

Income effect when the price of a good rises, consumers' purchasing power falls and so they purchase less of all normal goods.

Income elasticity of demand the percentage change in quantity demanded divided by the percentage change in income.

Increasing marginal returns when marginal physical product increases with each additional worker.

Increasing-cost industry an industry that faces higher resource prices as it expands.

Independent variable one whose value affects, but is not affected by, the value of other variables.

Indifference curve a curve showing all combinations of two goods that provide a consumer the same level of total utility.

Indifference map a set of indifference curves, one for each possible level of total utility.

Inferior good one for which demand decreases as income rises.

Interest the return to resource owners for the use of their capital.

Interest rate amount of money paid for the use of a dollar for one year.

Interlocking directorate a situation where the same individual serves on the boards of directors of competing firms.

Isocost line a line showing all combinations of two resources that a firm can purchase for a given total cost.

Isoquant A curve showing all technically efficient combinations of two resources that can produce a given amount of output.

Labor the physical and mental effort of humans.

Land plots of ground and other natural resources used in production.

Law of comparative advantage the individual with the lowest opportunity cost of producing a particular good should specialize in producing that good.

Law of demand the quantity of a good demanded is inversely related to its price, other things constant.

Law of diminishing marginal rate of substitution the amount of good Y a consumer is willing to give up to get one additional unit of good X declines as the consumption of X increases.

Law of diminishing marginal returns when more and more of a variable resource is added to a given amount of a fixed resource, the resulting changes in output will eventually diminish.

Law of diminishing marginal utility the more of a good consumed per period, the smaller the marginal utility, other things constant.

Law of increasing opportunity cost as more of a particular good is produced, the opportunity cost of production rises.

Logrolling the trading of support between voters.

Long run a time period during which all resources are variable.

Lorenz curve a curve showing the percentage of total income received by a given percentage of recipients arranged from smallest to largest.

Macroeconomics the study of the behavior of entire economies.

Marginal "extra" or "additional."

Marginal cost the change in total cost when output changes by one unit.

Marginal efficiency of capital the marginal rate of return on capital.

Marginal physical product the change in total physical product when the usage of a particular resource changes by one unit.

Marginal rate of substitution indicates how much of one good a consumer is willing to give up to get one more unit of another good, while remaining equally satisfied.

Marginal resource cost the change in total cost when an additional unit of a resource is hired.

Marginal revenue the change in total revenue after a one unit change in sales.

Marginal revenue product   the change in total revenue when an additional unit of a resource is hired.

Marginal utility   the change in total utility derived from a one unit change in consumption of a good.

Market   an arrangement through which buyers and sellers carry out exchange at mutually agreeable terms.

Market demand curve   a curve showing the quantity of a good demanded by all consumers at various possible prices.

Market power   the ability of one or more firms to maintain a price above the competitive level.

Market socialism   an economic system where the state owns resources other than labor but market forces are used to allocate the resources.

Market structure   the important features of a market, such as the number of firms, type of product, ease of entry, and forms of competition.

Market supply curve   a curve showing the quantity of a good supplied by all producers at various possible prices.

Market work   the sale of labor in return for a money wage.

Material balance system   a system of central planning designed to ensure a balance of supply and demand for important types of industrial output.

Median   the middle number in a series of numbers arranged from smallest to largest.

Mediation   the use of an impartial observer to help resolve differences between union and management.

Microeconomics   the study of the economic behavior of individual decision makers.

Minimum efficient scale   the lowest rate of output at which the firm takes full advantage of economies of scale.

Monetary policy   regulation of the money supply to influence aggregate economic activity.

Monopolistic competition   market structure characterized by a large number of firms selling products that are close substitutes.

Monopoly   the single producer of a product that has no good substitutes.

Monopsonist   the sole purchaser of a particular resource.

Natural monopoly   a situation where one firm can serve a market more cheaply than two or more firms can.

Negative income tax   a cash transfer program where benefits are reduced as earnings rise.

Negative (inverse) relationship   whenever one variable increases, the other decreases.

Negative-sum game   a game in which total losses exceed total winnings.

Normal good   one for which demand increases as income rises.

Normal profit   the accounting profit required to induce the firm's owners to employ their resources in the firm.

Normative economic statement   a statement that represents an opinion and is not capable of being proved or disproved.

Oligopoly   market structure with a small number of firms whose decisions are interdependent.

Open shop   a firm that hires both union and nonunion workers.

Opportunity cost   the benefit expected from the best alternative forgone.

Pareto optimal   a change to the status quo that makes at least one person better off while making no one worse off.

Partnership   a firm with multiple owners who share the firm's profits and bear unlimited liability for the firm's debts.

Perfect competition   market structure involving large numbers of fully informed buyers and sellers of a homogeneous product. There are no obstacles to entry or exit of firms.

Planned socialism   an economic system where the state owns resources other than labor and directs them through economic plans and central decision making.

Positive (direct) relationship   whenever two variables increase and decrease together.

Positive economic statement   a statement that can be supported by reference to facts.

Positive rate of time preference   a situation where present consumption is more highly valued than future consumption.

Positive-sum game   a game in which total winnings exceed total losses.

Present value   the value today of a payment to be received in the future.

Price discrimination   selling at different prices to different consumers or charging the same consumer different prices for different units of a good.

Price elasticity of demand   the responsiveness of consumers to a price change; the percentage change in quantity demanded divided by the percentage change in price.

Price elasticity of supply   the responsiveness of producers to a price change; the percentage change in quantity supplied divided by the percentage change in price.

Price leader   a firm whose prices are followed by the rest of the industry.

Price taker   any firm whose actions have no effect on the market price.

Principal   a person who makes an agreement with an *agent* in the expectation that the agent will act in the principal's behalf.

Product market   a market in which goods and services are exchanged.

Production function   shows the maximum amount of output that can be produced per period by specific combinations of resources, using the best available technology.

Production possibilities frontier   a curve showing all combinations of goods that can be produced when available resources are fully and efficiently utilized.

Productive efficiency   when output is produced with the least-cost combination of inputs and using the best available technology.

Profit   the return to resource owners for their entrepreneurial ability.

Public good   a good that is available for all to consume regardless of who pays and who does not.

Pure capitalism   the economic system characterized by private ownership of resources and the use of prices to coordinate economic activity in free, competitive markets.

Pure rate of interest   the rate on a risk-free loan.

Quota a legal limit on the quantity of a particular commodity that can be imported per year.

Real income income measured in terms of the goods and services it can buy.

Rent the return to resource owners for the use of their land.

Rent seeking the expenditure of resources to obtain favorable treatment from government.

Resource market a market in which resources are exchanged.

Roundabout production production of capital goods that can then be used to produce consumer goods.

Secondary effects effects of economic actions that develop slowly over time as people react to events.

Separation of ownership from control when no single stockholder has the incentive or ability to control the management of a corporation.

Shirking the tendency not to work as hard as required.

Short run a time period during which at least one resource cannot be varied.

Shortage an excess of quantity demanded over quantity supplied at a given price.

Signal a proxy for unobservable characteristics.

Slope a measure of the steepness of a line.

Social regulation measures designed to improve health and safety.

Sole proprietorship a firm with a single owner who has the right to all profits and who bears unlimited liability for the firm's debts.

Special-interest legislation legislation that involves concentrated benefits but widespread costs.

Specialization when individuals focus their efforts on the production of a single good or service.

Strike a union's attempt to withhold labor from a firm.

Substitutes a pair of goods such that an increase in the price of one leads to an increase in demand for the other.

Substitution effect when the price of a good rises, other goods will be substituted for it and the quantity demanded will fall.

Supply a schedule showing how much of a good a producer is willing and able to sell at various prices during a given time period, other things constant.

Supply curve a curve showing the quantity of a good supplied at various prices.

Surplus an excess of quantity supplied over quantity demanded at a given price.

Tangent a straight line that just touches, but does not cross, a curve at a particular point.

Tariff a tax on imports.

Tender offer an attempt to attain a controlling interest in a firm by purchasing shares at a premium over the market price.

Term structure of interest rates the relationship between the duration of loans and the interest rate charged.

Theory or **model** a simplification designed to capture the important elements of the relationship under consideration.

Time-series graph a graph showing the behavior of one or more variables over time.

Total revenue price multiplied by the quantity sold at that price.

Total utility the satisfaction from consuming a certain quantity of a good.

Transactions cost the cost of time and information required to carry out an exchange.

Transfer earnings what a resource could earn in its best alternative use.

Trust a merger or collusive agreement among competing firms.

Tying contract an arrangement where a seller of one good requires buyers to purchase other goods as well.

Union shop a firm where workers must join the union after being hired.

Utility the satisfaction received from consuming a good or service.

Variable any magnitude that can take on different values.

Variable cost any cost that increases as output increases.

Variable resource any resource that can be quickly varied to increase or decrease the level of output.

Vertical integration the expansion of a firm into earlier or later stages of production.

Vertical merger when one firm combines with another from which it purchases inputs or to which it sells output.

Wage bill employment multiplied by the wage rate.

Wages the return to resource owners for their labor.

World price the price determined by the world supply and demand for a product.

Zero-sum game a game in which total winnings just offset total losses.

INDEX